A HISTORY OF
ENGLISH DRAMA
1660–1900

A HISTORY OF
ENGLISH DRAMA
1660-1900

BY

ALLARDYCE NICOLL

VOLUME III
LATE EIGHTEENTH
CENTURY DRAMA
1750–1800

CAMBRIDGE
AT THE UNIVERSITY PRESS
1969

Published by the Syndics of the Cambridge University Press
Bentley House, 200 Euston Road, London N.W.1
American Branch: 32 East 57th Street, New York, N.Y. 10022

Standard Book Number: 521 05829 5

First edition 1927
Reprinted 1937
Second edition 1952
Issued as Volume III of
A History of English Drama 1660–1900
Reprinted 1955 1961 1966 1969

Printed in Great Britain
at the University Printing House, Cambridge
(Brooke Crutchley, University Printer)

CONTENTS

Chapter One
THE THEATRE

Chapter Two
TRAGEDY

Chapter Three
COMEDY

CONTENTS

Chapter Four

MISCELLANEOUS FORMS OF DRAMA

CHAPTER I

THE THEATRE

I. *Introductory*

IT is not to be denied that the great mass of late eighteenth century plays make today but dull reading. Countless are the trivial farces where a fair Clarissa or a fairer Celia is about to be married to an odious Squire Badger or a detestable Sir George Trifle and where a faithful Townly or a fascinating Lovemore arrives disguised as serving-man or as country clown to rescue her from the hated toils. Countless are the artificial and absurd comic operas; countless the weary tragedies and the lachrymose comedies of the period. There are, on the other hand, not a few considerations which must give us to pause ere we rashly dismiss this era of dramatic activity from serious investigation. After all, much of the minor work of even the most glorious theatrical decades has been of poor quality. Hardly anyone but the most blindly enthusiastic can profess to see in the lesser Elizabethan comedy and tragedy elements of greatness, and in our own days, with all the revival in the theatre, there is a vast amount of trivial, inartistic and uninteresting work produced. A period of literature cannot be judged on the total mass of its activity alone. It may seem at first as if Sheridan and Goldsmith, the twin stars which shine in the darkness of this era, stand entirely alone, and, in so far as no other dramatist quite reached their brilliance, this supposition is true; but there are many beside those two who came near at least to their mastery of dramatic dialogue and of dramatic situation. Colman gave two excellent comedies to the theatre, as did Macklin, the actor. Mrs Inchbald was a capable writer of sentimental comedy. Murphy has a comic sense all his own, and Holcroft possesses a sterling quality which makes his dramas rank as capable, if not brilliant, productions.

Mrs Cowley, Burgoyne, Foote, Kelly, Cumberland, Reynolds, Moore—in laughing comedy and in tearful comedy, in romantic tragedy and in domestic tragedy—all aided in providing for the stage genuine stock pieces, many of which have a more than ephemeral interest. It may be that few of these plays are consistently good, but most present at least some special scene or passage of dialogue which proves the existence yet of a true *vis comica* or of a genuine tragic spirit.

Over and beyond the presence of this, be it confessed all too rare, manifestation of dramatic excellence, this period of our drama has a paramount historical interest. This was the time when Dr Johnson's power, having risen to its height, was to wane rapidly under the increasing pressure of romantic sentiment. Chatterton, Percy and Macpherson were preparing the way for Blake and Burns, even as Blake and Burns were pioneers hacking a path for Wordsworth and Coleridge to pursue in their *Lyrical Ballads*. This was the time when murmurings of unrest fed by Rousseauesque theories of primitive virtue and of social corruption broke out into social ferment in France and aided in changing the atmosphere of literature throughout the entirety of Europe. Of these various movements in all their infinite ramifications and peculiar forms of expression much has been written, yet the movement of humanitarianism and of romance in the theatre has never been adequately dealt with. Sheridan and Goldsmith have had several biographers and many critics; a stray dramatist here and there has been politely favoured with a more or less scholarly study, but the larger development, the theatre as a whole, has remained unchronicled and unknown. It will be my endeavour here to present, in brief wise, some of the more important dramatic developments of these years, especially in so far as these developments harmonise with other literary activities of the period, and at the same time to throw some light on the minor and forgotten playwrights of the age.

A study of the dramatic literature of this period is complicated in various ways, and those complications are such as to increase with the passing on to later years. There is, first of all, the rapid establishment of the provincial theatres. It has been seen how, in the first half of the century, new playhouses were arising in Richmond, Bath, Tunbridge Wells and other fashionable localities. This tendency becomes deeply marked as we move onward from the year 1750. All over the country new audiences were springing into being, and bands of provincial actors emerged to form stock companies. The older strolling players still continued to trudge wearily from market-town to market-town, but the true days of strolling and of barn-acting were well-nigh over. Just as the performers of London had, nearly two centuries before, won for themselves a position of esteem, so these wandering "vagabonds" settled down to a life of comparative comfort and respectability[1]. The importance of these new theatres is to be seen in the number of dramas produced originally, or produced only, on provincial stages. The scope of English drama is, consequently, being widened in these years, and even begins to pass beyond the shores of the British Islands. The first American play, a tragedy called *The Prince of Parthia* by one Thomas Godfrey, was printed in Philadelphia in the year 1765, a fore-runner of many other works written exclusively for trans-Atlantic stages. It is, of course, utterly impossible to deal here with the development of the American stage, which, naturally enough, for many years followed the

---

[1] Many anecdotal works of the period deal incidentally with these provincial playhouses. Interesting side-lights on several, principally those of Norwich, Bath, York and Portsmouth, are given in Tate Wilkinson's *Memoirs of His Own Life* (York 1790) and *The Wandering Patentee* (1795). R. Crompton Rhodes has an interesting sketch of *The Theatre Royal, Birmingham*, 1774–1924 (1924). A valuable real-life record of the fortunes of a strolling company is preserved in the British Museum Add. MS. 33,488, f. 5; on this and other documents see Colby, E., *A Supplement on Strollers* (*Mod. Lang. Assoc. Amer.* xxxix. No. 28), *Strolling Players of the XVIII Century* (*Notes and Queries*, ix. Aug. 27, 1921) and *The Inchbalds strolling into Glasgow* (*id.* Nov. 1923), as well as Graves, T. S., *Strolling Players in the XVIII Century* (*id.* July 7, 1923). Other information may be obtained in S. W. Ryley's *The Itinerant; or Memoirs of an Actor* (3 series, 1808, 1816–7, 1827), Thomas Holcroft's *Memoirs* (1816), *A Dissertation of the Country Stage* in *The European Magazine* for Sept. 1792 (xxii. 230) and John Bernard's *Retrospections of the Stage* (1830).

main tendencies of London theatrical endeavour, but this American drama is, after all, drama in English, and as such must be kept in mind as the fortunes of the mother-drama are traced[1]. Nor must we forget that, as years passed years, theatres began to arise in the English colonies. Before the century closed the manager of the theatre at Calcutta was sending home to order a set of eight scenes to be painted by London's best scenic artists[2].

Contact with the continent, moreover, was becoming with every decade more close, and as a consequence the prevalence of adaptation and of translation increased. If Paris had a successful comedy, it was sure to be brought out on the London stage, so that for a large part of our period we seem to see nothing but a tissue of scenes hastily appropriated from French dramas and as hastily welded together. Indeed, the field of French influence is probably much wider than we now view it, for no exact endeavour has been hitherto made to determine its precise scope. We know now, more or less exactly, what the dramatists of the Restoration period took from Molière, but we have but a vague conception of what their successors borrowed from Regnard and Destouches, from Diderot and Favart. Other countries, too, were coming to have their influence on the development of the English theatre. With Metastasio and with Alfieri, Italy took a more important place in the international dramatic sphere, and these two writers, along with Goldoni, left their clear impress on several of our authors. Germany, also, was gradually becoming a force to reckon with. Lessing's *Hamburgische Dramaturgie* proved the most brilliant piece of dramatic criticism which the world had seen since the speculations of Castelvetro and the Italian Renascence critics. His own plays, and the plays of Goethe and of Schiller provided new models of artistic beauty. Kotzebue, less satisfactorily although more popularly, developed and

---

[1] For this subject see Quinn, A. H., *A History of the American Drama* (1923) and the bibliographies given in that volume.

[2] Odell, G. C. D., *Shakespeare from Betterton to Irving*, i. 444. An interesting account of *Early Halifax Theatres* is given by Mr A. R. Jewitt in *The Dalhousie Review* for 1925.

enlarged the sphere of sentimental and humanitarian drama. It can occasion no surprise, therefore, that the last decade of the century saw the influx of a large number of these German dramas in literal and adapted forms. With that influx the whole orientation of the English stage was altered.

These facts, added to the unparalleled number of plays produced yearly, obviously make the study of the theatre of this period much more complex and difficult than that of the earlier eras. It is less easy to secure adequate detailed information on the plays and the playwrights, and less easy to discern and to present clearly the main tendencies of the time.

II. *The Audience*

These main tendencies are, as always, to be related to the typical audiences in the theatres of London. Spectators in provincial theatres may have differed considerably from their metropolitan counterparts, but after all the provincial theatres merely followed the ruling tastes of London. Not until a full century had elapsed did there appear a definite school of dramatic writing outside of London, and even then it appeared only in the capital of a nation fundamentally separated, both in literary tradition and in outlook upon life, from the English.

No decided period of cleavage can be traced between the audiences of the early and those of the late eighteenth century; yet slowly the main features of the typical body of spectators was changing during those years. In spite of the recurring riots, in spite of rowdyism during and after the performance of plays, the playgoers of 1770 were quieter and less uproarious than their predecessors of 1730. Their tastes are reflected in the highly decorous comic operas of the age, in the more than decorous sentimental comedies and even in the moral melodramas which provided something of all worlds from spectacular show to poetic justice.

Disturbances, certainly, still broke this equitable calm. Five years after the opening of our period, we are confronted with the famous "Chinese Festival" riot of Nov. 8,

1755[1]. Barely four years had elapsed when another riot, on Oct. 31, 1759, broke out in the "Footmen's Gallery." Another is chronicled for Jan. 25, 1763[2], the notorious "Half-Price" riot which succeeded in destroying all previous records. Nor were these deliberate outbreaks of rowdyism confined to particular years. All through this period we learn of episodes which could not occur nowadays in any of our theatres. "Conversing about dramatic literature," Reynolds informs us,

Sheridan furnished us with some particulars relative to the first night's performance of *The Rivals*. During the violent opposition in the fifth act, an apple hitting Lee, who performed Sir Lucius O'Trigger, he stepped forward, and with a genuine rich brogue, angrily cried out,

"By the pow'rs, is it *personal?*—is it me, or the matter?[3]"

Among the Covent Garden newspaper cuttings in the British Museum is one from a paper of 1762, which gives some faint hint of what was happening regularly:

Thursday night there was a great riot at Covent Garden playhouse, without the least plea or pretence whatever, occasioned by the gentry in the upper gallery calling for a hornpipe, though

[1] For an account of this see Genest, J., *Some Account of the English Stage*, iv. 442–3, Fitzgerald, P., *A New History of the English Stage*, ii. 193–5 and *The Monthly Mirror*, Jan. 1802, pp. 43 ff. *The Dancers Damn'd; or, The Devil to Pay at the Old House* (1755) was a pamphlet occasioned by the disturbances.

[2] See *Theatrical Disquisitions: or a Review of the late Riot at Drury-Lane Theatre, on the 25th. and 26th. of January, with an Impartial Examen of the Profession and Professors of the Drama; Some few Hints on the Prerogative of an Audience, and, a Short Appendix, relative to the more flagrant Disturbance committed at Covent-Garden Theatre, on Thursday the 24th. of February. By a Lady* (1763). This pamphlet was followed by a number of others, notable among which are *Fitzgig, or the Modern Quixote, a Tale: relative to the late Disturbances* (1763), *An Appeal to the Public on behalf of the Managers* (1763), *An Historical and Succinct Account of the late Riots* (1763) and *Three Original Letters to a Friend in the Country, or the Cause and Manner of the late Riot....By an Old Man of the Town* (1763). These all refer to the famous "half-price" riot led by one Fitzpatrick. Having forced Garrick at Drury Lane to admit their claims, the rioters then made a massed attack on Covent Garden. See also B. Victor's *The History of the Theatres of London and Dublin* (1761–71), iii. 45–6 and Walpole's *Letters* (ed. Toynbee), v. 289, 291.

[3] *The Life and Times of Frederick Reynolds. Written by Himself* (1827), ii. 227–8.

nothing of the sort was expressed in the bills. They went so far as to throw a quart bottle and two pint bottles upon the stage, which happily did no mischief, but might have been productive of a great deal[1].

Catcalls still continued to play their noisy part in the evening's entertainment, as is indicated in Holcroft's *The German Hotel* (C.G. 1790). Fancy is aroused, in Jerningham's *The Welch Heiress* (D.L. 1795), from his profound slumber induced through witnessing Phrensy's play, "by a thousand cat-calls[2]," while the prologue to Moore's *Gil Blas* (D.L. 1751) is "*Spoken by Mr.* WOODWARD, *in the Character of a* Critic, *with a Cat-call in his Hand.*" The prologue to Murphy's *The School for Guardians* (C.G. 1767) is spoken by an actress, in a supposedly extempore strain:

May I intrude upon your patience for a minute?
Ladies and gentlemen, before the opening of the play,
Just to excuse an accident, which, I hope has no mischief in it....
I hope you'll not be angry; but we've got no prologue for to night;
And so I thought it was best to come and tell ye all the truth downright.
I went to Mr. Poet, and I spoke to him all I could,
But he said he had not leisure, tho' I know it's in his power if he would.
"A prologue, ma'am," says he!—"Yes, Sir, a prologue if you please."
And then I did so entreat the man, and beg, and pray, and teaze.
I told him, "You know, Sir, what a miserable plight we all are in,
To frown upon the performers, when pit, box, and gallery begin;
Whu—go the cat-calls—dub—dub—dub—each dreadful critick's stick
Prólog'—throw him over—won't ye ha some orange chips—
Prólógué—Cries o' London—Musick!

Several plays we know were damned by the wielders of these catcalls and of these critics' sticks. "It was said," declares Victor[3], "that Party interfered to condemn...very undeservedly" Murphy's *No One's Enemy but his Own* (C.G. 1764) and *What We must all Come to* (C.G. 1764). Kelly's *A Word to the Wise* (D.L. 1770) met with a severe

---

[1] Quoted in Alwin Thaler's *Shakespeare to Sheridan* (1922), p. 145.
[2] ii. i.   [3] iii. 66.

fate. It was painfully dragged through a Saturday's performance, and was announced for the Monday following. At
this, however, the author's opponents forced the actors to
give out instead the play of *Cymbeline*. Bitter strife waged in
the theatre during the early days of the ensuing week[1]. The
reason here was political, for Kelly had been accused of
servile trading with the Government. "The first Night's
Audience," Victor informs us, "were too conceited, and too
wise, to hear one Word of additional Wisdom from this
Performance; and therefore the Merits of the Play were not
attended to; nor any thing taken into Consideration, but the
private Conduct of the Author, who was charged by his
Opponents, with being a *ministerial* PARTY WRITER![2]"
Andrews, in the preface to his musical comedy *The Baron
Kinkvervankotsdorsprakingatchdern* (H.[2] 1781), speaks of "the
very extraordinary circumstances which attended the hearing,
or rather the not hearing of this piece." Supposed political
references in the same author's *The Reparation* (D.L. 1784)
caused disturbances[3], and the footmen, both in London and
in Edinburgh[4], showed lustily their disapprobation of
Townley's *High Life below Stairs* (D.L. 1759). Irish sentiment was aroused by Colman the Elder's *The Oxonian in
Town* (C.G. 1767) which "was violently opposed by a Party,
at whom the Satire of this Piece was supposed to be
levelled[5]," while Mrs Lennox' *The Sister* (C.G. 1769) "was
so ill treated by the Audience the first Night, that the
Authoress had spirit enough to withdraw it from the
Theatre[6]."

In spite of this, however, at least one writer could draw
attention to a new fair-play given to the dramatists:

> *'Twas once the mode inglorious war to wage*
> *With each bold Bard that durst attempt the Stage,*
> *And Prologues were but preludes to engage.*

[1] See the long preface attributed to the pen of Dr Johnson.
[2] iii. 161.
[3] See the *Biographia Dramatica*, iii. 201.
[4] For the latter see Victor, iii. 16–7.
[5] Victor, iii. 117; see also the advertisement to the play.
[6] Victor, *op. cit.* iii. 147.

Then mourn'd the Muse, not story'd Woes alone,
Condemn'd, with tears unfeign'd, to weep her own.
Past are those hostile days: and Wits no more
One undistinguish'd fate with Fools deplore[1].

It would seem from this that the old vice of the "First Nighters[2]" had passed away. Opposition to particular plays seems mainly to have arisen from political or social causes. Notwithstanding this quiescence of the livelier "bloods" eager to damn a new play, good or bad, the theatre had still somewhat a rough atmosphere, and playgoers were subjected to not a few discomforts. Reynolds has an account of a visit paid by him and his brother to Garrick's farewell performance of *Hamlet*:

The riot and struggle for places can scarcely be imagined.... Though a side box close to where we sat, was completely filled, we beheld the door burst open, and an Irish gentleman attempt to make entry, *vi et armis*—"Shut the door, box-keeper!" loudly cried some of the party—"There's room by the pow'rs!" cried the Irishman, and persisted in advancing. On this, a gentleman in the second row, rose, and exclaimed, "Turn out that blackguard!" "Oh, and is that your mode, honey?" cooly retorted the Irishman; "come, come out, my dear, and give me satisfaction, or I'll pull your nose, faith, you coward, and *shillaly* you through the lobby!" This public insult left the tenant in possession, no alternative; so he rushed out to accept the challenge; when, to the pit's general amusement, the Irishman jumped into his place, and having deliberately seated and adjusted himself, he turned round, and cried,

"I'll talk to you after the play is over[3]."

Perhaps we may make allowances here for this exceptional occasion, but the same confusions, the same struggles were there even on ordinary nights. In Colman's *Memoirs*[4] we are told how, in the struggle to secure places in the gallery, a man once pitched forward into the pit, injuring himself severely; and the "gentle Elia" has left on record memories of his earliest years when he was wont to battle his way into the same portion of the house. Holcroft, in the preface to his

---

[1] Prologue by William Melmoth to Dodsley's *Cleone* (C.G. 1758).
[2] See vol. ii, pp. 12–5, 17–9.
[3] *The Life and Times of Frederick Reynolds*, i. 90–1.   [4] i. 260.

comedy *Seduction* (D.L. 1787) speaks of "the nightly intrusion of unhappy and improper persons" into the theatre, in a state of extreme drunkenness. In every part of the house there were uncomfortable conditions, so that the prologue to Mrs Cowley's *The Town before You* (C.G. 1794) could point to the audience with the words:

> Ah! ah! you're here, and comfortably tight?
> Well squeez'd and press'd, I see—from left to right.

In the main, however, it does not seem to have been disturbance of the more violent sort or active opposition which troubled the dramatists of the time. What we do hear again and again during this period are complaints concerning the painful lack of attention on the part of the audience. The epilogue by M. P. Andrews to Reynolds' *The Dramatist* (C.G. 1789) chattily ridicules the "nightly Noise and Riot":

> What an overflowing House, methinks I see!
> Here, Box-keeper, are these my Places? No,
> Madam Van Bulk has taken all that Row;
> Then I'll go back—you can't—you can, she fibs,
> Keep down your Elbows, or you'll break my Ribs;
> Zounds, how you squeeze! Of what do you think one made is?
> Is this your Wig? No, it's that there Lady's.
> Then the Side-Boxes, what delightful Rows!
> Peers, Poets, Nabobs, Jews, and 'Prentice Beaux.
> Alderman *Cramp*, a gouty rich old Cit,
> With his young Bride, so lovingly will sit;
> While a gay Rake, who sees the happy Pair,
> A Bliss so wonderful resolves to share;
> He whispers, Madam, you've a charming Spouse,
> So neat in Limb, and then so smooth in Brows.
> Sir, I don't understand you.—What say, Dove?
> Nothing, my Duck—I'd only dropp'd my Glove.
> To morrow, at the Fruit Shop, will you come?
> At Twelve o'Clock—Lord, Sir, how you presume!
> Who's that scroudges? You shan't shove my wife,
> I shove her! A good Joke, upon my Life.
> Leave him to me; how dare you thus to treat me?
> *I dare do anything, if you'll but meet me.*
> Me, meet a Man! I shou'd'nt have thought of you;
> At Twelve indeed! I can't get out till Two.

So goes on the chatter, less highly fashionable, less witty than, but hardly different in kind from, the chatter in the side-boxes of Restoration theatres. A different kind of in-attention is hinted at in Kelly's *The School for Wives* (D.L. 1773) where we are told that

> *Some to yawn, some round about to look,*
> *Some to be seen, few come to mind their book:*
> *Some with high wit and humour hither run,*
> *To sweat their masters—and they call it fun.*
> *Some modish sparks, true stoicks, and high bred,*
> *Come, but ne'er know what's done, or sung, or said;*
> *Should the whole herd of criticks round them roar,*
> *And with one voice cry out, encore! encore!*
> *Or louder yet, off, off, no more! no more!*
> *Should Pit, Box, Gall'ry with convulsions shake,*
> *Still are they half asleep, nor t'other half awake*[1].

In order to combat this inattention dramatists were fre-quently forced to resort to the expedients already employed by Steele in the preceding half century. Again and again we find references to the "orderly Clapper-men and hir'd Puffers of Drury-Lane" and other theatres, who "deafen'd the Audience" with their "salaried" applause[2]. Reynolds, the author of the play, informs us how his *Eloisa* (C.G. 1786) was received. It

met with thunders of applause; not, however, owing to either its merit, or its fashion; but, in consequence of, at least, one hundred Westminster boys, rushing into the boxes, and pit, determined... to support the production of a brother Westminster. In addition, to this hearty, and tumultuous gang, my mother had sent our head clerk, Crouch, into the gallery, together with about fifty young sprigs of the law, to maintain a proper circulation of applause through all parts of the house[3].

It was no wonder that Harris, the manager, took the young author by the hand and congratulated him on having "more *real friends* than any other man in London." A similar phenomenon was witnessed at the production of Ayscough's *Semiramis* (D.L. 1776), when "the theatre...was filled with"

[1] Epilogue.
[2] Theophilus Cibber's *Dissertations* (1756), ii. 14–5.
[3] *Op. cit.* i. 321–2.

the author's "brother officers," who, however, were so dis-
gusted that they did not return a second time[1]. Other
writers, possibly feeling a natural repugnance to these
packed juries, or being unable to summon sufficient supporters, frankly drew the attention of the audience to the
fact that they had made no efforts to secure this party
applause[2]. Puffing, a companion art to hired clapping, was,
on the contrary, resorted to by almost all. The press, from
all accounts, was in a low and servile state during most of
these years. A little judicious payment could secure the
insertion of paragraphs true and false; and portraits of the
money-seeking printers and publishers of the news-sheets are
drawn for us again and again. Foote has several, scattered
through his numerous satirical farces, while the elder Colman
in *The English Merchant* (D.L. 1767) provides us with his
picture of Spatter, and in *The Spleen* (D.L. 1776) with that
of Rubrick. References to the art and science of theatrical
puffing are many. Perhaps Garrick was one of the first to
realise fully the power of the press, and how he made use of
it has been told repeatedly by his various biographers[3]. In
New Brooms (D.L. 1776) the elder Colman presents his
character of Catcall who writes as "*Dramaticus* in the
Chronicle, *the Observer* in the Post, *the Elephant* in the
Packet, the *Drury-Lane Mouse*, and *Covent-Garden Cricket*."
Three years later Sheridan brings forward in *The Critic*
(D.L. 1779) the more perfectly finished Mr Puff, who has
reduced this method of arousing public interest to scientific
proportions, and who recognises many subtle divisions and
species of the puff, direct and indirect. Still later, Bate in
The Dramatic Puffers (C.G. 1782) carries on the ridicule of
these agents of fame and provides an original touch in the
figure of Zephyr, who has invented a

play-house machine...an Applauder; a mechanical improvement
on the vulgar art of manucussion; by which one man, with the
simple winch of a barrel-organ, shall give a more mark'd and

---

[1] *Biographia Dramatica*, iii. 258.
[2] Cf. Murphy's *The Way to Keep Him* (D.L. 1760), prologue.
[3] On this particular aspect of Garrick's career, Colman's *Memoirs*,
i. 135–6, might also be consulted.

judicious applause, than can possibly be derived from any
stationary band of hireling clappers![1]

As for the general disposition of the audience in the playhouse, there seems to have been some slight rearrangement
from former days. Thus Richard Tickell, in the prologue to
Richardson's *The Fugitive* (H.[1] 1792) draws attention to the
altered state of the pit:

> And yet, in modern times, the aspiring Wit
> Braves but few perils from the well dress'd pit.
> Not as of old, when, train'd to frown and fret,
> In murky state, the surly synod met.
> Vain of half learning and of foreign rules,
> Vamp'd from the jargon of the antient schools,
> In black full-bottom'd wig, the Critic God
> Shook his umbrageous curls, and gave the nod!
> The pit was then all men—how shrunk the muse
> From those bleak rows of overhanging yews!
> Unlike the gay parterre we now salute.

If, however, the pit was no longer the abode of professional
critics, it was still that portion of the house which dramatists
most tried to interest. Cumberland, in *The Battle of Hastings*
(D.L. 1778)

> *Sues out a pardon from his Pope*—the Pit[2];

while his companion, Colman, recognised the predominance
of that portion of the theatre, choosing a political rather than
an ecclesiastical metaphor:

> *King, Lords, and Commons, o'er the nation sit;*
> *Pit, Box, and Gallery, rule the realms of wit*[3].

Francklin preferred to imagine the theatre a jury, which he
thus addressed,

> *Speak by your Foreman—what says Goodman Pit?*[4];

and Chalmers realised the all-predominance of the spectators there when he spoke of

> The Critic Bench! from which there's no appeal,

---

[1] In addition to these direct and indirect methods of securing applause,
there remained, of course, the older device of aristocratic patronage.
Victor (*op. cit.* iii. 34–9) informs us that *The Wishes* (D.L. 1761) was
pushed on the stage by this means. [2] Prologue.
[3] Kelly's *Clementina* (C.G. 1771), epilogue by Colman.
[4] *Matilda* (D.L. 1775). epilogue.

emphasising his words by appending a stage direction,
"*Looking into the Pit*[1]." From these allusions it would seem
that by the seventies of the century at least the pit, while still
retaining its professional and amateur critics, was patronised
as well by the more fashionable and intellectual parts of the
audience, leaving the first gallery for the middle classes and
the upper gallery for the poorer folk. This conclusion is
emphasised by Garrick's epilogue to Murphy's *All in the
Wrong* (D.L. 1761), where, addressing the various divisions
of the theatre, he endeavours to estimate their tastes:

> You *relish satire;* [to the pit] you *ragouts of wit;* [boxes]
> Your *taste is humour, and high season'd joke;* [1st gall.]
> You *call for hornpipes, and for Hearts of Oak!* [2nd gall.]

The same differentiation in the appreciation of serious
emotions is implied in Jephson's prologue to *The Count of
Narbonne* (C.G. 1781), where the author indicates the various
portions of the audience:

> *This beauteous circle, friends to polish'd verse,*
> *Admires soft sentiments in language terse;*
> *While the stern Pit all ornament disdains,*
> *And loves deep pathos, and sublimer strains.*
> *The middle order, free from critick pride,*
> *Take genuine nature for their faithful guide...*
> *While those above them, honest souls! delight in*
> *Processions, bustle, trumpets, drums, and fighting.*

For a certain number of years after 1750, of course, there
was another band of spectators to consider, as indeed there
had been, with a few spasmodic interruptions[2] since Elizabethan days. It was still permitted in the fifties of the century
for certain privileged gentlemen who had the wherewithal
to pay for it to come both upon the stage and behind the
scenes. If we may judge from the notices in bills and in
newspaper advertisements, attempts had been and were
being made to limit this abuse at the performances of operas
and of pantomimes where the presence of lounging gallants
would be likely to cause confusion to scene shifters and to

---

[1] MacNally's *Fashionable Levities* (C.G. 1785), prologue by Chalmers.
[2] See vol. i, pp. 11–12.

machinists, but they were not completely banished till in the
year 1763 Garrick, with a mighty stroke of courage, refused
to accept the money they proffered at the stage door. Peculiarly enough, no riot succeeded this innovation. The actors
thereafter, at regular performances, had and retained a clear
stage for their efforts. Only at benefit performances did the
custom linger on, till, with the enlarged theatres, the seating
capacity became such that there was no longer any necessity
for tiers of seats to be arranged, not only at the sides of the
stage, but even behind the actors as they played their parts.
Unquestionably it was good that these dandies and amorous
gallants should be prohibited from interfering with the
business of the dramatic performances, but we must ever
bear in mind that this final banishment of the stage audience
was the final blow delivered to the intimate theatre of earlier
days. The platform had given way to the apron; the apron
itself had gradually grown less; we are well on our way
towards the period when the picture frame stage erected its
invisible barrier between audience and actor. Ridiculous as we
may now think the presence of Elizabethan and of eighteenth
century gentlemen upon the stage, their presence was in a
way symbolical of an older and not wholly evil tradition when
actors and audience shared an intimacy denied to theatre-
goers and performers of a later day[1].

In this audience of the late eighteenth century there are
several general points which deserve to be noted. One of its
most outstanding features was an excessive sensibility, which
allied itself to a prudery unknown before. Colman, in his
prologue to Kelly's *Clementina* (C.G. 1771) speaks of "*these,
our moral and religious days*," a sufficiently striking contrast
to Bullock's reference, in 1715, to the then "vicious Age[2]."
His remark is paralleled by Murphy's emphasis upon "this
grave, this moral, pious age[3]," and many other writers drew
attention to the more refined and "genteel" emotions of their
contemporaries, although it must always be borne in mind

---

[1] See Odell, G. C. D., *Shakespeare from Betterton to Irving*, i. 408–11.
[2] See vol. ii, p. 160.
[3] *Three Weeks after Marriage* (C.G. 1776), epilogue.

that this sensibility was progressive, and that it was even stronger in the early nineteenth century than it had been in the latter parts of the century preceding. No better example of this could be found than the anecdote and reflections thereon given by Reynolds about 1827. He is speaking of his comedy, *How to grow Rich*, acted in 1793:

> In the epilogue was the following couplet:—
>
> "What lading brother?—why, the *pad*, Miss Sophy—
> I've made a seizure, and see, here's the trophy."
>
> As he thus spoke, Lewis produced from under his coat, this singular appendage to the female dress. The whole audience receiving this broad discovery with good humour, the effect was electrical. But *now* [i.e. in 1827], with our present *correct* spectators!—does the actor live who dares risk not only the loss of his profession, but of his life, by a similar exhibition?[1]

Notwithstanding this, the sensibility of 1790 was "correct" enough in all conscience. Then, "if the comedies of Congreve and Vanbrugh" were "acted at all," they were "acted almost without their dialogue." Many original English plays and plays taken from the German were deeply objected to. Thus Mrs Cowley's *A School for Greybeards* (D.L. 1786), a perfectly innocuous comedy, was damned for its "indecency," and quite a number of plays, equally innocent, had a similar fate. Much reprobation, too, was cast upon the German drama. Thomson, the translator of *Adelaide of Wulfingen*, thinks that "Some conclusion might have been found, not so offensive to sensibility," and the editors of the *Biographia Dramatica* do not hesitate to style this play "unnatural and disgusting in the highest degree" and "of an immoral tendency[2]." Schink altered part of *The Stranger* (1798) because he felt that this change would be "more congenial to the heart of an English audience[3]," while the editors of the *Biographia Dramatica* return to the attack when they come to Thompson's rendering of *The Virgin of the Sun* (1799). Their words may be quoted:

---

[1] *The Life and Times of Frederick Reynolds*, ii. 163.
[2] ii. 5. [3] Address to the Public.

Most of the characters, which the German dramatists have held up to view as objects of pity or admiration, have violated some of the moral duties. The hero of this play is a man who first deserts his country, and then seduces the object of his love; and the heroine is a woman who has not merely violated the purity of her sex, but has done it in defiance of a solemn vow. Yet, in contempt of every principle of morality, these characters are made happy, and that without their having shown the most trifling marks of contrition![1]

A terrible state of affairs, truly; but one which to us, who regard the dramatic strength rather than the abstract moral righteousness of the work, does not assume quite the same aspect it did in 1800. It is unquestionable that this sensibility had a deleterious effect upon the drama of the time. It kept the playwrights within one narrow circle; it prevented them from dealing with events natural and striking; it led towards artificiality in characterisation and in *dénouement*.

Besides this sensibility, the audience of the late eighteenth century was characterised, as had been that of the preceding fifty years, by extreme political emotions. It must not be lost sight of, in any outline of the drama of this period, that the French Revolution broke out in 1789 and that national feeling was rising to a fever heat in 1800. Holcroft, a "Liberty Boy" connected with the William Blake-Tom Paine group, had to bring out many of his works anonymously, although his sentiments would seem very tame and innocuous today. A typical example of the foolish wave of enthusiasm for the established order is provided in this writer's *Love's Frailties* (C.G. 1794). A particular sentence in this play gave considerable offence. We might have expected it to be some flaring revolutionary saying, but in reality it was only Craig's answer to Muscadel:

I WAS BRED TO THE MOST USELESS, AND OFTEN THE MOST WORTH- LESS, OF ALL PROFESSIONS; THAT OF A GENTLEMAN[2].

Reading them now we can but be amazed at the stupidity of contemporary audiences, and must subscribe to Holcroft's own defence. The words, he says, are

[1] iii. 216.   [2] Holcroft himself picks out the words in capitals.

pointed out that the reader, who in the heat of political zeal has not quite lost his understanding, may examine what there is in them injurious to truth, or the good of mankind, and find it, if he can. In different times and under different feelings, it will appear astonishing that any one of these passages were suppressed, from any apprehension of political resentment: but such was the fact. That the one unwarily retained should excite the anger which was testified is still more astonishing. A sentence so true as to have been repeated in a thousand different modes: for all strong moral truths are subject to such repetition. A sentence that, under a variety of forms and phraseology, is proverbial in all nations. It ought however to be remembered, that the persons offended, though violent, were few. Their intention doubtless was good: the same cannot be affirmed of their intellect[1].

Political prejudice, however, antedated by many years the outbreak of the Revolution. Home's *The Fatal Discovery* (D.L. 1769) ran successfully for some nights when its author was unknown, but as soon as it was discovered that it had been written by Home, an adherent of the Bute party, it was opposed and dismissed[2]. In a similar way, as we have seen[3], Kelly's *A Word to the Wise* (D.L. 1770) met with a bad reception because of the supposed political beliefs of its creator, so that Kelly was forced to bring forward his *Clementina* (C.G. 1771) anonymously. Andrews' *The Reparation* (D.L. 1784) caused a disturbance the first night because of a presumed political reference[4]; and it was only one of a large number which aroused similar enthusiasm, favourable and adverse. What we note most in these late eighteenth century dramas is the prevalent patriotic note, which takes form now as opposition to the French writers, now as martial ardour. The prologue to Jones' *The Earl of Essex* (C.G. 1753) emphasises the fact that it is a British audience to whom the dramatist is making his appeal. Murphy saw fit to append to *The Orphan of China* (D.L. 1759) a patriotic epistle to Voltaire, commenting unfavourably on that author's anti-English strictures, while Boaden felt that he could not permit his *Fontainville Forest* (C.G. 1794) to go before the public without an apology for having taken the theme from France

---

[1] Advertisement. [2] *Biographia Dramatica*, ii. 227.
[3] *Supra*, pp. 7–8. [4] *Biographia Dramatica*, iii. 201.

and without extolling in the epilogue the greatness of Shakespeare. The references to England's material glory outnumber
even these. Many are the occasional pieces, acted and unacted,
such as Pilon's *The Siege of Gibraltar* (C.G. 1780), A. L. G.'s
Courage Rewarded (1798) and the anonymous *The Battle of
the Nile* (1799), which show by their titles their inherent
purpose, and as many others, such as S. J. Arnold's *Auld Robin
Gray* (H.² 1794), which exist mainly for their patriotic sentiment.

Peculiarly enough, not many plays seem to have suffered,
because of political allusion, at the hands of the censor. We
learn from Reynolds that some drama entitled *The Bastille*,
then under rehearsal at C.G., was prohibited[1]; but the
few dramas stopped by the Lord Chamberlain's command
would seem to have been mainly satirical in the personal way.
In this period personal satire seems to have been relished by
the audience. Foote's many farces and comedies were nearly
all based on actual incidents and introduced living figures
on the stage, but the only one which met with opposition was
A Trip to Calais (H.² 1776), to secure the suppression of
which special pressure was brought to bear on the authori-
ties[2]. Macklin's *The Man of the World* (C.G. 1781) met with
similar opposition at first, as did Reed's *The Register Office*
(D.L. 1761). For some reason Lady Wallace's miserable
extravaganza *The Whim* (1795) was denied a licence—one
of the few examples of the powers of the censorship which,
on artistic grounds, can be heartily defended. In view of the
many occurrences of the Lord Chamberlain's veto both in
the fifty years which preceded and in the fifty years which
followed this period, the lack of an active censorship from
1750 to 1800 is almost inexplicable.

Before parting finally with the audience of this age, one
special feature, of considerable influence upon the drama
of the time, deserves to be noted. Many writers have left
on record the mania for private theatricals which stirred

---

[1] *Op. cit.* ii. 54
[2] F. Fowell and F. Palmer's *Censorship in England*, pp. 152–3; see also
pp. 150–1 and 155.

many hearts during those years. Reynolds puts it succinctly enough:

On my return from Switzerland, I found the whole town infected with another mania,—Private Theatricals. Drury Lane, and Covent Garden, were almost forgotten in the performances at Richmond House; and the Earl of Derby, Lord Henry Fitzgerald, Mrs. Hobart, and Mrs. Damer, in the "*Way to Keep Him,*" and "*False Appearances,*" were considered, by crowded, and fashionable audiences, equal, if not superior, to Kemble, Lewis, Mrs. Siddons, and the present Countess of Derby....

The Duke and Duchess of Marlborough, imitating and emulating the example of the Duke of Richmond, erected a splendid theatre at Blenheim, with the intention of there producing a theatrical representation, which should totally eclipse all previous attempts[1].

Blenheim, indeed, became one of the most favoured resorts of the aristocracy. The prologue spoken at the opening of the playhouse there has been preserved in *Poems by the late George-Monck Berkeley* (1797)[2], who recited his own verses to a brilliant audience. Other nobles vied with the Duke of Marlborough in giving shows of increasing brilliance and splendour. Richmond House was a favourite centre about 1787. Lady Craven, Margravine of Anspach, provided gorgeous festivals at Brandenburgh House from 1780 to the close of the century[3]. In the late eighties the Earl of Barrymore was an indefatigable enthusiast. He had theatres at Wargrave, Saville Row and Richmond. At Wynnstay Sir W. Williams Wynne produced a series of comedies and tragedies during Christmas and New Year from 1773 on to

[1] *Op. cit.* ii. 1–2; for a full account of a performance of *False Delicacy* at this theatre see also pp. 3–9. Valuable information concerning these private playhouses has been preserved by Dr Burney in a volume of newspaper cuttings, printed and manuscript playbills and invitation cards, now in the British Museum (939. i. 9). From this some of the details given above are taken. See also Bridge, Joseph, *Private Theatres in England* (*Notes and Queries*, xii. 112–3, Feb. 10, 1923) and R. L. C. on the same subject (*id.* xi. 457, Dec. 1922).

[2] It was also printed in *The World*, Nov. 12, 1787.

[3] *The Sleep-Walker* was given at Newberry in 1778, where also appeared for the first time *The Miniature Picture* (later, according to the authoress, "mis-*represented on the Stage*, at Drury Lane"). A prologue spoken to that play, written by Mr Jekyll, is printed in *The Gentleman's Magazine*, Dec. 12, 1780.

1790. Besides these, fully a dozen other centres are known to us; Audley End, Dover under William Fector[1], Dunkeld House, Eaton Hall, Gordon Castle, Grimsthorpe (under the Duke and Duchess of Ancaster), Guildford, Hall Place (under the Hon. Mrs Hobart)[2], Hinchingbrook (under the Earl of Sandwich), Kensington (under a Mr Craufurd), Privy Garden (under the Hon. Mrs Robinson), Wimpole, Seaton Delaval (under Lord Delaval), Bruce Castle (under Mr Townsend), and Norwich (under Mr Plumptree). The fashion was carried even to India where at Madras Lady Campbell organised her private theatre for the amusement of the English residents[3]. The new fashion naturally met with considerable ridicule. The aping by amateurs of the graces of professional actors, the aristocratic audiences and the servility of the newspapers, which gave special columns to this latest freak of fashion under the headings "Theatrical of Ton" or "Ton Theatrical"—all came under the lash of the satirists. In earlier times dramatists, such as Murphy in *The Apprentice* (D.L. 1756), had satirised the stage-struck youth; but from the eighties and nineties of the century when the fashion was at its height date the many references to this aristocratic craze. Thus Morris introduces ridicule of the new diversion in *False Colours* (H.[1] 1793)[4], and Sicklemore continues Murphy's travesty of amateur de-clamations in *The Dream* (Brighton, 1796). As an indication of the forms which these performances assumed reference might be made also to James Powell's otherwise uninteresting farce, *Private Theatricals* (1787). It was inevitable that this fashion should have a deleterious effect upon the public stage; "*ton*" ruled sufficiently in those days without this needless intensification of its effects in the realm of acting.

[1] Prologues spoken at his theatre are printed in the *Morning Chronicle*, Dec. 6, 1785, March 9, 1787, and *The World*, April 28, 1788, Nov. 25, 1788, and Feb. 13, 1789.

[2] See an epilogue written by M. P. Andrews in *The World*, Nov. 10, 1783.

[3] In addition to these there is to be noted the performances of French plays in the Lower Rooms at Bath. *Le Poulet* was given on Jan. 17, 1788, *Le Veuf* on Feb. 17 of the same year.

[4] I. i.

The private theatricals vogue is but another indication of a social atmosphere wide-spread in the age[1].

It is evident from this account of the late eighteenth century audiences that the main features of the auditorium are less distinct than they had been in previous times. This is precisely what might have been expected when we consider that the age itself was between two ideals, that of Augustanism and that of Romance. In large outline we see an audience less virile than before, more decorous outwardly and believing in morality and sensibility, full of patriotic sentiment and eager to welcome flamboyant expressions of that patriotism in the dramas put upon the stage. No longer had the dramatists and the performers to fight against uproarious tumult, unless on those occasions when riot was caused by some special innovation, but they had to combat now or to acquiesce in the prevalent indifference of the spectators. The dulness of the sentimental comedy reflects the latter method of escape; the weird and wonderful melodrama reflects the former.

III. *The Theatre*

Of fundamental importance there is comparatively little to chronicle concerning the late eighteenth century theatre, in so far as no epoch-making alteration was made in the general structure of the playhouses. Of gradual development, on the other hand, and slow alteration there was in this period a considerable amount, so that many minor innovations in scenery, in lighting and in costume have to be noted.

Possibly the most outstanding theatrical event in these fifty years was the enlarging of the patent houses. Drury Lane

[1] The fashion for private theatres almost certainly came from France. In the eighteenth century many "scènes princières" sprang into existence, notably those of Madame de Pompadour, of the court of Sceaux, of Marie Antoinette and of the Duc d'Orléans. On this subject see Adolphe Jullien, *Histoire du Théâtre de Madame de Pompadour dit Théâtre des petits cabinets* (Paris, 1874) and Eugène Lintilhac, *Histoire Générale du Théâtre en France* (vol. iv. *La Comédie: Dix-huitième Siècle*, Paris, 1909). The fashion passed over to Ireland also; an account of several playhouses there will be found in Richard Power's *The Private Theatre of Kilkenny, with Introductory Observations on other Private Theatres in Ireland, before it was opened* (1825).

in the year 1762 was remodelled so as to hold, in eighteenth century parlance, 337 guineas instead of only 220[1]. It
was again refashioned in 1780[2], and was entirely rebuilt in
1792/3, when it was calculated to hold 3611 persons, an audience of over £800[3]. Covent Garden was similarly altered
in 1782[4] and rebuilt in 1792[5], the rebuilding being designed
mainly to accommodate larger numbers of spectators. Provided sufficient audiences were gathered together, this must
have been well to the advantage of the management, but it had
grievous results upon acting and upon the type of performances given in the theatre. As the lighting was not as good
as it became after the introduction of gas and of electricity,
it was difficult for the audience in the furthest parts of the
house to have a clear view of the action upon the stage; and
as the acoustics were not all that could be desired, the hearing
of certain scenes was rendered more than difficult. The result
was, as indicated, twofold. The actors, in the first place, felt
the need for adapting themselves to the altered conditions,
and their performances became louder and more banal. The
finer lights and shades were lost; the delicacy of acting which
comes only from a *théâtre intime* disappeared because of the
necessity imposed upon the players to make their words
carry to the utmost galleries. In the second place, the
managers found that only the broadest effects could prove
successful, and accordingly intensified that tendency towards
spectacle in serious drama and towards farcical situation in
the more risible types which had been growing in power
ever since D'Avenant first introduced his scenes upon the
stage. "Damme," says Fustian in the younger Colman's
New Hay at the Old Market (H.[2] 1795), "I'll go home, turn
my play into a pageant, put a triumphal procession at the
end on't, and bring it out at one of the Winter Theatres,"
and no doubt many dramatists acted according to his recipe.
The song which concludes Colman's "occasional drama"
sums up well enough the general tendencies:

---

[1] Colman's *Memoirs*, i. 191. [2] *Walker's Hibernian Magazine*, Oct. 1780.
[3] See *The Annual Register* for 1794. [4] *Walker's Hib. Mag.*, Oct. 1782.
[5] Gilliland's *Dramatic Mirror*, i. 135-7.

Since the preference, we know,
Is for pageantry and shew,
'Twere a pity the publick to balk—
And when people appear
Quite unable to hear,
'Tis undoubtedly needless to talk.
Let your Shakespeares and Jonsons go hang, go hang!
Let your Otways and Drydens go drown!
Give us but Elephants, and white Bulls enough,
And we'll take in all the town.

Brave boys!

Or if, tardily, the sound
Travels all the house around,
'Twixt the action and words there's a breach:
And it seems as if Macbeth,
Half a minute after death,
On his back, made his last dying speech,
Let your Shakespeares, &c.

As a companion picture to this of the late eighteenth century, we might take Garrick's prologue, spoken at the opening of Drury Lane on Sept. 5, 1750:

Sacred to SHAKESPEARE, was this spot design'd
To pierce the heart, and humanize the mind.
But if an empty house, the actor's curse,
Shews us our *Lears*, and *Hamlets*, lose their force;
Unwilling, we must change the nobler scene,
And, in our turn, present you *Harlequin*;
Quit poets, and set carpenters to work,
Shew gaudy scenes, or mount the vaulting *Turk*.
For, tho' we actors, one and all, agree
Boldly to struggle for our——vanity;
If want comes on, importance must retreat;
Our first, great, ruling passion, is——to eat[1].

These are no exaggerations. We know how from all sides the pageantry and show was elaborated. A typical example is provided in the 1762 acting text of Shakespeare's *Henry VIII* as given at Drury Lane, where a full list is printed of the various characters introduced into the procession at act IV.

---

[1] This prologue is given in *The Gentleman's Magazine*, Sept. 1750, XX. 422.

Henry V was similarly diversified at Covent Garden in 1767 with a "Procession from the *Abbey* at the *Coronation*, with the Representation of *Westminster Hall*, and the *Ceremony of the Champion*," a ceremony which, apparently, also did duty for *King John*, while *Romeo and Juliet* was given a funeral procession at the end and a minuet danced by Juliet in act I[1]. Many plays won their success through devices of this kind. Perhaps the account provided by the *Biographia Dramatica* of Home's *Agis* (D.L. 1758) may serve for many another drama of the time:

It was performed with tolerable success, being strongly supported, not only by a party zeal in the author's favour, but also by the additional advantages of very fine acting, and two pompous and solemn musical processions[2].

All kinds of novelties were attempted. Animal performers seem to have been introduced freely. Murphy indulges in a satiric note on Lun's endeavours, announcing in his *Gray's-Inn Journal* a new pantomime at Covent Garden in which

the principal parts...will be performed by a wonderful *Armadillo* from *Brasil*, a *Serpent* from the river *Oronoque*, the famous *Lanthorn-Fly* from *Peru*, a *Mermaid* from the *Ladrones Islands*, a surprising *Camel*, a *Rhinoceras*, and many horrible animals, *being their first appearance on the English stage*[3].

Dancing, song, farcical harlequinade continued to amuse the audiences, and Murphy again provides us with a glimpse into the theatrical fare of the time when he mentions that "*Maddox*, the wire-dancer, continues to give great satisfaction to the *Goths* and *Vandals* who frequent" Covent Garden[4], and that Rowe's *Jane Shore*, as given at the same theatre, "concluded with the surprizing phænomenon of rope-dancing[5]." Everywhere, indeed, we find references to this tendency.

The prologue to Charlotte Smith's *What is She?* (C.G. 1799) traces the development of the stage from noise and

---

[1] See Odell, *op. cit.* i. 425–8.   [2] ii. 9.

[3] *Gray's-Inn Journal*, No. xiv. Sat. Jan. 20, 1752; see also No. v. Sat. Nov. 18, 1752.

[4] *Id.* No. vii. Sat. Dec. 2, 1752.   [5] *Id.* No. v. Nov. 18, 1752.

stage carpentry through good taste in Otway to decay
in stage carpentry again. Garrick is quite frank about
the matter. Concerning his *Cymon* (D.L. 1767) he informs
us:

> As for the Plot, Wit, Humour, Language—I
> Beg you such Trifles kindly to pass by;
> The most essential Part, which something means,
> As Dresses, Dances, Sinkings, Flyings, Scenes,—
> They'll make you stare[1].

"If it was not for us and the taylors," with justice declares
the carpenter in the elder Colman's *An Occasional Prelude*
(C.G. 1772), "you might shut up the theatre." Many plays,
such as Pearce's *Hartford-Bridge* (C.G. 1792), derived their
"Popularity from the decorative Aid, and animating Powers
of the Theatre[2]."

The result of all this upon the drama of the period will be
traced in the succeeding chapters. At present our object
must be to display its influence on the actual settings in the
theatre. We note, first of all, an increasing activity in the
preparation of new scenes. Instead of the stock scenery of
former times, fresh landscapes and architectural designs
were prepared to the order of the managers. Harris declared
in his *Observations on the Statement of Differences* (1800) that
since 1774 he had spent as much as £40,000 on scenery alone,
and his bill can hardly have been less than that of Drury
Lane's director. Of the actual painters who were engaged in
the theatres we know more than we do of the somewhat
misty figures of by-gone years. At Covent Garden Nicholas
Thomas Dall, a Dane, was working between 1760 and 1777.
He was succeeded by one Inigo Richards, who in his turn
gave way to William Capon, who prepared sets of entirely
new scenes about the year 1794[3]. At Drury Lane Hayman

---

[1] Prologue.

[2] Dedication to the manager, Harris.

[3] Odell, *op. cit.* ii. 86–90; W. J. Lawrence, *The Pioneers of Modern English Stage Mounting: William Capon* (*The Magazine of Art*, June 1895). Capon painted the scenery for the Royalty Theatre in 1787; rebuilt the King's Theatre in the Haymarket, 1789, and worked at Ranelagh Gardens, the Royal Circus and elsewhere.

and French worked as the chief painters, until in 1771 Garrick, at a dinner party given by the fencing master Angelo, discovered De Loutherbourg, an Alsatian who had already won fame in Paris[1]. Realising his genius, the actor-manager at once engaged him, and he continued working at the theatre until, in the year 1781, he left to open the Eido-phusikon, a scenic entertainment, at the Patagonian Theatre and at Panton Square. His work included designs for *A Christmas Tale* (D.L. 1773), *The Maid of the Oaks* (D.L. 1774)[2], *The Sultan* (D.L. 1775) and *Selima and Azor* (D.L. 1776). Observations gathered in a tour through parts of England were made use of in a spectacular pantomime, *The Wonders of Derbyshire* (D.L. 1779). Of several other scenic artists we have record besides these. Cipriani, possibly the "Italian master" who decorated *Cymon* (D.L. 1767)[3], aided Dall and Richards with the scenery for the elder Colman's *The Fairy Prince* (C.G. 1771)[4], and Kemble's *Lodoiska* (D.L. 1794) provides us with the names of Greenwood[5], who designed acts I and III, and Malton, with his assistants Lupino and Demaria, who were responsible for act II. This play also gives the first record of which I am aware of the names of costume designers; "The *Dresses* and *Decorations*," we are informed, "are designed and executed by Mr. JOHN-STONE, and Miss RHEIN." A melodrama such as this, of course, must have depended to a great extent on the effects secured by these costume designers and these scene painters, assisted by the efforts of "Mr. CABANEL," who "invented" the machinery. A whole page of stage direction in act III may serve as a typical example of what was served up regularly to the spectators:

---

[1] He was born in 1740. See W. J. Lawrence, *The Pioneers of Modern English Stage Mounting: De Loutherbourg* (*The Magazine of Art*, March 1895).

[2] The scenes for which are said to have cost £1500; see *The London Magazine* for that year.

[3] Victor, *op. cit.* iii. 99; although if this was so he must have been engaged at both theatres.

[4] All three are mentioned in the printed text.

[5] Greenwood's son, at the age of 19, provided scenes for the younger Colman's *Blue Beard* (D.L. 1798).

Shouts, Drums, Trumpets, and Cannon.
AN ENGAGEMENT COMMENCES BETWEEN THE
POLANDERS and the TARTARS;
The Tartars having stormed the Castle, which they fire in various
places, the battlements and towers fall in the midst of loud
explosions.
LUPAUSKI and LODOISKA
Are discover'd in a blazing tower;
FLORESKI *rushes through the flames, and rescues them.*
During this action
LOVINSKI and KERA KHAN
meet hand to hand, and, after a desperate conflict, the
Baron is killed.
The Tartars are victorious—Loud shouts of victory.

This must have taxed sufficiently the abilities of Messrs
Greenwood, Malton, Cabanel and Johnstone and of Miss
Rhein. No doubt Sanders, the earlier machinist at Drury
Lane, as well as Messink, machinist at the Theatre Royal,
Dublin, whose inventions for *The Elopement* were used in the
London theatres[1], attempted effects almost as grandiose.

The actual scenes utilised in these playhouses seem to
have been of various kinds. There were, of course, the
relics of the "Augustan" settings of Palace, Garden, Prison
and Temple[2], and these no doubt were used repeatedly for
plays of a non-spectacular class. That such were employed
even for some early pseudo-romantic dramas we learn from
a satirical notice of the first performance of Home's *The Fatal
Discovery* (D.L. 1769), given by the editors of the *Biographia
Dramatica*:

On the stage, we saw the youthful Ronan [acted by Barry]
bounding with all the vigour and alacrity that age, gout, and
rheumatism, usually inspire. The heroes of this truly Erse
performance
—*who never yet had being,*
Or, being, wore no breeches,

were invested in gold and purple, while a Grecian palace was
allotted to the monarch of a rock[3].

---

[1] Victor, *op. cit.* iii. 109.
[2] Which all appear in Arne's *Artaxerxes* (C.G. 1762). Note also the
"Wood" in Waldron's MS. stage directions to *The Devil to Pay* (1748
edn.; B.M. 643. g. 7).   [3] ii. 227.

These stock pieces of scenery, as well as more spectacular effects such as the creations of Servandoni[1], were freely made use of in the playhouses; but alongside of them other fresh scenes were being painted, and those fresh scenes showed an entirely new tendency. They are both romantic and realistic, striking well away from the conventional neo-classicism of former years. "A wild romantic Scene amidst overhanging Rocks" appears in II. i. of Murphy's *The Grecian Daughter* (D.L. 1772), and it may be paralleled by a whole group of settings which display either the dark grandeur of rugged mountains, or, more commonly, the gloomier mysteries of a ruined Gothic castle[2]. This tendency towards romance met with the realistic movement. The realistic movement itself assumes two forms, the one leading towards the attempt to secure complete illusion in the theatre, the other drawing manager and painter towards antiquarian efforts. Thus we find that De Loutherbourg endeavours to reproduce in *The Wonders of Derbyshire* (D.L. 1779)[3] actual scenes sketched by him in that county, while Pearce in the dedication to *Hartford-Bridge* (C.G. 1792) declares that "*For some of the Scenery the Writer must avow his Obligations, to the friendly Assistance of Mr.* WIGSTEAD; *who very politely visited the Place of Action, and collected every Locality that could embellish the Subject.*" This is the movement which leads later managers to give the audience a bird's-eye picture of Dover Cliff when they attempt a production of *King Lear*. It was but a step from this to the realism of antiquarian research. Boaden, in his *Life of Kemble*[4], presents us with a list of new settings provided by Capon for Covent Garden in 1794. These included "A chapel of the pointed architecture, which occupied the whole stage," as well as six chamber wings in the same style imitated from actual architecture; a view of New Palace Yard, Westminster, as it was in 1793; a view of

---

[1] Which Victor (iii. 165) says were stored in the theatre since 1739, to be brought forward for *The Rape of Proserpine* at Covent Garden in 1769.

[2] Such as actually appears in Andrews' *The Mysteries of the Castle* (C.G. 1795), I. iii.

[3] *Supra*, p. 27. Views of London were similarly shown in *Pigmy Revels* (D.L. 1772). [4] ii. 101.

the ancient palace of Westminster, as it was about three
centuries previously, studied from records of that building;
six wings showing a series of picturesque Elizabethan houses;
and a restoration of the Tower of London for Shakespeare's
Richard III[1]. Regarding a production of this play at Drury
Lane in 1814, a writer in *The Morning Chronicle* for Feb. 16,
1814, draws attention to the importance of Capon's original
scenes, which had been destroyed in the fire of 1809:

> The whole praise ought to be given to Mr. Capon alone, the
> view of the Tower having been originally composed and painted
> by him...whilst that exhibited at Drury Lane was copied in all
> its general forms from Mr. Capon's scene, but with injudicious
> alterations in detail. In the Drury Lane scene, there was no
> research; the research was Mr. Capon's, who, whilst preparing
> the original, went several times to the Tower for the purpose of
> studying the remaining buildings and fragments so as to form a
> correct idea of the ancient state of that fortress, in order that
> he might make the view to correspond as nearly as possible with
> the era of the play.

A new orientation, an orientation partly false and partly true,
had been given to the manager and to the scene designer.

Nor were these romantic and realistically antiquarian
effects the only innovations in regard to scenery of which the
late eighteenth century stage could boast. There was at least
a tentative movement during these years which led ultimately
to the establishment of the box-set, a form of *mise en scène*
which had been dreamed of by some scenic revolutionaries in
earlier decades but which obviously could not have come into
being until a new kind of drama had been born. This box-set
aided in the endeavours of the painters to secure realism.
Instead of the series of three side wings arranged laterally to
give the semblance of a room[2], instead of the antiquated convention by which characters in a drama could make their exits
and their entrances, ghost-wise, through walls intended to be

---

[1] Two of Capon's designs, now preserved in the Shakespeare Memorial
Library at Stratford, are reproduced by W. J. Lawrence in *The Magazine
of Art* (June 1895).

[2] Which, of course, still persisted even when the "box-set" was established towards the end of the century. On this subject see an article on
The Box Set by W. J. Lawrence (*The Stage*, 13 Aug. 1925).

solid, a back-scene and two side-scenes placed transversely across the stage provided as close an approximation to reality as could be obtained. These scenes were now provided with practicable doors. "*An elegant Apartment leading to Lady* SARAH's *Dressing-Room—the Door in the Flat,*" reads a stage direction in Reynolds' *The Rage* (C.G. 1794)[1]. Similar indications are provided in other plays. Andrews has "*A Room in* FRACTIOSO's *House—Large door in back Scene*" as well as "*An old room...two doors exactly alike in the back scene*[2]." "*An old Gothic Chamber, with Doors at each Wing— in the Flat another Door*" appears in Reynolds' *The Will* (D.L. 1797)[3], and Mrs Grace in Macnally's *Fashionable Levities* (C.G. 1785) "*goes to a door in the back scene*[4]." Murphy's *The Grecian Daughter* (D.L. 1772) provides a variation of this in calling for "*a cell in the back scene,*" the setting itself displaying "*the Inside of the Cavern*[5]." Already actors and actresses were moving away from the invariable employment of the proscenium doors[6] which were themselves to disappear in the following half-century.

If, however, new movements were on foot, many of the older conventions persisted almost untouched. Still the actors came down stage after their entries to speak to the audience on the attenuated apron. Zamti and Mandane, in Murphy's *The Orphan of China* (D.L. 1759), "*are brought forward on a couch*[7]," in the same author's *Zenobia* (D.L. 1768) several characters, in good old style, "*come forward*[8]," while in Bridges' *The Dutch-Man* (H.[2] 1775) Miss Sophy, after being "*discovered,*" "*rises, and advances to the Front of the Stage*" (I. i.). So, too, the old devices for changing scenes continued. The curtain certainly was coming more into use but with an irritating tardiness. Writing of the period about

[1] II. ii.
[2] *The Mysteries of the Castle* (C.G. 1795), I. ii. and II. i.
[3] IV. (ii.).   [4] I. i.
[5] II. (iii.).
[6] These, of course, were still used. Thus in Simpson's *The Patriot* (1785) we find a stage direction bidding Leotychides to enter "*at one Door, and* ANEXANDER *at the other*" (v. vi.). See also Odell, *op. cit.* i. 397–8.
[7] v. i.   [8] v. i.

1759 Dramaticus in *The Gentleman's Magazine* for May 1789[1] expresses a wish

that every dramatic author would so contrive the *denouement*...
as not to cover the stage with dead bodies, except in the *finale*,
or last scene of his play; whereby the specious representation
will be supported, and the curtain may drop, to leave us in the
full enjoyment of the prosimilitude.

Obviously, this is a precise implication that the curtain after
being raised when the prologue was spoken did not fall
during the performance of the play. On the other hand, the
drop scene was introduced in the early fifties of the century,
and, with the introduction of this drop scene, acts and even
scenes came to be closed more efficiently than before and the
value of the curtain was borne in upon the dramatists. Bate's
adaptation of Massinger as *The Magic Picture* (C.G. 1783)
provides at least three indications of its use. In I. i. "*The
Curtain rising, discovers* HILLARIO"; the second scene of that
act is heralded by "*The Scene rising to soft music, discovers*
HONORIA[2]"; while in II. iii. "*The Curtain rising, discovers*
LADISLAVS." Still, however, there are plentiful references to
the "closing" and the "opening" of scenes, in the time-
honoured Restoration style. In Murphy's *Zenobia* (D.L.
1768) Pharasmanes "*ascends his throne, and the back scene
closes*[3]"; and later "*The back scene draws, and discovers the
King's pavillion, with an altar, and fire blazing on it*[4]."
Simpson's *The Patriot* (1785) has "*Scene opens and discovers
the* Persian *Camp*[5]" while the anonymous *The Peruvian*
(C.G. 1786) provides us with the stage direction "SCENE
opens, and discovers an Apartment beautifully decorated[6]."
Even in the spectacular *Blue Beard* (D.L. 1798) of the younger
Colman an act ends with "*Scene closes*[7]," and in the same
decade, the last of the eighteenth century, the anonymous
author of *The Count de Villeroi* (1794) uses the same formula

[1] Quoted in Odell, *op. cit.* i. 400–1.
[2] It is probable here that we have to do with a drop scene revealed by
the raising of the front curtain at the beginning of the act.
[3] III. i.   [4] v. i.   [5] I. i.
[6] II. (ii.).   [7] I. iii.

that had been used by Dryden and Orrery—"SCENE...
opens and discovers Villeneuve[1]."

These scene-openings were also utilised for the two special
purposes for which they had been utilised in earlier times.
Dead bodies frequently were revealed by their means. This
device appears in v. i. of Murphy's *The Orphan of China*
(D.L. 1759) and may be paralleled by stage directions in
many other pseudo-classic tragedies. So, too, the scenes
could close and leave certain characters on the stage, mysteri-
ously conveyed to another locality. In Bate's *The Magic
Picture* (C.G. 1783) the "*Scene closes on* UBALDO *and*
RICARDO," permitting Hillario to remain and go out later in
an ordinary way. A similar scene occurs in Boaden's *Fontainville Forest* (C.G. 1794) where "*The phantom...glides
across the dark part of the Chamber, Adeline shrieks, and falls
back. The Scene closes upon her*[2]." The same convention
appears in I. ii. of Colman's *King Lear* (C.G. 1768) where
the "Scene opens" to discover the King while Gloucester
remains on the stage, as well as in the Bell edition of *Romeo
and Juliet*[3].

It must be quite clear that such conventions as those
described above must have been considerably modified and
finally destroyed completely by the introduction of the box-
set. Still more were they affected by the second special
feature of eighteenth century staging noted above. This was
the built-up set. Flat scenes, with of course a few practicable
properties, were all that had been known to this date. Now
was employed the more ornate device whereby solid or
seemingly solid hills and buildings were raised upon the
stage. It is said that Garrick brought over from Paris
a theatrical setting, wherein a palace was erected of
"painted stones...put together, with handles at the back."
A fire breaks out, and the stones are "drawn away from the
bottom" so that the whole comes down in ruins. De Loutherbourg proved the greatest genius of his time in the con-
triving of these effects, which, it will be observed, were

---

[1] II. iii.   [2] III. (iv.).
[3] See Odell, *op. cit.* i. 399–400.

eminently suited for the elaboration of those romantic settings beloved by a new school of dramatists.

Gradually, with these fresh scenic developments the theatre was moving towards present-day conditions. During this period we may notice two tendencies, the one moving counter to the other. Romantic and rich scenery helped to secure the success of many of the melodramas of the age, and the latest inventions in machinery were employed to ravish the spectators' gaze by swift changes and transformation scenes. Thus many of the romantic works produced during the half century abound in swiftly altering settings. Morton's *Columbus* (C.G. 1792), for example, presents us with a scene of only six lines[1], and, while this is almost unique, it is paralleled by countless scenes in other plays which extend to not more than twenty or thirty lines. On the other hand, even with the use of the drop-scene, managers were becoming suspicious of the multiplication of diverse settings, and we can trace the tendency, already visible in the Restoration period, towards the crystallisation of effects. Many of the plays of the time have but two or three separate settings, obviously more simple in manipulation than the crowded acts of the spectacular pieces. Moreover, while the managers, in order to gain custom, were prepared to expend large sums on the designing of new scenes, they still kept by them the stock flats and wings which had done duty in comedy or in tragedy during preceding years, and they were as ready to engage dramatists to write up plays for particular scenery as had been the King's Men in 1664[2]. Reynolds tells us in his *Life*[3] that the Covent Garden management in the year 1790 had put on rehearsal a topical piece called *The Bastille*. This was banned by the Lord Chamberlain, whereupon Reynolds was requested to prepare a drama which might allow the theatre to display the scenery painted for the prohibited play. *The Crusade* (C.G. 1790) was the result. In noting the development of more realistic and antiquarian settings, also, we must remember that frequently, as in the

[1] I. ii.   [2] See vol. i. p. 36.
[3] ii. 54.

past, sidewings and even back scenes were employed which hardly harmonised with the rest of the representation. Among the Burney newspaper cuttings[1] is a paragraph commenting on a Kemble production of *Coriolanus*. After praising the acting, the critic continues,

There were some *Anachronisms* of the scenery, however, which did what they could to break the illusion. A pretty exact representation of *Hanover-square*, and some very neat *Bond-street* shops appeared two, or three times, as parts of *Rome*....The dress of CORIOLANUS was entirely in the *costume* even to his sword; but those of his guards had served the heroes of other times and nations.

What happened at this playhouse no doubt happened at many. Still the theatre lies between the ancient and the modern.

It is the same with regard to costume. In his infancy Frederick Reynolds went to see Barry act in *Othello* when

the noble, the victorious warrior was personated by this great actor in a full suit of gold laced scarlet, a small cocked hat, knee breeches, and silk stockings conspicuously displaying a pair of gouty legs.

Still, as extant prints show, this was not Barry's only costume for the part, for Othello, like Bajazet and other Eastern heroes[2], was usually habited in a conventional dress of which the peculiar furred dressing-gown-like over-coat, broad sash, curved sword and plumed headgear were the most noticeable parts. Comparing prints with the accounts of contemporaries we must assume that there was a considerable clash during the early part of this period between the conventional tragic costumes and the fashions of the day. Thus Garrick still continued to use the tye-wig even in Shakespearian dramas; he himself draws attention to this in his pretendedly burlesque pamphlet, *An Essay on Acting: In which will be consider'd the Mimical Behaviour of a certain Fashionable*

[1] B.M. 936, g. vol. ii. I have failed to trace the particular paper of which this is an excerpt.

[2] See "M.̲ Barry in the Character of Othello" (published by I. Wenman, Feb. 1, 1777) and "M.̲ and M.̲̲ Barry in the Characters of Bajazet and Selima" (Bell's *British Theatre*, June 24, 1776).

Faulty Actor (1744). There the author is made to deliver himself as follows:

I must likewise observe, that in *Shakespear's* Time, the Actors wore their own Hair, and now, from the present Fashion of wearing Wigs, some Speeches are become absurd, such, for Instance, is this of *Macbeth*, *Never shake thy Goary Locks at me*; when at the same Time the Ghost is seen in a *Tye Wig*.

If, however, actors yet continued to habit the heroes of past time either in these fashionable garments or in conventional costumes, a new movement was on foot to revolutionise stage dressing as the settings had been revolutionised. Apparently the first performer who seriously thought of historical accuracy was the old Macklin who, in 1773, dared to bring *Macbeth* forward with Scots habits, but his effort was immediately rivalled by Garrick. Three years later, when he was about to retire from the stage, the latter performed in *Lear* and for the production ordered a new set of costumes, so that, as *The London Chronicle* declared[1], "the play received considerable improvement...from the characters being judiciously habited in old English dresses." Even before this, it is said, Garrick had consulted the painters Sir Joshua Reynolds and West so that he might the better be able to collaborate with the scenic artist De Loutherbourg in the improvement of settings[2]. From this date a gradual change is to be traced in the habiliments of the male performers. At first, no doubt, as in Kemble's *Coriolanus*, there existed a strange inconsistency in the dresses worn. Boaden informs us that for Delap's *The Captives* (D.L. 1786) "the parsimony of that day would consent" to provide only one Scottish dress (worn by Kemble)[3]. Even these stray historical garments, were they shown today, might seem to our eyes ridiculous enough; but at the same time an attempt was being made to secure that antiquarian realism which was aimed at by Capon and his followers. The old traditions still persisted

[1] May 21–3, 1776; quoted Odell, *op. cit.* i. 454.
[2] See *The Library of Fine Arts*, May 1831. Still earlier we find that *Richard III*, as acted at Drury Lane on Thursday, Sept. 20, 1764, was billed with dresses "in the Habits of the Times."
[3] *Memoirs of Mrs. Siddons* (1827), ii. 204–5.

but the way was being prepared for the actor-managers of the nineteenth century.

For some reason or other (perhaps because of a desire to avoid whatsoever might be unfashionable) the actresses lagged behind the actors. Glancing at the theatrical prints of the time we realise at once that the male costumes approximate far more closely to historical accuracy than do the female. When Macklin introduced his Scots habits for Macbeth in 1773, "Lady Macbeth's modern robes by no means accorded with the habits of the other personages[1]," and Mrs Bellamy in her *Apology* (1785) describes with some verve the dresses worn by her and her stage-sisters about the year 1750:

The Empresses and Queens were confined to black velvet, except on extraordinary occasions, when they put on an embroidered or tissue petticoat. The young ladies generally appeared in a *cast* gown of some person of quality[2].

At Dublin a "superb suit of cloaths formerly made for the Princess of Wales to be worn by her on the birthday" was purchased for the actress by the manager. This she was to wear in the character of Cleopatra, but unfortunately the dress was purloined by another actress who used it for the part of Octavia![3] The first woman, indeed, who would seem to have had a sense of historical propriety, was Mrs Siddons. Boaden in his *Memoirs* (1827) of that actress describes her attempts to restore to the stage a fitting decorum:

Her delight in statuary... directed her attention to the antique, and made a remarkable impression upon her, as to simplicity of attire and severity of attitude. The actress had formerly complied with fashion, and deemed the prevalent becoming; she now saw that tragedy was debased by the flutter of light materials, and that the head, and all its powerful action from the shoulder, should never be encumbered by the monstrous inventions of the hairdresser and the milliner.... What Mrs. Siddons had chosen remains in a great degree the standard of female costume to the present hour[4].

---

[1] *The London Chronicle*, Oct. 23–6, 1773.
[2] *An Apology for the Life of George Anne Bellamy* (1785), i. 130.
[3] *Id.*
[4] Boaden, *op. cit.* ii. 290–1.

By 1790, then, the actresses were endeavouring to come into line with the actors, who themselves were merely treading afar off the roads already travelled by the critics. Even as early as 1759 Wilkes in his *General View of the Stage* (1759) had uttered a warning to the theatre and had pleaded for a return to Roman traditions whereby "Actors were always habited according to the fashion of the country where their scene was laid."

Before leaving this question of the *mise en scène* and its appurtenances, a word must be said about a special feature of late eighteenth century staging which in its own way was to be of even greater importance than scenery itself. Up to 1750 the theatres had been regularly lighted in three ways, first by the footlights, which are to be seen as early as *The Wits* engraving of 1673, secondly by the "branches" or "hoops" fixed at the front of the proscenium pillars and presumably intended for the illumination of the apron stage, and thirdly by those rings of candles hung over the stage itself which can be plainly seen in so many theatrical prints of the period. It is probable that some of these at least were adjustable. From extant references the footlights appear to have been movable, and there is at least a possibility that some of the chandeliers were so arranged that they could be drawn up into the "flies" or lowered for night scenes[1]. Still, whatever arrangements were made for lighting effects, the system must have been both cumbrous and inartistic. When Romeo wooed Juliet, as he is seen doing in a contemporary print, with a couple of chandeliers floating over the balcony, when Rosalind wandered through a candle-lit forest of Arden, the effect must truly have been ludicrous; and, apart from that, there must have been a considerable strain on the eyes of the audience. Already the continental stage had moved in this question of lighting far beyond the English and it is to Garrick's credit that, in 1765, he introduced thence an

---

[1] In this connection Waldron's MS. stage directions, dated 1765, in *The Devil to Pay* (B.M. 643, g. 7) should be particularly noted. At the end of I. iv. we read, "Sink Lamps O Wood 1st Grove" (i.e. groove) and at the end of the scene, "Coblers Stool on O Jobsons House Lamps up."

entirely new principle. Although considerable doubt for
some time prevailed as to the precise nature of Garrick's
innovations it seems certain now that what he did was to
remove the circular chandeliers and substitute for them a
direct side-lighting. In other words "lengths" of perpen-
dicular candle battens were provided behind the proscenium
and the wings, the glare being removed from the stage itself
and the way opened up for new effects in realistic settings.
Undoubtedly little could be expected from candles as a
source of illumination, but to Garrick must be given the
credit of doing with his primitive materials all that could be
done. He was preparing the way for the more gorgeous effects
securable in present-day theatres by the aid of gas-filled
lamps, Schwabe-Haseit systems and all the gallimaufry of
twentieth century theatrical appurtenances.

IV. *Actors, Actresses and Managers*

All who have written on this period of our dramatic literature have emphasised the fact that the actor and not the
dramatist ruled the theatre. While this general dependence
of the playwright upon the performer is to a certain extent
true of all eras, the Quins and the Barrys, the Garricks and
the Kembles seem to have exercised more influence upon the
audiences than even a Betterton and a Cibber had done. Only
by taking into account the magnificent declamation of the
time can we explain the success of many dull tragedies and
of countless foolish farces. It is in this half century that we
meet with the clash between the old and the new styles of
acting, a clash which is to be intimately associated with the
old and new styles in scenic artistry and in costume designing. Garrick stands for the school of realism as Macklin
stands for the school of convention. The wide interest which
was taken in this conflict itself indicates the close attention
which contemporaries paid to the performance of plays. The
scores of pamphlets and the innumerable newspaper paragraphs attest fully to the popular enthusiasm.

Many are the plays which were damned because of poorly
cast *dramatis personæ*, many are those which held the boards

because of an actor or an actress. Mrs Cowley's preface to
her comedy, *The Town before You* (C.G. 1794), deals with
this subject:

An acute Critic lately said, in one of those assemblies where
conversation, though sometimes light, is seldom without meaning,
"A Comedy to please, in the present day, must be *made*, not
written." It requires no great expanse of comprehension to
perceive the meaning of this dogma; the truth of which I am equally
ready to acknowledge, and to deplore: But should it *want*
illustration, it may be found every week in a popular Piece, where
a great Actor, holding a sword in his left hand, and making
aukward pushes with it, charms the audience infinitely more
than he could do, by all the wit and observation which the
ingenious Author might have given him; and brings down such
applauses, as the bewitching dialogue of CIBBER, and of FARQUHAR
pants for in vain!

The pages of *A New Theatrical Dictionary* (1792) are full
of such entries as the following:

Almida. Trag. by Mrs Celisia....From the excellent performance of Mrs Crawford this play had a considerable run.

So Home's *Alonzo* (D.L. 1773) obtained a nine nights'
hearing "by the assistance of excellent acting"; Bickerstaffe's
Daphne and Amintor (D.L. 1765) won success through "the
excellent acting of Miss Wright (afterwards Mrs. Arne)[1]";
Mrs Bellamy brought approbation to Dodsley's *Cleone* (C.G.
1758)[2]; "probably through the aid that it received from good
acting," Pilon's *He would be a Soldier* (C.G. 1786) was
successful[3]; while Topham's *The Fool* (D.L. 1785) "owed
much of its applause to the excellent acting of Mrs. Wells
in the part of Laura[4]." These examples are typical of what
even less well-known performers could do in this way; the
power of a Barry or of a Garrick may be left to the imagination.

It is natural that, this being the position of affairs, many
playwrights should have penned their works for particular
actors and actresses. Home certainly wrote the part of
Ormisinda in *Alonzo* (D.L. 1773) for Mrs Barry, and Murphy

---

[1] *Biographia Dramatica*, ii. 152.
[2] *Id*. ii. 108.   [3] *Id*. ii. 300.   [4] *Id*. ii. 243.

had Miss Elliot in mind when he created *The School for Guardians* (C.G. 1767). It would, of course, be impossible to indicate the many tragedies and comedies similarly intended for Garrick and Mrs Siddons.

All this does not mean that the players were always perfect or were altruistic artists. Mrs Griffith's *A Wife in the Right* (C.G. 1772) was more or less of a failure, owing chiefly to the misdemeanours of the comedian Shuter, who confessed that he had been drunk for the three days preceding the production[1]. The Margravine of Anspach published *The Miniature Picture* (D.L. 1780) "*at the Request of several of her Friends, who saw it* mis-*represented on the Stage at* Drurylane[2]," and her complaint, although less sternly expressed, is uttered by many another. Rehearsals frequently became chaotic *conversazioni*, similar to that which Genest witnessed at Covent Garden in 1780:

Lewis interrupted the performance to show one of the actors a paragraph in the newspaper—Mrs. Mattocks requested the Prompter to take good care of her, as she was very imperfect—and Miss Younge did not attend at all[3].

In 1796 Colman the younger called "the loved shade of Garrick to witness that there never was one fair Rehearsal of" his *Iron Chest* (D.L. 1796)—"never one rehearsal wherein one, or two, or more, of the Performers, very essential to the piece, were not absent[4]," and although Garrick's shade is called upon we know from a letter of Miss Clive of 1765 that the star performers were quite as undutiful thirty years previously[5]. Add to this carelessness the quarrels which were constantly breaking out (mainly among the actresses, Truth is bound to record) concerning parts and dresses, and we may see into the life behind the scenes. "And the old story—" says Patent in Garrick's *A Peep behind the Curtain* (D.L. 1767),

Actresses quarrelling about parts; there's not one of 'em but thinks herself young enough for any part; and not a young one

---

[1] Preface.   [2] Advertisement.   [3] *Op. cit.* vi. 396.   [4] Preface.
[5] Quoted in A. Thaler's *Shakespere to Sheridan*, p. 116, from Garrick's *Private Correspondence*, i. 203.

but thinks herself capable of any part—but their betters quarrel about what they are not fit for, So our Ladies have at least great precedents for their folly[1].

Genest tells us of Mrs Hamilton's refusal to take the part of Lady Wronglove in Cibber's *The Lady's Last Stake*[2], and matters became strained at Covent Garden in 1799 for a similar reason. The quarrels over dresses are even pettier than those over parts. An instance, from Dublin, has been given above[3], and it can be paralleled by numerous others. Art in the theatre often became of less concern than self-aggrandisement, and beauty demanded its telling costumes and sympathetic lines.

Often the actors, counting on the support of a friendly public, indulged in "gagging." Reynolds tells a story of Edwin, famous for his "unrivalled *buffo* talent":

One night, while I was sitting in the front row of the balcony box at the Haymarket, during the performance of the *Son-in-Law*, in the excellent scene of equivoque, between *Cranky* and *Bowkit*, when the former, after making objections to the other's offer to marry his daughter, observes,

"Besides, you are such an ugly fellow!"

"Ugly," repeated Edwin, who played *Bowkit*: "ugly!" then coolly advancing towards the lamps, he cried, "Now, I submit to the decision of an enlightened British public, which is the ugliest fellow of the *three*—I, old *Cranky*, or," (he continued) pointing to me, "that gentleman in the front row of the balcony box[4]."

A similar anecdote is narrated of Foote, who, playing in *The Maid of Bath*, suddenly pointed to Mrs Baddeley as she sat in a box, and declared

Not even the beauty of the Nine Muses, nor even that of the divine Baddeley herself, who there sits...could exceed that of the Maid of Bath[5].

No wonder, with such practices, that the dramatists left much to the performers.

---

[1] I. ii.
[2] *Op. cit.* iv. 658–9; this was in 1762. Further details concerning this subject may be found in A. Thaler, *op. cit.* pp. 118–9.
[3] *Supra*, p. 37.
[4] *Memoirs*, ii. 60–1.   [5] Fitzgerald, *op. cit.* ii. 231.

A good deal is to be said, too, of the discourtesy and the duplicity of the actor-managers. The complaint had been made long ago that these gentlemen worked only for their own ends, but the complaint has possibly more force in this age than it had in the last. "In our days," says James Ralph, "all Access to 'the dramatic muse' is in a manner cut off. Those who have the Custody of the Stage claim also the Custody of the Muse....Hence the Preparatives from Season to Season so artfully laid, to keep the Relish of these stale Performances alive; as also to deaden every Wish for new ones![1]" Murphy in the Advertisement prefixed to *Alzuma* (C.G. 1773) comments on Garrick's discourtesy, and the younger Colman has an attack on John Kemble in the preface to *The Iron Chest* (D.L. 1796). The former manager was again reproached by Dodsley for refusing *Cleone* (C.G. 1758) and for having played a new part (Marplot) against it when it was produced at the other theatre. Holcroft's embittered cry in the preface to *Seduction* (D.L. 1787) is, on the other hand, against Harris, the manager of Covent Garden; he informs us that he received every courtesy from the management of Drury Lane. Harris, in his turn, is defended by Pilon, who declares he had every courtesy from him, and all discourtesy from Colman[2]. It is highly probable that, as in the previous half century, some germ of truth lies in these often exaggerated complaints, and there is a sting of sincerity in Andrews' semi-satirical words in the preface to his *Dissipation* (D.L. 1781):

Mr. Sheridan, it must be confessed, has taken away several *witty* things from this comedy, which probably would have had a *striking* and *very violent* effect; but should he, in his *great dearth* of genius, ever venture to introduce them in any future production of his own, and the audience should not immediately perceive the *difference*, the original author will certainly put in his claim to all the merit they possess.

A wide field of speculation, too, is opened up by R. Houlton's *A Review of the Musical Drama of The Theatre Royal*,

---

[1] *The Case of Authors Stated*, pp. 23–4.
[2] *He Would be a Soldier* (C.G. 1786), Preface. Pilon declares that Colman, through false bias, professed not to "*like a line*" of the play.

Drury Lane, for the Years 1797–98–99 & 1800 (1801), which
is one long attack on Michael Kelly, the composer and singer,
accusing him of securing the failure of works with which he,
personally, was not associated.

Not much need be said concerning that other aspect of
the theatrical managements which concerns the rivalry of
the various houses. Such rivalry we find in Elizabethan, in
Restoration and in modern days, the forms which it assumed
in the late eighteenth century not differing in principle from
those which have been already chronicled for the earlier
periods[1]. Richard Tickell, in the prologue to Richard Griffith's
Variety (D.L. 1782) sums up the conditions fairly succinctly:

> Amid the rivals of contending trade,
> That court variety's successive aid;
> Two neighbouring houses most exert their cares,
> To deck with novelty their *patent* wares;
> Both in their turns your *generous* custom gain,⎫
> For both a powerful *company* maintain, ⎬
> In Covent-garden, and at Drury-lane. ⎭
>   What emulation fires this rival pair—
> Variety their everlasting care!
> What choice assortments each presents to view!
> Now furbish'd remnants, now whole pieces—new;
> And now old patterns, by the scissors skill,
> Slice into safety—like a cut bank bill.
> Here all the sattin of Circassia shines,
> Or home-spun stuff, with Scottish plaid combines,
> There checquer'd Harlequin's, fair Virtue calls,
> To negro nymphs in linsey wolsey shawls:
> Chictaws and Tictaws, all the town entice,
> True Eastern splendour—"*Nothing but full price.*"
> Till good old Lun rebukes the haughty boast,
> Stalks from his tomb, and sinks a *half price ghost*.

Typical examples of this rivalry as expressed in concrete
fashion are not difficult to discover. In 1786 both Burgoyne
and MacNally wrote plays on *Richard Cœur de Lion* in
rivalry one to another. Already it has been seen that
Garrick played in a new character because of the production

---

[1] Theatrical rivalry in the period 1660–1700 is well attested; for the
period 1700–1750 see vol. ii, pp. 47–9.

of *Cleone* at the other house, and he hurriedly reworked
Wycherley's *The Country Wife* as *The Country Girl* (D.L.
1766) because he heard that Murphy was engaged on the
same task[1]. Kelly's *False Delicacy* (D.L. 1768) seems similarly to have been written to rival Goldsmith's *The Good
Natur'd Man* (C.G. 1768) while the elder Colman managed
to anticipate Garrick by introducing into his *Man and Wife*
(C.G. 1769) part of the Stratford Jubilee celebrations which
he knew the manager of Drury Lane intended to produce at
his house. If another example is needed, perhaps Birch's
Albert and Adelaide (C.G. 1798) and Hoare's *The Captive of
Spilburg* (D.L. 1798), both apparently taken from the same
play by Morsollier, might be cited. Again, as in the first half
of the eighteenth century, we have to take this rivalry into
consideration when we discuss the repertoires of the theatre
as a whole. Nor must we forget that revivals also owed
some of their success occasionally to the same source. In
1750 Garrick and Mrs Bellamy ran *Romeo and Juliet* against
the *Romeo and Juliet* of Barry and Mrs Cibber until the town
grew tired of the monotony:

> Well—what's to-night? says angry Ned,
>   As up from bed he rouses:
> *Romeo* again!...and shakes his head,
>   Ah! pox on both your houses[2].

The rivalry in *entr'acte* shows is, of course, infinite and often
not strictly analysable.

Finally, a note may be added on the playwright and the
conditions under which he worked. From the theatre the
successful writer could expect now to derive a fairly respectable income. Indeed we may almost say that the professional
dramatist has at last in this period fully established himself.
There were not many men in the earlier times who, like
Frederick Reynolds, were enabled to live comfortably on their

---

[1] Advertisement to *The School for Guardians* (C.G. 1767).
[2] *Life of G. A. Bellamy*, ii. 114; Davies, *The Life of David Garrick*,
i. 160–3; Murphy's *The Gray's Inn Journal*, No. 30, Sat. May 12, 1753.
The epigram is quoted from *The Gentleman's Magazine*, Oct. 1750, xx.
471, where also is given the satirical poem *Eel Pye* (p. 438) and a note on
this rivalry (p. 427).

playhouse incomes. A few authors might look back to the days when patronage secured the existence of some among the needy writers, and conversely complain of more modern conditions, but they were in the minority. I know of few complaints such as that expressed in Jodrell's *A Widow and No Widow* (H.[2] 1779), a play which the author dedicates to Nobody because "NOBODY respects an Author: NOBODY gives Authors any thing[1]." Plays now were much more marketable commodities than they had been before. To realise how true this statement is we have only to compare the records of John Downes with such accounts as are presented to us by Frederick Reynolds in his *Life and Times* (1827). Typical is the latter's remark concerning his *Cheap Living*, which was performed only eight nights—"my profits," he says, "amounted to no more than three hundred and twenty pounds[2]." From the same source we learn that Morton "received one thousand pounds for *Town and Country*, before it was acted; and Mrs. Inchbald...eight hundred pounds for *Wives as they were, and Maids as they are*, also, *previously* to representation[3]." It will be observed, from the last statement, that a return was being made in this time to old Elizabethan, pre-benefit, methods of buying plays outright. Again Reynolds suggests to us how this came about. He is speaking of his comedy, *The Rage* (C.G. 1794):

Fearing that a *benefit*, at Covent Garden, might prove a *loss*, and that I was more likely to receive a *call*, for my jokes, than a *dividend* (on account of the great attraction of the new theatre, in Drury Lane,) I proposed to Mr. Harris to make a new arrangement. To this, he willingly acceding, I was secured thirty-three pounds, six shillings, and eightpence, on each of the first nine nights, and one hundred pounds on the twentieth night. This, was the foundation of that bargain between manager, and author, which, I believe, exists to the present period. My whole profits on this piece amounted to five hundred pounds, and as it was acted forty nights, Mr. Harris had every reason to be satisfied with his bargain[4].

[1] This dedication has an interesting prototype in Day's *Humour Out of Breath* (1608).   [2] ii. 258.   [3] ii. 282.
[4] ii. 182–3. For further information on this point see Dibdin, *Reminiscences*, i. 277, 347, and *Observations on the Statement of Differences*, p. 36.

The dramatist, too, had now an additional source of in-come in the copyright of the printed play. In earlier times the value of this was infinitesimal; now writers like Kelly could secure as much as £200 from a bookseller for a work such as *Clementina* (C.G. 1771). Nor would this sum seem to have been exceptional, even although it is much higher than the record price of the period 1700–50[1]. O'Keeffe frequently received as much as £150 for his plays and the elder Colman paid £500 for the copyright of a number of Foote's comedies[2]. It is here that a comparatively new, yet essentially old, series of complications enters into the story of the production and publication of plays. We do not hear very much of play piracy in the early eighteenth century, although *Polly* was issued surreptitiously in 1729. In this period, on the contrary, in-numerable farces and musical dramas were issued without authority, and even Sheridan's *The School for Scandal* was first given to the reading world in a pirated edition[3]. It is the prevalence of this piracy that explains the frequent in-dication on title-page or fly-leaf of entry at Stationers' Hall. Sometimes this indication takes the form of a plain announce-ment, as in the first editions of Bickerstaffe's *The Maid of the Mill* (C.G. 1765), Mrs Inchbald's *Appearance is against Them* (C.G. 1785), Topham's *The Fool* (D.L. 1785) and Dudley's *The Travellers in Switzerland* (C.G. 1794), occasionally it assumes a more imperative form as in Arne's *The Sot* (H.[2] 1772) where we are informed that "*The Proprietors of this Pamphlet have entered it in the Hall-Book of the Company of Stationers; and whoever pirates it, or any Part of it, will be prosecuted with the utmost Severity of the Law.*" Verily we seem to have returned once more to the days of Shakespeare and Roberts and Danter. So, too, we find echoes of Shake-spearian days in the frequent theft by theatrical companies

---

[1] £180 paid to Southerne for the copyright of *The Spartan Dame*.

[2] A. Thaler, *op. cit.* p. 51, quoting from O'Keeffe's *Recollections* and Foote's *Works* as prepared for the press by Colman. Debrett gave £200 to Burgoyne for *The Heiress* (D.L. 1786).

[3] I have indicated in the Handlist of Plays appended to this volume many of those editions which seem to have been surreptitiously printed; see particularly under Foote.

of successful plays. The managements of Drury Lane and
of Covent Garden for the most part respected each other's
rights, but the provincial theatres made free use of the
popular metropolitan triumphs of the day. In 1795 Colman
endeavoured to bring the proprietors of the Richmond theatre
to task for their appropriation of two recent farces of O'Keeffe,
but, when he brought his case to the courts, he had the
mortification of losing it[1]. Exactly what arrangement of give
and take existed between the two London theatres has never
been satisfactorily determined, but we may judge from the
lack of undue friction that there still was preserved in essence
that mutual arrangement which is to be traced back to
Restoration days and thence even to the days of Elizabeth.

It is evident, even from this brief glance at some of the
conditions of the time that the late eighteenth century has
some interest because of its reflection of earlier dramatic
and theatrical conditions; it is probable that the full account
of sixteenth century playhouse life will not be written until
a minute investigation has been entered into of the relics of
Elizabethan theory and practice in the age of Sheridan and
of Goldsmith.

[1] O'Keeffe, *Recollections*, ii. 312-6.

CHAPTER II

TRAGEDY

I. *General Tendencies of the Period*

As the drama of the period 1700–1750 was characterised by the gradual growth and ultimate dominance of the pseudo-classic precepts, so this is marked out by the gradual emergence of romantic principles. Already it has been seen how the conflict between Augustan ideals and the newer spirit affected the settings, the costumes and the acting of plays; an effort must now be made to trace its influence on the dramatic literature of the period. Classicism, of course, even to the last years of the eighteenth century still held its own in spite of the revolutionary poetry of a Chatterton, a Burns and a Blake. The formal rules of the Augustan critics were still regarded by most as divinely inspired and even the writers of sentimental comedy bowed to their authority. It is perhaps natural that Dodsley should keep to a strict limitation of time in his *Cleone* (C.G. 1758), but we are somewhat surprised to find Cumberland indicating in *The Carmelite* (D.L. 1784) and in *The Natural Son* (D.L. 1785) that the "Time" is "that of the Representation," MacNally noting down "Time, One Day" in his *Fashionable Levities* (C.G. 1785) and Mrs Inchbald triumphantly drawing the attention of her readers to the fact that she has preserved the Unity of Time in *Lovers' Vows* (C.G. 1798). We are still more surprised to discover that Holcroft, most revolutionary of them all, saw the necessity of declaring in his *The Road to Ruin* (C.G. 1792) that the "Time" was "not twenty-four hours." There were but few dramatists of the age bold enough to pronounce openly against these fettering restrictions. Morgan certainly in his *Philoclea* (C.G. 1754) disregarded "the Unity of Place...because" he had "observed that such Regularity has seldom pleased the *English* Audience[1]," but in the fifties of the century his was a lonely voice. Some change may perhaps be discerned in the last decade when German drama was making its influence felt. Fitzgerald, obviously inspired by the author of the play, drew attention in the prologue to Morton's *Columbus* (C.G. 1792) that the Unities were there discarded, and the translator of *The Robbers* (1795) remarked on the worthlessness of these and similar rules, preferring a "certain wildness of fancy" to mechanical methods of composition. Indeed there were occasional writers in England who went even beyond the Germans. Johnstone, in presenting *The Disbanded Officer* (H.[2] 1786) to the public, wrote a preface on Lessing's art and suggested that the latter had sacrificed too much to pseudo-classic Unity. For all these criticisms, however, Augustanism held control of the stage and helped towards the suppressing of true dramatic emotion, and it was an Augustanism which had lost its first purpose and power. It had not the virile strength of the age of Pope, but feebly clutched with trembling fingers its long useless sceptre and its quivering crown. The elder Colman sums up the matter fairly accurately in the prologue to his adaptation of *Philaster* (D.L. 1763):

> Next, prim, and trim, and delicate, and chaste,
> A hash from Greece and France, came Modern Taste,

where

> Modern Tragedy, by rule exact,
> Spins out a thin-wrought fable, act by act.

At the same time, romance, in one or other of its many varied forms, was striving to win a place in the theatre. Colman, in the same prologue, dares to bring to the audience

> one of those bold plays
> Wrote by rough English wits in former days,

and his example was followed by others. Romanticism, of course, assumed countless diverse shapes in this period. For some it was that which "Monk" Lewis described in the prologue to *The Castle Spectre* (D.L. 1797) when he wrote:

[1] Preface.

Far from the haunts of men, of vice the foe,
The moon-struck child of genius and of woe,
Versed in each magic spell, and dear to fame,
A fair enchantress dwells, Romance her name.
She loathes the sun or blazing taper's light:
The moon-beam'd landscape and tempestuous night
Alone she loves; and oft, with glimmering lamp,
Near graves new-open'd, or 'midst dungeons damp,
Drear forests, ruin'd aisles, and haunted towers,
Forlorn she roves, and raves away the hours!
Anon, when storms howl loud and lash the deep,
Desperate she climbs the sea-rock's beetling steep;
There wildly strikes her harp's fantastic strings,
Tells to the moon how grief her bosom wrings,
And while her strange song chaunts fictitious ills,
In wounded hearts Oblivion's balm distills.

This is what romance meant to the author of the diablerie
surrounding "the false Imogene," but to the average writer
of the late eighteenth century it hardly bore this significance.
If it meant anything definite at all it meant "love and a
cottage[1]," or faithful love[2], or foolish altruism[3], or anything
not quite fashionable[4]. Generally, however, it was but an
unanalysable word, and was applied indiscriminatingly to
plays or characters or scenes or dresses or customs. Thus in
Murphy's *The Desert Island* (D.L. 1760) "CONSTANTIA *is
discovered at work at the inscription, in a romantic habit of
skins, leaves and flowers[5]*"; the younger Colman's *Blue Beard*
(D.L. 1798) introduces us to "*A Turkish Village—A Roman-*

---

[1] Cf. the elder Colman's *The Clandestine Marriage* (D.L. 1766), I. ii
Miss Sterling to Fanny: "Oh, my dear, grave, romantic sister!...Love
and a Cottage! eh, Fanny!"
[2] Cf. J. P. Kemble's *The Farm House* (D.L. 1789) II. i.: "*Modely.
What then you are really in love, that is a la romanski.*"
[3] Cf. Cumberland's *False Impressions* (C.G. 1797) where "romantic"
might be defined as "not looking for immediate personal gain."
[4] Cf. the elder Colman's *The Jealous Wife* (D.L. 1761), II. ii. Harriot
there objects to the fashionable levities of the town; Lady Freelove
answers her, "Romantick to the last degree! why, you are in the country
still, Harriot!" The same significance appears in Cumberland's *The West
Indian* (D.L. 1771), I. vi. In Holcroft's *Loves Frailties* (C.G. 1794)
"romantic" seems to mean "emotional and revolutionary"; cf. IV. ii.:
"*Lady Fancourt.* My views are rational, my motives dignified, and merit
success. Her's are romantic, fatal to order and the peace of families."
[5] I. i.

tick, Mountainous Country beyond it[1]"; "*a mountainous and romantic country*" as well as a "*romantic View*" appears in Cumberland's *Joanna of Montfaucon* (C.G. 1800)[2]; while Murphy's *The Grecian Daughter* (D.L. 1772) gives us "*A wild romantic Scene amidst overhanging Rocks*[3]." This was certainly a "romantic, sentimental age" as Topham defined it in his prologue to Andrews' *Dissipation* (D.L. 1781), but romance had as yet not given anything very outstanding to the theatre. We should, at the same time, be wrong to assume that this new movement was largely without its effect on the drama. The whole melodramatic movement of the last years of the century was a counterpart of the romantic element in poetry; it failed in its office mainly because of the spectacle demanded in the playhouse and because the dramatists had not made up their minds as the poets had done concerning what they desired to achieve in their art. The first of these causes led towards the production of the "closet-play" because of the poets' dissatisfaction with the theatre; the second led towards the general pessimism concerning the contemporary state of drama. Mrs Cowley's despairing preface to *The Town before You* (C.G. 1794) is typical of the general feeling that good literature could no longer hold a place on the boards. Its tones had been presented a few years before in the epilogue to Bicknell's *The Patriot King* (1788) and were repeated later by many another author who saw nothing in the playhouse but ruin and decay. Those writers of higher taste who penned dramas for the theatre frankly acknowledged that they set out deliberately to secure startling effects. Reynolds, for example, is nothing if not frank concerning his own work, *The Crusade* (C.G. 1790):

Thus, it will, I think, be allowed, that the piece was not weak from the want of efficient supports; yet, I am bound in justice, and in candour, to declare, that a more mawkish *hotch-potch*, a more sickening *melange*, than the *Crusade*, was never offered to the public.

In a similar fashion, Lewis frankly admitted his delinquencies in *The Castle Spectre* (D.L. 1797) and incontritely

[1] I. i.   [2] I and IV.   [3] II. (i.).

declared he would have done worse had that suited his purpose:

> That *Osmond* is attended by *Negroes* is an anachronism, I allow; but from the great applause which Mr Dowton constantly received in *Hassan* (a character which he played extremely well), I am inclined to think that the audience was not greatly offended at the impropriety. For my own part, I by no means repent the introduction of my *Africans*; I thought it would give a pleasing variety to the characters and dresses, if I made my servants black; and could I have produced the same effect by making my heroine blue, blue I should have made her[1].

These two confessions do much to explain the weakness of the romantic drama towards the close of the century. Not, of course, that every dramatist had the same end in view. There were many who endeavoured to resuscitate the dying embers of the tragic fire and to preserve the true tragic decorum. The success which attended, for example, the efforts of those who had endeavoured in previous years to banish the jesting epilogue after a serious play proves this fact[2]. Murphy had still to battle against this comic epilogue in his *Alzuma* (C.G. 1773)[3] and in *The Grecian Daughter* (D.L. 1772)[4], even as Home had done in *Douglas* (Edin. 1756; C.G. 1757), but by the later years of the century the fashion had been broken. Perhaps its disappearance is to be explained partly by that which took its place, the farcical afterpiece and the pantomimic display.

In tracing the fate of tragedy during these years, therefore, a balance must be kept between the attention paid to serious efforts made to support the serious drama and efforts made to secure spectacular effect, between a chronicle of pseudo-classic traditions and a chronicle of romantic revolt.

Before a more detailed examination is made of some of the main types of drama during these fifty years, a final note must

---

[1] To the Reader.

[2] For previous efforts in this direction see vol. ii, pp. 64–6.

[3] Of which a typical example occurs in Jones' *The Earl of Essex* (C.G. 1753).

[4] In the latter he introduced a jesting epilogue but displayed clearly his objection to the type.

be made concerning that greatest of all social upheavals in the eighteenth century, the French Revolution. Already some indication has been given of the patriotic reflex which came as a result of the grandiose schemes of the French revolutionaries, and once more our duty is to trace the conflict between the two forces. Numerous dramatic works of the nineties of the century are to be associated directly with the chaos in France. As early as 1789 a spectacular *Bastille* was in rehearsal at Covent Garden[1], while in August of that year the Royal Circus presented an "entertainment entitled *The Triumph of Liberty, or the Destruction of the Bastille,*" and the Royal Grove provided *Paris in an Uproar, or, the Destruction of the Bastille.* A year later, in Aug. 1790, both Sadlers Wells and the Royal Grove were performing *Champ de Mars, or, The Loyal Federation,* a "description of the Grand National Fête held at Paris on July 14th last," while the Royal Circus capped their efforts with *The French Jubilee.* Besides these, there are several dramas written either on the tragic events taking place on the continent or on the political consequences arising therefrom. An anonymous writer[2] gave in his *The Count de Villeroi* (1794) a story of conflicting democratic and humane motives. Bartholomew essayed an historical piece called *The Fall of the French Monarchy* (1794). Eyre brought the death of Marie Antoinette into *The Maid of Normandy* (Wolverhampton, 1794). Preston's *Democratic Rage: or, Louis the Unfortunate* (Dublin, Crow Street, 1793)[3] shows clearly its scope and purpose, as does Hey's *The Captive Monarch* (1794) which, however, is inclined to be revolutionary in aim. Coleridge's *The Fall of Robespierre* (1794) is to be included in this group of plays, along with the anonymous *Hezekiah* (1798), admittedly a political parallel. With the stirring events across the Channel audiences

---

[1] *Supra,* p. 19.

[2] Identified as the Rev. John Haggitt (*Biographia Dramatica,* iii. 473).

[3] This was reprinted at Philadelphia in 1794 as *Louis XVI* and acted under this title at Charleston, S.C., in 1795 and at Boston, Mass., in 1797. Seilhamer is mistaken in assuming that the author was an American and that the first production of the work was at Charleston (*History of the American Theatre,* iii. 283).

became unduly sensitive, and many authors, with no hidden meaning, had their works condemned because of supposed satirical or allegorical intent.

With this must be coupled the general atmosphere of humanitarianism which was spreading through all ranks of society, and which was to give the foundation on which the Romantic poets were later to work. In an extreme form this is expressed in the pretendedly extempore prologue spoken before Holcroft's *The Road to Ruin* (C.G. 1792). There Fawcet, the actor, feigns that he is detailing the sentiments of a prologue which has been mislaid, in which

The author had mounted on the stilts of oratory and elocution:
Not but he had a smart touch or two, about Poland, France, and the—the revolution;
Telling us that Frenchman, and Polishman, and every man is our brother:
And that all men, ay, even poor negro men, have a right to be free; one as well as another!
Freedom at length, said he, like a torrent is spreading and swelling,
To sweep away pride and reach the most miserable dwelling:
To ease, happiness, art, science, wit, and genius to give birth;
Ay, to fertilize a world, and renovate old earth!

But few, even in such a jesting strain, dared to be so explicit. The general movement is to be traced rather in those attacks made on the Inquisition by men such as Coleridge in England[1] and Schiller in Germany[2], or else in the praise of John Howard's self-sacrificing zeal in the cause of prison reform[3]. New ways were unquestionably being opened for the dramatists and new conceptions of character now were possible[4]; how the playwrights failed to take full advantage

---

[1] Cf. his *Remorse* (1797; D.L. 1813).

[2] Cf. *Don Carlos*; and also Kotzebue's *Adelheid von Wulfingen* (1789).

[3] This appears in Mrs Inchbald's *Such Things Are* (C.G. 1787) and in Kotzebue's *Üble Laune* (1799).

[4] Typical is the treatment of the Jew in drama. Foote represents the earlier point of view with his satirical portraits, carried on in Morton's *Zorinski* (H.² 1795). The fresh point of view appears in Cumberland's *The Jew* (D.L. 1794), a reflection of the same tendency in Kotzebue's *Das Kind der Liebe* (1790) and *Der Opfertod* (1798). This humanitarian sentiment is to be traced likewise in the same author's *Die Negersclaven* (1796) and in Ferriar's alteration of Southerne's *Oroonoko* as *The Prince of Angola* (1788).

of the opportunities offered to them may become apparent in the following sections of this chapter.

II. *English and Foreign Models*

As in the preceding two volumes of this history of post-Restoration dramatic endeavour, I wish again to emphasise my conviction that in essence the theatrical literature of this as of the other periods is thoroughly English in the sense that its chief sources of inspiration are to be discovered in the works of Shakespeare and of his successors. There is unquestioned French, German and Italian influence on this period, but after all the foundation of the dramatic work is to be sought for, not in continental, but in previous English example. In tracing this English influence it is not sufficient merely to look at the palpable borrowings; an examination must also be made of the repertoires of the playhouses. It is plainly evident when such a survey has been made that tragedy held still that low position which it occupied in previous years. Every season there were revivals of serious dramas and the production of new tragedies, but these were hopelessly outnumbered by the innumerable farces, comic operas and entertainments of the time. One thing is plain, too. Tragedy of the pseudo-classic sort was not popular. It was put on the stage through conventional prejudice, but the audiences manifestly preferred Shakespeare, manifestly preferred, as well, the romantic enthusiasm of the melodrama.

Shakespeare, then, was still popular; if anything, his popularity was growing. The Stratford Jubilee Festival of 1769 proves that that movement which had started about 1740 had by no means abated in the following thirty years. Many authors express in prologue and in preface their determination to follow Shakespeare's style. Murphy in his prologue to Jephson's *Braganza* (D.L. 1775) claims that the latter comes "warm from Shakespeare's school" and innumerable are the quotations from the works of the Elizabethan. Sometimes his themes were directly taken over, as in Hart's *Herminius and Espasia* (Edin. 1754); more frequently the eighteenth century writers showed their appreciation of his work by adapting his tragedies to the requirements of the more modern stage. A *Richard II* by Gentleman was performed at Bath about 1754, another by Goodhall was published in 1772[1]. Garrick's *Hamlet* appeared at Drury Lane in 1772 and Kemble's at the same theatre some twenty years later[2]. At Edinburgh in 1753 was produced Lee's poor alteration of *Macbeth*. *King Lear* was adapted by Garrick (D.L. 1756)[3], by Colman the elder (C.G. 1768)[4] and by Kemble (D.L. 1788). Dance produced a *Timon of Athens* in 1768 at Richmond; Cumberland's version appeared at Drury Lane in 1771[5]; and Hull's at Covent Garden in 1786. *Anthony and Cleopatra*, as altered by Capell and Garrick, was given at Drury Lane in 1759[6], and another version by Brooke appeared in 1778[7]. J. P. Kemble's version of *Coriolanus* was produced at Drury Lane in 1789[8]; and earlier, in 1754, had been acted at Covent Garden a *Coriolanus* which was a reworking of both Shakespeare's and Thomson's plays[9]. *Cymbeline*, too, proved popular, being altered no less than five times—by Marsh (1756), Hawkins (C.G. 1759)[10], Garrick (D.L. 1761)[11], Henry Brooke (1778)[12] and Eccles (1793). All of these versions, I believe, were made in sincere admiration of Shakespeare, and were destined to aid in the retention of his works as stock pieces. It may be said that Garrick only followed the tendency which we have seen in being before his time[13], and that he mangled Shakespeare; but the fact remains that both he and his companions genuinely respected the genius of Shakespeare's tragic works.

[1] See Odell, *op. cit.* i. 373.
[2] See Odell, *op. cit.* i. 385–9; ii. 51, 54, 205.
[3] See Genest, *op. cit.* iv. 475; Odell, *op. cit.* i. 377–9.
[4] See Odell, *op. cit.* i. 379–82.
[5] See Odell, *op. cit.* i. 382–4.
[6] An analysis is given in Genest, *op. cit.* iv. 544–6; see also Odell, *op. cit.* i. 366–7.   [7] Odell, *op. cit.* i. 367.
[8] See Odell, *op. cit.* ii. 50–1, 56–8.
[9] Genest, *op. cit.* iv. 417–8, analyses the plots of the three plays.
[10] See Genest, *op. cit.* iv. 561–4; Odell, *op. cit.* i. 367–71.
[11] Genest, *op. cit.* iv. 635–7; Odell, *op. cit.* i. 371–3.
[12] See Odell, *op. cit.* i. 373.
[13] See vol. ii, pp. 44, 111, 157.

Nor were other Elizabethan dramas completely forgotten. Professor G. H. Nettleton, in spite of his usual acumen in seizing on the main features of post-Restoration drama, errs when he declares that "an occasional adaptation like Garrick's *Gamesters* (D.L. 1757) altered from Shirley's *Gamester*, seems somewhat accidental[1]." There are numerous adaptations made during the period from Elizabethan comedies[2], and even in the realm of tragedy and of tragi-comedy several alterations testify to the interest taken in this early period of our dramatic literature. Among these might be noted the elder Colman's *Philaster* (D.L. 1763)[3], Lillo's *Arden of Feversham* (D.L. 1759), Victor's *The Fatal Error* (1776)[4], Gentleman's *Sejanus* (1752) and the anonymous play *The Favourite* (1770), taken from the same drama of Jonson's.

Restoration models were even more common than Elizabethan. Dryden's *Aureng-Zebe* gave Addington's *The Prince of Agra* (C.G. 1774) and *Don Sebastian* was worked by Bickerstaffe into *The Captive* (H.² 1769). Various adaptations of *King Arthur*, also, were made during the period, Garrick's appearing at Drury Lane in 1770, and an anonymous *Arthur and Emmeline* being produced at the same theatre in 1784[5]. Southerne proved fairly popular. His *The Fatal Marriage* was altered by Garrick as *Isabella* (D.L. 1757), and *Oroonoko* was taken over by Hawkesworth (D.L. 1759), Gentleman (Edin. *c.* 1760) and Ferriar (1788, as *The Prince of Angola*),

---

[1] *English Drama of the Restoration and Eighteenth Century* (1642–1780), p. 238.

[2] *Infra*, pp. 112–3.

[3] Although it must be noted that he testifies in his Advertisement to a changed taste. "It may be remembered," he says, "that the Spanish Curate, the Little French Lawyer, and Scornful Lady of our authors, as well as the Silent Woman of Jonson, all favourite entertainments of our predecessors, have, within these few years, encountered the severity of the pit, and received sentence of condemnation." In this preface he brings forward the critical view, usually associated with the Wartons, that "Gothic" and "Grecian" art must be judged each by its own laws.

[4] From Heywood's *A Woman Kilde with Kindnesse*.

[5] In this connection there is an interesting conversation in Mrs Griffith's *The Double Mistake* (C.G. 1766), ii. i.:

"*Lady Bridget.* I hope you are an admirer of Mr. Dryden, Miss Lawson?

"*Emily.* All persons of sense and taste, madam, I believe, admire his writings; and though I by no means pretend to either of those characters, I join my humble suffrage."

besides being adapted anonymously in 1760. Hoole's
Cleonice (C.G. 1775) seems to owe something to Mrs Behn's
The Young King; Lee's *The Rival Queens* was altered as
Alexander the Great and his *Theodosius* as *The Force of Love*
(by Tighe, 1786). The frequent revivals of other Restoration plays likewise tended to preserve in the drama of the
period some indefinable elements of heroic grandeur.

The tragedy of the early eighteenth century proved hardly
so rich a mine for adapters of the later decades although
Lillo's *Fatal Curiosity* was altered for the stage by Colman
(H.² 1782) and provided Mackenzie with *The Shipwreck*
(C.G. 1784), while Mitchell's *Fatal Extravagance* was re-
worked by Waldron as *The Prodigal* (H.² 1793). Many of the
earlier Augustan plays, on the other hand, were performed
regularly in the theatres and some, such as Addison's *Cato*
and Rowe's *Tamerlane*, saw almost yearly revivals.

One other thing may have held back the dramatists of
1750–1800 from making wholesale depredations on the
theatrical literature of the preceding fifty years and that was
the nearness in which they stood to that literature. The same
disadvantage hardly attended adaptation from the French.
Many testimonies besides the witness of the plays themselves exist to the popularity of Parisian drama in London.
Bicknell boasts in the prologue to *The Patriot King* (1788)
that his is no translated tragedy

> Though other Scenes, perchance,
> The new-translated Drama, warm from France,—
> Or flimsy Equivoque—or meteor Wit—
> The present lighter Taste might better hit,

while Vapid in Reynold's comedy, *The Dramatist* (C.G.
1789) gives his advice thus:

> I'll tell you,—write a play, and bad as it may possible be, say
> it's a translation from the French, and interweave a few com-
> pliments on the English, and my life on't, it does wonders.

Many playwrights followed the recipe and found it worked.
Only towards the end of the century, owing to the anti-Gallic
sentiments aroused by the Revolution, did the fashion abate.

Certainly then Boaden saw the necessity to prefix to his *Fontainville Forest* (C.G. 1794) a patriotic prologue in which he made apology for the French source of his plot:

> Caught from the Gothic treasures of Romance,
> He frames his work, and lays the scene in France.
> The word, I see, alarms—it vibrates here,
> And Feeling marks its impulse with a tear.

But before the nineties of the century such a disclaimer was entirely unnecessary. The record of borrowings proves this simply. It is difficult, of course, to distinguish here between pure translations and adaptations, and, as both had their influence on the dramatic productivity of the age, they shall be dealt with here together. Pierre Corneille's *Rodogune* (1646) was rendered by Aspinwall in 1765, while *Horace* (1639) provided Whitehead with the main part of *The Roman Father* (D.L. 1750). Lady Burrell's *Maximian* (1800) was taken from a play by the same author. The *Persée et Démétrius* of Thomas Corneille was certainly borrowed by Young for *The Brothers* (D.L. 1753)[1] and Racine's *Phèdre* (1677) was translated anonymously as *Phaedra* in 1776. Voltaire, too, still held his position of international eminence, and the lull in the adaptation of his works was broken by the appearance of Murphy's *The Orphan of China* at Drury Lane in 1759[2]. In 1761 started the translation of *The Works of M. de Voltaire* prepared by Smollett and Dr Thomas Francklin. This included the *Orestes*, taken from *Oreste* (1750), acted at Covent Garden in 1769. *Tancrède* (1760) was adapted by Mrs Celisia as *Almida* (D.L. 1771) and Francklin's version of *Le Duc de Foix* (1752) as *Matilda* was performed at Drury Lane in 1775. Ayscough's *Semiramis*, from *Sémiramis* (1748), appeared at the same theatre the following year. Besides the Francklin translations anonymous versions of *Socrate* (1759)

---

[1] For references see vol. ii, p. 113.

[2] On Voltaire's influence see vol. ii, pp. 71–3, and the works cited there. In addition to those consultation should be made of George Baumgärtner's *Voltaire auf der englischen Bühne des 18. Jahrhunderts* (Strassburg, 1913) and of R. S. Crane's *The Diffusion of Voltaire's Writings in England, 1750–1800* (*Mod. Phil.* Feb. 1923, xx. 3).

and *Sémiramis* were issued in 1760. It seems probable that
Logan's *Runnamede* (1784) was partly based on *Tancrède*.
Among numerous other alterations of and borrowings from
French serious plays apart from those mentioned above,
mention might be made of Graham's *Telemachus* (1763), a
masque based on a work of Fénelon's, Kemble's melodramatic
Lodoiska (D.L. 1794), taken from Dejaure's *Lodoiska* (1791),
Murphy's *The Desert Island* (D.L. 1760), which owes something to Collet's *L'Isle Déserte* (1758)[1], Francklin's *The Earl
of Warwick* (D.L. 1766) founded on the *Le Comte de Warwick*
(1763) of La Harpe, the anonymous *Alfred* (1789) taken from
D'Arnaud's play of the same title, and the younger Colman's
Blue Beard (D.L. 1798), filched from the popular Parisian
success, *Barbe Bleue*. Both Francis in *Eugenia* (D.L. 1752)
and one J. M. D. in *Cenia* (1752) borrowed from Madame
Graffigny's *Cénie* (1750). Such a list as this must obviously
be regarded as suggestive rather than as exhaustive; it pro-
fesses to do no more than indicate briefly some of the major
features of this French influence on tragic drama and hardly
takes into account the infinite number of scenes and characters which may, with more or less certainty, be traced back
to Gallic sources, nor does it delineate in any wise the broader
influence exerted by the classic drama of Paris.

After the French inspiration unquestionably that next in
importance is the German, but here an additional difficulty
arises because of the difficulty of classifying the plays. Nearly
all Kotzebue's dramas are "comedies" in the sense that they
do not end tragically, yet their influence on tragic drama in
England was almost as great as on comedy. A considerable
amount of latitude, therefore, will here be allowed as regards
the categories of plays included in this section. In the theatre
the German influence may be dated from the production of
Johnstone's *The Disbanded Officer* (H.[2] 1786), a free adaptation of Lessing's *Minna von Barnhelm, oder das Soldaten-
glück* (1763), although this had been preceded by Lloyd's
The Death of Adam (1763), a translation of Klopstock's *Der*

Tod Adams (1757). Of intrinsic value the chief among the eighteenth century German dramatists are, naturally, Schiller and Goethe, and both were brought to English readers in diverse versions[1]. *Die Räuber* (1781) was given a fairly satisfactory rendering by Alexander Fraser Tytler (1792), whose interest in German literature, like that of Sir Walter Scott, had sprung from Henry Mackenzie's paper read before the Royal Society of Edinburgh on April 21, 1788[2]. The same translation was adapted for private performance by the Hon. Keppel Craven and produced at Brandenburgh House in 1798; again altered, this time by Holman, it appeared at the Haymarket in 1799[3]. Once more Tytler's version was re-worked by Render (1799), in a none too satisfactory manner, and the original German was re-translated by Benjamin Thompson for his *German Theatre* in 1800. Clearly *Die Räuber* brought something new to the English stage and traces of its influence are to be discovered in many dramas of the time from Lewis' *The Castle Spectre* (D.L. 1797) to Cumberland's *Don Pedro* (H.² 1796). Of *Dom Carlos Infant von Spanien* (1787) there appeared likewise a number of renderings. An anonymous literal version was printed in 1798; this was followed by another, far more successful but still inadequate rendering, prepared under the direction of

---

[1] On Schiller's influence see particularly Thomas Rea's *Schiller's Dramas and Poems in England* (1906), Margaret W. Cooke's *Schiller's Robbers in England* (*Mod. Lang. Rev.* 1915, xi. 156 f.) and L. A. Willoughby's *English Translations and Adaptations of Schiller's "Robbers"* (*Mod. Lang. Rev.* 1921, xvi. 297 f.) and *Schiller's "Kabale und Liebe" in English Translation* (*Publ. of the English Goethe Society*, N.S. i. 44–66, 1924). Important studies also are those of A. Brandl, *Die Aufnahme von Goethes Jugendwerken in England* (*Goethe-Jahrbuch*, 1882, iii. 27) and W. Rullmann, *Die Bearbeitungen, Fortsetzungen und Nachahmungen von Schiller's "Räubern"* (1782–1802) (*Schriften der Gesellschaft für Theatergeschichte*, 1910, xv). On Lessing see Sydney H. Kenwood's *Lessing in England* (*Mod. Lang. Rev.* ix. 2, April 1914 and ix. 3, July 1914) and W. Todt's *Lessing in England* (Heidelberg, 1912). Consultation should also be made of Georg Herzfeld's article, *Goethe and Holcroft* (*Archiv*, cxlvi. 1923).

[2] See *Transactions*, 1790, II. ii. p. 180 f.

[3] Apparently a licence was denied to the original *Robbers* owing to supposed political dangers. *The Red Cross Knights* kept the main features of the German plot but toned down the language considerably. Another adaptation, by the Margravine of Anspach, entitled *The Gauntlet*, was acted at Brandenburgh House.

G. H. Noehden and J. Stoddart. Benjamin Thompson included the play in his *German Theatre* (1801). Noehden and Stoddart issued also a rendering of *Die Verschwörung des Fiesko zu Genua* (1783) as *Fiesco; or, The Genoese Conspiracy* (1798), a play which had already found an anonymous translator two years previously. *Kabale und Liebe* (1784) was adapted by M. G. Lewis as *The Minister* (1797) and literally Englished by an anonymous author[1] as *Cabal and Love* in 1795. Coleridge's *Wallenstein* (1800), with its two parts—*The Piccolomini* and *The Death of Wallenstein*—presents with tolerable accuracy and some poetic power the major portions of *Wallenstein* (1800), leaving out the one-act prelude of the *Lager*. Goethe's influence starts with the sentimentalism of *Werthers Leiden* (1774) which provided Reynolds with the theme of his first tragedy, *Werther* (Bath 1785; C.G. 1786). *Götz von Berlichingen* (1773) seized upon Scott's imagination, his version appearing in 1799, the same year which saw Mrs Lawrence's *Gortz of Berlingen*. Taylor of Norwich had already translated *Iphigenie auf Tauris* (1786) in 1793. *Clavigo* (1774) and *Die Geschwister* (1776) were both rendered into English before 1800. Besides these two major figures, a number of other German tragic writers were translated during these years. Franz Kratter's romantic tragi-comedies, *Alexander Menzikof* (1794) and *Das Mädchen von Marienburg* (*oder Die Liebschaft Peter des Grossen*) (1795) were rendered anonymously as *Natalia and Menzikof* (1798) and as *The Maid of Marienburg* (1798) respectively. The various translations of the plays of August Wilhelm Iffland might be mentioned along with these. *Verbrechen aus Ehrsucht* (1784) appeared as *Crime from Ambition* (1799) by Maria Geisweiler; *Die Jäger* (1785) as *The Foresters* (1799) by Bell Plumptre; *Bewustseyn!* (1786) as *Conscience* (1800) by Thompson; *Die Hagestolzen* (1793) as *The Batchelors* (1799) and *Die Advokaten* (1796) as *The Lawyers* (1799) by Ludger. Thompson gave a rendering of Lessing's *Emilia Galotti* (1772) in his *German Theatre*, his effort having been preceded

---

[1] Identified as J. J. K. Timäus (Karl Goedeke, *Grundriss zur Geschichte der deutschen Dichtung*, v. 173).

by an anonymous translation in 1794[1]. Raspe's *Nathan the Wise*, from *Nathan der Weise* (1779), had been issued as early as 1781. Joseph Marius Babo was represented in Benjamin Thompson's 1800 collection by *Dagobert*, from *Dagobert der Franken König* (1779), and by *Otto of Wittelsbach*, from *Otto von Wittelsbach Pfalzgraf in Bayern* (1782). Thompson also gave a specimen of the work of Karl Freiherr von Reitzenstein in *Count Koenigsmark* (1800) taken from *Graf von Königsmark* (1792). J. A. Gruttschreiber's *Siri Brahe, oder die Neugierigen* (1794), itself apparently an adaptation of Gustav III's *Gustaf Adolf* (1786), appeared as *Curiosity* (C.G. 1798), while Johann Christoph Unzer's *Diego und Leonore* (1775) was adapted by Andrews and Pye as *The Inquisitor* (1798) and was acted at the Haymarket the same year in Holcroft's rendering.

It has long been noted, however, that the influence of all the other German writers was as nothing during those years when compared with that of Kotzebue. His sentimentalism and humanitarian feelings added to his acknowledged skill in seizing upon theatrically effective incidents soon endeared him to the English dramatists. *Adelheid von Wulfingen* (1789) was translated by Thompson in 1798 as *Adelaide of Wulfingen*. Both Schink and Papendick issued renderings of *Menschenhass und Reue* (1789) as *The Stranger* in the same year, and this play, in an altered form, became a popular success on the stage (D.L. 1798). *Die Sonnen-Jungfrau* (1791) and its companion piece, *Die Spanier in Peru oder Rolla's Tod* (1796), were eagerly seized upon. Plumptre translated the former in 1799, and was followed by Thompson in 1800[2]. Plumptre also provided a literal rendering of the latter as *The Spaniards in Peru* (1799) and was accompanied in her task by many others. Sheridan's alteration as *Pizarro* (D.L. 1799) was an immense theatrical success, and other versions were issued by Dutton (1799), Heron (1799), West (1799) and Thomp-

---

[1] Some scenes of this play were given by Henry Maty in *The New Review*, ix. 1786. The acted version does not seem to have been printed. A reference to the play will be found in Boaden, J., *Memoirs of Mrs. Siddons* (1827), ii. 313-4.

[2] The title of both is *The Virgin of the Sun*.

son (1800). Besides these an anonymous rendering was printed in 1799 and in that year Constantin Geisweiler re-translated Sheridan's version into German. *Das Kind der Liebe, oder: der Strassenräuber aus kindlicher Liebe* (1790) may perhaps be included here among the serious dramas. It appeared in an English translation by A. Plumptre as *The Natural Son* in 1798, and the same year was published by Porter as *Lovers' Vows*, under which title it was altered by Mrs Inchbald and acted at Covent Garden in 1798. Maria Geisweiler rendered *Die edle Lüge...Fortsetzung von Menschenhass und Reue* (1792) as *The Noble Lie* (1799). *Graf Benjowsky oder die Verschwörung auf Kamtschatka* (1795) appeared in two English forms, one prepared by Render (1798) and the other by Thompson (1800). This play also provided a theme for Siddons' *Zelida* (Lancaster, 1799). As *Poverty and Nobleness of Mind* (1799) Maria Geisweiler Englished *Armuth und Edelsinn* (1795) and Prince Hoare used its situations for his *Sighs; or, The Daughter* (H.[2] 1799). An anonymous author provided a version of the humanitarian *Die Negersclaven* (1796) as *The Negro Slaves* (1796). Plumptre made a literal rendering of *Der Graf von Burgund* (1798) as *The Count of Burgundy* (1798), this work being utilised by both Pope and Smith for adaptations. *Falsche Schaam* (1798) appeared in Thompson's *The German Theatre* (1800) as *False Delicacy*; *La Peyrouse* (1798) was likewise included in that collection, and was, besides, Englished by A. Plumptre in 1799. Ludger's *Reconciliation* (1799) is a literal, though not very successful, version of *Die Versöhnung* (1798), while Neuman's *Self-Immolation* (1799) translates *Der Opfertod* (1798). *Die Corsen* (1799) appeared as *The Corsicans* (1799); *Üble Laune* (1799) as *The Force of Calumny* (1799; by A. Plumptre); *Johanna von Montfaucon* (1800) as *Joanna of Montfaucon* (1799, by Maria Geisweiler, and as altered by Cumberland, C.G. 1800); *Das Schreibepult, oder, die Gefahren der Jugend* (1800) as *The Writing Desk* (1799)[1] and, in Mrs Inchbald's adaptation, as *The Wise Man of the East* (C.G. 1799).

---

[1] Such is the date of the edition.

From this somewhat dry list of translations and adaptations, it is obvious that, while the German influence on our drama can be traced back to the early eighties of the century, the enthusiasm for the drama of Kotzebue and his companions did not reach a height until the years 1798–1800, coming to a culmination in the latter year with the publication of Benjamin Thompson's *The German Theatre*. It is equally obvious that on the stage the German drama never had such a hold as it had in the closet; comparatively few of the many translations were acted in the public theatres, and only one or two adaptations were produced during those years. A third point may be added; those plays most popular in the eighteenth century were, clearly, the dramas of Kotzebue. Schiller and Goethe, certainly, achieved some fame in England even before 1800, but it was a fame manifestly inferior to that held by the author of *Die Spanier in Peru*. Concerning these three points a word or two may be said. The localisation of the German furore in the last years of the century is due to romantic sentiment. It was those years which saw the arising of that first group of romantic poets who were to revolutionise the whole of English verse; 1798 witnessed the publication of *The Lyrical Ballads*. It is not surprising, therefore, to find a slow accumulation of interest in German literature, increasing, as it were by arithmetical progression, until the whole burst into flame in those very years which gave the first promise of nineteenth century poetic art.

That the stage did not so deeply reflect the current enthusiasm requires a lengthier comment. In the first place, the interest in things German was originally slightly "high brow" in the sense that it started in Royal Societies and among poets who had not yet made themselves definitely popular. The translators of these plays were by way of being missionaries, and, although considerable numbers must have bought their versions, even a few thousand purchasers of a printed play, scattered as they probably were throughout the length and breadth of Britain, were no guarantee that that same play would have been a success had it been produced at Drury

Lane or Covent Garden. It is, indeed, highly probable that the majority of these serious dramas would have been dismal failures on the stage; the audiences relished far other things than the heavy problem note in a Kotzebue or the higher tragic quality of a Schiller. To this must be added another fact of paramount importance. Within a few years of the appearance of the first German translations a wild storm of opposition arose. This opposition attacked both the political and moral tendencies of the plays in question. Republican feeling was in the air; many of the poets were known to hold extreme views[1], and no doubt the appreciation of German drama shown by men such as Coleridge aided in drawing attention to what came to be regarded as a tendency in it subversive to law and order. Canning issued his witty burlesque, *The Rovers* (1798), and others more seriously argued that a deliberate attempt was being made by secret societies to destroy the loyalty of British men and women. Perhaps a perusal of these plays today may cause us to deem such fancies ridiculous, yet there was sufficient of revolutionary sentiment in many of the continental works to provide ample justification for the alarm. A new world was here being introduced, and a new philosophy expounded. In the world of the theatre, at least, history repeats itself. Other critics attacked the moral nature of the German plays. The most important contribution to this side of the controversy, no doubt, appeared in Hannah More's *Strictures on the Modern System of Female Education* (1799)[2], but many joined her in her belief that Kotzebue and Goethe were atheists and libertines. In spite of current humanitarianism, such critics could not forget themselves so far as to sympathise with anyone who had broken the "moral law." Even Tytler, the translator of *Die Räuber*, found it necessary, after reading Hannah More's work, to declare that he wished "earnestly...that he had *left undone* what he *has done*[3]." The typical comment of the more

---

[1] See Landsberg, H., *Die französische Revolution im deutschen Drama* (*Nat. Zeit.* 1900), Mahrenholz, R., *Die französische Revolution auf der Schaubühne und in der Tagesdramatik* (*Archiv*, XCIV. i. 1895) and Dowden, E., *Goethe and the French Revolution* (*Fort. Rev.* xlvi. 1886).

[2] Especially i. 39–45.   [3] Postscript to the 2nd edn. of his translation.

conservative readers of the day may be found in the pages of
the *Biographia Dramatica*. The editors of this work, in
writing of *Crime from Ambition* (1799), find that here, "as is
too common in the generality of the German dramas, vice,
instead of meeting its just reward, is suffered to pass un-
punished[1]." Objection is taken to "the author's hatred of
kings and priests...visible in every scene" of *Don Carlos*
(1795)[2], and various other dramas are summarily damned
and dismissed. It is evident, therefore, that permission to
perform these works could have been obtained only with
difficulty and that the so-called anti-moral and anti-monar-
chical tendencies in them would have created more serious disturbances than those which accompanied the acting of some of
Holcroft's mildly sentimental and humanitarian productions.

Those plays which could appeal were the romantic and the
spectacular; *Pizarro* was the triumph of the German drama
in the world of the theatre. It should, therefore, occasion us
no surprise to find Kotzebue the favourite with the general
public even if Schiller was the master for the *élite*. That this
was unfortunate, none could deny. Kotzebue was a man
of consummate theatrical skill, but only too frequently he
employed his talents upon lesser themes, and he had no new
technique to offer to the stage. His romantic successes,
therefore, only served to intensify that spectacular melodrama which was all that the new movement had to offer in
the playhouse. The cheap situations of *Pizarro* were preferred to the genuine tragic note struck by the hand of a
genius in *Die Räuber* and in *Wallenstein*.

If therefore we are to appreciate this German influence
aright, we must note the two opposing camps who praised
and condemned it; we must note the general attitude of the
average audience; and we must attempt to trace the influence
of the new forms, not only in the regular translations and
adaptations, but in individual scenes and in individual
characters. What could not be done boldly and openly was
often achieved tentatively by partial borrowings and pale
imitations. Whatever else we do, moreover, we must recognise

[1] ii. 142.　　　　[2] ii. 170.

that a new element had come into the theatre; the German drama for good, as with Schiller's tragedies, and for evil, as with Kotzebue's spectacular pieces, had been acclimatised in England.

In thus discussing the introduction of the German drama to the London reading and play-going public, it may be fitting to draw attention to the first appearance in England of a translation from Scandinavian drama, itself an offshoot from the drama of Schiller's predecessors and contemporaries. This entry of Scandinavian drama is heralded by the publication of Wilson's *Poverty and Wealth* (1799). During these fifty years Italian influence was confined mainly to the realm of comedy and of opera, although a slight impression was made on English tragic drama by the drama of Italy. Pietro Metastasio was, naturally, the most noted of the writers in this connection. It should be observed how Metastasio, with his lyricism, his musical accompaniments, his insistence on *generosità*, on *magnanimità*, *grandezza di animo* and what not, proved a fore-runner of romantic melodrama. Reared under the strict pseudo-classicism of Vincenzo Gravina, he struck back to the spirit of Tasso and discovered a new medium which was destined to be one of the greatest forces in the theatre of the eighteenth and nineteenth centuries. A rendering of many of his operas and lyrical dramas was issued by Hoole in 1767, and several other English authors rendered individually a number of his works. Arne's *Artaxerxes* (C.G. 1762) follows the lines laid down in *Artaserse* (Rome 1730) and the same author's dramatic poem, *The Contest of Beauty and Virtue* (C.G. 1772), is a rendering of *La Pace fra la Virtù e la Bellezza* (Vienna 1738). *Didone Abbandonata* (Naples 1724) gave to Hoare his *Dido* (H.[1] 1792) and *Il Rè Pastore* (Schönbrunn 1751), to Rolt his *The Royal Shepherd* (D.L. 1764). Hamilton's *The Patriot* (1784) is based on *Temistocle* (Vienna 1736), as is Mrs Brooke's *The Siege of Sinope* (C.G. 1781) on an opera, *Mitridate a Sinope* (Florence 1779)[1]. *La Clemenza di Tito* (Vienna 1734) was rendered by

[1] This, however, is not by Metastasio, as the authoress and the editors of the *Biographia Dramatica* state.

Cleland as *Titus Vespasian* (1754) and Olivari issued three translations in 1797 of *Il Sogno di Scipione* (Vienna 1735), *Il Natal di Giove* (Vienna 1740) and *Astrea Placata* (Vienna 1739). Besides these we may note Hoole's *Timanthes* (C.G. 1770), founded on *Demofoonte* (Vienna 1733), as well as Murphy's *The Desert Island* (D.L. 1760), taken mainly from *L'Isola Disabitata* (Vienna 1752), a work which was translated literally by Anna Williams in 1766 (as *The Uninhabited Island*) and by Hoole in 1800[1]. Among works of a similar nature mention should be made of Stockdale's *Amyntas* (1770) from Tasso's *Aminta*, and the anonymous *The Faithful Shepherd* (1782) from Guarini's *Il Pastor Fido*. The latter pastoral gave a hint to Mrs Lennox for her *Philander* (1758). Apart from these, however, there is but one rendering from Italian serious or tragic drama during the period, Algarotti finding an anonymous translator for his *Ifigenia in Aulide* (1763) in the year 1787.

Spanish drama, too, was long out of favour. Quita's *Ignez de Castro* was translated by Thompson in 1800 and an anonymous author in 1770 gave a rendering of de Vega's *Castelvines y Monteses*, but beyond these we can trace hardly any signs of appreciation for that theatre which had excited the interest of Elizabethans and of Restoration cavaliers alike. This loss of one source of inspiration, however, was, as has been seen, amply compensated for by the new appreciation of Northern European drama, and this compensation was added to by a glimmering perception of dramatic excellence even without the boundaries of Europe. *Sacontalá, or, The Fatal Ring*, described as an Indian drama translated from the original Sanscrit and Pracrit by Sir William Jones, was published in 1789 and won some enthusiastic appreciation from English scholars. As the first rendering from the Danish is interesting because of its anticipation of Ibsen's coming, so this version of *Sakuntala* has value, not only in itself, but because it marks the origin of a new attention paid to the

---

[1] Note may also be taken of Hoole's translation of *Zenobia* (1740), issued in 1800, and of Hodson's *Arsaces* (1775) from *Arsace* (Venice 1768).

East—an attention which in our own days has culminated in the translations of the Japanese Nō-plays and in Yeats' short dramas for dancers.

Nor must it be forgotten that the classics still played their part in an age when pseudo-classicism warred with romantic sentiment. Æschylus' *Suppliants* was utilised along with Euripides' *Heraclidæ* for Delap's *The Royal Suppliants* (D.L. 1781). The *Persæ* of the former Greek author was used as a model by the anonymous writer of the ridiculous *Battle of the Nile* (1799) and Sophocles' *Electra* was adapted by Shirley in 1765 and by Francklin in 1759. The same play provided Murphy with the plot of his *Alzuma* (C.G. 1773), where the ancient theme was made to serve for an Indian subject. Whitehead borrowed his *Creusa* (D.L. 1754) from Euripides' *Ion* and the *Hecuba* was adapted by Delap (D.L. 1761). Of regular translations of *Agamemnon*, *Alcestis* and the rest of the Greek plays the period is full, while Murphy and others freely based character and situation on many of these works. An interesting relic of Senecan influence, too, is to be found in Glover's *Medea* (printed 1761; D.L. 1767). In noting this influence, however, we must always remember that romanticism was moving against the ancient veneration of the classics. Garrick pretended to find Murphy's *The Desert Island* (D.L. 1760)

> So very classic, and so very dull[1],

while even Whitehead could cry

> Enough of Greece and Rome. Th' exhausted store
> Of either nation now can charm no more:
> Ev'n adventitious helps in vain we try,
> Our triumphs languish in the public eye;
> And grave processions, musically slow,
> Here pass unheeded,—as a Lord Mayor's shew[2].

With the subject of foreign influence must be reckoned the impress made upon the drama by the increasingly popular novel. We have seen how, a few years before the opening of this half century, Richardson's *Pamela* had been adapted for

[1] Prologue.
[2] Prologue to Murphy's *The Orphan of China* (D.L. 1759).

the stage[1]. *Pamela* but marks the beginning of a long series of such dramatisations. During the period 1750–1800 we find innumerable plays taken from romance or novel themes. Boaden's *Fontainville Forest* (C.G. 1794) is based on Mrs Radcliffe's *The Romance of the Forest* (1791), Colman's *The Iron Chest* (D.L. 1796) comes from William Godwin's *Caleb Williams* (1794), Lewis' *The Castle Spectre* was partly suggested by Horace Walpole's *The Castle of Otranto* (1765)[2], Leland's *Longsword Earl of Salisbury* (1762) gave Hartson the materials for *The Countess of Salisbury* (Dublin 1765). Siddons' *The Sicilian Romance* (C.G. 1794) is taken from a novel of the same name by Mrs Radcliffe (1790), while Boaden's *Aurelio and Miranda* (D.L. 1798) is based on *The Monk* (1796) of M. G. Lewis. Samuel Richardson's widely-read *Clarissa* (1748) found an adapter in Porrett (*Clarissa*, 1788) while *Pamela* (1740), besides giving birth to a comedy, was adapted by Hull as *The Fatal Interview* (D.L. 1782). Metcalfe's *Julia de Roubigné* (Bath 1790) is a straightforward rendering of Mackenzie's novel (1777), Boaden's *The Italian Monk* (H.[2] 1797) is founded on Mrs Radcliffe's *The Italian* (1797), and *Edmond* (1799) on Clara Reeve's *The Old English Baron* (1777). Perhaps here too might be mentioned the various adaptations of Ossian. The most famous of these is Home's *The Fatal Discovery* (D.L. 1769), but several other plays owe their characters and atmosphere to the same source. Among their number Delap's *The Captives* (D.L. 1786), Lady Burrell's *Comala* (1793), the anonymous *Comala* (Hanover Square Rooms, 1792), *Oithona* (H.[2] 1768) and the pantomime *Oscar and Malvina* (C.G. 1791) deserve remembrance.

Before we pass from this question of outside influence on the tragedy of the period, note must be made of one tendency which was intensified by the many translations of German and other plays. We are approaching the era of the "closet-drama," and, while a fuller discussion of this literary activity may be deferred until a summary is made of the early nine-

[1] Vol. ii, pp. 183–4.
[2] This novel also gave suggestions to M. P. Andrews for *The Enchanted Castle* (C.G. 1786), and Jephson's *The Count of Narbonne* (C.G. 1781) owed to the same source.

teenth century theatre, it is necessary here to observe that the popularity of the reading, as distinct from the acting, play was fostered partly by the appearance in the nineties of the eighteenth century of those many versions from tragedies and *drames*, themselves unsuited to appeal to a general London audience. It is certainly true that the early eighteenth century provides us with many printed texts of dramas which never saw life on the stage, yet there was never such a sale of these works as there was during the last few years of the century. The romantic writers, in their enthusiasm for Schiller, were led to pen plays equally unactable, losing, in their desire to imitate *Die Räuber* or *Stella*, the true note of the theatre. Finding that Schiller and Goethe could not be performed in England, they were inclined to forget that there were theatres in Germany. Unquestionably, this tendency was for evil. More and more, as we trace the history of the nineteenth century theatre, we see the rift widening between the men of letters and the stage; so that the theatre became unliterary and the *littérateurs* undramatic and untheatrical. Vague reminiscences of Shakespeare's art and unthinking imitations of Schiller were not those things which could have saved the drama of the age. The poets, in the disdain which they displayed towards the theatre of their time, were guilty of fostering that decadence against which their cries were the loudest[1].

III. *The Relics of Augustan Tragedy*

It is not to be denied that the image of tragedy during the latter half of the eighteenth century makes but a sorry picture. No one writer seemed to know what he wanted. Classicism still was rife and gave to the outer form of drama a life-crushing chill. Rowe's pathos was not forgotten, and Shakespearian phraseology frequently intruded with grotesque effect. Sometimes, but rarely, heroics were applied to for some excitement, but the heroic drama of earlier years finds its true descendant in melodrama rather than in tragedy

---

[1] On the poetic drama see *infra*, pp. 208 ff.

proper. When we compare the true tragic note preserved even in the literal translations from the German with the average work done for the English theatre, we see how deep was the mire in which the London dramatists stood. Even Kotzebue, as for example in such a work as *Adelaide of Wulfingen*, has an atmosphere which we search for in vain among English writers. Almost the only tragedy I know of which seems to catch something of this true tragic note is Robert Dodsley's *Cleone* (C.G. Dec. 1758), which, in spite of a certain pseudo-classic formalism, tells a revenge theme in an arresting manner. The villain Glanville, traducing Cleone to her husband Sifroy, murdering the faithful friend Paulet and attempting Cleone's life, may be a trifle artificial, but Cleone herself has something of genuine beauty in her characterisation and Isabella, false through her love, is not only well drawn but presents a genuine tragic ἁμαρτία.

This work has been mentioned first, largely because it displays, by contrast, what is lacking in nearly all the tragedies of the age. It thus not only displays Dodsley's own power, but marks the weakness of the others. In dealing with these other dramatists, little attempt will be made here to distinguish pseudo-classic from what were described in *A History of Early Eighteenth Century Drama*[1] as "Augustan" tragedies. If the types were confused in the earlier period, they practically coalesce in this. In all, or in nearly all, we note the same uninspired features, we note the same continual decline. Pseudo-classicism in the early eighteenth century was, in its own way, a vital force; it had about it at least the charm of novelty. Now, on the other hand, it was something merely artificial and conventional, lingering on obstinately when men were pining for new emotions and new forms into which to cast their thoughts. It is hardly surprising, therefore, that we find among these pseudo-classic works no *Cato*, no tragedy where the classic movement achieves perfection of utterance and individuality of presentation.

Edward Young, whose earlier plays exhibited general classic features albeit with a slight movement towards romantic

[1] pp. 96–114.

theme and character[1], had his last tragedy, *The Brothers* (D.L. March 1753), produced in this era. Dealing with the love of Demetrius, son of Philip of Macedon, for the Thracian princess, Erixene, and with the intrigues of his brother, Perseus, it maintains that general high level of craftsmanship, fired at times with that genuine poetry, which was noted in his earlier plays. A peculiarity of this tragedy is the "happiness" dealt out to the "guilty[2]," Demetrius being executed and Perseus living to marry the fair Erixene. As a matter of fact, however, *The Brothers* may hardly be accounted an original play of this period. It was in the first place based fundamentally upon Corneille's *Persée et Démétrius*[3], with some few minor alterations, and, apart from that, had been written many years before its production at Drury Lane in 1753. Victor informs us that it was actually in rehearsal in the year 1726, but was withdrawn because of the author's assumption of Holy Orders[4].

A more typical tragic dramatist of the period was Arthur Murphy, who, after a certain success with four farces[5], brought out an adaptation of Voltaire, *The Orphan of China* (D.L. April 1759) and continued to produce a series of tragedies and comedies till near the end of the period. *The Orphan of China* is a not over-brilliant, yet an occasionally affecting, tragedy of mingled classic and romantic tendencies. The plot tells how Zamti and Mandane have reared, under the name of Etan, the rightful prince, Zaphimri. Their own son, Hamet, is mistaken by Timurkan to be the prince and

---

[1] See vol. ii, p. 113.

[2] This lack of poetic justice is noted in a serious epilogue, which, apparently, was not used. A comic epilogue was supplied at the last moment by Mallet.

[3] Young's indebtedness was first pointed out by a writer in *The London Magazine* (xxv. 433). See vol. ii, p. 113.

[4] *Op. cit.* ii. 129. The tragedy seems to have caused some considerable interest. A lengthy criticism of its merits and defects appears in *The Gray's-Inn Journal* (No. 21; March 10, 1752/3) and there was issued from the press in 1753 *The Story on which the New Tragedy, call'd, The Brothers ...is Founded.*

[5] *Infra*, pp. 179–81. Jessé Foot has an interesting *Life of Arthur Murphy* (1811). Murphy's own *Life of David Garrick* (1801) and the satirical *Murphiad* (1761) should be consulted.

Zamti would allow him to be sacrificed. When Mandane attempts to save him, the magnanimous Zaphimri-Etan reveals himself and with the aid of a faithful officer, Mirvan, slays Timurkan. The patriotic epistle to Voltaire appended to this play deserves notice; particularly important is its attack upon the love-motives in the original French drama, an attack which shows that Murphy had at least a glimmering of the true tragic temper[1].

For some years thereafter Murphy confined his energies to comedy, but *Zenobia* (D.L. Feb. 1768) marks a return to serious drama[2]. Here a Roman subject is chosen. Zenobia is the wife of Rhadamistus, but each thinks the other dead. Coming disguised to the camp of Pharasmanes, a cruel tyrant, that general and his son, Teribazus, fall in love with her. Amid a welter of conflicting emotions, Rhadamistus appears in the camp and flies with Zenobia. They are captured, and, to save her husband, Zenobia pledges herself to Pharasmanes, drinks from a poison cup, and dies. Much of the dialogue is uninteresting, but again some affecting scenes are introduced and the contrast between Armenian and Roman is not ill-managed. *The Grecian Daughter* (D.L. Feb. 1772) followed at an interval of four years. This tells the well-known story of Valerius Maximus, with the scene changed to Syracuse. The succour given to the imprisoned Evander by his daughter, Euphrasia, is capably dealt with, but the drama as a whole suffers from the dulness of conventional restraint. The slight note of romance apparent in *Zenobia* is, however, introduced here once more—even into the settings[3]. *Alzuma* (C.G. Feb. 1773) marks an increase of this slight element of romanticism. This play, which, according to the

[1] On the relationship between this drama and Voltaire's see Sandmann's thesis, *Voltaire's L'Orphelin de la Chine und Murphy's The Orphan of China* (*Neuphilologisches Centralblatt*, 1895, ix. 2). In Murphy's *Works*, it is said that the play was written in 1756. For contemporary interest in the production *A Letter from Mons. de Voltaire to the Author of the Orphan of China* (1759) should be consulted.

[2] This seems based on Crébillon's *Rhadamiste et Zénobie*.

[3] See the stage direction quoted *supra*, p. 29. The author notes that this theme had been dealt with previously in Belloy's *Zelmire*, but denies any indebtedness to the French play.

Advertisement, was written in 1762, turns to a Peruvian theme, but deals with that theme in a classic style. Voltaire's *Alzire* and *Sémiramis* have evidently furnished the author with some ideas (and that in spite of the attack on Voltaire in the preface), while the treatment is highly reminiscent of the Orestes-Clytemnestra story of Greek drama. Orellana, a Peruvian maiden, is loved by Don Carlos. Her brother, Alzuma, murders Pizarro and, unwittingly, his own mother. The scene in which the revenger comes to a realisation of his terrible deed reminds us irresistibly of Alfieri's *Oreste*, and indeed compares favourably with the brilliant scene in that drama. In this play Murphy reaches his highest tragic triumph. Neither *The Rival Sisters*, written in 1783, published in 1786 and acted at the Haymarket in March 1793, nor *Arminius* (1798), a political piece[1], deserves detailed attention.

Richard Cumberland's work in tragic drama is equally typical. This writer, most famous for his contributions to sentimental comedy, started his career with a grandiloquent play, *The Banishment of Cicero* (1761) and scattered a few other tragedies among his comedies, entertainments and masques[2]. *The Banishment of Cicero* is a well-written work, but by no means brilliant. The plot tells how Clodius aims at Cicero's downfall, and how Caius Piso Frugi, loving Tullia, remains in the latter's faction. Frugi, however, is loved by Clodia, and she, being rejected, burns for revenge. In the Capitol a general holocaust follows the internal dissensions. The tragedy as a tragedy has many faults, that which most affected contemporaries being no doubt the lack of poetic justice[3]. Cumberland's next essay in tragic realms was an

---

[1] It contains a dissertation on the war then entered into between England and France.

[2] Cumberland is one of the few dramatists of this period who has received adequate critical attention. Kurt Fehler's *Richard Cumberland. Leben und dramatische Werke, ein Beitrag zur Geschichte des englischen Dramas in* 18. *Jahrhundert* (Erlangen, 1911) is a suggestive study, and a thorough examination of this author's work is provided in S. T. Williams' *Richard Cumberland, His Life and Dramatic Works* (Yale Univ. Press, 1917). See also *Memoirs of Richard Cumberland, Written by Himself* (1806) and William Mudford's *The Life of Richard Cumberland* (1812).

[3] This play was patronised by Halifax but obstinately refused by Garrick.

adaptation of *Timon of Athens* (D.L. Dec. 1771), for which he wrote an entirely new fifth act and added an important new character in Evadne, Timon's daughter. Murphy's description of it as a "lame and wretched alteration[1]" is hardly too severe a criticism. A more original work, *The Battle of Hastings* (D.L. Jan. 1778), followed. This is a poor Augustan tragedy carried out on lines similar to those of Thomson's *Tancred and Sigismunda*. The tragic theme develops out of Edwin's refusal to allow Edwina, his sister, to marry the King, Edgar, because he believes that his monarch's union with Matilda would be of greater political benefit. At the conclusion Matilda commits suicide and a moderately happy ending is contrived with the marriage of Edgar and Edwina[2]. *The Princess of Parma*, staged at Mr Hanbury's private theatre at Kelmarsh in Northamptonshire in Oct. 1778, was never printed, nor has an account of it been preserved. An alteration of Massinger's *The Bondman* (C.G. Oct. 1779), and another of the same author, *The Duke of Milan* (C.G. Nov. 1779), have likewise perished[3]. These were succeeded by a domestic drama, *The Mysterious Husband*, in 1783[4], and by *The Carmelite* (D.L. Dec. 1784). The latter approaches romantic proportions in its old Norman setting, but the story is a rather foolish one of a long-lost husband (Saint Valori), an unknown son (Montgomeri) and jealousy mistaken. Elaborate spectacular accompaniments no doubt explain its contemporary success[5], for the dialogue is poor, and absurdities abound. Perhaps the following passage from the exposition,

[1] *Life of David Garrick*, ii. 89. For an analysis of the original and adapted plays see S. T. Williams, *op. cit.* 89–91; Genest, *op. cit.* v. 316–9; and Odell, *op. cit.* i. 382–4. The alteration was unsuccessful.

[2] The difficulties which Cumberland had to face in getting this play acted and the consequent criticisms are well summarised by S. T. Williams (*op. cit.* 136–43).

[3] The latter included portions of Fenton's *Mariamne*. For MS. copies of some unprinted plays see the Hand-list at the conclusion of this volume.

[4] *Infra*, p. 90.

[5] S. T. Williams, *op. cit.* 201–2; see particularly the quotation from *The Lady's Magazine*. The play was translated into German by W. H. von Dalberg as *Der Mönch von Carmel. Ein dramatisches Gedicht* (Berlin and Leipzig, 1787).

with its ridiculously inflated diction, may be taken as typical of the follies of Cumberland's style:

A rocky Shore, with a View of the Sea, at Break of Day.
Fitz-Allan *and* Raymond *meeting.*

RAYMOND.

Well met, Fitz-Allan; what's the time of day?

FITZ-ALLAN.

Broad morning by the hour.

RAYMOND.

Sleeps the sun yet?
Or has the stormy south, that howls so loud,
Blown out his untrimm'd lamp, and left us here
To be witch-ridden by this hag of night,
Out of time's natural course?

FITZ-ALLAN.

Methinks the winds,
Which peal'd like thunder thro' Glendarlock's towers,
Have lower'd their note a pitch; the flecker'd clouds,
Lifting their misty curtain in the east,
Unmask the weeping day.

A quotation such as this proves simply that on dramatists who could not realise the difference between the conditions of the Elizabethan and of the eighteenth century stages Shakespeare had as baneful an influence as had Kotzebue. This was, to all intents, Cumberland's last effort in Augustan tragedy, although in 1770 he was engaged on another tragedy, *Salome*, which was later reworked as *The Arab* (C.G. March 1785) and published among his posthumous works in 1813 as *Alcanor*, while *Don Pedro* (H.[2] July 1796) is fundamentally tragic. Later "dramas" from his pen were mainly, if not entirely, spectacular in the style of crude romanticism.

Cumberland's companion in the realms of sentimentalism, Hugh Kelly[1], likewise attempted tragedy in his *Clementina* (C.G. Feb. 1771), a poor dull pseudo-classic production, in

---

[1] Kelly's *Thespis: or, a Critical Examination into the Merits of all the Principal Performers belonging to Drury-Lane Theatre* (1766) with its companion for Covent Garden (1767) and the various counter-attacks make interesting reading.

spite of its Italian scene. The plot deals with Clementina's
marriage to Rinaldo, in opposition to her father's (Anselmo's)
wishes. Anselmo would have given his daughter to Palermo,
and at the conclusion of the play Rinaldo is slain by Palermo
while Clementina stabs herself. In spite of the high price
which Kelly received for the copyright and the esteem in
which some contemporaries held this drama we cannot in
any wise credit it among the even moderately successful
tragedies of its class.

William Whitehead, who had started his career earlier in
the century[1], after penning *Fatal Constancy* (1754), won a
moderate triumph in *Creusa* (D.L. April 1754)—a play not
entirely lacking in vital spirit. The plot is based on the *Ion*
of Euripides, the chief deviation lying in the marriage of
Creusa and Nicander, but the treatment is throughout in-
telligent and occasionally imaginative. This attempt to
rationalise Euripides' legendary drama must be accounted
one of the decided successes of the period.

The plays of John Delap, while not so well written, are of
a similar character. *Hecuba* (D.L. Dec. 1761), like *Creusa*, is
based on Euripides' play and is certainly "not devoid of
merit[2]," although the blank verse is dully uninteresting and
there is in almost every scene an undue tendency towards
that common failing of pseudo-classic dramatists, rhetorical
declamation. *The Royal Suppliants* (D.L. Feb. 1781) is
likewise founded on the Greek drama, Euripides' *Heraclidæ*
and Æschylus' *Suppliants* being here the models. This
tragedy shows an effort to escape from the trammels of
declamation, and this effort is continued in *The Captives*
(D.L. March 1786) where a departure has been made from
Greek themes in favour of a tale of Ossian. Delap's later
tragedies all belong to the nineteenth century.

Similar to these plays are the three dramas by Richard
Glover. *Boadicia* (D.L. Dec. 1753) is but a poor blank verse
tragedy with a theme borrowed from Tacitus' *Annals*.
Boadicia herself is shown as a frantic and murderous enthu-

---

[1] See vol. ii, p. 95.
[2] *Biographia Dramatica*, ii. 288.

siast, her character being contrasted with that of the magnanimous and princely Dumnorix. This Dumnorix is the real hero of the work, and his self-appointed death in the last act leads to the culmination of the tragic emotion. Again, as an example of the false diction which marred so much of the serious drama of those years, a few lines may be quoted from the sixth scene of the first act of this play. Dumnorix is addressing his lieutenant Tenantius:

> Do thou go forth this instant, and command
> Each ardent youth to gird his falchion round him,
> His pond'rous spear to loosen from the turf,
> And brace the target firmly on his arm.
> His car let ev'ry charioteer prepare,
> His warlike seat each combatant assume,
> That ev'ry banner may in battle wave,
> Ere the sun reaches his meridian height.

Reading such verses as these we are prepared to accept at its face value the modest statement of the epilogue, that in the play there is a

> *languid flow*
> *Of strains unequal to this theme of woe*[1].

Medea (published 1761; D.L. March 1767)[2] is, on the whole, more finely written, but is much more "classic" with its choruses, penned in cretics, iambics and trochaics, added to every act. The theme and treatment is taken mainly from Seneca, although the author introduces a good situation when he makes Medea kill her children in a moment of madness. *Jason*, a sequel to this tragedy, was printed in 1799, but the edition was suppressed[3].

Henry Crisp's *Virginia* (D.L. Feb. 1754) is a more capable production than any of Glover's plays. The story is that often dramatised tale of Appius and Virginia, with an addition in

---

[1] On this play see *Some Few Reflections on the Tragedy of Boadicia* (1753), *Female Revenge, or, the British Amazon, exemplified in the Life of Boadicea* (1753), *A Short History of Boadicea...Being the Story on which the new tragedy...is founded* (1754), and W. Rider's *A Comment on Boadicia* (1754).

[2] Victor, *op. cit.* iii. 101, says it was written as early as 1732.

[3] *Biographia Dramatica*, ii. 341.

the form of Marcia's love for Icilius[1]. The dialogue is good, and Virginius' strength well-drawn.

Richard Bentley's *Philodamus* (C.G. Dec. 1782; published 1767), in spite of the high praise given to it by Gray[2], hardly deserves more than brief mention here, but the tragedies of Dr John Brown are worthy of some attention. Both *Barbarossa* (D.L. Dec. 1754) and *Athelstan* (D.L. Feb. 1756) are Augustan in type. In the first is presented a story not unlike that given in Voltaire's *Mérope*, in which Selim, whose father has been murdered by Barbarossa, returns to take vengeance. The plot is complicated by the love of Selim for Barbarossa's daughter, Irene. Garrick's epilogue to this play is worthy of note because of its satirical references to the decay of tragedy, and its advice to

> *Banish your gloomy Scenes to foreign Climes,*
> *Reserve alone to bless these Golden Times,*
> *A Farce or two—and* Woodward's *Pantomimes*[3].

Athelstan likewise deals with the conflict between personal emotions and duty. The scene in which Athelstan stabs his daughter instead of Gothmund rises to a height rare in the tragedies of this time[4].

Mrs Celisia's *Almida* (D.L. Jan. 1771) is, like *Barbarossa*, based partly on Voltaire, with a fair intensification of the pathetic elements. In capable blank verse it tells the familiar story of how Tancred believes his Almida false, fights for her and finally dies in battle, but it displays no true dramatic sense. From Voltaire's *Sémiramis* George Edward Ayscough took his *Semiramis* (D.L. Dec. 1776), making of his adaptation only a dull classical drama of murder and revenge. The main development of the plot, as well as the names of the

---

[1] Otherwise the story as told by Livy (iii. 49) is followed.

[2] *Biographia Dramatica*, iii. 145.

[3] *Barbarossa* saw several revivals in the nineteenth century; at D.L. and C.G. in 1804 and at D.L. 1817. It was performed at New York in 1793 and was played as late as 1846 (see Davenport Adams' *A Dictionary of the Drama*, p. 109).

[4] See *Critical Remarks on the Tragedy of Athelstan. With Rules necessary to be observed by all Dramatic Poets. By the Author of the State-Farce* (1756).

characters (save that Arzace is Arzaces and Assur becomes Assures) is preserved.

John Hoole's three independent tragedies depend rather on Metastasio. *Cyrus* (C.G. Dec. 1768) and *Timanthes* (C.G. Feb. 1770) are both based on lyric dramas by that author and even *Cleonice* (C.G. March 1775), founded on Mrs Behn's *The Young King*, has a slight touch of the same influence. All are dully pseudo-classic, with mechanical blank verse breaking out at times into the foolish diction associated with contemporary opera[1].

In *Virginia* (1754) and in *The Siege of Sinope* (C.G. Jan. 1781) Mrs Frances Brooke showed, like Hoole, her appreciation both of pseudo-classicism and of the more lyric note in opera, but neither work can be esteemed a success. Nor was her fellow-authoress, Mrs Hannah Cowley, much more brilliant in tragic walks. *Albina, Countess Raimond* (H.[2] July 1779) deals rather dully with the intrigue of Gondibert and Editha against the unfortunate Albina, the verse rarely rising above mediocrity, and *The Fate of Sparta; or, The Rival Kings* (D.L. Jan. 1788) is as dull in its treatment of the villainy of Amphares and the innocence of Chelonice. It is noticeable, as marking the lack of inventive power among eighteenth century tragic dramatists, that the main elements in the plots of these two plays are identical. Sophia Lee's *Almeyda: Queen of Granada* (D.L. April 1796) has a more romantic theme, and indeed passes back to Shirley's *The Cardinal* for inspiration, but is no more successful.

Hugh Downman's classical tragedies deserve some notice because of the attempt made in them to unite freedom of blank verse movement with subject matter taken from Greece and Rome. *Lucius Junius Brutus; or, The Expulsion of the Tarquins* (1779) is the best of these, although *Belisarius* (Exeter; printed 1792) has some good scenes. *Editha; or, The Siege of Exeter* (Exeter *c.* 1784; printed 1784) marks an attempt

---

[1] With these dramas of Hoole's might be mentioned *Arsaces* (1775) by William Hodson, taken from Metastasio's *Ezio*. Hodson also wrote a poor independent tragedy, *Zoraida* (D.L. Dec. 1779).

to deal in a classical spirit with the English historical matter loved by many Augustan dramatists.

The historical play, indeed, found many to patronise it in this period. Apart from the few works of this character which have been noted above, there are quite a number of tragedies which deal with English history from Saxon times up to the days of Queen Elizabeth. Edward Jerningham, who had started his career with an "historical interlude," called *Margaret of Anjou* (D.L. March 1777), dealt with an early period in *The Siege of Berwick* (C.G. Nov. 1793), a wretched production in which pseudo-classic propriety mingles with turgid diction and plentiful effects of a spectacular nature[1]. Dr Thomas Francklin, translator of Sophocles and editor of the English version of Voltaire's works, dealt with similar themes in *The Earl of Warwick* (D.L. Nov. 1766) and in *Matilda* (D.L. Jan. 1775) although between the composition of these two works he wrote an adaptation of Voltaire's *Oreste* (C.G. March 1769). *The Earl of Warwick* is mournfully Augustan in spirit, treating in uninspired diction with the machinations of Margaret of Anjou connected with the love of the young Edward for Lady Elizabeth Gray[2]. A considerable advance on this play is marked in *Matilda*, the setting of which is Saxon. Here complications arise through Matilda's sense of indebtedness to Morcar and her love of Edwin. The conclusion is of the tragi-comic type, Morcar, after having aimed at Edwin's life, becoming duly repentant.

Henry Jones in *The Earl of Essex* (C.G. Feb. 1753) comes later in date to Elizabethan times, taking a theme which had been already dramatised by Banks in the seventeenth century. The author has laid chief stress upon the machinations of Burleigh and Raleigh against Essex, this giving him excuse for introducing considerable pathos in the scenes between Essex and Lady Rutland. The tragedy as a whole is good, although it lacks the genuine note of higher serious

---

[1] This tragedy, after the first night, was given a tragi-comic conclusion by which the heroine was permitted to live (*Biographia Dramatica*, iii. 270).

[2] The main treatment of this tragedy is indebted to the corresponding drama by de la Harpe, which was translated by Hiffernan in 1764.

drama[1]. The same theme was attempted also by Henry Brooke, who in *The Earl of Essex* (Dublin May 1750; D.L. Jan. 1761) produced a good historical drama which centred more on the figures of Elizabeth and of Essex than Jones' play had done. In spite of some rather foolish lines, *The Earl of Essex* shows that Brooke had a decided skill in dramatic construction.

The ever-popular story of Mary, Queen of Scots, attracted at least two writers during these years. Mrs Deverell's play, published in 1792, merits small attention, but the Hon. John St John's drama, produced at Drury Lane in March 1789, has some good features. His *Mary, Queen of Scots* traces the fortunes of the unhappy queen through her last days to her final execution. It is observable that, while the plan is strictly pseudo-classic, the unities have been completely broken.

Confessedly like Rowe's *Lady Jane Gray*, Mark Antony Meilan's *Northumberland* (1771) treats of approximately the same period of history in a classically pathetic fashion. Less definitely historical is Hall Hartson's *The Countess of Salisbury* (Dublin May 1765; H.[2] Aug. 1767), a not unaffecting Augustan drama taken from Dr Leland's novel of *Longsword, Earl of Salisbury*[2]. It tells how Grey and Raymond strive to seduce the Countess during the absence of her lord, Alwin, how she runs mad under her terror and finally recovers to be reunited to her lord.

Thomas Hull, amid a mass of farces, comedies, operas, musical entertainments and masques, succeeded in penning five tragedies, of which two were of this historical type. *Henry the Second; or, The Fall of Rosamond* (C.G. May 1773)

[1] Apparently considerable interest was taken in this work, both before and after its production. It was said that Colley Cibber and Lord Chesterfield assisted the author in preparing the tragedy for the stage. *The Gray's-Inn Journal* (No. 20, March 3, 1752/3) prints an epilogue by Jones, for which was substituted the comic epilogue printed with the play. Revivals of this drama were fairly frequent up to 1822, and the tragedy seems to have inspired H. Laube to write *Der Graf von Essex*.

[2] It is said that Leland aided Hartson in its composition (*Biographia Dramatica*, ii. 134). This may be so, but the evidence adduced is not of sufficient weight to permit acceptance of the attribution. Leland apparently was Hartson's tutor.

was apparently suggested by the poet Shenstone in 1761, who was responsible for the introduction of the character of the abbot[1]. The author's effort was, quite plainly, to produce a pathetic drama in the Rowe style. Henry is presented as sinning but repentant. The Abbot endeavours to inflame the Queen's mind against Rosamond, and this "fair frail one" along with Clifford, her father, dies. The Queen retires to a convent and Henry is left to reign on

> In solemn, sad, uncomfortable Woe.

Hull's second tragedy, *Edward and Eleonora* (C.G. March 1775), is but an alteration of Thomson's drama, and *Iphigenia* (C.G. March 1778) is no more than Boyer's *Achilles* with a changed name and some few minor alterations[2]. *The Fatal Interview* (D.L. Nov. 1782) is domestic in character, and in *Timon of Athens* (C.G. May 1786) a return is made to mere adaptation[3].

Dr James Hurdis, starting with a classically-themed tragedy in *Panthea*[4], turned to the historical drama in *Sir Thomas More* (1792) in which Anne Bullen plays the part of villainess. *Geralda; or, The Siege of Harlech* (Dublin 1777), later performed at Covent Garden in May 1778 as *The British Heroine*, by John Jackson, remained unprinted, as did his *Sir William Wallace, of Ellerslie; or, The Siege of Dumbarton Castle*, performed at Edinburgh in July 1780, but *Eldred; or, The British Freeholder* (Dublin, Capel Street, Dec. 1773; Edinburgh, Feb. 1774; H.[2] July 1775) has been preserved in printed form. It is a moderately enthusiastic treatment of early historical fact, and, in spite of many crudities, has some intrinsic value.

Sir Thomas Overbury (C.G. Feb. 1777), altered by William Woodfall from Savage's tragedy, continues the same tradition. It was brought out with a prologue by Sheridan and an epilogue by Cumberland, the former of which shows clearly

[1] Preface. The author declares he attempted to follow the story as told in the ballad printed in Percy's *Reliques*.
[2] This latter work does not seem to have been printed.
[3] This, likewise, was never printed.
[4] Unpublished in dramatic form. The Rev. Thomas Maurice also wrote a dull play called *Panthea; or, The Captive Bride* (1789).

the relationship still existing in the minds of eighteenth century audiences between this Augustan type of tragedy and the domestic species[1]. In *The Patriot King; or, Alfred and Elvida* (1788) Alexander Bicknell turned to an Anglo-Saxon theme, telling how Elvida, Alfred's wife, is taken prisoner and attempted by Haldane. The play is interesting because of its supernatural machinery, which includes the presence of an Attendant Spirit, a Magician and a Witch, and because of its utilisation of a Chorus of Furies in the Greek manner. More "Shakespearian," but still dominated by pseudo-classic sentiment, is Charles Hart's *Herminius and Espasia* (Edin. Feb. 1754), which takes a *Romeo and Juliet* theme and deals with it in the style of Addison. As in Shakespeare we are presented with two opposed houses, Herminius loving Espasia, daughter of Aristo. The plot is complicated by the fact that Aristo's wife, Marcella, an evil-woman type reminiscent of Dryden's Zempoalla, loves Herminius, and, on being rejected, employs Hernando to murder him. There is little that is intrinsically interesting in the play, but the evident desire to deal with "scenes of humble woe" makes it historically valuable. As a last specimen of this type George Watson's *England Preserved* (C.G. Feb. 1795) might be noted. Its theme is the protectorate of the Earl of Pembroke during the minority of Henry III.

Hardly any one of these plays has great literary or dramatic worth. A few present single scenes or single characters outlined with some power and skill, but in the main their tone is dull and monotonous. It is clear, when we survey them in the mass, that by 1750 pseudo-classicism was an outworn creed even although men as yet had found nothing definite to put in its place. *Cato*, after all, did bring something new to the theatre; these plays only repeat in ever-weakening tones the notes struck by the classicists at the beginning of the century. Neither those dramatists who dealt

----

[1] "Too long the Muse—attach'd to regal show,
    Denies the scene to tales of humbler woe,"
are Sheridan's words; cp. vol. ii, p. 11.

with Roman and Grecian history, nor those who treated of English monarchs rose above mediocre expression and theatrical hack-work. From the records of performances we may assume that the audiences accepted such plays as necessary evils; the very retention of tragedies in the repertoires had become a convention.

IV. *Domestic Tragedies*

The early eighteenth century had tentatively pointed the way towards one method of escape from pseudo-classicism. The domestic play, as adumbrated by Lillo and Moore, seemed to mark the beginning of a new and vital development in tragedy. Unfortunately, that suggestion of something fresh was not materialised in the following years. A few dramatists between 1750 and 1800 endeavoured to tread the path made ready for them by *The London Merchant*, but such dramatists were not numerous and their works lacked all enthusiasm and inner conviction. It is often hastily assumed that, after Lillo's first experiment, his prose domestic drama became to some extent popular among the audiences of the eighteenth century. Neither the repertoire lists nor the records of new plays give any countenance to this belief. If bourgeois settings were looked upon askance by pseudo-classicists in the early years of the century, they were no less condemned by those precursors of romanticism who desired scenery, spectacle and picturesque melodramatic situations. By both camps the domestic tragedy was neglected.

Just at the beginning of this period it seemed as if fresh life were to be given to the type when Edward Moore produced *The Gamester* (D.L. Feb. 1753), a truly excellent prose drama with a characteristically moral aim. This tragedy tells of the fate of the gambler, Beverley, who is led astray by his pretended friend, Stukely. After squandering all his money on cards he finally seizes his wife's jewels and loses them. Meanwhile Lewson, who loves Beverley's sister, Charlotte, discovers Stukely's villainy. The latter promptly hires Bates to murder Lewson, whose death is announced. Beverley is accused of murder, and, in his misery, he takes poison, dying just at the moment when news is brought to him that he is the recipient of a handsome legacy. In spite of a certain artificiality in the situations, the general atmosphere of this play is arresting. The character of the gambler is well-drawn, and the lesser figures have all a certain vitality. The dialogue, like the dialogue of *The London Merchant*, is occasionally too poetical to appear real[1], but usually it has a more convincing temper than corresponding conversations in earlier domestic dramas. There is, too, cast over the whole play that atmosphere of fate which Lillo first introduced to eighteenth century theatrical literature, so that the action is raised a trifle above the somewhat sordid levels of ordinary bourgeois tragedy. Probably because of political and personal associations[2], *The Gamester* was not a contemporary success, but it was frequently revived in later years and became one of the models of its particular class[3].

Unfortunately hardly any dramatist of talent followed Moore in his endeavour to establish definitely the domestic type on the English stage. George Lillo's *Arden of Feversham*, of course, was first performed at Drury Lane in July 1759, but this adaptation of the anonymous Elizabethan play[4] was hardly calculated to further the development of the species, and in any case had been written many years before

---

[1] It is said that the play was originally written in blank verse.

[2] For the first four nights the Rev. Joseph Spence permitted the play to be thought his.

[3] It may be noted that the interview between Stukely and Lewson was attributed in eighteenth century circles to Garrick, who took the title-character of Beverley. The performance at D.L. in 1783 had Kemble as Beverley and Mrs Siddons as his wife. During the nineteenth century the play was revived at C.G. in 1803, 1814 and 1836, at D.L. in 1842 and 1861; at Sadler's Wells in 1845; and at the Marylebone Theatre in 1847. It had been performed in New York as early as 1754, one year after its London production. It is said that Diderot's translation, published in 1819, was written in 1760. A rendering by the Abbé Brute de Loirelle was issued in 1762, and an adaptation as *Beverlei ou le Joueur* was acted at Paris in 1786. As *De Dobbelaar* it appeared in the *Spectatoriaale Schouwburg* (1775), vol. iv, and as *Beverley, oder der Spieler* in the *Neue Sammlung von Schauspielen* (1764). In 1753 was issued *The Gamester, a True Story; on which the Tragedy of that Name, now acting at the Theatre Royal in Drury-Lane, is founded. Translated from the Italian.*

[4] For an examination of Lillo's alterations see Genest, *op. cit.* iv. 553.

it appeared on the stage[1]. All that can be said for Lillo's effort is that he draws the attention of contemporaries to the little school of early seventeenth century bourgeois dramatists.

Nor did Henry Mackenzie, the novelist, succeed in furthering the progress of this form of tragedy. After having a worthless *Prince of Tunis* performed at Edinburgh in 1773, he turned to alter an earlier drama of Lillo's as *The Shipwreck: or Fatal Curiosity* (C.G. Feb. 1784). In this alteration he has succeeded only in rendering some fine passages in Lillo's original sentimentally mawkish. Much more effective in its own way is George Colman's stage version of the same play, performed at the Haymarket in June 1782[2].

In *The Fatal Interview* (D.L. Nov. 1782) Thomas Hull tried a new experiment by adapting Richardson's *Pamela* to the stage, making the action tragic, but the work seems to have been of a slender texture[3]. Like Lillo, Benjamin Victor essayed the task of popularising the work in domestic tragedy of the early seventeenth century, but with little success. His drama, *The Fatal Error* (1776), taken from Heywood's *A Woman Killed with Kindness*, was never performed.

Almost the only work of note, indeed, written in this style during the later years of the period is Richard Cumberland's *The Mysterious Husband* (C.G. Jan. 1783), which, as the prologue shows, was based on the efforts of Lillo and Moore. The author (thinking probably of *The Critic*) hoped that now parodies had ceased, and "*Pageants and pantomimes*" had "*spent their rage*," genuine tragic emotion might rise again, but his drama was to remain almost unique. The story here tells how Lord Davenant has, through treachery, succeeded in marrying a girl beloved of Dormer. Dormer still continues his addresses, but is faced by Lady Davenant's virtue.

---

[1] It was completed by Dr John Hoadly. A revival occurred at C.G. in 1790 and Lillo's alteration was used for the Sadler's Wells performance in 1852.

[2] *The Fatal Curiosity. An Affecting Narrative, founded on Facts. To which is annex'd, A Letter from the Unfortunate and famous Sir Walter Ralegh to his Lady* (1767) is based on the story of Lillo's play.

[3] This was not printed. Lillo and Moore seem to have been the masters of Hull in this effort.

Meanwhile Lord Davenant has gone through another ceremony of marriage, abroad, with Mariamne, Dormer's sister.
She, believing this husband of hers dead, marries Davenant's
son, Captain Davenant. The tangle of complications is
loosened only by the father's suicide. This drama shows
clearly the weakening processes at work. There is, on the
one hand, the love of rococo situations such as appealed to
many of the early romanticists; there is, on the other, the
spirit of sentimentalism ill-calculated to harmonise with a
sterner tragic spirit. *The Mysterious Husband* is but slenderly
connected with *Fatal Curiosity* or *The Gamester*; its prose
dialogue and domestic setting are largely fortuitous. Here
was nothing that could lead to permanent advance in the
future.

By neglecting to follow along the paths of Lillo and Moore
the English dramatists of the late eighteenth century lost
one of their greatest opportunities. They might have led
the van of continental playwrights in the common search for
something vital and expressive of modern conditions. As it
was, they and their followers allowed first France and then
Germany and Scandinavia to assume the generalship of the
more progressive forces, and sank themselves "to the rear and
the slaves" with a withered pseudo-classicism and a false type
of romance[1].

V. *Pseudo-Romantic Tragedy*

This false type of romance is exemplified during the period
in two distinct ways. On the one hand, there are tragedies
which, in spite of the retention of some features evidently
borrowed from the pseudo-classic conventions, yet show an
appreciation of that vague something which we call romantic.
On the other there are the numerous melodramas, both with
and without music, which display the cruder and wilder
elements of the same spirit. Unquestionably the latter were

[1] Among the bourgeois dramas might be noted the wholly untheatrical
but interesting two-act piece of Maria Barrell, *The Captive* (1790),
written in prison. The story tells, in a would-be affecting manner, of
Captain Heartley's afflictions and death. Hannah More's *The Fatal
Falsehood* (G.G. May 1779) also belongs to this group of plays.

more popular; the former seemed constantly to fall between
two stools, satisfying neither classicist nor romanticist,
descending into bathos in their attempt to secure something
of the best of both worlds.

The earliest on the field with this new form of drama was
John Home, famous for his Scots tragedy of *Douglas*. *Douglas*
was produced first in Edinburgh in Dec. 1756; after its
enthusiastic reception there it was brought down to London
and performed at Covent Garden in March of the following
year[1]. *Douglas*, it must be confessed, has many fine qualities,
even although it does not succeed, as a compatriot thought,
in rising superior to the plays of "Wully Shakespeare." The
story is one of mistaken identity. In a stranger youth Lady
Randolph recognises her long-lost son, Douglas. As she
meets him frequently, her husband, Lord Randolph, grows
jealous, and, fired by the arguments of Glenalvon, finally gets
him murdered. The truth is revealed and the unhappy mother
commits suicide[2]. We can see now that the Scots spectator's
enthusiastic remark, as well as the chaster encomia of Gray[3]
and Hume[4], were not entirely merited by the author; flaws
are only too apparent in every scene of *Douglas*. At the same
time there is a genuine passion in many lines, and a distinct
love of nature, which show that Home had passed beyond
the chiller forms of pseudo-classic tragedy. This obscure
Scots writer had struck a new note, which but expressed
certain latent tendencies in the spirit of his time. *Douglas*
was a success and remained a stock play for many years to
come[5].

---

[1] There were some slight changes in the London production, the chief
of which was the substitution of Lady Randolph for Lady Barnard among
the *dramatis personæ*.

[2] As is obvious the plot is borrowed from the well-known ballad of
Gil Morrice, a version of which was included in Percy's *Reliques of Ancient
English Poetry* (1760).

[3] See *The Letters of Thomas Gray* (ed. D. C. Tovey), i. 335.

[4] See *The Philosophical Works of David Hume* (ed. Green and Grose),
iii. 67.

[5] See *Advice to the Writers in Defence of Douglas* (1757). On its first
production the play caused not a little excitement in the camp of pamphlet
writers. Various Scots religious fanatics came forward with their attacks,
among which the most notable were: *An Argument to prove that...Douglas*

Unfortunately Home never rose again to the heights he achieved in this tragedy. *Agis* (D.L. Feb. 1758), which apparently had been written before the inception of *Douglas*, is but a dull pseudo-classic drama with a Spartan setting and owed whatever measure of success it received to the fame of the other play[1]. *The Siege of Aquileia* (D.L. Feb. 1760) carries on the same outworn tradition. In *The Fatal Discovery* (D.L. Feb. 1769), on the other hand, Home reverted to his pseudo-romantic atmosphere, taking his subject matter from Ossian and dealing with it according to classical rule and precept. Here we are introduced to Kathul, Lord of the Isles, who has betrothed his daughter, Rivine, to Durstan, King of the Picts. In order to oversway her desires, it is given out that her love, Ronan, Prince of Morven, is dead, but the trick is pierced through by her brother, Conan. Baffled, Durstan determines to capture Rivine by treachery; in the mêlée that follows he and Ronan are slain, while Rivine commits suicide. The contemporary setting of this play, an account of which has been given above[2], is symbolic of the general atmosphere. We hardly recognise these Ossianic heroes in their eighteenth century court dress, and must come to the decision that the tragedy possesses little save historical value. Perhaps the compromise was near to the heart of the period; at any rate, it seemed as though *The*

---

ought to be *Publickly Burnt at the Hands of the Hangman; The Players Scourge: or a Detection of the Ranting Prophanity and Regnant Impiety of Stage Plays...and especially against the Nine Prophane Pagan Priests, falsely called Ministers of the Gospel, who countenanced the Thrice Accursed Tragedy called Douglas; The Morality of Stage Plays seriously considered* (by Adam Ferguson, answered by the Rev. Mr Harper in *Some Serious Remarks*); *Apology for the Writers against the Tragedy of Douglas; A Letter to the Reverend the Moderator, and Members of the Presbytery of Haddington; Douglas...weighed in the Balances, and found wanting; The Immorality of Stage-Plays in General, and of...Douglas, in Particular, briefly illustrated; The Philosopher's Opera; The Deposition, or Fatal Miscarriage; The Seven Champions of the Stage* (all published in Edinburgh during the year 1757). *A Letter to Mr David Hume, on the Tragedy of Douglas* was issued in London the same year. There are a few other less important pamphlets besides those mentioned above.

[1] See *The Story of the Tragedy of Agis. With Observations on the Play, the Performance and the Reception* (1758) and *The Dramatic Execution of Agis* (1758).

[2] *Supra*, p. 28.

Fatal Discovery would have been successful had not political associations entered in to break its initial run[1].

Alonzo (D.L. Feb. 1773) has something of the same atmosphere although here the subject matter is placed in a Spanish setting. Ormisinda, a part deliberately written for Mrs Barry, is presented to us as deserted by her husband Alonzo, who, however, has just arrived in disguise. Misled by idle stories, he accuses his wife and is opposed by Alberto, really the son of Ormisinda. Death comes to the couple on the "fatal discovery." There is nothing in the tragedy to attract our attention, and we need not question the statement that "by the assistance of Mrs Barry's excellent acting" it had a short run, "and then sank, as it deserved, into oblivion[2]."

Home's last tragedy was *Alfred* (C.G. Jan. 1778), but neither subject matter nor treatment entitles it to independent consideration. In the enthusiasm of his youth he produced one good play; his later efforts were merely pitiful attempts to catch something of his own earlier style, of his own "first fine, careless rapture."

Apart from Home, the most notable among the pseudo-romantic playwrights was Robert Jephson, whose first tragedy, *Braganza*, appeared at Drury Lane in Feb. 1775. The prologue written by Arthur Murphy claims that the author of this play comes "warm from Shakespeare's school," and, while we may be disposed now to substitute Otway's name for Shakespeare's, we recognise that Jephson had in him a temper above the ordinary. The story of the play tells of the revolt headed by Don Juan, Duke of Braganza, against the usurping Velasquez and Pizarro in Portugal. The tale is one with many similarities to that given in *Venice Preserv'd*, with the difference that there is here, instead of a vacillating Belvidera, a staunch Duchess who proves a fit mate for her husband. Sometimes the Otway and Shakespeare phraseology so plentifully scattered throughout the drama strikes

---

[1] Home at this time was a follower of the Earl of Bute, and, lest odium due to this should injure the chances of his play, it was brought out anonymously. After a fair run the secret leaked out and *The Fatal Discovery* was hurriedly withdrawn.

[2] *Biographia Dramatica*, ii. 21.

a false note, but there are occasional scenes, such as that in which Velasquez tempts Ramirez to poison Don Juan, which are truly excellent. These well deserved the applause they received at the original production of the tragedy.

For the story of *The Law of Lombardy* (D.L. Feb. 1779) Jephson went to *Much Ado about Nothing*, and conducted the theme in a quite successful manner. Here Paladore loves and is loved by the Princess of Lombardy, whose father destines her for Bireno. The last-mentioned, using Alinda as a tool, makes Paladore believe the Princess false. Fortunately, however, Alinda's dying confession is heard by Paladore, and Bireno's machinations are revealed. The blank verse of this play is truly excellent in places, although in others it is too clearly imitative of the peculiar ring of late Shakespearian dialogue. The characterisation, too, albeit marred by the usual conventional features, has some strength and subtlety. Jephson's next work, *The Count of Narbonne* (C.G. Nov. 1781), founded on Walpole's *The Castle of Otranto*, continues in the same strain. The characters are stereotyped—a cruel usurper in Raymond, a hero in Theodore and a heroine in Adelaide—but the dialogue in places rises well above the ordinary tragic diction of the period.

For the next few years Jephson devoted himself to farce and comic opera, returning to tragedy with *Julia; or, The Italian Lover* (D.L. April 1787), a definitely romantic piece with a certain inclination towards the domestic type. The failure of this play rests in the fact that the whole plot concerns the tracing of a murderer, so that the primal tragic emotions are supplanted by those which are associated with the detective play. The characters of Mentevole and of Julia are, however, well drawn, and the incidents are handled with a true skill and adroitness. This play was followed by Jephson's last tragic work, *Conspiracy* (D.L. Nov. 1796), taken from Metastasio's *La Clemenza di Tito*, and naturally displaying less of the realistic romanticism visible in his earlier plays. In general, one might say that Jephson struck as surely as any in his age the true chords of tragic romantic sentiment. Something in his work, however, failed to appeal largely to his contem-

poraries and as a force in contemporary dramatic literature
he is accordingly negligible.

In dealing with Jephson it has been noted that one of his
plays was derived from a novel of Walpole's. Horace Walpole
himself, of course, provided in this period one of the most
characteristic romantic dramas in *The Mysterious Mother*
(1768), a work which, while it never saw stage representation,
was widely read and commented on. The story which it tells,
albeit horrible, has many literary and historical parallels[1].
The Countess of Narbonne, awaiting the arrival of her husband, is smitten with a fatal and frenzied passion for her son,
Edmund. The last mentioned returns after a long absence to
his ancestral castle and falls in love with the orphan Adeliza,
who is really his own daughter and sister. They are married,
and the Countess in semi-madness reveals the terrible secret
before she commits suicide. The tale is one which well might
delight the hearts of the crude romanticists of the late eighteenth century, and in the main the treatment of the subject
is good. The blank verse shows Walpole's power over a
lower kind of poetry and the last scenes have a nervous
intensity which mark him out as something of a true
dramatist. Judged by highest standards, of course, the play
is ridiculous and weak, but, tested by the drama of its time,
it is by way of being a masterpiece.

More in the style of Home's *Douglas* (C.G. 1757), Hannah
More wrote her *Percy* (C.G. Dec. 1777). This tragedy had
been preceded three years previously by an uninteresting
Regulus drama entitled *The Inflexible Captive*, performed at
Bath in the year 1774. *Percy*, which is admittedly based on a
French play, is wrought out according to pseudo-classic
plan, but the subject matter is thoroughly romantic. The
tragic issue comes from the fact that Douglas has married
Elwina, whose real love is Percy. The marriage is a forced
one, brought about through the machinations of Elwina's
father, Raby, but it is not only external events which entail
the tragic catastrophe. Douglas himself has a fatal flaw in his
extreme jealousy, so that we are made to feel that unhappi-

---

[1] A list of these is given in the *Biogrobhia Dramatica*, iii. 66.

ness and death are inevitable for the principal characters. This play of *Percy* is unquestionably the *chef-d'œuvre* of Hannah More. *The Fatal Falsehood*, which followed at Covent Garden in May 1779, is an infinitely weaker drama[1].

Not many other romantic tragedies of this period deserve independent mention. Each one is interesting as showing the break-down of classical chill; each one points out the path which later poets were to follow more gloriously in the sphere of pure poetry. For the audiences of the time, however, as we have seen, they inevitably fell between two stools. On the one hand, they often failed to preserve the fitting decorum of pseudo-classicism; on the other, they did not give to spectators those rich, if crude, scenes introduced into the more flamboyant sister-form of melodrama.

VI. *Melodrama*

It is an exceedingly unfortunate thing for literary historians that the regular nomenclature of criticism has never had that precision and definiteness shared by the terms of scientific research. We still quarrel over the meaning of romantic and classic; the word renascence signifies one thing for one man and another thing for another man; even the types of literature, sonnet, ode, lyric, elegy, have a variety of different interpretations put upon them in different ages and by different *littérateurs*. The term melodrama has shared the fate of most of the other type-classifications. The word, of course, came to us in 1802 from the French *mélodrame*, the first example of which, theoretically, was *Victor, ou l'enfant de la forêt*, written by Guilbert de Pixérécourt, and performed in 1798 at the Ambigu Comique in Paris[2]. Theory and fact,

---

[1] On Hannah More's work and life in general the critical biography by Annette Meakin should be consulted.

[2] On the *mélodrame* see Paul Ginisty's *Le Mélodrame* (Paris, 1910) and James F. Mason's uncompleted *The Melodrama in France from the Revolution to the Beginning of Romantic Drama* (Baltimore, 1910). Valuable details are given also in W. G. Hartog's *Guilbert de Pixérécourt* (Paris, 1913). See also E. B. Watson's *Sheridan to Robertson* (1926), pp. 349–355.

however, do not always move together, and it is essential
to note, first, that the fundamental features of the *mélodrame*
were in existence in the French theatres long before 1798,
and, secondly, that the same features can be traced in English
plays from 1770 onwards. Originally, the term melodrama
was applied to a serious play accompanied by music, and in
this sense the French type springs naturally from the *ballet
d'action* and the *scène lyrique*; but we cannot apply the
term only to those plays which were provided with incidental
music. If the *mélodrame* took something from the lyrical
comedy which preceded it, the *drame* also contributed to its
development, so that we can trace truly "melodramatic"
features in dramas not associated with orchestral harmonies.
In general, one might hazard as a definition of these melodramatic features the spectacular nature of the setting, the
love of gloom and mystery, the excess of artificial sentimentalism, the hopelessly unnatural poetic justice and the general
air of pathetic morality. Added to these should go the
presence of a set of stage figures—villain, heroine distressed
but thoroughly virtuous, hero guarding and alert, servant or
friend honest but full of comic pranks—figures without
which no later example of the type could be considered complete. In this section an attempt is made to deal with these
elements together. The "Dramatic Romance" is thus treated
as a kind of melodrama, and the inclusion of songs and
incidental music has not been taken as a *sine qua non*. It is
rather the spirit of melodrama that we have to think of than
the more formal characteristics of the species. The various
titles given to these pieces are of minor importance; whether
they are styled "Plays[1]," or "Dramas[2]," or "Musical
Dramas[3]," or "Dramatic Romances[4]," or "Musical Dramatic
Romances[5]," or "Historical Romances[6]," or "Historical

---

[1] Morton's *Zorinski* (H.[2] 1795), Boaden's *Fontainville Forest* (C.G.
1794), Lee's *The Mysterious Marriage* (1798).
[2] Lewis' *The Castle Spectre* (D.L. 1797).
[3] Birch's *The Smugglers* (D.L. 1796) and *The Adopted Child* (D.L.
1795), Cross' *The Purse* (H.[2] 1794).
[4] Colman's *Blue Beard* (D.L. 1798).
[5] Cross' *The Apparition!* (H.[2] 1794).
[6] Burgoyne's *Richard Cœur de Lion* (D.L. 1786).

Plays[1]," or "Operas[2]"—this does not matter; the point of importance is the general tone and atmosphere of each play[3].

All of these dramas make free use of spectacular effects. Matthew Gregory Lewis, or, more familiarly, "Monk" Lewis, realised fully what could be done with a few outlandish costumes and striking scenery. He points out in his epilogue to Holcroft's *Knave or Not?* (D.L. 1798) that that comedy had nothing of this sort to recommend it:

Your canvas presents neither Dæmons nor Witches;
And your Villains appear in coat, waistcoat, and breeches!

and he proceeded to indicate the recipe for success:

That his Play must succeed, may the Bard safely boast,
Who opens the piece with a Song by a Ghost;
But in popular plaudits unbounded he revels,
If he follows the Song with a Dance by two Devils...
Give us Lightning and Thunder, Flames, Daggers and Rage;
With events that ne'er happened, except on the Stage.

This recipe Lewis himself followed in his most famous play, *The Castle Spectre* (D.L. Dec. 1797), a brilliant example of the more thrilling type of melodrama, accompanied by music by Michael Kelly. The story tells how Osmond, the villain, captures Angela, whose father has been long immured in his dungeons. Just at the apparently fatal moment the valorous hero, Percy, partly aided by the portly and humorous Father Philip, succeeds in rescuing them both. Many of the component episodes and characters are derived from previous originals. Thus Father Philip is based on Juliet's nurse and on Sheridan's Father Paul; a scene has been taken from *The Castle of Otranto*, and another from a German play written round a certain Landgrave of Thuringia; while a vision is derived from the dream of Francis in Schiller's *Die Räuber*. The whole play, indeed, is a tissue of spectacular "romantic" episodes and devices, confessedly gathered together, not for

[1] Morton's *Columbus* (C.G. 1792).

[2] Siddons' *The Sicilian Romance* (C.G. 1794), Scawen's *New Spain* (H.[2] 1790).

[3] While the use of the term melodrama for English plays before 1802 may be anachronistic, the presence of "melodramatic" features in the dramas of this time justifies the use of the term here.

the sake of art but for that of effect[1]. To our eyes, the atmosphere is ridiculous, with its conventionalised bombastic language and lack of subtlety. This lack of subtlety is nowhere more apparent than in the last act when Osmond, pursuing Angela, is forcibly detained by an exceedingly solid ghost:

OSM. [*employed with* Hassan *in retaining* Angela, *while* Reginald *defends himself against* Muley *and* Alaric.]—Down with him! Wrest the sword from him!—[Alaric *is wounded, and falls*; Muley *gives back*; *at the same time* Osmond's *Party appears above, pursued by* Percy's.]—Hark! They come!—Dastardly villains!—Nay then my own hand must—[*Drawing his sword, he rushes upon* Reginald, *who is disarmed, and beaten upon his knees*; *when at the moment that* Osmond *lifts his arm to stab him*, Evelina's *Ghost throws herself between them*: Osmond *starts back, and drops his sword.*]

OSM. Horror!—What form is this?

ANG. Die!—[*Disengaging herself from* Hassan, *she springs suddenly forwards, and plunges her dagger in* Osmond's *bosom, who falls with a loud groan, and faints. The Ghost vanishes*; Angela *and* Reginald *rush into each other's arms.*]

ANG. Father, thou art mine again!

No doubt contemporary audiences were duly thrilled and melted with soft pity, but we cannot today esteem Lewis any other than a mediocre dramatist intent upon the cheapest of effects.

Very similar in general spirit is *The Mysteries of the Castle* (C.G. Jan. 1795), written nominally by Miles Peter Andrews but partly composed by Frederick Reynolds[2], in which, as we are informed by the prologue, the "Bard"

> *this night makes up,*
> *Of various beverage...a kind of* cup;
> *Of Music, Pantomime, and graver scenes,*
> *Perhaps a dash of terror intervenes.*

The ancient ruins of a castle and the horrors of a dungeon are there as in *The Castle Spectre* to awe the audience, and the plot runs along the same lines. Here Julia, distressful heroine, is immured by the villain, Count Montoni, and is

---

[1] *Supra*, p. 53.
[2] See the latter's autobiography, ii. 198–9.

discovered by the valorous hero, Carlos, who, aided by the humorous old Fractioso, his friend Hilario and Cloddy the clown, succeeds in effecting her rescue. Again the same story and the same typical serious and humorous characters.

One of the first to come on the stage with this new type of drama was Thomas Morton, whose *Columbus* was performed at Covent Garden in December 1792. *Columbus* is a truly amusing piece, derived ultimately from Marmontel's tale of the Incas and traversing the same ground covered by Kotzebue's *Die Spanier in Peru*[1]. The highly spectacular plot centres on the love of Alonzo and of Cora and is full of the artificialities typical of the species. Thus in i. iii. Columbus, newly arrived in America, can converse at once with the Indian Orozimbo, who has never before seen a white man.

Zorinski[2], which followed at the Haymarket in June 1795, is fundamentally similar. Here the theme, taken from contemporary Polish history, tells how Radzano and O'Curragh return from England and are received by Casimir, at a moment when the latter's life is being aimed at by Rodomsko. Rodomsko succeeds in persuading the wronged Zorinski to aid in the plot, but loyalty is eventually victorious. The noble but offended Zorinski marks the introduction of a new and popular stock character into the melodrama, but, after all, his features are but those of Brutus conventionalised. Here again are spectacular scenes set in a not very historical Cracow relieved by comic episodes surrounding the breezy Irishman O'Curragh and the Jew Amalekite.

Another writer of similar calibre was Samuel Birch, who provided the stage with two melodramas, *The Adopted Child* (D.L. May 1795) and *The Smugglers* (D.L. April 1796), besides the later "romance" of *Albert and Adelaide; or, The Victim of Constancy* (C.G. Dec. 1798). The first of these tells

---

[1] John Thelwall, who had submitted a play called *The Incas; or the Peruvian Virgin* to Harris in 1792, accused Morton of plagiarism. The general theme, however, was so popular that no doubt each author discovered it independently.

[2] See *Mr Morton's Zorinski and Brooke's Gustavus Vasa compared. Also a Critique on Zorinski* (1795).

of the honesty of Michael, a loyal ferryman, who has reared
the true heir to Milford Castle, and who dutifully exposes
the villainy of Sir Bertrand and his tool Le Sage. In spite of
artificiality in language and character-drawing it had, like
The Smugglers, a decided success. In the latter the hero is
Captain Pendant who, with his man Trim, is rescued on the
English coast by his daughter, Stella, and the villains are a
band of evil smugglers who, of course, are defeated in the
end.

Henry Siddons likewise attempted this type of drama in
several pieces, starting with *The Sicilian Romance: or, The
Apparition of the Cliffs*, produced at Covent Garden in May
1794. It abounds in "Gothic Halls" and in would-be
pathetic pictures, as that in which through a doorway in an
"*internal Rock*" (whatever that may be) we are shown "*a
lady, pale, her hair dishevel'd, &c. sleeping on a stone*[1]."
Neither this nor any of Siddons' later pieces has the slightest
literary value.

The work of James C. Cross has possibly a little more
individuality. The first melodrama by this writer was *The
Purse: or, Benevolent Tar* (H.[2] Feb. 1794) and he reverted to
the type several times in his long career as purveyor of pantomimes, entertainments and spectacles. *The Purse* may be
taken as a specimen of one-act melodrama. In it Theodore
robs a Baron and then accuses Page. Edmund and Will
Steady—true $\theta\epsilon o\grave{\iota}\ \grave{\alpha}\pi\grave{o}\ \mu\eta\chi\alpha\nu\hat{\eta}s$—arrive just in time to set
everything to rights. *The Apparition!* (H.[2] Sept. 1794) is
even more in the typical strain with its "*Thunder, Light'ning,
Rain, &c.*" which (to harmonise with the success of the hero)
"*gradually clear up*[2]."

Lieutenant-General John Burgoyne's *Richard Cœur de
Lion* (D.L. Oct. 1786) and the similarly named play by
Leonard MacNally (C.G. Oct. 1786), both taken from the
successful play by Sedaine[3], are of the same group, affording
plentiful scenes of distressed virtue and faithful love. *New
Spain, or, Love in Mexico* (H.[2] July 1790), ascribed to John

---

[1] II. i.   [2] II. i.
[3] The two translations seem to have been executed in rivalry.

Scawen, is more of a comic production, showing two girls, Leonora and Flora, who masquerade as soldiers for love of Fabio and Don Garcias, and tempering their folly by the picture of true adoration in the persons of the "noble savages," Alkmonoak and Iscagli. Harriet Lee's *The Mysterious Marriage, or The Heirship of Roselva* (1798) is wholly serious and is by no means lacking in sterling merit. The play seems to have been written in 1795, so that, as the authoress points out, the ghost of Constantia was then a novelty, although three years later, when the theatre had become "a land of apparitions," it was already time-worn. The plot here deals with the usurper, Count Roselva, who knows that Constantia is the real heiress. The latter loves Albert, who, villain in his heart, gives her a lingering poison. This he does because he wishes to marry the Countess, who, in turn, dotes on Sigismond, discovered later to be the brother of Constantia and the real heir. It is evident that the theme of this play is tragic in essence, but the lack of any subtle character-drawing, the distressful heroine, the ghost and the spectacular "Gothic" scenes necessitate its being included in this rather than in the preceding sections. In its own way it displays clearly enough the gradual disappearance of the true tragic spirit in the illogicalities of melodrama.

Before passing to the work in this kind of one or two more important writers, it may be well to pause for a moment on James Boaden's *Fontainville Forest* (C.G. March 1794), one of many similar pieces contributed by him to the stage, and itself thoroughly representative of current theatrical fare. Based on *The Romance of the Forest*, it takes as its setting a dim Gothic abbey of the fifteenth century where Lamotte is living in dismal poverty. In the woods one day he rescues a maiden named Adeline. Driven on by poverty he robs the Marquis of Montault, who promises to forgive him on condition that he acts as pandar between himself and Adeline. Before matters reach a crisis, however, it is discovered that Adeline is really the daughter of his murdered brother, and his love consequently turns to fear and hate. In the nick of time she is saved. The play contains a phantom which "*glides across the dark part of the Chamber*[1]," and rejoices in similar romantic spectacle. Its happy ending and presentation of forced brigandage in Lamotte tell at once of its mixed French and German origin; and the stock characteristics of the principal persons are all in accordance with the "rules" of the type.

It were vain, of course, to pass the whole of the efforts in this style under review. Hardly any have even the dimmest glimmerings of poetry in them, and all are marred by the same elements of cheap sensationalism. It may, however, be of interest to turn for a moment to the cognate efforts of two capable dramatists, George Colman the Younger and Richard Cumberland. The former first attempted the true melodramatic style in *The Iron Chest* (D.L. March 1796) and continued his efforts in *Blue Beard; or, Female Curiosity* (D.L. Jan. 1798), two of the most outstanding successes of the eighteenth century, but perhaps *The Mountaineers* (H.[2] Aug. 1793) might be included also in this category. The last-mentioned, written in excellent blank verse, tells how Count Virolet, a slave in Granada, wins the love of Zorayda. Along with Kilmallock, the ever-popular Irishman, Agnes, the duenna, and Sadi, a converted Moor, they fly for safety and are met by Floranthe, Virolet's sister, who has come to seek for her hermit lover, Octavian. All the characters of pure melodrama are there but the villain; the omission of this character as well as the truer romance in the general atmosphere of the play lifts it a trifle above the ordinary productions of this class[2]. *The Iron Chest* has its villain all complete in Sir Edward Mortimer, a head-keeper of the New Forest, who has been acquitted on a charge of murder some years previously. The dire secret of his real guilt is learnt by Wilford, the hero, who is consequently persecuted by Sir Edward and is accused of robbery. In an old iron chest the documentary evidence of the latter's guilt is discovered. The artificial character of the plot and the stock features in hero

---

[1] III. iv.
[2] The story, as is obvious, is partly based on the Cardenio tale in *Don Quixote.*

and in villain make this a typical, although successful, melodramatic production[1]. *Blue Beard* is even more spectacular
and thrilling. The scene here is "*A Turkish Village*" and we
are presented to Blue Beard and his latest wife in person[2].
What the play depends on, however, is not the characters,
but the effects. In I. iii. we are confronted with "*A Blue
Apartment*" which has a mysterious "*Large door in the middle
of the Flat*" and "*Over the door, a Picture of* ABOMELIQUE,
Kneeling in amorous supplication to a beautiful woman."
Shacabac puts the key into the lock, and

> *The Door instantly sinks, with a tremendous crash, and the* Blue
> Chamber *appears streaked with vivid streams of Blood. The figures
> in the Picture, over the door, change their position, and* ABOMELIQUE
> *is represented in the action of beheading the Beauty he was, before,
> supplicating. The Pictures, and Devices of Love, change to subjects
> of Horror and Death. The interior apartment (which the sinking
> of the door discovers,) exhibits various Tombs, in a sepulchral
> building;—in the midst of which ghastly and supernatural forms are
> seen;—some in motion, some fixed—In the centre, is a large Skeleton,
> seated on a Tomb, (with a Dart in his hand) and, over his head, in
> characters of Blood, is written*
>
> "THE PUNISHMENT OF CURIOSITY."

Can we not almost hear the gasp of "Oh!" sent forth by
these eighteenth century audiences? These spectacles continue to the end in a regular succession. In the last act
Fatima

> *struggles with* ABOMELIQUE, *who attempts to kill her; and, in the
> struggle, snatches the Dagger from the pedestal of the Skeleton.
> The Skeleton rises on his feet, lifts his arm which holds the Dart,
> and keeps it suspended...* SELIM *and* ABOMELIQUE *fight with
> Scimitars.—During the Combat, Enter* IRENE *and* SHACABAC. *After
> a hard contest,* SELIM *overthrows* ABOMELIQUE *at the foot of the*

---

[1] The first and second editions contain a fierce attack on John Kemble
for his acting in the play and for his general conduct towards the playwright. This attack Colman wisely suppressed in later issues. See *Remarks
on Mr Colman's Preface. Also a summary comparison of the Play of the
Iron Chest with the Novel of Caleb Williams. Originally written for, and
inserted in, the Monthly Mirror; and now re-published...with Alterations
and Additions. By a Gentleman of the Middle Temple* (1796); and *The
Preface to the Iron Chest. A Satirical Poem. Written by Thinks-I-to-
Myself—Who?* (1796).

[2] The plot is partly founded on the French play, *Barbe-Bleue.*

Skeleton. The Skeleton instantly plunges the Dart, which he held suspended, into the Breast of ABOMELIQUE, *and sinks with him beneath the earth.—(A volume of Flame arises, and the earth closes.)*

Whereupon, of course, "SELIM *and* FATIMA *embrace*" and the former brings the play to a conclusion on a familiar moral note:

Come, Fatima. Let us away from this rude scene of horror: and bless the Providence which nerves the arm of Virtue to humble Vice, and Oppression.

The other writer mentioned above who helped on the development of the melodrama was Richard Cumberland, an author more famous perhaps for his sentimental comedies than for his tragic or would-be tragic productions. It was in the year 1796 that this author turned to the sphere of the "dramatic romance," writing in *The Days of Yore* (C.G. Jan. 1796) a prose drama obviously influenced by the example of earlier melodrama. The scene is placed in Anglo-Saxon times, and there we meet Voltimar, son of the Danish Hastings, in love with Adela, daughter of Oddune, Earl of Devonshire. This Voltimar is faced with a problem, because his mother, Oswena, desires to have him chosen as the Danish leader. To escape this undesirable position he feigns that he is only half-witted, but springs to action in order to save King Alfred, who had already listened to Adela's confession of their mutual love. It must be confessed that *The Days of Yore* is but a dull play, but it displays an interesting attempt, possibly not uninfluenced by German example, to introduce an historical setting for more or less melodramatic devices.

Cumberland's other eighteenth century play in this style, *Joanna of Montfaucon* (C.G. Jan. 1800), described as "A Dramatic Romance of the Fourteenth Century," is admittedly based on the German of Kotzebue, or, rather, on Maria Geisweiler's English rendering of that original. The story tells, in sentimental melodramatic wise, how Albert, Lord of Thurn, is smitten with conscience because his father had taken away the castle of Thurn from its real owner. In the midst of this torment, Lazarra, who loves Albert's wife, Joanna, causes a diversion by making an attack on the castle.

After many exciting scenes, Albert proves victorious, Lazarra is slain, and the play ends on a setting of mutual reconciliation and new-found happiness. The language hardly ever rises above mediocrity and only the spectacular effects could have made the drama as a whole appeal to spectators. Even with this show, it does not seem to have won over-much approval. "It was a grand spectacle," says the editor of the *Biographia Dramatica*[1], "full of noise and bustle; but was not very successful"; the rich settings were specially noted by the reviewer in the *Lady's Magazine*, who described the whole play as "a vehicle for the charms of music, scenery, decoration, and stage effect." Cumberland himself seems to have remained in no doubt about what he was doing. In his Preface he expresses himself boldly and unreservedly concerning the main features of the German drama he was thus helping to introduce on the English stage:

I also perceive I have lived to see the time, when not content with the eccentricities of our own stage, we have gone to that of the Germans for fresh supplies of what we were overstocked with —false writing and false moral.

This last quotation shows well the weakness of the melodrama as a form of art. This was the type of serious play which most appealed to the audiences of the time, but hardly any author entered into its spirit whole-heartedly. Nearly all were writing with their tongues in their cheeks, with the consequence that none of their plays has the genuine mark of sincerity. Here there was nothing but writing for effect; here there was a total lack of any dominant purpose or urgent artistic necessity.

[1] ii. 346.

CHAPTER III

COMEDY

I. *The Main Types*

IN the preceding chapter we have seen how the serious drama completely broke down in the late eighteenth century. The literary men for the most part clung to the outworn ideals of pseudo-classicism, but pseudo-classicism had long ago passed by its era of vitality and had become a mere fetish; it had, moreover, but a scanty following in the auditorium of the theatre. A few men, certainly, endeavoured to bring true romanticism into the playhouse, but their efforts were both sporadic and amateurish. Others, too, appealed to the audiences, but they did so through the more blatant and artistically vulgar medium of the melodrama.

When we study the repertoires of these years, therefore, it is not surprising to find that tragedy rapidly loses the position it held in the first half of the century. As season passes season we can see the nightly performances growing more heterogeneous and absurd. Farces, pantomimes, short melodramas, comic operas fill up the majority of the playbills; if a tragedy or a finer comedy is acted, it is accompanied by a mass of other less dignified attractions. At the same time a certain section of the audience at least called for more serious works of dramatic art, obtaining the revival of many of the best among the older plays. Shakespeare is well represented, not only with *Henry IV* and *The Merry Wives of Windsor*, but with the romantic comedies as well. The comedies of manners, still popular in 1750, continued to appear for a few years, but then were dismally altered or vanished completely. Early eighteenth century sentimental comedy flourished, as, of course, did the sentimental comedies newly produced in the later years of the century.

From these repertoire lists we see clearly that the older types of comedy no longer held the position accorded to them from 1700 to 1750. Wycherley and Congreve are not merely cut but entirely altered; everything becomes decorously moral and genteel. The hey-day of the Sentimental Muse has arrived. Sufficient has been said perhaps concerning the nature of sentimentalism in the relevant sections of the two preceding volumes of this *History of English Drama*, but attention might be drawn here to the development of new types of this all-pervading atmosphere. Sentimentalism can be both sincere and hypocritical; it can be both revolutionary and conservative; and all its varied aspects are well shown in the comedies of this time. The spirit of Richardson's *Pamela*, essentially lower middle class and vulgarly moral, appears in many a work of the age. Sterne's fantastic sentimentalism is not so common, its place being taken by the lamentable sensibility of Mackenzie's style. Sentimental humanitarianism is evident in Cumberland's *The Jew* (D.L. 1794) and in Holcroft's many dramas, while the hypocritical sentimentalism breathes in countless dramas of the time. The fact that this mood in one or another of its many forms penetrates into almost every play of the age explains to a certain extent the failure of late eighteenth century comedy. Many an otherwise brilliant drama is ruined by a conclusion essentially mawkish and artificial. Many a stroke of wit loses its point because of the repression caused by a sentimentalised conscience.

As in tragedy, then, it is difficult to distinguish the various movements in comedy during these years. The spirit of Congreve was still alive, but it was never allowed free expression. The audiences loved to see the follies and vices of fashionable life put upon the stage, but they were not content to witness the inevitable consequences of that folly and vice. A typical form of comedy, then, was what we might call the sentimentalised play of manners, which alternates the mood of Steele with the mood of Etherege. Other considerations entered in as well. The playwrights had to please, not only the People of Quality, but the middle-class section of the

audience as well. Fine comedy would appeal to the one but
not to the other, and as a consequence many good comedies
of the time are spoilt by the intrusion of farcical elements
designed to attract the less fashionable spectators. The
"comedy-farces" of Frederick Reynolds are, in this way,
thoroughly typical of the period. The influence of melodrama, too, must be noted. Coalescing with the force of
sentimentalism, it frequently led comedy far astray. Figures
conceived in the comic spirit move alongside of villains and
heroes delineated in those strong hues of black or of white
which are the *beau idéal* of the melodrama, and the plays
end in a welter of tears and laughter. Music will enter in, and
the gay witticism be capped, not by another stroke of comic
genius, but by an unlyrical and sentimental ditty.

All this, and more, was happening to comedy in this age;
yet we have to note how many writers succeeded in rising
above the rapidly degenerating standards of the time.
Laughter still holds its place in the works of Goldsmith and
Sheridan, and they had many, unfortunately neglected, companions in their own style. It must be our object in the
succeeding pages of this book to delineate both the typically
inartistic movements of the time and the genuine success of
those who retained something of that refined polish and perfection of comic utterance which marked out the comedies
of the Restoration period.

II. *English and Foreign Models*

Already an indication has been given of the indebtedness of
the century both to French and to German tragedy and melodrama, but the adaptations of serious dramas are im-
measurably fewer in number than the borrowings made from
the farces and comedies of the continent, as well as of previous
ages in England itself. Most of the comic dramatists seem to
have had their heads filled with a tissue of situations, characters and *bons mots* which they wove into their most original
productions. It is not too much to say that not a single comedy
written between 1750 and 1800 is free entirely from passages

or conceptions taken from some continental or earlier English playwright. The record given in this section is one of direct adaptation only; it must be regarded as symbolic merely of a vast influence which will perhaps remain for ever unchronicled.

It must be remembered that from 1744 onwards Shakespeare's romantic comedies were rapidly coming into fashion. The age unconsciously felt a sympathy for this art which, in the period of classicism, had been almost completely neglected, so that we need feel no surprise that these romantic comedies formed a happy hunting-ground for the lazy or the uninventive dramatist of the time. *The Comedy of Errors* was put on at York in 1780 as altered by J. P. Kemble. The same year Edinburgh saw another anonymous version called *The Twins*, a production evidently distinct from Hull's earlier rendering, *The Twins: or, The Comedy of Errors*, produced at Covent Garden in 1762. *The Two Gentlemen of Verona* was altered and added to by Victor (D.L. 1762)[1], and later by Kemble (D.L. 1790). *A Midsummer-Night's Dream* gave, in an adapted form, Garrick's *The Fairies* (D.L. 1755)[2] with "Songs from Shakespeare, Milton, Waller, Dryden, Lansdown, Hammond, &c." and Colman's *A Fairy Tale* (D.L. 1763), altered from Garrick's version[3]. Bayley's *The Forester; or, The Royal Seat* (1798) might also be noted as a drama almost certainly suggested by Shakespeare's comedy. *As You Like It* was altered by Smith into *The Noble Foresters* (1776) and probably, along with *Cymbeline*, gave Holcroft the basis for *The Noble Peasant* (H.[2] 1784). It may be noted that Holcroft anticipated by six years Burgoyne's recommendation that Shakespeare's plays should be turned into comic operas[4].

The later comedies proved equally popular. Garrick wrote an adaptation of *The Tempest* (D.L. 1756) and another of *A Winter's Tale* as *Florizel and Perdita* (D.L. 1756). The latter may be compared with Morgan's *The Sheep-Shearing: or, Florizel and Perdita* (C.G. 1754)[5]. *Catharine and Petruchio*

[1] Odell, *op. cit.* i. 374–5.   [2] *Id.* i. 358.   [3] *Id.* i. 376.
[4] See *infra*, p. 202.   [5] Odell, *op. cit.* i. 357, 361.

(D.L. 1756) is a very similar attempt to reduce Shakespeare's own farce to still slighter proportions[1].

Everywhere the influence of Shakespeare penetrated. It need not surprise us that Bewley in *What is She?* (C.G. 1799) enters carolling

Merrily, merrily shall I live now![2]

nor that Garrick could organise a highly successful Jubilee in the year 1769. At the same time we must not suppose that this admiration of Shakespeare was greater than it was in reality. There is much of truth in Mezzetin's words in Colman's *New Brooms* (D.L. 1776):

> Vat signify your *triste* Sha-kes-peare? Begar, dere was more moneys got by de gran spectacle of de Sha-kes-peare Jubilee, dan by all de *comique* and *tragique* of Sha-kes-peare beside, *ma foi!* —You make-a de danse, and de musique, and de pantomime of your Sha-kes-peare, and den he do ver well.

We have to put against one another the newly awakened interest in Shakespeare's comedies and this more trivial propensity of the age.

Shakespeare, however, does not stand alone in appealing to the late eighteenth century. Jonson, Beaumont and Fletcher, Shirley and others were eagerly ransacked, for Dodsley's collections were not published without authority from contemporary taste. *Epicœne* was altered by Colman (D.L. 1776) and by Gentleman (*The Coxcombs*, H.[2] 1771). The latter likewise provided a version of *The Alchemist* (as *The Tobacconist*, H.[2] 1771), while the former gave a stage version of the masque *Oberon* as *The Fairy Prince* (C.G. 1771). The "Beaumont and Fletcher" series presents even a greater list of renderings. *The Coxcomb* provided a theme for Richardson's *The Fugitive* (H.[1] 1792), and suggested part of Colman's *The Suicide* (H.[2] 1778). An anonymous adaptation of *The Tamer Tamed* appeared at Drury Lane in 1757; *The Female Duellist* (H.[1] 1793) is simply a rendering of *Love's Cure*; and *The Greek Slave* (D.L. 1791) as clearly

---

[1] Genest, *op. cit.* iv. 446–51; Odell, *op. cit.* i. 358, 360.
[2] ii. iii.

goes back to *The Humorous Lieutenant*. *The Two Noble Kinsmen* was revived in an altered form as *Love and Valour* (Richmond 1779) and gave a theme to Waldron for *Love and Madness* (H.² 1795). Mrs Booth has a *Little French Lawyer* (C.G. 1778); an anonymous *Knight of Malta* appeared at Covent Garden in 1783; Kemble rewrote *The Pilgrim* (D.L. 1787); in 1783 an anonymous writer brought forward a version of *The Spanish Curate* (C.G. 1783); Hull's *The Royal Merchant* (C.G. 1767) is based on Norton's alteration of *The Beggar's Bush*; while *The Triumph of Honour* (H.² 1783) is founded on one of the *Four Plays in One*.

Other authors came in for their due share of rifling. Middleton's *A Mad World my Masters* provided themes for MacNally's *April Fool* (C.G. 1786) and for Kenrick's *The Spendthrift* (C.G. 1778). Cumberland's *The Duke of Milan* (C.G. 1779) was apparently taken from Massinger, whose *The Bashful Lover* appeared as Hull's *Disinterested Love* (C.G. 1798). Kemble altered *The Maid of Honour* (D.L. 1785), *The Fatal Dowry* appeared as *The Insolvent* (H.² 1758), *The Picture* as Bate's *The Magic Picture* (C.G. 1783) and *A New Way to Pay Old Debts* gave something to *The Peruvian* (C.G. 1786). Mayne's *The City Match* was altered by Bromfield as *The Schemers* (D.L. 1755). Garrick similarly dealt with Tomkis' *Albumazar* (D.L. 1773) and with Shirley's *The Gamesters* (D.L. 1757). Mrs Lennox' *Old City Manners* (D.L. 1775) is a considerably cut-down version of Jonson and Chapman's *Eastward Hoe*; Stephen Kemble's *The Northern Inn* (H.² 1791) preserves the main plot and much of the dialogue of Heywood's *The Fair Maid of the West*; Dance's *The Ladies Frolick* (D.L. 1770) is but another of the many eighteenth century versions of Brome's *The Jovial Crew*; while *George a Green* (York 1775) presents an interesting attempt to revive a long-forgotten Elizabethan drama.

Restoration plays, too, remained popular even although their subject matter was often regarded as morally vicious. Dryden's *Amphitryon* appeared in Dibdin's version as *Jupiter and Alcmena* (C.G. 1781), and had been used earlier by Hawkesworth (D.L. 1756). The anonymous *Jealous Husband* (C.G.

1777) was but an alteration of *The Spanish Fryar*, and the
narrative poem *Cymon and Iphigenia* suggested Garrick's
Cymon (D.L. 1767). Mrs Behn was remembered in her
The Emperor of the Moon, which provided a similarly named
entertainment (Patagonian 1777), in *The False Count*, which
was reduced to a farce as *The Merry Counterfeit: or, The
Viscount à la Mode* (C.G. 1762), in *The Rover*, which pro-
vided Kemble with *Love in Many Masks* (D.L. 1790) and
was also adapted anonymously (C.G. 1757), and in *The
Lucky Chance*, which suggested part of Mrs Cowley's *A
School for Greybeards* (D.L. 1786). Sedley's *The Grumbler*
was produced in an altered version at Drury Lane in 1754.
Crowne's *Sir Courtly Nice* appeared as *Sir Thomas Callicoe*
(C.G. 1758) and as *Opposition* at the Haymarket in 1790.
Among the minor Restoration plays favoured with alteration
might be noted Cokain's *A Duke and No Duke* (at D.L.),
Howard's *The Committee* (adapted as *The Honest Thieves*
by Knight, C.G. 1797), Shadwell's *Epsom Wells* (used by
Foote for *The Mayor of Garratt*, H.[2] 1763), D'Avenant's
The Man's the Master (altered by Woodward, C.G. 1775),
Tuke's *The Adventures of Five Hours* (used by Hull for *The
Perplexities*, C.G. 1767), Dennis' *A Plot and No Plot* (which
probably gave a hint to Foote for a device in *The Orators*,
H.[2] 1762), Ravenscroft's *The Anatomist* (D.L. 1771), Better-
ton's *The Amorous Widow* (adapted anonymously as *Barnaby
Brittle*, C.G. 1781), Durfey's *Don Quixote* (used by Pilon in
Barataria, C.G. 1785), *Love for Money* (made into a farce
as *The Counterfeit Heiress*, C.G. 1762) and *The Richmond
Heiress* (altered by Waldron, Richmond 1777), and Digby's
Elvira (used for part of Mrs Griffith's *The Double Mistake*,
C.G. 1766). So far, of course, no mention has been made of
the dramatists of the manners school, but these also found
their admirers. Wycherley's *The Country Wife* was regularly
altered by Garrick as *The Country Girl* (D.L. 1766) and also
by Lee (D.L. 1765). *The Gentleman Dancing Master* suggested a character in Bickerstaffe's *Love in a Village* (C.G.
1762). Congreve's *The Old Bachelor* was reduced to a farce
as *Fondlewife and Letitia* (Dublin 1767). Vanbrugh's *Æsop*

suggested *The Fabulist* (York) and also *Esop* (D.L. 1778), while *The Relapse* was freely utilised by Sheridan in *A Trip to Scarborough* (D.L. 1777). It is certainly true that the enthusiasm for these dramatists was waning in the last years of the eighteenth century, for "Congreve and Vanbrugh seldom" filled "the house[1]," but these records, added to the evidence of the repertoire lists and to the many undoubted reminiscences in plays other than those cited above, prove that the Restoration influence was still potent in the theatre.

Peculiarly enough the early eighteenth century comic dramatists were more frequently adapted than the tragic playwrights of those years[2]. One hardly knows what to suggest as the reason for this, but the fact unquestionably remains. Here, of course, we have to reckon with the last relics of the true manners style, and must add a part of the influence at least to that of the Restoration. Thus Farquhar's *The Beaux Stratagem* was used by Cumberland for *The Impostors* (D.L. 1789), and *The Twin Rivals* was adapted by Horde as *It was Right at the Last* (1787). Vanbrugh's *The Mistake* gave *Lovers' Quarrels* (C.G. 1790) and Ryder's *Like Master like Man* (Dublin 1766), while *The False Friend* was altered by Kemble (D.L. 1789) and by an anonymous author[3]. Mrs Centlivre's *The Stolen Heiress* was taken by Mrs Cowley for *Who's the Dupe* (D.L. 1779), *The Artifice* was used for part of Foote's *The Englishman returned from Paris* (C.G. 1756), *The Gamester* was reduced to *The Faro Table* (C.G. 1789) and *The Man's Bewitched* was similarly cut down to *The Ghost* (Dublin 1767). *Celadon and Florimel* (D.L. 1796) is based on Cibber's *The Comical Lovers*[4], Bickerstaffe's *The Hypocrite* (D.L. 1768) on *The Nonjuror*, Forde's *The Miraculous Cure* (1771) on *The Double Gallant*, and Oliphant's *A Sop in the Pan* (Liverpool 1790) on *The Refusal*. Charles Johnson's *The Country Lasses*, a long popular play and often suggesting portions of plot and

---

[1] Epilogue by Conway to Jerningham's *The Welch Heiress* (D.L. 1795).
[2] Cp. *supra*, p. 59.
[3] As *Friendship à la Mode* (Dublin, S.A. 1766).
[4] The same play was used for *The School for Indifference* (1787) mentioned in the *Biographia Dramatica*.

dialogue, was adapted by Kemble as *The Farm House* (D.L. 1789) and by Kenrick as *The Lady of the Manor* (C.G. 1778), while *The Village Opera* suggested some points in Bicker-staffe's *Love in a Village* (C.G. 1762). Fielding also seems to have formed a treasure-house for the adapters. *The Intriguing Chambermaid* gave suggestions for Dibdin's *Liberty Hall* (D.L. 1785); Murphy's *The Upholsterer* (D.L. 1758) and Hodson's *The Adventures of a Night* (D.L. 1783) are both based on *The Coffee House Politician*; Arne's *Squire Badger* (H.² 1772) seems to owe something to *Don Quixote in England*, and there are several other characters and situations in the plays of diverse authors which suggest the influence of this piece; a few scenes in Theophilus Cibber's *The Auction* (1757) are modelled on *The Historical Register*; while *The Life and Death of Commonsense* (H.² 1782) clearly is an alteration of *Pasquin*. It is impossible here to present a full list of these many borrowings, but as an indication of the influences exerted by the minor dramatists of the early eighteenth century the following plays may be noted: Mac-ready's *The Bank Note* (C.G. 1795; based on Taverner's *The Artful Husband*), Colman's *The Female Chevalier* (H.² 1778; altered from the same play), Wignell's *Love's Artifice* (1762; taken from Taverner's *The Maid the Mistress*), *Marriage à la Mode* (D.L. 1760; evidently an adaptation of Boden's *The Modish Couple*), *Wives in Plenty* (H.² 1793; a version of the same author's *The Coquet*), Colman's *Achilles in Petticoats* (C.G. 1773; taken from Gay's *Achilles*), Thompson's *The Beggar's Opera* (C.G. 1777; an alteration of the earlier *Beggar's Opera*), Lloyd's *The Capricious Lovers* (D.L. 1764; taken from Odingsells' play of the same name), *The Female Officer* (Dublin, 1763; altered from Charles Shadwell's *The Humours of the Army*), Thompson's *The Fair Quaker* (D.L. 1773; altered from *The Fair Quaker of Deal*), Williams' *The Unfortunate Beau* (Dublin, Capel St, 1784; a version of Bullock's *Woman is a Riddle*, a play which was altered again as *The Invisible Mistress*, D.L. 1788), *The Man of Taste* (D.L. 1752; an abridgement of Miller's play), *The Spaniards Dis-mayed* (C.G. 1780; taken from Carey's *Nancy*), Dibdin's *Poor*

Vulcan (C.G. 1778; based on Motteux' *The Loves of Mars and Venus*), and the four separate versions of Ramsay's *The Gentle Shepherd*[1].

It is quite evident, then, that the dramatists of this period paid due attention to the English theatre from Elizabethan times to 1750. The alterations show that constant endeavours were made to keep the older stock plays up to date, and the imitations prove that, whatever was the continental influence, an English substratum of character delineation and of sentiment was always present in the drama of the time. Not that that continental influence can be minimised. The French playwrights, from Molière to the authors of contemporary Paris, were eagerly ransacked and provided many a theme and suggestion. Molière himself received more adequate translation in these years, and still the dramatists found his comedies fruitful of suggestions. *L'Étourdi*, along with *L'École des Femmes* and *L'École des Maris*, was used by Murphy for *The School for Guardians* (C.G. 1767). *Le Dépit amoureux* was adapted as *The Amorous Quarrel* (1762). *Le Mariage forcé* provided Garrick with *The Irish Widow* (D.L. 1772). Lewis' *The East Indian* (D.L. 1799) has caught an idea from *Le Festin de Pierre*[2]; Colman's *Spleen* (D.L. 1776) and Bickerstaffe's *Dr Last in his Chariot* (H.[2] 1769) are both based on *Le Malade imaginaire*; Murphy's *All in the Wrong* (D.L. 1761) is likewise adumbrated in *Le Cocu imaginaire*; *No Wit like a Woman's* (D.L. 1769) and Dibdin's *The Metamorphoses* (H.[2] 1775) go back to *George Dandin*. Pierre Corneille's *Le Menteur* proved the ultimate basis of Foote's *The Lyar* (C.G. 1762), although the original situations were freely modified, while *Mélite* was translated in 1776, and *Don Sanche d'Aragon* adapted as *The Conflict* (1798) by Brand. Dancourt's *La Femme d'Intrigue* (1692) was used, along with Molière's *Le Bourgeois Gentilhomme*, by Foote for *The Commissary* (H.[2] 1765) and *Le Besoin de l'Amour* was adapted by Warboys as *The Preceptor* (1777). Warboys' *The Rival Lovers* (1777) is

[1] For which see the Hand-list of late eighteenth-century plays.
[2] This was also given as Craven's *The Statue Feast* (Benham House 1782).

a version of Regnard's *La Sérénade* (1694) and King's *Wit's Last Stake* (D.L. 1768) is founded on *Le Légataire universel* (1708). *Crispin rival de son maître* (1707) of Lesage gave Garrick the theme for *Neck or Nothing* (D.L. 1766). The same French author was used freely in Boaden's *Ozmyn and Daraxa* (H.[1] 1793), and *Gil Blas* provided material for *The Female Adventurer* (C.G. 1790), *The Knights of the Post* (Newcastle 1797) and Reed's *The Impostors* (C.G. 1776). Destouches was utilised in Murphy's *The Citizen* (D.L. 1761; taken from *La Fausse Agnès*, 1759, which also gave part of the plot of Colman's *Man and Wife*, C.G. 1769), in the same author's *Know your own Mind* (C.G. 1777, based on *L'Irrésolu*, 1713), in Mrs Inchbald's *The Married Man* (H.[2] 1789, adapted from *Le Philosophe marié*, 1727), in Holcroft's *The School for Arrogance* (C.G. 1791, based on *Le Glorieux*, 1732), in *Cross Partners* (H.[2] 1792) and Francklin's *The Contract* (H.[2] 1776; both from *L'Amour usé*, 1741), in Obeirne's *The Generous Impostor* (D.L. 1780) and Mrs Inchbald's *Next Door Neighbours* (H.[2] 1791; both from *Le Dissipateur*, 1736), and in Brand's *Adelinda* (1798; from *La Force du Naturel*). Marivaux likewise was freely borrowed from. *Le Jeu de l'Amour et du Hasard* (1730) was adapted as *The Mutual Deception* (Dublin 1785) by Atkinson, and again was used in Bickerstaffe's *Love in a Village* (C.G. 1762); *La Joie imprévu* (1738) was altered by Rule as *The Agreeable Surprise* (school production, 1766); the tale of *Le Paysan Parvenu* was used by Victor as *The Fortunate Peasant* (1776); while *L'Isle des Esclaves* (1725) was translated twice (once anonymously and once by Mrs Clive, D.L. 1761 and D.L. 1781). Naturally, in this age of comic opera Favart was also popular. *La Fée Urgèle* (Fontainebleau 1765) "gave a hint" to Garrick for *A Christmas Tale* (D.L. 1773), *Le Caprice amoureux* (1755) was liberally used for Lloyd's *The Capricious Lovers* (D.L. 1764), *La Bohémienne* (1755) was similarly borrowed from for Dibdin's *The Gipsies* (H.[2] 1778), and *Annette et Lubin* (1762) was directly adapted by the same author. Beaumarchais, equally naturally, gripped the imaginations of those dramatists who indulged in the satiric comedy. *Le Barbier de Séville ou la Précaution inutile* (1775) was translated by Mrs Griffith (1776) and was adapted by Colman as *The Spanish Barber* (H.² 1777). Holcroft attended early performances of *Le Mariage de Figaro* (1784) in Paris, jotted down the plot and some of the dialogue, hurried back to England, and produced *The Follies of a Day* (C.G. 1784). *Les deux Amis* (1770) suggested Colman's *The Man of Business* (C.G. 1774) and was translated by C. H. as *The Two Friends* (1800). *Eugénie* (1767) gave a portion of Mrs Griffith's *The School for Rakes* (D.L. 1769) and *Tarare* was rendered by James in 1787.

Various other French authors besides these specially popular figures exercised an influence on the comedy of the time. Voltaire was fully translated during these years, and several of his plays were influential in moulding characters and situations of individual English comedies. *L'Indiscret* (1725) was thus made use of by Murphy for *No One's Enemy but his Own* (C.G. 1764), while *L'Écossaise* (1760) provided Colman with the theme for *The English Merchant* (D.L. 1767). La Font's *Les Trois Frères rivaux* (1713) provided material for *Cross Purposes* (C.G. 1772) by O'Brien, and *Le Naufrage* (1710) was utilised by Dodd for *Gallic Gratitude* (Dublin 1772). Fagan's *L'Étourderie* (1737) was copied closely in Murphy's *The Old Maid* (D.L. 1761), and *La Pupille* (1734) in Garrick's *The Guardian* (D.L. 1759). *L'Isle Sauvage* (1743) of Saint-Foix and *La Colonie* (1775) of Framéry were used by Dibdin for *The Islanders* (C.G. 1780). Sedaine's *La Gageure imprévue* (1768) was made into a farce as *A Key to the Lock* (H.² 1788), *Blaise le Savetier* (1759) was similarly handled by Dibdin in *The Cobler* (D.L. 1774) and *Le Philosophe sans le Sçavoir* (1765) by O'Brien in *The Duel* (D.L. 1772). Poinsinet's *Tom Jones* (1765) gave part of Reed's *Tom Jones* (C.G. 1769), de Boissy's *Le Français à Londres* (1727) was translated as *The Frenchman in London* (1755), Gresset's *Le Méchant* (1745) suggested Mrs Inchbald's *Young Men and Old Women* (H.² 1792). Several of Rousseau's works provided English dramatists with materials for plot and character. *Le Devin du Village* (Fontainebleau 1752) was freely adapted by Burney as *The Cunning Man* (D.L. 1766), besides being translated as *The Village Conjurer* (1767), *La Nouvelle Héloïse* (1767) gave Reynolds' *Eloisa* (C.G. 1786), *Narcisse, ou l'amant de lui-même* (1752) was rendered into English in 1767, and *Pigmalion* (1775) in 1779. Diderot, too, still exercised his old fascination. *Le Fils naturel* (1757) was translated as *Dorval* (1767), while on *Le Père de famille* (1761) were based Burgoyne's *The Heiress* (D.L. 1786), Miss Lee's *The Chapter of Accidents* (H.² 1780), *The Father* (1770, a modified translation), Jenner's *The Man of Family* (1771) and *The Family Picture* (1781). De Moissy's *La Nouvelle École des Femmes* (1758) was utilised by Murphy for *The Way to Keep Him* (D.L. 1760) besides being translated by Lloyd as *The New School for Women* (1762). Fontanelle's *Le Testament* (1758) became Whitehead's *The School for Lovers* (D.L. 1762), Patrat's *L'Heureuse Erreur* (1783) gave both Atkinson's *A Match for a Widow* (Dublin, T.R. 1786) and Mrs Inchbald's *The Widow's Vow* (H.² 1786), Count de Pont de Vesle's *Le Somnambule* (1739) was rendered by Lady Craven as *The Sleep-Walker* (private, 1778) and de Launay's *Le Complaisant* (1752) as *He's Much to Blame* (C.G. 1798), Fenouillot de Falbaire's *Les deux Avares* (1770) appeared as O'Hara's *The Two Misers* (C.G. 1775), Delisle's *Arlequin Sauvage* (1721) as Cleland's *Tombo-Chiqui* (1758). Mercier's *L'Indigent* (Dijon 1773) was translated as *The Distressed Family* (1787), and Sedaine's *Le Déserteur* (1769) was adapted by Dibdin as *The Deserter* (D.L. 1773), besides giving suggestions to at least two other dramatists[1]. Florian's *La Bonne Mère* (1785) provided material for Robson's *Look before You Leap* (H.² 1788). In tracing this French influence, notice must be taken, too, of the various lesser pieces imitated here and of the *contes* which provided much matter for the dramatists. Thus Marmontel's *Silvain* (1770) gave some suggestions to Burgoyne for *The Lord of the Manor* (D.L. 1780), another tale provided the plot of Colman's *The Deuce is in Him* (D.L. 1763), another that of Morton's *Columbus* (C.G. 1792), another (*Coralie, ou l'Amitié à l'Épreuve*) that of Kelly's *The Romance of an Hour* (C.G. 1774), another

---

[1] It was used too for the ballet, *The Deserter of Naples* (Royalty 1788).

(*L'heureux Divorce*) that of Mrs Griffith's *The Platonic Wife* (D.L. 1765), and there are several other works wherein influence exerted by the same author may strongly be suspected. Madame de Genlis, with her *Théâtre d'éducation* (1780) and her *Théâtre de société* (1782), had likewise a certain influence. The former was literally translated in 1781, *Zélie* was used by Mrs Inchbald for *The Child of Nature* (C.G. 1788) and Holcroft in 1786 issued a set of her sacred dramas. Lesser works were plentifully used. *Le Tableau parlant* (1769), a Franco-Italian farce, by Anseaume, was utilised by Colman for *The Portrait* (C.G. 1770), *Le Tonnelier* (1765) of N. M. Audinot became Arne's *The Cooper* (H.[2] 1772), *Le Prisonnier* (1798), an opera by A. Duval, was put on the stage by Heartwell as *The Castle of Sorrento* (H.[2] 1799), Dumaniant's *La Ruse contre Ruse, ou La Guerre ouverte* (1786) was used by Lady Wallace for *Diamond cut Diamond* (1787), and by Mrs Inchbald for *The Midnight Hour* (C.G. 1787), de Boissy's *Dehors Trompeurs* (1740) became Conway's *False Appearances* (D.L. 1789), *Le Comte d'Albert et sa Suite* (Fontainebleau 1786) by Sedaine was used by Hoare in *A Friend in Need* (D.L. 1797), Dorvigny's *La Fête de Campagne* (1784) by Bonnor in *The Manager an Actor* (C.G. 1785), *L'Aveugle prétendu* by Dibdin in *None so Blind* (H.[2] 1782), Favart's *Les Moissonneurs* (1768) was translated as *The Reapers* (1770), while countless comedies confess in preface or in advertisement to a French source, now difficult to identify. Few could declare with Murphy in the prologue to *The Apprentice* (D.L. 1756):

> To-night no smuggled scenes from France we shew,
> 'Tis ENGLISH, ENGLISH, Sirs, from top to toe.

It is natural that the French influence in comedy during this period should have been considerably weightier than the corresponding influence of Germany, although it must be borne in mind that many of the serious plays mentioned above[1] were, not tragedies, but *drames* and so are partly connected with the comic theatre. Goethe's *Clavigo* (1774) gave a hint to the author of *He's Much to Blame* (C.G. 1798)

---

[1] *Supra*, pp. 61–5.

and was translated twice (1790 and 1798). Kotzebue's *Die
Indianer in England* (1789) was translated as *The Indians in
England* (1796, by A. Thomson) and as *The Indian Exiles*
(1800, by Thompson), besides suggesting part of the theme of
Lewis' *The East Indian* (D.L. 1799). The same author's *Die
Witwe und das Reitpferd* (1796) was rendered literally by
Plumptre as *The Widow and the Riding Horse* (1799), which was
adapted for the stage by Dibdin as *The Horse and the Widow*
(C.G. 1799). Dibdin's *The Birth-Day* (C.G. 1799) is similarly
altered from *Der Bruderzwist* (1797). *Die Corsen* (1799) was
translated as *The Corsicans* (1799) and *Das Schreibepult, oder
die Gefahren der Jugend* (1800), translated as *The Writing
Desk* (1799), was used by Mrs Inchbald for *The Wise Man
of the East* (C.G. 1799). Lessing's *Minna von Barnhelm*
(1763) first found an adapter in Johnstone (*The Disbanded
Officer*, H.[2] 1786), and was literally rendered later as *The
School for Honour* (1799). Holcroft's *The German Hotel*
(C.G. 1790) is based on Brandes' *Der Gasthof, oder Trau',
schau' wem!* (1769), Thompson's *The Ensign* (1800) is a
rendering from F. L. Schröder, and *The Set of Horses* (1792)
is a version of C. H. von Ayrenhoff's *Der Postzug, oder die
nobeln Passionen* (1769).

Italian influence, on the other hand, is stronger in the
realm of comedy than in that of tragedy. Goldoni had established out of the old *commedia dell' arte* a new form of
farcical intrigue comedy, and his style was eagerly watched
by dramatists in London. *La Serva Amorosa* (1752) and *Il
Padre di Famiglia* (1750) were worked together by Holcroft
into *Knave or Not?* (D.L. 1798). *Il Servitore di due Padroni*
(1749) was taken along with the Franco-Italian *Arlequin
Valet de deux Maîtres* by Vaughan for *The Hotel* (D.L. 1776).
Il Padre di Famiglia was directly translated in 1757, and *La
Buona Figliuola* (1760; as *The Maid of the Vale*) in 1775.

Among other plays reminiscent of Italian may be noted
Don Juan (D.L. 1790) with its indebtedness to the *scenarii*
of the *commedia dell' arte*, and Dibdin's *The Wedding Ring*
(D.L. 1773)[1]. Great success was attained by G. A. Federico's

---

[1] An alteration of *Il Filosofo di Campagna* (Venice 1754).

La Serva Padrona (Naples 1733), which was translated directly as *The Servant Mistress* (1770), adapted by Bickerstaffe as *He Wou'd if he Cou'd* (D.L. 1771) and by O'Keeffe as *The Maid the Mistress* (C.G. 1783), besides being performed at Marylebone Gardens in a version set by Storace. Many other comedies, such as Bentley's *The Wishes* (D.L. 1761), seem based either on literary Italian comedy of the eighteenth century or on the lingering traditions of the *commedia dell' arte*.

Spanish literature had but small influence on the stage of this time. Lope de Vega provided materials for *The Father Outwitted* (1784), Calderon's *El Escondido y la Tapada* was utilised for Bickerstaffe's *'Tis Well it's no Worse* (D.L. 1770), Cervantes' tale of the *Curioso Impertinente* provided the plot of *The Padlock* (D.L. 1768) and the same author's *Don Quixote* was used by Colman for *The Mountaineers* (H.² 1793), but apart from these we can trace but little reminiscence in this period of that comedy which had laid such a powerful hand upon Restoration playwrights.

The classical influence is also rather meagre. More or less scholarly translations of Terence were issued from the press; Cumberland used *Heautontimoroumenos* for *The Choleric Man* (D.L. 1774); Colman based part of *The Man of Business* (C.G. 1774) on various suggestions both in Terence and in Plautus; but the fact remained that the classic authors had been drained dry. Little was left which could prove of value to playwrights of the time.

It will be seen from this brief and necessarily dull summary that, in the realm of comedy, English and French models were all predominant. The romantic comedy of the Elizabethan age was once more coming into favour. The age still enjoyed the wit of the Congreve school although it despised the peculiar morals of the Restoration period. In France it found a social comedy excellently suited to contemporary taste and at the same time a didactic and sentimental note easy to admire and to imitate. It cannot, of course, be denied that often what was borrowed lost its point in the process. The wit of the manners style frequently disappeared in the purifying treatment of the dramatists, and the polish of French utterance was dulled. Take, for example, the scene in Destouches' *La Fausse Agnès*, in which Angélique pretends to simplicity in order that she may drive off her unwanted suitor, M. des Mazures. Let this be compared with the corresponding scene in Murphy's *The Citizen* (D.L. 1761) where Maria meets the awkward George, and at once it will be seen that in the transmutation from French to English much of the temper of the original has been lost. The same phenomenon will be evident in a consideration of other works of the time. The age, in purifying its manners outwardly, had lost the grace of wit and of *badinage*.

III. *Sentimental Comedy*

Owing to the fact that the whole of the dramatic literature of this time is influenced, directly or indirectly, by sentimentalism, it will be well to start with a brief sketch of the fortunes of this type of comedy before the year 1800. Included in this section will be found the more pronounced examples of the school as well as the non-comic *drames* or "plays," but it must be ever borne in mind that quite a number of the comedies dealt with in the following sections display a marked colouring of sentimentality. Indeed, many of them, had they been written before 1750, would certainly have been included in the sentimental group. Sentimentalism, therefore, extended in the theatre further during this period than the record of plays in this section would suggest[1].

Of all the sentimental writers of this time, partly because of their inclusion in Goldsmith's *Retaliation*, Richard Cumberland and Hugh Kelly have been remembered, by name at least, in the following centuries. There is a certain justice in taking these as the two most important sentimental dramatists of the era. While other playwrights may have penned individual comedies of greater intrinsic value, these two gave the stage the widest range of sentiments and were

[1] On the sentimentalism of the eighteenth century Ernest Bernbaum's excellent study of *The Drama of Sensibility* should be consulted.

imitated closely by a host of followers. Cumberland's dramatic career started in 1761 with the publication of *The
Banishment of Cicero*, a tragedy, which was immediately
followed by a couple of musical pieces[1]. Neither in tragedy
nor in musical comedy, however, lay Cumberland's forte,
and it was not until the production of *The Brothers* (C.G. Dec.
1769) that he discovered his true *métier*. *The Brothers* is
not a brilliant piece of work, but its pathetic situations and
artificialised characters were such as appealed to the time.
We cannot believe in Belfield Senior, who is secretly married
to Violetta, nor can we believe in the plot which presents this
gentleman seeking the love of Sophia, the adored of Belfield
Junior. The only really good parts of the play are the comic
scenes which deal with Sir Benjamin Dove's subjugation of
his wife, but even these comic scenes are deeply coloured by
reminiscences of earlier plays. A greater literary and theatrical
success Cumberland secured in the famous comedy of *The
West Indian* (D.L. Jan. 1771), which might be taken as typical
of a whole school of dramatic writing. Belcour in this play,
a good-hearted rake, became a regular stock figure. Like one
of Farquhar's heroes he makes attempts on Louisa Dudley
under the misapprehension that she is Charles Dudley's
mistress. At the same time as his libertinism is shown, he
is presented as relieving the distress of old Dudley and
generally behaving himself as a true disciple of the sentimental school. It is strange to note here that Fielding,
avowed enemy of sentimentalism though he was, has given
us in Tom Jones a character of fundamentally similar characteristics. The other figures in *The West Indian* are planned
on the same style. Miss Rusport, who loves Charles Dudley,
is a vapid second heroine; Lady Rusport is the usual grasping
old dowager; Mrs Fulmer represents the odious side of
humanity and is paralleled by Fulmer, through whom
Cumberland aims a blow at the press of the day. Last, but
hardly least, comes Major O'Flaherty, a 'sentimental' stage

---

[1] On Cumberland see Williams, S. T., *The Dramas of R. C.*, 1779–1785
(*Mod. Lang. Notes*, xxxvi. 403–8, Nov. 1921) and *The Early Sentimental
Dramas of R. C.* (*ib.* xxxvi. 160–5, March 1921).

Irishman, irascible, generous, foolish and wise by turns. As is well known, *The West Indian* proved an extremely popular play and at once its author found himself at the summit of fame. It is not to be denied that his comedy possesses intrinsic merit, but even here, where Cumberland has produced a thoroughly creditable work of art, we cannot but stand amazed at the artificiality of both character-drawing and of dialogue, and the subjugation of all to the requirements of a sentimental moral[1].

The Fashionable Lover (D.L. Jan. 1772) followed, with a confessed "attempt upon" the reader's "heart[2]," a year later. Here the sentimental muse is once more called upon. Augusta Aubrey, the heroine, is ill-treated as a ward in Bridgemore's house. Accused of lightness, she makes her escape, and would have been seduced by Lord Abberville, had the latter's servant, Colin Macleod, not proved an able *deus ex machina.* Besides this sentimental story, we are treated to a variety of "humours" types, including Mortimer, the generous surly man, Naphtali the Jew, and Doctor Druid, the Welsh virtuoso. Perhaps the *Biographia Dramatica* is right in assuming that the failure of the comedy was due to the re-exploitation of sentimental features so soon after the production of *The West Indian.*

Between 1772 and 1785, amid his tragedies, farces and entertainments, Cumberland twice attempted the sentimental style, in *The Choleric Man* (D.L. Dec. 1774)[3] and *The Walloons* (C.G. April 1782), but neither has any permanent or historic value. In *The Natural Son* (D.L. Dec. 1784), however, we have a play which has considerable affinities with *The West Indian.* The plot is slight, but the dialogue at times rises well above mediocrity, and we are reintroduced

---

[1] On this play see Williams, S. T., *Richard Cumberland's "West Indian"* (*Mod. Lang. Notes*, xxxv. 7, Nov. 1920). The play was translated as *Der Westindier, ein Lustspiel...aus dem Englischen* by J. J. C. Bode (Hamburg, 1772) and as *L'Américain, comédie...en prose* by F. G. J. S. Andrieux (*Chefs-d'œuvre des Théâtres étrangers*, 1822).

[2] Preface. The play seems to have been very coolly received. A German version as *Miss Obre oder die gerettete Unschuld, ein Lustspiel...aus dem Englischen* written by C. C. H. Rost appeared at Leipzig in 1774.

[3] This play Ernest Bernbaum treats as non-sentimental, but the preface shows clearly Cumberland's sympathies.

to a Tom Jones hero in Blushenly and are favoured with a reappearance of the popular figure of Major O'Flaherty. From this time on, Cumberland held more strictly to the sphere he had made his own. After producing *The Country Attorney* (H.² July 1787), an unsuccessful effort, he won some applause for *The Impostors* (D.L. Jan. 1789), the plot of which is taken from Farquhar's *The Beaux Stratagem* and which shows Cumberland in a less sentimental strain. Here Harry Singleton masquerades as Lord Janus and is finally unmasked by Sir Charles Freemantle, who, after saving Eleanor, marries her in the end. The comedy is notable for the witty dialogue and for the excellently drawn "humour" of Sir Solomon Sapient. In *The School for Widows* (C.G. May 1789) and *The Box-Lobby Challenge* (H.² Feb. 1794), the latter a fairly bright comedy of lower-class manners, Cumberland seemed to be moving still further away from true sentimentalism, but he returned with renewed fervour to his old love in *The Jew*, produced at Drury Lane in May 1794. This play is frankly propagandist. The prologue makes a direct appeal to the audience:

> If to your candour we appeal this night
> For a poor Client, for a luckless Wight,
> Whom Bard ne'er favour'd, whose sad fate has been
> Never to share in one applauding scene,
> In Souls like your's there should be found a place
> For every Victim of unjust disgrace.

The logic of the verses is shaky but their purpose is plain. The story is written obviously in the endeavour to establish the Jew in a position of praise and esteem. Cumberland tells how Frederick, son of Sir Stephen Bertram, secretly marries Eliza Ratcliffe and how Charles, her brother, quarrels with Frederick. The plot would be a perfectly simple one were it not for the presence of Sheva the Jew, who is a kind of vilified *deus ex machina*. He succours the distressed and tries to bring peace and concord into troubled hearts. He is cast, that is to say, in the same mould as that from which the West Indian came. As the latter, in Cumberland's eyes, had the misfortune to be a libertine, so Sheva has the misfortune to be a Jew; but both are sympathetic and kindly and generous in their hearts. There can be no question that Cumberland did a fine thing in thus defending a race which long had suffered the taunts and jeers of professing Christians; our only doubt lies in the way he executed his self-appointed task. The portrait, as all Cumberland's portraits, is artificial and highly improbable. No man, Jew or Gentile, ever acted as Sheva did. At the same time we must remember that this exaggeration was in its own way necessary at the time when *The Jew* was written, and the "moral" was keenly appreciated by contemporary spectators and critics[1].

Immediately after this success came *The Wheel of Fortune* (D.L. Feb. 1795), which deals with a theme of repentance. Roderick Penruddock plans revenge on an old enemy, Woodville, who, years before, had married through trickery the girl he loved. Just at the crucial moment he meets Henry Woodville, and, seeing the mother's features in the son, foregoes his revenge. This play is by way of being a triumph for Cumberland. Penruddock, in spite of the sentimentalising of his nature, is an excellently drawn character and a good acting part[2], while the plot, reminiscent though it be of Kotzebue's style, has both probability and originality. From the point of view of dramatic technique, too, the play is worthy of notice, the various episodes being skilfully welded together and successfully developed.

First Love (D.L. May, 1795) followed within a month or two, but in it we see a decided falling off. Here sentimentalism colours more deeply both the episodes and the characters.

---

[1] The record of performances tells its own tale. This moral was praised in *The Analytical Review* for Dec. 1794 and in *The Universal Magazine* for May 1794. For a full account of the play and consequent incidents see S. T. Williams' interesting study of *Richard Cumberland* (Yale, 1917), pp. 231–8. Cumberland's character comes out hardly so well from an examination of his personal attitude towards critics and friends as it does from an analysis of his object in writing the play. He was a man with a good heart who, unfortunately, wished praise for his goodness. *The Jew* was rendered into German as *Der Jude* (by one Dengel; Königsberg, 1798; Stuttgart, 1868) and into Czech as *Žid, aneb, Dědicové Bělohoršti* (by E. Peškové; Prague, 1880).

[2] For records of later actors who won success in this rôle see S. T. Williams, *op. cit.* pp. 238–44.

Frederick Mowbray, who appears as the protector of Sabina Rosny, abandoned by Lord Sensitive, and Lady Ruby, Frederick's first love, are both unnatural creations, while the quarrels of Mr and Mrs Wrangle, who have been married by parental command, become unduly monotonous and wearisome. Propaganda has laid a heavy hand on Cumberland's comic spirit. Only one other play of Cumberland's comes near to the tone of *The Wheel of Fortune*. Fully five comedies he wrote before 1800, but of these *False Impressions* (C.G. Nov. 1797) alone possesses real intrinsic excellence. The prologue confesses that it was written to gain popular applause, and the whole is but a dramatisation of the author's own novel, *Henry*. At the same time the dialogue is good and there are many effective situations. Historically, too, this comedy is interesting as showing how the sentimental play and the melodrama came to coalesce towards the end of the century. The plot tells how Algernon has been traduced by Earling. Aided by Scud, he enters Lady Cypress' house disguised as a servant, and finally clears his name before the honest Sir Oliver Montrath, winning thereby the fair Emily Fitzallan. There is little of comedy here and several of the situations have the true melodramatic tinge.

As a dramatist Cumberland was not a great master, but he was a man of literary talent by no means to be despised. Many of his plays may seem nowadays to be absurd and ridiculous, yet the fact that he was able, at least once or twice, to make a propaganda story live shows that he had a decided power over his pen. Many of his scenes are well contrived, and, if we consider his work in the light of the dramatic technique of his time, we must confess that he had a true *flair* for the theatre. Plagiarist he may have been, but a plagiarist who made good use of what he stole and always coloured the borrowed ideas or characters of others with the light of his own vision. Several of his plays, if slightly adapted, would play well today, a fact alone which shows that he was no mean rival of Goldsmith and Sheridan.

His chief companion, Hugh Kelly, has not such a list of plays to show as Cumberland. A tragedy and five comedies only has he left us. The first of these comedies was *False Delicacy* (D.L. Jan. 1768), a highly moral work written in rivalry to Goldsmith's *The Goodnatur'd Man* (C.G. 1768)[1]. The title shows clearly its general scope. Lady Betty has rejected Lord Winworth through a false delicacy. Through false delicacy Miss Marchmont, out of gratitude to Lady Betty, is prepared to marry him, although she really loves Sidney, who is destined to marry Miss Rivers, who loves Sir Harry. As is evident, there would have been a nice tangle of broken hearts and loveless marriages had Cecil, an unconventional gentleman, and the gay Mrs Harley not resolved matters. In judging the play, we must remember of course that this " false delicacy " was a curse of the time, but no amount of historical defence will take away from its inherent artificiality.

Two years later appeared *A Word to the Wise* (D.L. March 1770), a play the success of which was ruined because of the political faith of the author[2]. This comedy deals with the familiar theme of parental commands. Sir John Dormer desires his daughter to marry Sir George Hastings, a sentimental fop. She, however, dotes on Villars, the sentimental hero who believes all will eventually turn out for the best, and whose belief is justified to the extent that he is discovered to be the long-lost son of Willoughby. This portion of the plot is solved by Sir George's renunciation of the heroine when he hears of her firmly fixed affections. Beside this story runs another. Sir John desires his son, who is a sentimental libertine, to marry Miss Montague, an interestingly cheery character. He, on the contrary, loves and is just saved from seducing Miss Willoughby. Happily, Miss Montague herself adores Sir George, so that there is a pretty little trio of weddings in the fifth act. Obviously the comedy is deeply influenced by French sentimentalism.

---

[1] It was an immense success. The publisher declared he sold 3000 copies on the day of publication before 2 p.m. Over 10,000 were disposed of during the season, the author's profits being upwards of £700. It was translated into French by M. J. Riccoboni as *La Fausse Délicatesse* (*Œuvres complètes*, 1818, vi) and was imitated in *L'Amour Anglais* (1788).

[2] *Supra*, pp. 7–8, 18.

Willoughby himself is likened to Candide—"Candide to perfection," says Dormer—and the moral is clearly that nature should dictate the bonds of marriage.

Kelly's next comedy was *The School for Wives* (D.L. Dec. 1773), which presents more of the atmosphere of the comedy of manners, and so may be dealt with in another section. Perhaps sufficient of Kelly's style has been seen in these two plays to make detailed mention of *The Romance of an Hour* (C.G. Dec. 1774) unnecessary[1]. It will have been observed that Kelly took a path distinct from that traversed by Cumberland. He has no "problems" to present to us, and while he is a propagandist he does not allow his sentimentalism to colour so heavily his conception of character and his construction. He veers away, moreover, from the *drame*. In *The School for Wives*, indeed, he has a hit at the current style patronised by Cumberland, when he makes Lady Rachel remark that the managers "alledge that the audiences are tired of crying at comedies[2]." He represents, not so much the pure sentimental spirit as given by Cumberland, but the mingling together of vague French "philosophic" precepts and the relics of the comedy of manners. His style is sprightlier than that of his companion and his delineation of types is freer and more natural.

It is difficult to select among the other sentimental authors one or two for preferential treatment, but possibly we shall not be wrong in choosing Frederick Reynolds as the next in importance. Reynolds' association with the sentimental school is at once proved by his first production, *Werter*, produced at Bath in Nov. 1785. In his comedies this author approaches more nearly to Kelly than to Cumberland. *The Dramatist: or, Stop Him Who Can!* (C.G. May 1789) is a fairly well written sentimental comedy of manners somewhat in the style of the former, although more influenced by incipient melodramatic tendencies. The chief character here is the villainess, Lady Waitfor't, who tries to hinder the loves of Louisa and Harry Neville. They are rescued partly through

---

[1] *The Man of Reason* (C.G. Feb. 1776) remained unprinted.
[2] I. ii. and see *infra*, p. 155.

the aid of Floriville, Neville's good-natured fop of a brother[1], and partly through that of Vapid, a would-be dramatist ever on the look-out for telling situations. This last-mentioned character, who gives the title to the play, was immensely popular and proved the ancestor of a numerous progeny of similar personages of like tempers. In the revival of 1925[2] the excellence of the character delineation and the amusing situations in which Vapid finds himself were fully demonstrated. The play is amongst those which, if carefully cast, might prove successful on the present-day stage.

Again, as in dealing with Kelly, it may be sufficient merely to select a few of Reynolds' works for special treatment. Such plays as *Notoriety* (C.G. Nov. 1791), *Speculation* (C.G. Nov. 1795), *Laugh when you can* (C.G. 1798) and *Management* (C.G. 1799) may be omitted here. *How to Grow Rich* (C.G. April 1793) was one of this author's greatest successes in the theatre[3], although it is by way of being his poorest comedy. The story tells how Lady Henrietta is nearly ruined by the gamblers, Sir Charles Dazzle and his sister, but is ultimately saved by her lover, Warford. While the scenes are plentifully scattered with sometimes witty satire—at gamblers, at country justices in the person of Sir Thomas Roundhead and at would-be get-rich-quicks in that of Small Trade —and while one or two characters, such as the engagingly criminal Pavè and Latitat, the latter of whom might have sat to Dickens for the portrait of Jingle, are skilfully and even delightfully drawn, the comedy is full of artificialities and exaggerated features.

Much finer intrinsically is *The Rage* (C.G. Oct. 1794) which again mingles manners, sentimentalism and satire. Here Darnley and Mrs Darnley live in retirement, until the former is drawn from his seclusion by Sir George Gauntlet and Lady Sarah Savage. The husband is rescued from degradation just in time. This, like Reynolds' other plays,

---

[1] A character probably taken from Sir George Hastings in *A Word to the Wise* (D.L. 1770).

[2] Apart from burlesques this is one of the first plays to make a dramatist a central figure.

[3] Reynolds tells in his *Life* (ii. 161–4) that it brought him in fully £620.

presents an extremely entertaining picture of the age. The mannish Lady Sarah, the money-lender Flush, the brainless aristocrat Savage, the old beau Sir Paul Perpetual, the opera-singer Signor Cygnet, as well as the unconventional Gingham, child of two fathers, show that Reynolds, in spite of his sentimentalism, was the Thomas Shadwell of his age. Novelists might well find here as much material for a picture of the social life of the late eighteenth century as Scott found in *The Squire of Alsatia* for a picture of seventeenth century manners.

Fortune's Fool (C.G. Oct. 1796) is also a fair comedy in which "humours" types, wit, social satire and sentimentalism are mingled once more. The main *vis comica* in the play comes from the eternally unlucky Ap-Hazard and from Tom Seymour, the sailor, but the author stresses chiefly the "interesting" sentimental poverty of Sir Charles Danvers and the intrigue by which Miss Union endeavours to lead his wife into the arms of Orville. In *The Will* (D.L. April 1797) Reynolds turned to a more melodramatic story, in which Mrs Rigid stops the letters sent by Mandeville to her daughter, Albina. Here an effort is made to secure the double effect of sentimentalised drama of contemporary manners and of romantic thrill. "*An old Gothic Chamber*" provides the setting for one of the acts[1]. With *Cheap Living* (D.L. Oct. 1797), Reynolds returned to his more usual type, introducing in Sponge a fairly well-drawn character[2]. In this, as in his other plays mentioned above, Reynolds stands forward as an excellent delineator of contemporary manners, and as one possessed of a peculiar skill in the drawing of farcical, but not unreal, figures. Vapid in *The Dramatist*, Pavè in *How to Grow Rich*, Gingham in *The Rage*, Ap-Hazard in *Fortune's Fool* and Sponge in *Cheap Living* are all characters who bring the plays in which they appear above the levels of mediocrity.

Miles Peter Andrews, who was closely associated with

[1] IV. (ii.).
[2] In *The School for Ingratitude* (1798) one Fisher accused Reynolds of having stolen from his play.

Reynolds in his efforts, was also a purveyor of this distinctly mixed dramatic repast. His most typical work was done in the operatic style, but one or two of his plays were regular comedies. Of these the first was *Dissipation* (D.L. March, 1781)[1]. The main atmosphere here is sentimental, encircling the loves of Harriet and Charles Woodbine, but Andrews is not sufficiently imbued with the Cumberland strain to avoid making satiric game of the Jew, Ephraim Labradore. Like Shylock, this Labradore has a daughter who runs off with a French servant, Coquin. The main defect of the comedy is its lack of unity. There are many witty passages in it, but the whole is but a series of more or less disconnected scenes. *Reparation* (D.L. Feb. 1784) had a somewhat chequered career. Written for Mrs Siddons, it was rejected by the Covent Garden management, and when eventually it was produced at the rival theatre a political reference caused some disturbance. The sentimental note is here deeply stressed. Loveless' remorse over Julia is the principal thing in this "comedy," and the moral reflections which the former metes out to his friend Belcour are full of the best approved lachrymose morality of the day.

Most of Thomas Holcroft's plays[2] belong rather to the sphere of the *drame* than to that of comedy, but two of his productions are of the latter type—*Duplicity* (C.G. Oct. 1781) and *The German Hotel* (C.G. Nov. 1790). The first of these is particularly interesting because of the testimony in it of the force of Goldsmith's attack on the sentimental type. Holcroft, however, remains impenitent. He "would rather have the merit of driving one man from the gaming-table, than of making a whole theatre merry[3]," and he proceeds to concoct his lecture. Apparently, in this his second play, Holcroft

---

[1] The *Biographia Dramatica* traces the origin of this comedy to *Bon Ton*. I confess that I can see no resemblance between the two plays.

[2] On Holcroft's works see Colby, Elbridge, *A Bibliography of T. H.* (Bulletin of the New York Public Library, xxvi. June–Sept. 1922). Colby, E., *Thomas Holcroft—Man of Letters* (*S. Atlantic Quarterly*, xxii. Jan. 1923).

[3] Preface. In this preface the author denies any indebtedness either to Destouches' *Le Dissipateur* or to Mrs Centlivre's *The Gamester*. There is no marked borrowing from either.

had decided to take upon himself the Cumberland mantle, for

> Our bard, who full of antiquated notions,
> Intends to cure the world by scenic potions,
> Gravely resolves to set the nation right,
> If your applause should crown his hopes to-night,

are the words of the epilogue spoken by Miss Younge. The comedy introduces us to a gamester, Sir Harry Portland, who is enticed on by his friend Osborne to lose his all. This friend, however, has merely been deceiving him so that he should not let his wealth go into the hands of the rascals surrounding him. In the end Osborne reveals his real motives, Sir Harry marries Clara, and Melissa, Sir Harry's sister, rewards his friend by giving him her hand. The more purely comic element in the play is provided by the humours of 'Squire Turnbull and Miss Turnbull. Altogether this is an excellent comedy of sentimentalised manners and would be worthy of a revival[1].

The German Hotel, based on a German drama by Brandes, was at first attributed to one Marshall, but there seems no doubt that it was really written by Holcroft[2]. Here once more the latter takes his stand against the reactionaries, Goldsmith and Sheridan. The play is preluded by a conversation between a Scots author and several wits:

Frankly. Ay! Where is he? Where does Genius live?
M'Carnock. Genius leves, Sir—he leves at the sign of the School for Scandal!
Frankly. Granted: but he never lives at the sign of sentiment and drama.
M'Carnock. Bagging yeer pardon, Sir, yeer wrong—yeer wrong—Drama is the legeetimate child of the Muses.

Drama certainly *The German Hotel* is. Dorville has married a daughter of Count Werling, but Baron Thorck, the villain, has forged letters which lead to a complete estrangement between Dorville and his father. At an hotel, through a

---

[1] It was reduced in the nineteenth century to three acts after having been revived at Covent Garden as *The Mask'd Friend* (C.G. 1796).
[2] See Genest, *op. cit.* vii. 23-4.

fortuitous series of coincidences, fate unmasks the Baron and
all ends well.

Holcroft, of course, is much better known for his serious
drama, *The Road to Ruin* (C.G. Feb. 1792) than for any of
these comedies. We cannot deny now that this play is
artificial, that it shows many melodramatic features, that the
psychological delineation of the characters is unconvincing.
At the same time, judged by reference to other plays of the
same kind, it is found to be a dramatically effective production
and by no means wholly unworthy of praise. Again the theme
is one of gambling, but more gloomily told. Harry Dornton
has ruined himself, and his losses threaten to bring his father's
bank to disaster. In his misery and remorse he proposes to
marry Mrs Warren, an old widow, but is saved from this in
the end. The drama is well diversified with a collection of
interesting types, among them Sulky, Dornton's blunt out-
spoken clerk, a figure familiar later, both in dramatic and in
fictional literature, and Silky, a rascally usurer who conspires
with Mrs Warren and Goldfinch (who reminds us at times of
Jingle both in deeds and language) to cheat Jack Milford and
Sophia. It is in this play that Holcroft shows his real feelings
most clearly. As a companion of Blake and Tom Paine he
prefaced the drama with a supposedly extempore utterance,
in which he displays his intense enthusiasm for the French
Revolution and his millennium dreams[1].

Famous as *The Road to Ruin* is, it is decidedly questionable
whether it rises in dramatic worth above *Love's Frailties*
(C.G. Feb. 1794), a sentimental comedy based on Gem-
mingen's *Der deutsche Hausvater*. The story here is one of
true love and false, and possibly it is a sign of Holcroft's
weakness that in the fundamental situation of his play he
repeats the main theme of his previous drama. Here it is
Seymour who is faced with the dilemma of marrying his
love, Paulina, and so being cast off by Sir Gregory Oldwort,
his guardian, or of marrying Lady Fancourt and saving his
sister from want. Happily, love and the virtue of Paulina
triumphs, Sir Gregory's hypocrisy is exposed and Lady

[1] *Supra*, p. 55.

Fancourt welcomes again her sensible, but outwardly foppish admirer, Muscadel. *Love's Frailties* is notable for an excellently drawn character and for one brilliant scene. Craig Campbell, gentleman and painter, is a type new to the theatre who gives life to the production, while the scene where the poor Paulina rushes raving into Lady Fancourt's boudoir passes away from the mawkishly pathetic and becomes truly appealing. There is a strength here and a power over the human passions lacking in Cumberland's work.

The Deserted Daughter (C.G. May 1795) is even more serious. Here Morden will not recognise his daughter Joanna, who has been brought up by the faithful Donald. The girl gets into the clutches of Mrs Enfield, a bawd. At the house of the last mentioned, Lennox sees and falls in love with her, saving her from ruin. At this point Morden discovers that Item has been cheating him for many years, Donald is praised and rewarded, and Joanna is taken back by her father. There are only one or two passages of a comic strain in the drama, and some scenes definitely approach the tragic[1]. Similar to it in aim is *Knave or Not?* (D.L. Jan. 1798), a play written to show up the evils of people of apparent respectability. Taking these plays as representative, we may say that Holcroft's work was among the most notable in the last years of the century. He has a genuine sincerity lacking in many writers of the time, and his literary ability is by no means to be despised. He had, moreover, the gift of conceiving problem situations of a general and an interesting type. In many ways he is a predecessor of Robertson and of Robertson's followers more than a century later.

Numerous other writers followed in the Kelly, Cumberland, Reynolds and Holcroft strains, some veering towards the *drame*, some confining their efforts more purely to the world of comedy. Prince Hoare, an enterprising adapter, gave in this style his *Sighs; or, The Daughter* (H.[2] July 1799) and *Indiscretion* (D.L. May 1800). The first is an adaptation

---

[1] A poor alteration was performed at Covent Garden in Sept. 1819 as *The Steward*. It may be assumed that part of the theme was suggested to Holcroft by Cumberland's *The Fashionable Lover* (D.L. 1772).

of Maria Geisweiler's *Poverty and Nobleness of Mind* (1799),
a literal translation of Kotzebue's *Armuth und Edelsinn* (1795).
Several important changes have been made in the plot.
Fabian Stopsel becomes the "calculating" Totum[1], and the
rich Peter Plum is transmogrified into the peevish Von
Snarl. The English author, moreover, introduces the cause
of liberty in the character of Adelbert, a Pole who has sacrificed his all for his country. *Indiscretion*, in spite of one or
two borrowed episodes, is more original. The general spirit
is obviously taken from Kotzebue, but the various episodes
are Hoare's own. The "indiscretion" of the characters is
shown in the elopement of Julia Burly and in the matrimonial advertisement of Sir Marmaduke Maxim. It may
be fitting here to call attention to the many comedies of the
late eighteenth century which have abstract titles such as
this one of Hoare's. *Reparation*, *Dissipation*, *Duplicity*,
Reconciliation, *False Shame*—such were the titles beloved in
these years. The tendency must, of course, be related to the
similar movement in the realm of tragedy, where, as we have
seen, Joanna Baillie's *Plays on the Passions*, followed by
Coleridge's *Remorse*, displayed a leaning towards the philosophic rather than the concrete, with a consequent loss of
realism and dramatic value.

Among the other authors who adopted this style, Edward
Morris also deserves an important place. *False Colours* (H.[1]
April 1793) is one of the typical sentimental-manners
comedies of the time. The risible element is provided by
Sir Paul Panick and Lady Panick, by Lord Visage who
believes in Lavater, and by Grotesque. Amid these "humours" figures, Montague and Harriet plot together, and
Sir Harry Cecil and Constance display their true sentimental
adoration. *The Secret* (D.L. March 1799) is a poorer drama,
again trading largely in "humours." It is of decided
interest, however, because of its clear presentation of a familiar
sentimental situation. Mr Torrid is a man who has made his
wealth by cheating others, including his ward Rosa, who is

---

[1] Who, it may be observed, speaks in the "Jingle" strain used by
Goldfinch in Holcroft's *The Road to Ruin* (C.G. 1792).

loved by his son Henry. Rosa, believing herself penniless, rejects Henry's offers partly through pride, partly through disinterested love. Meanwhile Henry finds that most of their money really should belong to Rosa. This fact he reveals to her and now in his turn rejects her. Happily Rosa discovers her father in the tender-hearted Dorville, and all ends happily. This serious plot is tempered by the arrival of Lizard and his numerous progeny who settle on the Torrid estate and impolitely blackmail the unfortunate villain.

Mrs Frances Sheridan's *The Discovery* (D.L. Feb. 1763) is more vivacious. Here a certain return has been made to the style of the writers of the comedy of manners. Lord Medway who, having designs on Lady Flutter, succeeds in counselling Sir Harry Flutter to an estrangement, is conceived much in the earlier manner. The intrigue, however, is not allowed to go far. Lady Medway steps in as the *deus ex machina* to save the half-erring wife. The sub-plot, dealing with Col. Medway and Miss Richly, is more definitely sentimental in character. This comedy is a good one, although its contemporary success was due initially to the acting of Garrick as Sir Anthony Branville, of O'Brien as Sir Harry Flutter and of Miss Pope as Lady Flutter[1]. Among late eighteenth century comedies this has had the distinction of belonging to the small group thought worthy of professional revival on the modern stage.

The Fugitive (H.[1] April 1792) by Joseph Richardson is also a good play and once more has certain features which remind us of the earlier drama. Wingrove, Larron, O'Donnel and Cleveland all recall the Jonsonian type, while the episode which introduces the drunkenness of Manly and the distress of Julia seems borrowed from Fletcher and Massinger's *The Coxcomb*. The aim of the play is obviously to show natural goodness and virtue as superior to birth and caste pride, but the author has not always allowed his didactic aim to run away with him. His comedy in many ways is as deserving of revival as *The Discovery* and might well have a certain

[1] For the success of the last two see *The Companion to the Playhouse* (1764).

success on the modern stage. The characters are well conceived and some of the episodes are unquestionably ludicrous.

Important among these sentimental dramas, although at
the same time darker and coarser in texture, Charles Macklin's *The Man of the World* (C.G. May 1781) stands out
robustly. Produced first at Crow Street, Dublin, in July,
1764, as *The True-born Scotsman*, *The Man of the World*
was long banned by the censor, and party voices were not
silent when the play was put on in London[1]. Read now with
impartiality, it is seen to be an excellent and mordant satire
on the times. The character of Sir Pertinax Macsycophant is
powerfully drawn, his ideas and social conventions being
presented before us with a masterly touch. Sentimentalism
is amply apparent in the relations between Charles Egerton
and Lady Rodolpha Lumbercourt, and between Charles'
brother and Constantia. Pathos, too, is freely introduced
through Sidney's hopeless love of the last-named. This
comedy, however, does not exist for plot alone. Its characterisation proves Macklin one among the better dramatists
of his time.

George Colman the Elder, in spite of some satire directed
at the sentimental school, did not entirely refrain from the
current style. Indeed, in *The English Merchant* (D.L. Feb.
1767), a play taken from Voltaire's *L'Écossaise*[2], he may be
thought to have given one of the most representative sentimental dramas of the age. The plot is a good one. Amelia is
the daughter of the proscribed Sir William Douglas. She is
befriended by Freeport, an eccentric merchant, as she is also
by Lord Falbridge, who loves her. These two save both
father and daughter when the life of the former is imperilled

---

[1] A full account of this matter is related in William Cooke's *Memoirs
of Charles Macklin, comedian, with the dramatic characters, manners,
anecdotes, &c. of the age in which he lived* (1804). See also J. T. Kirk-
man's *Memoirs of the Life of Charles Macklin, Esq.* (1799, 2 vols.) and
F. A. Congreve's *Authentic Memoirs of the late Mr Charles Macklin,
Comedian* (1798). There are many pamphlets on various stormy periods
of this actor-dramatist's life, for a list of which see R. W. Lowe's *A
Bibliographical Account of English Theatrical Literature* (1888) and J. J.
O'Neill's *A Bibliographical Account of Irish Theatrical Literature* (Dublin
1920).

[2] See Colman's *Memoirs*, i. 191. The comedy is dedicated to Voltaire.

by the machinations of the jealous Lady Alton and the journalist Spatter. Both characterisation and dialogue in this play are excellent, and pathos is blended with comedy more successfully than in the majority of the similar plays of the type[1].

Colman's other sentimental play is *The Man of Business* (C.G. Jan. 1774) which is admittedly indebted to Plautus, Terence, Marmontel and Beaumarchais. In spite of obvious borrowings, however, whether from *Phormio* or from another source, the comedy has Colman's individual touch. In general outline the plot reminds us of *The Road to Ruin* and also of *Duplicity*. Indeed, both these later dramas may have drawn inspiration from this source. The riotous Beverley recalls the heroes of both these Holcroft plays, and the faithful clerk, Fable, who pretends he is ruined, shows the features of Sulky and the actions of Osborne. On hearing that Beverley is ruined, all his erstwhile friends turn from him, including Denier, his Macchiavellian friend. Seeing this, the hero is struck with remorse and sees the goodness of Lydia. Wedding bells as usual take the place of the merry jingle of guineas at the gaming-house.

A decade later than these plays by Colman, Mrs Hannah Cowley produced, in the midst of her more purely comic works, an excellent sentimental play in *Which is the Man?* (C.G. Feb. 1782). If Holcroft took anything from *The Man of Business*, he certainly pretended to rectitude, for he accused Mrs Cowley of having copied Bobby Pendragon and his sister from *Duplicity* (C.G. 1781). It is probable that the authoress was innocent of the charge. There is a good deal of gaiety in this play, concentrating mainly on the figure of Lady Bell Bloomer, who is attracted by Lord Sparkle, but who finds in the end she rather prefers the honester and humaner Beauchamp. This once more is a decidedly good play and deserves to be placed alongside of Mrs Sheridan's *The Discovery* (D.L. 1763) as a reviveable comedy. In

---

[1] *The English Merchant* was revived at New York in June, 1795 as *The Benevolent Merchant* (see Davenport Adams, *A Dictionary of the Drama*, p. 462).

looking at these dramas, indeed, it may be said without exaggeration that there is more of worth in this half century than there was in the period from 1700 to 1750 if we omit from both the major figures—Farquhar and Vanbrugh, Goldsmith and Sheridan. The excess of sentimentalism to be found in so many plays should not cause us to ignore the numerous gay scenes and amusing characters which animate at least some of the comedies of the time.

It is impossible here to single out all the many authors who approached this type of comic drama during the period. Again, it may be deemed sufficient to cast a rapid glance on one or two individual plays which may be taken as typical of the general movements of the time. In the sentimental-manners strain Richard Griffith's *Variety* (D.L. Feb. 1782) may be noted as a fairly well developed play with some good dialogue and successfully drawn types. Charles Steady is the hero in this drama, befriending Harriet Temple (really his own sister) in a magnanimous manner. When the latter discovers her consanguinity with Charles, she also finds that she is niece to Commodore Broadside and is thus enabled to marry Captain Seafort, her lover. With this main plot go two others. In the first Lord Frankly is presented to us. He is devoted to his wife, but, believing her to be jealous, is inclined to return to an old flame in the person of Lady Courtney. The domestic difficulties are satisfactorily, if sentimentally, settled, and Lady Courtney consents to marry the somewhat wooden philosopher, Morley. The second sub-plot concerns almost entirely the lazy bored knight, Sir Frederick Fallal, and his vivacious Irish wife. *Variety*, as is evident from this brief outline of the plot, is preserved from dullness and inanity by the attempt to delineate contemporary types and contemporary follies.

Thomas Morton, already noted for his work in the realm of melodrama[1], provided the stage with one or two similar productions, *The Way to Get Married* (C.G. Jan. 1796), *A Cure for the Heart-Ache* (C.G. Jan. 1797), *Speed the Plough* (C.G. Feb. 1800) and *Secrets Worth Knowing* (C.G. Jan. 1798). Each

---

[1] *Supra*, p. 101.

of these has independent value, although the second and the third are undoubtedly superior to the others. In *A Cure for the Heart-Ache* two plots are run together. Vortex, a rich "Nabob," has cheated his niece Ellen of her estates. The latter is in love with Stanley Hubert whose father is in imminent danger of being ruined by the wealthy scoundrel. Into this darker element strolls Young Rapid, honest enough but apt to be led astray by the aping of fashion. Through his means Ellen recovers her estates and old Hubert's ruin is averted. Stanley consequently marries Ellen, Young Rapid, reformed, comes back to his old love Jessy Oatland, and Vortex completes the happy family by declaring that he is, on the whole, rather relieved, as his conscience has been troubling him considerably. In spite of the lameness of this conclusion and the frequently farcical situations introduced, the plea against fashionable viciousness and heartlessness contained in *A Cure for the Heart-Ache* is by no means to be despised.

Speed the Plough is no less noteworthy. The play itself is a kind of sentimental melodramatic comedy presenting as chief character Farmer Ashfield, one who "behaves pratty" and honestly. His daughter Susan loves Bob Handy who in the end rejects Miss Blandford in her favour. Alongside of this largely comic plot runs a more serious one. Sir Philip Bland-ford thinks he has killed his erring brother whose son, Henry, has been reared by Ashfield. In the end the brother reveals himself alive, and Henry is paired off happily to Sir Philip's daughter. Whatever of artificial sentiment appears in this part of the plot is made up for by the humours of Sir Abel Handy and his wife, Lady Handy. The latter, a former servant of the Ashfields, discovers to her own confusion and to Sir Abel's unconcealed delight that her former spouse is yet alive. Interesting as the comedy is from its dialogue and character, that which gives it historical importance is none of these things. When in the first scene we hear Ashfield exclaiming:

Be quiet, woolye? aleways ding, dinging Dame Grundy into my ears—what will Mrs Grundy zay? What will Mrs Grundy think?

we recognise that we are in the presence of one who was later to become so dismal a presence both in life and in literature.

A similar union of didacticism, emotionalism and the portrayal of contemporary types is to be discovered in the plays of Mrs Elizabeth Inchbald, an authoress who, considered from the historical point of view, is one of the most interesting figures of her time. Born in 1753, adopting the stage as her profession under her married name, graced with the acquaintance of nearly all the prominent *littérateurs* of her time and with the friendship of Mrs Siddons, Kemble and Godwin, producing plays at the London theatres regularly from 1784 to 1805, issuing novels in 1791 and in 1796, editing several valuable collections of the most classical of English tragedies and comedies, sought as an honoured contributor to *The Edinburgh Review* when that periodical was in its greatest glory, she is as symptomatic as any writer of her period[1]. Her forte lies in the writing of that peculiar type of sentimental play which was created "par le parti philosophique pour attendrir et moraliser la bourgeoisie et le peuple en leur présentant un tableau touchant de leurs propres aventures et de leur propre milieu"—in other words the humanitarian comedy. Many of her works, certainly, are but alterations of contemporary French or German sentimental plays. Thus *The Widow's Vow* (H.[2] 1786) is an adaptation of *L'heureuse Erreur* of Patrat; *The Midnight Hour* (C.G. 1787) is from Dumaniant's *La Ruse contre Ruse*; *The Child of Nature* (C.G. 1788) is derived from the *Zélie* of the Countess of Genlis, *The Married Man* (H.[2] 1789) from Néricault-Destouches' famous sentimental comedy *Le Mari, honteux de l'être ou Le Philosophe marié*, which had already, in 1732, appeared on the English stage as translated by Kelly[2]. *L'Indigent* of Mercier and *Le Dissipateur* of Destouches gave most of the plot of *Next Door Neighbours* (H.[2] 1791) while

[1] On her life and works see James Boaden's *Memoirs of Mrs Inchbald*, 2 vols., 1833; Littlewood, S. R., *Elizabeth Inchbald and her Circle* (1921). Some of the matter given in this account of her dramatic activity is repeated from an article contributed by the present writer to *The Times' Literary Supplement*, Aug. 4, 1921.

[2] See vol. ii, p. 145.

Lovers' Vows (C.G. 1798) and *The Wise Man of the East*
(C.G. 1799) are both free renderings of plays of Kotzebue.
Apart from this, moreover, her best works of individual
inspiration are more nearly allied to the French and German
humanitarian dramas than to the sentimental English plays
immediately preceding them. They are full of the same air of
serious purpose, the same *naïveté*, the same earnestness, the
same improbabilities. *The True Briton*, although it was
ably silenced by the authoress, was not more wrong in
finding the germs of revolution in her work than Burke was
in discovering a great part of the French upheaval due to
the continuous and seemingly innocuous stream of fanciful
plays and romances that flowed from the time of *Le Fils
Naturel* to the last years of the century. Mrs Inchbald,
like Diderot, was serious, humanitarian and sincere. She
was destructive in her attacks on contemporary foibles of
society, as, for example, the ill-judged vanity and flaunting
ambition of Lady Tremor in *Such Things Are* (C.G. Feb.
1787), the corrupt libertinism of Count Cassel in *Lover's
Vows* (C.G. Oct. 1798)[1], the foolish faithlessness of Sir
Robert Ramble in *Every One has his Fault* (C.G. Jan. 1793),
the giddy thoughtlessness of Miss Dorillon in *Wives as they
Were, and Maids as they Are* (C.G. March 1797). All these
are meant with a serious purpose—a purpose usually emphasised by prologue and by epilogue. Mrs Inchbald, however, is not always wholly destructive in this way. All but
the worst of her characters are amenable to reason, all are
capable of being touched by conscience or by good counsel.
In her first real comedy, *I'll Tell You What* (H.[2] Aug. 1785)
it is the goodness of Anthony Euston that is brought to light[2];
in *Wives as they Were, and Maids as they Are* Miss Dorillon,
apparently a giddy girl of fashion going the primrose way
to perdition, falls into a debtor's prison, but is willing to

[1] The character is of her own imagining and differs from the original
of Kotzebue.
[2] The *Biographia Dramatica* ii. 319 asserts that the principal incident
of this play is derived from Colman's *The English Merchant*. The situations in the two plays are entirely different, and admit of no comparison
in this way.

forego a gift of £1000 when she believes that her father, whom she has never seen since her infancy, is in want; in *Such Things Are* the heart of an apparently cruel Sultan is touched by the nobility of Haswell[1], and primitive virtue is seen in Zedan, the Indian "savage[2]"; in *Every One has his Fault* Mr Harmony succeeds in drawing forth the good qualities of everyone, even reconciling the bickering pair of Mr and Mrs Placid; in *Lovers' Vows* the old Baron Wildenhaim repents and marries the girl he has betrayed in his youth. All which is very pretty and nice, and displays the sincerity of the authoress, even if, like so much of the other sentimental work of the age, it leaves us rather cold. As those of Cumberland, her

> Fools have their follies so lost in a crowd
> Of virtues and feelings, that folly grows proud.

The French Revolution was in the air; minds had been softened and emotions were on edge. Hence we find Mrs Inchbald's work crammed with impossibilities and with scenes of dubiously pathetic tendency. She freely borrowed the French loving-couple-and-irate-father theme, particularly when that could be emphasised by the introduction of unfortunate children. Lord Norland, in *Every One has his Fault*, has rejected his daughter, Lady Eleanor Irwin, and Irwin, driven half-mad by hunger and despair, robs him and is arrested[3]. Lord Norland, in spite of his harshness, has secretly adopted Irwin's son Edward, and, when the mother comes to her father's house, the child recognises her by instinct and cleaves to her. In the same way, Miss Dorillon in *Wives as they Were, and Maids as they Are*, feels by nature that the man whom she knows only as Mandred (and who is in reality her father) is nearly related to her. In *I'll Tell You*

---

[1] An acknowledged portrait of John Howard, the prison reformer.

[2] The "noble savage" was, of course, a stock type among the sentimentalists. Mrs Inchbald's portrait reminds us of the similar pictures in the plays of Kotzebue, such as Malvina in *La-Peyrouse* (1798), Rolla and Cora in *Die Sonnen-Jungfrau* (1791) and Mistivoi in *Adelheid von Wulfingen* (1789).

[3] It may be suggested that this episode was taken from the similar scene in *Das Kind der Liebe* (1790).

What Charles Euston has married without his father's consent, and the latter unwittingly saves his own daughter-in-law from shame at the hands of Lord Layton. A slightly similar situation occurs in *To Marry or not to Marry* (C.G. Feb. 1805), where Hester, the daughter of his greatest enemy, succeeds in breaking down the anti-matrimonial philosophy of Sir Oswin, the crabbed recluse.

There are, too, the free presentation of misfortune and the extraordinary discoveries. In *Such Things Are* we are introduced to a prison in Sumatra, where one of the women prisoners turns out to be the long-lost bride of the Sultan, who has kept her, unwittingly, for long years in captivity. In *Lovers' Vows* the scene opens with Agatha Friburg fainting by the roadside and rescued by her long absent son, who afterwards just escapes murdering his own father. There is no horror here, as in some of the contemporary French dramatists of a similar cast, but misfortune and pathos are heaped on with a free hand.

> No dreadful cavern, and no midnight scream,
> No rosin flames, nor e'en one flitting gleam,
> Nought of the charms so potent to invite
> The monstrous charms of terrible delight—

none of these does her Muse employ; it "rather aims to soften than surprise." The authoress herself esteems it as one of the proofs of success of one of her dramas that "some of the audience were seen to weep[1]." She would have agreed with Diderot in part of his definition of sensibility that

la sensibilité, selon la seule acception qu'on ait donnée jusqu'à présent à ce terme, est...cette disposition,...qui incline à compatir, à frissonner, à admirer, à craindre, à se troubler, à pleurer, à s'évanouir, à sécourir.

While Mrs Inchbald thus reflects, probably more precisely than any of the other dramatists of her time, the prevailing continental social consciousness, in her comedies she keeps, in many ways, true to the national tradition. There

[1] It must be remembered that weeping was a characteristic of the late eighteenth century. W. J. Lawrence draws attention to the fact that even military men indulged in tears when attending the playhouse.

are many affinities she shares with those authors who, before her, carried on the style of Jonson and the style of Congreve. Many of her characters are "humours," while in *I'll Tell You What* the domestic relations of Major Cyprus and of his wife differ little from the domestic relations of Restoration husbands and wives, and Sir Harry Harmless is much like a fop of 1700. The picture of Sir Robert Ramble in *Every One has his Fault*, a man divorced from his wife and marrying her again, at once owes a great deal to the work of men like Etherege and Congreve, and bears a strangely modern note. It might have been created by one of our contemporaries on the other side of the Atlantic, steeped in the style of the Restoration. As Mrs Inchbald advanced in life the atmosphere of Jonson came to usurp that of Congreve. *I'll Tell You What* contains only one artificial "humour" in Col. Downwright, and he, after all, has no very serious part to play in the development of the plot. In *Such Things Are*, on the contrary, we find that at least half the *dramatis personæ* are abstract, or at best only semi-real. There are here Sir Luke Tremor, Lord Flint, and Twineall, the last a figure "formed on the plan of Chesterfield's finished gentleman." In *Every One has his Fault* the very basis of the play rests on the clash and interaction of the various "humorous" types. Mr Harmony acts as a neutralising agent in the company of Sir Robert Ramble, Solus, Miss Spinster and Mr and Mrs Placid. Even to the end, however, and particularly when we consider her portraits of women, she still preserved just that touch of life which makes almost all her characters interesting, if not always psychological, studies.

The social ideas presented in Mrs Inchbald's comedies have been dealt with here at modest length, largely because this authoress is so typical of the many other writers who adopted this more advanced style of sentimental humanitarian drama. Noticeable in her work, as in the work of her companions, is the stress laid upon domestic problems. All her best studies are studies of domestic life, whether that domestic life be "romantic" but unfortunate, as with Irwin and Lady Eleanor Irwin or as with Charles Anthony and his wife; whether it be troublesome and annoying, as with Mr and Mrs Placid, Major and Mrs Cyprus, Sir Luke and Lady Tremor; whether it be based on old-fashioned rudeness, as with Lord and Lady Priory. In general we feel that Mrs Inchbald's tendencies, in spite of the romantic glow which she received from the *drame*, wherein love is the one vitalising and beautifying emotion of life, were towards a more "old-fashioned" conjugal relationship. She seems to have loved liberty, yet at the same time she seems to have felt that in the hypocritical fashionable life she saw around her lay too many temptations for any woman left to her own devices. Hence in *Wives as they Were, and Maids as they Are*, she displays in Miss Dorillon a good-hearted girl led astray by fashionable gaieties, in the absence of paternal or maternal counsels, while in Lady Priory she shows a woman kept in subjection by her husband, but made kind and loving and homely by her subjection. The test is made of Lady Priory, and she passes it with colours flying. She is allowed to be taken by the rake Bronzely to his country residence, and there vanquishes the libertine by her calm purity. "A Tarquin is impossible without a Lucrece," and "A maid of the present day" should "become a wife like those of former times," seem to be the two texts running through all her work.

This, as is evident, is one of the pictures that does not quite tally with the usual themes of the *drame*, and is due entirely to the authoress' realisation of the follies and vices of her age. She was too practical, perhaps, for idealism to carry her over-far; her English common sense pointed out to her one way, what seemed to her the only way, out of a position degrading and obnoxious—more degrading than the old-fashioned subjection she would, no doubt temporarily, have substituted for it. The practical nature of Mrs Inchbald's mind is revealed, too, in one other minor matter where she again deviated slightly from her models. In her presentation of feminine innocence she kept much nearer to life as she knew it than did the authors of the French or German sentimental comedies. She saw that her period was a hypocritical and coquettish period. She saw, for example, that no girl would act as the original of Amelia in Kotzebue's drama acted, with a fearless sort of sincerity, boldly asking her tutor to marry her. This, she realised quite plainly, "would have been revolting to an English audience." Accordingly she has kept Amelia as an unspoilt child, while presenting her with just those coquettish touches, with just those little hints of civilised hypocrisy which would make her conform with life. A similar figure, this time entirely of her own invention, is to be seen in the Hester of *To Marry or not to Marry*, supposedly innocent, almost lisping in many a scene, yet able to insinuate in a very artful and experienced manner to Sir Oswin that she would not object to marry him.

In surveying Mrs Inchbald's work as a whole, we cannot deny the fact that her plays are as good as any of her time, and that one, at least, *I'll Tell You What*, has quality sufficient in its situations and characters to warrant revival. Her sense of construction is excellent. Scene follows scene with absolute precision. Nor are her plots simple. She usually manages to confuse and mingle two or three themes delightfully, disentangling the webs at the end with a skilful hand. Towards this her own love of situation led her surely. She has little comedy of character, but she excels in the comedy of situation. In *I'll Tell You What* Major Cyprus has boasted that Sir George Euston's former wife (now his own) once put him into a closet to hide him from the eyes of her husband. In the last act he himself finds Sir George there, on which his friend Col. Downright remarks, "Did not I tell you to keep the *key* of that closet?" A situation of like nature occurs in *Such Things Are*, where Twineall, after being privately informed that Sir Luke Tremor (a coward) prides himself on his bravery and soldiership, that Lady Tremor (a wig-maker's daughter) boasts of being descended from the ancient Kings of Scotland and of possessing a wig that belonged to Malcolm III, and that Lord Flint (a confidential spy of the Sultan) is inwardly a rebel, speaks to them all under their supposed characters. While trying to ingratiate himself, he drives Sir Luke from the room after mentioning a battle—"He generally runs away on these occasions," comments his loving spouse—sends Lady Tremor into convulsions by asking for the wig, and gets himself arrested for talking sedition to Lord Flint. On his arrest, "Gentlemen," he cries, "you are mistaken—I had all my clothes made in England, and 'tis impossible the bill can have followed me already." This comic element, well-calculated for stage success, is ably woven into the scenes of pathos and distress. We are in the realm of Dickens, fifty years before *The Pickwick Papers* startled the world into tears and laughter. The one thing that seriously mars her work, even as it marred Dickens', is the purpose element— good, when subordinated to the plot; bad, when usurping almost all of the attention. The moral is aimed at us again and again:

> Look to the hero, who this night appears,
> Whose boundless excellence the World reveres;
> Who, friend to nature, by no blood confin'd,
> Is the glad relative of all mankind.

It is enforced by the time-honoured "sentimental sentences" introduced artificially into the body of the plays. "The good," says Harmony in *Every One has his Fault*, "even in the very grasp of death, are objects of envy; it is the bad who are the only sufferers. There, where no internal consolation cheers, who can refuse a little external comfort?"—*à propos* of very little. On the other hand, the serious intent frequently strikes a note that is fresh and honest and thoughtful. We are listening to Major Cyprus' cynical and brutal account of his gallantries, especially his gallantries with his own wife at the time when she had been married to another, when suddenly he turns to his companion—"But laugh!—why the devil don't you laugh?" to which comes a reply, brief and to the point—"I was thinking...." It startles us, it arouses us, it awakes our consciences better than any pages of philosophy could have done. It is a kind of symbol of all that was best in the comedy of sentiment, and shows clearly the foundation of that theory of the sentimental which takes as the basis of the new type the quality of *thought*.

After Mrs Inchbald, thus taken as typical of what was finest in at least one stream of the new humanitarian movement, not many other writers need be mentioned. Of these Lieutenant-General John Burgoyne deserves a moderately prominent place for his sprightly comedy, *The Heiress* (D.L. Jan. 1786)[1], taken partly from Diderot's *Le Père de Famille*. The portrait of the poor Miss Alton, fittingly contrasted by the upstart heiress, Miss Alscrip, is well drawn, and the sentimental portions of the play are ably blended with the comic. Matthew Gregory Lewis, more famous for *The Castle Spectre* (D.L. 1797), also came forward with a fair specimen of the type in *The East Indian* (D.L. April 1799)[2]. Here Beauchamp has run off with Zorayda, and the death of his own wife enables him to marry her in the end. There is satire of fashionable callousness and slander in Lady Clara Modish, Lord Listless and Miss Chatterall, while Mrs Slip-Slop makes fritters of English in the regular Malaprop style, sometimes not without effectiveness as in I. i. where she cries for her

Chariot and servants!—Lud! Lud! how I detest and extricate that conceited trollop! She affects to contemnify me too, and why? Sure my figure and hidication an't anterior to hers; and as to birth, I hope my contraction's as extinguished as Mrs Tiffany's, or truly I should be sorry for it!

Charlotte Smith's comedy, *What is She?* (C.G. April 1799), likewise contains scenes of excellence[3]. Here, too, is satire of fashionable follies in the figure of Lady Zephyrine Mutable, who is contrasted with the modest Mrs Derville. In the midst of the social satire appears Period, a would-be writer who is preparing a volume of his "Tours." Sentimentalism cer-

---

[1] This play won some success abroad, being translated into French by A. F. Villemain as *L'Héritière* (*Chefs-d'œuvre des Théâtres étrangers*, 1822, vol. iii) and into German by W. Schenk as *Die Erbin* (*Deutsche Schaubühne*, 1788, vol. iii; *Neueste Deutsche Schaubühne*, 1803, I. i). It is said that Debrett, the original publisher, gave the author no less than £200 for the copyright.

[2] The main plot has been suggested by the story on which *The School for Scandal* (D.L. 1777) was based, but is developed in an individual manner.

[3] Hitherto this comedy has been regarded as anonymous; see the appendix.

tainly colours this comedy, but satire is one of its pre-
dominating traits. Perhaps one of the best touches is that
which girds at the Mrs Radcliffe type of romance. Says
Mrs Gurnet to her spouse, "And didn't I strive to correct
you, by drawing your character as a jealous German Baron
in my romance of 'The Horrid Concavity' or 'The Sub-
terraneous Phantom'?[1]"

Five Thousand a Year (C.G. March 1799) by Thomas
Dibdin is a slighter, but similarly planned, work, based on
the legacies of £5000 each left to George and Frederick
Fervid. George makes many vows which he constantly
breaks, and eventually succumbs to the fascinations of Julia
Maxim. He has, however, all honest feelings, for, when
Hastings seduces Aurelia in Frederick's name, he challenges
this gentleman to a duel and forces him to marry the injured
maid. This comedy has been dealt with here because it
shows a typical portrait of the careless hero beloved by the
Cumberland school of sentimentalists. Typical, too, in its
own way is Mrs Elizabeth Griffith's *The Double Mistake*
(C.G. Jan. 1766), which may be singled out from among her
several comedies. The tale here is one of jealousy. The true
love of Sir Charles Sommerville for Emily is first painted,
and then his suspicions of Young Freeman are luridly depicted. Protected by Lord Belmont, the lady is eventually
piloted through to safety. This comedy has been chosen here
because in the prologue we have an indication that though
the medium might be prose and the aim ostensibly comedy,
the writers of these plays often looked to tragedy and rime
as their true and natural sphere:

> To lead attention through five acts of prose,
> Where to soft notes no tuneful couplet flows,
> To please each heart, each judgment, eye and ear,
> The attempt how bold! the labour how severe!

In this summary of the sentimental movement in the second
half of the eighteenth century, it has become plentifully
evident that three distinct tendencies are to be traced in the

[1] II. i.

comic literature of this type. There are the relics of the Cibberian genteel comedy, aiding in the intensification of that "high" note in comedy against which Goldsmith raised the flag of rebellion; there is the often mawkishly pathetic theatre of Cumberland, intent upon raising a sigh and calling forth a tear; and there is the more revolutionary humanitarian drama which is seen at its best in the plays of Mrs Inchbald and of Thomas Holcroft. All of these three types are "sentimental," but each approaches the problems of life in a different way, and it is only the last-mentioned which formed a basis on which the nineteenth century poets reared their larger and wider standards of humanitarian sympathy.

IV. *Comedies of Manners*

The appearance of Goldsmith and of Sheridan in the midst of this galaxy of emotional softness is not in itself strange. Already it has been noted that the sentimental comedy itself often bound together scenes which recalled those of Congreve with others savouring of episodes in Steele. It is assuredly true that the sentimental note nearly always prevented the full expression of these "manners" tendencies, but, at the same time, the tradition had been preserved from the last years of the seventeenth century. Along with this perfectly progressive movement went the reaction. Many writers during this period realised that sentimentalism, if allowed to progress too far, would crush out entirely the spirit of laughter, and, accordingly, they raised their voices in protest, sometimes through satirical references in prologue and in epilogue, sometimes in critical essays, sometimes in creative artistry. In 1770 William Whitehead allowed a genial lash to fall on the sentimental tendencies of his time when, in *A Trip to Scotland* (D.L. 1770), he presented the character of Sotherton, a strolling actor, who, after having eloped with Miss Flack, finds her moneyless and packs her off, taking pride in the fact that he has not ruined her. "So that you perceive, Sir," he says, "at least the good company will perceive, that whatever effect the late run of sentimental comedies may have had upon their audiences, they have at least made the players men of honour." The same year even Kelly, the chief companion of Cumberland, could not resist a sly reference to the folly of the type in *A Word to the Wise* (D.L. 1770) when he makes Miss Dormer comment on a gorgeous phrase of her friend's:

Upon my word, Harriot, a very florid winding up of a period, and very proper for an elevated thought in a sentimental comedy[1].

Even from the mouths of its professors the type was being condemned. A few years later, Garrick took up the satirical pen in his dialogue between Tragedy and Comedy in *The Theatrical Candidates* (D.L. 1775):

Tragedy. You can be wise too; nay a *thief* can be!
        Wise with stale sentiments all stol'n from me:
        Which long cast off, from my heroic verses,
        Have stuff'd your motley, dull sententious farces:
        The town grew sick!
Comedy. For all this mighty pother,
        Have you not laugh'd with one eye, cry'd with t'other?
Tragedy. In all the realms of nonsense, can there be,
        A monster, like your comic—tragedy?
Comedy. O yes, my dear!—your tragic-comedy.

This satire, of course, merely repeated what Garrick had already written seven years previously in his rather awkward prologue to Kelly's *False Delicacy* (D.L. 1768)[2]:

I'm vex'd—quite vex'd—and you'll be vex'd—that's worse;
To deal with stubborn scribblers! there's the curse!
Write moral plays—the blockhead!—why, good people,
You'll soon expect this house to wear a steeple!
For our fine piece, to let you into facts,
Is quite a Sermon,—only preach'd in Acts.
You'll scarce believe me, 'till the proof appears,
But even I, Tom Fool, must shed some tears.

---

[1] I. i.

[2] A note in the first edition of this play states that "Mr Kelly originally intended the prologue to be grave, and accordingly wrote a serious one himself; but as Mr King was to speak it, Mr Garrick, with great propriety, thought a piece of humour would be best suited to the talents of that excellent actor, and therefore very kindly took the trouble of putting it into a form so entirely different from the first, that it cannot, with the least justice, be attributed to any other author."

This laughter at tears shed in comedy was repeated again and again. M. P. Andrews refers to it when he speaks of

this Age of *Theatric change*, when TRAGEDIES have found themselves to be COMEDIES, and COMEDIES have bordered upon PANTOMIME[1].

So, too, Murphy, in his prologue to Jephson's *Braganza* (D.L. 1775) remarks that

> In these days of sentiment and grace
> Poor comedy in tears resigns her place,
> And smit with novels, full of maxims crude,
> She, that was frolic once, now turns a prude.

Burgoyne thought that

continued uninterrupted scenes of tenderness and sensibility (*Comedie larmoyante*) may please the very refined, but the bulk of an English audience, including many of the best understanding, go to a comic performance to laugh in some part of it at least[2].

Foote, through the medium of his character of Bever in *The Patron* (H.[2] 1764), girds at the same tendency when he imagines a play of which the second act shows "the fatal effects of disobedience to parents; with, I suppose, the diverting scene of a gibbet; an entertaining subject for a comedy[3]." Others attached their satire to the more mawkish and hypocritical movements in the sentimental camp. "Heyday!" cries Young Whimsey in Cobb's *The First Floor* (D.L. 1787), when Furnish orders him to be arrested:

What's become of the exquisite luxury of a feeling mind in relieving distress?
Furn. It may do very well for people of fortune; but a tradesman shou'd never indulge in luxury.
Y. Whim. Consider, generosity is part of the business of man.
Furn. And a d—d losing trade it is—therefore it shan't be a part of *my* business[4].

"The title, I think will strike," declares the dramatist in Colman the Younger's *New Hay at the Old Market* (H.[2] 1795):

[1] Preface to *The Enchanted Castle* (C.G. 1786).
[2] *The Lord of the Manor* (D.L. 1780), Preface, p. xviii.
[3] III   [4] II. i.

The fashion of Plays, you know, now, is to do away old pre-judices; and to rescue certain characters from the illiberal odium with which custom has mark'd them. Thus we have a generous Israelite, an amiable Cynic, and so on. Now, Sir, I call my play— *The Humane Footpad*[1].

All of these latter attacks are, of course, interesting, and they must be taken into account when we consider the tendencies of the age. They serve to illustrate that greater attack which is symbolised in the figures of Oliver Goldsmith and of Richard Brinsley Sheridan. Through the peculiar blight which has fallen on late eighteenth century dramatic literature, these two men have tended to be considered the sole opponents of the sentimental play. It is as if they, and they alone, stemmed the torrent of a weeping age and taught men how to laugh once more. As a matter of fact they were but two among a large number of others who passed on to the nineteenth century the traditions of the comedy of earlier times. In dealing with their works, therefore, the background against which they ought to stand relieved should ever be borne in mind.

It was in the year 1759 that Goldsmith, himself senti-mentally inclined, as both *The Vicar of Wakefield* (1766) and *The Deserted Village* (1770) amply prove, came forward against the sentimental dramatists in his essay on *The Present State of Polite Learning*[2]. Some years later came the putting into practice of the theories in the well-known comedy, *The Good-Natur'd Man* (C.G. Jan. 1768). Written several years before, it was put on after some considerable difficulty, and was directly rivalled by Kelly's *False Delicacy* (D.L. 1768), produced by Garrick at his theatre one week pre-

[1] p. 11.

[2] There are many critical and biographical works dealing with Gold-smith. The following are probably the more important: W. Black, *Goldsmith* (English Men of Letters Series, 1878), Austin Dobson, *Life of Goldsmith* (Great Writers Series, 1888), J. Forster, *Life and Adventures of Oliver Goldsmith, A Biography* (latest edition, 1877), Washington Irving, *Life of Oliver Goldsmith* (2nd edition, 1849), R. Ashe King, *Oliver Gold-smith* (1910), F. Frankfort Moore, *The Life of Oliver Goldsmith* (1910). Much information is also to be obtained in critical editions of Goldsmith's plays (e.g. the Belles Lettres series) and Arthur Mendt has a dissertation on *Goldsmith als Dramatiker* (1911).

viously. Tersely, but pointedly, the author prefaced the printed play with a statement of his aims:

When I undertook to write a comedy, I confess I was strongly prepossessed in favour of the poets of the last age, and strove to imitate them. The term, *genteel comedy*, was then unknown amongst us, and little more was desired by an audience, than nature and humour, in whatever walks of life they were most conspicuous. The author of the following scenes never imagined that more would be expected of him, and therefore to delineate character has been his principal aim. Those who know anything of composition, are sensible, that in pursuing humour, it will sometimes lead us into the recesses of the mean; I was even tempted to look for it in the master of a sponging-house: but in deference to the public taste, grown of late, perhaps, too delicate, the scene of the bailiffs was retrenched in the representation. In deference also to the judgment of a few friends, who think in a particular way, the scene is here restored. The author submits it to the reader in his closet; and hopes that too much refinement will not banish humour and character from our's, as it has already done from the French theatre. Indeed the French comedy is now become so very elevated and sentimental, that it has not only banished humour and *Moliere* from the stage, but it has banished all spectators too.

This preface must be considered very carefully, because it indicates, not only the point of departure between Goldsmith and Sheridan, but also the differences in their comic aims. By "the last age" Goldsmith means the age of Shakespeare; to Shakespeare he looked when Sheridan sported with Congreve. Goldsmith's real objection to the sentimental comedy is that it is too "genteel" and does not admit of "nature" and "humour." Sheridan preferred to see wit on the boards of the theatre. Goldsmith endeavours to revive the spirit of *As You Like It* where Sheridan strives to create another *Way of the World*. The only justification, therefore, for including the former's work in this section is that he joined issue with the latter against one common enemy.

Judged by the highest dramatic standards *The Good-Natur'd Man* cannot be accounted a great play. Elements of sentimentalism mar its general tone, so that the conclusion is forced and vapid. Many of the characters seem to be hastily sketched in, and the plot is frankly impossible. Nor does a true *vis comica* breathe from the dialogue. There is indeed sometimes less of genuine laughter in Goldsmith's scenes than there is in many of the plays dealt with in the last section of this book. Perhaps, were *The Good-Natur'd Man* to be judged frankly and honestly, if we could dissociate it from its author, we should not place it in that niche of fame to which fortune, often inexplicable in its judgments, has exalted it.

Such a lukewarm criticism of Goldsmith's first play must, of course, give way to honest praise when we consider his second comedy, *She Stoops to Conquer, or, The Mistakes of a Night* (C.G. March 1773), produced, like its predecessor, after considerable trials. Colman and Garrick both rejected the manuscript; the very title was fixed on only at the last moment, after *The Novel, The Old House or New Inn* and *The Belle's Stratagem* had been dismissed as infelicitous. Assuredly the first-night applause, stoutly led by Dr Johnson himself, made up for these trials, but the sting remained. Goldsmith wrote no more for the theatres. Immediately before the production of this play the author had continued his earlier assault by *An Essay on the Theatre; or, A Comparison between Laughing and Sentimental Comedy*, contributed to *The Westminster Magazine* of Dec. 1772. Rarely have critical theory and creative practice been so ably wielded by the one writer. We may cavil at the construction of the comedy; we may describe certain of the incidents as farcical; we may criticise some of the characterisation, but always Goldsmith's "humour" and his "nature" prevail. With a breezy sweep of enthusiasm he carries us forward, rarely introducing any of that *esprit* which distinguishes the true comedy of manners, but full of those *mots de caractère* and *mots de situation* in which Shakespeare had delighted. Goldsmith has been compared to Farquhar[1], but his spirit is earlier still. Without the romantic pastoralism, it is close to the mood which is prevalent in the works of Greene and Lyly and the young

[1] Cf. G. H. Nettleton's *English Drama of the Restoration and Eighteenth Century* (1914), p. 286.

Shakespeare. Sir Toby Belch and the Gravediggers seem to take life again in this Augustan writer's conversations.

If Goldsmith marks an attempt to return to Elizabethan comedy, an attempt wherein he stood almost alone, Richard Brinsley Sheridan shows the movement back to the Restoration masters[1]. Only two dramas, if we except *A Trip to Scarborough* (D.L. Feb. 1777) as a fairly poor effort to make Vanbrugh's *The Relapse* fit for the audiences of the time, fall within the purview of this section. Of these, *The Rivals* (C.G. Jan. 1775), was Sheridan's first play[2], a comedy which, because of some satirical references to the Irish, was greeted with somewhat riotous disapproval on the first and second nights of performance. *The Rivals* is a good, but by no means a brilliant, comedy. The continuous stream of infelicitous verbiage which flows from the mouth of Mrs Malaprop begins after a time to pall, and the idiosyncrasies of Lydia Languish are over-emphasised. The satire of sentimental self-torture in Faulkland is well carried out, but again, as with Goldsmith, the last scene of the play introduces a form of sentimentalism which is no longer burlesque, and which clashes rather hopelessly with the rest of the play. Seen on the stage as read in the study, *The Rivals* is found to be a thing of shreds and patches, and even if those patches were once parts of royal garments their juxtaposition can hardly be regarded as harmonious. The play is an amusing essay in light comedy but hardly a flawless masterpiece.

[1] As with Goldsmith, there is a large critical literature surrounding Sheridan. Thomas Moore's *Memoirs of the Life of the Right Honourable Richard Brinsley Sheridan* (3rd edition, 2 vols., 1825) is important for its date; consultation should also be made of W. Fraser Rae's *Sheridan, a Biography* (2 vols., 1906), Walter Sichel's *Sheridan, from new and original material* (2 vols., 1909) and Lloyd C. Sanders' *Life of R. B. Sheridan* (Great Writers Series, 1890). The problems presented by the texts of Sheridan's plays have never been fully worked out. The best bibliographical studies are those by Iolo Williams (*Six Eighteenth Century Bibliographies*, 1923) and by Crompton Rhodes (*Times' Literary Supplement*). Rival claims are made for the "Moore" text (1821) and the "Rae" text (1902). See also the Handlist of Plays appended to this volume.

[2] See H. Hartmann's *Über die Vorlagen zu Sheridan's Rivals* (Königsberg, 1888); J. Q. Adams in *The Nation*, xc. 2337 and *Mod. Lang. Notes*, xxv. 171–3. The play was translated as *Die Nebenbuhler* by J. A. Englebrecht (*Hamburgisches Theater*, 1776, i).

The farce of *St Patrick's Day: or, The Scheming Lieutenant* (C.G. 1775), the comic opera *The Duenna* (C.G. 1775) and *A Trip to Scarborough* (D.L. 1777) followed before the appearance of *The School for Scandal* (D.L. May 1777)[1]. This play, as has long been recognised, marks the acme of Sheridan's comic achievement. Here the sentimental flavour is hardly for a moment felt, save in the concluding lines of the drama, and we are treated to a direct satirical portrait of hypocritical sensibility in the person of Joseph Surface. For the most part, however, the comedy is free from surrounding influences and their action; the spirit that animates it is the spirit of Wycherley's *Love in a Wood* and Congreve's *Love for Love*, without, of course, the moral liberty which characterises all the works of the Restoration writers. Sheridan has even the failings of the earlier masters of the comedy of manners. His plot is so involved that only a brilliant *tour de force* in the screen scene—so brilliant that it has become a kind of *locus classicus* for comic invention—enables him to unweave the web he has so closely entangled round his characters. The wit, too, colours all of the dialogue and, scintillating as it is, it seems to obscure the personalities of the various dramatic figures. Everyone, in this world of refined manners, is able to say something that is brilliant. Never for a moment does the sparkle disappear; so that sometimes we are inclined to be surfeited with too much of these intellectual fireworks. We pine occasionally for some of Goldsmith's "humour" and homely "nature," feeling that this comedy of Sheridan's possesses that "high" tone against

---

[1] See H. Hartmann's *Sheridan's the School for Scandal* (Königsberg, 1900). The original title of the comedy was *The Slanderers*, and the play was but slowly put together. On the bibliography, reference should be made to Rhodes, R. Crompton, *The Early Editions of Sheridan*. II. "*The School for Scandal*" (*Times' Literary Supplement*, 24 Sept. 1925). In this article Mr Rhodes announces the discovery of a 1799 Dublin edition which he takes to be the *editio princeps* of the genuine text. This play was translated several times, a list of the principal versions being given below:

German: Leonhardi (1782); C. Meissner (1863).

French: anonymous (1788); B. Delille (1789); P. N. Famin (1807); A. F. Villemain (1822); A. H. Châteauneuf (1824); M. A. Pichot (1852).

Italian: anonymous (1796); M. Leoni (1818).

which the former did battle. In many ways, indeed, *The School for Scandal* is to be related to contemporary comedies. The very satire of scandal-mongering is a contemporary picture which so many of the semi-sentimental dramatists loved to depict, and, although in spirit Sheridan looks back over a period of eighty years, he is in touch in this way with his own time. *The School for Scandal* is not, as so many critics have implied, entirely a miracle in the year 1777.

Nor is it only the manners' portions of sentimental dramas which approach Sheridan's style. There are many comedies of the time which move even closer to his spirit. A selection of typical examples of these will be outlined in this section. Among the many dramatists who thus perpetuated the style of Congreve, one of the most important was Arthur Murphy, an author who has already been noted for his activities in the realm of tragedy. It was with farces and tragedies that Murphy started his dramatic career, but in 1760 he discovered a new *métier* when he wrote *The Way to Keep Him* (D.L. Jan. 1760)[1]. Unquestionably sentimentalism is to be traced both in the conduct of the plot and in the dialogue, but this element is not more marked than it is, for example, in *The Good-Natur'd Man* and in *The Rivals*. The story, in good old Restoration wise, tells how Lovemore, tired of home, pays attentions to Mrs Bellmour, disguising himself for this purpose as Lord Etheridge. In his range of pleasure-seeking he also includes a flirtation with Lady Constant, whose husband, Sir Bashfull Constant, is afraid, lest he be laughed at, of loving his own wife. All comes well in the end, and the women are duly virtuous, but the general resemblances between Murphy's theme and the themes of the Restoration masters are plainly evident. While Murphy has not that refinement of dialogue which was Sheridan's, there

---

[1] This was first performed in three acts, but later expanded to five acts and so produced at Drury Lane in Jan. 1761. It is probable that Murphy was inspired to write his comedy through reading De Moissy's *Nouvelle École des Femmes*. This was translated by Robert Lloyd and printed in *The St James's Magazine* for 1762 in order to show Murphy's indebtedness. The play was adapted by M. J. Riccoboni as *The Way to Keep Him, ou, la Façon de le Fixer* (Riccoboni, *Œuvres complètes*, 1818, vol. v).

is no question that he belonged to the same school. "That would be the impolitest thing," says Mrs Lovemore, "A married couple to be interfering and encroaching on each other's pleasures. Oh hideous! it would be Gothic to the last degree[1]." Have we not there the tones of Congrevian heroines?

All in the Wrong (D.L. June 1761) followed within a year[2]. This once more is manners in tendency. Sir John Restless suspects his wife with Beverley, while Lady Restless suspects him with Belinda. Belinda and Beverley join the jealous crew by suspecting one another. This quartette forms the centre of the drama, but the plot is further complicated by the fact that Belinda's parents plan their daughter for Bellmont. Again everything is solved satisfactorily, the story being excellently developed to a happy conclusion, but the atmosphere is that of earlier times.

After these two decidedly talented productions, Murphy once more turned his attention to farce, moving back to truly comic realms only five years later, when he produced *The School for Guardians* (C.G. Jan. 1767). Here the manners spirit is testified to by the inception of the play. Apparently the author attempted first to alter Wycherley's *The Country Wife*, but turned from that comedy to its original, Molière's *L'École des Femmes*. Finally, he wrote a new work which utilised parts of Wycherley's drama as well as portions of *L'École des Femmes*, *L'École des Maris* and *L'Étourdi*[3]. The new plot tells how Brumpton loves Mary Ann, and how Belford loves her sister Harriet. Oldcastle, the guardian of the two girls, is cheated by Harriet into carrying their *billets-doux*, and eventually the pair of marriages duly takes place. If we mean by the term, comedy of manners, nothing but "immoral comedy," then assuredly Murphy's play is not in this

---

[1] v. i.

[2] Part of the plot is confessedly based on Molière's *Le Cocu Imaginaire*, a familiar hunting-ground for English dramatists. Murphy's comedy was translated into German as *Die Eifersüchtigen, oder: Keiner hat Recht* (*Deutsche Schaubühne*, 1788, vol. xxiv).

[3] The Advertisement to the play expresses the author's astonishment when he found that he had been forestalled by Garrick's *The Country Girl* (D.L. 1766).

style; but if we signify by the phrase a certain method
of comic treatment of life, then we have in this work, as in
the others, examples of that art form which is developed first
by Fletcher and finds its heyday of popularity at the close of
the seventeenth century.

Once more was Murphy's development as a writer of
comedy interrupted, by the penning both of tragedy and of
farce, but in *Know Your Own Mind* (C.G. Feb. 1777) he
returned to the manners' style. Basing his play on Destouches' *L'Irrésolu* he tells of Millamour's indecision in
matters of love, thus giving opportunity to Mrs Bromley,
who, using Malvil as a tool, herself aims to capture the way-
ward lover's attentions. The plot is complicated, not only
by Lady Bell's delightful modishness, but by the unfortunate
plight of Miss Neville, who is only just rescued from seduction
at the hands of Malvil, and who marries in the end the honest
Harry Lovewit. Among the minor characters Dashwould,
the railing cynic with a good heart, deserves remembrance.
In spite of the fact that he may have been girded at in Colman
the Younger's *New Hay at the Old Market* (H.[2] 1795)[1], neither
this character, nor his companions are cast in the sentimental
mould. Murphy's full importance can be appreciated only
when we take his work as a whole into consideration, for some
of his farces are among the best that were written in this age
of good farces, but we may note here his real skill in this
revived activity of manners' writing.

The close ties that undoubtedly existed during this time
between the so-called sentimental dramas and the dramas
written in the manners' tradition are attested by Hugh Kelly's
The School for Wives (D.L. Dec. 1773)[2], which relates how
Belville, who is a rake in spite of the fact that he loves his
wife, tries to run off with Miss Leeson and makes attempts on
Miss Walsingham. The latter is beloved by Captain Savage,
whose father, General Savage, imagines that her heart is
fixed on himself. There are, it is true, many scenes in the

---

[1] *Supra*, p. 157.

[2] A German translation of this play by J. C. Brock appears in Schröder's
Hamburgisches Theater, 1776, vol. iii. The comedy was originally brought
out under the name of Addington, owing to political complications.

Steele moralising strain, but Kelly shows clearly his realisation that sentimentalism as a force was losing ground. The managers, declared Lady Rachel, "alledge that the audiences are tired of crying at comedies[1]," and the author is evidently desirous in this play of providing something written in another style.

Nor was Kelly alone in thus approaching the spirit of the comedy of manners from the standpoint of a sentimentalist. Mrs Inchbald's two comedies, *I'll Tell You What* (H.[2] 1785) and *Every One has his Fault* (C.G. 1793) contain many episodes which are directly reminiscent of the Congreve style, and the plots of both are cast in the intrigue social strain beloved by Restoration dramatists[2]. Mrs Inchbald's feminine companion in the realm of comedy, Mrs Hannah Cowley, likewise shared her interest in the earlier atmosphere. *The Belle's Stratagem* (C.G. Feb. 1780) is an excellent comedy of manners, slightly sentimentalised. Doricourt is the handsome gallant, destined to wed Letitia Hardy. Thinking that she is a fool, he will have nothing to do with the match, but he is agreeably surprised when he finds that she is none other than a fair unknown who had flirted wittily with him at a masked ball. This part of the plot is carried forward with a gaiety which at once recalls previous times, and the sense of spontaneous wit is not dissipated even when we turn to the much more sentimental sub-plot in which the loving Sir George and Lady Touchwood play their more solemn parts. This play is particularly interesting for its subtle insistence on the changing conditions of the time. Although the particular passage has a slightly more sentimental colouring than many scenes in the comedy, the third scene in the first act shows us perfectly the way in which the Restoration spirit was being adapted to meet the requirements of the new age. Doricourt, the fop and man of fashion, is speaking to his friend Saville:

Doric. Why, she's *only* a fine girl; complexion, shape, and features; nothing more.
Sav. Is not that enough?

[1] I. ii.   [2] *Supra*, p. 148.

Doric. No! she should have spirit! fire! *l'air enjoue!* that something, that nothing, which every body feels, and which no body can describe, in the resistless charmers of Italy and France.

Sav. Thanks to the parsimony of my father, that kept me from travel! I would not have lost my relish for true unaffected English beauty, to have been quarrell'd for by all the Belles of Versailles and Florence.

Doric. Pho! thou hast no taste. *English* beauty! 'Tis insipidity; it wants the zest, it wants poignancy, Frank! Why, I have known a Frenchwoman, indebted to nature for no one thing but a pair of decent eyes, reckon in her suite as many Counts, Marquisses, and *Petits Maîtres*, as would satisfy three dozen of our first-rate toasts....

Sav. And has Miss Hardy nothing of this?

Doric. If she has, she was pleased to keep it to herself. I was in the room half an hour before I could catch the colour of her eyes; and every attempt to draw her into conversation occasioned so cruel an embarrassment, that I was reduced to the necessity of news, French fleets, and Spanish captures, with her father....

Sav. Come, I detain you—you seem dress'd at all points, and of course have an engagement.

Doric. To St James's. I dine at Hardy's, and accompany them to the masquerade in the evening: but breakfast with me tomorrow, and we'll talk of our old companions; for I swear to you, Saville, the air of the Continent has not effaced one youthful prejudice or attachment.

Sav. —With an exception to the case of Ladies and Servants.

Doric. True; there I plead guilty:—but I have never yet found any man whom I could cordially take to my heart, and call Friend, who was not born beneath a British sky, and whose heart and manners were not truly English.

Again, for those who look in the comedy of manners for immoral dialogue and lubricity alone, this passage can have not the slightest touch of the Restoration flavour, yet, if we consider it carefully it is seen to derive in spirit only from that period. Patriotic sentiment had come to give that last concluding sentence; moral deportment had come to make Doricourt a strangely sober gallant; but the basic purpose below this picturing of Doricourt and that below the delineation of Mirabel are the same.

Mrs Cowley's next important play, *Which is the Man?*

(C.G. 1782) is much more sentimentally inclined, and accordingly has been dealt with elsewhere[1], but in *A Bold Stroke for a Husband* (C.G. Feb. 1783) the manners' note once more predominates. The plot has a family likeness to that of *The Belle's Stratagem* in that Olivia, the heroine, not desiring to marry the choice of her father, pretends she is a termagant and later that she is a fool. In the end, of course, she succeeds in uniting herself to her own fancy, young Julio. Beside this there is a sub-plot which tells how Carlos, having abandoned his wife Victoria, is aided by, and eventually reconciled to, her. All through, the dialogue is neat and occasionally rises to the true height of wit. Rarely does one come across the typical "sentimental sentences"; such for Mrs Cowley were clearly *démodé*; "Yes," says Julio in the play, "And when she unveil'd her Gothic countenance, to render the thing completely ridiculous, she began moralising[2]."

More Ways than One (C.G. Dec. 1783) has something of the same tone, a tone which is deeply stressed in *The Town before You* (C.G. Dec. 1794), the last comedy by this authoress. The main plot here concerns Fancourt, a villain, who, with the aid of Tippy, imposes on Sir Robert Floyer and is eventually exposed. There is certainly much sensibility in the presentation of Mrs Fancourt, and the declaration of Lady Horatia Horton's love to Asgill is cast in the Cumberland strain; yet these are but incidental. Sentimentalism tinctures all the works of this age; it appears even in *She Stoops to Conquer*. No one, however, would call Goldsmith's comedy a typical sentimental production, and Mrs Cowley's works have as good a claim to be exempted from association with that type of drama.

So far no word has been given to what were truly among the dramatic masterpieces of this time, George Colman the Elder's *The Jealous Wife* (D.L. Feb. 1761) and *The Clandestine Marriage* (D.L. Feb. 1766). The former was one of the greatest successes of its own time[3], and continued as a

---

[1] *Supra*, p. 141.　　　　　　　　　　[2] III. i.
[3] See Colman's *Memoirs*, i. 64–7.

stock piece until well into the nineteenth century[1]. This is
an excellent comedy of manners, full of telling situations and
well-drawn characters[2]. Charles Oakly loves Harriot, who,
in order to escape a marriage with Sir Harry Beagle, flies
from her father, Russet. Lady Freelove, a lady of quality
not unlike the *grandes dames* of late seventeenth century
comedy, tries to throw her into the clutches of Lord Trinket,
but she finds a haven, if a troubled one, in Oakly's house.
Mrs Oakly becomes duly jealous, but is finally stormed into
submission. With brilliance and verve the story is carried
through from an excellent opening to a humorous conclusion. There is here something of Vanbrugh's breezy
laughter, and occasionally not a little of Wycherley's wit.
Truly the comic spirit in the late eighteenth century was not
so dormant when it could produce a work such as this is.

Concerning the authorship of *The Clandestine Marriage*
there has been some doubt. Garrick collaborated with Colman
in its preparation, but possibly his share in the composition
was merely that of reviser. In any case his association with
Colman need not take from the latter's claim to be considered
its main author. Garrick's facile genius had not the strength
to create *The Clandestine Marriage*[3]. The plot tells of the

---

[1] It was translated by M. J. Riccoboni as *The Jealous Wife, ou, La
Femme Jalouse* (*Œuvres complètes*, 1818, vol. vi) and by J. J. C. Bode as
Die eifersüchtige Ehefrau (1764). A satirical attack on the play appears in
*George Colman, Esq.; analysed; being a vindication of his Jealous Wife,
against his malicious aspersions* (1761).

[2] Colman's indebtedness to the Restoration masters was not confined
to general atmosphere. While much of the plot is taken from Fielding's
Tom Jones, resemblances have been traced to Congreve's *Love for Love*
and to Shadwell's *The Squire of Alsatia*. Colman himself acknowledged
some "hints" taken from *The Spectator* and the *Adelphi* of Terence.

[3] On this subject see *Posthumous Letters, from various celebrated Men;
addressed to Francis Colman, and George Colman, the Elder: with...papers
tending to elucidate the question relative to the proportional shares of authorship to be attributed to the Elder Colman and Garrick, in the Comedy of the
Clandestine Marriage* (1820). See also Beatty, J. M., *Garrick, Colman, and
The Clandestine Marriage* (*Mod. Lang. Notes*, xxxvi. 129–41, March,
1921). The play was a great success. It was regularly acted in the
eighteenth century and saw many revivals from 1800 to 1870. In May
1871, Phelps gave it at the Princess's and brought it forward again at the
Gaiety in April 1874. It was performed at the Strand in May 1887, and
at the Haymarket in March 1903. A French translation as *Le Mariage
Clandestin* appeared in 1768 and a German as *Die heimliche Heirath* in

secret union of Fanny Sterling and Lovewell. Sir John Melvil, who had proposed to marry her affected elder sister, falls in love with her, as does the foppish Lord Ogleby. Eventually all is satisfactorily explained, and Lovewell and Fanny settle down to more happy times. The play abounds in telling situations, of which the finest perhaps is that in which Mrs Heidelberg in curling-pins and Miss Sterling rouse the house in order to expose the delinquencies of Fanny. Deservedly, this was reckoned by contemporaries as one of the most brilliant of the "modern" comedies. It stands the test of time, preserving its freshness even yet, when the manners depicted have long since disappeared.

The only play of Garrick's written in this style, if we except his rather poor *Country Girl* (D.L. 1766), is *Bon Ton* (D.L. March 1775), which, in spite of its two short acts, rises to the levels of comedy. The picture of the outraged moralist, Sir John Trotley, is an excellent one, and the intrigues of Lord Minikin, Miss Tittup, Colonel Tivy and Lady Minikin are managed with distinct skill. The dialogue as a whole lacks brilliance but is certainly above the levels of mediocrity.

A few other typical plays may be singled out from among the numbers of similar comedies. Holcroft's *Seduction* (D.L. March 1787) is a very good example of the sentimentalised manners' style. Fairly well written, it tells how Lady Morden, neglected by Lord Morden, pretends to gaiety, and, after cheating Sir Frederic Fashion, succeeds in winning back the attentions of her husband. The close may teem with highly moral sentences, but the way in which this theme is treated is decidedly in the older strain.

Edward Jerningham's *The Welch Heiress* (D.L. April 1795) is still more completely in the Restoration style, even

---

1769. The comedy was also turned into an Italian comic opera as *Il Matrimonio Segreto*. The inspiration of the work seems to have come from one of Hogarth's *Marriage à la Mode* series, but Roberdeau brought forward an accusation in *Fugitive Verse and Prose* (1801) that the three main characters were stolen from James Townley's farce, *False Concord*. The accusation has justice, but there can be no comparison between Townley's farcical characters and Colman's finished portraits.

although Conway in the play notes that "Congreve and Vanbrugh seldom fill the house." The character of Lord Melcourt, who, in his impoverishment, is about to marry Miss Plinlimmon, half-idiot and half-wit, has decided brilliance, as has that of Phrensy, the unsuccessful poet, who pretends to die in order to obtain subscriptions for his collected works. Jerningham had more than ordinary talent, and this is unquestionably his brightest play.

Perhaps among these plays might be noted the one good comedy of Lady Craven, Margravine of Anspach, *The Miniature Picture* (D.L. May 1780)[1]. In fair dialogue it deals with the love of the lively Eliza for Belvil, and that of Camply for Miss Loveless. The theme is a hackneyed one, but the spirit with which the somewhat unoriginal episodes are clothed is deserving of critical praise.

A reasonably good comedy is Leonard Macnally's *Fashionable Levities* (C.G. April 1785), a play slightly reminiscent of Wycherley's *The Country Wife*. The story is one of love and intrigue. Ordeal keeps Clara from contact with the world, but Douglas, disguised as a Scots pedlar, wins her heart. Welford, a good-hearted rake, loves Constance, but pursues in the meanwhile both Lady Flippant Savage and Widow Volatile. Such a bare outline of the two main themes shows how deeply these dramatists of the eighties were in the debt of the masters of a preceding generation.

Finally, we may take William Macready's *The Bank Note, or, Lessons for Ladies* (C.G. May 1795), which is usually said to have been based on Taverner's *The Artful Husband*. As a matter of fact it is a tissue of reminiscences of previous dramas, skilfully bound together and well expressed. While the method adopted by Bloomfield to frighten his wife from extravagance has something in it of sentimental morality, the way in which the witty Miss Russel dresses as a man and regains her money from Lady Supple is quite apart from the usual sentimental strain. In its brightness and risibility *The Bank Note*, like the other comedies mentioned in this

---

[1] It seems to have been produced first at a private theatre, but was re-written for public performance.

section, stands far away from the *comédie larmoyante* beloved of Cumberland.

It may be repeated here that no claim is made that in these comedies we have the unadulterated finesse of Restoration drama; such a claim would be more than foolish. What is suggested is that in these works we find exemplified a tradition which passes straight from Etherege to Sheridan, and to Sheridan's successors; that those writers on our dramatic literature who class all the comedies between 1750 and 1800 as "sentimental" (always excepting the works of Goldsmith and Sheridan) are building a hasty theory on an incomplete foundation of fact. Indeed, when we look at the typical dramatic fare of the period, we may be inclined to wonder whether, after all, it was not sentimentalism which was the fashion insecurely planted in the theatre, whether Sheridan was not merely carrying on a movement which can be traced from Elizabethan times to the present day.

V. *The Comedy of Humours and of Intrigue*

In considering what is usually styled the "reaction to sentimentalism[1]" we must not, of course, forget that it was not only the comedies of manners that moved against the spirit of the Cumberland school. Both comedies of humours and comedies of intrigue presented those risible features which formed a fitting contrast to the pathos of the "tearful comedy." Indeed, those few critics who do strive to suggest that the spirit of laughter did not die out completely in the eighteenth century have recourse mainly to the Jonsonian pieces of this time, and in particular to the satirical works of that strange hobbling figure, Samuel Foote. Beginning his dramatic work just before 1750[2], Foote continued to pour out a series of highly libellous plays until the year of his death, 1777. The start was made by a series of imitations of prominent actors and actresses, but soon advances were made into the realm of social satire. Not only were the general types of the age depicted in his comedies—the Frenchified

---

[1] Cf. Nettleton, *op. cit.* p. 277.
[2] See vol. ii, p. 329.

Englishmen, the doctors, the bawds and the cullies—but particular persons were held up to ridicule. Amazingly enough, Foote escaped with little chastisement. His physical injury perhaps saved him a trifle, but, even apart from that, he, the "English Aristophanes" as sometimes he is styled, occupied a unique position of licence among the playwrights of the time. While other managers could not battle with the patent theatres, he kept the doors of the Haymarket open; while other dramatists suffered at the hands of indignant audiences or of a no less indignant Censor's Office, he pursued his biting, bitter, satiric way[1].

Many of Foote's plays are purely farcical, but several may be singled out as regular satiric comedies, most of them carelessly constructed but all displaying in some scenes at least a true *vis comica*. The first of sterling excellence, for we may pass over *Taste* (D.L. Jan. 1752)[2], *The Englishman in Paris* (C.G. March 1753), *The Knights* (revised form, D.L. Feb. 1754)[3], *The Englishman returned from Paris* (C.G. Feb. 1756), and *The Author* (D.L. Feb. 1757), is *The Minor* (Crow Street, Dublin, Jan. 1760; H.[2] June 1760)[4]. Like the majority

---

[1] Particular attention should be paid to *Memoirs of the Life and Writings of Samuel Foote, Esq.; the English Aristophanes: to which are added the bons mots, repartees, and good things said by that great wit and excentrical genius* (1777) and *Memoirs of Samuel Foote, Esq...By William Cooke, Esq.* (1805). Foote's life has been retold by Percy Fitzgerald (*Samuel Foote,* 1910) and additional anecdotes will be discovered in *Wit for the Ton; or, Sam Foote's last Budget opened* (1777). Several of Foote's non-dramatic satirical pamphlets have a certain value. *The Roman and English Comedy consider'd and compar'd. With Remarks on the Suspicious Husband* (1747) is of importance, while *A Treatise on the Passions* (1747), answered in *A Letter of Compliment to the ingenious Author of a Treatise on the Passions* (1747), is interesting for its contemporary account of Garrick, Quin and Barry.

[2] See *Whipping Rods for trifling, scurrhill Scribblers; as Mr F——t on Taste* (1752).

[3] See *A New Scene for the Comedy called the Knights. Or, fresh Tea for Mr Foote* (1758).

[4] On its first Dublin production it was uncompromisingly damned. Then in two acts, it lacked the character of Smirk (see Tate Wilkinson's *Memoirs* (Dublin 1791), ii. 72 ff.). It was expanded to three acts and so given at the Haymarket. It was said that Mrs Cole was a portrait of a certain Mother Douglas, and that Smirk took off the person of Langford the auctioneer. The epilogue satirises Whitfield. The play aroused a vast amount of controversy owing to the attack on the Methodists. In 1760 appeared *Christian and Critical Remarks on a Droll, or Interlude, called the*

of Foote's works, the plot of this play, which concerns a
trick played on the good-hearted libertine, Sir George, by
his father, Sir William Wealthy, does not matter. It is the
vigorous dialogue, the ceaseless bustle, the mordant satire
which call for our attention.

The Orators (H.[2] Aug. 1762) is a duller production, but the
idea of having actors speaking from the boxes is a novel one.
Possibly it was of Foote's own invention, although there
was a precedent in Dennis' A Plot and No Plot[1]. Turning for
inspiration to Spanish intrigue, Foote's next play, The Lyar
(C.G. Jan. 1762), is reminiscent of Steele's The Lying Lover,
itself taken from de Vega through the intermediate channels
of Corneille's Le Menteur and the anonymous Restoration
comedy, The Mistaken Beauty. Here personal satire is not
so apparent, the author seemingly losing himself in his enjoyment over Young Wilding's hopeless propensity towards
mendacity. In The Patron (H.[2] 1764) a return is made to
direct satire. The story tells of a Sir Thomas Lofty who
writes a play, Robinson Crusoe, and gets Bever to father it.
In order to keep the latter from revealing the secret, the noble
author is forced to consent to a marriage between his daughter
Juliet and his "ghost." The "patron" was said to have been
Lord Melcombe, and the comedy as a whole must be teeming
with now untraceable references to contemporaries. Dr Arne

Minor....By a Minister of the Church of Christ (answered by Foote in
A Letter...to the Reverend Author of the Remarks), A Letter to Mr
F - - - te, another Letter to Mr Foote, A. P.'s A Letter to David Garrick,
Esq. After the Haymarket production Pottinger issued The Methodist,
a Comedy: being a Continuation and Completion of the Plan of the Minor
(1761), and other pamphlets appeared including An Additional Scene to
the comedy of the Minor (1761), Observations, Good or Bad, Stupid or
Clever, Serious or Jocular, on Squire Foote's...The Minor (1761) and A
Letter of Expostulation from the Manager of the Theatre in Tottenham-
Court, to the Manager of the Theatre in the Haymarket. Relative to a New
Comedy, called the Minor (1761). Ten years later the play roused a storm
in Edinburgh. James Baine published a tract on The Theatre Licentious
and Perverted (1770), answered by Foote in an Apology (1771) and by an
anonymous writer ("Simplex") in A Letter to Mr James Baine (1771).
Another attack on the play appears in Belinda's Account of a Comedy, called
the Minor (1770).

[1] This was one of the plays that brought Foote into trouble. Faulkner,
the publisher, assumed he was being aimed at and brought a legal action
against the author. The full story is told in Biographia Dramatica, iii. 99.

came in for his share of ridicule in *The Commissary* (H.² 1765) where he is pictured as Dr Catgut and associated with none too genteel a set of companions, the subtle Mrs Mechlin, the stupid Zachariah Fungus and their kin[1]. *The Lame Lover* (H.² June 1770) deals with more general types, and must have been written with a distinct eye on Foote's own infirmity. Sir Luke Limp and Mrs Circuit here are excellent types. This general humours atmosphere reappears once more in *The Bankrupt* (H.² July 1773) which tells how Lady Riscounter puts false information into the newspapers concerning Lydia in order to favour her own daughter Lucy, and accordingly gives the author ample opportunity for indulging in satire of what was one of his *bêtes noires*, the contemporary journalist.

For modern readers Foote's next comedy, *The Maid of Bath* (H.² June 1771), forms one of his most interesting works, not only for its humorous scenes but for the light it sheds on Sheridan's bride-to-be, Miss Linley. This songstress is figured in the play as Miss Linnet and the plot is said to have been founded on an actual event immediately prior to Sheridan's famous duel of July 1772. The story relates how Flint would marry Miss Linnet but is eventually persuaded to abandon her, she preferring herself to remain a celibate. This comedy contains one of Foote's best drawn stage characters, Sir Christopher Cripple, an aged rake desperately anxious to lead henceforth a reformed existence.

On the doctors Foote turned in *The Devil upon Two Sticks* (H². May 1768), a play not connected with Le Sage's famous *Le Diable Boiteux*. The doctors introduced were portraits of living men and the author-actor made himself up to resemble no less a person than Sir William Browne, President of the College of Physicians. Wisely the latter, instead of entering into a legal action, revenged himself by complimenting Foote on his skill in mimicry, an action which

---

[1] The main idea seems to have been derived from Molière's *Le Bourgeois Gentilhomme* with perhaps a suggestion from D'Ancourt's *La Femme d'Intrigue*.

seems to have reached even to the author's shallow sense of shame. There is a certain fantasy in this play, which tells how Harriet and Invoice elope and succeed in rescuing an embottled devil. This spirit, in return, reveals to the lovers the follies of English physicians. Typically inconsequent, the satire contains some of the dramatist's best work. Ridicule of evil forces in society is given in *The Cozeners* (H.[2] July 1774) and personal satire is fully evident in *A Trip to Calais*, later altered as *The Capuchin* (H.[2] Aug. 1776). Apparently the Duchess of Kingston recognised herself in the thoroughly vicious Lady Kitty Crocodile, and succeeded through her influence in preventing the performance of the comedy in its original form[1]. The love of depicting evil seems to have grown on Foote, and, in spite of the extenuating characters of Colonel Crosby and Miss Lydell, the drama is over-weighted with bitterness. The same is true of *The Nabob* (H.[2] June 1772) in which Sir Matthew Mite is said to have been intended for General Richard Smith and another character for Sir Thomas Robinson[2]. Again, there are good elements here in Sophy, Thomas Oldham and Young Oldham, but the greater part of the play is taken up with bitter reflections on the vulgar rich (Sir Matthew Mite), parasitic servants (Janus and Conserve), antiquarians and social hangers-on (Rapine, Moses and Nathan).

As a whole Foote's dramatic work was a failure. He had little constructive power and little true insight into character. Assuredly he made up for the lack of both by his fine eye for theatrical effectiveness in situation and by his skill in dealing with contemporary society. At their best, however, his most noted comedies are largely farcical and his delineation of character suffers from the same defects as those which marred his power of acting. Foote could never have been a Garrick; he could only mimic the oddities of Garrick's style. Similarly as a dramatist he could create nothing great and

---

[1] See *The Case of the Duchess of Kingston, and her Letters to Samuel Foote* (1775).
[2] See Pickering and Chatto's Catalogue (No. 196) which quotes from MS. notes on a copy of the play belonging to Horace Walpole.

strong and original in comedy; he could only limn certain peculiarities of speech and of physical appearance.

"If Foote," says Hazlitt, "has been called our English Aristophanes, O'Keefe might well be called our English Molière. The scale of the modern writer was smaller, but the spirit is the same. In light, careless laughter, and pleasant exaggerations of the humorous, we have had no one equal to him. There is no labour or contrivance in his scenes, but the drollery of his subject seems to strike irresistibly upon his fancy, and run away with his discretion as it does with ours[1]." What prompted Hazlitt thus to eulogise so highly that prolific writer of farces, comic operas, operatic farces, interludes and pantomimes, can hardly be decided, but assuredly, while John O'Keefe or O'Keeffe deserves a place of importance in any account of the comic opera of his time he hardly merits much space in this account of regular comedy[2]. Almost the only work from his pen which can be included here is *Life's Vagaries* (C.G. March 1795) which, after all, is but a confused jumble of varying styles and ill-conceived characters. The rakish old Lord Torrendel has perhaps some claim to praise, but apart from this one portrait there is little of true strength in the play.

Another writer of marked variety of styles was Miles Peter Andrews, who turned in *Better Late than Never* (D.L. Nov. 1790) to the humours atmosphere, not, it must be confessed, with any marked success[3]. One of Richard Cumberland's plays, *The Impostors* (D.L. Jan. 1789), belongs to this group. Although most of the characters are conceived in the Jonsonian strain, the play is interesting as showing that Cumberland could, at least for a time, escape from his prevailing sentimental mood and present dialogue designed for the single purpose of raising laughter[4]. Fair dialogue

[1] *Lectures on the English Comic Writers*. Lecture VIII, "On the Comic Writers of the Last Century."

[2] See *Recollections of the Life of John O'Keeffe, written by Himself* (1826).

[3] In writing the play Andrews collaborated with Frederic Reynolds, and the pair received occasional aid from Edward Topham (Reynolds' *Life*, ii. 79).

[4] See *supra*, p. 127.

likewise distinguishes Lady Craven's *The Sleep-Walker* (private theatre at Newberry, 1778), based on Count de Pont de Vesle's *Somnambule*. The heavy Dutch Clipman is good, and the title part, Mr Devasthouse, is pictured with some considerable skill.

With these specimens of the satiric strain and of the tendency towards "humours" portraiture might be taken a few examples of the comedy of intrigue during these years. This type was not nearly so popular as the others dealt with above, although many of the comedies of manners make free use of intrigue material. Of the few pure specimens of the species Mrs Cowley's *A School for Greybeards; or, The Mourning Bride* (D.L. Nov. 1786) is the most noticeable. Based on Mrs Behn's *The Lucky Chance*, it presents to us the well-known Spanish figures—a Don Gaspar, his affianced bride Antonia and a banished lover Don Henry. The last-mentioned, by the aid of a disguise and not a little effrontery, gets into Don Gaspar's house, pretending that he is his nephew, Don Julio. By the side of this plot moves another which relates how the gay young wife of Don Alexis, Seraphina by name, occupies the attentions of Octavio in order that her step-daughter Viola may escape with Don Sebastian. Without vulgarity, this comedy does succeed in capturing some of that verve which characterised in previous eras the plays of Mrs Behn and of Mrs Centlivre.

Another good comedy of intrigue is Joseph Atkinson's *The Mutual Deception* (S.A., Dublin, March 1785), later altered by Colman as *Tit for Tat* (H.² Aug. 1786). The theme, already utilised by Popple in *The Double Deceit*, was confessedly based on *Le Jeu de l'Amour et du Hasard*, the ever-popular Franco-Italian comedy by Marivaux. Audiences can hardly tire of witnessing the laughable situations which must arise from the interchange of position between a Florinda and her servant Letty, and that between an Amorveil and his servant Skipwell. There is not the moral freedom here that there is in Popple's play, but the freshness of Atkinson's style cannot be denied.

The third example of this type of comedy is Isaac Bicker-

staffe's *'Tis Well it's no Worse* (D.L. Nov. 1770), taken from
Calderón's *El Escondido y la Tapada*, a fair comedy of un-
sentimental tendencies and written also with a certain freshness[1]. As is evident, the comedy of intrigue does not count
for much in this time, but, taking the few examples of this
type along with the comedies of manners and the comedies
of humours, we can well see that the "reaction" to sentimentalism—if so it is doomed to be called—had distinguished
supporters and at times succeeded in producing dramatic
work not entirely to be despised.

VI. *Farce*

Finally, in discussing the power of this reaction, we must
not overlook the innumerable farces of the time. While the
word "farce" itself seems to have fallen into disrepute, as
Garrick notes in *A Peep Behind the Curtain* (D.L. Oct. 1767)
when he observes that

> *Bold is the man, and compos mentis, scarce...*
> *Who, in these nicer times, dares write a Farce;*
> *A vulgar long----forgotten taste renew;*
> *All now are Comedies, five acts, or two*[2]

there can be not the slightest doubt that some of our best
farces belong to this period. Men might print the more
imposing title "Comedy" on their printed works, but it is
the spirit and not the name that counts. The age lacked
guiding principles, but it had a certain comic power, and that
comic power is expressed most felicitously in the hearty
careless sketches which O'Keeffe and Bickerstaffe and Murphy
so well knew how to write.

Farce, after all, is a roughened form of comedy, and the
farces of this period repeat the atmospheres of the main types

---

[1] What Bickerstaffe means when in the Preface he declares "that the
Maid of the Mill, a piece written by himself...was the first sentimental
Drama that had appeared on the English stage for near forty years" is
apparently now unexplainable. His round date would carry us back to
about 1722. Perhaps he was thinking of Steele's *The Conscious Lovers*,
but he must have been sadly ignorant of the dramatic literature of his
own age.

[2] Prologue.

of comic drama we have already glanced at. The majority deal with characters cast in the Jonsonian mould, but others are of the intrigue type and in some we catch glimpses of the manners style. A few, but very few, are sentimental.

The Jonsonian farces may well be introduced by an examination of the plays of this nature written by Arthur Murphy. Murphy's first work indeed was a piece of this kind, *The Apprentice* (D.L. Jan. 1756), designed to satirise in Dick Wingate the stage-struck tradesmen of its time. The way in which the author has contrasted the infatuated amateur and the worthy citizen is not unamusing. Here, for instance, the puzzled father, Wingate, confronts his theatrically-minded son:

WINGATE

Do you think I am to fall in love with your face? Must I bear with you, because I am your father?

DICK

"A little more than kin, and less than kind."

WINGATE

What a pretty figure you cut now?...I would not give a farthing for all you know. If you have a mind to thrive in this world, study figures, and make yourself usefull.

DICK

"How weary, stale, flat and unprofitable seem to me all the uses of this world!"

WINGATE

Mind the scoundrel now!

GARGLE

Do, Mr Wingate, let me speak to him. Softly, softly; I'll touch him with a gentle hand, Come, young man, lay aside this sulky humour, and speak as becomes a son.

DICK

"O Jeptha, judge of Israel, what a treasure hadst thou!"

WINGATE

What does the fellow say?

GARGLE

He relents, Sir; come, come, young man, make peace with your father.

DICK

"They fool me to the top of my bent." Egad, I'll bamboozle 'em, and so get out of the scrape...."A truant disposition, good my lord."....No, no, stay, stay, that's not right: my friend *Ranger* can supply a better speech...."It is as you say, when we are sober, and reflect but ever so little on our follies, we are ashamed and sorry; and yet, the very next minute, we rush again into the very same absurdities.'

WINGATE

Well said, lad, well said; that's very good sense; I like you when you talk sense[1].

Murphy's next effort in this style was *The Upholsterer, or, What News?* (D.L. March 1758)[2], taken partly from Fielding's *The Coffee-House Politician.* Quidnunc here is an eager seeker for news. He can, in his own opinion, secure the financial stability of England, yet he himself goes bankrupt. Beside him are kindred humours figures, Pamphlet, Razor, Feeble and Codicil, as well as a charming Mrs Termagant, who seems, it may be suggested, to have directly inspired Sheridan. The following speech is unquestionably reminiscent of Mrs Malaprop:

By my troth you're in the right on't;...there's ne'er a she in all Old England, (as your father calls it) is mistress of such *phisiology*, as I am. Incertain as I am, as how you does not know nobody that puts their words together with such a *curacy* as myself. I once lived with a *mistus*, Ma'am,...*mistus!*...she was a lady; a great tallow-chandler's wife! and she wore as fine cloaths as any person of quality, let her get up as early as she will; and she used to call me...Tarmagant, says she, what's the *signification* of such a word? and I always told her; I told her the *importation* of all my words, though I could not help laughing, Miss Harriet, to see so fine a lady, such a downright *ignoranimus*.

---

[1] i. i.
[2] *The Spouter or The Triple Revenge* (1756) was a personal attack on Sir John Hill, Theophilus Cibber and Samuel Foote; *The Englishman from Paris* (D.L. April 1756) was never printed.

With her "*curacy*" Mrs Termagant seems nearer to Mrs Malaprop than the many originals which have been discovered for the latter.

A fair farce of the humours type was provided by Murphy in his next work of this kind, *The Old Maid* (D.L. July 1761), the excellence of which is marred only by the rather lame conclusion[1]. The theme is a clever one. Clerimont sees Mrs Harlow and Miss Harlow; he falls in love with the former but assumes that she is the "Miss" and unmarried. Obviously, however, this general situation does not lend itself to a regularly logical outcome, and the last speeches are thoroughly unnatural and forced.

The Citizen (D.L. July 1761), which seems to have suffered transformations in 1763 and in 1786, is not so original in development, many scenes being directly adapted from *La Fausse Agnès* of Destouches. The plot runs in the hackneyed direction. Old Philpot plans George, his son, for Maria, daughter of Sir Jasper Wilding. Maria pretends that she is a fool and George casts her off. Eventually she succeeds in wedding Beaufort, while Philpot and George confront one another in the house of Corinna, a courtesan[2]. *No One's Enemy but his Own* (C.G. Jan. 1764), founded on Voltaire's *L'Indiscret*, is slightly brighter and full of humours. Careless, tiring of Lucinda, has captured the heart of Hortensia, but he can keep no secret, so that Lucinda exposes him and Hortensia gives her hand to Wisely. All these types are well drawn and are aptly contrasted with the figures of Sir Philip Figurein, Crib and their crew.

Murphy's next, and last farce, was *Three Weeks after Marriage; or, What we must all come to* (C.G. March 1776), which had been damned in an earlier form acted under the subtitle in 1764[3]. The daughter of the old virtuoso Drugget

---

[1] Portions of the plot seem to be taken from Fagan's *L'Étourderie*. Murphy's play was translated into German in J. C. Nossek's *Komische Schaubühne der Engländer* (1842), vol. ii.

[2] The theme, of course, was not so hackneyed in 1761 as it became later. Mrs Cowley's *The Belle's Stratagem* (C.G. 1780) and *A Bold Stroke for a Husband* (C.G. 1783) both work along lines similar to those in *The Citizen*.

[3] In its later form it was a huge success. A German translation was published in 1786 as *Drei Wochen nach der Hochzeit*.

has been married to Sir Charles Rackett. The couple lead
an unholy life of quarrelling, and, shocked at their behaviour,
the parents give their other daughter, Nancy, to the low-
born Woodley rather than to the richer and more aristocratic
Lovelace. Such is the bare theme, obviously with a sentimental tinge, of this farce, but the quarrel scenes and the
excellent farcical situations make it undoubtedly a theatrical
success, well rounding off Murphy's efforts in this style.

One of the most notable contributors to this species apart
from Murphy was the elder Colman, who brought to it that
peculiar verve and wit which irradiates both *The Jealous Wife*
and *The Clandestine Marriage*. The "Dramatic Novel,"
Polly Honeycombe (D.L. Dec. 1760), marks his start in this
style[1], the satire being directed against those novels which
later set the heart of Lydia Languish a-fluttering. So full
of romantic sentiment is Polly after perusing those volumes
from that "evergreen tree of diabolical knowledge," the
lending library, that she is only just prevented from eloping
with the wretched attorney's clerk, Scribble. *The Musical
Lady* (D.L. March 1762) followed. Being merely a discarded
portion of the original *Jealous Wife*[2], it is natural that it
should have little organic unity. The Italian opera meets
here with plentiful satire, Mask winning Sophy by his
pretence to "*virtù*." Much finer is *The Deuce is in Him*
(D.L. Nov. 1763), which, the author says, was first suggested
by a "hint" taken from *Scrupule* and *Alcibiade ou le Moi*
in Marmontel's *Tales*[3]. The scenes in which Emily and
Mdlle Florival laugh the jealous Colonel Tamper out of
court have decided merit. *The Oxonian in Town* (C.G. Nov.
1767) met with but a dubious reception, it being "violently
opposed by a Party, at whom the Satire...was supposed to
be levelled[4]." Written in a free strain reminding us of

---

[1] The play was thought at first to be Garrick's, who wrote the Prologue
and Epilogue. These were printed in *The Public Advertiser* for Dec. 12,
1760.

[2] See Colman's *Memoirs*, i. 69.

[3] It was translated by M. J. Riccoboni as *The Deuce is in Him; ou, Il est
possédé* (*Œuvres complètes*, 1818, vol. v).

[4] Victor, *op. cit*. iii. 117.

Restoration times, it tells how Knowell saves Careless from
the clutches of Rook, Shark and McShuffle. Lacking in
unity, it makes up for this defect by the strength of the
dialogue and the living nature of the characters. For *Man
and Wife; or, The Shakespeare Jubilee* (C.G. Oct. 1769)
Colman turned to the ever-popular *Fausse Agnès* of Destouches,
creating his Sally from Babet. The main *raison d'être* of this
piece was the desire to forestall Garrick, who had produced
the Jubilee procession at Stratford-upon-Avon in September
and who was then preparing to bring the whole "production"
to Drury Lane. In this desire Colman seems to have been
successful; whether his farce deserves remembrance is
another matter. Finally, before the composition of a long line
of pantomimes, adaptations and entertainments, we reach
The Spleen; or, Islington Spa (D.L. Feb. 1776), derived
from *La Malade Imaginaire*. This is, like *Man and Wife*,
a rather poor work, interesting mainly for its ridicule of
newspaper men and for its presentation of the hypochondriac
D'Oyley. It seems unfortunate that Colman did not stop
with *The Deuce is in Him*, for his early farces have the same
power we see in *The Jealous Wife*, a true zest and crude
strength often lacking in the genteel finesse of late eighteenth
century dramatic literature. Perhaps managerial toils distracted Colman's mind in the later years, perhaps his inspiration passed away, but, whatever the cause, his plays of
1765 onwards never showed the same free tumultuous-
ness and sincere naturalism which distinguished his first
efforts.

Distinctly of the "humours" type also is Charles Macklin's
Love À-la-Mode (D.L. Dec. 1759)[1], a production notable
for its character of Sir Archy MacSarcasm. Representatives of
various races are here introduced—in MacSarcasm himself (a
Scotsman), Squire Groom (an Englishman), Sir Callaghan
O'Brallaghan (an Irishman, the hero) and Mordecai (a Jew).
All are suitors for the hand of Charlotte, the ward of Sir

---

[1] Not printed in full till 1793. One act was given in *The Court Miscellany* for April 1766. See *A Scotsman's Remarks on the Farce of Love à
la Mode* (1760).

Theodore Goodchild, and it is the Irishman who successfully passes the test that is imposed.

Sheridan deserves an important place for *St Patrick's Day: or, The Scheming Lieutenant* (C.G. May 1775), a short piece written for the benefit of the actor Clinch. There are genuinely witty portions in this drama, but as a whole its style does not rise to any great heights and often falls below the upper level of late eighteenth century farcical work. Much better from this point of view are some of Mrs Inchbald's similar farces. *Appearance is against Them* (C.G. Oct. 1785) is a rather vivacious production which might have been styled *Much Ado about a Shawl*[1]. Walmsley gives a friend of his a present of a shawl. Miss Angle, aided by Mrs Fish, takes it and sends it to Lord Lighthead, thinking he will return it. He gives it to Lady Loveall, who is arrested. In the end Miss Angle confesses to vanity, and laughter concludes the play. Cleverness likewise marks *The Widow's Vow* (H.[2] June 1786), derived partly from Patrat's *L'Heureuse Erreur*. The scene in which the amorous but somewhat timorous Antonio is confronted by the Marquis disguised as a woman is in the true spirit of the best comic work in this style. This story had been adapted before in English, first as *The Ambiguous Lover* (Crow-street, Dublin, March 1781), ascribed to Miss Sheridan, and later by Joseph Atkinson as *A Match for a Widow: or, The Frolics of Fancy* (S.A. Dublin, April 1786). The latter is a comic opera, but may be considered here. The characters are English, instead of the Spanish figures favoured by Mrs Inchbald, and the play has decided interest in that Jonathan seems to be the first "Yankee" put upon the stage.

Mrs Inchbald's *The Midnight Hour* is a fairly sprightly farce, but not so dramatically effective as the anonymous play of the same title which, taken from Dumaniant's *La Ruse contre Ruse*, narrates the love of Sir Charles Dashwood for Lucinda and his outwitting, with the aid of the astute Bronze, of his rival, Colonel Ambush. As the preface to the 1787

---

[1] It was revived in 1804 as *Mistake upon Mistake*.

Dublin edition states, its "chief merit...consists in pantomimical situations."

The Wedding Day (D.L. Nov. 1794), Mrs Inchbald's last
work of this kind, has more brilliance. The story is a poor one
—Sir Adam Contest's marriage with a country-reared girl
and the reappearance of his former wife, the love of young
Contest for her mother, he not knowing of the relationship
—but the brightness of the dialogue and the general risibility
of the situations entitles it to what has hitherto been denied,
modern revival.

Perhaps it may be thought that John O'Keeffe's plays
ought largely to be considered in this section, but the farces
of this writer seem to have no great claim to attention, in
spite of Hazlitt's discovery in them of Molièresque qualities.
The Prisoner at Large (H.[2] July 1788) is one of the best, but
it rivals in no way the sparkling nature of Mrs Inchbald's
work. The tale, relating how Lord Esmond, for long a
prisoner in France, returns to greet his love Adelaide and
reward his faithful steward, is a dull one, and the dialogue
does nothing to revive the piece from mediocrity. Instead
of dealing with his work in detail, or indeed with the work of
any outstanding dramatist, it may be best to examine a few
individual farces as typical of larger tendencies in the time.
David Garrick's *Neck or Nothing* (D.L. Nov. 1766), "an
imitation of the *Crispin Rival de Son Maître* of LE SAGE[1]"
is a fair specimen of the humours-intrigue type. The devices
of the servant Martin are full of good fun, and the dialogue
teems with sentences which, if, like Cibber's, are not wit,
sound very much like it. Humour of a lower kind occurs in
Lord Hailes' *The Little Freeholder* (1790), in W. C. Oulton's
Botheration: or, A Ten Years' Blunder (C.G. May 1798)[2]
and in Thomas Vaughan's *The Hotel; or, The Double Valet*
(D.L. Nov. 1776). The latter is based partly on Goldoni's
Il Servitore di due Padroni and partly on a Franco-Italian piece,

---

[1] Advertisement.
[2] The chief point in this play is that an adventurer reads a matrimonial
advertisement in a newspaper ten years old without noticing the date.
Similar in style is another work by Oulton, *As it Should Be* (H.[2] June 1789).

Arlequin Valet de deux Maîtres. All of these are representative of the more mediocre farcical fare of the time. Of the same type, though much more finely constructed, is Isaac Bickerstaffe's *The Absent Man* (D.L. March 1768), in which Flavia succeeds in escaping a union with the absent-minded ass, Shatterbrain. As in many of these farces, good situations atone for the tameness of the plot. Similar, too, is Edward Topham's *The Fool* (D.L. April 1785), where Beaufort, newly married to Laura, is horrified to find that she is a fool. Excellent situations follow one another until it is discovered that the folly is merely assumed in order that the bride may unmask an old lecherous Abbé.

Devices of a like nature are made use of in Mrs Cowley's *Who's the Dupe?* (D.L. May 1779), which tells how Doiley, an uneducated man, desires to have a scholar for his son-in-law. Gradus arrives but is cheated into taking up the pose of a beau, while the modish Granger assumes the guise of a learned man. It is he, of course, who in the end wins the hand of the fair Elizabeth.

In Isaac Jackman's *All the World's a Stage* (D.L. April 1777) we approach the common satire of amateur theatricals. Wooing Kitty Sprightly in play-fashion, Charles Stanley succeeds in winning that flighty young lady in the end. *The Divorce* (D.L. Nov. 1781), by the same playwright, is more sentimentally inclined, but well shows the cleverness of the author. Sir Harry and Lady Trifle really love one another, but, to gain notoriety, they decide to sue for a divorce. Approaching Qui Tam for this purpose, they are cheated by this attorney's clerk, the versatile Dennis Dogherty, who succeeds in running off with the elderly Mrs Anniseed and her fifty thousand pounds.

Satire of private theatricals is continued in one of the two farces of James Powell. *The Narcotic* (1787) deals with an adventure of Don Juan, and *Private Theatricals* (1787) burlesques the current mania. Equally satirical, although along different lines, is the anonymous "Dramatic Piece," *The Adventurers* (1777) and Frederick Pilon's *Aerostation; or, The Templar's Stratagem* (C.G. Oct. 1784). The latter ridicules the *virtuosi* of the time and, in particular, the current passion for ballooning[1]. The same author's *The Deaf Lover* (C.G. Feb. 1780)[2] is not unamusing, and works on a fairly good theme. Old Wrongward and Young Wrongward have been intercepting the letters of Meadows sent to Sophia. With the aid of Betsy Blossom, a clever little flower-seller, he disguises himself as a deaf old man and pretends to take their house for an inn. In the end, of course, the villains are exposed and the lovers triumph.

Poorer on the whole is Paul Joddrell's *A Widow and No Widow* (H.[2] July 1779), which follows Foote in an indulgence in personal satire. Macfable, Dr Alfred and Jenny Daisy have historic interest from this point of view, and the manner in which they are pictured testifies to the impress made by Foote's style upon contemporaries[3].

Other farces experiment mainly in the style of intrigue. Of this type is Morris' *The Adventurers* (D.L. March 1790) as is also *The Wandering Jew: or, Love's Masquerade* (D.L. May 1797) by Andrew Franklin. In the latter Atall's disguise as the Wandering Jew is not ill-managed. For material for his intrigue farce *The Peckham Frolic: or Nell Gwyn* (1799) Edward Jerningham passed to historical persons, telling of a trick by which Sir Oliver Luke is forced to marry Ann Killigrew. Among these farces William Whitehead's *A Trip to Scotland* (D.L. Jan. 1770) deserves honourable mention. In spite of the fact that the author refers to it as a "little whimsical trifle[4]," it is a well-constructed piece and well merits the high commendation of the editors of the *Biographia Dramatica*. The story of Miss Griskin's elopement with Jemmy Tweedle, and the consequent pursuit by Griskin and his housekeeper Filigree is told with manifest zest and great good humour.

A few, but, as has been noted, a very few, of these farces

---

[1] Similar works were appearing on the continent; cf. the *Nicodème de la Lune*.

[2] In its original form *The Device; or, The Deaf Doctor* (C.G. Sept. 1779).

[3] A special point of interest in this play lies in the Dedication, addressed to Nobody, because "NOBODY respects an Author"; cf. *supra*, p. 46.

[4] Dedication to Garrick.

were sentimental in character. It is fairly easy to unite some forms of laughter with sensibility, but farcical situation, abounding in hilarious merriment, rarely allows of the close juxtaposition of serious aims. As a consequence, but a small number of the sentimental dramatists turned to farce, and those who did for the most part left their moral preoccupations behind them. J. P. Kemble tried his hand at this style of serious farce when he adapted Charles Johnson's *The Country Lasses* as *The Farm House* (D.L. May 1789). The story of Modely and Heartwell, of Aura and Flora, is left largely as Johnson planned it, but there has been an attempt to intensify the more serious aspects of their relationships. Richard Sicklemore's *The Dream* (Brighton, Aug. 1796), described as "A Serio-Dramatic Piece," has a similar tendency. The device of the "spouting-club" with the admixture of Shakespearian and colloquial terms seems to have been taken from Murphy's *The Apprentice* (D.L. 1756)[1] and the trick played by Dr Fortville and Miss Willoughby on the ranting Alfred seems to savour a little of the early eighteenth century farce, *The Hypocondriac*. *Fortune's Frolic* (C.G. May 1799) by John Till Allingham is equally sentimental, introducing a curmudgeonly villain in Snacks and a generous child of fortune in Robin Roughhead. Ridiculous situations mingle with highly sentimental situations in Leonard MacNally's *Retaliation* (C.G. May 1782), which tells of a plot by old Rebate to ruin the house of Trueman and which abounds in sentimental sentences such as that which Trueman rhetorically enunciates, "What would the world say, should a British merchant act with such dishonour[2]?"

Apart from the main types indicated above, the eighteenth century farces are nondescript affairs. If we are able to single out some two score of excellently devised pieces, we can put alongside of them innumerable little one- or two-act pieces of practically no real dramatic value whatsoever. Elopements and nauseous marriages just escaped, as in Charles Shillito's *The Man of Enterprise* (Norwich 1789)[3],

---

[1] *Supra*, p. 179–80.   [2] I. i.
[3] Genest, *op. cit.* x. 198, places this amongst the unacted plays.

were as popular in 1780 and 1790 as they are to cinema-
frequenters of our own time. So too astute servants owing
a distant descent from Italian ancestors—Harlequin, Bri-
ghella and their peers—proved successful. One such, culled
from among many others, may be found in Pinch of *The
Family Party* (H.[2] July 1789), who contrives the marriage of
Jack Spriggins and Laura. What might be called the farcical
complications of locality likewise found many admirers. Thus
in Cobb's *The First Floor* (D.L. Jan. 1787) Whimsey and his
daughter Charlotte arrive at his son's lodgings—lodgings
which Monfort believed he had taken for the latter. It is
said that this piece received "great applause[1]," but its
literary value is almost nothing. Situations of a kindred
nature occur in Thomas Dibdin's *The Horse and the Widow*
(C.G. May 1799), a farce which is, however, saved by the
presence in it of Killruddery, the Irishman.

As in other fields of eighteenth century theatrical work,
we must strive to set against these many poorer pieces the
true successes of the period. The comparison with the present-
day cinema holds good in this connection. While there are
some excellent films shown every year throughout the world
we should do ill were we to forget them because of a too great
attention paid to the vacuous farcical pictures hastily rushed
through at some obscure studio. No doubt thousands enjoy
those films, even as thousands in the late eighteenth century
enjoyed the poorer farces of the time, but in a true estimation
of the period we must ever strive to hold the balance between
over-praising the few genuine successes of the age and over-
emphasising the unquestioned poverty of many of the playwrights and the stupid tastes of at least large sections of the
audience.

The importance of the late eighteenth century farce is
twofold. In the first place, as has been indicated, some of the
brightest and most truly theatrical things in the period took
this form, and, while farce as such cannot be accorded a
place level with that occupied by the finest tragedy and

---

[1] *The Theatrical Dictionary* (1792). The farce was translated into
German as *Hier ist eine Wohnung zu vermiethen* (1792).

comedy, skill and talent, sometimes genius, go to the making of a perfect example in this kind. Farce in the late seventeenth century may generally have been but a debased form of Jonsonian or Molièresque comedy; here we have often something distinct, a type of dramatic literature obeying its own laws and instinct with independent vitality. In the second place, save for the very few of a sentimental nature, the farces of this time exist solely for the purpose of arousing laughter, and in so far are to be taken as indicating that the cult of the *comédie larmoyante* was by no means universal. To the dignified critic it may seem to be preposterous that Mrs Inchbald's *The Wedding Day* (D.L. 1794) should in any way be considered with Sheridan's *The School for Scandal* (D.L. 1777), but the truth remains that both have many tendencies in common. They present two different fronts to the attack of sensibility. They are not forces of "reaction," but rather show the regular development of comic drama as it had been passed down from *Gammer Gurton's Needle* through *Every Man in His Humour*, *The Way of the World*, *The Comical Gallant* and *The Suspicious Husband*. As in the realm of narrative fiction there was a conflict between the *Pamelas* and the *Tom Joneses*, so in the realm of dramatic art there was a struggle between a *West Indian* and a *School for Scandal*. When we take into consideration, not merely the works which have, rightly or wrongly, been singled out for critical praise and academic reading, we find that in the drama the older traditions were too strong to be lost. The spirits of Jonson, of Congreve and of Fielding were so deeply implanted that no wave even of French sensibility could destroy the laughter and the tumultuous merriment.

CHAPTER IV

MISCELLANEOUS FORMS
OF DRAMA

I. *Definitions*

IN the discussion of the conflict between sentimentalism
and what we might style the older traditions we must
not lose sight of the fact that we must take into account
many other forms besides the regular comedy and the
already long-established farce[1]. Already in the early eighteenth century new forms of dramatic literature, such as the
ballad-opera and the pantomime, were springing into birth,
and this tendency towards the development of fresh species
continued in the years after 1750. Pantomime continued on
its triumphal career, now taking the form of pantomimic
opera as it had done in the time of Lewis Theobald, now
moving towards the region of the pure "entertainment"—
little more than a spectacular harlequinade. So, too, burlesques,
pastorals, "dramatic poems" and similar pieces helped to
fill out the body of dramatic workmanship in the age.

Of all these miscellaneous forms unquestionably the most
popular were the comic opera, the operatic farce, the burletta
and the "interlude"; it is concerning the significance of each
of these terms that something must be said in this section.
In the previous volume of this history of English drama[2] it was
noted that the ballad-opera, as created in 1728 by John Gay,
ran its course within a few years and suddenly disappeared.
After 1750 a few regular ballad-operas made their appearance,
but a critical distinction must be made between *The Beggar's
Opera* and the many works which surround *The Duenna*

---

[1] On the introduction of farce to the English theatre see vol. i, pp.
247–8 and 257–63.
[2] Pp. 237–51.

(C.G. 1775). The ballad-opera is essentially an operatic comedy of which the words have been written to fit certain more or less traditional airs. Thus most of the music for *The Beggar's Opera* dated from the seventeenth century; none of it was specially written for Gay's own lyrics. Part of the worth of a ballad-opera, therefore, comes from the subtle juxtaposition in the mind of the auditor of the *original* tune and words and of the new words written for the music. *The Beggar's Opera* would not have been the success it was had it not been that the audience realised the delicious parody of songs they could hear daily in market-place or in country lane. Obviously, the store of popular melodies is limited, and the failure of ballad-opera after 1732 is that the dramatists repeated or wrote awkwardly because of the impress made on the tunes by their predecessors. To this ballad-opera corresponds *la comédie en vaudevilles*, which has "couplets à chanter sur des airs connus, sur des *timbres* populaires[1]," otherwise known as *vaudevilles dramatiques* or, more simply, *vaudevilles*. With this in French literature is contrasted the *comédie à ariettes*, which has "couplets à chanter, *sur des airs nouveaux*[2]," and which gradually developed into the *opéra comique*. In English literature this *comédie à ariettes* is perhaps suggested in Settle's early *The World in the Moon*, which undoubtedly reminds us of the comic opera, but the full development of the type comes not until after 1750.

The comic opera as such corresponds to the serious opera; it is *la comédie musicale* or *la comédie lyrique* as the serious opera is *la tragédie musicale* or *la tragédie lyrique*. This type of comic opera in its full development was first made popular through the famous *La Serva Padrona* performed at the Opéra in Paris on August 1, 1752. A year later Vadé and Dauvergne collaborated in the production of *Les Troqueurs* and so set the fashion in France for native comic opera. Naturally the mode passed over to England and became duly popular. Perhaps no better illustration could be found

---

[1] Eugène Lintilhac, *Histoire Générale du Théâtre en France* (vol. iv, *La Comédie: Dix-huitième siècle*, pp. 19–20).

[2] Eugène Lintilhac, *op. cit.* p. 20.

of its success than a passage culled from the elder Colman's
New Brooms (D.L. 1776):

Crotchet. No—but plays are worn out, Sir. Otway's a rag,
Jonson obsolete, and Shakespeare worn threadbare. Plays!—
plays might do well enough formerly indeed; but quite out of
fashion now, Sir. Plays and little Roscius left the stage together,
Sir!

Phelim. What will the stage do then?

Crotchet. Do!—Musical pieces, to be sure—Operas, Sir—our
only dependance now.—We have nothing for it now but wind,
wire, rosin and catgut. This is the thing—this is the thing
[*thrumming on the harpsichord*]. Have you any voice? Can you
sing, Sir?

Phelim. Voice! Oh, by my sowle, voice enough to be heard
across the Channel, from the Gate or the Hid, to ould Dublin:—
And then I can sing, *Arrah my Judy, Arrah my Judy!* and the
Irish howl—*Hubbub-o-boo!* [*howling*]—oh, it would do your heart
good to hear it.

Crotchet. Should be glad of that pleasure, Sir; a little song now,
by way of specimen!

Phelim. Oh, you're as welcome as the flowers in May, my jewel.
Him! him! [*Sings*.

Crotchet. Well, Sir, that may do very well, introduced into a
Comick Opera.

Phelim. An Irishman in an Opera! Oh, my dear!

Crotchet. And why not, Sir!—Operas are the only real entertainment. The plain unornamented drama is too flat, Sir. Common dialogue is a dry imitation of nature, as insipid as real conversation; but in an opera, the dialogue is refreshed by an air
every instant.—Two gentlemen meet in the Park, for example,
admire the place and the weather; and after a speech or two the
orchestra take their cue, the musick strikes up, one of the characters takes a genteel turn or two on the stage, during the
symphony, and then breaks out—

> When the breezes
> Fan the trees-es,
> Fragrant gales
> The breath inhales,
> Warm the heart that sorrow freezes.

[*Singing and walking, as described in his speech*[1].

---

[1] Scene ii.

Though many, like Colman, may have laughed at it, the type proved immensely popular, and there is truth in the criticism that "the plain, unornamented drama" proved "too flat." The distinction already made between the ballad-opera and the comic opera, however, is not quite sufficient for our purposes. As the comic opera is largely musical comedy (using that phrase in its literal sense) it is obvious that a sub-species would be musical farce. Indeed the operatic farces of this time are almost as numerous as the more highly finished comic operas, and certainly were as popular. The distinction is, of course, not a fundamental one, but in considering the development of the type it must be taken duly into account. With this operatic farce goes what must be called the "musical interlude." There is little difference between the two, save that the interlude is frequently merely an episode, whereas the true operatic farce presents a short plot. It has been found impossible here to maintain a strict distinction, and many individual pieces may seem to some readers wrongly placed. It may be noted that many of these "interludes" are styled "musical entertainments" and frequently introduce little more than a few lyrics roughly placed in a semi-farcical setting. From these, too, must be separated the burletta, another type of no very decided characteristics. Technically the term burletta ought to be confined to burlesque comic operas, to those for example which deal in a ludicrous way with classic legend or history, but there is no such sharp distinction in the eighteenth century usage of the word. An illustration of the confusion reigning in the minds of contemporaries in regard to this type is presented in Mrs Clive's *The Rehearsal; or, Bays in Petticoats* (D.L. 1750):

WITLING

But pray Madam, you say you are to call your new Thing, a Burletto; what is a Burletto?

MRS HAZARD

What is a Burletto? why havn't you seen one at the Haymarket?

WITLING

Yes; but I don't know what it is for all that.

MRS HAZARD

Don't you! why then, let me die if I can tell you, but I believe it's a kind of poor Relation to an Opera.

As a "poor Relation to an Opera" it remained, and, if eighteenth century audiences defined it at all, they thought of it as connected with recitative and aria. If this recitative is in ridicule of the recitative of serious opera, the application of the test seems justified, but in practice no such method or rule seems to have been employed[1].

II. *Opera, Comic Opera and Kindred Forms*

From Colman's *New Brooms* (D.L. 1776) it has already been seen how popular any form of musical drama was in this latter half of the eighteenth century. The Italian opera proceeded on its destined path, and although there is no necessity here to discuss in detail the chief manifestations of its activity[2], we must remember the popularity of the type and the rivalry between it and the English drama. That the opera, both Italian and English, was a fashionable amusement is proved by many satirical references of the time. Such

[1] A discussion concerning the significance of the term burletta will be found in Peake's *Memoirs of the Colman Family* (1841) ii. 397-9. Noting how the term had been widened in meaning in the nineteenth century, Colman declares that it is difficult for him "to consider a burletta otherwise than as a diama in rhyme, and which is entirely musical; a short comic piece, consisting of recitative and singing, wholly accompanied, more or less, by the Orchestra." As typical burlettas he cites *Midas, The Golden Pippin, Poor Vulcan* and *The Portrait*. The extension in meaning of the term after 1800 was due entirely to the activities of the minor theatres and their efforts to elude the provisions of the Patent Theatre Acts. On the type see also W. J. Lawrence's essay on *Early Irish Ballad Opera and Comic Opera* in *The Musical Quarterly*, July 1922.

[2] The reason being that after its establishment in the early eighteenth century, little that was truly new was introduced. Librettists followed one another and new composers came to replace the old, but the chief features of the operatic type remained. See vol. ii, pp. 225-37.

a reference is to be found in IV. i. of Jerningham's *The Welch Heiress* (D.L. 1795); the passages there may be paralleled with others written thirty years earlier in the elder Colman's *The Musical Lady* (D.L. 1762). Morris commends his auditors not to

> *Join fashion's circle, where my lady doats*
> *On the soft warblings of Italian throats...*

but to

> *Prefer the scene where native passions glow,*
> *To Vestris turning on the pivot toe.*
> *Not led by Fashion's varying taste to seek*
> *Refin'd amusement in a puppet squeak*[1].

These dictates of fashion are attested to likewise in Burgoyne's epilogue to Richardson's *The Fugitive* (H.[1] 1792), which is partly addressed

> To those who bear not from mere tril of tongue,
> Words of soft nothing, by soft nothing sung,
> [*Sings.*] But one dull chime in *Solo, Duo, Trio,*
> Ah! *Mio Bel*, to—Ah, Bel Idol Mio.
> Why by no sorcery of fashion bound,
> Listen for sense e'er they applaud the sound.

Finally there must be noted Sheridan's contribution to the satire. The first episode in the second scene of act I of *The Critic* (D.L. 1779) introduces an "*Italian Family*" who are patronised by "LA CONTESSA RONDEAU" and by "mi LADI FUGE" and who "*sing trios &c.*" before Dangle and Sneer. Once more the fashionable nature of the operatic furore is hinted at[2].

Not many of the serious English operas are worth individual mention, although a word here must be said of the influence exerted by Metastasio on the dialogue and plan of such works. Already have been noted the many translations and adaptations of Metastasio's musical dramas. Although Apostolo Zeno (1668–1750) had preceded him, Metastasio

---

[1] Prologue, "by a friend," to *The Adventurers* (D.L. 1790).
[2] Note may be taken also of G. S. Carey's satire in *The Old Women Weatherwise* (1770).

brought a new breath of life to the opera libretto. He had a fine sense of the theatre and he was a true poet. Such an air as

> Ne giorni tuoi felici
> Ricordati di me!

could have been written only by one who had the genuine poetic feeling for the music of words. In imitating Metastasio, therefore, English dramatists were following a master, and we must admit that his influence was for the good. In spite of many follies in Dr T. A. Arne's *Artaxerxes. An English Opera* (C.G. Feb. 1762), there is something of the spirit of the original *Artaserse* left. The same is true of Richard Rolt's *The Royal Shepherd* (D.L. 1764) taken from *Il Rè Pastore*, and of the same author's *Almena*. Nor can the influence of Metastasio's style be limited to the field of opera; we have to take into account such works as Hoole's *Cyrus* (C.G. 1768), based on *Ciro, Timanthes* (C.G. 1770), based on *Demofoonte*, and *Cleonice, Princess of Bithynia* (C.G. 1775), obviously influenced by Metastasio's manner.

When all is said and done, however, the record of English serious opera in the late eighteenth century is but a sorry one; it shares the fate of the tragedy of that age. If we would look for sparks of brilliance we must turn to the comic operas and the operatic farces, where, amidst a welter of mediocre work, we may discern a few elements of greatness.

There are many writers who here call for our attention. Numbers, such as George Saville Carey, author of *The Cottagers* (1766), Prince Hoare, author of *My Grandmother* (H.² Dec. 1793) and *The Italian Villagers* (C.G. April 1797), and Robert Merry, author of *The Magician no Conjuror* (C.G. Feb. 1792), may be completely neglected, but others must be carefully considered with the major dramatists of the time. From the point of view of influence, and perhaps also of intrinsic importance, the most outstanding person here is Isaac Bickerstaffe, who, commencing his career in 1756 with a dramatic poem called *Leucothoè*, soon found his true *métier*. A "Musical Entertainment" entitled *Thomas and Sally: or, The Sailor's Return* (C.G. Nov. 1760), devised in recitative and aria, paved the way for his first important comic opera, *Love in a Village* (C.G. Dec. 1762) taken partly from Wycherley's *The Gentleman Dancing Master* and Marivaux' *Le Jeu de l'Amour et du Hasard* which proved an enormous success. It is highly probable that Bickerstaffe was led towards this musical path by John Beard who had, with Bencroft, become co-lessee of the theatre at Covent Garden. He was himself a singer, and, it is said, devoted himself mainly to the encouragement of musical drama[1]. To him *Love in a Village* is dedicated. It must be confessed that this comic opera deserved its success. The plot, certainly, is not very original, relating, as it does, how Young Meadows disguises himself as a gardener and how Rossetta poses as a maid, but the dialogue is often sprightly and the lyrics sometimes have true merit. There could be no doubt that in the author of the play was a true mastery of his craft[2].

The Maid of the Mill (C.G. Jan. 1765), founded on Richardson's *Pamela*, followed soon after. Its somewhat mawkish development of Lord Aimworth's love for, and marriage to, Patty Fairfield lacks the sparkle of the earlier work. Based on Mrs Cibber's *The Oracle* (C.G. 1752), *Daphne and Amintor* (D.L. Oct. 1765), Bickerstaffe's next play, did little more to advance his fame, but *Love in the City* (C.G. Feb. 1767), with music by the author, again captured the grace of *Love in a Village*. The characters, as is noted in the Preface, are "Low," but there is no vulgarity in the piece, and the dialogue is frequently witty. In spite of this, of the presence of some truly engaging lyrics, and of the character of Priscilla, a wild West Indian girl, the opera was damned, it is said by city folk.

More successful in every way was *Lionel and Clarissa* (C.G. Feb. 1768), a work of intrigue tendencies with a sentimental note at the conclusion. The characters are well drawn, particularly those of the loquacious Lady Mary Oldboy, the foppish Jessamy and the two pairs of lovers, Clarissa and

[1] Cf. Victor, *op. cit.* iii. 113–4.

[2] The music to this opera was by various composers. As some of the airs were old the piece is a kind of compromise between the ballad-opera and the true comic opera.

Lionel, Diana and Harman[1]. Relying on Charles Dibdin as composer, Bickerstaffe next turned to the famous "jealous husband" theme of Cervantes, and so created *The Padlock* (D.L. Oct. 1768). Diego is about to marry Leonora, but, suddenly realising that 16 and 60 ill go together, abandons her to Leander. There are a few good scenes in the piece, but as a whole the texture is but slight.

During this period, Bickerstaffe was also occupied with comedy and farce; his next musical piece was "A Comic Serenata, After the Manner of the *Italian*" entitled *The Ephesian Matron* (Ranelagh House, 1769) followed by a poor adaptation of scenes from the *Don Sebastian* of Dryden, *The Captive* (H.[2] June 1769). Before 1800 this was his last comic opera. *The Recruiting Serjeant* (Ranelagh; D.L. 1770) is "A Musical Entertainment" in recitative and aria; *He Wou'd if he Cou'd* (D.L. April 1771) but a slight adaptation of *La Serva Padrona*. Still, if these latter pieces are of small account, Bickerstaffe had, in the seventies, set his seal on the comic opera of his time. He was flattered sincerely by many an imitator.

Dr Thomas Augustine Arne also patronised this type of drama with his attentions. His musical farce, *Don Saverio*, appeared at Drury Lane in Feb. 1750, and this early effort was followed by *The Guardian Outwitted* (C.G. Dec. 1764), suggested by Goldoni[2]. The editors of the *Biographia Dramatica* dismiss this piece with the adjective "contemptible," but the dialogue is clever, and the characters of Flirtilla and La Finesse are exceedingly sprightly. *The Cooper* (H.[2] June 1772), "A Musical Entertainment" derived from *Le Tonnelier*, is a much poorer production, and *The Rose* (D.L. Dec. 1772), while aiming at higher things, lacks both spirit and grace. The "burletta" of *Squire Badger* (H.[2] March 1772),

---

[1] The opera was later altered by the author and acted at D.L. in Feb. 1770 as *The School for Fathers*. The Lyric Theatre, Hammersmith, revival under Mr Nigel Playfair has well shown the interest the period may have for modern playgoers.

[2] The play is regularly ascribed to Arne, who, however, denied the authorship according to Victor (*op. cit.* iii. 66). While we cannot be certain that he wrote the libretto, it is convenient to assume that it was his.

or, as it appeared later, *The Sot*, is a more interesting production. Taken from Fielding's *Don Quixote in England*, it transforms the original dialogue into recitative and creates one or two fresh characters. This, save for an "operetta," *Phœbe at Court* (1776), was Arne's last effort in this style.

The irritating figure of John O'Keeffe intrudes once more, into this section as into others. From *The Dead Alive* (H.[2] June 1781), called variously "A comic Opera" and a "Musical Farce," to his last musical play, *The Wicklow Mountains* (C.G. Oct. 1796), O'Keeffe turned out many of these dramas, leaving eventually nearly a score behind him. Some of these have remained unprinted, others, such as *The Maid the Mistress* (C.G. Feb. 1783) are mere translations or adaptations; few show real touches of individual talent. *The Farmer* (C.G. Oct. 1787), for example, is an exceedingly poor sentimental farce with airs. It tells how Valentine, after a rakish life, is brought back to his wife Louisa, but neither characterisation nor dialogue preserves it from mediocrity[1]. The same mediocrity mars another work which has found contemporary praise, *Sprigs of Laurel* (C.G. May 1793). In these, and they are thoroughly typical of O'Keeffe's productivity, there is nothing that calls for critical attention. If further evidence be required of the worthlessness of O'Keeffe's musical farces, the ridiculous dialogue of *Peeping Tom of Coventry* (H.[2] Sept. 1784), supposed to be set in the time of the Danes, may be referred to; while a short quotation from the opening scene of *The Agreeable Surprise* (H.[2] Sept. 1781) will show at once the poverty of his invention and the perennial curse of mawkish artificiality which has ever clung to musical comedy:

Sir Felix Friendly *and* Compton *discovered sitting.* John *and* Thomas *waiting behind, country lads and lasses at a distance, singing chorus as the curtain rises.*

CHORUS
Here we sing, dance and play....

---

[1] This was apparently written first in five acts and called *The Plague of Riches*. Colman disapproved of it, and the author, after abridging the play, sent it to Harris.

Sir Felix: There there, get you gone all to the lawn, and be as merry as good cheer, strong beer, and the pipe and tabor can make you.

Peasants: Long life and happy days to our master Sir Felix!

There is precious little of a Molièresque character in this, but there is much that goes to prove O'Keeffe responsible for countless inanities in nineteenth century musical drama.

Lieutenant-General John Burgoyne's *The Maid of the Oaks* (D.L. Nov. 1774) and *The Lord of the Manor* (D.L. Dec. 1780), poor as many scenes are, demand more notice. The first was apparently occasioned by a Fête Champêtre at the Oaks in Kent to celebrate the marriage of the Earl of Derby and Lady Betty Hamilton[1]. Its dialogue is on the whole better than that of *The Lord of the Manor*, concerning the authorship of which, it must be confessed, we have no sure evidence[2]. The plot, taken from Marmontel's *Silvain*, tells how Rashly, really the elder son of Sir John Contrast, lives on a humble farm with his daughters Annette and Sophia. Sir John Contrast arrives on the scene, and his son attempts to ruin Sophia. She is defended by Trumore her lover, and in the end the heart of Sir John is softened into receiving back his long-estranged son. The play is undoubtedly sentimental, introducing a generous and tender-hearted steward who reminds us of the Trusty of Steele's imagination, a certain amount of moralised patriotic fervour and a contrast between the fashionable follies of society and country innocence. Perhaps the most interesting part of the production is the Preface written in defence of English comic opera[3].

---

[1] This occurred on June 9, 1774. The play of Burgoyne's ran into many editions, and was translated into German as *Das Mädchen im Eichthale* (by J. C. Bock in F. L. Schröder's *Hamburgisches Theater*, 1776, vol. iii).

[2] The author of the *Theatrical Dictionary* (1792) did not know the author of this "flimsy piece." As far as can be made out the ascription to Burgoyne was made by the editors of the *Biographia Dramatica*. There is no real reason for doubting this.

[3] This preface decides "that the adopting what is called recitative into a language, to which it is totally incongruous, is the cause of failure in an English serious Opera much oftener than the want of musical powers in

David Garrick himself, apart from his operatisations of Shakespearian dramas, approached the comic opera in *Cymon* (D.L. Jan. 1767) and in *May-Day* (D.L. Oct. 1775). The first is styled a "Dramatic Romance," and is derived from Dryden's poem of *Cymon and Iphigenia*. There is hardly any merit in it to call for praise[1]. *May-Day; or, The Little Gipsy*, while trivial in character, is a fairly successful farce written for the confessed object of introducing a Miss Abrams to the stage.

Uniting skill in music with a fairly facile pen, Charles Dibdin proved one of the most prolific in the production of comic operas. Well over a score of such pieces he wrote between *Damon and Phillida* (D.L. Feb. 1769), "Altered from Cibber....With the Addition of New Songs and Chorusses," to the musical entertainment called *The Regions of Accomplishment* (R.C.). Few of these require individual attention, and once more a bare two or three must stand symbolic of the rest. *The Wedding Ring* (D.L. Feb. 1773) is a fair example of his usual work—theme hackneyed, dialogue lacking distinction, but development of plot showing a true theatrical sense[2]. Ballad opera saw a revival in *The Waterman: or, The First of August* (H.² Aug. 1774), a slight sketch introducing a number of "humours" characters—Bundle and the termagant Mrs Bundle, Wilhelmina and her two swains, Tug and Robin. At this time, Dibdin seems to have come under the influence of Sedaine, both *The Deserter* (D.L. Nov. 1773) and *The Cobler; or, A Wife of Ten Thousand* (D.L. Dec. 1774) being based on his work. Favart, too, came to give

the performers," and that music in such productions ought to be subordinate. In this connection the author makes a distinction between comic opera and musical comedy, and concludes by begging his friend Sheridan to operatise *As You Like It*, thus carrying on the tradition set by Garrick, who had introduced music into the final Lear-Cordelia scene in *King Lear*, and who had retained the musical tendencies in the adaptations of *Macbeth* and *The Tempest*.

[1] It was turned into an opera in 1792 when at the Haymarket there was added to it a "Grand Procession of" a "Hundred Knights of Chivalry, and" an "Ancient Tournament." See Appendix B, under Unknown Authors.

[2] The idea of this play was taken from *Il Filosofo di Campagna*. Produced anonymously, it was first attributed to Bickerstaffe. To the first edition Dibdin appended an affidavit that he was the real author.

him inspiration; *The Gipsies* (H.² Aug. 1778) is but a free translation of *La Bohémienne*. Indeed, most of his comic operas and operatic farces either are directly rendered from the French, or can be traced back to a French source. One of the few apparently independent plays is *Liberty-Hall: or, A Test of Good Fellowship* (D.L. Feb. 1785) which tells how Rupee riots away his money in the midst of a crowd of parasites, Nettle, Fidgit and Ap Hugh. Through the agency of English he is reformed and is fully established in sobriety on the arrival of his father, Sir Ephraim Rupee and his sister Aurelia¹. *The Harvest-Home* (H.² May 1787) is less original and less sentimental, dealing with one of the very ordinary love themes of the time. The above are only a few among Dibdin's similar productions, but they will show generally the tendencies of his dramatic work.

Thomas Holcroft, towards the beginning of his career, gave the theatre two of these comic operas. The first, called *The Noble Peasant* (H.² Aug. 1784), is more or less romantic in tone, recalling both *As You Like It* and *Cymbeline*. The second, *The Choleric Fathers* (C.G. Nov. 1785), is a fairly pleasing comedy of love and intrigue in the Spanish style. It tells how Don Pimiento, a philosopher, and Don Salvador agree to the marriage of Don Fernando and Donna Isabel, but quarrel because of their irascibility. In vain Pedro, the servant, dresses as an inquisitor and as a philosopher in order to cheat them; he is arrested and suffers for his ingenuity. Eventually Pimiento falls into bad hands and Salvador, gaining his release, is able to restore the erstwhile pact. While both of Holcroft's operas are pleasant productions they hardly add anything very original to the type.

Another somewhat mediocre writer in this style was William Pearce, who started his career with a (unprinted) comic opera called *The Nunnery* (C.G. April 1785) and continued to produce several kindred works in the succeeding years. *The Midnight Wanderers* (C.G. Feb. 1793)

¹ The sentimental and humanitarian tendency in this work is to be clearly seen in the strangely un-eighteenth century lyric directed against hunting (p. 12), a lyric which raises the author in our esteem.

is a poor farcical romantic opera, which deals with the adventures of some French refugees in a Spanish village. Its sole interest lies in the topical subject-matter. The same is true of the "Operatic Drama," *Arrived at Portsmouth* (C.G. Oct. 1794), designed in honour of Lord Howe's victory. *Netley Abbey* (C.G. April 1794) is a poor operatic farce, which, it is said, was well received. More pleasing is *Hartford-Bridge: or, The Skirts of the Camp* (C.G. Nov. 1792). This introduces, alongside of the habitual love theme, a few military characters of some interest.

Miles Peter Andrews, versatile as he was, approached the comic opera type from various angles. *Belphegor: or, The Wishes* (D.L. March 1778) is a peculiar fantastic piece, followed by what seems to have been a realistic operatic farce, *Summer Amusement; or, An Adventure at Margate* (H.² July 1779)[1]. The peculiar *Fire and Water!* (H.² July 1780) succeeded. The usual love theme is here in the mutual adoration of Nancy and Frederick, but what gives the piece its value is the character of Sulphur, who, with his man Firebrand, is reminiscent of Jonson's Alchemist. This Sulphur is presented as attempting to perfect an electrical machine which will destroy all England—a strange anticipation of more modern instruments of devilry[2].

Still more peculiar is *The Baron Kinkvervankotsdorsprakingatchdern* (H.² July 1781), a play damned because of its reputed vulgarity. This was due, no doubt, to the chamber scene when Franzel, mistaking his room, enters Cecil's and remains there all night. It is certainly true that there is more than a touch of cynicism in this work, and there is no need to blame eighteenth century audiences for a mawkish and hypocritical morality because of their action in condemning the piece[3].

[1] Written in collaboration with Miles, but not printed.
[2] The author draws attention to the fact that his opera was written before the disturbances which fluttered London society in 1780.
[3] Here might also be noted Andrews' earlier "Musical Interlude" called *The Election* (D.L. Oct. 1774), a trivial afterpiece. The comment of the editors of the *Biographia Dramatica* (ii. 188) is not inappropriate: "What nauseous potions will not music wash down the throat of the public!"

In this section must, of course, be considered what proved the greatest success of this time, R. B. Sheridan's *The Duenna* (C.G. Nov. 1775), an opera which had the then extraordinary run of seventy-five performances. If only qualified acquiescence could be given to that verdict which placed Sheridan's and Goldsmith's comedies as something entirely apart from the ordinary dramatic activity of the time, it must be conceded that *The Duenna* surpasses in lyric brilliance, in skill of dialogue and in plot construction almost all its companions. There is a genuine vitality in the scenes which present Isaac Mendoza and the Duenna together, which is totally unlike the usual artificiality evident in this type. There is, too, a definite theatricality in the play; it is a work designed primarily for performance in the playhouse. No better instance of this could be found than those last scenes where Louisa and Clara, veiled, befool their lovers. Read in the study, this scene has no mirth; put into action on the stage, it is excellent comedy. Various "sources" have been found for Sheridan in the writing of this play—Wycherley's *The Country Wife*, Molière's *Le Sicilien*, Mrs Centlivre's *A Wonder!* and *Il Filosofo di Campagna*—but the wit is his own, and the characters bear the stamp of his individuality.

Among other writers, James Cobb, for his prolific production, if not for his intrinsic merit, deserves mention. Most of his many comic operas are of French origin and few rise above mediocrity. *The Strangers at Home* (D.L. Dec. 1785) has some little value, and there are some rattling scenes in *Ramah Droog* (C.G. Nov. 1798)[1]. The Irishman Liffey, who poses as Dr O'Liffey and saves the Rajah's life by means of a potato, is a good character, and Margaret, his Amazonian wife, has true comic vitality. Apparently spectacular show eked out the dialogue of this work, real elephants being introduced on the stage. Most of Cobb's works are of a similarly trivial nature. The quality of his "lyrics" may be inferred from a not untypical specimen verse culled

[1] The "book" of songs gives the title as *Ramah Droog; or, Wine does Wonders*. It was reduced to one act and so performed in May 1805.

out of *The Siege of Belgrade* (D.L. Jan. 1791) where Ghita
sings:

> How the deuce I came to like you,
> I am sure I cannot tell;
> Had my face not chanc'd to strike you,
> I'd been pleas'd, Sir, just as well—.

which shows that the popularity of such songs as "You made
me love you" has a very respectable ancestry. Samuel
James Arnold likewise patronised this musical drama with
fervour before 1800. Perhaps his first piece, *Auld Robin
Gray* (H.[2] July 1794), partly a ballad-opera, may be taken
as typical of his productions. The story, like so many of
these stories, is a trivial one, and the lovers, Jemmy and
Jenny, never take independent life. The play, however, is
rescued by the presence in it of Jerry the piper who comes
triumphantly through, reminding us dimly of Padraic Colum's
more recent itinerant musician in *The Fiddler's House*. The
semi-"pastoral" element in this piece is paralleled in Mrs
Brooke's *Rosina* (C.G. Dec. 1782), where, too, appear definitely
sentimental tendencies. The plot tells of an evil brother,
Captain Belville, who tries to seduce the young Rosina,
and of an honest brother, Belville himself, who protects
and marries her. Perhaps it were to consider too curiously
to follow the authoress in her speculation that the source of
the story lies in the Book of Ruth. A French opera was
probably better known to her.

The anonymous author of *The Peruvian* (C.G. March
1786) confessed definitely to a French source for his work[1],
and has succeeded in giving it a fairly bright and independent colouring. The characters of Clara and Coraly are
by no means ill drawn, and that of Sir Gregory Graveall,
in spite of a family likeness to Justice Greedy in Massinger's
A New Way to Pay Old Debts, has true life and spirit. French
inspiration, too, may be discerned in the comic operas written
by Sir Henry Bate Dudley (the reverend Henry Bate), but
the tracks are carefully concealed. *The Flitch of Bacon* (H.[2]
Aug. 1778) and *The Travellers in Switzerland* (C.G. Feb.

---

[1] Marmontel's tale of *Coralie, ou L'Amitié à l'Épreuve*.

1794) are the best among his somewhat ordinary productions. A few operatic farces by various writers may be taken now as a conclusion to this necessarily scattered account of so many diverse plays. Lloyd's *The Romp* (C.G. March 1778) shows the manner in which regular comic operas were reduced to trivial after-pieces. Here Bickerstaffe's *Love in the City* (C.G. 1767) has been abridged, it is said for the actress Mrs Jordan, Priscilla Tomboy still retaining her central part, but the rest of the characters having been woefully cut down[1]. Satirical tendencies of a low kind are exemplified in Harry Rowe's *No Cure No Pay: or, The Pharmacopolist* (1797), directed against quack doctors. Frederick Pilon's *The Siege of Gibraltar* (C.G. April 1780) and the actor Benson's *Britain's Glory; or, A Trip to Portsmouth* (H.[2] Aug. 1794) are representative of the patriotic farces of the age, both poor uninteresting productions. The latter has a more finely finished "Musical Farce" to his credit in *Love and Money; or, The Fair Caledonian* (H.[2] Aug. 1795) which has an exciting plot wherein smugglers, hired by the lewd Lord Rakish, attempt to carry Drowsy off to sea. This hero adroitly turns the tables on his enemies, and Rakish, with his tool Pliant, is borne off in his stead. Spanish intrigue is freely employed by M. Lonsdale in *The Spanish Rivals* (D.L. Nov. 1784) in which Don Fernandez, pretending to be the old Don Narcisso de Medicis, wins the proud beauty Roxella. Sentimentalism steals into Isaac Jackman's *The Milesian* (D.L. March 1777) as it does into Kane O'Hara's *The Two Misers* (C.G. Jan. 1775), confessedly taken from Falbaire's *Les deux Avares*.

None of the comic operas or operatic farces mentioned in the last paragraphs contains anything of true intrinsic merit. They are mentioned here solely because an endeavour is being made to present, not only the major dramatic works of the age, but, as well, the general theatrical fare of the period under discussion. Nor can it be claimed that the contemporary burlettas and kindred plays have much more value. The elder Colman's *The Portrait* (C.G. Nov. 1770), taken from an Italian-French piece called *Le Tableau Parlant*, has,

---

[1] For Bickerstaffe's play see *supra*, p. 198.

thus, some taking songs, but the story of Leander and Isabella, of Pantaloon and Colombine has no worth save that it illustrates the continued popularity of the *commedia dell' arte* tradition. Kane O'Hara's *The Golden Pippin* (C.G. Feb. 1773) and *April-Day* (H.² Aug. 1777) lack even the distinction of possessing taking songs, although *Midas* (C.G. Feb. 1764) is a sprightly and amusing piece, rising superior to most of the efforts in this kind. There is no hope that any of these plays should ever come again into fame; they are among the withered leaves on the green slopes of Parnassus. They will always possess, on the other hand, a true historic value; just as the revue and the musical comedy of to-day, they permit us glimpses into the tastes of the average spectators of the time.

III. *Pantomimes, Preludes, Dramatic Poems and Masques*

The general lack of fixity in the dramatic types of the time and the innumerable petty playwrights led towards the cultivation of many miscellaneous forms of drama during the half-century. Pantomime continued on its triumphal career, receiving fresh impetus from the fact that the minor London theatres, such as those at Sadler's Wells and the Royal Grove, were permitted by authority to present only musical and pantomimic shows. Cries Garrick in the epilogue to Browne's *Barbarossa* (D.L. 1754):

> *Banish your gloomy Scenes to foreign Climes,*
> *Reserve alone to bless these Golden Times,*
> *A Farce or two—and* Woodward's *Pantomimes!*

Among the "True Intelligence" which Murphy appended to *The Gray's-Inn Journal* for Jan. 6, 1753, we read that

Two new tragedies have been offered to the Manager, but the run of *Harlequin Sorcerer* has only left room for one of them. The contending poets, it is said, have determined the precedence by tossing up, when fortune declared in favour of the *Earl of Essex*, written by Mr *Jones. Constantine*, by the Rev. Mr Francis, is deferred till next season.

The "True Intelligence" is, of course, satiric, but below the
satire lies a foundation of truth. There were more plays
besides *Constantine* which were crushed out because of
pantomimic successes. The pantomimes of this period do not
show sufficient originality to warrant more than passing
mention here; fundamentally their styles follow the lines
laid down in the early eighteenth century. For the most part
the *commedia dell' arte* tradition remained predominant. There
are thus among them a regular string of Harlequinades—
Harlequin and Faustus, or, The Devil will have his Own
(C.G. 1793), *Harlequin Peasant; or, A Pantomime Rehearsed*
(H.[2] 1793), *Harlequin's Museum; or, Mother Shipton Triumphant* (C.G. 1792), to mention only two or three of those
which found their way into print—and those Harlequinades
had their definite influence on the drama of the time. Even
when planning a political satire, one anonymous author saw
fit to frame his work as *The Harlequins. A Comedy. After
the Manner of the Theatre Italien. As it is now acting with
great Applause, by a Company of Gentlemen, for the Entertainment of their Friends at the Great Room in Drumcondra-
Lane* (1753). Several "composers" were, naturally, specially
noted for their skill in the devising of these shows, and among
them Henry Woodward undoubtedly stands the chief.
Fortunatus, presented at Drury Lane in 1753 is his, as are
Harlequin Ranger (D.L. 1751), *The Genii* (D.L. 1752),
Queen Mab (D.L. 1750)[1], *Proteus or Harlequin in China*
(D.L. 1755), *Mercury Harlequin* (D.L. 1756), *Harlequin Dr.
Faustus* (C.G. 1766) and *Harlequin's Jubilee* (C.G. 1770),
designed to ridicule Garrick's *Jubilee*[2]. Others, too, won some
kind of contemporary popularity or notoriety through their
efforts in this style. James Love, or Dance, author of the
pre-1750 *Pamela,* devised quite a number, including *The
Witches; or, Harlequin Cherokee* (D.L. 1762), *The Rites of
Hecate; or, Harlequin from the Moon* (C.G. 1763)[3] and *The*

---

[1] R. W. Lowe (*Theatrical Literature*) mentions a pamphlet he had not
been able to see: *The History of Queen Mab, the story on which the Entertainment was founded.* 8°, 1751.
[2] Cf. Victor, *op. cit.* iii. 169.
[3] Cf. Victor, *op. cit.* iii. 56–7.

Hermit; or, Harlequin at Rhodes (D.L. 1766)—all titles indicative of the nature of the productions. Even the elder Colman could leave the atmosphere of *The Jealous Wife* (D.L. 1761) to prepare *The Genius of Nonsense* (H.[2] 1780), O'Keeffe could turn to pantomime in *Harlequin Teague; or, The Giant's Causeway* (H.[2] 1782), while Garrick could endeavour to kill two birds with one stone, by presenting pantomimic spectacle and ridiculing it in *Harlequin's Invasion* (D.L. Dec. 1759)[1]. Among the fully printed specimens of this type[2] attention should be given to the anonymous *Don Juan; or, The Libertine Destroyed* (D.L. Oct. 1790) where Don Juan moves alongside of the characters of the Italian comedy, served by his man Scaramouch. It is instructive to compare this text with that of the more ancient *scenario* of Domenico Biancolelli's comedy on the same subject, noting the intensely traditional nature of this peculiar dramatic development of the eighteenth century[3].

At the same time changes were coming into even this realm of theatrical art. The various productions at the minor theatres did not keep strictly to the realm of the harlequinade. Historical "spectacles" abounded, some going back to Mary, Queen of Scots and Joan of Arc, others presenting current events such as were occurring in France. These spectacles aided in bringing the old pantomimic tradition to its death. We note, also, that new themes are creeping in. The Arabian Nights are ransacked. There are pantomimes on Aladdin and other Eastern heroes. Robinson Crusoe and Friday are pantomimatised and, along with these two favourites, other heroes of popular legend. The way is being slowly prepared for the Christmas shows of the succeeding century.

Another form of play which became specially popular in the late eighteenth century was the prelude. These preludes were usually designed for the opening of a new theatre or for the opening of a season, and generally took the form of

---

[1] Said to have been borrowed from an earlier pantomime given at Covent Garden.

[2] Many are non-extant, and some are preserved only fragmentarily.

[3] For Biancolelli's *scenario* see L. Moland's *Molière et la Comédie italienne.* There Harlequin instead of Scaramouch is Don Juan's servant.

satirical and sometimes burlesque interludes. Generally a manager is introduced *in propria persona*, and his conversations with playwrights or with actors give occasion for many comments upon the state of the theatres at the time. That which appealed in these preludes was the intimate tone as of conversation which could so easily be evoked; perhaps they may be regarded as expressions of a reaction to that gradual cleavage, which was ever becoming wider and wider, between audience and actor. Maybe the spectators were unconsciously pining for the conditions of 1610 and of 1670.

Many of the preludes have been irretrievably lost, and of those extant we may select some half a dozen as representative of the whole field. The first of these is David Garrick's *The Theatrical Candidates* (D.L. Sept. 1775). In this Mercury descends upon the stage to introduce Tragedy, Comedy and Harlequin, the last-mentioned as typical of pantomime. The trio wrangle together concerning their respective claims to honour; some of their argumentation has already been quoted[1]. Before the appearance of Garrick's clever little playlet, George Colman the Elder had brought at least one similar work on the stage. *An Occasional Prelude, Performed at the Opening of the Theatre Royal, Covent Garden, on the Twenty-First of September*, 1772, is a rather trivial example of the manager-actor type of prelude. It was followed by *New Brooms, An Occasional Prelude performed at the Opening of the Theatre-Royal in Drury-Lane, September* 21, 1776. This is an excellent piece, introducing Catcall, a dramatic puffer[2], Crotchet, Phelim, a manager, and one Mezzetin. It is the last-mentioned who proposes that Shakespeare should be made into "pantomime[3]," and many of the dramatists of the age seemed to act on his advice; doing, we may presume, very well on it, or, at least, doing on the whole better than those who strove to uphold the dignity of tragedy and of comedy. Colman later wrote a third prelude for the Haymarket called *The Manager in Distress* (H.[2] May 1780),

[1] See *supra*, p. 155.   [2] See *supra*, p. 12.
[3] See *supra*, p. 112.

but its dialogue has little of the value that attaches to the words of the interesting characters figured in *New Brooms*. Colman's son, George Colman the Younger, also took up this style in *New Hay at the Old Market; An Occasional Drama, In One Act: Written...on opening the Hay-Market Theatre. On the 9th of June,* 1795[1]. This shows Fustian and Daggerwood waiting in the manager's office, and abounds in highly interesting topical references, some of which have already been quoted[2]. The value of these preludes for a study of the literature of the period is not to be overlooked, while, like the farces of the time, some possess intrinsically amusing scenes. The late eighteenth-century authors and audiences loved these trivialities.

Other various miscellaneous types must also be considered here. It has already been noted how in the period 1700–1750 there was a recrudescence of interest taken in the masque[3], and this interest was carried on to the succeeding half century. George Graham's *Telemachus* (1763) won a certain amount of fame in its time, but this was probably due to the fact that his "Mask" is planned as a classical tragedy with full chorus and lyric *intermedii*. George Colman the Elder was happier in selecting Ben Jonson's *The Masque of Oberon* as the basis for *The Fairy Prince* (C.G. Nov. 1771). Although the insertion of songs from Shakespeare, Gilbert West and Dryden hardly adds to its unity of conception, the resultant work is by no means lacking in beauty and in theatrical effectiveness. Most of the masques of the time, however, hardly reach this standard. The only one that approaches it is the very similar production of Mrs Susannah Cibber, *The Oracle* (C.G. March 1752), derived from the French. Here, too, Oberon makes his appearance, and, pretending deafness and dumbness, wins Cynthia's love, so fulfilling the oracle.

Few of the pastorals and "dramatic poems" have much intrinsic value. Jeanette Marks in her *English Pastoral Drama*

---

[1] Later styled *Sylvester Daggerwood*, see Appendix B.
[2] *Supra*, p. 23.
[3] See vol. ii. pp. 258–62.

*from the Restoration to the Date of the Publication of the
"Lyrical Ballads"* (1660–1798) has covered this field with
some thoroughness, if not with duly co-ordinated effort, and
among the various examples cited by her there are not many
which add anything to the wealth of our literature. Garrick's
Florizel and Perdita (D.L. Jan. 1756) may here be mentioned as a pleasing attempt to preserve some of the
enchanting scenes in Shakespeare's *Winter's Tale*. Contrary
to what is asserted in Jeanette Marks' volume[1], acknowledg-
ment was made in the title of Garrick's play to his original.
More has been retained in it of Shakespeare's scenes than
has been done in McNamara Morgan's kindred "pastoral,"
The Sheep-Shearing: Or, Florizel and Perdita (C.G. March
1754), which, however, may have provided Garrick with the
suggestion for his work[2]. Perhaps James Harris' *The Spring*
(1762), reissued in 1766 as *Daphnis and Amaryllis*, deserves
mention for its pleasant songs. Hannah More's *A Search after
Happiness* (private performance *c.* 1765) also merits some
attention in spite of the unduly moral tone of its not very
enlivening couplets, as does William Mansell's *Fairy Hill;
Or May-Day* (1784) which mingles the world of contemporary society with the conventions of pastoralism. The truth
is, however, that pastoralism as a vital force was dead by
1750. It had become decadent already in the hands of Pope
and of Phillips in the early eighteenth century; there was no
life and vitality left in it, and all the writers could do was
copy and imitate a Tasso, a Spenser, a Guarini, a Fletcher.
The age, too, was moving towards a new naturalism. Burns
already was singing his songs of Lowland fields and peasant
sorrows or joys; Wordsworth was slowly gathering strength
of utterance. The age of pastoral had gone, and such few
relics as remained breathed of artificial sentiment and musty
antiquity.

[1] P. 100. For a detailed analysis of the relationship between Garrick's
production and the original see Genest, *op. cit.* iv. 446–8.
[2] See Genest, *op. cit.* iv. 398.

IV. *Burlesques*

No account of late eighteenth century dramatic literature can omit a section on the burlesque and the rehearsal. If such a section seems unduly short, it is only because the skill in burlesque was suffering at the time a slight relapse. Fielding had run his course and Planché was yet to come. It must, therefore, be confessed that the burlesques of this period are not nearly so good (with one exception) as the burlesques of the previous half century, but once more they serve to throw a flood of light on the conditions of the period. Mrs Clive's *The Rehearsal: or, Bays in Petticoats* (D.L. March 1750) casts the cloak of ridicule on the woman writer and the Italian opera. Garrick also laughs at the Burletta in his *A Peep behind the Curtain; or, The New Rehearsal* (D.L. Oct. 1767), which contains an excellent burlesque of the popular type. The dialogue of these foolish productions is well caught in the opening lines of the rehearsed play:

The Curtain rises to soft Musick after the Overture, and discovers ORPHEUS *asleep upon a Couch with his Lyre near him—after the Symphony—*

RECITATIVE *accompanied*

ORPHEUS (*dreaming*.)
I come—I go—I must—I will.

(*half awake*.)
Bless me!—Where am I?—Here I'm still—

(*quite awake*.)
Tho' dead, she haunts me still, my wife!
In death my torment, as in life;
By day, by night, whene'er she catches
Poor me asleep—she thumps and scratches;
No more she cries with Harlot's revel,
But fetch me, ORPHEUS, from the Devil.

The triumph of this style in the period is, naturally, Sheridan's *The Critic: or, A Tragedy Rehearsed* (D.L. Oct.

1779), a work which has attained to continental fame[1]. There
may be some debate concerning the relative merits of Buckingham's *The Rehearsal* and this gay piece of Sheridan's, but,
whatever our final judgment, we are bound to agree that *The
Critic* does on the whole deserve the high esteem in which it
is held. There are many good contemporary thrusts in it as
where Puff explains:

O,—if they had'nt been so devilish free with their cutting here,
you would have found that Don Whiskerandos has been tampering
for his liberty, and has persuaded Tilburina to make this proposal
to her father—and now pray observe the conciseness with which
the argument is conducted. Egad, the *pro & con* goes as smart
as hits in a fencing match. It is indeed a sort of small-sword
logic, which we have borrowed from the French.

"TILBURINA

"A retreat in Spain!

"GOVERNOR

"Outlawry here!

"TILBURINA

"Your daughter's prayer!

"GOVERNOR

"Your father's oath!

"TILBURINA

"My lover!

"GOVERNOR

"My country!

"TILBURINA

"Tilburina!

"GOVERNOR

"England!

"TILBURINA

"A title!

[1] Revivals of this burlesque continue to our own day. The contem-
porary success of the work is well attested. A couple of pamphlets should
be noted: *The Critic Anticipated; or, The Humours of the Green-Room, a
Farce. As rehearsed behind the Curtain of the Theatre Royal, Drury-Lane.
By R. B. S. Esq. &c.* (1779) and *The Critick, or, A Tragedy Rehearsed, a
Literary Catchpenny! by way of Prelude to a Dramatic After-piece, by
R. B. Sheridan, Esq.* (1780).

> "GOVERNOR
>
> "Honor!
>
> "TILBURINA
>
> "A pension!
>
> "GOVERNOR
>
> "Conscience!
>
> "TILBURINA
>
> "A thousand pounds!
>
> "GOVERNOR
>
> "Hah! thou hast touch'd me nearly!

PUFF

There you see—she threw in *Tilburina*, Quick, parry cart with *England!*—Hah! thrust in teirce a title!—parried by honor.—Hah! a pension over the arm!—put by by conscience.—Then flankonade with a thousand pounds—and a palpable hit egad!

> "TILBURINA
>
> "Canst thou—
> "Reject the *suppliant*, and the *daughter* too?
>
> "GOVERNOR
>
> "No more; I wou'd not hear thee plead in vain,
> "The *father* softens—but the *governor*
> "Is fix'd! [*Exit*

DANGLE

Aye, that antithesis of persons—is a most establish'd figure.

That Sheridan was not merely talking in the air may be proved by a glance at almost any sentimental comedy of the period. At random one might take as representative IV. vi. of Holcroft's *Seduction* where Lady Morden, Sir Frederic and Lord Morden meet:

Lord *Morden*. I cannot resist the impulse which—How!—Sir Frederic!
Sir *Frederic* [*rising*]. My Lord [*with perfect indifference*].
Lord *Morden*. So, madam!
Lady *Morden*. So, Sir.
Lord *Morden*. You can listen to *morality* from *others*, madam, if not from *me*[1].

---

[1] With the exception of "*morality*" the words italicised are not so distinguished in the original.

Lady *Morden*. Oh! I—I have no dislike to a *sermon*, when I—
admire the *preacher*.

Lord *Morden*. Madam—If you have no respect for my *honour*,
you might have some for my *feelings*.

Truly Sheridan had seized on a dramatic vice of the period.
The Critic is full of such good things; but, unhappily, it is
companioned by but few burlesques of an equally vivacious
character. Perhaps the age was suffering from incipient
romantic self-conscious seriousness, but, whatever the reason,
The Critic stands almost completely alone.

V. *Dramatic Poems and Unacted Plays*

In the preceding sections there have been included several
tragedies and comedies, such as Horace Walpole's *The
Mysterious Mother* (1768), which had never seen the boards
of the stage. Most of the pastorals are of this class; even
A Search after Happiness was presented only privately, and
Fairy Hill, intended for private performance, was laid aside
for the publisher. In dealing with these unacted plays among
the theatrical repertoires the assumption was, naturally, that
the majority were at least vaguely intended by the authors
for public performance, and that consequently they deserved
to be included among their more fortunate brethren. This is
true, not only of many plays of this period under discussion,
but of the vast majority of unacted dramas written from 1600
to 1750, and in the two preceding volumes of these dramatic
histories no special section has been laid aside for their consideration. We are, however, approaching the period of
Wordsworth and Shelley and Keats, while already Coleridge
and Southey had tried their hands at playwriting, a period
when the "poetic play" becomes firmly separated from the
"theatre play"; when publishers deliberately issue dramas
for the "closet," as they would issue novels and poems. It
may be argued that there is no really new development here,
that political plays and even "poetic" plays were freely
issued during the first half of the eighteenth century, that
many of the "poetic" dramas, such as those of Coleridge and

Byron and Tennyson, found their way into the theatres. This is undeniably true, yet the mere noting of external phenomena does not alter the facts that, during this period, there developed a distinct cleavage between the acting and the "poetic" play, and that the publishing of dramas began to develop along entirely new lines. In this age it became more or less universally understood that certain types of drama were fundamentally unactable, and "closet" and "theatre" appreciation were made the starting points from which a play was to be viewed.

There seems not the slightest doubt that the main cause contributing to this development was the unprecedented activity in the realm of translation—particularly of translation from the German—which extended from 1790 onwards. As has been seen[1], the majority of these German dramas made but small appeal in the theatre; but the many editions into which the majority ran proves conclusively that there was an enormous demand for them among the reading public, while the unquestioned reminiscences in the works of the English poets show how eagerly and attentively they were read. While the majority of the German plays chosen for translation were originally stage pieces with a very definite theatrical career, the English renderings were, almost unanimously, regarded as quite unfitted for representation in a London playhouse[2], and appealed only to a few adapters and to the larger reading public. It has already been seen how they aided in intensifying the spectacular melodrama and the humanitarian *drame* of the time, but, in addition to this, they had a very wide influence upon the poets and upon a certain section of the public, an influence which ultimately led to the composition of those many poetic and would-be poetic dramas in the succeeding century.

From this point of view, the impress of the German drama upon English literature is seen to have had both good and bad results. The poets were able to gain real strength from

[1] See *supra*, pp. 61–8.
[2] See *supra*, pp. 66–7, where these German plays are considered from the point of view of the contemporary theatre.

the continental playwrights, but they were led, through a
mistaken conception, to regard the theatre as such an author
as Kotzebue never regarded it. In an attempt to follow the
style of their originals, they forgot that the one essential
law which governed dramatic writing was that the author
should adapt himself to the requirements of his age, of his
race and of the theatres in his time. What could prove a
success in Dresden or Hamburg obviously might be a vast
failure in London; but this fact the English poetic dramatists
completely failed to realise. They were as obtuse in this
connection as had been their predecessors, the Augustan
pseudo-classicists, who endeavoured to establish on a picture
frame stage the antiquated traditions of the Greek choral
tragedy.

On the other hand, if indirectly the German writers led
English poets astray, they provided them with many ideas
and with many intimate suggestions. Among the German
dramas were to be found examples of a true tragic spirit
which had been lost in England since Otway wrote *Venice
Preserv'd*. Schiller's *Die Räuber*, with its fine portrait of
Karl Moor and its carefully developed fable, was such
an example, and the same author's *Don Carlos*, presenting
its complex figures of the Marquis Posa, the King Philip
and Carlos himself, was another. This fundamental tragic
spirit is apparent, too, in Schiller's *Kabale und Liebe*, where
Präsident von Walter, Ferdinand and Lady Milford play
their fatal parts, in *Die Verschwörung des Fiesko zu Genua*,
with its fine historical atmosphere, in Goethe's *Götz von
Berlichingen*, even in Kotzebue's *Adelheid von Wulfingen*.
Through such plays as these the poets were taught how to
throw rich tragic emotion into their scenes and how to
adapt historical material for dramatic purposes. The pity
was that the poets knew not the theatre, and the stage
writers left unheeded the admonitions of Schiller and of
Goethe.

This spirit of pure tragic emotion, however, was not all
that the poets learned from Germany. They took from there
as well a tendency towards a kind of humanitarian and sen-

timental melodrama which, in the nineteenth century, did much to weaken the dramas of Wordsworth and of Byron. Kratter's *Natalia und Menzikow* is of this type, with its generous and humane Tsar Peter and its sudden saving from death of Natalia. Similar to this are a number of other German dramas translated during this period. Kratter's own sequel, *Das Mädchen von Marienburg*, carries on the tradition of the generous and feeling monarch, and pleases vague democratic sentiment by its introduction of the poor-born Chatinka who will become later the Tsaritsa Catherine I. Kotzebue's *Graf Benjowsky oder die Verschwörung auf Kamtschatka* deals with cognate subject matter. Here is a brave and altruistic nobleman, a conspiracy, a hopeless love, a departure fraught with happiness and tears. Parts of *Graf Benjowsky* have a truly stirring appeal, but this can hardly be said of *Die Corsen*, a poor romantic drama set in Hungary, with its theme of hidden parentage and peculiar love conflicts. The more humanitarian side of the German drama is to be traced in a score or so of translated plays, mainly of originals by Kotzebue. Some of these are domestic problem dramas by nature, others veer to the side of the melodrama proper. One of the best, and certainly one of the best known, is Kotzebue's *Menschenhass und Reue*, translated and performed as *The Stranger* (D.L. 1798). The theme of the sinning wife is here treated with some considerable strength, and the play abounds in telling situations. It shows that sincerity of humanitarian sentiment which was unfortunately lacking in so many productions of a similar kind, even in the sequel to this particular play, *Die edle Lüge*, where Baron Meinau pretends to sin in order that he may ease the tormented conscience of his wife[1].

It is useless here entering into the niceties of German drama of the late eighteenth century, but enough has been said perhaps to indicate the main tendencies of that move-

---

[1] The English attitude towards plays of this kind is well seen in Genest's condemnation (*op. cit.* x. 216). This distinguished historian of the drama, who had seen fit to praise even minor Restoration comedy, decided that Kotzebue's play was immoral because no lie could be noble. Truly our standards of morality are hard to fathom! Cp. *supra*, pp. 67–8.

ment which came to impress itself so deeply on our literature.
Perhaps the whole subject ought to have been left until the
field of early nineteenth century drama lay open, but, even
though the full force of the German influence is not apparent
before the first decades of the succeeding century, its mark
was already made on the literature of 1790–1800. In many
ways, the German drama, thus destined to be for Englishmen
a closet drama, harmonised with a movement which had been
growing in force during the early years of the transitional
romantic movement. The tendency towards the purely
poetic play is to be traced in William Mason's *Caractacus*
(written and published 1759; acted Crow Street, Dublin,
March 1764, and C.G. Dec. 1776). Written on the plan of
Æschylean tragedy, the theme is taken from Druidic Britain,
and there is a certain enthusiasm in the work which puts it
apart from the average pseudo-classical productions of the
age. Indeed, the classicism here is in many ways nearer to
the classicism of Shelley than to that of Pope. The choruses
in this work have special value because of their inherent
power and because of their intimate relationship to the
contemporary Pindaric odes of Gray. This, for example, is
undoubtedly reminiscent of the more famous verses:

> Mute 'till then was ev'ry plain,
> Save where the flood 'mid mountains rude
> Tumbled his tide amain;
> And echo from th' impending wood
> Resounded the hoarse strain;
> While from the north the sullen gale
> With hollow whistlings shook the vale;
> Dismal notes, and answer'd soon
> By savage howl the heaths among,
> What time the wolf doth bay the trembling moon,
> And thin the bleating throng.

> *   *   *   *   *   *   *

> Thou spak'st, imperial Lyre,
> The rough roar ceas'd, and airs from high
> Lapt the land in extasy:
> Fancy, the fairy, with thee came;
> And Inspiration, bright-ey'd dame,

Oft at thy call would leave her sapphire sky;
And, if not vain the verse presumes,
Ev'n now some chast Divinity is near:
For lo! the sound of distant plumes
Pants thro' the pathless desart of the air.
'Tis not the flight of her;
'Tis sleep, her dewy harbinger,
Change, my harp, O change thy measures;
Cull, from thy mellifluous treasures,
Notes that steal on even feet,
Ever slow, yet never pausing,
Mixt with many a warble sweet,
In a ling'ring cadence closing,
While the pleas'd power sinks gently down the skies,
And seals with hand of down the Druids slumb'ring eyes[1].

A similar union of classicism and romanticism in a poetic framework is to be seen in Arthur Murphy's *The Desert Island* (D.L. Jan. 1760), taken from Metastasio's *L'Isola Disabitata* with some suggestions from the French adaptation by Collet entitled *L'Isle Déserte*[2]. The story is a simple one, but there is an evident desire on the part of the author to produce rather a closet than a stage drama.

With this play might be considered another example culled from the sixties of the century, *The Muse of Ossian* (Edinburgh 1763) written by D. Erskine Baker around Macpherson's tales. Neither this, nor any of the others mentioned above, is a work of sterling excellence, but these "dramatic poems" may be taken as representative of a movement which was ultimately to lead to the writing of Byron's and Browning's dramas. In this period, it may be repeated, there were various tendencies all leading towards a similar end.

[1] J. W. Draper has an excellent study of Mason's career and historical importance (*William Mason; A Study in Eighteenth Century Culture*, 1924).

[2] See *supra*, p. 61. Metastasio's play was written at Vienna in 1750 and was produced with music by Bonno. The French adaptation appeared at the Comédie Française in August 1758. Both seem to have been before Murphy when he produced his text, and the engraved design given as a frontispiece to the octavo French edition of 1758 (designed by C. Cochin and engraved by N. le Mire) was copied in the first English octavo (designed and engraved by A. Walker). Murphy's rendering was translated into Dutch as *Het Onbewoonde Eiland. Tooneelspel gevolgd naar't Engelsch van A. Murphy* (in L. Pater's *Poëzy*, 1774).

The growth of the poetic play was one of these; another was the interest taken in the German drama in a translated form. To this we must add the dissatisfaction felt by writers of promise when they surveyed the typical theatrical fare of the time, and probably we might include the extraordinary furore over the private performances, the "Theatrical of Ton," noted in a preceding chapter[1]. Everything conspired to lead the men of thought and of poetic genius to pen plays which were designed, not for the storm and stress of the public stage, but for the quiet contemplation of the study. The weakness of these plays is obvious, even to one who has little knowledge of the workings of the theatre or but slight acquaintanceship with the problems of dramatic theory. This weakness is to be seen most deeply displayed in the dramas of 1800 to 1850, but it makes its appearance even in this half century.

The authors, not writing for the theatre, paid little attention to the requirements of the playhouse. They indulged in long unnatural soliloquies. They left their characters standing aimlessly and silent on the stage, simply because they had forgot to indicate an *exit*. There are poetic plays where characters suddenly spring from the void to speak, no direction having bidden them enter before the audience. Drama, if it is to be great, must be theatrical, and of true stage quality the romantic poetic plays have practically none. Action is sacrificed to talk, and everything seems to move in a haze of obscurity. Apart from this, there were certain things which prevented the appearance even of good literary plays in this time. Romantic criticism was then coming into being, and the Elizabethan dramatic activity was being eagerly appraised. This criticism was, of course, of inestimable value in some fields of literary work, but it had a definitely evil effect upon the poetic dramatists. Coleridge had no idea as to what constituted a good play. He could estimate the value of poetry and he could, in his rather metaphysical manner, analyse character; but he had not the slightest conception of the problems that faced the Elizabethan dramatist, simply

[1] See *supra*, pp. 19–21.

because he had not endeavoured to visualise the Globe or the Blackfriars. The researches of Malone he passed by, unheeding. The consequence was that he, and other dramatists of the time, wholly neglected the practical side of those very masterpieces which were chosen as his models. Instead of endeavouring to separate the permanent from the temporary in Shakespeare, instead of striving to give to their age something which should combine that eternal tragic emotion which is present in Æschylus, in Schiller, in Ibsen, with the moods and desires of their own time, these dramatists slavishly followed the unessential in Shakespeare and in Schiller, unthinkingly and, naturally, without effect. Nearly all the poets, too, were would-be philosophers, and abstract emotions became to them of more importance than concrete presentation of character. Perhaps misled partly by Kotzebue (*Menschenhass und Reue*, *Die edle Lüge*, *Armuth und Edelsinn*, *Falsche Schaam*), they wrote their dramas round one emotion, valiantly opposing the introduction of antagonistic sentiments in their plays. Even Byron and Browning in the nineteenth century suffer from this preoccupation with the one ideal or the one passion.

There are but few unacted dramas of this time which call for serious mention, for Coleridge's *Osorio*, written before the end of the century, was not published till long afterwards, and did not come to the stage until, several years later, it appeared in an altered form as *Remorse*. The only truly important documents of this type produced during the period were the three dramas by Joanna Baillie, included in *A Series of Plays: in which it is attempted to delineate the stronger passions of the mind. Each passion being the subject of a tragedy and a comedy* (1798)[1]. This collection includes two tragedies, *Count Basil* and *De Monfort*, as well as a comedy, *The Tryal*. The preface to the series has several points which call for our critical attention. Emphasis is laid on the fact that passion, and passion alone, can form the basis for true tragedy, while a plea is offered against the introduction of love as a tragic emotion[2].

---

[1] See Carhart, M. S., *The Life and Work of Joanna Baillie* (1923).
[2] Cf. vol. ii. pp. 62–4.

The authoress here can win only our sincere admiration and agreement, but when she proceeds to remark that the passion rather than the character is the important thing in drama, we begin to wonder whether perhaps some logical error has not been committed. Joanna Baillie, peculiarly enough, shares the views of her contemporary, William Blake, concerning the existence of "states" through which men pass and thus begs "it may be considered that it is the passion and not the man which is held up to our execration." The whole tendency of her plays, therefore, is towards the romantically abstract. Instead of tragedy springing from character and circumstance as in Shakespeare, achieving grandeur of spirit and more universal tone through its basis in actuality, Joanna Baillie's plays start from the vague generalisation and rarely succeed in capturing our appreciation for the rather shadowy figures of her imagination.

Joanna Baillie's plays as a whole are by no means negligible; the blank verse is fair, and the dialogue in parts is vigorous. At the same time neither *Count Basil* nor *De Monfort* is a great tragedy. The authoress, in spite of the fact that she thinks

A King driven from his throne, will not move our sympathy so strongly, as a private man torn from the bosom of his family,

is overawed by somewhat uncritical admiration for Shakespeare. She has not studied the subtler intricacies of dramatic technique. The primitive question and reply which appears in the exposition to *Count Basil* with the echoes of Shakespearian verse is thoroughly typical:

An Open Street, crouded with People, who seem to be waiting in expectation of some Show.

Enter a CITIZEN.

First Man. Well friend, what tidings of the grand procession?
Cit. I left it passing by the northern gate.
Second Man. I've waited long, I'm glad it comes at last.
Young Man. And does the Princess look so wondrous fair
　As fame reports?

> *Cit.* She is the fairest lady of the train,
> And all the fairest beauties of the court
> Are in her train.

> *Old Man.* Bears she such off'rings to Saint Francis' shrine,
> So rich, so marvellous rich as rumour says?
> 'Twill drain the treasury.

> *Cit.* Since she in all this splendid pomp, returns
> Her publick thanks to the good patron Saint,
> Who from his sick bed hath restor'd her father,
> Thou wouldst not have her go with empty hands?

So it continues—a diction false because unnatural and imitative, an exposition lumbering and weak, a wealth of words without that intimate touch which in the hands of the major dramatists makes the language a key to the innermost reaches of the spirit. In these plays the weakness of the nineteenth century poetic dramatists is seen in embryo.

Dramas of a similar kind appear in William Hayley's *Plays of Three Acts written for a Private Theatre* (1784), a collection which contains two tragedies and three comedies[1]. The latter are interesting experiments because of their medium. Perhaps inspired by Aristophanes, Hayley has here tried the effect of rime in comic scenes. It cannot be denied that the rollicking rhythm which the author has chosen, added to his multiplicity of double rimes, is at times rather effective. Take for example Mr Varnish's words in *The Two Connoisseurs*:

> Dear Madam, observe what a delicate touch!
> See how finely 'tis pencil'd! and what preservation!
> There is not, I know, such a gem in the nation;
> And Italy has not a brighter, I'm sure.
> The figures so glowing! the story so pure!—
> Good ladies would never have wandering spouses,
> If they'd only hang subjects like this in their houses.

The weakness of Hayley's comedies lies not in their couplet form, which seems fully justified by the event, but in their flimsiness of plot. The story of *The Happy Prescription; or, The Lady Relieved from her Lovers* is thus trivial in the ex-

---

[1] Of which some, of course, were acted. See Appendix B.

treme, while the characters, Sir Nicholas Oddfish, Sapphic, Decisive, Morley and Selina, are mere figureheads. The tragedies are penned in blank verse, but betray similar weaknesses. *Marcella*, the plot of which Hayley declared he took from a theme suggested by Richardson to Young, is nothing but a reworking of the story of that terrible seventeenth century play, Middleton's *The Changeling*. A comparison between the two is fatal to the later romantic drama. Hernandez is but a feeble echo of De Flores, and there is none of that complicated character delineation in the treatment of the heroine which vivified the Elizabethan drama.

One other play of this type may be noted, not for any intrinsic excellence, but simply for a point of historical interest. In *The Distressed Family* (1787)[1], translated most sentimentally from Le Mercier, there appear what seem to be the first long descriptive stage directions which have become so fashionable in our own times. In many ways they are a premonition of Mr Bernard Shaw's introductory disquisitions and are a result, of course, of the tendency towards the production of the "closet" or reading play.

It is this closet play which is at once the manifestation of dramatic debility in the age, and the cause of that debility. The slightest examination of early nineteenth century literature amply reveals the fact that the stage declined largely owing to the strict line of demarcation established between the "theatre-writers" and the poets. While it is assuredly true that Byron and Browning succeeded in getting their dramas produced, the vast majority of their companions either failed to secure recognition from the managers, or did not seek it. The more pernicious effects of this separation of theatre and literature become visible only in the next century, but their traces are clearly to be seen in this period as well. Melodrama on the one hand and would-be poetic grandeur on the other are but sorry substitutes for the true dramatic grandeur of the Shakespearian age.

At the same time, even when we have to end thus on a note of failure, it is necessary to emphasise once more the true

[1] Later acted at the Haymarket.

excellence of late eighteenth century drama in several directions. If melodrama spreads its blighting influence over many of the serious plays of the time, we are still left with a masterly portraiture of manners in the comedies of Holcroft, Mrs Cowley, Mrs Inchbald, Colman, Cumberland and a host of others, we have still the excellent farces and the bustling "farcical comedies" of Reynolds and Murphy. Sheridan and Goldsmith, great as their triumph may have been, are only two out of a goodly number of playwrights gifted with skill and verve. It has been the fate of those playwrights to be neglected because of critical prejudice, but an impartial reading of their works will serve to display clearly their vivacity and their charm. If this book has any purpose beyond the mere tracing of historical fact, it is that of vindicating many authors who have been dismissed unheard. Whether the judgments set forward in the preceding pages will be accepted or not, it is only just that these comedies of the Georgian era should be taken from their dusty shelves, or, still better, favoured with occasional revival in our theatres.

APPENDIX A

The Theatres, 1750–1800

THE contractions used for the various theatres in the previous volume on early eighteenth-century drama have been employed in this survey as well. It has not been thought necessary here to enter into the *minutiæ* of the stage history of the period; those may be studied in the many volumes of theatrical reminiscences which abound at this time.

Drury Lane (D.L.). This theatre was under the management of Garrick until his retirement in 1776, when his share was sold for £35,000 to Linley, Sheridan and Dr Ford. Although Sheridan was nominally manager of the Company till 1809, J. P. Kemble was the actual director from 1788 onwards. The old D.L. theatre was abandoned on 4/6/1791, the company playing first at the King's Theatre in the Haymarket and later (19/9/1793) at the Little Theatre in the Haymarket. A new Theatre Royal at D.L. was built by Holland and opened on 12/3/1794. It was a much larger structure, capable of holding over 2500 spectators. The proscenium opening was 43 feet wide and the height 38 feet.

Covent Garden (C.G.). Under the management of John Rich till his death in 1761, when it passed into the hands of Bencroft and John Beard, who devoted himself to comic opera. In Aug. 1767 the shares passed to Thomas Harris, John Rutherford, George Colman and William Powell. In 1777 this arrangement was broken through the departure of George Colman, who took over the management of the Little Theatre in the Haymarket. The theatre was altered in 1782, and greatly enlarged for the season 1792–3.

The Little Theatre in the Haymarket (H.²). The earlier history of this theatre has been outlined in the preceding volume. A few pieces, mostly of a musical kind, were given in it up to 1766 when, in July of that year, Foote obtained a summer licence for plays. He pulled down the old 1720 structure and reopened a new building on the same site as a Theatre Royal. The management passed to George Colman in 1777, and the theatre was used from Sept. 1793 to March 1794 by the D.L. company.

The King's Theatre in the Haymarket (H.¹). This house was used regularly for Italian operas, under a variety of managements. On 17/6/1789 the old structure was completely gutted by fire, but a new theatre was erected in 1790. From Sept. 1791 to June 1793 it was used by the D.L. company.

Royalty. On 20/6/1787 John Palmer endeavoured to open a new theatre in Wellclose Square on the site of the old playhouse in Goodman's Fields. The patent theatres vigorously opposed it, and eventually the idea of giving plays there was abandoned. Pantomimes, however, and musical shows appeared on its boards.

Pantheon. Opened in 1790 for operas. Situated in Oxford-street. Burnt 14/1/1792.

Royal Circus (R.C.). Used for pantomimes and musical pieces under Charles Dibdin. Renamed in the nineteenth century as the *Surrey Theatre.*

Royal Grove (R.G.) and *Royal Saloon* (R.S.). In the spring of 1777 Astley started an equestrian entertainment on a piece of ground near Westminster Bridge. Till 1783 the ring was called *Astley's Amphitheatre Riding School* ; after 1784 *Astley's Amphitheatre and Ambigu-Comic* was used as the title; after 1787 *Royal Grove, and Astley's Amphitheatre*; after 1792 *Royal Saloon, and New Amphitheatre*; and after 1796 *Amphitheatre of Arts, Astley's* or simply *Astley's* (contracted as Ast.).

Theatre of Varieties (Th. of Var.), Saville Row.

Sadler's Wells (S.W.). A brick building, the walls of which still stand, was erected in 1765, by one Rosoman. The house was used for entertainments of a musical and pantomimic nature.

Marylebone Gardens (M.G.).

Smock Alley (S.A. Dublin). The other Dublin theatres are given in uncontracted forms.

APPENDIX B

Hand-list of Plays, 1750–1800

THE following list of plays has a number of additions, and a few corrections, presented in the supplementary notes. No doubt some of the new titles do not represent new plays, but where any doubt remains they have been included. Thus, for example, James Love's pantomime *The Rites of Hecate; or, Harlequin from the Moon* was produced in 1763: it seems impossible to determine whether *Harlequin Emperor of the Moon* (1784), *Harlequin from the Moon* (1775), *Harlequin in the Moon* (1799) and *The Cave of Hecate* (1797) are or are not connected with this original piece, but for completeness all these titles have been included.

The method of citing plays is as follows:

1. An initial asterisk indicates that a copy of the play has not been seen by the compiler. Such asterisks have, however, been omitted from the supplementary notes.

2. An indication of the type of play is given by contractions:

T.	Tragedy	M.D.	Melodrama
C.	Comedy	Int.	Interlude
T.C.	Tragi-comedy	Ent.	Entertainment
F.	Farce	P.	Pantomime
M.	Masque	Ball.	Ballet
O.	Opera	Burl.	Burletta
C.O.	Comic opera	Prel.	Prelude
B.O.	Ballad-opera	Ser.	Serenata
O.F.	Operatic farce	Past.	Pastoral
D.	Drama	Pol.	Political play
D.O.	Dramatic opera	Sat.	Satirical piece

3. The date in round brackets after the title is that of first production. Days of the week are given in the main hand-list but, in accordance with the practice adopted in the later volumes of this series, are omitted in the supplementary notes.

4. Records of printed editions follow, with other references to manuscripts or printed copies in the Larpent collection. When I first drew attention to the resources of this collection only a manuscript catalogue was available, but that has now been super-

seded by Dougald MacMillan's excellent *Catalogue of the Larpent Plays in the Huntington Library* (1939). Naturally, I should have preferred to alter all the former references so as to accord with his renumbering of the plays, but such a procedure would have involved an almost completely fresh setting of the following pages. The original catalogue press-marks have, therefore, been allowed to stand, although all new references, whether inserted in the text or included in the supplementary notes, adopt MacMillan's numbers. Little confusion, if any, can result, since the original press-marks take such forms as "25. M." or "8. L.", whereas MacMillan's have a simple numeral. It should be noted, however, that in all the new references the Larpent collection is indicated, not by "Larpent," but by a simple "L" ("Larpent 66. M." thus refers to an entry in the manuscript catalogue, whereas "L. 863" gives MacMillan's numbering). In most instances the dates given immediately after the Larpent press-marks are those of the managers' applications for licence but some give the dates marked on the manuscripts by the Examiner himself: since nowhere is there a difference of more than a few days between these dates I have allowed the manuscript catalogue entries to remain. Further information, of course, can be obtained in MacMillan's work.

I. *English Plays and Operas*

ADDINGTON, *Sir WILLIAM*.
*T. The Prince of Agra (C.G. Th. 7/4/1774) MS. Larpent 11. L. [21/3/1774].
[This alteration of Dryden's *Aureng-Zebe* is sometimes ascribed to *HUGH KELLY*. It does not seem to have been printed.]

ALDERSON, *Miss* [*Mrs OPIE*].
*T. Adelaide (Plumptre's private theatre, Norwich, Jan. 1791).

ALLEN, ——.
Int. Hymen (D.L. 20/1/1764).
[Printed only in *The Gentleman's Magazine*, Jan. 1764, xxxiv, 38–9.]
*Sacred D. Hezekiah, King of Judah 8° 1798.

ALLINGHAM, *JOHN TILL*.
F. Fortune's Frolic (C.G.S. 25/5/1799) 8° 1799; 16° 1799 [*Dublin*]; 8° 1805 [4th]; MS. Larpent 36. S. [9/5/1799].
F. 'Tis All a Farce (H.¹ June 1800) 8° 1800.
[For his later works see the Hand-list of Plays, 1800–50.]

ANDREWS, *JAMES PETIT* [*and PYE, HENRY JAMES*].
T. The Inquisitor....Altered from the German 8° 1798.
[An adaptation of Johann Christoph Unzer, *Diego und Leonore*.]

ANDREWS, *MILES PETER*.
*F. The Conjuror (D.L. F. 29/4/1774) MS. Larpent 11. S. [16/4/1774].

M. Int. A New Musical Interlude, called The Election (D.L. W. 19/10/1774) 8° 1774; 8° 1780; MS. Larpent 11. L. [15/10/1774].

C.O. Belphegor; or, The Wishes (D.L. M. 16/3/1778) 16° 1788 [Dublin]; Songs, Chorusses, &c. in...Belphegor, or The Wishes 8° 1778; MS. Larpent 14. S. [6/3/1778].
[Music François Hippolyte Barthélémon.]

C.O. Songs, Trios, Duetts, and Chorusses, in the Comic Opera of Summer Amusement; or, An Adventure at Margate (H.² Th. 1/7/1779) 8° 1780 [bis]; 8° 1781 [3rd]; MS. Larpent 14. L. [1779].
[Andrews was assisted in the writing of this opera by W. A. MILES; music Dr Arnold, with selections from Arne, Giordani and Dibdin.]

C.O. Fire and Water! (H.² S. 8/7/1780) 8° 1780; Songs, Duetts, Trios, &c. &c. in...Fire and Water! 8° 1780; MS. Larpent 23. M. [12/5/1780].
[Music Samuel Arnold.]

C. Dissipation (D.L. S. 10/3/1781) 8° 1781 [bis]; MS. Larpent 25. M. [1781].

[C.O.] The Baron Kinkvervankotsdorsprakingatchdern. A New Musical Comedy (H.² M. 9/7/1781) 8° 1781; Songs, Duets, Chorusses, &c. in...The Baron 8° 1781; MS. Larpent 27. M. [6/6/1781].
[Music ascribed to Dr Arnold.]

*F. The Best Bidder (D.L. W. 11/12/1782) MS. Larpent 28. M. [22/11/1782].

C. The Reparation (D.L. S. 14/2/1784) 8° 1784 [bis]; MS. Larpent 37. M. [31/1/1784].

P. The Songs, Recitatives, Airs, Duets, Trios, and Chorusses, Introduced in the Pantomime Entertainment, of the Enchanted Castle (C.G. T. 26/12/1786) 8° 1786.
[Music W. Shield.]

C. Better late than Never (D.L. W. 17/11/1790) 8° 1790; 12° 1791 [Dublin]; MS. Larpent 53. M. [25/3/1790].
[In this Andrews was assisted by FREDERICK REYNOLDS.]

[M.D.] The Mysteries of the Castle: A Dramatic Tale (C.G. S. 31/1/1795) 8° 1795; MS. Larpent 66. M. [Jan. 1795].
[In this Andrews was assisted by FREDERICK REYNOLDS. Music selected and composed by William Shield.]

ARMSTRONG, Dr JOHN.
T. The Forced Marriage [in Miscellanies 8° 1770].

ARNE, Dr THOMAS AUGUSTINE.
[C.O.] Don Saverio (D.L. Th. 15/2/1750) 4° 1750.
[It is probable that the libretto as well as the music was by Arne. For this work see the Hand-list of Plays, 1700–50 and supplementary notes.]

O. Artaxerxes. An English Opera (C.G. T. 2/2/1762) 8° 1762; 12° 1762 [Dublin]; 8° 1763; 8° 1764; 12° 1764 [Dublin]; 8° 1787.
[Music by T. A. Arne; words apparently paraphrased by him from P. Metastasio, Artaserse.]

C.O. The Guardian Out-witted (C.G. W. 12/12/1764) 8° 1764; 12° 1765 [Dublin]; M.S Larpent 8. L. [21/11/1764].
[Music T. A. Arne; the libretto is ascribed to him, although Victor (op. cit. iii. 66) declares that he himself denied the attribution.

[O.F.] The Cooper. A Musical Entertainment (H.² W. 10/6/1772) 8° 1772; MS. Larpent 12. M. [26/5/1772].
[Music T. A. Arne; the libretto, an adaptation of *Le Tonnelier*, is regularly ascribed to him.]

C.O. The Rose (D.L. W. 2/12/1772) 8° 1773; MS. Larpent 9. S. [23/11/1772; as *The R., or The Female Contest*].
[Music T. A. Arne; the libretto is ascribed to him.]

*M. The Contest of Beauty and Virtue (C.G. 1772) 4° 1773.
[Music by the author. Based on P. Metastasio, *La Pace fra la Virtù e la Bellezza*.]

Burl. The Sot...Altered from Fielding (H.² March 1772) 8° 1775; MS. Larpent 13. M. [6/3/1772; as *Squire Badger*].
[Based on H. Fielding, *Don Quixote in England*.]

*— A Pasticcio (C.G. 1773) 4° 1773.

*Operetta. Phoebe at Court 4° 1776.
[Based on R. Lloyd, *The Capricious Lovers*.]

ARNOLD, CORNELIUS.
*T. Osman [in *Poems* 4° 1757].

ARNOLD, SAMUEL JAMES.
[C.O.] Auld Robin Gray: A Pastoral Entertainment (H.² T. 29/7/1794) 8° 1794; MS. Larpent 27. S. ["Musical Piece" 22/7/1794].
[Music Dr Arnold.]

*M. Ent. Who Pays the Reckoning? (H.² Th. 16/7/1795) MS. Larpent 68. M. [11/7/1795].
[Music Dr Arnold.]

C.O. The Shipwreck (D.L. M. 19/12/1796) 8° 1796; 12° 1797; 8° 1807; MS. Larpent 70. M. [9/12/1796].
[Music Dr Arnold.]

*O.F. The Irish Legacy (H.² M. 26/6/1797).
[Music Dr Arnold.]
[For his nineteenth century works see the Hand-list of Plays, 1800–1850.]

ASPINWALL, STANHOPE.
T. Rodogune: or The Rival Brothers...Done from the French of Mons. Corneille 8° 1765.
[A literal translation of P. Corneille, *Rodogune*.]

ATKINSON, JOSEPH.
C. The Mutual Deception (S.A. Dublin W. 2/3/1785) 8° 1785.
[Suggested by Marivaux, *Le Jeu de l'Amour et du Hasard*.]

C.O. A Match for a Widow: or, The Frolics of Fancy (S.A. Dublin M. 17/4/1786) 8° 1788; 12° 1788 [*Dublin*].
[Music Charles Dibdin. An adaptation of Patrat, *L'Heureuse Erreur*.]

*C.O. Love in a Blaze (Crow-street, Dublin W. 29/5/1799) 12° 1800 [*Dublin*].
[Music Sir John Stevenson.]

AVERAY, ROBERT.
[M.] Britannia and The Gods in Council; A Dramatic Poem: Wherein Felicity is predicted to Britain, the Causes of the present Disputes in Europe and America are debated, and their Issue prophetically determined 4° [1756].

AYSCOUGH, GEORGE EDWARD.
>T. Semiramis (D.L. S. 14/12/1776) 8° 1776; MS. Larpent 16. M. [2/12/1776].
>>[An adaptation of Voltaire, *Semiramis.*]

BACON, JAMES.
>[D.] The American Indian; or, Virtues of Nature. A Play, in Three Acts. With Notes. Founded on an Indian Tale 8° 1795.
>>[The "Death Song" is by Mrs Morton, on whose *Ouâbi; or, The Virtues of Nature* this play is founded.]

BACON, Dr PHANUEL.
>[Sat.] The Taxes, A Dramatic Entertainment 8° 1757.
>[Sat.] The Insignificants. A Comedy 8° 1757.
>[Sat.] The Tryal of the Time-Killers. A Comedy 8° 1757.
>[Sat.] The Moral Quack. A Dramatic Satire 8° 1757.
>[Sat.] The Oculist. A Dramatic Entertainment 8° 1757.

BAILLIE, JOANNA.
>A Series of Plays: in which it is attempted to delineate the stronger passions of the mind. Each passion being the subject of a tragedy and a comedy 8° 1798; 8° 1799.
>>[Contains: 1. *Count Basil: A Tragedy*; 2. *The Tryal: A Comedy*; 3. *De Monfort: A Tragedy.*]
>>[For her later works see the Hand-list of Plays, 1800–50.]

BAKER, DAVID ERSKINE.
>Dr. Poem. The Muse of Ossian...Selected from the Several Poems of Ossian the Son of Fingal (Edinburgh 1763) 12° 1763 [*Edinburgh*].
>[C.O.] La Serva Padrona, Comedia in due Atti. The Maid the Mistress, A Comedy (Edinburgh 1763) 12° 1763 [*Edinburgh*; Ital. and Eng., the latter a translation of *La Serva Padrona* by Gennaro Antonio Federico].

BALL, EDMUND.
>C. The Beautiful Armenia; or, The Energy and Force of Love 12° 1778 [*Chesham*].
>>[An adaptation of Terence, *Eunuchus.*]

BANISTER, Rev. JAMES.
>*— The Plays of Euripides 8° 1780.

BARETTI, JOSEPH.
>[Sat.] The Sentimental Mother. A Comedy...The Legacy of an Old Friend, and his last Moral Lesson to Mrs Hester Lynch Thrale, now Mrs Hetser [*sic*] Lynch Piozzi 8° 1789.

BARNARD, EDWARD.
>Virtue the Source of Pleasure 8° 1757.
>>[Contains: 1. *The Somewhat*; 2. *Edward VI.*]

BARRELL, MARIA.
>[D.] The Captive 8° 1790.

BARTHOLOMEW, JOHN.
>T. The Fall of the French Monarchy, or Louis XVI 8° 1794 [priv.].

BATE, Rev. HENRY [later Sir HENRY BATE DUDLEY].
>Int. Henry and Emma (C.G. W. 13/4/1774) 8° 1774.
>C.O. The Rival Candidates (D.L. W. 1/2/1775) 8° 1775; 12° 1775 [*Dublin*]; MS. Larpent 12. S. [21/1/1775].
>>[Music Thomas Carter.]

C.O. Airs, Ballads, etc. in The Blackamoor wash'd White (D.L. Th. 1/2/1776) 8° 1776; MS. Larpent 14. S. [22/1/1776].

C.O. The Flitch of Bacon (H.² M. 17/8/1778) 8° 1779; 12° 1779 [*Dublin*]; MS. Larpent 18. M. [1/8/1778].
[Music William Shield.]

Prel. The Dramatic Puffers (C.G. S. 9/2/1782) 8° 1782.

[T.C.] The Magic Picture, A Play. [Altered from Massinger.] (C.G. S. 8/11/1783) 8° 1783.
[An adaptation of P. Massinger, *The Picture*.]

C.O. The Woodman (C.G. S. 26/2/1791) 8° 1791 [*bis*]; 8° 1794; Songs ...in...The Woodman 8° 1791; MS. Larpent 55. M. [25/2/1791].
[Music Shield.]

C.O. The Travellers in Switzerland (C.G. T. 25/2/1794) 8° 1794 [*bis*]; Airs, Duets, Trios, Glees, Chorusses, &c. in the Opera of the Travellers in Switzerland 8° 1794 [5 editions]; MS. Larpent 62. M. [14/2/1794].
[Music selected and composed by Shield.]

BATES, ——.
P. Harlequin Mungo; or, A Peep into the Tower: A New Panto-mimical Entertainment (Royalty, T. 17/6/1788) 8° [1788].
[Music W. Reeve.]

BAYLEY, JOHN.
D. The Forester; or, The Royal Seat 8° 1798.

BELLAMY, THOMAS.
[Int.] The Benevolent Planters. A Dramatic Piece (H.² W. 5/8/1789, as *The Friends*; M. 10/8/1789, as *The B.P.*) 8° 1789; MS. Larpent 21. S. [29/7/1789].

BENSON, ——.
[O.F.] Britain's Glory; or, A Trip to Portsmouth, A Musical Enter-tainment (H.² W. 20/8/1794) 8° [1794]; 8° [1798]; MS. Larpent 27. S. [18/8/1794].
[Music S. Arnold.]

[O.F.] Love and Money; or, The Fair Caledonian. A Musical Farce (H.² S. 29/8/1795) 8° [1798]; MS. Larpent 65. M. [24/8/1795]. For another *Love and Money* see under *UNKNOWN AUTHORS.*
[This and the above were issued together in 1798 with a general title page. Music S. Arnold.]

BENTLEY, RICHARD.
*C. The Wishes; or, Harlequin's Mouth Open'd (D.L. M. 27/7/1761); MS. Larpent 5. M. [1761].

T. Philodamus (C.G. S. 14/12/1782) 4° 1767; MS. Larpent 28. M. [1767; printed copy].

C.O. Airs, Duetts, Trios, and Chorusses, Etc., in The Prophet (C.G. M. 15/12/1788) 8° 1788.

BERGUIN, M.
*D. The Honest Farmer 12° 1791.

BERKELEY, GEORGE MONCK.
C. Nina, or the Madness of Love...Translated from the French (as published by Mr Le Texier) 8° [1787; 3 editions].

*[Int.] Love and Nature (Dublin, March 1789) 4° 1797.
[Music Shield.]

BICKERSTAFFE, ISAAC.
*Dr. Poem. Leucothoe 8° 1756.
[Int.] Thomas and Sally: or, The Sailor's Return. A Musical Enter-
    tainment (C.G. F. 28/11/1760) 8° 1761; 8° 1765 [3rd]; 12° 1767
    [*Dublin*]; 8° [1780; with many alterations].
    [Music T. A. Arne.]
C.O. Love in a Village (C.G. W. 8/12/1762) 8° 1763 [7 editions]; 8°
    1764; 8° 1765; 8° 1767; 8° 1776.
    [Music by various composers.]
C.O. The Maid of the Mill (C.G. Th. 31/1/1765) 8° 1765 [6 editions].
    [Music selected by the author in collaboration with S. Arnold.]
C.O. Daphne and Amintor (D.L. T. 8/10/1765) 8° 1765 [5 editions];
    8° 1766.
    [Music pasticcio from Piccinni, Vento, Cocchi and others.
    Based on Susanna-Maria Cibber, *The Oracle.*]
C. The Plain Dealer...With Alterations from Wycherley (D.L.
    S. 7/12/1765) 8° 1766; MS. Larpent 8. L. [25/11/1765].
C.O. Love in the City (C.G. S. 21/2/1767) 8° 1767 [*bis*].
    [Music selected and composed by the author and Charles Dibdin.]
C.O. Lionel and Clarissa (C.G. Th. 25/2/1768) 8° 1748 [*sic, for* 1768];
    8° 1768 [3rd]; MS. Larpent 9. M. [16/2/1768].
    [Music Charles Dibdin.]
F. The Absent Man (D.L. M. 21/3/1768) 8° 1768; 12° 1768 [*Dublin*];
    MS. Larpent 9. M. [15/3/1768].
C.O. The Padlock (D.L. M. 3/10/1768) 8° 1768 [3 editions]; 8° [1769];
    MS. Larpent 9. L. [19/9/1768].
    [Music Charles Dibdin.]
Int. The Royal Garland. A New Occasional Interlude (C.G. M.
    10/10/1768) 8° 1768.
    [Music S. Arnold.]
C. The Hypocrite...taken from Moliere and Cibber (D.L. Th.
    17/11/1768) 8° 1769 [*bis*].
    [Mainly an alteration of C. Cibber, *The Non-Juror.*]
C. Doctor Last in his Chariot (H.² W. 21/6/1769) 8° 1769.
    [A scene in act 1 was written by *SAMUEL FOOTE.* Based on
    Molière, *Le Malade Imaginaire.*]
C.O. The Captive (H.² W. 21/6/1769) 8° 1769.
    [Music Charles Dibdin with selected airs. Based on scenes in
    J. Dryden, *Don Sebastian.*]
[Int.] The Ephesian Matron. A Comic Serenata, After the Manner
    of the Italian [Ranelagh House; H.² Th. 31/8/1769] 8° 1769.
    [Music Charles Dibdin.]
C.O. The School for Fathers (D.L. Th. 8/2/1770) 8° 1770; 8° 1773.
    [An alteration of *Lionel and Clarissa, supra.*]
C. 'Tis Well it's no Worse (D.L. S. 24/11/1770) 8° 1770 [3 editions];
    MS. Larpent 9. L. [17/11/1770].
    [An adaptation of Calderon, *El Escondido y la Tapada.*]
[Int.] The Recruiting Serjeant, A Musical Entertainment [Ranelagh
    House; D.L. 1770] 8° 1770; 8° 1787 [as at Royalty].
    [Music Charles Dibdin.]
Burl. He Wou'd if he Cou'd: or, an old Fool worse than any (D.L.
    F. 12/4/1771) 8° 1771; 12° 1792 [Edinburgh Collection of Farces].
    [An adaptation of G. A. Federico, *La Serva Padrona.* Music
    C. Dibdin.]

[O.F.] The Sultan, or, A Peep into the Seraglio. A Farce (D.L. T. 12/12/1775) 8° 1787 [*bis*]; MS. Larpent 12. S. [30/11/1775].

F. The Spoil'd Child (D.L. M. 22/3/1790) 12° 1799 [*Dublin*]; 8° [1800]; MS. Larpent 53. M. [15/3/1790].

[This farce has been ascribed to *Mrs JORDAN*, *FORD* and Bickerstaffe.]

BICKNELL, ALEXANDER.

T. The Patriot King; or, Alfred and Elvida. An Historical Tragedy 8° 1788.

BIDLAKE, JOHN.

*T. Virginia; or The Fall of the Decemvirs [private, Plymouth *c.* 1800] 8° 1800.

BIRCH, SAMUEL.

[Int.] Songs, Duets, Trio and Choruses, in The Mariners, A Musical Entertainment [H.¹ F. 10/5/1793] 8° 1793; MS. Larpent 61. M. [4/5/1793].

[Music selected and composed by T. Attwood.]

*[Int.] The Packet Boat; or, A Peep behind the Veil (C.G. S. 17/5/1794) MS. Larpent 27. S. [7/5/1794].

[M.D.] The Adopted Child, A Musical Drama (D.L. F. 1/5/1795) 8° 1795; MS. Larpent 29. S. [25/4/1795].

[Music T. Attwood.]

[M.D.] The Smugglers; A Musical Drama (D.L. W. 13/4/1796) 8° 1796 [*bis*]; MS. Larpent 30. S. [8/4/1796].

[Music T. Attwood.]

*[Int.] Fast Asleep (D.L. M. 27/11/1797).

[Music T. Attwood.]

*[M.D.] Albert and Adelaide; or, The Victim of Constancy (C.G. T. 11/12/1798).

[The bills state that this is taken "from the German"; music Steibelt.]

BISHOP, SAMUEL.

*Int. The Fairy Benison (in *Poems* 8° 1796).

BLAKE, WILLIAM.

T. Edward the Third [in *Poetical Sketches* 8° 1783].

BLAND, JOHN.

D. The Song of Solomon 8° 1750.

BOADEN, JAMES.

[M.D.] Songs and Chorusses in Ozmyn and Daraxa, A Musical Romance (H.¹ Th. 7/3/1793) 8° 1793; MS. Larpent 60. M. [12/2/1793].

[M.D.] Fontainville Forest, A Play...(Founded on the Romance of the Forest) (C.G. T. 25/3/1794) 8° 1794 [*bis*].

[M.D.] The Secret Tribunal: A Play (C.G. W. 3/6/1795) 8° 1795; MS. Larpent 28. S. [11/5/1795].

[M.D.] The Italian Monk, a Play (H.² T. 15/8/1797) 8° 1797 [*bis*].

[M.D.] Cambro-Britons, an Historical Play (H.³ S. 21/7/1798) 8° 1798; MS. Larpent 35. S. [12/7/1798].

[M.D.] Aurelio and Miranda: a Drama...with Music (D.L. S. 29/12/1798) 8° 1798; 8° 1799 [3rd]; MS. Larpent 73. M. [as "Aurelio...A Play"; 7/11/1798].

[M.D.] The Voice of Nature: a Play (H.² July 1802) 8° 1803.

[M.D.] The Maid of Bristol, a Play (H.² Aug. 1803) 8° 1803.

BOISSY, MICHAEL.

*C. The Miser [see Biographia Dramatica, ii. 40].

BONNOR, CHARLES.

*Int. The Manager an Actor in spite of himself (C.G. M. 14/6/1784); MS. Larpent 37. M. [1784; as "First Performed in Paris"].
[Based on Dorvigny, La Fête de Campagne.]

P. The Airs, Duetts, & Chorusses, Arrangement of Scenery, and Sketch of the Pantomime, entitled The Picture of Paris (C.G. M. 20/12/1790) 8° 1790.
[Music W. Shield; songs by ROBERT MERRY.]

BOOTH, Mrs.

F. The Little French Lawyer...Taken from Beaumont and Fletcher (C.G. M. 27/4/1778) 8° 1778.

BOULTON, THOMAS.

C. The Guinea Outfit; or, The Sailor's Farewell (D.L.) 12° 1768 [Bristol]; 12° 1800; 12° [N.D.; Liverpool].

BOWES, MARY ELEANOR, Countess of STRATHMORE.

T. The Siege of Jerusalem 8° 1774.

BOYCE, SAMUEL.

Past. The Rover; Or, Happiness at Last: A Pastoral Drama, As it was intended for the Theatre 4° 1752.

BOYCE, Rev. THOMAS.

T. Harold 4° 1786.

BOYD, HENRY.

Poems, chiefly Dramatic and Lyric 8° 1793 [Dublin].
[Contains: 1. The Helots; 2. The Rivals; 3. The Temple of Vesta; 4. The Royal Message. The last was reprinted in The Woodman's Tale...and The Royal Message 8° 1805.]

BRAND, HANNAH.

Plays and Poems 8° 1798 [Norwich].
[Contains: 1. Adelinda; 2. The Conflict; or, Love, Honour, and Pride; 3. Huniades; or, The Siege of Belgrade. The last was acted at H.¹ W. 18/1/1792, and, in an altered form, as Agmunda, at H.¹ Th. 2/2/1792. Adelinda is an alteration of Destouches, La Force du Naturel, The Conflict an alteration of P. Corneille, Don Sanche d'Aragon. The Larpent collection [57. M.] has the last scene of Agmunda, as well as Huniades [56. M.; 26/3/1791, sent from Norwich].

BRENAN, ——.

[Sat.] The Painter's Breakfast. A Dramatick Satyr 12° 1756 [Dublin].

BREWER, GEORGE.

F. The Dinner Party [in How to be Happy, or The Agreeable Hours of Human Life...A Series of Essays 8° 1814. How to be Happy was acted at H.² S. 9/8/1794. It is preserved in MS. Larpent 63. M. Aug. 1794].

[Int.] Bannian Day, A Musical Entertainment (H.² S. 11/6/1796) 8° 1796; MS. Larpent 30. S. [7/6/1796].
[Music S. Arnold.]

*[Int.] The Man in the Moon [ascribed to Brewer; advertised for the opening of the Haymarket 1799, but apparently not acted]; MS. Larpent 74. M. [30/5/1799].

BRIDGES, THOMAS.
   C.O. Dido (H.² W. 24/7/1771) 8° 1771; MS. Larpent 10. L. [19/6/1771].
   [Int.] The Dutch-Man, A Musical Entertainment (H.² M. 21/8/1775)
      8° 1775; MS. Larpent 12. L. [15/8/1775].

BROMFIELD, WILLIAM.
   C. The Schemers; or, The City Match (D.L. T. 15/4/1755) 8° [1755].
      [An alteration of Jasper Mayne, The City Match.]

BROOKE, FRANCES.
   T. Virginia 12° 1754 [Dublin]; 8° 1756.
   T. The Siege of Sinope (C.G. W. 31/1/1781) 8° 1781; 12° 1781
      [Dublin]; MS. Larpent 24. M. [24/1/1781].
      [Based on Mitridate a Sinope (1779).]
   C.O. Rosina (C.G. T. 31/12/1782) 8° 1783 [6 editions]; 8° 1784
      [7th]; 12° 1785 [Dublin]; 8° 1786 [11th]; 8° 1788 [12th]; 8° 1790
      [13th]; 8° 1796 [14th] etc.; MS. Larpent 27. M. [27/12/1782].
      [Music W. Shield.]
   [O.F.] Airs, Songs, Duetts, Trios, and Chorusses in Marian. A Comic
      Opera (C.G. Th. 22/5/1788) 8° 1788; Marian: A Comic Opera
      8° 1800; MS. Larpent 48. M. [1788; as Marian of the Grange].
      [Music W. Shield.]

BROOKE, HENRY.
   [For his earlier works see the Hand-list of Plays, 1700–1750.]
   M. The Triumph of Hibernia (S.A. Dublin 4/11/1748; C.G. S.
      18/4/1752).
      [Music N. Pasquali.]
   T. The Earl of Essex (Dublin, S.A. May 1750; D.L. S. 3/1/1761)
      8° 1761; 12° 1761 [Dublin]; 8° 1761 [Edinburgh]; MS. Larpent 6. L.
      [31/12/1760].
      Works of H. B. 8° 1778.
         [Contain: 1. The Earl of Essex (q.v.); 2. The Female Officer
         (Dublin, S.A. March 1740); 3. The Victims of Love and Honour
         (Dublin, Crow-street M. 24/5/1762); 4. The Vestal Virgin; 5. The
         Marriage Contract; 6. Montezuma; 7. The Impostor; 8. The Con-
         tending Brothers; 9. The Charitable Association; 10. Cymbeline;
         11. Antony and Cleopatra. The Works were reprinted in 1792.]

BROWN, ——.
   *F. Alive and Merry (D.L. T. 17/5/1796) MS. Larpent 70. M.
      [12/5/1796].
      [Ascribed to one Brown and another GRUBB.]

BROWN, JAMES.
   *[F.] The Frolic 8° 1783 [Edinburgh].

BROWN, Dr JOHN.
   T. Barbarossa (D.L. T. 17/12/1754) 8° 1755 [bis]; 8° 1770 [4th];
      8° 1770 [5th]; MS. Larpent 3. M. [3/12/1754].
   T. Athelstan (D.L. F. 27/2/1756) 8° 1756; MS. Larpent 4. M.
      [18/2/1756].

BRUNTON, ANNA (Miss ROSS).
   C.O. The Cottagers 8° 1788 [3 editions].

BURGESS, Mrs.
   [O.F.] The Oaks; or, The Beauties of Canterbury. A Comedy (Can-
      terbury 12/5/1780) 12° 1780 [Canterbury].

BURGOYNE, Lieutenant General JOHN.
[C.O.] The Maid of the Oaks: A New Dramatick Entertainment
(D.L. S. 5/11/1774) 8° 1774 [*bis*]; 8° 1775; 8° 1777; 8° 1788;
12° 1794 [*Dublin*]; Songs, Choruses...in...the Maid of the
Oaks 8° 1774; MS. Larpent 11. S. [20/10/1774].
[Music selected and composed by F. H. Barthélémon.]
C.O. The Lord of the Manor...with a Preface by the Author
(D.L. W. 27/12/1780) 8° 1781; Airs, Duets, Trios...in the Lord
of the Manor 8° 1780; MS. Larpent 27. M. [1781].
[Music William Jackson.]
C. The Heiress (D.L. S. 14/1/1786) 8° 1786 [7 editions]; 12° 1786
[*Dublin*]; 8° 1787 [7th]; 8° 1787 [8th]; 8° 1787 [9th]; 8° 1787
[10th]; 8° 1787 [11th]; 12° 1801 [*Dublin*]; MS. Larpent 43. M. [1786.]
[Based partly on Diderot, *Le Père de Famille*.]
[M.D.] Richard Cœur de Lion. An Historical Romance. From the
French of Sedaine (D.L. T. 24/10/1786) 8° 1786 [*bis*]; 12° 1786;
8° [N.D. 6th]; 8° 1804; 12° 1806; Songs, Chorusses, &c. of...
Richard Cœur de Lion 8° 1786; 8° 1787 [5th]; MS. Larpent 42.
M. [16/10/1786].
[Music Grétry adapted by Thomas Linley.]
[See also his *Dramatic Works*, 2 vols. 8° 1808.]

BURKE, Miss.
*C.O. The Ward of the Castle (C.G. Th. 24/10/1793) MS. Larpent
60. M. [1793].

BURNEY, Dr CHARLES.
[Int.] The Cunning-Man, A Musical Entertainment...Originally
written and composed by Mr J. J. Rousseau (D.L. F. 21/11/1766)
8° 1766 [*bis*]; F. [1766]; MS. Larpent 8. S. [13/11/1766].
[An adaptation of Rousseau, *Le Devin du Village*.]

BURNEY, FANNY [see under *D'ARBLAY*].

BURRELL, Lady SOPHIA RAYMOND.
Dr. Poem. Comala...Taken from a Poem of Ossian [in *Poems* 8°
1793].
T. Maximian...Taken from Corneille 8° 1800.
T. Theodora; or, The Spanish Daughter 8° 1800.

BURTON, PHILIPPINA.
*C. Fashion Displayed (H.² F. 27/4/1770) MS. Larpent 10. M.
[20/3/1770].

BUSHE, AMYAS.
Dr. Poem. Socrates 4° 1758; 4° [1759; *Kilkenny*; corrected]; 8° 1762
[*Glasgow*].

BYRNE, JAMES.
*Ball. Dermot and Kathlane; or, The Irish Wedding (C.G. F.
18/10/1793).

CANNING, GEORGE.
[Burl.] The Rovers [in *The Anti-Jacobin* (1798) xxx and xxxi; reprinted
in *The Spirit of the Public Journals*].

CAPELL, EDWARD.
[T.] Antony and Cleopatra: An Historical Play...fitted for the Stage
by abridging only (D.L. W. 3/1/1759) 12° 1758.
[Prepared by Capell and *DAVID GARRICK*.]

CAREY, GEORGE SAVILLE.
    C.   The Inoculator 8° 1766.
          [Ascribed to Carey; this volume contains also *The Cottagers,*
          an opera [C.O.], reprinted in *Analects* 1770.]
    *[Pol.] Liberty Chastised 8° 1768.
    M.   Shakespeare's Jubilee 8° 1769 [reprinted in *Analects*].
    Int.   The Old Women Weatherwise (D.L. 1770) 8° 1770; The Three
          Old Women Weatherwise...To which is added A Dialogue in the
          Register Office 12° [1825?; *Hull*].
          [This was reprinted in *Analects*, but all three texts vary con-
          siderably.]
    *Burl. The Magic Girdle (M.G.).
          Analects in Verse and Prose, chiefly Dramatical, Satirical, and
          Pastoral, 2 vols. 12° 1770.
          [Contain: 1. *Thorney, Laben and Dobin, A Pastoral*; 2. *The*
          Cottagers; 3. *Shakespeare's Jubilee*; 4. *The Old Women Weather-*
          wise.]
    Burl. The Noble Pedlar: or, The Fortune Hunter (M.G.; D.L
          M. 13/5/1771) 8° 1771 [*bis*].
          [Music F. H. Barthélémon.]
    F.   The Dupes of Fancy, or Every Man his Hobby; A New Farce
          (H.¹ T. 29/5/1792) 8° 1792; 12° 1792 [*Dublin*]; MS. Larpent
          24. S. [10/5/1792].

CARR, Rev. JOHN.
    [T.] Epponina: A Dramatic Essay. Addressed to the Ladies 8° 1765.

CARR, ROBERT [and SAMUEL HAYES].
    T.   Eugenia 8° 1766.

CARTER, JOHN.
    T.   Alberta, A New Tragedy 8° 1787.
    [Int.] The Constant Couple; or, Though out of Sight, ne'er out of
          Mind. A Musical Entertainment [Royalty, 1788] 8° 1788.

CAWDELL, JAMES.
    *[Prel.] An Appeal to the Muses; or, Apollo's Decree (Sunderland,
          18/11/1778).
          [See *Apollo's Holiday*, which is probably an altered version of
          this.]
    Burl. Melpomene's Overthrow; or, The Comic Muse Triumphant
          (in *Miscellaneous Poems* 8° 1778).
    *C. The Triumph of Genius; or, The Actor's Jubilee (Scarborough
          1785).
    *Prel. Apollo's Holiday; or, A Petition to the Muses (Durham 1792).
          [See *An Appeal to the Muses, supra.*]
    *Ent. Battered Batavians; or, Down with the Dutch (Scarborough
          1798).

CELISIA, Mrs DOROTEA (MALLET).
    T.   Almida (D.L. S. 12/1/1771) 8° 1771; MS. Larpent 12. M.
          [1/1/1771].
          [*DAVID GARRICK* made some additions to this play; it is an
          adaptation of Voltaire, *Tancrède*.]

CHATTERTON, THOMAS.
          [There are some semi-dramatic verses among the Rowley
          poems, but these hardly necessitate inclusion in this list.]

Burl. The Revenge...With Additional Songs (M.G. 1770) 8° 1795.
[Reprinted in *Works* of T.C. 8° 1803. Music S. Arnold.]
Burl. The Woman of Spirit [in *Works* 8° 1803].

CHERENSI, B. FRERE.
C. The Prejudices (Hoy's Co., Hereford Dec. 1798) 12° 1796 [*Hereford*].

CHERRY, ANDREW.
*P. Harlequin in the Stocks; or, A Pantomime Launched (Hull 1793).
*C.O. The Outcasts; or, Poor Bess and Little Dick (Crow-street, Dublin F. 1/3/1796; later Manchester).
[For his later works see the Hand-list of Plays, 1800–1850.]

CHRISTIAN, Lieutenant T. P.
[D.] The Revolution. An Historical Play 8° 1791.
Int. The Nuptials 8° 1791.

CIBBER, Mrs SUSANNA-MARIA.
[M.] The Oracle. A Comedy (C.G. T. 17/3/1752) 8° 1752; 8° 1763; 8° [1778]; MS. Larpent 4. L. [25/2/1752].
[An adaptation of St. Foix, *L'Oracle*.]

CIBBER, THEOPHILUS.
[For his earlier works see *A History of Early Eighteenth Century Drama*, pp. 313–4.]
F. The Auction 8° 1757.

CLARKE, GEORGE SOMERS.
T. Œdipus, King of Thebes...translated into prose 8° 1790.

CLELAND, JOHN.
T. Titus Vespasian 8° 1754.
[Int.] The Ladies' Subscription. A Dramatic Performance 8° 1755.
[Int.] Tombo-Chiqui: or, The American Savage. A Dramatic Entertainment 8° 1758.

CLIVE, CATHARINE.
[Burlesque.] The Rehearsal: or, Bays in Petticoats. A Comedy (D.L. Th. 15/3/1750) 8° 1753.
[Music Dr Boyce.]
*F. Every Woman in her Humour (D.L. Th. 20/3/1760) MS. Larpent 5. S. [1760].
*F. The Island of Slaves (D.L. Th. 26/3/1761) MS. Larpent 6. S. [9/3/1761].
*F. The Sketch of a Fine Lady's Return from a Rout (D.L. M. 21/3/1763) MS. Larpent 7. M. [12/3/1763].
*F. The Faithful Irishwoman (D.L. M. 18/3/1765) MS. Larpent 7. S. [9/3/1765].

COBB, JAMES.
*F. The Contract; or, The Female Captain (D.L. M. 5/4/1779; as *The Female Captain* H.² 1780) MS. Larpent 21. M. [29/3/1779].
[Attributed to J. C.]
*[O.F.] The Wedding Night (H.² S. 12/8/1780) MS. Larpent 24. M. [21/7/1780].
[Music Dr Arnold.]
*F. Who'd have thought it? (C.G. S. 28/4/1781) MS. Larpent 24. M. [1781].

*Int. Kensington Gardens; or, The Walking Jockey (H.² F. 31/8/1781)
MS. Larpent 16. S. [16/8/1781].

*F. The Humourist (D.L. W. 27/4/1785) MS. Larpent 35. M. [1784;
as *The H., or Who's Who*].

P. Hurly Burly; or, The Fairy of the Well (D.L. 1785) 8° [1785]; MS.
Larpent 39. M. [1785].
[Written in collaboration with *T. KING*.]

C.O. The Strangers at Home (D.L. Th. 8/12/1785) 8° 1786 [*bis*]; 12°
1786 [*Dublin*]; 12° 1787 [*Dublin*]; Songs in the Strangers at Home
8° [1786]; 8° 1791; MS. Larpent 39. M. [28/11/1785].
[Music Thomas Linley.]

F. The First Floor (D.L. S. 13/1/1787) 8° 1787 [3 editions]; 12° 1787
[*Dublin*]; 8° 1789 [4th]; MS. Larpent 47. M [1787].

[Sat.] English Readings. A Comic Piece (H.² T. 7/8/1787) 8° 1787;
16° 1788 [*Dublin*]; MS. Larpent 45. M. [25/6/1787].

C.O. Love in the East; or, Adventures of Twelve Hours (D.L. M.
25/2/1788) 8° 1788 [*bis*]; 12° 1788 [*Dublin*]; 8° [1789; *Dublin*];
Songs and Chorusses in... Love in the East 8° 1788.
[Music Thomas Linley.]

[O.F.] The Doctor and the Apothecary. A Musical Entertainment
(D.L. S. 25/10/1788) 8° 1788; 8° 1792; Songs...in...the Doctor
and the Apothecary 8° 1788.
[Music Stephen Storace.]

C.O. The Haunted Tower (D.L. T. 24/11/1789) 12° [1790, *Dublin*;
pirated]; 12° 1793 [pirated]; 12° 1819 [pirated]; Songs, Duets,
Trios, and Chorusses, in the Haunted Tower 8° 1789; 8° 1790;
8° 1791; MS. Larpent 49. M. [18/11/1789].
[Music Stephen Storace.]

C.O. The Siege of Belgrade (D.L. S. 1/1/1791) 16° [1792, *Dublin*;
pirated]; 12° [1815]; 12° 1818; Songs, Duets, etc., in the Siege of
Belgrade. An Opera 8° 1791; 8° 1796; MS. Larpent 52. M.
[26/12/1790].

*Prel. Poor Old Drury!!! (H.¹ Th. 22/9/1791) MS. Larpent 24. S.
[20/9/1792, probably in error for 1791].

*[Int.] The Algerine Slaves (H.¹ S. 17/3/1792).
[This seems to have been an abridgment of *The Strangers at
Home*.]

[C.O.] Songs, Duets, Trios, Chorusses, etc., in The Pirates. An
Opera (H.¹ W. 21/11/1792) 8° 1792; MS. Larpent 56. M.
[12/11/1792].
[Music Stephen Storace.]

[C.O.] The Cherokee, An Opera (D.L. S. 20/12/1794) 8° 1795
[pirated]; Songs, Duetts, Trios, Chorusses, etc., in The Cherokee
8° 1794; MS. Larpent 64. M. [18/12/1794].
[Music Stephen Storace.]

*[O.F.] The Shepherdess of Cheapside (D.L. S. 20/2/1796) MS.
Larpent 70. M. [16/2/1796].
[Songs and Finale in *The Shepherdess of Cheapside*. 8° 1796.]

C.O. Ramah Droog (C.G. M. 12/11/1798) 8° 1800; Songs, Duets,
Trios, and Finales in Ramah Droog; or, Wine does Wonders 8°
1798; MS. Larpent 33. S. [3/11/1798].
[Music Mazzinghi and Reeve]; 12° 1776 [*Dublin*].

[O.F.] Paul and Virginia. A Musical Entertainment (C.G. May

1800) 12° [1800, *Dublin*; pirated]; Songs, Duets, Trios, Chorusses, etc., in Paul and Virginia, A Musical Farce 8° 1800.
[Music Mazzinghi and Reeve.]
[For his later works see the Hand-list of Plays, 1800–50.]

COCKINGS, GEORGE.
T. The Conquest of Canada; or, The Siege of Quebec. An Historical Tragedy 8° 1766; 8° 1773 [*Albany*].

COLERIDGE, SAMUEL TAYLOR.
[T.] The Fall of Robespierre. An Historic Drama 8° 1794 [*Cambridge*].
[Act I by Coleridge; acts II and III by *ROBERT SOUTHEY.*]
T. The Piccolomini 8° 1800.
T. The Death of Wallenstein 8° 1800.
T. Osorio...now first printed 8° 1873.
T. Remorse (D.L. Jan. 1813) 8° 1813 [3 editions].

COLLIER, Sir GEORGE.
[M.D.] Selima and Azor, A Persian Tale, in Three Parts (D.L. Th. 5/12/1776) 8° 1784; Songs, Duets, Trios, Etc., in the Dramatic Romance of Selima and Azor 8° 1776; 8° 1777; MS. Larpent 13. S. [2/12/1776].
[Music Thomas Linley, based on Grétry.]

COLLINGWOOD, Dr.
*[F.] The Agreeable Separation. A Comic Entertainment 12° [N.D.; *Berwick*].
*[F.] The Dead Alive Again. A Tragi-Comical Farce 12° [N.D.; *Berwick*].

COLLS, J. H.
O. Theodore [in *Poems; and Theodore in Opera* 8° [N.D.; *Norwich*].
*F. The World as it Goes; or, Honesty the Best Policy (Norwich 1792).
*F. The Loyal Salopian; or, The King in the Country (Shrewsbury 1795).
*C. The Honest Soldier 8° 1805.

COLMAN, GEORGE, The Elder.
[F.] Polly Honeycombe; A Dramatic Novel (D.L. F. 5/12/1760) 8° 1760; 12° 1761 [*Dublin*]; 8° 1761; 8° 1762 [3rd; with alterations]; 8° 1778; MS. Larpent 5. M. [1760].
C. The Jealous Wife (D.L. Th. 12/2/1761) 8° 1761 [*bis*]; 12° 1761 [*Dublin*]; 8° 1763 [*Oxford*, 3rd]; 8° [N.D.; 4th]; 12° 1775 [*Dublin*]; 8° 1789; 8° 1790 [5th]; 12° 1816.
F. The Musical Lady (D.L. S. 6/3/1762) 8° 1762; 12° 1762 [*Dublin*]; 8° 1778; MS. Larpent 6. M. [3/3/1762].
T. Philaster...Written by Beaumont and Fletcher, with Alterations (D.L. S. 8/10/1763) 8° 1763; 12° 1763 [*Dublin*]; 8° 1764; 8° 1780.
F. The Deuce is in Him (D.L. F. 4/11/1763) 8° 1763; 8° 1764 [2nd]; 12° 1764 [*Dublin*]; 8° 1769; 8° 1776; MS. Larpent 7. M. [23/9/1763].
[Int.] A Fairy Tale...Taken from Shakespeare (D.L. S. 26/11/1763) 8° 1763; 8° 1777 [altered]; MS. Larpent 7. L. [Jan. 1761].
[A version of *A Midsummer Night's Dream*, executed along with *DAVID GARRICK*, and taken partly from the latter's adaptation,

presented D.L. W. 23/11/1763. Music chiefly by Michael Arne and Charles Dibdin.]

The Comedies of Terence translated into familiar blank verse 4° 1765; 12° 1766; 8° 1768; 8° 1810.

C.   The Clandestine Marriage (D.L. Th. 20/2/1766) 8° 1766 [3 editions]; 12° 1766 [Dublin]; 8° 1766 [Edinburgh]; 8° 1770; 8° 1778; 12° 1788 [Dublin]; 8° 1800.

   [Written in collaboration with DAVID GARRICK.]

C.   The English Merchant (D.L. S. 21/2/1767) 8° 1767 [bis].

[F.] The Oxonian in Town. A Comedy (C.G. S. 7/11/1767) 12° 1769 [Dublin]; 8° 1770; MS. Larpent 10. M. [1770].

T.   The History of King Lear (C.G. S. 20/2/1768) 8° 1768.

C.   The Merchant [in Comedies of Plautus 8° 1769].

[F.] Man and Wife; or, The Shakespeare Jubilee. A Comedy (C.G. S. 7/10/1769) 8° 1770 [3 editions]; 12° 1770 [Dublin].

   [In the Larpent collection is Ye Jubilee of Covent Garden Theatre dated 1769 (9. S.) and also this play Man and Wife (10. M.) dated 3/10/1769.]

Burl. The Portrait (C.G. Th. 22/11/1770) 8° 1770 [bis]; 8° 1772; MS. Larpent 10. M. [1770; as The P., or A Painter's Easel].

   [Music Dr Arnold.]

M.   The Fairy Prince (C.G. T. 12/11/1771) 8° 1771; MS. Larpent 11. M. [28/9/1771].

   [Music Dr Arne.]

Prel. An Occasional Prelude (C.G. M. 21/9/1772) 8° 1776; MS. Larpent 12. M. [10/9/1772].

M.   Comus...Altered from Milton (C.G. S. 16/10/1773) 8° 1772; 8° 1774; 8° 1780; 8° 1815.

   [Music Dr Arne.]

[C.O.] Achilles in Petticoats. An Opera...Written by Mr Gay, with Alterations (C.G. Th. 16/12/1773) 8° 1774; The Overture, Songs, etc., in the Opera of Achilles in Petticoats. F. [1774].

   [Music Dr Arne.]

C.   The Man of Business (C.G. S. 29/1/1774) 8° 1774 [bis]; 12° 1774 [Dublin]; 8° 1775; MS. Larpent 15. M. [1774].

C.   Epicœne; or, The Silent Woman...written by Ben Jonson... With Alterations (D.L. S. 13/1/1776) 8° 1776.

[F.] The Spleen; or, Islington Spa, A Comick Piece (D.L. S. 24/2/1776) 8° 1776; MS. Larpent 13. S. [17/2/1776].

Prel. New Brooms! An Occasional Prelude (D.L. S. 21/9/1776) 8° 1776.

[B.O.] Polly, An Opera. Being a Sequel to the Beggar's Opera, written by Gay, with Alterations (H.² Th. 19/6/1777) 8° 1777.

Past. The Sheep Shearing: A Dramatic Pastoral (H.² F. 18/7/1777) 8° 1777.

*C. The Spanish Barber; or, The Fruitless Precaution (H.² S. 30/8/1777) MS. Larpent 16. S. [25/8/1777].

*C. The Female Chevalier (H.² M. 18/5/1778).

   [An alteration of W. Taverner, The Artful Wife.]

*C. The Suicide (H.² S. 11/7/1778) MS. Larpent 19. M. [29/6/1778].

T.   Bonduca...Written by Beaumont and Fletcher, with Alterations (H.² Th. 30/7/1778) 8° 1778; 8° 1801; 8° 1808.

*C. The Separate Maintenance (H.² T. 31/8/1779) MS. Larpent 13. L. [20/8/1779].

Prel. The Manager in Distress (H.² T. 30/5/1780) 8° [1780]; 8° 1820; 12° 1854; MS. Larpent 16. S. [21/5/1780].

*P. The Genius of Nonsense (H.² S. 2/9/1780) MS. Larpent 22. M. [25/8/1780].

    [Attributed to G. C., and called an "Extravaganza" in the bills.]

*Prel. Preludio to the Beggar's Opera (H.² W. 8/8/1781). See *UN-KNOWN AUTHORS*.

T. Fatal Curiosity: A True Tragedy...with Alterations (H.² S. 29/6/1782) 8° 1783.

*Prel. The Election of the Managers (H.² W. 2/6/1784) MS. Larpent 34. M. [1784].

C. Tit for Tat (H.² T. 29/8/1786) 8° 1788; 4° 1788; MS. Larpent 20. S. [1786; as *Tit for Tat, or The Mutual Deception*].

    [See Atkinson's *Mutual Deception*, of which this is an alteration.]

[Int.] Ut Pictura Poesis! or, The Enraged Musician. A Musical Entertainment founded on Hogarth (H.² M. 18/5/1789) 8° 1789.

COLMAN, GEORGE, *The Younger*.

    [For *The Castle of Sorrento* see under *HENRY HEARTWELL*.]

C.O. Two to One (H.² S. 19/6/1784) 8° 1784; 12° 1785 [*Dublin*; pirated]; Songs, Duets, Trios, etc., in the New Comedy of Two to One 8° 1784; MS. Larpent 32. M. [14/8/1783].

    [Music Samuel Arnold.]

*[C.O.] A Turk and No Turk (H.² S. 9/7/1785) MS. Larpent 39. M. [18/6/1785]. Songs, Duetts, Trios, &c. in A Turk and No Turk 8° 1785.

C. Ways and Means; or, A Trip to Dover (H.² Th. 10/7/1788) 8° 1788 [*bis*]; 8° 1805; 8° 1806.

[C.O.] Inkle and Yarico: An Opera (H.² S. 4/8/1787) 8° [1787]; 8° 1788 [2nd]; 12° 1788 [*Dublin*]; 12° 1789 [*Dublin*]; 8° 1792; 8° 1806; 12° 1807 [*Dublin*]; Songs, Duets, Trios, etc. in...Inkle and Yarico 8° 1787; MS. Larpent 44. M. [25/7/1787].

    [Music Samuel Arnold.]

[M.D.] The Battle of Hexham. A Comedy (H.² T. 11/8/1789) 12° 1790 [pirated]; Songs, Choruses, etc., in the Battle of Hexham; or, Days of Old. A Play 8° 1789; MS. Larpent 50. M. [3/8/1789].

    [Music S. Arnold.]

[M.D.] The Surrender of Calais. A Play (H.² S. 30/7/1791) 12° 1792 [*Dublin*; pirated]; 8° 1808; Songs, Duets, Choruses, &c., in the Surrender of Calais 8° 1791 [3 editions]; 8° 1792 [4th]; MS. Larpent 23. S. [23/7/1791].

    [Music S. Arnold.]

*Prel. Poor Old Haymarket; or, Two Sides of the Gutter (H.² F. 15/6/1792) 8° 1792; MS. Larpent 24. S. [11/6/1792].

[M.D.] The Mountaineers. A play (H.² S. 3/8/1793) 12° 1794 [*Dublin*; pirated]; 8° 1795 [3 editions]; 12° 1806 [*Dublin*]; Songs, Duets, Chorusses, etc., in The Mountaineers 8° 1793 [4 editions]; MS. Larpent 18. L. [30/7/1793].

    [Music S. Arnold.]

[Prel.] New Hay at the Old Market; An Occasional Drama (H.² T. 9/6/1795) 8° 1795; Sylvester Daggerwood; or, New Hay at the Old Market 8° 1808 [altered]; MS. Larpent 66. M. [4/6/1795].

    [As *Sylvester Daggerwood* this was played at H.² S. 16/7/1796.]

[M.D.] The Iron Chest: A Play...With a Preface and a Postscript

(D.L. S. 12/3/1796) 8° 1796 [*bis*]; 12° 1796 [*Dublin*]; 8° 1798 [3rd]; 8° 1808 [4th]; MS. Larpent 69. M. [11/3/1796].

[Music S. Storace.]

C. The Heir at Law (H.² S. 15/7/1797) 12° 1800 [*Dublin*; pirated]; 12° 1806 [*Dublin*; pirated]; 8° 1808; MS. Larpent 32. S. [7/7/1797].

[M.D.] Blue-Beard; or, Female Curiosity! A Dramatick Romance (D.L. T. 16/1/1798) 8° 1798 [4 editions]; 12° 1798 [*Dublin*]; 8° 1799 [5th]; 8° [1800; 6th]; 8° 1811; MS. Larpent 73. M. [2/1/1798].

[Music M. Kelly.]

F. Blue Devils (C.G. T. 24/4/1798) 8° 1808; 12° 1854; MS. Larpent 73. M. [17/4/1798].

[M.D.] Feudal Times; or, The Banquet-Gallery. A Drama (D.L. S. 19/1/1799) 8° [1799]; 12° [1799, *Dublin*]; 8° 1808; Songs, Duets, Trios, and Chorusses, in a New Musical Drama: called Feudal Times 8° [1799]; MS. Larpent 37. S. [2/1/1799].

[Music M. Kelly.]

[For his later works see the Hand-list of Plays, 1800–50.]

CONWAY, *Field-Marshal the Rt. Hon. HENRY SEYMOUR.*

C. False Appearances...altered from the French (Richmond House 1788; D.L. M. 20/4/1789) 8° 1789; 12° 1789 [*Dublin*]; MS. Larpent 49. M. [April 1789].

[Music M. Kelly.]

COOKE, *ADAM MOSES EMANUEL.*

*C. The King cannot Err 12° [1762].

[C.] The Hermit Converted; or, The Maid of Bath Married 8° [1771].

COOKE, *WILLIAM.*

C. The Capricious Lady...Altered from Beaumont and Fletcher (C.G. F. 17/1/1783) 8° 1783; MS. Larpent 30. M. [1783].

CORNELYS, *Mrs TERESA.*

*C. The Deceptions (Crow-street, Dublin, W. 14/3/1781).

COWLEY, *Mrs HANNAH.*

C. The Runaway (D.L. Th. 15/2/1776) 8° 1776 [*bis*]; MS. Larpent 13. S. [5/2/1776].

[It is said that *DAVID GARRICK* made some additions to this play.]

F. Who's the Dupe? (D.L. S. 10/4/1779) 8° 1779 [*bis*]; 8° 1780 [3rd]; 8° 1812; MS. Larpent 15. S. [29/3/1779].

T. Albina, Countess Raimond (H.² S. 31/7/1779) 8° 1779 [*bis*]; 8° 1780 [4th]; 8° 1812 [2nd, *sic*]; MS. Larpent 21. M. [10/7/1779].

C. The Belle's Stratagem (C.G. T. 22/2/1780) 12° 1781 [*Dublin*; pirated; two editions]; 8° 1782; 8° 1787 [2nd]; 8° 1806; 8° 1812; MS. Larpent 22. M. [15/2/1780].

*Int. The School for Eloquence (D.L. T. 4/4/1780) MS. Larpent 22. M. [30/3/1780].

*C. The World as it Goes; or, A Party at Montpellier (C.G. S. 24/2/1781) MS. Larpent 25. M. [17/2/1781].

*C. Second Thoughts are Best (C.G. S. 24/3/1781).

[An alteration of the above.]

C. Which is the Man? (C.G. S. 9/2/1782) 8° 1782; 8° 1783 [2nd]; 8° 1783 [3rd]; 8° 1784 [4th]; 8° 1785 [5th]; 8° 1812; MS. Larpent 28. M. [7/2/1782].

C. A Bold Stroke for a Husband (C.G. T. 25/2/1783) 8° 1784 [5 editions]; 8° 1812 [2nd, *sic*]; MS. Larpent 31. M. [1783].

C.   More Ways than One (C.G. S. 6/12/1783) 8° 1784 [3 editions].
C.   A School for Greybeards; or, The Mourning Bride (D.L. S.
     25/11/1786) 8° 1786; 12° 1787 [*Dublin*]; 8° 1787 [2nd]; MS. Lar-
     pent 41. M. [1786].
T.   The Fate of Sparta; or, The Rival Kings (D.L. Th. 31/1/1788)
     8° 1788 [*bis*]; 12° 1788 [*Dublin*]; MS. Larpent 47. M. [1788].
[C.O.] A Day in Turkey; or, The Russian Slaves (C.G. S. 3/12/1791)
     8° 1792 [4 editions]; Airs, Duets...in...A Day in Turkey 8° 1781
     [*sic*]; MS. Larpent 54. M. [29/11/1791].
C.   The Town before You (C.G. S. 6/12/1794) 8° 1795 [*bis*]; 12°
     [1799;*Dublin*] MS. Larpent 64. M. [25/11/1794; as *The Town as it is*].

CRADOCK, JOSEPH.
T.   Zobeide (C.G. W. 11/12/1771) 8° 1771; 8° 1772 [2nd]; 12° 1772
     [*Dublin*].
T.   The Czar, an Historical Tragedy 8° 1824.
     [This play was offered to Garrick in June 1776, was accepted for
     production by Sheridan in July 1780 but was, however, never acted.]

CRANE, EDWARD.
     Poetical Miscellanies 8° 1761.
     [Contains: 1. The Female Parricide; 2. Saul and Jonathan.]

CRANKE, ——.
*F. The True Briton (D.L. W. 17/4/1782).

CRAVEN, ELIZABETH, Baroness CRAVEN, afterwards Margravine
     of ANSPACH.
C.   The Sleep-Walker...Translated from the French (private,
     Newberry) 8° 1778.
C.   The Miniature Picture (private, Newberry; D.L. W. 24/5/1780)
     8° 1781; MS. Larpent 16. S. [22/5/1780; printed copy].
*O.F. The Silver Tankard; or, The Point at Portsmouth (H.² W.
     18/7/1781) MS. Larpent 17. S. [30/6/1781].
*[Int.] The Arcadian Pastoral (private, Burlington Gardens 1782).
*[C.] The Statue Feast (private, Benham House 1782).
C.   Le Philosophe Moderne 16° 1790.
*C. The Yorkshire Ghost (private, Brandenburgh House 1794).
*O. The Princess of Georgia (private, Brandenburgh House; C.G.
     F. 19/4/1799).
*P. Puss in Boots (private, Brandenburgh House 1799).
Past. Love Rewarded 8° [1799; Italian and English].
*Int. Nourgad (private, Brandenburgh House 1803).
*C. Love in a Convent (private, Brandenburgh House, July 1805).

CRISP, HENRY.
T.   Virginia (D.L. M. 25/2/1754) 8° 1754; MS. Larpent 3. M.
     [18/2/1754].

CROSS, JAMES C.
*[Int.] The Divertisement (C.G. T. 23/11/1790) MS. Larpent 53. M.
     [1790].
*[Int.] The Humours of Brighton; or, The Cliff, Steine, and Level
     (Brighton F. 7/9/1792).
[M.D.] The Purse; or, Benevolent Tar: A Musical Drama (H.² S.
     8/2/1794) 8° 1794; 12° 1794 [*Dublin*]; 8° 1794 [new]; 8° 1797; MS.
     Larpent 27. S. [22/1/1794].
     [Music W. Reeve.]

[Int.] British Fortitude, and Hibernian Friendship; or, An Escape from France. A Musical Drama (C.G. T. 29/4/1794) 8° 1794; MS. Larpent 27. S. [as *British Gratitude and H. F.*].

[Music W. Reeve.]

[M.D.] The Apparition! A Musical Dramatic Romance (H.² W. 3/9/1794) 8° 1794; Songs, Choruses, &c. in The Apparition! 8° 1794.

[Music W. Reeve.]

Parnassian Bagatelles: being a Miscellaneous Collection of Poetical Attempts 8° 1796.

[Contains: 1. *The Way to get Un-Married, a Comic Sketch* (C.G. W. 30/3/1796); 2. *The Village Doctor, or Killing no Cure; a Favourite Burletta* (Jones's Royal Circus, St George's Fields, March 1796, music by Saunderson). The first is in the Larpent collection 29. S. 18/3/1796. With music by Reeve it was given at H.² on Th. 1/9/1796 as *Married and Unmarried; or The Widow'd Wife.*]

[Int.] Songs, Choruses, &c. in The Charity Boy, A Musical Entertainment (D.L. S. 5/11/1796) 8° 1796; MS. Larpent 69. M. [2/8/1796].

[Music W. Reeve.]

[O.F.] Airs, Duets, and Chorusses, in a New Musical Farce, called An Escape into Prison (C.G. M. 13/11/1797) 8° 1797.

*P. Niobe; or, Harlequin's Ordeal (R.C. T. 20/6/1797).

P. Airs, Duets, and Chorusses in a New Pantomime, called Harlequin and Quixotte, or The Magic Arm (C.G. Th. 28/12/1797) 8° 1797.

*Mus. D. In Love, in Debt, and in Liquour; or, Our Way in Wales (R.C. W. 28/6/1797) 8° 1797.

*P. The Nymph of the Fountain (R.C. 1797).

*Ball. Joan of Arc; or, The Maid of Orleans (C.G. M. 12/2/1798) MS. Larpent 34. S. [30/1/1798].

[Int.] The Raft; or, Both Sides of the Water. A Musical Drama (C.G. S. 31/3/1798) 8° 1798; Songs...in the new Musical Piece of the Raft 8° 1798; MS. Larpent 34. S. [13/3/1798].

[Music W. Reeve.]

*P. Harlequin's Return (C.G. M. 9/4/1798) MS. Larpent 35. S. [April 1798].

*P. The Genoese Pirate; or, Black Beard (C.G. M. 15/10/1798) MS. Larpent 34. S. [12/10/1798].

[See below under *Works*. It is called a "Ballet" in the advertisements.]

Spectacle. The Songs...in the New Splendid Serious Spectacle called Cora; or, The Virgin of the Sun...Principally taken from Marmontel's Incas of Peru and the German Drama of The Virgin of the Sun, by Kotzebue, being the first part of his Popular Play of the Death of Rolla (R.C. 15/7/1799) 8° [1799].

[Reprinted in *Works*; music Saunderson.]

Spectacle. Halloween, or Castles of Athlin and Dunbaine (R.C. 24/9/1799) 8° [1799], Songs...in the New Grand Scotch Spectacle.

[Reprinted in *Circusiana* and *Works*; music Saunderson.]

Circusiana 8° 1809 and The Dramatic Works of J. C. Cross 8° 1812.

[Contain: 1. *The Round Tower; or, The Chieftains of Ireland. A New Ballet Pantomime* (C.G. T. 24/11/1795; music Reeve); 2. *Blackbeard; or, The Captive Princess* (R.C. April 1798; music

Saunderson; reprinted 12° N.D.); 3. *Cora; or, The Virgin of the Sun* (*q.v.*); 4. *Julia of Louvain; or, Monkish Cruelty. A New Dramatic Spectacle* (R.C. Th. 18/5/1797; music Cross and Saunderson); 5. *Halloween; or, The Castles of Athlin and Dunbane*—besides a number of nineteenth century productions.]

[For his later works see the Hand-list of Plays, 1800–1850.]

CULLUM, Mrs.

[D.] Charlotte: or One Thousand Seven Hundred and Seventy Three A Play 8° 1775.

CUMBERLAND, RICHARD.

[Int.] Shakespeare in the Shades [selections in R. C.'s *Memoirs* 1806, i. 56–64; written *c.* 1744].

T.   The Banishment of Cicero 4° 1761; 12° 1741 [*sic*, for 1761; *Dublin*; pirated].

[C.O.] The Summer's Tale. A Musical Comedy (C.G. F. 6/12/1765) 8° 1765; MS. Larpent 8. L. [25/11/1765].
[Overture Karl Friedrich Abel; T. A. Arne, S. Arnold and J. S. Bach aided in choosing the music. See *Amelia, infra*.]

[C.O.] Amelia. A Musical Entertainment (C.G. T. 12/4/1768) 8° 1768; 8° 1771 [with alterations].
[This is a shortened version of *The Summer's Tale*.]

C.   The Brothers (C.G. S. 2/12/1769) 8° 1770; 12° 1775 [2nd]; 8° 1777; 8° 1778; MS. Larpent 10. M. [22/11/1769].

C.   The West Indian (D.L. S. 19/1/1771) 8° 1771 [several editions]; 8° 1773; 8° 1774; 8° 1775; 12° 1775 [*Dublin*]; 12° 1790 [*Perth*]; 8° 1792; MS. Larpent 11. M. [1/1/1771].

T.   Timon of Athens, Altered from Shakespear (D.L. W. 4/12/1771) 8° 1771; 12° 1772 [*Dublin*]; MS. Larpent 11. M. [23/11/1771].

C.   The Fashionable Lover (D.L. M. 20/1/1772) 8° 1772 [*bis*]; 8° 1772 [new]; 8° 1774; MS. Larpent 13. M. [10/1/1772].

F.   The Note of Hand, or Trip to Newmarket (D.L. W. 9/2/1774) 8° 1774; MS. Larpent 15. M. [31/1/1774].

C.   The Choleric Man (D.L. M. 19/12/1774) 8° 1775 [3 editions]; 12° 1775 [*Dublin*]; MS. Larpent 11. S. [7/12/1774].

T.   The Battle of Hastings (D.L. S. 24/1/1778) 8° 1778.

*T.   The Princess of Parma (private, Kelmarsh, Northamptonshire, Th. 21/10/1778).

*[Int.] The Election (private, Kelmarsh, Th. 21/10/1778).

M.   Calypso (C.G. S. 20/3/1779) [in *Miscellaneous Poems* 4° 1778]; 8° 1789; MS. Larpent 20. M. [15/3/1779].
[Music T. Butler.]

*T.C. The Bondman (C.G. W. 13/10/1779).

*T.   The Duke of Milan (C.G. W. 10/11/1779).

[C.O.] The Songs in the Widow of Delphi: or, The Descent of the Deities, A Musical Drama (C.G. T. 1/2/1780) 8° 1780; MS. Larpent 22. M. [24/1/1780].
[Music Thomas Butler.]

C.   The Walloons (C.G. S. 20/4/1782) MS. Larpent 30. M. [8/4/1782].
[See *Posthumous Dramatick Works, infra*.]

T.   The Mysterious Husband (C.G. T. 28/1/1783) 8° 1783; 8° 1785; MS. Larpent 33. M. [1783, "Prompt Copy"].

T.   The Carmelite (D.L. Th. 2/12/1784) 8° 1784 [*bis*]; 8° 1785 [3rd]; 12° 1785 [*Dublin*]; MS. Larpent 35. M. [1784].

C. The Natural Son (D.L. W. 22/12/1784) 8° 1785 [*bis*]; 16° 1785 [*Dublin*]; MS. Larpent 35. M. [1784].

T. The Arab (C.G. T. 8/3/1785) MS. Larpent 39. M.
  [See *Posthumous Dramatick Works, infra*, under *Alcanor*.]

*F. The Country Attorney (H.² S. 7/7/1787).

C. The Impostors (D.L. M. 26/1/1789) 8° 1789 [3 editions]; 12° 1789 [*Dublin*]; MS. Larpent 48. M. [17/1/1789].

*C. The School for Widows (C.G. F. 8/5/1789) MS. Larpent 50. M. [25/4/1789].
  [An alteration of *The Country Attorney*.]

*Prel. An Occasional Prelude (C.G. M. 17/9/1792).

C.O. Songs and Chorusses in...The Armourer (C.G. Th. 4/4/1793) 8° 1793; MS. Larpent 60. M. [16/3/1793].
  [Music said to be by Captain Warner.]

C. The Box-Lobby Challenge (H.² S. 22/2/1794) 8° [1794; 7 editions]; 12° [1794; *Dublin*]; M.S. Larpent 27. S. [14/2/1794].

C. The Jew (D.L. Th. 8/5/1794) 8° 1794 [*bis*]; 12° 1794 [pirated]; 8° 1795 [3rd]; 8° 1795 [4th]; 8° 1795 [5th]; 12° 1796 [*Dublin*]; 8° 1797 [5th]; 8° 1797 [6th]; 8° 1801 [7th]; MS. Larpent 62. M. [1/5/1794].

C. The Wheel of Fortune (D.L. S. 28/2/1795) 8° 1795 [4 editions]; 12° 1795 [*Dublin*]; 8° 1796 [4th]; 12° 1801 [*Dublin*]; 8° 1805; MS. Larpent 66. M. [Feb. 1795].

C. First Love (D.L. T. 12/5/1795) 8° 1795 [*bis*]; 8° 1796 [3rd]; 12° 1795 [*Dublin*]; 8° 1799 [3rd, *sic*]; MS. Larpent 29. S. [2/5/1795].

*C. The Dependant (D.L. T. 20/10/1795) MS. Larpent 68. M. [10/10/1795].

[M.D.] The Days of Yore: A Drama (C.G. W. 13/1/1796) 8° 1796; MS. Larpent 28. S. [17/12/1795].

[D.] Don Pedro; A Play (H.² S. 23/7/1796) MS. Larpent 30. S. [4/7/1796].
  [See *Posthumous Dramatick Works, infra*.]

C. The Last of the Family (D.L. M. 8/5/1797) MS. Larpent 32. S. [25/4/1797].
  [See *Posthumous Dramatick Works, infra*.]

*Int. The Village Fete (C.G. Th. 18/5/1797) MS. Larpent 71. M. [10/5/1797].
  [Ascribed to R. C.]

C. False Impressions (C.G. Th. 23/11/1797) 8° 1797; 12° 1798 [*Dublin*].

C. The Clouds of Aristophanes 8° [1797].

C. The Eccentric Lover (C.G. M. 30/4/1798) MS. Larpent 35. S. [4/1798].
  [See *Posthumous Dramatick Works, infra*.]

C. A Word for Nature (D.L. W. 5/12/1798) MS. Larpent 73. M. [Nov. 1798].
  [See *Posthumous Dramatick Works, infra*, under *The Passive Husband*.]

[M.D.] Joanna of Montfaucon: A Dramatic Romance of the Four-teenth Century...Formed upon the Plan of the German Drama of Kotzebue, and Adapted to the English Stage (C.G. Jan. 1800) 8° 1800 [*bis*]; The Songs and Chorusses in...Joanna of Mont-faucon 8° [1800]; 8° 1800 [2nd].
  [Music T. Busby.]

The Posthumous Dramatick Works of R.C. 8° 1813.
[Contains: 1. *The Walloons*; 2. *Alcanor*; 3. *Don Pedro*; 4. *The Last of the Family*; 5. *The Eccentric Lover*; 6. *A Word for Nature.*]
[For his later works see the Hand-list of Plays, 1800–1850.]

CUNNINGHAM, JOSIAS.
Past. The Royal Shepherds 8° 1765.

CUTHBERTSON, Miss.
*C. Anna (H.¹ M. 25/2/1793) MS. Larpent 61. M. ["T.R. Haymarket" 9/2/1793].

DALLAS, ROBERT CHARLES.
T. Lucretia [in *Miscellaneous Writings* 4° 1797].
[Int.] Not at Home: A Dramatic Entertainment (Lyceum Nov. 1809) 8° 1809.

DALTON, JOHN, of CLIFTON.
F. Honour Rewarded: or, The Generous Fortune Hunter 8° 1775 [*York*].

D'ARBLAY, FRANCES [FANNY BURNEY].
*T. Edwy and Elgiva (D.L. S. 21/3/1795) MS. Larpent 28. S. [10/3/1795].

D'AUBERVAL, ——.
P. Le Cocq du Village; or, The Ingenious Lottery. A Pantomime Ballet, in the Rural Style (D.L. 1784) 8° 1784.
*P. Ball. Le Volage Fixe (H.¹ S. 10/3/1792).
*P. Ball. La Foire de Smirne; ou, Les Amans reunis (H.¹ S. 14/4/1792).

DAVIDSON, Rev. ANTHONY.
*C.O. Maria; or, The Maid of the Rock (Bigg's Co. at Lymington].

DAVIES, WILLIAM.
Plays written for a Private Theatre 8° 1786.
[Contains: 1. *News the Malady*; 2. *The Mode*; 3. *The Generous Counterfeit*; 4. *Better late than Never*; 5. *The Man of Honour.*]

DELAP, JOHN.
T. Hecuba (D.L. F. 11/12/1761) 8° 1762; 12° 1762 [*Dublin*]; 16° 1782 [*Dublin*]; MS. Larpent 6. M. [28/11/1761].
T. The Royal Suppliants (D.L. S. 17/2/1781) 8° 1781 [3 editions]; MS. Larpent 27. M. [26/1/1781; as *The R.S., or Macaria*].
T. The Captives (D.L. Th. 9/3/1786) 8° 1786; MS. Larpent 41. M. [For his later works see the Hand-list of Plays, 1800–1850.]

DELL, HENRY.
[F.] The Spouter, or the Double Revenge. A Comic Farce...As it was intended to be Acted 8° 1756 [2 issues].
T. Minorca 8° 1756 [*bis*].
C. The Mirrour...With the Author's Life, and an Account of the Alterations 8° 1756; 8° 1757 [2nd].
F. The Frenchified Lady Never in Paris, taken from Dryden and Colley Cibber (C.G. M. 23/3/1756) 8° 1757.

DELPINI, CARLO.
P. Don Juan; or, The Libertine Destroy'd. A Tragic Pantomimical Entertainment (Wargrave 1790) 8° 1790.
[Songs, etc. by Reeve; instrumental music Gluck.]

DENIS, CHARLES.
    T. The Siege of Calais. A Tragedy, from the French of Mr De
        Belloy, with Historical Notes 8° 1765.

DENT, JOHN.
    F. The Candidate (H.² M. 5/8/1782) 8° 1782 [*bis*]; MS. Larpent
        28. M. [1/8/1782].
 *F. The Statesman [advertised for D.L. in 1782, but apparently never
        acted].
    F. Too Civil by Half (D.L. T. 5/11/1782) 8° 1783; MS. Larpent
        30. M. [17/10/1782].
    F. The Receipt Tax (H.² W. 13/8/1783) 8° 1783; MS. Larpent 19. S.
        [5/8/1783].
 *Prel. The Lawyers' Panic (C.G. S. 7/5/1785) MS. Larpent 37. M.
        [1785].
   Ent. The Bastille (R.C. M. 19/10/1789) 8° [1789]; 8° 1790 [2nd].
   [F.] The Telegraph, or, A New Way of Knowing Things. A Comic
        Piece (C.G.W. 8/4/1795) 8° 1795; MS. Larpent 66. M. [26/3/1795].
 *F. The Tarantula [mentioned in *Biographia Dramatica*, iii. 321].

DERRICK, SAMUEL.
   [O.] Sylla. A Dramatic Entertainment...Translated from the French
        of the King of Prussia 8° 1753.
        [Translated from *Silla. Drama per Musica*.]

DEVERELL, Mrs M.
    T. Mary, Queen of Scots; An Historical Tragedy, or, Dramatic Poem
        8° 1792.

DIBDIN, CHARLES.
   Past. The Shepherd's Artifice. A Dramatic Pastoral (C.G. M.
        21/5/1764) 8° 1765; MS. Larpent 7. M. [28/4/1764].
        [Music by the author.]
   C.O. Damon and Phillida. Altered from Cibber into a Comic Opera.
        With the Addition of New Songs and Chorusses (D.L. Th.
        23/2/1769) 8° 1768; 12° 1769 [*Dublin*].
        [Music by the author.]
 *[Int.] The Mischance (S.W. 1772).
        [I can find record of this at S.W. only on M. 18/5/1789.]
 *[Int.] The Ladle (S.W. 1773) 8° 1773.
   C.O. The Wedding Ring (D.L. M. 1/2/1773) 8° 1773; The Songs in...
        The Wedding Ring 8° 1773; MS. Larpent 10. S. [14/1/1773].
        [Based on Goldoni, *Il Filosofo di Campagna*.]
   Burl. La Zingara; or, The Gipsy (M.G. W. 11/8/1773).
        [Music Barthélémon; an adaptation of Favart's *La Bohémienne*.]
  [Int.] The Deserter. A New Musical Drama (D.L.T. 2/11/1773) 8° 1773
        [*bis*]; 8° 1776; 12° 1789 [*Dublin*]; MS. Larpent 11. L. [18/10/1773].
        [An adaptation of Sedaine's *Le Déserteur*; music Monsigny.]
   B.O. The Waterman: or, The First of August (H.² M. 8/8/1774) 8°
        1774; 8° 1776; 8° 1777; 8° 1783; 12° 1785 [*Dublin*]; MS. Larpent
        11. L. [2/8/1774].
        [Music selected and composed by the author.]
   B.O. The Cobler; or, A Wife of Ten Thousand (D.L. F. 9/12/1774)
        8° 1774; 12° 1775 [*Dublin*]; 12° 1776 [*Dublin*].
        [Music by the author.]
   C.O. The Metamorphoses (H.² M. 26/8/1775) 8° 1776.

[Music by the author. Partly based on Molière, *George Dandin* and *Le Sicilien*.]

C.O. The Seraglio (C.G. Th. 14/11/1776) 8° 1776; Airs, Chorusses, etc., in the New Musical Entertainment of The Seraglio 8° 1776; MS. Larpent 16. M. [9/11/1776].
[Music by the author.]

C.O. The Quaker (D.L. T. 7/10/1777) 8° 1777; 8° 1778 [2nd]; 8° 1780 [3rd]; 12° 1782 [*Belfast*]; 12° 1784 [5th]; Songs, Duets, and Trios, in...the Quaker 8° 1777.
[Music by the author.]

Burl. Poor Vulcan (C.G. W. 4/2/1778) 8° 1778 [*bis*]; 12° [1789; *Dublin*; "by John O'Keefe"]; MS. Larpent 17. M. [31/1/1778].
[Music by the author with two airs by Dr Arne and Dr Arnold.]

C.O. The Gipsies (H.² M. 3/8/1778) 8° 1778.
[Music S. Arnold.]

C.O. Rose and Colin (C.G. F. 18/9/1778) 8° 1778; MS. Larpent 18. M. [7/11/1778].
[Music by the author.]

C.O. The Wives Revenged (C.G. F. 18/9/1778) 8° 1778; 12° 1780 [*Dublin*]; MS. Larpent 18. M. [7/11/1778].
[Music by the author.]

C.O. Annette and Lubin (C.G. F. 2/10/1778) 8° 1778; MS. Larpent 18. M. [7/11/1778].
[Music by the author. Adapted from *Annette et Lubin*, attributed to Favart and Santerre, with music by Adolphe Blaise.]

P. The Songs, Chorusses etc., in The Touchstone, or, Harlequin Traveller; an Operatical Pantomime (C.G. M. 4/1/1779) 8° 1779 [4 editions]; 8° 1780; MS. Larpent 17. M. [1778].
[Another contemporary MS. is extant in private hands; see Pickering and Chatto's *Book Lover's Leaflet*, No. 220, 1925. Music by the author.]

C.O. The Chelsea Pensioner (C.G. Th. 6/5/1779) 8° 1779 [*bis*]; 12° 1779 [*Dublin*]; MS. Larpent 21. M.
[Music by the author.]

P. The Mirror; or, Harlequin Every-where. A Pantomimical Burletta, in Three Parts (C.G. T. 30/11/1779) 8° 1779 [*bis*]; MS. Larpent 21. M. [26/11/1779].
[Music by the author.]

C.O. The Shepherdess of the Alps (C.G. T. 18/1/1780) 8° 1780; MS. Larpent 22. M. [6/1/1780].
[Music by the author; based on J. F. Marmontel, *La bergère des Alpes*.]

C.O. Songs, Duetts, Trios etc., in The Islanders (C.G. S. 25/11/1780) 8° 1780 [*bis*]; MS. Larpent 23. M. [23/11/1780].

P. The Songs...in...Harlequin Freemason (C.G. F. 29/12/1780) 8° 1780; MS. Larpent 23. M. [27/12/1780].
[The pantomimical business by Messink; the songs by Dibdin. Quotations are given in Northcott, R., *Charles Dibdin's Masonic Pantomime "Harlequin Freemason"* 8° 1915.]

F. The Marriage Act (C.G. M. 17/9/1781) 8° 1781.
[An abridgment of *The Islanders, supra*.]

*Burl. Jupiter and Alcmena (C.G. S. 27/10/1781) MS. Larpent 25. M. [25/10/1781].
[The *Biographia Dramatica* states that the songs were printed Based on J. Dryden, *Amphitryon*.]

*[O.F.] None so Blind as those who won't see (H.² 2/7/1782).

[Int.] The Graces: an Intermezzo (R.C. 1782) 8° 1782.
  [Music by the author.]

*Ser. The Cestus (R.C. 1783) 8° 1783.

*P. Harlequin the Phantom of a Day (R.C. 1783) 8° 1783.

*P. The Lancashire Witches; or, The Distresses of Harlequin (R.C. 1783).
  [The *Biographia Dramatica* states that the songs were printed.]

*Ser. The Long Odds (R.C. 1783) 8° 1783.

*Int. Clump and Cudden; or, The Review (R.C. 1785) 8° 1785.

C. A Game at Commerce, or, The Rooks Pigeoned.
  [This play was rejected both under the above title and under that of *The Two Houses*.]

C.O. Liberty-Hall: or, A Test of Good Fellowship (D.L. T. 8/2/1785); 8° 1785; The Songs in Liberty-Hall 8° 1785; MS. Larpent 40. M. [1785].
  [Music by the author.]

C.O. Harvest Home (H.² W. 16/5/1787) 8° 1787; 12° 1788 [*Dublin*]; Songs, Duets, etc., in Harvest Home 8° 1787; MS. Larpent 47. M. [30/4/1787].
  [Music by the author.]

*Ent. The Fortune Hunters; or, You May Say That (S.W. M. 13/4/1789).

*Ent. The Wags, or The Camp of Pleasure (Lyceum 1790).

*Ent. The Quizes, or A Trip to Elysium (Sans Souci 1795).

*Ent. Will of the Wisp (Sans Souci S. 10/10/1795).

*[Int.] A Loyal Effusion (C.G. 4/6/1794) MS. Larpent 63. M. [1794].

*[Int.] Hannah Hewitt; or, The Female Crusoe (D.L. M. 7/5/1798) MS. Larpent 35. S. [30/4/1798].
  [For his later works see the Hand-list of Plays, 1800–1850.]

DIBDIN, THOMAS JOHN.

F. The Mad Guardian: or, Sunshine after Rain. To which are added Fugitive Pieces in Prose and Verse by T. Merchant (Manchester 1794; C.G. T. 16/4/1799 as *Sunshine after Rain*) 8° [1795; *Huddersfield*]; MS. Larpent 69. M. [1795; as *S. after R., or The M. G.*].

[Int.] The Mouth of the Nile: or the Glorious First of August, a Musical Entertainment (C.G. Th. 25/10/1798) 8° 1798.
  [Music Thomas Attwood.]

F. The Jew and the Doctor (C.G. F. 23/11/1798) 8° 1800; MS. Larpent 34. S. [17/11/1798].

P. Songs, Recitations, etc., in The Volcano, or, The Rival Harlequins. A Serio-Comic Pantomime (C.G. 1799) 8° 1799; MS. Larpent 37. S. [12/12/1799].
  [Written in collaboration with *FARLEY*.]

C. Five Thousand a Year (C.G. S. 16/3/1799) 8° [1799]; 12° 1799 [*Dublin*]; MS. Larpent 36. S. [6/3/1799].

C. The Birth-Day...Altered from the German of Kotzebue, and adapted to the English Stage (C.G. M. 8/4/1799) 8° 1800; MS. Larpent 36. S. [16/2/1799].

F. The Horse and the Widow...Altered from the German of F. von Kotzebue (C.G. S. 4/5/1799) 8° 1799; 8° 1799 [*Dublin*; styled

A Dramatic Piece]; MS. Larpent 74. M. [30/4/1799; as *The Widow and the Riding Horse, or The Paradox An Interlude*].

*Int. Tag in Tribulation (C.G. T. 7/5/1799) MS. Larpent 74. M. [26/4/1799; as *T. in T., or The Benefit Night*].

[Int.] The Naval Pillar, A Musical Entertainment (C.G. M. 7/10/1799) 8° 1799; Songs...in the Naval Pillar: or, Britannia Triumphant, A New Musical Piece 8° 1799; MS. Larpent 74. M. [21/9/1799; as *The N.P., or Britannia's Triumph*].

[Overture by John Moorhead. H. C. Porter in his *History of the Theatres of Brighton* p. 20 mentions a performance of Dibdin's *The Glorious First of August, or British Tars Triumphant* on T. 9/10/1798, which may be this play, but see also *SICKLEMORE'S Aboukir Bay*.]

[For his later works see the Hand-list of Plays, 1800–1850.]

DOBBS, FRANCIS.

T. The Patriot King; or, Irish Chief (S.A. Dublin, M. 26/4/1773) 8° 1774.

DODD, JAMES SOLAS.

C.O. Gallic Gratitude; or, The Frenchman in India (S.A. Dublin 1772 as *The Funeral Pile*; C.G. F. 30/4/1779) 8° 1779; MS. Larpent 15. S. [24/4/1779].

[Based on La Font, *Le Naufrage*.]

DODSLEY, ROBERT.

[For his earlier works see the Hand-list of Plays, 1700–1750.]

T. Cleone (C.G. S. 2/12/1758) 8° 1758; 12° 1759 [*Belfast*]; 8° 1765 [4th]; 8° 1771 [4th]; 8° 1781; 8° 1786 [5th]; MS. Larpent 4. M. [23/11/1758].

DOSSIE, ROBERT.

[O.F.] The Statesman Foil'd. A Musical Comedy (H.² F. 8/7/1768) 8° 1768.

[Music Rush.]

DOUGLAS, Rev. ——.

*T. Edwin, the Banished Prince 8° [1784].

DOW, ALEXANDER.

T. Zingis (D.L. S. 17/12/1768) 8° 1769 [*bis*]; 8° 1773 [new]; MS. Larpent 8. M. [3/12/1768].

T. Sethona (D.L. S. 19/2/1774) 8° 1774; MS. Larpent 14. M. [4/2/1774].

DOWNING, GEORGE.

C. Newmarket; or, The Humours of the Turf (D.L. S. 25/4/1772) 8° 1774; 8° 1774 [*Coventry*, 2nd].

T. The Parthian Exile (Coventry and Worcester *c.* 1773) 12° 1774.

[O.F.] The Volunteers; or, Taylors, to Arms! A Comedy (C.G. 19/4/1780) 8° 1780; MS. Larpent 16. S. [1780; as *The Loyal V., or T. to A.*]. [Music Hook.]

DOWNMAN, HUGH.

[T.] Lucius Junius Brutus; or, The Expulsion of the Tarquins; an Historical Play 8° 1779; 8° 1792 [in *Tragedies*].

T. Editha (Exeter *c.* 1784) 8° 1784 (*Exeter*); 8° 1792 [in *Tragedies*].

T. Belisarius (Exeter 1786) 8° 1792 [in *Tragedies*].

DUBOIS, Lady DOROTHEA.
  Ent. The Magnet (M.G. 1771) 4° 1771; 8° 1771.
  [Int.] The Divorce. A Musical Entertainment (M.G. 1771) 8° 1771.
      [Music Hook.]
  *C.O. The Haunted Grove (Crow-street, Dublin, 16/4/1773).

DUNCAN, GED.
  *Past. The Constant Lovers; or, The Sailor's Return 8° 1798.

DUNLOP, ——.
  *——. Darby's Return [mentioned in *Biographia Dramatica*, ii. 152, and
      there dated 1789].

DUNSTER, CHARLES.
  C. The Frogs...Translated from the Greek of Aristophanes 8°
      [*Oxford*, 1785].

DUTTON, THOMAS.
  T. Pizarro in Peru, or the Death of Rolla...Translated from the last
      German Edition of Augustus von Kotzebue. With Notes etc.
      8° [1799].
          [The running title is *The Spaniards in Peru*.]

EARLE, WILLIAM Jun.
  C. Natural Faults...as written by William Earle Junr: so like First
      Faults...that the Reader will immediately conclude it is the same
      8° 1799.
  *[Int.] The Villagers [mentioned in the preface to the above, but
      probably never printed].

ECCLES, ——.
  *T. Cymbeline 8° 1793.

EDMEAD, Miss.
  *C. The Events of a Day (Norwich 1795) MS. Larpent 65. M.
      [28/3/1795].

EDWARDS, ANNA MARIA.
  [Int.] The Enchantress, or The Happy Island. A Favourite Musical
      Entertainment (Capel-street, Dublin, F. 31/12/1783) 12° 1787
      [*Dublin*, in *Poems on Various Subjects*].
          [Music T. Giordani.]

EDWARDS, Miss.
  Dr. Tale. Otho and Rutha 16° 1780 [*Edinburgh*].

EGVILLE, J. d'.
  *Ball. Le Jaloux Puni (H.¹ S. 1/6/1793).
  *P. Alexander the Great (D.L. 1795).
      [Music Krazinski Miller.]

ERSKINE, Hon. ANDREW.
  F. She's not Him, and He's not Her (Edinburgh T. 6/2/1764) 8°
      1764 [*Edin.*].

EWING, Capt. PETER.
  *C.O. The Soldier's Opera; or, Life Without a Mask 8° [1792]; MS.
      Larpent 55. M. [2/4/1791].
      [Music C. Dibdin.]

EYRE, EDMUND JOHN.
  F. The Dreamer Awake; or, Pugilist Matched (C.G. F. 6/5/1791) 8°
      1791 [Shrewsbury]; M.S Larpent 24. S. [4/5/1791].

T. The Maid of Normandy; or, The Death of the Queen of France (Wolverhampton 1794) 8° 1794.

C. Consequences; or, The School for Prejudice (Worcester *c.* 1794) 8° 1794.

M.D. The Fatal Sisters; or, The Castle of the Forest. A Dramatic Romance 8° 1797.

M.D. The Discarded Secretary; or, The Mysterious Chorus. An Historical Play 8° 1799.

[For his later works see the Hand-list of Plays 1800–1850.]

FARRER, ——.
Dr. Poem. The Trial of Abraham 8° 1790 [*Stamford*].

FEILDE, MATTHEW.
*Past. Vertumnus and Pomona (C.G. Th. 21/2/1782); MS. Larpent 29. M. [11/2/1782]. Songs, Duets, &c. in Vertumnus and Pomona 8° 1782.

FENNELL, JAMES.
C. Lindor and Clara; or, The British Officer (provinces *c.* 1790) 8° 1791; MS. Larpent 53. M. [18/8/1790, as for Richmond].
*F. The Advertisement (H.¹ March 1791) MS. Larpent 56. M. [1791; as *The Advertisement, or A New Way to get a Husband*].

FERRAR, JOHN.
*T. The Orphan; or, The Happy Marriage 8° 1765 [*Limerick*, in *Poems on Several Occasions.*]

FERRIAR, Dr JOHN.
T. The Prince of Angola...altered from the Play of Oroonoko, and adapted to the Circumstances of the Present Time 8° 1788.

FINNEY, ——.
*Prel. The Green Room (H.² W. 27/8/1783) MS. Larpent 30. M. [25/8/1783].

FISHER, ——.
C. The School for Ingratitude...So like, in many Points—in one, so Unlike, "Cheap Living" 8° [1798; *bis*].

FITZGERALD, MICHAEL.
*T. Elwina (Crow-street, Dublin, Th. 29/3/1792).

FOOTE, SAMUEL.
[For his earlier works see the Hand-list of Plays, 1700–1750, and for *Doctor Last in his Chariot* (H.² 1769) see under *ISAAC BICKERSTAFFE.*]

C. Taste (D.L. S. 11/1/1752) 8° 1752; 8° 1753 [2nd]; 12° 1762 [*Dublin*]; 8° 1765 [3rd]; 8° [1772]; 8° 1778 [4th]; 8° 1781 [4th]; 8° 1799; MS. Larpent 6. M. [1761].

C. The Englishman in Paris (C.G. S. 24/3/1753) 8° 1753; 12° 1753 [*Dublin*]; 8° 1763; 8° 1765; 8° 1778.

C. The Knights (H.² 1749; in revised form D.L. S. 9/2/1754) 8° 1754; 12° 1754 [*Dublin*]; 12° 1758 [*Glasgow*]; 8° [1778]; 8° 1787; MS. Larpent 3. M. [16/1/1754].

F. The Englishman returned from Paris. Being the Sequel to the Englishman in Paris (C.G. T. 3/2/1756) 8° 1756; 8° [1780]; 8° 1780 [3rd]; 8° 1788.

C. The Author (D.L. S. 5/2/1757) 8° 1757; 12° 1757 [*Dublin*]; 8° [1760]; 8° [1778]; 8° 1782; 8° 1794; MS. Larpent 5. L. [27/1/1757].

[An extra scene intended for this play was printed in *The Monthly Mirror*.]

C. The Minor (Crow-street Dublin M. 28/1/1760; H.² S. 28/6/1760), 8° 1760 [4 editions]; 12° 1760 [*Dublin*]; 8° 1762 [5th]; 8° 1764 [6th]; 8° 1767 [7th]; 8° 1778; 8° 1781 [9th]; 8° 1792; MS. Larpent 5. M. [1760].

[As produced in Dublin this play was in two acts and did not contain the character of Smirk.]

*[F.] The First Act of Taste. Connected with a new additional Act call'd Modern Tragedy (D.L. M. 6/4/1761).

C. The Lyar (C.G. T. 12/1/1762) 8° 1764; 12° 1764 [*Dublin*]; 8° 1769; 8° 1776; 8° 1780; 8° 1786; 12° 1793 [*Dublin*]; 8° 1805; MS. Larpent 7. L. [16/9/1761].

C. The Orators (H.² M. 30/8/1762) 8° 1762; 12° 1762 [*Dublin*]; 8° 1767; 8° 1777; 8° 1780.

C. The Young Hypocrite, or the Country Poet [in *The Comic Theatre* 12° 1762, vol. i].

C. The Mayor of Garret (H.² M. 20/6/1763) 8° 1764; 12° 1764 [*Dublin*]; 8° 1769 [2nd]; 12° 1774 [*Dublin*]; 8° 1776; 8° 1780; 8° 1783; 8° 1797; MS. Larpent 7. L. [20/6/1763].

F. The Tryall of Samuel Foote, Esq. for a Libel on Peter Paragraph (H.² 1763). [Printed in Tate Wilkinson's *The Wandering Patentee*, 1795, vol. iv.]

C. The Patron (H.² T. 26/6/1764) 8° 1764 [*bis*]; 12° 1764 [*Dublin*]; 8° 1774 [3rd]; 8° 1780.

C. The Commissary (H.² M. 10/6/1765) 8° 1765 [*bis*]; 12° 1765 [*Dublin*]; 8° 1773 [3rd]; 8° 1779; 8° 1782 [4th].

Prel. An Occasional Prelude (H.² 1767).

[Printed in *The Monthly Mirror*, xvii. 44, where it is wrongly headed a "Prologue." Portions were given in *The London Magazine* of 1767 and were copied into *The Theatrical Recorder* 1806.]

C. The Devil upon Two Sticks (H.² M. 30/5/1768) 8° 1778; 8° 1794; MS. Larpent 9. L. [1768].

C. The Lame Lover (H.² F. 22/6/1770) 8° 1770; 12° 1770 [*Dublin*]; 12° 1794; MS. Larpent 10. L. [7/6/1770].

C. The Maid of Bath (H.² W. 26/6/1771) 8° 1778; 8° 1778 [pirated]; 12° 1778 [*Dublin*]; 8° [1780]; MS. Larpent 10. L. [12/6/1771].

C. The Nabob (H.² M. 29/6/1772) 8° 1778; 8° 1795; MS. Larpent 10. L. [17/6/1772].

*C. Piety in Pattens (H.² M. 15/2/1773) MS. Larpent 10. L. [15/2/1773].

[A full account of this work will be found in the *Biographia Dramatica*, iii. 150–156.]

C. The Bankrupt (H.² W. 21/7/1773) 8° 1776 [*bis*]; 8° 1782; MS. Larpent 10. L. [8/7/1773].

C. The Cozeners (H.² F. 15/7/1774) 8° 1778; 8° 1778 [pirated]; 8° 1795; MS. Larpent 11. L. [28/6/1774].

C. A Trip to Calais... To which is annexed, The Capuchin... Altered from the Trip to Calais (H.² M. 19/8/1776) 8° 1778; 8° 1795; *Capuchin* MS. Larpent 12. L. [8/8/1776].

Burlesque, Lindamira; or, Tragedy A-la-Mode 8° 1805. [See above, *The First Act of Taste*.]

FORDE, BROWNLOW.
  F. The Miraculous Cure; or, The Citizen Outwitted 8° 1771 [*Newry*].
    [Based on C. Cibber's *The Double Gallant.*]

FORREST, THEODOSIUS.
  [O.F.] The Weathercock, A Musical Entertainment (C.G. T. 17/10/1775) 8° 1775; MS. Larpent 15. M. [4/10/1775].

FRANCIS, ——.
  Legendary Drama. The Enchanted Wood (H.² W. 25/7/1792) 8° 1792; MS. Larpent 58. M. [13/7/1792].

FRANCIS, PHILIP.
  T. Eugenia (D.L. M. 17/2/1752) 8° 1752.
  T. Constantine (C.G. S. 23/2/1754) 8° 1754; MS. Larpent 3. M. [15/2/1754; as *Constantine the Great*].

FRANCKLIN, Dr THOMAS.
  T. The Orphan of China 8° 1756 [*bis*]; 12° 1761 [6th].
    The Tragedies of Sophocles 4° 1759.
  T. The Earl of Warwick (D.L. S. 13/12/1766) 8° 1766 [*bis*]; 12° 1767; 8° 1769 [4th].
    The Works of Mr de Voltaire 12° 1761–1765 [vols. i–xxv]; 12° 1778–81 [vols. i–xxxviii].
    [Contains *Orestes* (C.G. M. 13/3/1769) and *Electra* (D.L. S. 15/10/1774).]
  T. Matilda (D.L. S. 21/1/1775) 8° 1775; 12° 1775 [*Dublin*].
  [F.] The Contract: A Comedy (H.² W. 12/6/1776) 8° 1776; MS. Larpent 15. M. [10/8/1775].
  T. Tragopodagra; or, The Gout 4° 1780 [in *The Works of Lucian*].
  [T.] Mary, Queen of Scots, An Historical Play 8° 1837.

FRANKLIN, ANDREW.
  *Int. The Hypocondriac (S.A. Dublin 4/1/1785).
    [Music T. Giordani.]
  F. The Mermaid (C.G. M. 26/3/1792) 8° 1792; 12° 1792; MS. Larpent 58. M. [24/3/1792].
  [F.] The Wandering Jew: or, Love's Masquerade. A Comedy (D.L. M. 15/5/1797) 8° 1797 [4 editions]; MS. Larpent 32. S. [25/4/1797].
  [Int.] A Trip to the Nore. A Musical Entertainment (D.L. Th. 9/11/1797) 8° 1797; Songs, Duetts, Chorusses...in A Trip to the Nore 8° 1797; MS. Larpent 71. M. [5/11/1797].
  [M.D.] Songs...in The Outlaws. A Music Drama (D.L. T. 16/10/1798) 8° 1798; MS. Larpent 73. M. [6/10/1798].
    [Music Florio.]
  *F. Gander Hall (H.² M. 5/8/1799) MS. Larpent 36. S. [1/8/1799].
  [Int.] Songs...in the New Music Entertainment of the Embarcation (D.L. Th. 3/10/1799) 8° 1799; MS. Larpent 74. M. [27/9/1799].
    [Music Reeve.]
  [C.O.] The Egyptian Festival; An Opera (D.L. March 1800) 8° 1800; Songs, Duets, Trios, Chorusses, etc., in The Egyptian Festival. An Opera 8° 1800.
  F. The Counterfeit (D.L. March 1804) 8° 1804 (*bis*).

GAMBOLD, JOHN.
  T. The Martyrdom of Ignatius...written in the year 1740 8° 1773.

GARDNER, Mrs [Miss CHENEY].
  *C. The Advertisement; or, A Bold Stroke for a Husband (H.¹ S. 9/8/1777) MS. Larpent 13. L. [26/7/1777; as *The Matrimonial Advertisement, or A Bold Stroke for a Husband*].
  *[O.F.] The Female Dramatist (H.² F. 16/8/1782) MS. Larpent 29. M. [3/8/1782].
      [A contemporary MS. record of Haymarket productions (Widener Library, Harvard) has a note to this play: "This was young Colman's first attempt."]

GARRICK, DAVID.
      [For his earlier works see the Hand-list of Plays, 1700–1750. For *Antony and Cleopatra* see under *E. CAPELL*; for *Almida* see under *Mrs CELISIA*; for *A Fairy Tale* see under *G. COLMAN*; for *False Delicacy* see under *H. KELLY*.]
  C. Every Man in his Humour...With Alterations and Additions (D.L. F. 29/11/1751) 8° 1752; 8° 1755; 12° 1774 [*Edinburgh*]; 8° 1777.
  C. The Chances...with Alterations (D.L. Th. 7/11/1754) 8° 1773.
  [D.O.] The Fairies. An Opera. Taken from A Midsummer Night's Dream...The Songs from Shakespeare, Milton, Waller, Dryden, Lansdowne, Hammond, &c. (D.L. M. 3/2/1755) 8° 1755.
      [Music J. C. Smith.]
  [F.] Catharine and Petruchio. A Comedy (D.L. W. 18/3/1756) 8° 1756; 12° 1786.
  Past. Florizel and Perdita; or The Winter's Tale. A Dramatic Pastoral (D.L. W. 21/1/1756) 8° 1758; 8° 1762; MS. Larpent 5. L. [14/1/1756].
  [D.O.] The Tempest...Taken from Shakespeare (D.L. W. 11/2/1756) 8° 1756; MS. Larpent 4. M. [9/2/1756].
      [Music J. C. Smith.]
  T. King Lear...Altered from Shakespeare (D.L. Th. 28/10/1756) 12° 1786 [the text is in Bell's *Shakespeare*].
  [Int.] Lilliput. A Dramatic Entertainment (D.L. F. 3/12/1756) 8° 1757.
  *F. The Modern Fine Gentleman (D.L. Th. 24/3/1757) MS. Larpent 5. S. [14/3/1757].
      [At the second performance entitled *The Male Coquette*.]
  [T.] Isabella: or, The Fatal Marriage. A Play. Alter'd from Southern (D.L. F. 2/12/1757) 8° 1757; 8° 1758 [2nd]; 8° 1779; 8° 1783; 12° 1800.
  F. The Male Coquette; or, Seventeen Hundred Fifty Seven (D.L. S. 3/12/1757) 8° 1757; 12° 1758 (*Dublin*).
  C. The Gamesters...Alter'd from Shirley (D.L. Th. 22/12/1757) 8° 1758; MS. Larpent 5. L. [12/12/1757].
  [F.] The Guardian. A Comedy (D.L. S. 3/2/1759) 8° 1759 [*bis*]; 12° 1771; 8° 1773 [4th]; 8° 1779; MS. Larpent 5. S. [17/1/1759].
  *[Sat.] Harlequin's Invasion. A Christmas Gambol, after the Manner of the Italian Comedy (D.L. M. 31/12/1759) MS. Larpent 4. M. [1759].
  [Int.] The Enchanter; or, Love and Magic. A Musical Drama (D.L. S. 13/12/1760) 8° 1760; MS. Larpent 5. M. [Nov. 1760].
      [Music J. C. Smith.]
  T. Cymbeline...By Shakespear. With Alterations (D.L. S 28/11/1761) 12° 1762; 12° 1767; 12° 1770; 8° 1784.

Int. The Farmer's Return from London (D.L. S. 20/3/1762) 8° 1762;
4° 1762 [2nd]; MS. Larpent 6. S. [1762; as *The Farmers Return*].

C. A Midsummer Night's Dream...With Alterations and Additions
and Several New Songs (D.L. W. 23/11/1763) 8° 1763; MS.
Larpent 6. S. [1763].

C. The Clandestine Marriage [see under *GEORGE COLMAN*].

C. The Country Girl...Altered from Wycherley (D.L. S. 25/10/1766)
8° 1766; 8° 1790; 12° 1791; MS. Larpent 8. S. [20/10/1766].

F. Neck or Nothing (D.L. T. 18/11/1766) 8° 1766; 12° 1767; 8°
1774.

[D.O.] Cymon. A Dramatic Romance (D.L. F. 2/1/1767) 8° 1767
[3 editions]; 8° 1768; 8° 1770; 8° 1778; F. [1784]; 12° [1786];
MS. Larpent 8. M. [Dec. 1766].
[Music Michael Arne.]

Int. Linco's Travels (D.L. M. 6/4/1767) MS. Larpent 8. M. [2/4/1767].
[Music Michael Arne.]

[Burlesque.] A Peep Behind the Curtain; or, The New Rehearsal (D.L.
F. 23/10/1767) 8° 1767 [3 editions]; 8° [N.D.]; 12° 1767; 8° 1772.
[Music of "The Burletta of *Orpheus*," F. H. Barthélemon.]

[Int.] Songs, Chorusses, &c. which are introduced in the New Enter-
tainment of The Jubilee (D.L. S. 14/10/1769) 8° 1769; 8° 1776; 8°
1778; Shakespear's Garland; or, The Warwickshire Jubilee, being
a Collection of Ballads, Catches, and Glees, as performed in the
Great Booth at Stratford-upon-Avon F. [1769]; Shakespeare's
Garland, being a Collection of New Songs...performed at the
Jubilee at Stratford upon Avon 8° 1769.
[Music C. Dibdin, Dr Arne, Barthélémon and Attwood.]

[D.O.] King Arthur; or, The British Worthy. A Masque, by Mr Dryden (D.L. Th. 13/12/1770) 8° 1770 [*bis*]; 8° 1781.
[Music Purcell and Arne.]

M. The Songs, Chorusses, and Serious Dialogue of the Masque
called, The Institution of the Garter, or Arthur's Round Table
Restored (D.L. M. 28/10/1771) 8° 1771; MS. Larpent 9. S.
[15/10/1771; as *The Order of the Garter*].
[Music C. Dibdin.]

C. The Irish Widow (D.L. F. 23/10/1772) 8° 1772 [*bis*]; 8° 1773; 8°
1774; 8° 1781; 8° 1787.

*T. Hamlet (D.L. F. 18/12/1772).

M. Alfred (D.L. S. 9/10/1773) 8° 1773.
[An alteration of the play by James Thomson and David
Mallet. Music by Dr Arne.]

C. Albumazar. A Comedy...with Alterations (D.L. T. 19/10/1773)
8° 1773 [*bis*]; MS. Larpent 11. L.

[Ent.] A New Dramatic Entertainment, called a Christmas Tale, in
Five Parts (D.L. M. 27/12/1773) 8° 1774 [3 editions]; 12° 1774
[*Dublin*]; 8° 1776 [in 3 acts]; The Songs, Chorusses, etc., in...A
Christmas Tale 8° [1773]; MS. Larpent 10. S. [13/12/1773].
[Music Charles Dibdin. Based on *La Fée Urgèle*, attributed to
Favart, and with music originally composed by Egidio Romualdo
Duni.]

*Prel. The Meeting of the Company; or, Bayes's Art of Acting (D.L.
S. 17/9/1774).

[F.] Bon Ton; or, High Life Above Stairs. A Comedy (D.L. S.

18/3/1775) 8° 1775; 8° 1776; 8° 1781; 8° 1784; 12° 1785 [*Dublin*]; 8° 1793; MS. Larpent 12. S. [7/3/1775].

[O.F.] May-Day; or, The Little Gipsy. A Musical Farce...To which is added, The Theatrical Candidates, A Musical Prelude (1. D.L. S. 28/10/1775; 2. D.L. 23/9/1775) 8° 1775; Songs...in the New Musical Entertainment, May-Day 8° 1775; 8° 1776; 12° 1777; MS. of *May Day* Larpent 11. S. [14/10/1775].

> [Music T. A. Arne; *The Theatrical Candidates* is also printed separately in *The British Stage* 12° 1786, vol. vi.]

C. The Alchymist...As Altered from Ben Jonson (? D.L. Oct. 1774) 8° 1777.

GAY, JOHN.

C. The Rehearsal at Goatham 8° 1754.

GEISWEILER, CONSTANTIN.

T. Pizarro 8° 1800 [Eng. and German, the latter being a translation of Sheridan's play].

GEISWEILER, MARIA.

D. Crime from Ambition: a Play...Translated from the German of Wilhelm Augustus Iffland 8° 1799.

*D. Joanna of Montfaucon 8° 1799.

D. The Noble Lie; A Drama...Being a Continuation of Misanthropy and Repentance, or The Stranger 8° 1799.

[D.] Poverty and Nobleness of Mind: A Play 8° 1799.

GENTLEMAN, FRANCIS.

T. Sejanus...As it was intended for the Stage. With a Preface, wherein the Manager's Reasons for refusing it are set forth 8° 1752.

*T. Osman (Bath 25/11/1754).

*T. Zaphira (Bath 18/1/1755).

T. The Sultan, or Love and Fame. A New Tragedy (Bath, York and Scarborough *c.* 1754; H.² 1769) 8° 1770.

*T. Richard II (Bath 1754).

*Sat. The Mentalist (Manchester *c.* 1759).

*Int. The Fairy Court (Chester 1761).

C. The Tobacconist...Altered from Ben Jonson (Edinburgh *c.* 1760; H.² M. 22/7/1771) 8° 1771.

C. The Modish Wife (Chester 1761; H.² S. 18/9/1773) 8° [1774]; 8° [1775].

*T. Oroonoko; or, The Royal Slave (Edinburgh *c.* 1760; D.L. S. 11/3/1769 as *The Royal Slave*) 12° 1760 [*Glasgow*].

[F.] The Stratford Jubilee. A New Comedy...As it has been lately exhibited at Stratford upon Avon, with Great Applause. To which is prefixed Scrub's Trip to the Jubilee 8° 1769.

*F. The Coxcombs (H.² M. 16/9/1771).

Past. Cupid's Revenge. An Arcadian Pastoral (H.² M. 27/7/1772) 8° 1772; MS. Larpent 12. M.

> [Music Hook.]

Ent. The Pantheonites. A Dramatic Entertainment (H.² F. 3/9/1773) 8° 1773; MS. Larpent 14. M. [1773].

*O. Orpheus and Euridice (S.A. Dublin 1783).

GIBSON, FRANCIS.

[T.C.] Streanshall Abbey; or, The Danish Invasion. A Play (Whitby Dec. 1799) 8° 1800.

GILLUM, WILLIAM.
F.   What Will the World Say? [in *Miscellaneous Poems* 8° 1787].

GLOVER, RICHARD.
T.   Boadicia (D.L. S. 1/12/1753) 8° 1753; 12° 1753 [*Dublin*]; MS.
     Larpent 3. M. [21/11/1753].
     [This tragedy had "new pieces of music between the Acts,
     adapted to the Play, and composed by Dr Boyce."]
T.   Medea (D.L. T. 24/3/1767) 4° 1761; 12° 1761 [*Dublin*]; 4° 1762
     [2nd]; 8° 1762 [3rd]; 8° 1762 [4th]; 8° 1777.
T.   Jason 8° 1799.

GOLDSMITH, OLIVER.
C.   The Good Natur'd Man (C.G. F. 29/1/1768) 8° 1768 [6 editions];
     12° 1784 [*Dublin*]; 8° 1792; 12° 1792 [*Perth*].
C.   She Stoops to Conquer: Or The Mistakes of a Night (C.G. M.
     15/3/1773) 8° 1773 [4 editions]; 8° 1786; 8° 1791; 12° 1792 [*Perth*];
     12° 1793 [*Dublin*]; MS. Larpent 13. M. [1773; as *The Novel, or
     Mistakes of a Night*].
*F. The Grumbler (C.G. S. 8/5/1773).

GOODALL, THOMAS.
*C. The Counterplot (Bath *c.* 1787).

GOODENOUGH, RICHARD JOSCELINE.
[O.F.] The Cottagers. A Musical Entertainment (C.G. F. 12/11/1779, as
     William and Nanny) 8° 1768; William and Nanny: A Ballad Farce
     8° 1779; The Songs in William and Nanny. A Dramatic Pastoral
     8° 1779; MS. Larpent 21. M. [11/11/1779; as *William and Nancy*].
     [Music Baumgarten.]

GOODHALL, JAMES.
T.   Florazene: or, the Fatal Conquest 8° [*Stamford*, 1754].
T.   King Richard II...Alter'd from Shakespear and the Style
     Imitated 8° 1772 [*Manchester*].

GOODWIN, T.
Past. Poem. The Loyal Shepherds; or, The Rustic Heroine. A
     Dramatic Pastoral Poem...To which is affixed, Several Sonnets,
     Ballads, Acrostics 8° [1779].

GORDON, ——.
     The Comedies of Terence 12° 1752.

GRAHAM, Rev. GEORGE.
M.   Telemachus 4° 1763; 12° 1763 [*Dublin*].

GRAVES, RICHARD.
[Ent.] Euphrosyne: or, Amusements on the Road of Life 8° 1776
     [includes *Echo and Narcissus*, a pastoral].
C.   The Coalition; or, The Opera Rehears'd (Bath *c.* 1793) 12° 1794.

GREATHEED, BERTIE.
T.   The Regent (D.L. S. 29/3/1788) 8° 1788 [2 editions]; MS. Larpent
     47. M. [15/3/1788].

GREEN, GEORGE SMITH.
[T.] Oliver Cromwell. An Historical Play. To which is Prefix'd An
     Extract or Journal of the Rise and Progress of Oliver Cromwell 8°
     1752.
C.   The Nice Lady 8° 1762.

GREEN, RUPERT.
*T. The Secret Plot 12° 1777.

GREENFIELD, ANDREW.
T. Henrique, Prince of Sicily...Left Unfinished [in *Poems* 8° 1790].

GREGORY, Dr GEORGE.
*T. The Siege of Jerusalem. [See *Memoirs of Gilbert Wakefield* mentioned in *Biographia Dramatica*, iii. 272.]

GRIFFITH, Mrs ELIZABETH.
Dr. Poem. Amana 4° 1764.
C. The Platonic Wife (D.L. Th. 24/1/1765) 8° 1765; 12° 1765; MS. Larpent 8. L. [12/1/1765].
C. The Double Mistake (C.G. Th. 9/1/1766) 8° 1766 [3 editions]; MS. Larpent 8. L. [24/12/1765].
C. The School for Rakes (D.L. S. 4/2/1769) 8° 1769 [3 editions].
C. A Wife in the Right (C.G. M. 9/3/1772) 8° 1772; MS. Larpent 13. M. [20/2/1772; as *Patience the Best Remedy, or A W. in the R.*].
C. The Barber of Seville; or, The Useless Precaution 8° 1776.
C. The Times (D.L. Th. 2/12/1779) 8° 1780; MS. Larpent 14. L. [29/11/1779].

GRIFFITH, RICHARD.
C. Variety (D.L. M. 25/2/1782) 8° 1782 [*bis*]; MS. Larpent 17. S. [5/2/1782].

GROVE, WILLIAM.
Past. The Faithful Shepherd. A Dramatic Pastoral 12° 1782.

HAILES, Lord.
[F.] The Little Freeholder, A Dramatic Entertainment 12° 1790.

HALL, ROBERT.
[O.F.] The Old Quizzes: or, What's the News? (Crow-street, Dublin, May 1797) 8° 1799 [*Dublin*].

HAMILTON, CHARLES.
T. The Patriot...Altered from the Italian of Metastasio 8° [1784].

HARDHAM, JOHN [pseud. ABEL DRUGGER].
[F.] The Fortune Tellers: or, The World Unmask'd. A Medley 8° [N.D. ?1750].

HARPLEY, T.
Dramas and Poems 8° 1790 [*Liverpool*].
[Contains: 1. *The Milliners, or Female Revenge*; 2. *The Triumph of Fidelity*; 3. *The Genius of Liverpool*. All these were performed at Liverpool. The last is in the Larpent collection 48. M. 21/12/1789.]

HARRIS, JAMES.
Past. The Spring (D.L. F. 22/10/1762) 8° 1762; Daphnis and Amaryllis 8° [1766].
[Music Händel and others.]

HARRISON, ELIZABETH.
*T. The Death of Socrates [in *Miscellanies* 8° 1756].

HARRISON, Lieutenant NICHOLAS BACON.
C. The Travellers...As read with Applause at the English Readings 8° 1788.

HARROD, W.
  *T. The Patriot 8° 1769.

HART, CHARLES.
  T. Herminius and Espasia (Edinburgh M. 25/2/1754) 8° 1754
      [Edinburgh].

HARTSON, HALL.
  T. The Countess of Salisbury (Crow-street, Dublin F. 2/5/1765;
      H.² M. 31/8/1767) 8° 1767 [3 editions]; 8° 1769 [4th]; 12° 1775
      [Dublin]; 8° 1784; 12° 1793; MS. Larpent 9. L. [1767].
      [The date of production is given as F. 21/8/1767 in a contem-
      porary MS. record of Haymarket productions, now in the Widener
      Library, Harvard.]

HARWOOD, THOMAS.
  T. The Death of Dion 8° 1787.
  T. The Noble Slave 8° 1788 [Bury St Edmunds].

HAVARD, WILLIAM.
      [For his earlier works see the Hand-list of Plays, 1700–1750.]
  *F. The Elopement (D.L. W. 6/4/1763) MS. Larpent 7. M. [26/3/1763].

HAWKESWORTH, JOHN.
  C. Amphitryon: or, The Two Sosias... altered from Dryden (D.L.
      W. 15/12/1756) 8° 1756; 8° 1780; MS. Larpent 1. S. [printed copy of
      Dryden's play altered].
  T. Oroonoko... with Alterations (D.L. S. 1/12/1759) 8° 1759; 8°
      1775; MS. Larpent 5. S. [20/11/1759].
  [Ent.] Edgar and Emmeline, A Fairy Tale in a Dramatic Entertainment
      (D.L. S. 31/1/1761) 8° 1761; 8° [1777].
      [Music Michael Arne.]

HAWKINS, W.
  *Past. The Enlisted Shepherds [in Poems 8° 1786].

HAWKINS, WILLIAM.
      [For his earlier works see the Hand-list of Plays, 1700–1750.]
  *T. The Siege of Aleppo [in Miscellanies 8° 1758].
  [T.C.] Cymbeline, A Tragedy, Altered from Shakespeare (C.G. Th.
      15/2/1759) 8° 1759; MS. Larpent 4. M. [2/2/1759].

HAYES, SAMUEL [and ROBERT CARR].
  T. Eugenia 8° 1766.

HAYLEY, WILLIAM.
      Plays of Three Acts written for a Private Theatre 4° 1784; 8° 1784
      [Dublin]; also Plays and Poems 8° 1785; 8° 1788.
        [Contains: 1. The Happy Prescription; or, The Lady Relieved
      from her Lovers; 2. Marcella; 3. The Two Connoisseurs; 4. Lord
      Russell; 5. The Mausoleum.]
      Marcella D.L. S. 7/11/1789.
      The Two Connoisseurs H.² Th. 2/9/1784.
      Lord Russell H.² W. 18/8/1784.
      Larpent collection MS. 34. M. Lord Russell [24/6/1784]; Marcella
      49. M. [4/11/1789]; The Two Connoisseurs 36. M. [1784].
  *T. Eudora (C.G. F. 29/1/1790) 8° 1811; MS. Larpent 52. M. [1790].
      [For his later works see the Hand-list of Plays, 1800–1850.]

HAZARD, JOSEPH.
  *M. Redowald 12° 1767 [Chelmsford].

HEARD, WILLIAM.
  [F.] The Snuff Box; or, A Trip to Bath. A Comedy (H.² 1775) 8° 1775.
    [Music J. Hook.]
  [O.F.] Valentine's Day. A Musical Drama (D.L. S. 23/3/1776) 8°
    1776; MS. Larpent 12. L. [2/3/1776].

HEARTWELL, HENRY.
  *C.O. The Prisoner; or, The Resemblance. Translated from the
    French 8° 1799.
    [Acted later as The Castle of Sorrento (H.² W. 17/7/1799) and
    taken from Alex. Duval, Le Prisonnier, ou La Ressemblance, with
    music by Domenico della Maria.]
  C.O. The Castle of Sorrento... Altered from the French, and adapted
    to the English Stage (H.² W. 17/7/1799) 8° 1799; 8° 1812; MS.
    Larpent 36. S. [26/6/1799].
    [In this alteration Heartwell was aided by GEORGE COLMAN.
    Music Thomas Attwood.]

HENDERSON, ANDREW.
  T. Arsinoe; or, The Incestuous Marriage 8° [1752].

HERON, ROBERT.
  *[O.F.] St. Kilda in Edinburgh; or, News from Camperdown (Edin-
    burgh W. 21/2/1798) 8° 1798; MS. Larpent 73. M. [Feb. 1728].
  *T. Pizarro; or, The Death of Rolla 8° 1799.

HEY, RICHARD.
  T. The Captive Monarch 8° 1794.

HIFFERNAN, Dr PAUL.
  C. The Self-Enamoured, or The Ladies Doctor 8° 1750 [Dublin].
  *[F.] The Lady's Choice. A Petite Piece (C.G. F. 20/4/1759); MS.
    Larpent 6. L. [31/3/1759].
  Dr. Poem. The Wishes of a Free People 8° 1761.
  *[F.] The New Hippocrates; Or, A Lesson for Quacks. A Dramatic
    Satire (D.L. W. 1/4/1761) MS. Larpent 5. M. [March 1761].
  T. The Earl of Warwick; or, The King and Subject 8° 1764; 8° 1767.
  *C. National Prejudice (D.L. W. 6/4/1768).
  [Sat.] The Philosophic Whim: or, Astronomy a Farce. In the Old
    Thespian Manner. Being a New and Humorous Display of the
    Universe, with Proper Elucidations 4° 1774.
  T. The Heroine of the Cave (D.L. S. 19/3/1774) 8° 1775; MS. Lar-
    pent 15. M. [11/3/1774].
    [This play was a revision by Hiffernan of a tragedy called The
    Cave of Idra, left unfinished by HENRY JONES.]

HILL, AARON
  [For his earlier works see the Handlist of Plays, 1700–1750.]
  T. The Insolvent: or Filial Piety... Partly on a Plan of Sir William
    Davenant's and Mr Massenger's (H.' M. 6/3/1758) 8° 1758.
  The Dramatic Works of Aaron Hill, 2 vols. 8° 1760.
    [Contain, besides earlier plays: 1. The Muses in Mourning;
    2. Merlin in Love; 3. The Snake in the Grass; 4. Daraxes; 5. The
    Roman Revenge (Bath c. 1753); 6. Saul; 7. The Insolvent: or, Filial
    Piety.]

HILL, Sir JOHN.
  O. Orpheus, An English Opera...With a Preface, appealing to the
       Publick for Justice, and laying before them a Fair and Impartial
       Account of the Quarrel between the Author and Mr Rich, who
       intends in a few weeks to perform such an Entertainment without
       his Concurrence F. 1740.
 *F. The Maiden Whim; or, The Critical Minute (D.L. S. 24/4/1756).
  F. The Rout (D.L. W. 20/12/1758) 8° 1758; MS. Larpent 5. L.
       [12/12/1758].

HILL, RICHARD.
  C. The Gospel Shop...With a New Prologue and Epilogue, originally
       intended for Public Representation, but suppressed at the particular
       desire of some eminent Divines 8° [c. 1770].

HILTON, WILLIAM.
       The Poetical Works of William Hilton 8° 1776.
       [Contains: 1. Arthur, Monarch of the Britons; 2. The Siege of
       Palmyra.]

HITCHCOCK, ROBERT.
  C. The Macaroni (York c. 1773; H.² Sept. 1773) 8° 1773 [2 editions];
       12° 1774; MS. Larpent 10. S. [Feb. 1773, as for T. R. York].
 *C. The Ladies Stratagem (York 1775).
  C. The Coquette: or, The Mistakes of the Heart (York and Hull c.
       1776; H.² Th. 9/10/1777) 8° 1777 [Bath]; MS. L. 395.

HOADLY, Dr BENJAMIN.
       [For an earlier work see the Hand-list of Plays, 1700–1750.]
 *C. The Tatlers (C.G. S. 29/4/1797) MS. Larpent 71. M. [12/4/1797].
       [This had remained in MS. and was acted posthumously.]

HOARE, PRINCE.
 *T. Such Things Were (Bath, 1/1/1788; D.L. M. 2/5/1796 as Julia;
       or S. T. W.) MS. Larpent 46. M. [1787; as The Tears of Virtue,
       or S. T. W.].
 [O.F.] No Song, No Supper. An Opera (D.L. F. 16/4/1790) 8° 1792
       [Dublin; pirated]; Songs, Duets, Trio and Finales in No Song
       No Supper 8° 1790; 8° 1792; 8° 1795; 8° 1798; MS. Larpent 52. M.
       [9/4/1790].
       [Music S. Storace.]
 *[Int.] The Cave of Trophonius (D.L. T. 3/5/1791) MS. Larpent
       54. M. [as "An Opera"; 26/4/1791].
       [Music S. Storace.]
  O. Dido, Queen of Carthage...With the Masque of Neptune's
       Prophecy (H.¹ W. 23/5/1792) 8° 1792.
       [Music S. Storace.]
 [O.F.] The Prize, or, 2, 5, 3, 8. A Musical Farce (H.¹ M. 11/3/1793)
       16° 1793 [Dublin; pirated]; 8° 1798 [pirated]; Songs, Duets, and
       Chorus in The Prize...A Farce 8° 1793; MS. Larpent 59. M.
       [5/3/1793].
       [Music S. Storace.]
 [O.F.] My Grandmother. A Musical Farce (H.² M. 16/12/1793) 12°
       1794 [pirated]; 12° 1795 [Dublin; pirated]; 12° 1796 [pirated];
       8° 1796 [pirated]; Songs, Trio and Finale of My Grandmother
       8° 1793; 8° 1794; MS. Larpent 25. S. [12/12/1793].
       [Music S. Storace.]

[O.F.] The Three and the Deuce: A Comic Drama (H.² W. 2/9/1795) 8° 1806; 8° 1809; 8° 1823; MS. Larpent 68. M. [25/8/1795].
[Music S. Storace.]

[O.F.] Lock and Key. A Musical Entertainment (C.G. T. 2/2/1796) 8° 1796; 8° 1797 [2nd]; Songs, Duets and Finales in Lock and Key. A Musical Farce 8° 1796; MS. Larpent 30. S. [19/1/1796; as *L. & K., or Bamboozell*].
[Music W. Shield.]

[M.D.] Songs, Duets, Trios, Finales, &c., in Mahmoud, a Musical Romance (D.L. S. 30/4/1796) 8° 1796; MS. Larpent 70. M. [28/4/1796].
[Music S. Storace, with a few selections from Sarti and Haydn, prepared for performance by Michael Kelly.]

*[C.O.] A Friend in Need Is a Friend Indeed (D.L. Th. 9/2/1797) MS. Larpent 33. M. [2/2/1797]. Songs, Trios, &c. and Finales in A. F. in N. 8° 1797.
[Music M. Kelly.]

*C.O. The Italian Villagers (C.G. T. 25/4/1797) MS. Larpent 31. S. [10/4/1797]. Airs, Duets, Trios, &c. &c. in the I.V. 8° 1797.
[Music Shield.]

[M.D.] The Captive of Spilburg...Altered from the...French Drama called Le Souterrain, with a Preface by the Translator (D.L. W. 14/11/1798) 8° 1799; MS. Larpent 73. M. [7/11/1798].
[Adapted from Marsollier, *Camille ou le Souterrain* (Paris, 1791). Music by M. Kelly and Dussek.]

C. Sighs; or, The Daughter...Taken from the German Drama of Kotzebue, with Alterations (H.² T. 30/7/1799) 8° 1799 [*bis*]; 12° 1802 [*Dublin*].

*[O.F.] Children; or, Give Them their Way (April 1800).
[Music Kelly; the *Biographia Dramatica* says the songs were printed.]

C. Indiscretion (D.L. May 1800) 8° 1800 [3 editions]; 12° 1803 [*Dublin*].
[For his later works see the Hand-list of Plays, 1800–1850.]

HODSON, WILLIAM.

T. Arsaces 8° 1775.

T. Zoraida...To which is added, A Postscript, containing Observations on Tragedy (D.L. M. 13/12/1779) 8° 1780; MS. Larpent 22. M. [26/11/1779].

F. The Adventures of a Night (D.L. M. 24/3/1783) 8° 1783; MS. Larpent 31. M. [28/2/1783].

HOLCROFT, THOMAS.

*C.O. The Crisis; or, Love and Fear (D.L. F. 1/5/1778).

C. Duplicity (C.G. S. 13/10/1781) 8° 1781 [2 editions]; 8° 1782 [3rd]; 12° 1782 [*Dublin*]; MS. Larpent 26. M. [9/10/1781].

C.O. The Noble Peasant (H.² M. 2/8/1784) 8° 1784; 12° 1784 [Dublin]; Songs, Duets, Glees, Choruses, &c. in...the Noble Peasant 8° 1784; MS. Larpent 34. M. [17/7/1784].
[Music chiefly William Shield.]

C. The Follies of a Day; or, The Marriage of Figaro...From the French of M. de Beaumarchais (C.G. T. 14/12/1784) 8° 1785 [*bis*];

8° 1811 [reduced to 3 acts]; MS. Larpent 34. M. [1784; as *The Marriage of Figarro*].

C.O. The Choleric Fathers (C.G. Th. 10/11/1785) 8° 1785; 12° 1786 [*Dublin*]; MS. Larpent 38. M.
[Music William Shield.]
Sacred Dramas; written in French, by Madame la Comtesse de Genlis. Translated into English 8° 1785; 12° 1786.
Theatre of Education. Translated from the French 8° 1781; 8° 1787.

C. Seduction (D.L. M. 12/3/1787) 8° 1787 [3 editions]; 12° 1787 [*Dublin*]; MS. Larpent 44. M. [1787].

*D. Louis in the Elysian Fields [in *Posthumous Works of Frederick II* 8° 1789, which also contains *The School of the World* and *Tantalus at Law*].

C. The German Hotel (C.G. Th. 11/11/1790) 8° 1790 [2 editions]; MS. Larpent 51. M. [2/11/1790].
[Attributed to Marshall on the first production.]

C. The School for Arrogance (C.G. F. 4/2/1791) 8° 1791 [2 editions]; 12° [*Dublin*; 1791]; MS. Larpent 55. M. [2/2/1791].

C. The Road to Ruin (C.G. S. 18/2/1792) 8° 1792 [10 editions]; 12° 1792 [*Dublin*]; 8° 1802; MS. Larpent 56. M. [7/2/1792].

C. Love's Frailties (C.G. W. 5/2/1794) 8° 1794; MS. Larpent 62. M. [4/1/1794; as *L. F., or Precept against Practice*].

*Prel. The Rival Queens, or Drury Lane and Covent Garden (C.G. M. 15/9/1794) MS. Larpent 63. M. [10/9/1794].

C. The Deserted Daughter (C.G. S. 2/5/1795) 8° 1795 [4 editions]; 8° 1806 [5th]; MS. Larpent 66. M. [17/4/1795].

C. The Man of Ten Thousand (D.L. S. 23/1/1796) 8° 1796 [3 editions]; MS. Larpent 68. M. [19/1/1795].

*C. The Force of Ridicule (D.L. T. 6/12/1796) MS. Larpent 30. S. [23/11/1796].

C. Knave or Not? (D.L. Th. 25/1/1798) 8° 1798; 12° 1798 [*Dublin*]; MS. Larpent 35. S. [8/1/1798].

C. He's Much to Blame (C.G. T. 13/2/1798) 8° 1798 [4 editions]; MS. Larpent 34. S. [Feb. 1798].

[D.] The Inquisitor; A Play (H.[1] S. 23/6/1798) 8° 1798; MS. Larpent 34. S. [21/6/1798].

*Int. The Old Clothesman (C.G. T. 2/4/1799) MS. Larpent 36. S. [Jan. 1799].
[Music T. Attwood; the play is attributed to Holcroft.]
[For his later works see the Hand-list of Plays, 1800–1850.]

HOLFORD, GEORGE.
Dramatic Poems 8° 1799.
[Contains: 1. *The Cave of Neptune*; 2. *The Storm*.]

HOLFORD, Mrs MARGARET.
C. Neither's the Man (Chester *c.* 1798) 8° [*Chester*; 1799]; MS. Larpent 33. S. [31/10/1798].

HOLMAN, JOSEPH GEORGE.
C.O. Abroad and at Home (C.G. S. 19/11/1796) 8° 1796 [5 editions]; 12° 1797 [*Dublin*]; 8° 1801; Songs, Duets, Trios,· Choruses, &c. in Abroad and at Home 8° 1796; MS. Larpent 70. M. [14/11/1796; as *The King's Bench*].
[Apparently the original title was *The King's Bench*, but this,

it is said, was objected to by the Lord Chamberlain. Music W. Shield.]

C.   The Votary of Wealth (C.G. S. 12/1/1799) 8° 1799 [4 editions]; 12° 1799 [*Dublin*]; MS. Larpent 37. S. [Jan. 1799].

[M.D.] The Red-Cross Knights. A Play...Founded on the Robbers of Schiller (H.² W. 21/8/1799) 8° 1799; Songs, Duets, and Choruses, in the Red-Cross Knights 8° 1799; MS. Larpent 36. S. [7/8/1799].
[Music T. Attwood.]

C.O. What a Blunder! (H.² Aug. 1800) 8° 1800.
[For his later works see the Hand-list of Plays, 1800-1850.]

HOME, JOHN.

T.   Douglas (Edinburgh, Dec. 1756; C.G. M. 14/3/1757) 8° 1757 [*Edinburgh*]; 8° 1757; 8° 1783.

T.   Agis (D.L. T. 21/2/1758) 8° 1758; 8° 1758 [*Dublin*]; MS. Larpent 6. L. [2/2/1758].
[Music Dr Boyce]

T.   The Siege of Aquileia (D.L. Th. 21/2/1760) 8° 1760; MS. Larpent 5. S. [7/2/1760].

T.   The Fatal Discovery (D.L. Th. 23/2/1769) 8° 1769; 12° [*Dublin*; 1769]; MS. Larpent 10. M. [14/2/1769].

T.   Alonzo (D.L. S. 27/2/1773) 8° 1773 [*bis*]; 12° 1773 [*Dublin*]; MS. Larpent 11. S. [29/1/1773].

T.   Alfred (C.G. W. 21/1/1778) 8° 1778 [*bis*]; MS. Larpent 19. M. [13/1/1778].

HOOK, Mrs JAMES [HARRIET HORNCASTLE].

[O.F.] The Double Disguise, A Comic Opera (D.L. M. 8/3/1784) 8° 1784; Songs in The Double Disguise 8° 1784; MS. Larpent 37. M. [6/2/1784].
[Music James Hook.]

HOOK, Rev. Dr JAMES.

*C.O. Jack of Newbury (D.L. W. 6/5/1795) Songs, Choruses, &c. in J. of N. 8° 1795. MS. Larpent 67. M. [9/4/1795].
[Music James Hook.]

*C.O. Diamond cut Diamond; or, Venetian Revels (C.G. T. 23/5/1797). L. 1172 [as *A Venetian Tale (UA)*.]

HOOLE, JOHN.

T.   Cyrus (C.G. S. 3/12/1768) 8° 1768; 8° 1772 [3rd]; MS. Larpent 9. M. [20/11/1768].

T.   Timanthes (C.G. S. 24/2/1770) 8° 1770 [3 editions]; MS. Larpent 11. M. [31/1/1770].

T.   Cleonice, Princess of Bithynia (C.G. Th. 2/3/1775) 8° 1775; MS. Larpent 15. M.
The Works of Metastasio. Translated from the Italian, 2 vols. 8° 1767.
Dramas of the Abbé Pietro Metastasio. Translated from the Italian 8° 1800.

HORDE, THOMAS, Junior.

T.   Leander and Hero 8° 1769.

T.   Zelida 8° 1772 [*Oxford*].

*C. Dramatic Love 8° 1773 [*Oxford*].

[Int.] Damon and Phebe; a Musical Entertainment 8° 1774 [*Oxford*].
Ent. Disappointed Villainy 8° 1775 [*Oxford*].
F.   The Pretended Puritan 8° 1779 [*Oxford*].
F.   The Whimsical Serenade 8° 1781 [*Oxford*].
F.   The Female Pedant 8° 1782 [*Oxford*].
F.   Intrigue in a Cloyster 8° 1783 [*Oxford*].
*F. Nature Will Prevail 8° 1784 [*Oxford*].
*F. Love in a Mystery 8° 1786.
F.   It was Right at the Last 8° [*Oxford*; 1787].
     [The *Biographia Dramatica* mentions the titles of three other
     plays, *As the World Goes*, *The Empirick* and *A Paradise of Fools*,
     but the editors do not appear to have seen copies of these works.]

HOUGH, J.
   [C.O.] Second Thought is Best...in which is introduced the Song
   rejected by the Lord Chamberlain (D.L. M. 30/3/1778) 8° 1788
   [in error for 1778].

HOULTON, ROBERT.
   *C.O. The Contract (S.A. Dublin 14/5/1782; revived in altered form
   as *The Double Stratagem*, Capel-street, May 1784).
      [Music Cogan and Stevenson; the songs are included in the
      Haliday collection of pamphlets, no. 451, Library of the Royal Irish
      Academy.]
   *Int. The Female Angler; or, A Sure Bait for a Good Husband (S.A.
   Dublin, 24/5/1783; called in the *Biographia Dramatica*, *A Dialogue
   between a Mother and a Daughter*).
   *C.O. Gibraltar (Capel-street, Dublin, 18/12/1783).
      [Music T. Giordani.]
   *Burl. Orpheus and Eurydice (Capel-street, Dublin, 14/6/1784).
      [Music T. Giordani.]
   [C.O.] Songs, Duets, Trios, Chorusses and Finales, in Calypso, a
   serio-comic Opera (S.A. Dublin, 9/4/1785, as *Calypso, or, Love
   and Enchantment*) 8° 1785 [*Dublin*].
      [Music T. Giordani.]
   C.O. Wilmore Castle: a new Comic Opera (D.L. Oct. 1800) 8° 1800.
   [Music James Hook.]

HOUSTON, Lady.
   *C. The Coquettes; or, The Gallant in the Closet (Scotland?).

HOWARD, FREDERIC, Earl of CARLISLE.
   T.   The Father's Revenge 4° 1783.
   T.   The Step-Mother 8° 1800.

HOWARD, GEORGES EDMOND.
   T.   Almeyda, or, The Rival Kings *12° 1769; 8° 1769 [*Dublin*; 2nd
        with alterations]; 8° 1769 [3rd].
   T.   The Siege of Tamar (S.A. Dublin, 26/4/1774) *8° 1773; 8° 1773
        [*Dublin*; 2nd]; 8° 1773 [3rd].
        [It is said that the author received some aid from *HENRY
        BROOKE* in the lyric portions.]
        Miscellaneous works, in Verse and Prose 8° 1782 [*Dublin*].
        [Contains: 1. *Almeyda*; 2. *The Siege of Tamar*; 3. *The Female
        Gamester*.]

HUDSON, WILLIAM.
   T.   Zoraida (D.L. M. 13/12/1779) 8° 1780 [*bis*].

HUGHES, Mrs ANNE.
   Moral Drama's, intended for Private Presentation 8° 1790.
   [Contains: 1. *Cordelia*; 2. *Constantia*; 3. *Aspacia*.]

HULL, THOMAS.
   *C. The Twins; or, The Comedy of Errors (C.G. S. 24/4/1762).
      L. 212 [as *The Comedy of Errors*] 8° 1793.
   *F. The Absent Man (C.G. S. 28/4/1764).
   O. Pharnaces...altered from the Italian (D.L. F. 15/2/1765) 8° 1765;
      MS. Larpent 7. S. [26/1/1765].
      [Music William Bates. Altered from *Farnace* (Bologna, Theatro
      Malvezzi, spring 1731) by Antonio Maria Lucchini.]
   [Int.] The Spanish Lady, A Musical Entertainment...Founded on the
      Plan of the Old Ballad (C.G. Th. 2/5/1765) 8° [1765]; MS. Lar-
      pent 7. M. [22/1/1763].
   *F. All in the Right (C.G. S. 26/4/1766) MS. Larpent 9. L.
   C. The Perplexities (C.G. S. 31/1/1767) 8° 1767; MS. Larpent 9. L.
      [16/1/1767].
   M. The Fairy Favour (C.G. S. 31/1/1767) 8° 1766; MS. Larpent 8. M.
      [16/10/1766].
   C.O. The Royal Merchant. An Opera. Founded on Beaumont and
      Fletcher (C.G. M. 14/12/1767) 8° 1768; 12° 1768 [Dublin]; MS.
      Larpent 8. M. [2/12/1767].
      [Music Thomas Linley.]
   T. Henry the Second; or, The Fall of Rosamond (C.G. S. 1/5/1773)
      8° 1774 [3 editions]; 8° 1795; MS. Larpent 10. S. [1773].
   T. Edward and Eleonora...Altered from James Thomson (C.G. S.
      18/3/1775) 8° 1775.
   C.O. Airs, Duets, Trios, &c., in the New Comic Opera, called, Love
      Finds the Way (C.G. T. 18/11/1777) 8° 1777 [*bis*].
      [An alteration of A. Murphy, *The School for Guardians*. Music
      Dr Arne, Sacchini and Dr Fisher.]
   *T. Iphigenia; or, The Victim (C.G. M. 23/3/1778).
   C. The Comedy of Errors (C.G. F. 22/1/1779). [See *Shakespeare's
      Comedy of Errors. Adapted to the Stage by Thomas Hull. Revised
      by J. P. Kemble* 8° 1811; and above *The Twins*.]
   *T. The Fatal Interview (D.L. S. 16/11/1782) MS. Larpent 28. M.
      [12/10/1782].
   *[Int.] The True British Tar; or, A Friend at a Pinch (1786).
   *T. Timon of Athens (C.G. S. 13/5/1786).
   *C. Disinterested Love (C.G. W. 30/5/1798) MS. Larpent 72. M.
      [19/5/1798].
      [An alteration of P. Massinger, *The Bashful Lover*.]

HUNTER, GEORGE M.
   *T. Louis and Antoinette 8° 1794.

HURDIS, Dr JAMES.
   *T. Panthea [see *Biographia Dramatica*, iii. 126].
   T. Sir Thomas More 8° 1792; 8° 1793 [2nd].

HURLSTONE, THOMAS.
   C.O. Just in Time (C.G. Th. 10/5/1792) 8° [1792]; 8° 1792; 12° 1793
      [*Dublin*]; 8° 1798; MS. Larpent 58. M. [1/5/1792].
      [Music T. Carter.]

Int. To Arms! or, The British Recruit. A Musical Interlude (C.G.
   F. 3/5/1793) 8° 1793; MS. Larpent 26. S. [1793; printed copy].
   [Music W. Shield and T. Giordani.]
F. Crotchet Lodge (C.G. S. 14/2/1795) 8° [1795]; 8° 1796; MS.
   Larpent 28. S. [7/2/1795].

HYDE, HENRY, Lord HYDE and VISCOUNT CORNBURY.
C. The Mistakes; or, The Happy Resentment 8° 1758.

INCHBALD, Mrs ELIZABETH.
[Int.] A Mogul Tale (H.² T. 6/7/1784; as *A M.T.; or The Descent of the
   Balloon*) 12° 1824; MS. Larpent 37. M. [29/5/1784].
C. I'll Tell You What (H.² Th. 4/8/1785) 8° 1786; 8° 1787 [2nd];
   12° 1787 [*Dublin*]; MS. Larpent 38. M. [30/4/1785].
F. Appearance is against Them (C.G. S. 22/10/1785) 8° 1785; 12°
   1786 [*Dublin*]; MS. Larpent 19. S.
F. The Widow's Vow (H.² T. 20/6/1786) 8° 1786.
[D.] Such Things Are. A Play (C.G. S. 10/2/1787) 8° 1788 [*bis*]; 12°
   1788 [*Dublin*]; 8° 1800 [12th]; MS. Larpent 44. M. [1787].
F. The Midnight Hour; or, War of Wits...Translated from the
   French (C.G. T. 22/5/1787) 8° 1787; 12° 1787 [*Dublin*]; 8° 1788;
   12° 1788 [*Dublin*]; MS. Larpent 46. M. [10/5/1787].
   [This farce was advertised for T. 22/5/1787.]
*C. All on a Summer's Day (C.G. S. 15/12/1787) MS. Larpent
   46. M.
[F.] Animal Magnetism (C.G. T. 29/4/1788) 12° 1792 [*Dublin*;
   pirated]; 12° [1789]; MS. Larpent 47. M.
[D.] The Child of Nature, a Dramatic Piece...from the French of
   Madame the Marchioness of Sillery, formerly Countess of Genlis
   (C.G. F. 28/11/1788) 8° 1788; 8° 1789 [2nd]; 12° 1789 [*Dublin*];
   12° 1790; 8° 1794; 8° 1800 [6th]; 8° 1806 [7th].
C. The Married Man...from Le Philosophe Marie of Mr Nericault
   Destouches (H.² W. 15/7/1789) 8° 1789; 12° 1789 [*Dublin*]; MS.
   Larpent 50. M. [2/7/1789].
*F. The Hue and Cry (D.L. W. 11/5/1791) MS. Larpent 54. M.
   [26/4/1791].
C. Next Door Neighbours...From the French Dramas L'Indigent
   & Le Dissipateur (H.² S. 9/7/1791) 8° 1791; MS. Larpent 23. S.
   [4/7/1791].
*F. Young Men and Old Women (H.² S. 30/6/1792).
C. Every One has his Fault (C.G. T. 29/1/1793) 8° 1792; 12° 1793
   [*Dublin*]; 8° 1793 [5 editions]; 8° 1794 [7th]; MS. Larpent 61. M.
   [12/1/1793].
[F.] The Wedding Day. A Comedy (D.L. S. 1/11/1794) 8° 1794; MS.
   Larpent 65. M. [31/10/1794].
C. Wives as they Were and Maids as they Are (C.G. S. 4/3/1797)
   8° 1797 [6 editions]; MS. Larpent 32. S. [10/2/1797; as *The
   Primitive Wife and Modern Maid*].
[D.] Lovers' Vows, A Play...From the German of Kotzebue (C.G.
   Th. 11/10/1798) 8° 1798 [11 editions]; MS. Larpent 35. S.
   [28/9/1798].
[D.] The Wise Man of the East, a Play...from the German of Kotze-
   bue (C.G. S. 30/11/1799) 8° 1799 [3 editions]; MS. Larpent 19. L
   [14/11/1799].
C. To Marry, or Not to Marry (C.G. Feb. 1805) 8° 1805.

IRELAND, SAMUEL WILLIAM HENRY.
T.   Vortigern, an Historical Tragedy (D.L. 2/4/1796) 8° 1799; 8° 1832;
     MS. Larpent 70. M. [4/2/1796].
[T.] Henry the Second, an Historical Drama 8° 1799.
        [Both these plays were issued in 1799 with a general title
        page.]
[T.] Mutius Scaevola; or, The Roman Patriot. An Historical Drama
     8° 1801.

JACKMAN, ISAAC.
[O.F.] The Milesian, A Comic Opera (D.L. Th. 20/3/1777) 8° 1777
       [*bis*]; Songs and Duets in...The Milesian 8° 1777; MS. Larpent
       14. S. [14/3/1777].
        [Music T. Carter.]
F.   All the World's a Stage (D.L. M. 7/4/1777) 8° 1777 [3 editions];
     MS. Larpent 14. S. [31/3/1777].
[O.F.] The Divorce. A Farce (D.L. S. 10/11/1781) 8° 1781; 8° 1782
       [2nd]; 12° 1790 [*Dublin*]; MS. Larpent 17. S. [2/11/1781].
F.   The Man of Parts: or, A Trip to London (S.A. Dublin, Dec. 1785)
     12° 1795 [*Dublin*, as at Crow-street].
Burl. Hero and Leander (Royalty 1787) 8° [1787]; 8° 1787 [with title:
     *Royal and Royalty Theatres. Letter to Phillips Glover, Esq. of
     Wispington, in Lincolnshire; in a Dedication to the Burletta of Hero
     and Leander*].
*Burlesque. Almirina (Royalty M. 23/6/1788).

JACKSON, JOHN.
T.   Eldred; or The British Freeholder (Capel-street, Dublin 2/12/1773;
     Edinburgh, 19/3/1774; H.² F. 7/7/1775) 8° 1782; MS. Larpent 12.
     L. [1775; as *E., or the B. Father*].
*T. The British Heroine (C.G. T. 5/5/1778; this had been acted at
     Dublin on M. 13/1/1777 as *Geralda; or, The Siege of Harlech*);
     MS. Larpent 13. L. [28/4/1778].
*T. Sir William Wallace, of Ellerslie; or, The Siege of Dumbarton
     Castle (Edinburgh W. 26/7/1780).

JACKSON, WILLIAM.
[Int.] Lycidas: A Musical Entertainment...The Words altered from
       Milton (C.G. W. 4/11/1767) 8° 1767; MS. Larpent 8. M.
       [3/11/1767].
        [Music by the author.]
C.O. Songs, Duets, &c., in The Metamorphosis (D.L. F. 5/12/1783)
     8° 1783; MS. Larpent 33. M. [25/11/1783].
        [Music by the author.]

JAMES, C.
O.   Tarare 8° 1787.
        [A version of Beaumarchais, *Tarare*, with music by A. Salieri.]

JENNER, CHARLES.
*[Int.] Lucinda [in *Letters from Lothario to Penelope* 12° 1770].
C.   The Man of Family: A Sentimental Comedy 8° 1771; 12° 1771.

JEPHSON, ROBERT.
T.   Braganza (D.L. F. 17/2/1775) 8° 1775 [*bis*]; 8° 1776.
T.   The Law of Lombardy (D.L. M. 8/2/1779) 8° 1779; 12° 1779
     [*Dublin*]; MS. Larpent 20. M. [26/1/1779].

T.   The Count of Narbonne (C.G. S. 17/11/1781) 8° 1781; MS. Larpent 25. M. [12/11/1781].

F.   The Hotel: or, The Servant with Two Masters (S.A. Dublin, 8/5/1783) 12° 1784 [*Dublin*].

C.O. Songs, Chorusses, &c., in The Campaign, or Love in the East Indies (S.A. Dublin, Jan. 1784; C.G. Th. 12/5/1785) 8° 1785; MS. Larpent 40. M.

*[Int.] Love and War (C.G. Th. 15/3/1787).
   [An abridgment of *The Campaign, q.v.*]

T.   Julia; or, The Italian Lover (D.L. S. 14/4/1787) 8° 1787 [*bis*]; 8° [1802]; MS. Larpent 45. M. [1787].

F.   Two Strings to Your Bow (C.G. W. 16/2/1791) 8° 1791 [*bis*]; 8° 1806.

T.   Conspiracy (D.L. T. 15/11/1796) 8° 1796 [*Dublin*; probably pirated]; MS. Larpent 70. M. [30/3/1796].

JERNINGHAM, EDWARD.
   Poems and Plays... In Four Volumes 8° 1806.
   [Contains, besides the other plays published separately: *Margaret of Anjou* (D.L. T. 11/3/1777).]

T.   The Siege of Berwick (C.G. W. 13/11/1793) 8° 1794; MS. Larpent 60. M. [10/11/1793].

C.   The Welch Heiress (D.L. F. 17/4/1795) 8° 1795 [*bis*]; 8° 1796 [3rd]; 8° 1798 [4th]; MS. Larpent 28. S. [9/4/1795].

[F.] The Peckham Frolic: or Nell Gwyn. A Comedy 8° 1799.

JODRELL, RICHARD PAUL.
   [F.] A Widow and No Widow. A Dramatic Piece (H.² S. 17/7/1779) 8° 1780; 12° 1780 [*Dublin*]; MS. Larpent 13. L. [1779].

   [F.] Seeing is Believing: A Dramatic Proverb (H.² F. 22/8/1783) 8° 1786; MS. Larpent 32. M. [16/8/1783].

T.   The Persian Heroine 8° 1786; 4° 1786 [2nd].
   Select Dramatic Pieces, some of which have been acted in Provincial Theatres, others written for Private Performance and Country Amusement: viz., The Boarding School Miss, One and All, The Disguise, The Musico, Who's Afraid, and The Bulse 8° 1787.

JOHNSTONE, JAMES.
   C.   The Disbanded Officer; or, The Baroness of Bruchsal (H.² M. 24/7/1786) 8° 1786; 12° 1786 [*Dublin*]; MS. Larpent 41. M. [29/6/1786].

JONES, HENRY.
   T.   The Earl of Essex (C.G. W. 21/2/1753) 8° 1753; 12° 1753 [*Dublin*]; 8° 1754 [2nd]; MS. Larpent 4. L. [14/2/1750].
   [The epilogue as written by the author, but not spoken, is given in *The Gray's-Inn Journal* No. 20, March 3, 1753.]
   [For *The Cave of Idra* see under *PAUL HIFFERNAN.*]

JONES, HENRY [*Shoemaker*].
   [M.] Lucy. A Dramatic Poem 8° [1780?].

JONES, LINDESIUS.
   *Sat. The Authors 8° 1755.

JONES, Sir WILLIAM.
   [T.C.] Sacontalá, or The Fatal Ring, an Indian Drama by Calidas. Translated from the original Sanscrit and Pracrit 8° 1789 [*Calcutta*]; 8° 1789; 4° 1790; 8° 1792; 8° 1796.

KEATE, GEORGE.
Dr. Poem. The Monument in Arcadia 4° 1773.
*T. Semiramis [see the *Biographia Dramatica*, iii. 257].

KELLY, HUGH.
F. L'Amour A-la-Mode; or, Love-a-la-Mode 8° 1760.
   [Attributed to Kelly.]
C. False Delicacy (D.L. S. 23/1/1768) 8° 1768 [4 editions]; MS. Lar-
   pent 9. M. [16/1/1768].
   [Additions to the play are said to have been made by *DAVID
   GARRICK*.]
C. A Word to the Wise (D.L. S. 3/3/1770) 8° 1770; 8° 1773; 8° 1775;
   MS. Larpent 9. S. [15/2/1770].
T. Clementina (C.G. S. 23/2/1771) 8° 1771 [*bis*]; MS. Larpent 11. M.
   [14/2/1771].
C. The School for Wives (D.L. S. 11/12/1773) 8° 1774 [4 editions];
   8° 1775; MS. Larpent 14. M. [29/11/1773].
C. The Romance of an Hour (C.G. F. 2/12/1774) 8° 1774 [*bis*]; MS.
   Larpent 14. M. [24/9/1774].
*C. The Man of Reason (C.G. F. 9/2/1776).

KEMBLE, JOHN PHILIP.
*T. Belisarius or Injured Innocence (Liverpool and Hull 1778; York
   1779) MS. Larpent 13. L. [27/7/1778, for Liverpool].
*F. The Female Officer (Manchester 1778) MS. Larpent 14. S.
   [1/1/1778].
   [Acted at D.L. S. 18/2/1786 as *The Projects*; MS. Larpent 41. M.
   1786.]
*C. Oh! It's Impossible (York 1780) MS. Larpent 15. L. [4/2/1780].
*C. The Maid of Honour (D.L. Th. 27/1/1785) MS. Larpent 40. M.
   [1785].
*C. The Pilgrim (D.L. F. 26/10/1787) 8° 1787.
T. Shakespear's King Lear. As Altered by N. Tate, Newly Revised
   by J. P. Kemble (D.L. M. 21/1/1788) 8° 1788.
F. The Pannel. An Entertainment...Altered from the Comedy of
   "'Tis Well it's no Worse" (D.L. F. 28/11/1788) 8° 1789; The
   Pannel. As Altered...from Bickerstaff's Translation of Calderon's
   El Escondido y la Tapada 8° [1789].
*T. Coriolanus (D.L. S. 7/2/1789) 8° 1789.
[F.] The Farm House. A Comedy (D.L. F. 1/5/1789) 8° 1789 [*bis*];
   12° 1789 [*Dublin*].
T. King Henry V, or The Conquest of France (D.L. Th. 1/10/1789)
   8° 1789.
C. The Tempest; or, The Enchanted Island...with Additions from
   Dryden (D.L. T. 13/10/1789) 8° 1789; Shakespeare's Tempest, or,
   The Enchanted Island. A Play. Adapted to the Stage, with
   Additions from Dryden and Davenant 8° 1806.
*C. The False Friend (D.L. S. 24/10/1789).
   [An alteration of Vanbrugh's comedy.]
[C.] Love in Many Masks. As Altered...from Mrs. Behn's Rover
   (D.L. M. 8/3/1790) 8° [1790]; MS. Larpent 51. M. [8/3/1790].
T. Macbeth (D.L. M. 21/4/1794) 8° [1794].
M.D. Lodoiska. An Opera (D.L. M. 9/6/1794) 8° [1794; *bis*]; 8° 1801
   [3rd]; Songs in Lodoiska. A Musical Romance 8° 1794 [*bis*].
   [Music Cherubini, Kreutzer, Andreozzi, selected by S. Storace.]

C. Shakespeare's All's Well that Ends Well. With Alterations (D.L. F. 12/12/1794) 8° 1793.

*[T.] The Roman Actor. A Piece in Two Acts (D.L. 23/5/1796) MS. Larpent 27. S. [16/10/1794].
[An alteration from Massinger.]

T. Lees Tragedy of Alexander the Great (D.L. M. 23/11/1795) 8° 1796.

*C. The Plain Dealer (D.L. S. 27/2/1796) 8° 1796.

C. The Merry Wives of Windsor (D.L.) 8° 1797.

*C. Celadon and Florimel; or, The Happy Counterplot (D.L. M. 23/5/1796) MS. Larpent 31. S. [12/5/1796].

*C. Much Ado about Nothing (C.G. F. 6/10/1797).
[For his later works see the Hand-list of Plays, 1800–1850.]

KEMBLE, Mrs MARIE-THERESE [Miss DE CAMP].
*C. First Faults (D.L. F. 3/5/1799) MS. Larpent 37. S. [29/4/1799].
[For her later work see the Biographia Dramatica.]

KEMBLE, STEPHEN.
*F. The Northern Inn; or, The Good Times of Queen Bess (H.² T. 16/8/1791) MS. Larpent 24. S. [23/7/1791; as The Northern Lass, or The Days of Good Queen Bess].

KENRICK, WILLIAM.
Sat. Fun: A Parodi-Tragi-Comical Satire. As it was to have been Perform'd at the Castle-Tavern, Pater-noster-Row, on Thursday, February 13, 1752, But suppressed, By a Special Order from the Lord-Mayor and Court of Aldermen 8° 1752.

C. Falstaff's Wedding...Being a Sequel to the Second Part of the Play of King Henry the Fourth. Written in Imitation of Shakespeare (D.L. S. 12/4/1766) 8° 1760 [evidently in error for 1766, the preface being dated Jan. 1, 1766]; 8° 1766 [bis]; 8° 1773; 8° 1781; MS. Larpent 8. L. [4/4/1766].

C. The Widow'd Wife (D.L. S. 5/12/1767) 8° 1767; 12° 1768 [Dublin]; MS. Larpent 8. M. [28/11/1767].

C. The Duellist (C.G. S. 20/11/1773) 8° 1773 [3 editions]; MS. Larpent 11. L. [1/11/1773].

C.O. The Lady of the Manor (C.G. M. 23/11/1778) 8° 1778 [3 editions]; MS. Larpent 18. M. [19/11/1778].
[Music Hook.]

*F. The Spendthrift; or, A Christmas Gambol (C.G. M. 21/12/1778) MS. Larpent 18. M. [Dec. 1778].

KING, THOMAS.
[B.O.] Love at First Sight: A Ballad Farce (D.L. M. 17/10/1763) 8° 1763; MS. Larpent 7. M. [1763].

F. Wit's Last Stake (D.L. Th. 14/4/1768) 8° 1769 [bis]; 8° 1803 [4th]; MS. Larpent 9. M. [5/4/1768].

KNAPP, HENRY.
*F. The Exciseman (C.G. S. 4/11/1780).

[O.F.] The Musical Farce of Hunt the Slipper (H.² S. 21/8/1784) 12° 1792 [Dublin; pirated]; MS. Larpent 34. M. [20/5/1784].

KNIGHT, THOMAS.
*[Sat.] Thelyphthora; or, The Blessings of Two Wives at Once (Hull 1783).

*Prel. Trudge and Wowski (Bristol 1790).

F. The Honest Thieves...Altered from The Committee (C.G. T. 9/5/1797) 12° 1797; 8° 1820; MS. Larpent 71. M. [26/4/1797].

[C.O.] The Turnpike Gate; A Musical Entertainment (C.G. Th. 14/11/1799) 8° 1799 [bis]; 8° 1801 [5th]; 8° 1806 [6th]; Songs, Duets, and Chorusses, in The Turnpike Gate. A Comic Opera 8° 1799; MS. Larpent 19. L. [17/10/1799].
[Music J. Mazzinghi and W. Reeve.]

LANGHORNE, Dr JOHN.
The Poetical Works of John Langhorne, 2 vols. 12° 1766.
[Contains: *The Fatal Prophecy, a Dramatic Poem.*]

LATHOM, FRANCIS.
C. All in a Bustle *8° 1795 [*Norwich*]; 8° 1800 [*Norwich*; 2nd].
F. Holiday Time; or, The School Boy's Frolic (Norwich *c.* 1799) 8° 1800.
[D.] Orlando and Seraphina; or, The Funeral Pile. An Heroic Drama (Norwich *c.* 1799) 12° [1799].
C. The Dash of the Day (Norwich *c.* 1799) 8° 1800 [Norwich; *bis*].

LATTER, MARY.
T. The Siege of Jerusalem, By Titus Vespasian...To which is prefixed, by Way of Introduction, An Essay on the Mystery and Mischiefs of Stage-Craft 8° 1763.

LAWRENCE, ROSE.
[D.] Gortz of Berlingen, with The Iron Hand. An Historical Drama, Of the Fifteenth Century. Translated from the German of Goethe 8° [1799].

LEAPOR, MARY.
Poems upon Several Occasions, 2 vols. 8° 1751.
[Contains: *The Unhappy Father, a Tragedy.*]

LEARMONT, JOHN.
Poems Pastoral, Satirical, Tragic and Comic 8° 1791 [*Edinburgh*].
[Contains: *The Unequal Rivals, a Pastoral.*]

LEE, [HENRY?].
[O.F.] Songs...in a new Musical Farce, called Throw Physic to the Dogs! (H.¹ F. 6/7/1798) MS. Larpent 34. S. [29/6/1798; as *T. P. to the D., or Jack of all Trades*].
[Music S. Arnold.]

LEE, HARRIET.
C. The New Peerage; or, Our Eyes may deceive us (D.L. S. 10/11/1787) 8° 1787 [*bis*]; 12° [1787; *Dublin*]; 12° 1788 [*Dublin*]; MS. Larpent 45. M. [1787].
[M.D.] The Mysterious Marriage, or the Heirship of Roselva: A Play 8° 1798.

LEE, JOHN.
T. The Historical Tragedy of Macbeth (Written originally by Shakspear). Newly adapted to the Stage. With Alterations (Edinburgh *c.* 1753) 8° 1753 [*Edinburgh*].
[F.] The Country Wife. A Comedy...Altered from Wycherley (D.L. F. 26/4/1765) 8° [1765]; 8° 1786.
F. The Man of Quality...Taken from the Comedy of The Relapse (C.G. T. 27/4/1773) 8° [1773].
*T. Romeo and Juliet (C.G. M. 29/9/1777).

LEE, R. G.
*[D.] The Ransom of Manilla; or England's Ally. An Historical Play
8° 1793.

LEE, SOPHIA.
C. The Chapter of Accidents (H.² S. 5/8/1780) 8° 1780 [bis]; 8°
1781 [3rd]; 8° 1782 [4th]; 8° 1792 [5th]; MS. Larpent 16. S.
[23/5/1780].
T. Almeyda: Queen of Granada (D.L. W. 20/4/1796) 8° 1796; 12°
1796 [Dublin]; MS. Larpent 70. M. [19/2/1796].
*C. The Assignation (D.L. Jan. 1807).

LEFANU, PETER.
Prel. Smock Alley Secrets; or, The Manager Worried (S.A. Dublin
W. 1/11/1780). A MS. of this prelude was in the theatrical collection
of H. Houdini at New York.

LENNOX, CHARLOTTE.
Past. Philander. A Dramatic Pastoral 8° 1758.
[An edition of 1757 is mentioned in the Biographia Dramatica;
this I have never met with.]
C. The Sister (C.G. S. 18/2/1769) 8° 1769 [bis]; MS. Larpent 10. M.
[31/1/1769].
C. Old City Manners...Altered from the Original Eastward Hoe
(D.L. Th. 9/11/1775) 8° 1775; MS. Larpent 12. L. [3/11/1775].

LEWIS, EDWARD.
[T.] The Italian Husband: or, The Violated Bed Avenged. A Moral
Drama 8° 1754.

LEWIS, MATTHEW GREGORY ["MONK" LEWIS].
*Sat. Village Virtues 4° 1796.
T. The Minister...Translated from the German of Schiller 8° 1797;
8° 1798.
[M.D.] The Castle Spectre: A Drama (D.L. Th. 14/12/1797) 8° 1798
[7 editions]; 12° 1798 [Dublin]; 8° 1799 [8th]; MS. Larpent 72. M.
[27/11/1797].
[Music chiefly M. Kelly.]
T. Rolla; or, The Peruvian Hero. Translated from the German ot
Kotzebue 8° 1799 [4 editions].
*F. The Twins; or, Is it He or his Brother? (D.L. M. 8/4/1799) MS.
Larpent 19. L. [28/3/1799].
C. The East Indian (D.L. M. 22/4/1799) 8° 1800 [bis]; Rivers or
The East Indian 12° 1800 [Dublin].
[For his later works see the Hand-list of Plays, 1800–1850.]

LILLO, GEORGE.
[For his earlier works see the Hand-list of Plays, 1700–1750.]
[T.] Arden of Feversham. A New Historical Play...Taken from
Holingshead's Chronicle (D.L. Th. 12/7/1759) 8° 1775 [in Works];
MS. Larpent 6. L. [29/6/1759].
[Completed by Dr JOHN HOADLY.]

LINLEY, WILLIAM.
*C.O. Songs...in...The Honey Moon (D.L. S. 7/1/1797) 8° 1797;
MS. Larpent 30. S. [31/12/1796].
[Both words and music seem to have been by Linley.]

[Int.] Songs, Duets, &c., in The Pavilion, a Musical Entertainment
(D.L. W. 16/11/1799) 8° [1799]; MS. Larpent 37. S. [29/3/1799].
[Music Linley.]

*[Int.] The Ring; or, Love me for Myself (D.L. Jan. 1800) 8° 1800;
MS. Larpent 38. S. [13/1/1800].
[An alteration of *The Pavilion, q.v.*]

LINNECAR, RICHARD.
The Miscellaneous Works of Richard Linnecar of Wakefield 8°
1789 [*Leeds*].
[Contains: 1. *The Lucky Escape*; 2. *The Generous Moor*; 3. *The
Plotting Wives*. The last was acted at York *c.* 1789, and *The
Generous Moor* was performed at Wakefield in Sept. 1792.]

LLOYD, ——.
[O.F.] The Romp. A Musical Entertainment...Altered from Love in
the City (C.G. S. 28/3/1778) 8° 1786; 8° 1789.
[Music C. Dibdin.]

LLOYD, HANNIBAL EVANS.
[D.] The Nephews: A Play...Freely Translated from the German of
William Augustus Iffland 8° 1799 [*Oxford*].

LLOYD, ROBERT.
*M. The Tears and Triumphs of Parnassus (D.L. 1760) 4° 1760.
[Music Stanley.]
Past. Arcadia; or, The Shepherd's Wedding. A Dramatic Pastoral
(D.L. M. 26/10/1761) 8° 1761; 8° [1778].
[Music Stanley.]
C.   The New School for Women...from the French of Mr. De
Moissy [in *The St James's Magazine*, 1762, i. 162].
T.   The Death of Adam...From the German of Mr. Klopstock 12°
1763.
[It is said that part of Act II was written by *GEORGE COLMAN,
The Elder.*]
C.O. The Capricious Lovers (D.L. W. 28/11/1764) 8° 1764; 12° 1764
[*Dublin*]; MS. Larpent 7. S. [16/11/1764].
[Music Rush. Based on Favart, *Le Caprice amoureux ou Ninette
à la Cour.*]

LOGAN, JOHN.
T.   Runnamede 8° 1784; MS. Larpent 36. M. [1784].
[An adaptation of Voltaire, *Tancrède.*]
*C. The Wedding Day [a translation of Mercier, *Le Déserteur*; see
Biographia Dramatica, iii. 394].

LONSDALE, MARK.
[O.F.] The Spanish Rivals. A Musical Farce (D.L. Th. 4/11/1784)
8° 1784; Songs...in...The Spanish Rivals 8° 1784; MS. Larpent
35. M. [1784].
[Music T. Linley.]
*P. Mago and Dago; or, Harlequin the Hero (C.G. F. 26/12/1794).

LOVE, JAMES [JAMES DANCE].
[For his earlier works see the Hand-list of Plays, 1700–1750.]
*P. The Witches; or, Harlequin Cherokee (D.L. T. 23/11/1762).
*P. The Rites of Hecate; or, Harlequin from the Moon (D.L. M.
26/12/1763) MS. Larpent 7. M. [1764].

*P. The Hermit; or, Harlequin at Rhodes (D.L. M. 6/1/1766).

Past. The Village Wedding: or, The Faithful Country Maid, a Pastoral
Entertainment (Richmond S. 18/7/1767) 8° 1767.

T.C. Timon of Athens...Altered from Shakespear and Shadwell
(Richmond *c.* 1768) 8° 1768 [*bis*]; 8° 1780.

*C.O. The Ladies Frolick (D.L. 7/5/1770).
[An alteration of Brome, *The Jovial Crew.*]

*C. The City Madam (Richmond 1771).
[An alteration of Massinger.]

C. Beaumont and Fletcher's Rule a Wife, and Have a Wife...
adapted to the Stage by James Love; revised by J. P. Kemble
(D.L. W. 14/2/1776) 8° 1811.

LUCAS, HENRY.

*C.O. Love in Disguise (S.A. Dublin, Th. 24/4/1766).
[Music T. Giordani.]

*C.O. The Triumph of Variety (Crow-street, Dublin, W. 8/4/1772).
[Music Tenducci.]

T. Poems to Her Majesty; to which is added a new tragedy, entitled
the Earl of Somerset, literally founded on History: with a Pre-
fatory Address 4° 1779.

M. Coelina...With Songs, Chorusses, and a Grand Finale; com-
memorative of the Nuptials of Their Royal Highnesses the Prince
of Wales and Princess Caroline 4° 1795.

LUDGER, C.

D. The Lawyers...Translated from the German of Augustus
William Iffland 8° 1799.

D. The Peevish Man...By Augustus Kotzebue. Being his last
Production. Translated 8° 1799.

D. The Reconciliation; or, The Birth-Day 8° 1799.

LUND, JOHN.

F. Ducks and Green Pease; or, The Newcastle Rider...Founded in
Fact 12° 1785; 12° 1788; 12° [1793]; 12° [1800]; 8° [1810]; 12°
[1820]; 12° [1838].

MACARTHUR, SAMUEL.

T. The Duke of Rothsay 8° 1780 [*Edinburgh*].

MACARTNEY, CHARLES JUSTIN.

C.O. The Vow 8° [1800?; *Sheffield*].

MACAULAY, JOHN.

M. The Genius of Ireland (Capel-street, Dublin, W. 4/2/1784) 8°
1785.
[Music T. Giordani.]

M^cDERMOTT, JOHN.

*C.O. The Milesian (S.A. Dublin Th. 26/11/1772).

M^cDONALD, ANDREW.

T. Vimonda (H.² W. 5/9/1787) 8° 1788; 12° 1788 [*Dublin*]; 8° 1791
[in *Miscellaneous Works*]; MS. Larpent 21. S. [23/8/1787].
The Miscellaneous Works of A. McDonald 8° 1791.
[Contains: 1. *Vimonda*; 2. *Love and Loyalty, an Opera*; 3. *The
Fair Apostate, a Tragedy*; 4. *The Princess of Tarento: a Comedy*.]

MACKENZIE, HENRY.

T. The Prince of Tunis (Edinburgh M. 8/3/1773) 8° 1773 [*bis*].

T. The Shipwreck: or Fatal Curiosity...Altered from Lillo (C.G.
    T. 10/2/1784) 8° 1784; MS. Larpent 16. L. [1784].
      [An adaptation of George Lillo, *Fatal Curiosity*.]
*C. The Force of Fashion (C.G. S. 5/12/1789) MS. Larpent 17. L.
    [2/12/1789].
*[T.?] The White Hypocrite [see *Biographia Dramatica*, iii. 401–2].

MACKLIN, CHARLES.
      [For his earlier works see the Hand-list of Plays, 1700–1750.]
*Sat. Covent Garden Theatre; or, Pasquin turn'd Drawcansir, Censor
    of Great Britain (C.G. W. 8/4/1752) MS. Larpent 4. S.
[F.] Love A-la-Mode. A Comedy (D.L. W. 12/12/1759) 8° 1793; 12°
    1784; 16° 1785; 12° 1786.
      [One act was printed in *The Court Miscellany* for April 1766.]
*C. The Married Libertine (C.G. W. 28/1/1761).
*C. The True-born Irishman (Crow-street, Dublin, F. 14/5/1762).
      [Printed in Jones' *British Theatre*, 1795.] MS. Larpent 8. M.
      [21/11/1767].
*C. The True-born Scotsman (Crow-street, Dublin, W. 10/7/1764).
      [Later altered as *The Man of the World*, *infra*.]
*F. The Whim; or, A Christmas Gambol (Crow-street, Dublin, W.
    26/12/1764).
*F. The Irish Fine Lady (C.G. S. 28/11/1767).
      [Apparently a slightly altered version of *The True-born Irishman*,
      supra.]
C. The Man of the World (C.G. Th. 10/5/1781) 12° 1785 [*Dublin*];
    8° 1786; 12° 1791 [*Dublin*]; 8° 1793; 8° 1809; MS. Larpent 26.
    M. [1781; see also under *UNKNOWN AUTHORS*].
      [A revised version of *The True-born Scotsman*, *supra*.]

M^cLAREN, ARCHIBALD.
*F. The Conjuror; or, The Scotsman in London 12° 1781 [*Dundee*].
Ent. The Coup de Main, or The American Adventurers. A Musical
    Entertainment (Dundee *c.* 1783) 8° 1784 [*Perth*].
Int. The Humours of Greenock Fair, or The Taylor made a Man.
    A Musical Interlude (Greenock *c.* 1788) 12° 1790 [*Paisley*].
*C.O. American Slaves; or, Love and Liberty (Dumfries 1792).
*Ent. The Siege of Perth; or, Sir William Wallace the Scots Champion
    (Dumfries 1792).
[O.F.] The Highland Drover.—The Scottish Volunteers, A Musica
    Farce 8° 1795 [*Paisley*].
C.O. What News from Bantry Bay; or, The Faithful Irishman (St
    Peter's, Guernsey *c.* 1794) 8° 1798 [*Dublin*].
C.O. Old England for Ever! or A Fig for the Invasion 12° 1799
    [*Bristol*].
[Int.] The Negro Slaves, or, The Blackman and the Blackbird (Edin-
    burgh *c.* 1799) 8° 1799; 12° 1799 [2nd].
C.O. The Humours of the Times; or, What News Now? 8° 1799.
Ent. The Soldier's Widow; or, The Happy Relief. A Musical Enter-
    tainment 8° 1800.
Ent. The Monopolizer Outwitted! A Musical Entertainment 12° 1800;
    12° 1801.
*F. The First Night's Lodging 12° [? 1800].
      [For his later works see the *Biographia Dramatica*.]

MACLAURIN, JOHN, Lord DREGHORN.
*T.   Hampden 8° 1799.
T.   The Public [in *Works* 8° 1798, *Edinburgh*].
*[C.O.]   The Philosopher's Opera [see the *Biographia Dramatica*, iii. 145].

MACNALLY, LEONARD.
*C.O.   The Ruling Passion (Capel-street, Dublin, T. 24/2/1778).
   [Music Cogan.]
M.   The Apotheosis of Punch; A Satirical Masque (Patagonian 1779)
   8° 1779.
*Prel.   A New Occasional Prelude (C.G. M. 16/9/1782).
F.   Retaliation (C.G. T. 7/5/1782) 8° 1782 [3 editions]; 12° 1782
   [*Dublin*].
[C.]   Tristram Shandy: A Sentimental, Shandean Bagatelle (C.G. S.
   26/4/1783) 8° 1783 [*bis*]; MS. Larpent 31. M. [1783].
*[O.F.]   Coalition. A Musical Piece (C.G. M. 19/5/1783) MS. Lar-
   pent 31. M.
C.O.   Robin Hood; or, Sherwood Forest (C.G. S. 17/4/1784) 8° 1784;
   8° 1787 [with alterations]; 12° 1788 [*Dublin*; with additional
   songs]; 8° 1789; Sonnets, Ballads, Glees, Duettos, etc., in...
   Robin Hood 8° 1784; Music and words 8° [1784]; MS. Larpent
   34. M. [1784].
   [Music W. Shield.]
C.   Fashionable Levities (C.G. S. 2/4/1785) 8° 1785 [*bis*]; 12° 1786
   [*Dublin*]; MS. Larpent 38. M. [1785].
*F.   April Fool; or, The Follies of a Night (C.G. S. 1/4/1786) MS.
   Larpent 41. M.
C.O.   Richard Coeur de Lion...Taken from the French Comedy of
   the Same Name, by M. Sedaine (C.G. M. 16/10/1786) 8° 1786;
   Songs, Duettos, Trios, Quartettes, Quintettos, and Musical
   Dialogues...in...Richard Cœur de Lion 8° 1786; 8° [?1787];
   MS. Larpent 43. M.
   [An adaptation of M. J. Sedaine, *Richard Cœur de Lion* (Paris,
   1784).]
[F.]   Critic upon Critic: a Dramatic Medley 8° 1788 [2nd]; 8° 1792
   [2nd, as at C.G.].
   [On this satirical piece, its probable date of composition and the
   possibility that it was never acted, see Genest, *op. cit.* x. 197.]
*O.F.   The Cottage Festival; or, A Day in Wales (Crow-street, Dublin,
   S. 29/11/1796).
   [Music T. Giordani.]

MACREADY, WILLIAM.
F.   The Village Lawyer (H.¹ T. 28/8/1787) *8° 1795; 8° 1801; MS.
   Larpent 44. M. [22/8/1787].
F.   The Irishman in London; or, The Happy African (C.G. S.
   21/4/1792) 8° 1793; 8° 1799; 8° 1800 [3rd]; MS. Larpent 58. M.
   [1792].
   [Said to be an alteration of *The Intriguing Footman*; *q.v.* under
   J. WHITELEY.]
C.   The Bank Note, or, Lessons for Ladies...Partly an Alteration
   (C.G. F. 1/5/1795) 8° 1795; 8° 1802 [3rd]; MS. Larpent 19. L.
   [April 1795].
   [Largely based on W. Taverner, *The Artful Husband*.]

MALLET, DAVID.
[For his earlier plays see the Hand-list of Plays, 1700–1750.]
M. Alfred, a Masque (D.L. S. 23/2/1751) 8° 1751.
[This is an alteration of the earlier *Alfred* (1740) prepared by Mallet and James Thomson.]
M. Britannia (D.L. F. 9/5/1755) 8° 1755.
[Music Dr Arne.]
T. Elvira (D.L. W. 19/1/1763) 8° 1763; 8° 1763 [*Edinburgh*]; MS. Larpent 6. M. [7/12/1762].

MAN, HENRY.
*[Sat.] Cloacina. A Comi-Tragedy 4° 1775.
[Ascribed to Henry Man.]
F. The Elders (C.G. F. 21/4/1780) [in *Miscellaneous Works* 8° 1802] MS. Larpent 24. M. [1780].

MANSELL, WILLIAM.
Past. Fairy-Hill; or May Day. A Pastoral Opera...As it was originally written for a Private Theatre 8° 1784.

MARSH, CHARLES.
[For his earlier works see the Hand-list of Plays, 1700–1750.]
T. Cymbeline. King of Britain...written by Shakespear. With some Alterations 8° [1756]; 8° 1762.
[T.C.] The Winter's Tale, a Play altered from Shakespear 8° 1756 [reissued with fresh title page 1756 as the 2nd edition].
*T. Romeo and Juliet [see the *Biographia Dramatica*, iii. 223].

MARSHALL, Mrs JANE.
C. Sir Harry Gaylove: or, Comedy in Embryo 8° 1772 [*Edinburgh*].

MASON, WILLIAM.
Dr. Poem. Elfrida...Written on the Model of the Antient Greek Tragedy (C.G. S. 21/11/1772) 4° 1752; 8° 1752 [2nd]; 8° 1752 [3rd]; 8° 1753 [4th]; 12° 1755 [*Edinburgh*]; 8° 1757 [5th]; 8° 1759 [6th]; 8° 1773 [3 editions; 7th, 8th, and 9th]; 8° 1779; MS. Larpent 12. M. [9/10/1772].
[Music Dr Arne.]
Dr. Poem. Caractacus...Written on the Model of the Ancient Greek Tragedy (Crow-street, Dublin, F. 30/3/1764; C.G. F. 6/12/1776) 4° 1759; 8° 1759 [2nd]; 8° 1760 [3rd]; 8° 1777 [*York*, acting edition].
[Music Dr Arne.]
[*Argentile and Curan* and *Sappho* appear in the *Poems* of 1796–7. *Cupid and Psyche*, if ever completed, seems to be lost.]

MATY, HENRY.
T. Emilia Galotti [in *The New Review*, ix. 1786].
[A partial translation of Lessing, *Emilia Galotti*.]

MAURICE, THOMAS.
Poems...with a Free Translation of the Œdipus Tyrannus of Sophocles 4° 1779.
*T. Panthea; or, The Captive Bride 8° 1789.
T. The Fall of the Mogul...founded on an interesting portion of Indian History and attempted partly on the Greek Model 8° 1806.

MAXWELL, JOHN.
    [For his earlier works see the Hand-list of Plays, 1700–1750.]
  *T. The Loves of Prince Emilius and Louisa 8° 1755 [York].
   T. A New Tragedy call'd The Distressed Virgin 8° 1761 [York].

MEILAN, MARK ANTONY.
   T. Emilia 8° [1771].
   T. Northumberland 8° [1771].
   T. The Friends 8° 1771.

MENDEZ, MOSES.
    [For his earlier works see the Hand-list of Plays, 1700–1750.]
  M.Ent. The Chaplet (D.L. S. 2/12/1749) 8° 1749; 8° 1750; 8° 1753;
    8° 1756 [2nd]; 8° 1759 [3rd]; 12° 1767.
    [Music Dr Boyce.]
  [M.] Robin Hood, a new Musical Entertainment (D.L. Th. 13/12/1750)
    8° 1751; MS. Larpent 4. L. [19/11/1750; as "An English Bur-
    letta"].
    [Music Dr Burney.]
  [M.] The Shepherd's Lottery. A Musical Entertainment (D.L. T.
    19/11/1751) 8° 1751.
    [Music Dr Boyce.]

MERRY, ROBERT.
    [For A Picture of Paris see under CHARLES BONNOR.]
  *T. Ambitious Vengeance [in Bell's British Album 8° 1790].
   P. The Airs, Duetts, & Chorusses, Arrangement of Scenery, and
    Sketch of the Pantomime, entitled The Picture of Paris (C.G. M.
    20/12/1790) 8° 1790; MS. Larpent 52. M. [11/12/1790].
    [Music W. Shield.]
   T. Lorenzo (C.G. T. 5/4/1791) 8° 1791; MS. Larpent 18. L.
    [25/3/1791].
  *C.O. The Magician no Conjuror (C.G. Th. 2/2/1792) MS. Larpent
    59. M. [Jan. 1792; as The Magician].
   D. Fénelon: or, The Nuns of Cambray. A Serious Drama 8° 1795.
    [An adaptation from the French.]

METCALFE, CATHARINE.
  *T. Julia de Roubigné [Bath, Th. 23/12/1790] MS. Larpent 23. S.
    [16/12/1790; as Julia].

MEYERS, ——.
  *[M.D.] Zelma; or, The Will o' the Wisp (C.G. T. 17/4/1792) MS.
    Larpent 58. M. [12/4/1792].
    [An adaptation from the German prepared for the stage by
    WILLIAM HAYLEY.]

MICKLE, WILLIAM JUNIUS.
   T. The Siege of Marseilles [in Poems and a Tragedy 4° 1794].

MILES, WILLIAM AUGUSTUS.
    [For Summer Amusement (H.² 1779) see under M. P. ANDREWS.]
  C.O. The Artifice (D.L. F. 14/4/1780) 8° 1780; MS. Larpent 22. M.
    [16/3/1780].
    [Music M. Arne.]

MONCRIEFF, JOHN.
   T. Appius (C.G. Th. 6/3/1755) 8° 1755; MS. Larpent 4. S. [17/2/1755].

MOORE, EDWARD.
    [For his earlier works see the Hand-list of Plays, 1700–1750.]
  C. Gil Blas (D.L. S. 2/2/1751) 8° 1751; MS. Larpent 4. L. [3/1/1751].
  T. The Gamester (D.L. W. 7/2/1753) 8° 1753 [*bis*]; 12° 1763 [*Dublin*];
      8° 1771 [5th]; 12° 1784; MS. Larpent 4. L. [9/1/1753].
    [One scene is attributed to *DAVID GARRICK*.]

MOORE, S.
  *F. The World as it Wags (Chesterfield S. 1/12/1792).

MORE, Mrs HANNAH.
  Past. A Search after Happiness 4° [1765; *Bristol*]; 8° 1775 [6th]; 8°
      1796 [11th with alterations].
  T. The Inflexible Captive (Bath 1774) 8° 1774 [*Bristol*]; 12° 1775.
  T. Percy (C.G. W. 10/12/1777) 8° 1778 [*bis*]; 8° 1784 [3rd]; MS. Lar-
      pent 17. M. [2/12/1777].
  T. The Fatal Falsehood (C.G. Th. 6/5/1779) 8° 1779; MS. Larpent
      21. M. [1779].
  Sac. D. Sacred Dramas: chiefly intended for Young Persons: the Sub-
      jects taken from the Bible 8° 1782 [*bis*]; 8° 1783 [3rd]; 8° 1785
      [4th]; 8° 1789 [6th]; 8° 1802 [13th]; 12° 1812 [17th]; 12° 1815 [18th].
      [Contains: 1. *Moses in the Bulrushes*; 2. *Belshazzar*; 3. *David
      and Goliath*; 4. *Daniel*.]

MORELL, Dr THOMAS.
    [For his earlier works see the Hand-list of Plays, 1700–1750.]
  *T. Prometheus in Chains 8° 1773.
    [A translation from Æschylus.]

MORGAN, MᶜNAMARA.
  T. Philoclea (C.G. T. 22/1/1754) 8° 1754; 12° 1754 [*Dublin*]; MS.
      Larpent 3. M. [9/1/1754].
  Past. The Sheep-Shearing: Or, Florizel and Perdita. A Pastoral
      Comedy. Taken from Shakespeare (C.G. M. 25/3/1754) 12° 1767
      [*Dublin*]; MS. Larpent 3. M. [18/3/1754].
    [Attributed to Morgan; an alteration of *The Winter's Tale*.]

MORISON, DAVID.
  *C.O. The Fortunate Sailor [see *Biographia Dramatica*, ii. 246].

MORRIS, EDWARD.
  F. The Adventurers (D.L. Th. 18/3/1790) 8° 1790; 8° 1807; MS.
      Larpent 53. M. [as *The Adventurers, or Mutual Deception*;
      11/2/1790].
  C. False Colours (H.¹ W. 3/4/1793) 8° 1793 [*bis*]; MS. Larpent 61. M.
      [27/3/1793].
  C. The Secret (D.L. S. 2/3/1799) 8° 1799 [3 editions]; 12° 1799
      [*Dublin*]; MS. Larpent 74. M. [2/2/1799].

MORTON, E.
  *Ent. The Register Office 12° 1758 [*Salop*].

MORTON, THOMAS.
  [M.D.] Columbus; or, A World Discovered. An Historical Play
      (C.G. S. 1/12/1792) 8° 1792 [*bis*]; 8° 1799; MS. Larpent 59. M.
      [23/11/1792].

[Int.] The Children in the Wood. A Musical Piece (H.² T. 1/10/1793)
12° 1794 [Dublin; pirated]; MS. Larpent 25. S. [26/9/1793].
[Music S. Arnold.]

[M.D.] Zorinski. A Play (H.² S. 20/6/1795) 8° 1795; 8° 1800; Songs,
Duets, Chorusses, &c., in Zorinski 8° 1795.
[Music S. Arnold.]

C. The Way to Get Married (C.G. S. 23/1/1796) 8° 1796; 8° 1805;
MS. Larpent 70. M. [7/1/1796].

C. A Cure for the Heart-Ache (C.G. T. 10/1/1797) 8° 1797 [bis]; MS.
Larpent 30. S. [24/12/1796].

C. Secrets Worth Knowing (C.G. Th. 11/1/1798) 8° 1798; 12° 1798
[Dublin]; 8° 1802; MS. Larpent 71. M. [26/12/1797].

C. Speed the Plough (C.G. Feb. 1800) 8° 1800 [9 editions]; 8° 1805;
MS. Larpent 38. S. [29/1/1800].
[For his later plays see the Hand-list of Plays, 1800–1850.]

MOUBRAY, ——.
*[O.F.] The Devil of a Lover (C.G. S. 17/3/1798) MS. Larpent 35. S.
[20/2/1798].
[Music T. Attwood.]

MOULTRU, Rev. ——.
[C.] False and True. A Play (H.² S. 11/8/1798) 8° 1798 [4 editions];
12° 1798 [Dublin]; MS. Larpent 33. S. [9/8/1798].
[The 2nd and later editions have as the title F. and T.; or, The
Irishman in Italy. Music by Dr Arnold.]

MOZEEN, T.
F. The Heiress; or, The Antigallican (D.L. M. 21/5/1759) [in A
Collection of Miscellaneous Essays 8° 1762] MS. Larpent 4. M.
[May 1759].

MURDOCH, JOHN.
D. The Double Disguise [in Pictures of the Heart...and the Double
Disguise 12° 1783].

MURPHY, ARTHUR.
F. The Apprentice (D.L. F. 2/1/1756) 8° 1756 [bis]; 12° 1756
[Dublin]; 8° 1764; 12° 1773 [Belfast]; 8° [c. 1803].
F. The Spouter; or, The Triple Revenge 8° 1756.
*F. The Englishman from Paris (D.L. S. 3/4/1756).
F. The Upholsterer, or, What News? (D.L. Th. 30/3/1758) 8° 1758;
8° 1765 [2nd]; 8° 1769 [3rd with additions]; 12° 1786 [Newry];
MS. Larpent 5. L. [16/3/1757]; additions to 23. S. [25/1/1791].
T. The Orphan of China (D.L. S. 21/4/1759) 8° 1759 [bis]; 12° 1759
[Dublin]; 12° 1761 [Dublin]; 8° 1772 [3rd]; 12° 1787 [Dublin];
8° [c. 1803]; MS. Larpent 6. L. [4/4/1759].
Dr. Poem. The Desert Island (D.L. Th. 24/1/1760) 8° 1760; 8° 1762;
12° 1786.
[An adaptation of Metastasio, L'Isola Disabitata with suggestions from L'Isle Déserte.]
C. The Way to Keep Him (D.L. Th. 24/1/1760, in 3 acts; D.L. S.
10/1/1761, in 5 acts) 8° 1760 [bis]; 12° 1760 [Dublin]; 8° 1761
[4th]; 12° 1765 [Dublin]; 8° 1765 [5th]; 8° 1770 [6th]; 8° 1785;
8° 1787; 12° 1802; MS. Larpent 5. M. [8/1/1760].
[A song by DAVID GARRICK appears in editions after the
revival of 1761.]

C. All in the Wrong (D.L. M. 15/6/1761) 8° 1761; 12° 1762 [*Dublin*]; 12° 1765 [*Cork*]; 12° 1765 [*Dublin*]; 8° 1775; 8° 1787; 8° 1797; MS. Larpent 6. L. [5/6/1761].

[C.] The Old Maid, A Comedy (D.L. Th. 2/7/1761) 8° 1761 [*bis*]; 12° 1762 [*Dublin*]; 12° 1769 [*Belfast*].

F. The Citizen (D.L. Th. 2/7/1761) 8° 1763; 12° 1763 [*Dublin*]; 8° 1766 [2nd]; 8° 1770 [3rd]; 12° 1774 [*Dublin*]; 12° 1784; 8° [*c*. 1803].

C. No One's Enemy but his Own (C.G. M. 9/1/1764) 8° 1764; MS. Larpent 7. L. [10/12/1763].

C. What We Must All Come To (C.G. M. 9/1/1764) 8° 1764; MS. Larpent 7. L. [10/12/1763].

*C. The Choice (D.L. S. 23/3/1765) 8° 1786; MS. Larpent 7. S. [9/3/1765].

C. The School for Guardians (C.G. S. 10/1/1767) 8° 1767; MS. Larpent 8. L. [1/12/1766].

T. Zenobia (D.L. S. 27/2/1768) 8° 1768 [4 editions]; 12° 1784; MS. Larpent 9. M. [19/2/1768].

T. The Grecian Daughter (D.L. W. 26/2/1772) 8° 1772 [*bis*]; 8° 1776; 8° 1777; 12° 1802; MS. Larpent 12. M. [8/2/1772].

[Burlesque.] Hamlet with Alterations (written in 1772; in Foot's *Life of Murphy* (1810), pp. 256–74).

T. Alzuma (C.G. T. 23/2/1773) 8° 1773 [3 editions]; 8° 1774; MS. Larpent 14. M. [27/1/1773].

[F.] Three Weeks after Marriage; or, What we must all come to (C.G. S. 30/3/1776) 8° [1776]; 8° 1776; 8° [1778]; 8° [1784].
    [An alteration of *What We Must All Come to, supra*.]

*Prel. News from Parnassus (C.G. M. 23/9/1776) 8° 1786; MS. Larpent 16. M. [9/9/1776].

C. Know Your Own Mind (C.G. S. 22/2/1777) 8° 1778; 12° 1787; 8° [1800]; MS. Larpent 16. M. [4/2/1777].
    [Based on Destouches, *L'Irrésolu*.]

T. The Rival Sisters (H.[1] M. 18/3/1793) 8° 1786 [in *Works*]; 8° 1793.

T. Arminius 8° 1798.

MURRAY, CHARLES.
F. The Experiment (Norwich 10/5/1779) 8° 1779 [*Norwich*]; MS. Larpent 19. M.

MYLNE, JAMES.
Poems, consisting of Miscellaneous Pieces and Two Tragedies 8° 1790.
    [Contains: 1. *Darthula*; 2. *The British Kings*.]

NATION, WILLIAM, Junior.
The Dramatic Pieces, and Poetry, of W. Nation, Jun. 8° 1789 [*Plymouth*].
    [Contains: 1. *The School for Diffidence*; 2 *Old Love Renewed*.]

NELSON, JAMES.
C. The Affectionate Father: A Sentimental Comedy: Together with Essays on Various Subjects 8° 1786.

NEVILLE, EDWARD.
[O.F.] Plymouth in an Uproar; A Musical Farce (C.G. W. 20/10/1779) 8° 1779 [3 editions]; MS. Larpent 20. M. [19/10/1779].
    [Music Charles Dibdin.]

NEUMAN, H.
[D.] Self-Immolation...a Play...Translated from the German 8°

1799; Family Distress; or Self-Immolation. A Play...By Augustus von Kotzebue. As it is now performing...Faithfully translated from the German 8° 1799.
[*Family Distress* (H.² S. 15/6/1799).]

NOEHDEN, GEORG HEINRICH and STODDART, J.
T. Fiesco; or, The Genoese Conspiracy...Translated from the German of Frederick Schiller 8° 1796; 8° 1798 [*bis*].
T. Don Carlos...from the German 8° 1798.

NORTH, FRANCIS, 4th Earl of GUILFORD.
[M.D.] The Kentish Barons; A Play...Interspersed with Songs (H.² S. 25/6/1791) 8° 1791; MS. Larpent 23. S. [1/8/1790].

NORVAL, JAMES.
*T. The Generous Chief (Montrose *c.* 1792) 8° 1792 [*Montrose*].

NOVERRE, JEAN GEORGES.
*Ball. The Chinese Festival (D.L. S. 8/11/1755).

O'BEIRNE, THOMAS LEWIS, Bishop of MEATH.
C. The Generous Impostor (D.L. W. 22/11/1780) 8° 1781; MS. Larpent 23. M. [6/11/1780].
  [Based on Destouches, *Le Dissipateur*.]

O'BRIEN, WILLIAM.
F. Cross Purposes (C.G. S. 5/12/1772) 8° [1772; *bis*]; 8° [1773]; 8° 1783; MS. Larpent 13. M. [26/11/1772].
[D.] The Duel, a Play (D.L. T. 8/12/1772) 8° 1772; 8° 1773 [2nd]; MS. Larpent 9. S. [25/11/1772].

O'BRYEN, DENIS.
*C. A Friend in Need is a Friend Indeed (H.² S. 5/7/1783).

OGBORNE, DAVID.
C. The Merry Midnight Mistake, or Comfortable Conclusion, A New Comedy 8° 1765 [*Chelmsford*].

O'HARA, KANE.
Burl. Midas, an English Burletta (Crow-street, Dublin, F. 22/1/1762; C.G. W. 22/2/1764) 8° 1764 [*bis*]; 8° 1766; 8° 1767; 8° 1768; 12° 1770 [*Cork*]; 12° 1770 [*Dublin*]; 8° 1771 [6th]; 12° 1777 [*Perth*]; 12° 1795; 8° 1812; Midas. A comic Opera...For the Harpsichord, Voice, German Flute, Violin, or Guitar F. [1764]; MS. Larpent 7. S. [1764, printed copy] and 8. L. [1764].
  [See *An Improved Edition of the Songs in...Midas, adapted to the Times* 8° 1789. A pasticcio.]
Burl. The Golden Pippin: An English Burletta (C.G. S. 6/2/1773) 8° 1773 [*bis*]; 8° 1776; 8° 1777; 8° 1787; MS. Larpent 12. M. [dated 5/2/1772 and marked "Forbid"] and 13. M. [dated 9/10/1772].
  [A pasticcio.]
[O.F.] The Two Misers: A Musical Farce (C.G. S. 21/1/1775) 8° 1775.
  [Based on F. de Falbaire, *Les Deux Avares* (Paris 1770). Music C. Dibdin.]
Burl. April-Day (H.² F. 22/8/1777) 8° 1777; 8° 1778.
  [Music Dr Arnold.]
Burl. Tom Thumb...Altered from Henry Fielding (C.G. T. 3/10/1780) 8° [1805]; 8° 1806 [*Cawthorne's Minor Theatre*]; 12° 1810; 12° 1830.
  [Based on Henry Fielding, *Tom Thumb*.]

O'KEEFFE, JOHN.

[The following list of plays is based partly on *Recollections of the Life of John O'Keeffe written by Himself* (1826), ii. 359–62.]

**C. The Generous Lover.

[F.] The She Gallant; or, Square-Toes Outwitted, A New Comedy (S.A. Dublin, W. 14/1/1767) 8° 1767.

*F. The India Ship (Cork).

*Past. Colin's Welcome (Belfast, Th. 26/7/1770).
[Music set from Rini, Purcell, Clagget and Tenducci.]

*F. The Comical Duel (acted at Cork and Dublin).

*C.O. The Shamrock; or, St. Patrick's Day (Crow-street, Dublin, T. 15/4/1777; C.G. M. 7/4/1783) MS. Larpent 31. M. [1783; as *The S., or Anniversary of St. Patrick A Pastoral Romance*].

F.   Tony Lumpkin in Town (H.² Th. 2/7/1778) 8° 1780; 8° 1780 [*Dublin*].
[See *Tony Lumpkin's Ramble* under *UNKNOWN AUTHORS.*]

[O.F.] The Son-in-Law (H.² S. 14/8/1779) 12° 1783 [*Dublin*, pirated]; 8° 1788 [*Dublin*]; Airs, Duetts, Trios, &c., in the Musical Farce of The Son-in-Law 8° 1780; MS. Larpent 14. L. [1779].
[Music S. Arnold.]

[O.F.] The Dead Alive; A Comic Opera (H.² S. 16/6/1781) 12° 1783 [*Dublin*, pirated]; 12° 1784 [*Belfast*]; Songs, Duets, Trios, &c. &c., in the New Musical Farce of The Dead Alive 8° 1781; MS. Larpent 16. S. [10/5/1781; as *Edward and Caroline, or The Dead Alive. A Farce*].
[Music S. Arnold.]

[O.F.] The Agreeable Surprise, A Comic Opera (H.² M. 3/9/1781) 12° 1784 [*Dublin*, pirated]; 16° 1785 [*Dublin*]; 8° 1786 [*Dublin*]; 12° 1787 [*Dublin*]; 12° 1792 [*Dublin*]; Songs, Choruses, &c. in…the Agreeable Surprise 8° 1781; MS. Larpent 24. M. [as a "Musical Entertainment"].
[Music S. Arnold.]

C.O. Songs, Duetts, and Trios in…The Banditti; or, Love's Labyrinth (C.G. W. 28/11/1781) 8° 1781; MS. Larpent 25. M. [23/11/1781].
[Music S. Arnold.]

F.   The Positive Man (C.G. S. 16/3/1782) 8° 1800; MS. Larpent 28. M. [9/3/1782].
[An alteration of *The She Gallant, supra.* Music S. Arnold and M. Arne.]

P.   Songs, Airs, Etc., in the Entertainment of Harlequin Teague; or, The Giant's Causeway (H.² S. 17/8/1782) 8° 1782; MS. Larpent 29. M. [15/8/1782].
[Music S. Arnold.]

C.O. The Castle of Andalusia (C.G. S. 2/11/1782) 8° 1783 [*Dublin* "with Additional Songs by Sig. Tenducci," pirated]; 12° 1788 [*Dublin*]; 12° 1794 [*Dublin*]; 8° 1794 [authorised]; Songs, Duets, Trios…in…The Castle of Andalusia 8° 1782 [5 editions]; 8° 1783; 8° 1788; 8° 1791; MS. Larpent 28. M. [28/10/1782].
[An alteration of *The Banditti, supra.* Music S. Arnold. The play was itself altered for a performance at C.G. T. 1/4/1788.]

P.   Songs, Duets, &c., in the New Pantomime called Lord Mayor's Day, or, A Flight from Lapland (C.G. M. 25/11/1782) 8° 1782; MS. Larpent 29. M. [1782].
[Music W. Shield.]

Burl. Songs, Airs, etc., in The Maid the Mistress (C.G. F. 14/2/1783)
8° 1783; MS. Larpent 31. M. [1783; as *The Servant Mistress*].
[An adaptation of G. A. Federico, *La Serva Padrona*.]

C.   The Young Quaker (H.² S. 26/7/1783) 12° 1784 [*Dublin*, pirated];
12° 1788 [*Dublin*]; MS. Larpent 31. M. [19/7/1783].

[O.F.] The Birth-Day; or, The Prince of Arragon. A Dramatick
Piece, with Songs (H.² T. 12/8/1783) 8° 1783 [*Dublin*, pirated];
MS. Larpent 33. M. [31/7/1783].
[Music S. Arnold.]

C.O. The Poor Soldier (C.G. T. 4/11/1783) 12° 1785 [*Dublin*, pirated];
12° 1786 [*Dublin*]; 12° 1788 [*Dublin*]; 8° 1800 [authorised]; The
Songs, Duets, and Chorusses in the two favourite Farces of
Rosina and the Poor Soldier 12° 1786; MS. Larpent 31. M. [1783].
[Music W. Shield. An alteration of *The Shamrock, supra*.]

*Int. The Definitive Treaty.

*P. Friar Bacon; or, Harlequin's Adventures in Lilliput, Brobdignag
etc. (C.G. T. 23/12/1783) MS. Larpent 30. M. [1783].
[The pantomime is said to have been contrived by *CHARLES
BONNOR*, with words by O'Keeffe.]

C.O. Peeping Tom of Coventry (H.² M. 6/9/1784) 12° 1786 [*Dublin*,
pirated]; 8° 1787 [*Dublin*]; 12° 1792 [*Dublin*]; MS. Larpent 36. M.
[29/5/1784].
[Music S. Arnold.]

C.O. Fontainebleau; or, Our Way in France (C.G. T. 16/11/1784) 12°
1785 [*Dublin*, pirated]; 8° 1787 [*Dublin*]; 12° 1790 [*Dublin*]; 8°
1791; Songs, Duets, Trios, &c., in Fontainebleau 8° 1784; 8°
1791; MS. Larpent 36. M. [11/11/1784].
[Music W. Shield.]

[O.F.] Songs and Duets in The Blacksmith of Antwerp (C.G. M.
7/2/1785) 8° 1816 [altered]; MS. Larpent 38. M. [8/1/1785].

[O.F.] A Beggar on Horseback (H.² Th. 16/6/1785) MS. Larpent
16. L. [30/4/1785].
[Printed in O'Keeffe's *Works*.]

*P. Omai; or, A Trip round the World (C.G. T. 20/12/1785) MS.
Larpent 39. M. [1785].
[Music W. Shield.]

[O.F.] Patrick in Prussia; or, Love in a Camp. A Comic Opera...
With all the Original Songs (C.G. F. 17/2/1786) 8° 1786 [*Dublin*,
pirated]; 12° 1792 [*Dublin*]; 8° 1800 [authorised]; MS. Larpent
42. M. [1786].
[A sequel to *The Poor Soldier, supra*. Music W. Shield.]

C.O. Songs, Duets, Trios, &c., in The Siege of Curzola (H.² S.
12/8/1786) 8° 1786; MS. Larpent 16. L. [17/5/1785].

[O.F.] The Man Milliner (C.G. S. 27/1/1787) MS. Larpent 44. M.
[1787].
[Printed in O'Keeffe's *Works*.]

[O.F.] The Farmer; A Comic Opera (C.G. W. 31/10/1787) 12° 1788
[*Dublin*, pirated]; 12° 1789 [*Dublin*]; 12° 1792 [*Dublin*]; 8° 1800
[authorised]; Songs, Duets, Chorusses, &c., in the Musical
Entertainment of The Farmer 8° 1787 [*bis*].
[Music W. Shield. Originally called *The Plague of Riches*
(*Recollections*, ii. 128).]

F.   Tantara-Rara, Rogues All (C.G. S. 1/3/1788) MS. Larpent 48. M.
[1788; as *Sing Tantara Rara R.A.*].
[Later advertised as *T.-R., R.A., or Honesty the Best Policy*.]

[F.] The Prisoner at Large. A Comedy (H.² W. 2/7/1788) 8° 1788;
    12° [1789; *Dublin*; pirated]; 12° 1792 [*Dublin*]; 8° 1806.
C.O. The Highland Reel (C.G. Th. 6/11/1788) 8° 1789 [*Dublin*,
    pirated]; 8° 1790 [*Dublin*]; 8° 1800 [authorised]; Songs, Duetts,
    &c., in the Highland Reel. A Comic Romance 8° 1789 [5 editions].
    [Music W. Shield.]
*P. Aladdin; or, The Wonderful Lamp (C.G. F. 26/12/1788).
    [Music W. Shield.]
C. The Toy; or, The Lie of the Day (C.G. T. 3/2/1789; as *The T.,
    or Hampton Court Frolics*) MS. Larpent 49. M. [Jan. 1789].
    [See O'Keeffe's *Works*.]
F. The Little Hunch-Back; or, A Frolic in Bagdad (C.G.T. 14/4/1789)
    8° 1789; MS. Larpent 50. M. [March 1789].
*C.O. The Loyal Bandeau (C.G.).
Ent. Le Grenadier [see *Works*].
    [Cp. under *UNKNOWN AUTHORS*.]
C.O. Airs, Duets, Trios, Chorusses, in The Czar (C.G. M. 8/3/1790)
    8° 1790; MS. Larpent 52. M.
    [Music W. Shield.]
[Int.] Songs...in The Basket-Maker, a Musical Piece (H.² S. 4/9/1790)
    8° 1790; MS. Larpent 22. S. [24/8/1790].
    [Music S. Arnold.]
*[Int.] The Fugitive (C.G. Th. 4/11/1790) MS. Larpent 52. M.
    [2/11/1790].
    [An alteration of *The Czar, supra*.]
F. Modern Antiques; or, The Merry Mourners (C.G. M. 14/3/1791)
    12° 1792 [*Dublin*; 2 editions, both pirated]; 8° 1800 [authorised].
C. Wild Oats: or, The Strolling Gentleman (C.G. S. 16/4/1791)
    12° 1791 [*Dublin*, pirated]; 12° 1792 [*Dublin*]; 8° 1794 [authorised];
    8° 1806; MS. Larpent 54. M. [12/4/1791].
*D. Alban and Aphanasia.
*A Pageant.
C.O. Sprigs of Laurel (C.G. S. 11/5/1793) 8° 1793; 8° 1804; MS. Lar-
    pent 60. M. [1793; as *S. of L., or Royal Example*].
C. The World in a Village (C.G. S. 23/11/1793) 8° 1793; MS. Larpent
    60. M. [21/11/1793].
C. The London Hermit, or, Rambles in Dorsetshire (H.² S. 29/6/1793)
    8° 1793 [4 editions]; 8° 1798 [5th]; MS. Larpent 26. S.
    [27/6/1793].
*F. Jenny's Whim; or, The Roasted Emperor [advertised at H.² 1/9/
    1794, but withdrawn] MS. Larpent 27. S. [25/8/1794].
C. Life's Vagaries (C.G. Th. 19/3/1795) 8° 1795 [*bis*]; 8° [1810]; MS.
    Larpent 66. M. [12/3/1795].
Ent. The Irish Mimic: or, Blunders at Brighton (C.G. Th. 23/4/1795)
    8° 1795; 8° 1797; Songs, Duets, Choruses, &c., in the Irish Mimic
    ...A Musical Piece 8° 1795.
    [Music W. Shield.]
*Ent. The Siege of Troy (Ast. T. 21/7/1795).
*Ent. Valentine and Orson; or, The Wild Man of Orleans (S.W. T.
    8/9/1795).
P. Airs, Duets, and Chorusses in the Operatical Pantomime of Merry
    Sherwood or Harlequin Forrester (C.G. M. 21/12/1795) 8° 1795;
    MS. Larpent 28. S. [14/12/1795; as *The Merry Forrester*].
    [Music W. Reeve.]

C.   The Lie of the Day (C.G. S. 19/3/1796, as *The L. of the D.; or,
     A Party at Hampton Court*) 8° 1800.
     [An alteration of *The Toy, supra.*]

[C.O.] The Wicklow Gold Mines; or, the Lads [*sic*] of the Hills
     (C.G. W. 13/4/1796) 12° 1814 [*Dublin*]; Airs, Duets, Glees,
     Chorusses, &c., in the Opera of The Lad of the Hills, or Wicklow
     Gold Mines 8° 1796; MS. Larpent 29. S. [13/3/1796].

F.   The Doldrum; or, 1803 (C.G. S. 23/4/1796) MS. Larpent 31. S.
     [12/4/1796; as *The Sleeper, or A.D.* 1803].
     [Printed in O'Keeffe's *Works*.]

D.   Alfred: or, The Magic Banner (H.[2] W. 22/6/1796) 12° 1796
     [*Dublin*]; MS. Larpent 30. S. [17/6/1796; as *The Magick Banner,
     or Two Wives in a House*].

C.O. The Wicklow Mountains (C.G. F. 7/10/1796).
     [Printed in O'Keeffe's *Works*. An alteration of *The Wicklow
     Gold Mines, supra*. Music W. Shield.]

*Burl. Olympus in an Uproar; or, The Descent of the Deities (C.G.
     S. 5/11/1796) MS. Larpent 70. M. [20/10/1796].
     [Based largely on *The Golden Pippin* of *KANE O'HARA*.]

*[O.F.] The Rival Soldiers (C.G. W. 17/5/1797) 8° 1798.
     [An alteration of *Sprigs of Laurel, supra*.]

*C. She's Eloped (D.L. S. 19/5/1798).

*F. The Eleventh of June; or, The Daggerwoods at Dunstable (D.L.
     T. 5/6/1798) MS. Larpent 73. M. [2/6/1798].
     [A sequel to *Sylvester Daggerwood* by *GEORGE COLMAN*.]

*Int. All to St. Paul's.

*Ent. William Tell.
     [Cp. *William Tell* under *UNKNOWN AUTHORS*.]

*F. A Nosegay of Weeds; or, Old Servants in New Places (D.L. W.
     6/6/1798) MS. Larpent 72. M. [2/6/1798].
     [For some other plays, mostly unacted, see *Recollections*, ii. 362.]

OLDMIXON, *Sir JOHN*.

[Ent.] Apollo turn'd Stroller; or, Thereby hangs a Tale. A Musical
     Pasticcio (Royalty M. 3/12/1787) 8° 1787.
     [Music G. F. Händel.]

OLIPHANT, *ROBERT*.

*C. The Learned Lady (Liverpool 1789) MS. Larpent 22. S. [6/8/1789].

*F. A Sop in the Pan; or, The Beau Outwitted (Liverpool 1790).
     [Based on Colley Cibber, *The Refusal*.]

OLIVARI, *FRANCIS*.

Three Dramatic Pieces of Metastasio. The Dream of Scipio. The
     Birth of Jupiter. Astrea Appeased 12° 1797.
     [Translations of *Il Sogno di Scipione, Il Natal di Giove* and
     Astrea Placata.]

OSWALD, *JOHN*.

*Poems 8° 1789.
     [Contains *The Humours of John Bull*.]

OULTON, *WALLEY CHAMBERLAINE*.

*Int. The Haunted Castle (Capel-street, Dublin, Th. 18/12/1783).
     [Music T. Giordani.]

*C.O. The Happy Disguise; or, Love in a Meadow (Capel-street,
     Dublin, W. 7/1/1784).

*F. The New Wonder—A Woman Holds her Tongue (Capel-street, Dublin, W. 14/1/1784).

*Ent. The Mad House (Capel-street, Dublin, W. 5/5/1784) 12° 1785 [Dublin].

    [Music T. Giordani.]

*Int. Poor Maria (Crow-street, Dublin, 1785).

*F. A New Way to Keep a Wife at Home (S.A. Dublin, Th. 20/1/ 1785) 12° 1787 [Dublin].

    [Altered from Henry Fielding, *The Letter Writers*.]

*Prel. The Recruiting Manager (Fishamble-street, Dublin, 1785).

*C. Curiosity; or, A Peep through the Keyhole (S.A. Dublin, M. 27/3/1786).

*Burl. Hobson's Choice; or, Thespis in Distress (Royalty T. 3/7/1787).

*Int. Perseverance; or, The Third Time the Best (Crow-street, Dublin, Th. 12/3/1789; C.G. T. 2/6/1789) MS. Larpent 51. M. [18/5/1789].

    [Music T. Giordani.]

[Int.] As it Should Be; A Dramatic Entertainment (H.² T. 2/6/1789) 8° 1789; 12° 1789 [Dublin]; MS. Larpent 21. S. [9/4/1787, corrected to 1789].

*Burl. What's the Matter? 12° 1789.

[Int.] All in Good Humour. A Dramatic Piece (H.² S. 7/7/1792) 8° 1792; MS. Larpent 58. M. [25/6/1792].

*Int. The Irish Tar; or, Which is the Girl? (H.² Th. 24/8/1797) MS. Larpent 31. S. [19/8/1797].

F. Botheration: or, A Ten Years' Blunder (C.G. T. 8/5/1798) 8° 1798; MS. Larpent 33. S. [30/4/1798].

*P. Pyramus and Thisbe (Birmingham 1798).

*P. The Two Apprentices; or, Industry and Idleness Rewarded (Birmingham 1798).

    [For his later works see the *Biographia Dramatica*.]

PAPENDICK, GEORGE.

D. The Stranger; or, Misanthropy and Repentance...Faithfully translated, entire, from the German of Augustus von Kotzebue 8° 1798 [4 editions].

    [A rendering of A. v. Kotzebue, *Menschenhass und Reue*, prepared for the press by Stephen Jones.]

PARSONS, Mrs ELIZA.

[F.] The Intrigues of a Morning (C.G. W. 18/4/1792) 8° 1792; MS. Larpent 57. M. [16/4/1792].

    [Based on Molière, *Monsieur de Pourceaugnac*.]

PATON, ——.

*[B.O.] William and Lucy. An Opera 8° 1780 [Edinburgh].

PATSALL, ——.

T. Marcus Tullius Cicero [see the *Biographia Dramatica*, iii. 19].

PAUL, GEORGE.

[Pol.] The Antichristian Opera, or, Mass Unmask'd [advertised as published Jan. 1755; see the *Biographia Dramatica*, ii. 30].

PEARCE, WILLIAM.

C.O. The Words of the Songs...in The Nunnery (C.G. T. 12/4/1785) 8° 1785; MS. Larpent 39. M. [1785].

[O.F.] Hartford-Bridge: or, The Skirts of the Camp (C.G.S. 3/11/1792)
8° 1793; 12° 1793 [*Dublin*]; 8° 1796; Songs, Duets, Choruses...
in...Hartford Bridge 8° 1792; MS. Larpent 56. M. [1792].
[Music partly W. Shield.]

C.O. The Midnight Wanderers (C.G. M. 25/2/1793) 8° 1793; 12° 1793
[*Dublin*]; The Words of the Songs...in The Midnight Wanderers
8° 1793 [*bis*]; MS. Larpent 59. M. [9/2/1793].
[Music partly W. Shield.]

[O.F.] Netley Abbey (C.G. Th. 10/4/1794) 8° 1794; MS. Larpent 63.
M. [28/3/1794].
[Music partly selected, partly composed by Baumgarten, W.
Parke, Paisiello, Howard and W. Shield.]

[O.F.] Arrived at Portsmouth! An Operatic Drama (C.G. Th.
30/10/1794) 8° 1794; The Words of the Songs...in...Arrived at
Portsmouth 8° 1794; MS. Larpent 64. M. ["Operatic Drama";
21/10/1794].
[Music W. Shield.]

[M.D.] Songs, Choruses, &c., in the New Drama of Windsor Castle;
or, The Fair Maid of Kent, in Two Parts (C.G. M. 6/4/1795)
8° 1795 [*bis*]; MS. Larpent 29. S. [17/2/1795].
[Music J. P. Salomon and R. Spofforth.]

PENN, JOHN.
T. The Battle of Eddington; or, British Liberty (H.² W. 10/5/1797)
8° 1792; 8° 1796; 8° 1832 [2nd *sic*]; MS. Larpent 19. L. [as from
Theatre Royal Richmond, 1796].

PENNY, Mrs ANNE.
Poems, with a Dramatic Entertainment 4° 1771; 4° 1780.
[Contains *The Birth-Day*.]

PERCY, Dr THOMAS.
Miscellaneous Pieces relating to the Chinese 8° 1763.
[Contains *The Little Orphan of the House of Chao*.]

PIERSON, THOMAS.
*T. The Treacherous Son-in-Law (Stokesley *c.* 1785) 8° 1786
[*Stockton*].

PIGUENIT, D. J.
Ent. Don Quixote. A Musical Entertainment (C.G. 1774) 8° 1774; 8°
1776.
[Music S. Arnold.]

PILON, FREDERICK.
F. The Invasion; or, A Trip to Brighthelmstone (C.G. W. 4/11/1778)
8° 1778 [*bis*]; MS. Larpent 18. M. [29/10/1778].
F. The Liverpool Prize (C.G. M. 22/2/1779) 8° 1779; MS. Larpent
20. M. [Feb. 1779].
Prel. Illumination; or, The Glazier's Conspiracy (C.G. M. 12/4/1779)
8° 1779; MS. Larpent 14. L. [7/4/1779].
*F. The Device; or, The Deaf Doctor (C.G. M. 27/9/1779); MS.
Larpent 19. M. [23/9/1779].
[Taken from the French; see *infra*, The Deaf Lover.]
F. The Deaf Lover (C.G. W. 2/2/1780) 8° 1780 [*bis*]; 8° 1781 [3r d];
8° 1793 [4th]; 12° 1802 [*Dublin*]; 8° 1811 [6th].
[An alteration of *The Device, supra*.]

[O.F.] The Siege of Gibraltar; A Musical Farce (C.G. T. 25/4/1780) 8° 1780 [bis].
    [Music William Shield.]
F. The Humours of an Election (C.G. Th. 19/10/1780) 8° 1780 [bis]; MS. Larpent 22. M. [11/10/1780; as The Close of the Poll].
*F. Thelyphthora; or, More Wives than One (C.G. Th. 8/3/1781) MS. Larpent 24. M. [7/3/1781].
C.O. The Fair American (D.L. S. 18/5/1782) 8° 1785; 12° 1785 [Dublin]; Songs, Duets, etc., in the Fair American 8° 1782; MS. Larpent 18. S. [14/5/1782].
    [Music T. Carter.]
F. Ærostation; or, The Templar's Stratagem (C.G. F. 29/10/1784) 8° 1784; 12° 1785 [Dublin]; MS. Larpent 37. M.
F. Barataria; or, Sancho turn'd Governor (C.G. T. 29/3/1785) 8° 1793 [new edition].
*C. All's Well that Ends Well (H.² T. 26/7/1785).
    [Alteration from Shakespeare.]
C. He Would be a Soldier (C.G. S. 18/11/1786) 8° 1786 [bis]; 8° 1787 [3rd]; 12° 1787 [Dublin]; MS. Larpent 45. M. [1786].

PLUMPTRE, ANNE.
    [D.] The Count of Burgundy, A Play...By Augustus von Kotzebue... Translated from the Genuine German Edition 8° 1798 [3 editions]; 12° 1799 [Dublin].
    [D.] The Natural Son; A Play...by Augustus von Kotzebue...Being the Original of Lovers' Vows...Translated from the German 8° 1798 [4 editions]; 12° 1798 [Dublin].
    [D.] The Force of Calumny. A Play...By Augustus von Kotzebue. Translated from the German 8° 1799 [bis].
    D. La-Peyrouse, A Drama...By Augustus von Kotzebue. Translated from the German 8° 1799.
    T. The Spaniards in Peru; or, The Death of Rolla. A Tragedy...By Augustus von Kotzebue. The Original of the Play performed... under the Title of Pizarro. Translated from the German 8° 1799 [6 editions, the last being "revised"].
    [D.] The Virgin of the Sun. A Play...By Augustus von Kotzebue. Translated from the Genuine German Edition 8° 1799 [5 editions].
    [F.] The Widow and the Riding Horse. A Dramatic Trifle...By Augustus von Kotzebue. Translated from the German 8° 1799.

PLUMPTRE, BELL.
    [D.] The Foresters, A Picture of Rural Manners, A Play...By William Augustus Iffland. Translated from the German 8° 1799.

PLUMPTRE, JAMES.
    C. The Coventry Act (Norwich 16/1/1793) 8° 1793 [Norwich]; MS. Larpent 25. S. [29/12/1792].
    T. Osway 4° 1795 [Norwich].
    C.O. The Lakers 8° 1798.

POPE, Miss.
    *F. The Young Couple (D.L. T. 21/4/1767).
    [An alteration of Mrs Frances Sheridan, The Discovery.]

POPE, ALEXANDER [Actor].
    *T. The Count of Burgundy (C.G. F. 12/4/1799).
    [An adaptation of Anne Plumptre's The Count of Burgundy (1798), translated from Kotzebue; see supra.]

PORRETT, ROBERT.

T. Clarissa: or, The Fatal Seduction...Founded on Richardson's celebrated novel of Clarissa Harlowe 8° 1788.

PORTAL, ABRAHAM.

T. Olindo and Sophronia...The Story taken from Tasso 8° 1758 [bis].

C. The Indiscreet Lover (H.² 1768) 8° 1768 [bis].

C.O. Songs, Duets, and Finale, in the Cady of Bagdad (D.L. Th. 19/2/1778) 8° 1778 [bis]; MS. Larpent 18. M. [as The Cady; 9/2/1778].

T. Vortimer; or, The True Patriot 8° 1796.

PORTER, STEPHEN.

[D.] Lover's Vows: or, The Child of Love. A Play...translated from the German of Augustus von Kotzebue with a Brief Biography of the Author 8° 1798.

   [A literal translation from A. v. Kotzebue. See *supra* Mrs Elizabeth Inchbald, *Lovers' Vows* and Anne Plumptre, *The Natural Son*.]

PORTER, WALSH.

C.O. Songs, Duetts...in The Chimney Corner (D.L. S. 7/10/1797) 8° [1797]; MS. Larpent 71. M. [30/9/1797].
   [Music M. Kelly.]

*Int. Voluntary Contributions (Bath 1798; and C.G. S. 12/5/1798) MS. Larpent 33. S. [27/2/1798].

POTT, JOSEPH HOLDEN.

T. Selmane [in Elegies: With Selmane 8° 1782].

POTTER, JOHN.

*Ser. The Choice of Apollo (H.² M. 11/3/1765) 4° 1765.
   [Music William Yates.]

POTTER, ROBERT.

The Tragedies of Æschylus, translated 4° 1777; 8° 1779 etc.
The Tragedies of Euripides, translated 4° 1781; 8° 1808 etc.

POTTINGER, ISRAEL.

C. The Methodist...being a Continuation and Completion of the Plan of the Minor, written by Mr. Foote 8° [1761].
   [See Samuel Foote, *The Minor*.]

*F. The Humorous Quarrel; or, The Battle of the Greybeards (Southwark Fair, 1761) 8° [1761].

[Sat.] The Duenna: a Comic Opera 8° 1776 [bis]; 8° [?1779].
   [See R. B. Sheridan, *The Duenna*.]

POWELL, JAMES.

The Narcotic and Private Theatricals Two Dramatic Pieces 8° [1787].

PRATT, SAMUEL JACKSON.

*F. Joseph Andrews (D.L. M. 20/4/1778).

T. The Fair Circassian (D.L. T. 27/11/1781) 8° 1781 [3 editions].

C. The School for Vanity (D.L. W. 29/1/1783) [in *Miscellanies*, 4 vols. 8° 1785] MS. Larpent 32. M. [15/1/1783].

*C. The New Cosmetic; or, The Triumph of Beauty 8° 1790 [under pseudonym of C. Melmoth].

   [For his later works see the Hand-list of Plays, 1800–1850.]

PRESTON, ——.
*F. The Rival Father 8° 1754 [*Dublin*].

PRESTON, WILLIAM.
 T. Offa and Ethelbert; or, The Saxon Princes 8° 1791 [*Dublin*].
  The Poetical Works of William Preston, 2 vols. 8° 1793 [*Dublin*].
  [Contain: 1. *Messene Freed* (Crow-street, Dublin, Th. 12/1/1792);
  2. *Rosimunda*. Besides this there is a song for a tragedy (unprinted)
  called *The Adopted Son.*]
 T. Democratic Rage: or, Louis the Unfortunate (Crow-street,
  Dublin, June 1793) 8° 1793 [*bis*]; 8° 1793 [*Dublin*].
 T. The Siege of Ismail...An Historical Tragedy 8° 1794.

PRICE, JOHN.
 O.F. The Seaman's Return, or, the Unexpected Marriage (Worcester,
  Shrewsbury, Ludlow and Wolverhampton) 8° 1795 [*Ludlow*].
  [This is said to be an adaptation from the German.]

PYE, HENRY JAMES.
  [For *The Inquisitor* (1798) see under *J. P. ANDREWS*.]
 T. The Siege of Meaux (C.G. M. 19/5/1794) 8° 1794.
 T. Adelaide (D.L. Jan. 1800) 8° 1800.
 C. A Prior Claim (D.L. Oct. 1805) 8° 1805.
  [Written in collaboration with *SAMUEL JAMES ARNOLD*.]

PYE, Mrs J. HENRIETTA.
*F. The Capricious Lady (D.L. F. 10/5/1771) MS. Larpent 12. M.
 [30/4/1771].

RANNIE, JOHN.
  Musical Dramas, with Select Poems, and Ballads 8° [*c*. 1806].
  [Contains: 1. *The Cottage of the Cliffs*; 2. *The Exiles*; 3. *The
  Deserted Tower*; 4. *The Convent, or the Forc'd Vow*; 5. *The Lowland Lassie; or, A Trip from Kinghorn*. The first of these was
  certainly written before 1800, and it is probable that most of the
  others were eighteenth century productions.]

RASPE, RUDOLPH ERICH.
 D. Nathan the Wise. A Philosophical Drama. From the German of
  G. E. Lessing 8° 1781.
  [A translation of G. E. Lessing, *Nathan der Weise*.]

REED, JOSEPH.
*F. The Superannuated Gallant (Newcastle) 12° 1745 [*Newcastle*].
  [Burlesque] Madrigal and Trulletta. A Mock-Tragedy...With Notes
  by the Author, and Dr. Humbug, Critick and Censor-General
  (C.G. Th. 6/7/1758) 8° 1758; MS. Larpent 5. S. [2/6/1758].
  [Evidently re-written for H.[2] W. 18/9/1771.]
 F. The Register-Office (D.L. S. 25/4/1761) 8° 1761; 8° 1771; MS.
  Larpent 6. S. [1761].
 T. Dido (D.L. S. 28/3/1767) 8° 1808; MS. Larpent 8. S. [6/3/1767].
 C.O. Tom Jones (C.G. S. 14/1/1769) 8° 1769 [*bis*]; 12° 1769 [*Dublin*];
  music and words F. [1769]; MS. Larpent 8. S. [22/12/1768].
  [Partly based on Poinsinet, *Tom Jones*. A pasticcio.]
*F. The Impostors; or, A Cure for Credulity (C.G. F. 19/3/1776]
  MS. Larpent 16. M. [11/3/1776; as *The Impostors, or The Credulous
  Don*].

REES, THOMAS DAVID.
    [M.D.] Iver and Hengo; or, The Rival Brothers; a Dramatic Romance
       4° 1795.

REEVES, JOSEPH.
    *T. Cato 8° 1764.
       [An alteration of Joseph Addison, Cato.]

RENDER, Dr WILLIAM.
    T.C. Count Benyowsky; or, The Conspiracy of Kamtschatka...By
       Baron Kotzebue...Translated from the German 8° 1798 [bis].
    T. The Robbers 8° 1799.
       [A translation of Schiller, Die Räuber.]

REYNOLDS, FREDERICK.
    [For Better Late than Never (D.L. 1790) and The Mysteries of the
       Castle (C.G. 1795) see under M. P. ANDREWS.]
    T. Werter (Bath F. 25/11/1785; C.G. T. 14/3/1786) 8° 1786 [Dublin;
       pirated]; 8° 1796; 8° 1802; MS. Larpent 39. M. [29/11/1785].
    *T. Eloisa (C.G. W. 20/12/1786) MS. Larpent 41. M. [1786].
    C. The Dramatist: or, Stop Him who Can! (C.G. F. 15/5/1789) 12°
       1790 [Dublin; pirated]; 8° 1793; MS. Larpent 51. M. [7/5/1789].
    [M.D.] Songs, Duets, Chorusses, &c., in the Historical Romance of
       The Crusade (C.G. Th. 6/5/1790) 8° 1790; MS. Larpent 51. M.
       [21/4/1790].
    C. Notoriety (C.G. S. 5/11/1791) 8° 1792 [Dublin; pirated]; 12° 1792
       [Dublin; pirated]; 8° 1793; MS. Larpent 54. M. [3/11/1791].
       [Based partly on Fletcher, Monsieur Thomas.]
    C. How to Grow Rich (C.G. Th. 18/4/1793) 8° 1793 [4 editions];
       12° 1793 [Dublin]; MS. Larpent 61. M. [27/3/1793].
    C. The Rage (C.G. Th. 23/10/1794) 8° 1795 [3 editions]; 8° 1795
       [Dublin]; 8° 1797; MS. Larpent 63. M. [10/10/1794].
    C. Speculation (C.G. S. 7/11/1795) 8° 1795; 8° 1796 [2nd]; 8° 1800;
       MS. Larpent 67. M. [29/9/1795].
    C. Fortune's Fool (C.G. S. 29/10/1796) 8° 1796; 12° 1797 [Dublin];
       MS. Larpent 69. M. [12/10/1796].
    C. The Will (D.L. W. 19/4/1797) 8° 1797 [3 editions]; 12° 1797
       [Dublin; 3rd]; 8° 1806 [4th]; 8° 1815 [5th].
    C. Cheap Living (D.L. S. 21/10/1797) 8° 1797 [3 editions]; 12° 1798
       [Dublin]; MS. Larpent 72. M. [9/10/1797].
       [See Fisher, The School for Ingratitude (1798).]
    C. Laugh When You Can (C.G. S. 8/12/1798) 8° 1799; 12° 1799
       [Dublin]; 8° 1802.
    C. Management (C.G. Th. 31/10/1799) 8° 1799 [4 editions]; 8° 1800
       [5th]; MS. Larpent 74. M. [18/10/1799].
       [For his later works see the Hand-list of Plays, 1800–1850.]

REYNOLDS, G. N.
    Ent. Airs and Chorusses in the Musical Entertainment called Bantry
       Bay (C.G. M. 20/2/1797) 4° 1797; MS. Larpent 71. M. [10/2/1797].

RHODES, THOMAS.
    *C.O. The Sailor's Opera 8° 1789.

RICH, JOHN.
    C. The Spirit of Contradiction, A New Comedy (C.G. Th. 6/3/1760)
       8° 1760; MS. Larpent 6. S. [1760; as The S. of C., or Domestick
       Tyrant].

RICHARDS, ——.
　*C.O. The Device; or, The Marriage Office (C.G. M. 5/5/1777) MS.
　　Larpent 17. M. [29/4/1777].
RICHARDSON, ELIZABETH.
　*C. The Double Deception (D.L. W. 28/4/1779) MS. Larpent 21. M.
　　[23/4/1779; as *The D.D., or Lovers Perplexed*].
RICHARDSON, JOSEPH.
　C. The Fugitive (H.¹ F. 20/4/1792) 8° 1792 [3 editions]; 8° 1792
　　[*Cork*]; MS. Larpent 57. M. [16/3/1792].
RICHARDSON, Professor WILLIAM.
　T. The Indians (Richmond *c.* 1790) 8° 1790.
　[M.D.] The Maid of Lochlin: A Lyrical Drama 8° 1801.
ROBERDEAU, JOHN PETER.
　*F. The Point of Honour (advertised for C.G. Th. 10/5/1792, but never
　　acted) MS. Larpent 58. M. [24/4/1792].
　*Sat. St Andrew's Festival; or, The Game at Golf (D.L. 29/5/1795)
　　MS. Larpent 68. M. [23/5/1795].
ROBERTS, JAMES.
　[Int.] Rule Britannia: a Loyal Sketch (H.² M. 18/8/1794) 8° 1794; MS.
　　Larpent 28. S. [11/8/1794].
ROBERTS, Miss R.
　T. Malcolm 8° 1779.
ROBERTS, WILLIAM [Schoolmaster].
　*T. Abradates and Panthea (St Paul's School, 1770).
ROBERTS, WILLIAM [Barrister].
　C. The Fugitives 8° 1791 [*Warrington*].
ROBERTSON, ——.
　*[Int.] The Heroine of Love 8° 1778.
ROBERTSON, Mrs.
　*[M.D.] Ellinda; or, The Abbey of St. Aubert. A Dramatic Romance
　　(Newark 1800).
ROBINSON, ——.
　*Ent. The Test of Love (H.² F. 17/8/1787) MS. Larpent 46. M.
　　[15/8/1787].
　　　[Taken from the French.]
ROBINSON, ——.
　*F. A Trip to Plymouth Dock; or, The Launch of the Caesar
　　(Plymouth 1793).
ROBINSON, MARY.
　C.O. The Songs...in The Lucky Escape (D.L. Th. 30/4/1778) 8°
　　[1778]; MS. Larpent 15. S. [23/4/1778].
　*C. Nobody (D.L. S. 29/11/1794) MS. Larpent 62. M. [28/11/
　　1794].
　T. The Sicilian Lover 8° 1796.
ROBSON, HORATIO.
　*Int. Too Loving by Half (C.G. M. 10/5/1784) MS. Larpent 35. M.
　　[1784].
　C. Look before You Leap...Translated from the Celebrated La
　　Bonne Mere of De Florian (H.² F. 22/8/1788) 8° 1788.
　[O.F.] Money at a Pinch; or, The Irishman's Frolics (C.G. Th.
　　25/4/1793) MS. Larpent 62. M. [12/4/1793; as a comic opera].

RODD, THOMAS.
   T. Zuma 8° 1800.
      [A translation from the French of P. F. A. Le Fevre.]

ROGERS, ROBERT.
   T. Ponteach: or the Savages of America 8° 1766.

ROLT, RICHARD.
   [Int.] Eliza; a New Musical Entertainment (H.² W. 29/5/1754; D.L.
      F. 21/1/1757) 8° 1754; 8° 1757.
      [Music M. Arne. This Interlude is said to have been given first
      at Dublin in 1743 or 1756.]
   O. The Royal Shepherd, An English Opera (D.L. F. 24/2/1764) 8°
      1764 [3 editions]; 12° [1765].
      [Music Rush. An adaptation of Metastasio, Il Rè Pastore. It
      was later altered as Amintas (C.G. F. 15/12/1769).]
   O. Almena: An English Opera (D.L. F. 2/11/1764) 8° 1764; 12°
      [1764; Dublin]; MS. Larpent 7. S. [27/10/1764].
      [Music M. Arne and Battishill.]
   O. Amintas, an English Opera (C.G. F. 15/12/1769) 12° 1786 [in a
      Collection of Farces].
      [See The Royal Shepherd, supra; alteration by F. TENDUCCI.]

ROSE, Rev. JOHN.
   [F.] A Quarter of an Hour before Dinner; or, Quality Binding. A
      Dramatic Entertainment (H.² S. 2/8/1788) 8° 1788.
   *F. The Family Compact (H.² Th. 6/9/1792) MS. Larpent 24. S.
      [30/8/1792].
   [M.D.] The Prisoner. A Musical Romance (H.¹ Th. 18/10/1792) 8°
      [1792]; 8° 1793 [Dublin]; Songs, Choruses, &c., in The Prisoner
      8° 1792; MS. Larpent 57. M. [10/10/1792].
      [Music T. Attwood.]
   [M.D.] Caernarvon Castle; or, the Birth of the Prince of Wales, an
      Opera (H.² M. 12/8/1793) 8° 1793; MS. Larpent 25. S. [6/8/1793].
      [Music T. Attwood.]

ROSS, Miss ANNA.
   C.O. The Cottagers 8° 1788 [bis].

ROSS, Lieutenant WILLIAM.
   *C. What Would She Not? or, The Test of Affection (Portsmouth
      1790).

ROUGH, WILLIAM.
   D. Lorenzino di Medici...and other Poems 12° 1797.

ROWE, HARRY.
   [O.F.] No Cure no Pay: or, The Pharmacopolist. A Musical Farce 8°
      1797 [York].

RULE, JOHN.
   *C. The Agreeable Surprise (school performance, Islington) [in
      Poetical Blossoms 12° 1766].
      [A translation from Marivaux, La joie imprévue (1738).]

RYDER, THOMAS.
   C. Like Master, Like Man...Altered from Sir John Vanbrugh
      (S.A. Dublin W. 30/4/1766; H.² M. 21/9/1767) 12° 1799 [Dublin].
      [An alteration of The Mistake.]

*Int. Such Things Have Been (C.G. T. 31/3/1789) MS. Larpent
17. L. [25/3/1789].
[An alteration of Jackman, *The Man of Parts*.]

RYLEY, SAMUEL WILLIAM.
Roderick Random, A Comic Opera and The Civilian, A Musical
Farce (Manchester *c.* 1790) 8° [*c.* 1798]; MS. of *The Civilian*
Larpent 17. L. [15/4/1789] and of *Roderick Random* 22. S.
[12/4/1790].

RYVES, ELIZABETH.
Poems on Several Occasions 8° 1777.
[Contains: 1. *The Prude*; 2. *The Triumph of Hymen*.]
*C. The Debt of Honour [see the *Biographia Dramatica*, ii. 156].

SADLER, THOMAS.
F. Poems on Various Subjects—To which is added, The Merry
Miller 8° 1766 [*Salop*].

ST JOHN, Hon. JOHN.
T. Mary, Queen of Scots (D.L. S. 21/3/1789) 8° 1789; 12° 1789
[*Dublin*]; MS. Larpent 49. M. [March 1789].
O. The Island of St. Marguerite (D.L. F. 13/11/1789) 8° 1789
[3 editions]; 8° 1790 [4th]; MS. Larpent 48. M. [21/10/1789].
[Music Thomas Shaw.]

SARGENT, JOHN.
Dr. Poem. The Mine 4° 1785.

SAWYERS, Dr. FRANK.
Poems, containing Sketches of Northern Mythology *4° 1789;
8° 1803 [3rd]; 8° 1807 [4th *Norwich*].

SCAWEN, JOHN.
*F. The Girl in Style (C.G. W. 6/12/1786) MS. Larpent 43. M. [1786].
[C.O.] New Spain, or, Love in Mexico: An Opera (H.² F. 16/7/1790)
8° 1790; 12° 1790 [*Dublin*]; Songs, Chorusses, &c., in the Opera
of New Spain 8° 1790; MS. Larpent 53. M. [6/7/1790].
[Music S. Arnold.]

SCHINK, A.
[D.] The Stranger: A Comedy. Freely Translated from Kotzebue's
German Comedy of Misanthropy and Repentance 8° 1798 [5
editions]; 8° 1799 [6th]; 8° 1799 [7th].
[An altered version of A. v. Kotzebue, *Menschenhass und Reue*.]

SCHOMBERG, RALPH.
*Burlesque. The Death of Bucephalus (Edinburgh *c.* 1765).
Burl. The Judgment of Paris (H.¹ W. 24/8/1768) 8° 1768; MS. Larpent
9. M. [1768].
[Music Barthélémon.]
T. Romulus and Hersilia [see the *Biographia Dramatica*, iii. 224].

SCOTT, THOMAS.
T. Edwin and Catherine; or The Distressed Lovers 8° 1793 [*Paisley*];
8° 1793 [in *Poems*].

SCOTT, Sir WALTER.
T. Goetz of Berlichingen, With the Iron Hand...Translated from
the German of Goethe 8° 1799.
[A translation of Goethe, *Götz von Berlichingen*.]

SEALLY, JOHN.
*Burlesque O The Marriage of Sir Gawaine [in *The European Magazine*, May and July, 1782].

SHAPTER, THOMAS.
Past. The Fugitive; or, Happy Recess 8° [1790].

SHARPE, JOHN.
*C.O. Laura; or, Who's to Have Her? (Sheffield 1791).
*F. Too Learned by Half; or, The Philosopher Outwitted 12° [1793].

SHEPHERD, HENRY.
O. The Orphans; or, Generous Lovers 8° 1800 [*bis*].

SHEPHERD, Dr RICHARD.
Dr. Poem. The Nuptials 4° 1761.
Dr. Poem. Hector 4° 1770; *8° 1775.
T. Bianca 8° 1772 [*Oxford*].

SHERIDAN, Miss.
*F. The Ambiguous Lover (Crow-street, Dublin, Th. 5/3/1781).

SHERIDAN, Mrs FRANCES.
C. The Discovery (D.L. Th. 3/2/1763) 8° 1763 [*bis*]; 8° 1763 [*Edinburgh*]; 12° 1763 [*Dublin*]; MS. Larpent 6. M. [24/1/1763].
C. The Dupe (D.L. S. 10/12/1763) 8° 1764; MS. Larpent 7. M. [22/11/1763].

SHERIDAN, Rt. Hon. RICHARD BRINSLEY.
C. The Rivals (C.G. T. 17/1/1775) 8° 1775 [3 editions]; 12° 1775 [*Dublin*]; 8° 1776 [3rd]; 8° 1776 [4th]; 8° 1791 [5th]; 12° 1793 [*Dublin*]; 8° 1798 [6th]; 8° 1797; MS. Larpent 12. L. [9/1/1775].
[F.] St. Patrick's Day: or, The Scheming Lieutenant. A Comic Opera (C.G. T. 2/5/1775) 12° 1788 [*Dublin*; pirated]; MS. Larpent 15. M. [24/4/1775].
C.O. The Duenna (C.G. T. 21/11/1775). The Duenna: or, The Double Elopement 8° 1783; 12° 1785 [*Dublin*]; 12° 1787 [*Dublin*]; The Duenna 8° 1794; 12° [1795; *Dublin*]; 8° 1797; Music and words F. [1775]; 12° 1783; 8° 1785; Songs, Duets, Trios, &c. in The Duenna; or, The Double Elopement 8° 1775 [6 editions]; 8° 1776 [at least 10 editions]; 8° 1777 [23rd]; 8° 1780 [27th]; 8° 1783 [29th].
  [On the whole question of Sheridan bibliography and on the relations between *The Duenna* and *The Governess* 12° 1777 see R. Crompton Rhodes' bibliographical essay in his edition of the plays. Music T. Linley.]
C. A Trip to Scarborough...Altered from Vanbrugh's Relapse (D.L. M. 24/2/1777) 8° 1781; 12° 1781 [*Dublin*]; MS. Larpent 17. M. [17/2/1777].
C. The School for Scandal (D.L. Th. 8/5/1777).
  [The complicated text of this play is dealt with by R. Crompton Rhodes in his edition of Sheridan's works (1928). See also G. H. Nettleton (*Times Literary Supplement*, Oct. 11, 1934; March 28, 1935), M. J. Ryan (*id.* March 22, 29, April 19, May 10, June 7, 1928; Oct. 25, 1934) and F. W. Bateson (*id.* Nov. 28, Dec. 5, 1929). See supplementary notes.]
Ent. The Camp, A Musical Entertainment (D.L. Th. 15/10/1778) 8° 1795; MS. Larpent 18. M. [13/10/1778].
  [Tate Wilkinson (*The Wandering Patentee*, iv. 124) denies

Sheridan's authorship, although the title-page declares it to be his; it has been attributed to *RICHARD TICKELL*. Music T. Linley.]

[Burlesque.] The Critic or A Tragedy Rehearsed A Dramatic Piece (D.L. S. 30/10/1779) 8° 1781 [3 editions]; 12° 1785 [*Dublin*]; 8° 1781 [*sic*, but *c.* 1796]; 8° 1808; 8° 1811; MS. Larpent 15. S. [29/10/1779].

Ent. Songs, Duetts, Choruses, &c. In a New and Appropriate Entertainment, Called The Glorious First of June... For the Benefit of the Widows and Orphans of the Brave Men who fell in the late Engagements under Lord Howe (D.L. W. 2/7/1794) 8° [1794]; MS. Larpent 64. M. [1/7/1794].

[Dialogue by Sheridan and *JAMES COBB*; many songs by the Duke of Leeds, Lord Mulgrave, Mrs Robinson, etc. See *Cape St Vincent, infra.*]

Ent. Songs, Duetts, Chorusses, &c., in an Occasional Entertainment called Cape St. Vincent; or, British Valour Triumphant. Altered from a Dramatical Performance performed in 1794 (D.L. March 1797) 8° 1797.

[An alteration of *The Glorious First of June, supra.*]

T. Pizarro...Taken from the German Drama of Kotzebue; And adapted to the English Stage (D.L. F. 24/5/1799) 8° 1799 [26 editions]; 8° 1804 [27th]; 8° 1807 [28th]; 8° 1811 [29th]; 8° 1814 [30th].

SHERIDAN, THOMAS.

[For his earlier works see the Hand-list of Plays, 1700–1750; a few pre-1750 plays are included here.]

T. Coriolanus: or, The Roman Matron...Taken from Shakespear and Thomson (C.G. T. 10/12/1754) 8° 1755; 8° 1786.

*T. The Loyal Subject [S.A. Dublin M. 2/3/1741; an alteration of the eponymous play by Beaumont and Fletcher].

*T. Romeo and Juliet [S.A. Dublin M. 15/12/1746].

*F. Æsop (D.L. S. 19/12/1778).

[An alteration of Sir John Vanbrugh's comedy.]

SHILLITO, CHARLES.

F. The Man of Enterprise (Norwich 1789) 8° 1789 [*Colchester*]; 12° 1790 [*Dublin*]; MS. Larpent 50. M. [Jan. 1789].

SHIRLEY, WILLIAM.

[For his earlier works see the Hand-list of Plays, 1700–1750.]

Burlesque O. King Pepin's Campaign (D.L. M. 15/4/1745) 8° 1755. [Music Dr Arne.]

T. Edward the Black Prince; or, The Battle of Poictiers: An Historical Tragedy. Attempted after the Manner of Shakespear (D.L. S. 6/1/1750) 8° 1750; MS. Larpent 2. M. [3/11/1749].

T. Electra 4° 1765.

[An adaptation from Sophocles. Written 1745 and in rehearsal at C.G. Jan. 1763, but refused a licence by the Lord Chamberlain.]

M. The Birth of Hercules 4° 1765 [printed with above]; MS. Larpent 6. S. [11/1/1763 as from C.G.].

[This piece was in rehearsal at C.G. in 1763 but was put off owing to the Half Price Riots. Music Dr Arne.]

*T. The Roman Sacrifice (D.L. Th. 18/12/1777).

*T. The Roman Victim [see *Biographia Dramatica*, iii. 220].

SHIRREFS, ANDREW.
  Past. Jamie and Bess, or the Laird in Disguise, a Scots Pastoral
    Comedy...in imitation of The Gentle Shepherd (Edinburgh,
    Aberdeen, Elgin, Inverness) 8° 1787 [Aberdeen]; 8° 1790 [in
    Poems].
  *Int. The Sons of Britannia (Edinburgh 1796).

SHRAPTER, THOMAS.
  *Past. The Fugitive; or, The Happy Recess 8° 1790.

SICKLEMORE, RICHARD.
  [F.] The Dream. A Serio-Dramatic Piece (Brighton, T. 23/8/1796)
    8° 1797 [Lewes].
  Int. Quarter Day (Dover c. 1797) 8° 1798 [Lewes]; MS. Larpent 73. M.
    [30/4/1798].
  [C.O.] Saltimbanco; or, The Disagreeable Surprise. An Opera
    (Brighton S. 5/8/1797) 8° 1798 [Lewes].
    [Music Prince.]
  *C.O. The Cottage Maid; or, The Customs of the Castle (Brighton
    T. 2/10/1798).
  [M.D.] Aboukir Bay; or, the Glorious First of August. A Musical
    Drama (Brighton 1799) 8° 1799 [Lewes].
    [For his later works see the Hand-list of Plays, 1800–1850.]

SIDDONS, HENRY.
  Int. Modern Breakfast: or, All Asleep at Noon (H.¹ W. 11/8/1790) 8°
    1790; MS. Larpent 53. M. [3/8/1790].
  [M.D.] The Sicilian Romance: or, The Apparition of the Cliffs, An
    Opera (C.G. W. 28/5/1794) 8° 1794; MS. L. 995 [as The Castle of
    Otranto (UA)].
    [Music W. Reeve.]
  *F. The Adventures of Tom Trip; or, The Wounded Sailor (New-
    castle 1796).
  *F. What We Have Been, and What We May Be; or, Britain in her
    Glory (Newcastle 1796).
  *O. Zelida; or, The Pirates (Lancaster 1799).
    [Partly based on A. v. Kotzebue, Graf Benjowsky.]
    [For his later works see the Handlist of Plays, 1800–1850.]

SILVESTER, ——.
  *C. Ranger in Wedlock; or, The Amiable Mistake (H.² 1788).

SIMON, ——.
  *C. National Prejudice (C.G. T. 10/5/1791) MS. Larpent 54. M.
    [9/5/1791].
  *F. The Village Coquette (H.¹ M. 16/4/1792) MS. Larpent 58. M.
    [9/4/1792].
    [Taken from the French.]

SIMPSON, JOSEPH.
  T. The Patriot...From a Manuscript of the Late Dr. Samuel John-
    son, Corrected by Himself 8° 1785.
    [Corrections apparently were made in the play by Johnson. The
    tragedy was written about 1764.]

SLADE, JOHN.
  T. Love and Duty (H.² 1756) 8° 1756.

SMART, CHRISTOPHER.
[For his earlier works see the Hand-list of Plays, 1700–1750.]
*M. The Judgment of Midas [in *Poems* 8° 1752].

SMITH, ADAM.
*Int. The Noble Foresters [in *The Theatrical Museum* 8° 1776].
[Based on *As You Like It*.]

SMITH, CHARLES.
Ent. Songs, Duetts, Chorusses, &c., in A Day at Rome. A Musical
Entertainment (C.G. Th. 11/10/1798) 8° 1798; MS. Larpent 33. S.
[9/4/1798].
[Music T. Attwood.]
[A Charles Smith issued a three volume translation of the
Dramatic Works of Kotzebue at New York in 1798.]

SMITH, CHARLOTTE.
C. What is She? (C.G. S. 27/4/1799) 8° 1799 [*bis*]; 8° 1800 [3rd];
12° [*Dublin*; ?1800; "by Charlotte Smith"].

SMITH, E.
C. The Contrast, or the Mayoralty of Trueborough 8° [*Plymouth*;
?1790].

SMITH, J.
F. Sir John Butt 8° 1798 [*Edinburgh*].

SMITH, JAMES.
O.F. The Cottage 8° [*Tewkesbury*; 1796].

SMOLLETT, TOBIAS GEORGE.
[For his earlier works see the Hand-list of Plays, 1700–1750.]
C. The Reprisal; or, The Tars of Old England (D.L. S. 22/1/1757) 8°
1757; 8° 1758; 12° 1758 [*Glasgow*]; 12° 1761 (*Dublin*); 8° 1777 [in
Plays and Poems].
*C. The Israelites; or, The Pampered Nabob (C.G. F. 1/4/1785) MS.
Larpent 39. M. [1785].
[Ascribed to Smollett.]

SMYTHE, GEORGE.
C. The Generous Attachment 8° 1796.

SOTHEBY, WILLIAM.
T. The Siege of Cuzco 8° 1800.
[For his later works see the Hand-list of Plays, 1800–1850.]

STANFIELD, JAMES FIELD.
*C.O. The Fishermen (York *c.* 1786).

STANLEY, EDWARD.
Dr. Poem. Elmira 8° 1790 [*Norwich*].

STARKE, MARIANA.
C. The Sword of Peace; or, A Voyage of Love (H.² S. 9/8/1788) 8°
1789; 12° 1790 [*Dublin*].
*T. The British Orphan (Mrs Crespigny's private theatre at Camber-
well, F. 7/4/1790).
T. The Widow of Malabar (Mrs Crespigny's private theatre at

Camberwell 1790; C.G. W. 5/5/1790) 8° 1791; 12° 1791 [*Dublin*];
8° 1791 [3rd]; MS. Larpent 51. M. [21/4/1790].
[An adaptation of A. M. Lemierre, *La Veuve de Malabar*.]
T. The Tournament... imitated from the celebrated German Drama
entitled Agnes Bernauer 8° 1800.
[An adaptation of J. A. von Törring und Kronsfeld, *Agnes
Bernauer*.]

STAYLEY, GEORGE.
Ent. The Court of Nassau; or, the Trial of Hum-bug. A Comedy not
worth acting 8° 1753 [*Dublin*].
F. The Rival Theatres; or, A Play-House to be Let... To which is
added, The Chocolate-Makers; or, Mimickry Exposed, an Interlude (S.A. Dublin May 1759) 8° 1759; 12° 1759 [*Dublin*].

STEELE, ARCHIBALD.
*Past. The Shepherd's Wedding 8° 1789 [? *Edinburgh*].

STEVENS, GEORGE ALEXANDER.
Burlesque. Distress upon Distress: or, Tragedy in True Taste. A
Heroi-Comi-Parodi-Tragedi-Farcical Burlesque... With all the
Similes, Rants, Groans, Sighs, &c., entirely new. With Annota-
tions, Dissertations, Explanations, Observations, Emendations,
Quotations, Restorations, &c. By Sir Henry Humm. And Notes,
Critical, Classical, and Historical, by Paulus Purgantius Pedas-
culus. Who has carefully Revised, Corrected and Amended it;
Expurged the several Errors and Interpolations; Reconciled the
various Readings, and Restored the Author to Himself 8° 1752;
8° 1752 [*Dublin*].
*Int. Hearts of Oak (D.L. 15/1/1762) [see *Biographia Dramatica*, ii. 286]
MS. Larpent 7. L. [13/1/1762].
F. The French Flogged, or, British Sailors in America (Bartholomew
Fair 1767; C.G. 20/3/60) 8° 1767; MS. Larpent 6. L. [28/2/1760].
Burlesque O. The Court of Alexander (C.G. F. 5/1/1770) 8° 1770 [*bis*];
12° 1770 [*Dublin*].
[Music J. A. Fisher.]
[O.F.] The Trip to Portsmouth: A Comic Sketch (H.² W. 11/8/1773)
8° [1773]; Songs in the Trip to Portsmouth 8° [1773]; MS. Lar-
pent 11. L. [3/8/1773].
[Music C. Dibdin.]
[O.F.] The Songs... in The Cabinet of Fancy : or, Evening's Exhibi-
tion (H.² 1780) 8° 1780; MS. Larpent 15. L. [2/10/1780].

STEWART, JAMES.
C. The Two English Gentlemen; or, The Sham Funeral (H.² 1774)
8° 1774; MS. Larpent 11. L. [21/3/1774].
F. The Students, or The Humours of St. Andrews (H.² 1779) 8°
1779; MS. Larpent 13. L. [24/9/1777].

STEWART, THOMAS.
T. Valentia; or, The Fatal Birth-Day 8° 1772.

STILLINGFLEET, BENJAMIN.
Orat. Medea 8° [1765]. See *ITALIAN OPERAS.*

STOCKDALE, Rev. PERCIVAL.
Past. The Amyntas of Tasso. Translated from the Original Italian
8° 1770.
T. Ximenes 8° 1788.

STORACE, STEPHEN.

Ent. La Serva Padrona; or, The Servant Mistress, translated from the Italian (M.G. 8/6/1758) 4° 1761.
[A translation of *La Serva Padrona* by S. A. Federico.]

Ent. The Coquet. A Musical Entertainment... Translated from the Italian of Signor Goldoni, and adapted to the original Music of Signor Galuppi (M.G. 1771) 8° 1771.
[An adaptation from Goldoni.]

STRATFORD, Dr THOMAS.

T.   Lord Russel (amateurs at D.L. 1784) 8° [*Dublin*; ?1794].

STREATFIELD, T.

C.   The Road to Ridicule... Written for the L.D.I. and performed January 9, 1799 8° [1799; *Oxford*].

STREETER, F.

F.   The Physical Metamorphosis; or, A Treble Discovery (Rochester *c.* 1778) 8° 1778 [with *Hampton Court*, a poem].

STUART, CHARLES.

F.   The Experiment (C.G. W. 16/4/1777) MS. Larpent 17. M. [8/4/1777].
[Ascribed to Stuart.]

Ent. The Cobler of Castlebury. A Musical Entertainment (C.G. T. 27/4/1779) 8° [1779].
[Music partly W. Shield.]

*Int. Damnation; or, The Playhouse hissing Hot (H.² W. 29/8/1781) MS. Larpent 16. S. [27/8/1781].

*Int. Ripe Fruit; or, The Marriage Act (H.² W. 22/8/1781) MS. Larpent 16. S. [16/8/1781]. This was the "3rd Course" in *The Feast of Thalia*; see p. 327.

O.F. Gretna Green (H.² Th. 28/8/1783) 8° [N.D.; *Dublin*]. Songs, Airs, &c. in... G.G. 8° 1783. L. 634, as *The New Gretna Green*. See *UA*.
[Music S. Arnold]

*Prel. The Box-Lobby Loungers (D.L. W. 16/5/1787) MS. Larpent 45. M. [12/5/1787].

F.   The Distress'd Baronet (D.L. F. 11/5/1787) 8° 1787 [*bis*]; 12° 1788 [*Dublin*]; MS. Larpent 45. M. [1787].

Int. The Stone Eater (D.L. W. 14/5/1788) 8° 1788; MS. Larpent 48. M. [10/5/1788].

F.   The Irishman in Spain... taken from the Spanish (H.² S. 13/8/1791) 8° 1791; MS. Larpent 54. M. [30/8/1791].
[This is confessedly an adaptation of another play called *She Would be a Duchess*, banned by the Lord Chamberlain. The Larpent collection shows that the play with the original title had been suppressed on 13/8/1791.]

SULLIVAN, WILLIAM FRANCIS.

*F. The Rights of Man (Buxton 1791; H.² F. 9/8/1792).
[Printed in *The Thespian Magazine*, 1792, vol. i.]

[Pol.] The Test of Union and Loyalty, or the Long-threatened French Invasion 8° 1797; 8° 1803 [4th].

SYMMONS, Rev. CHARLES.

T.   Inez 8° 1796.

TASKER, WILLIAM.

T.   Arviragus (Exeter *c.* 1795) 8° 1796 [*Exeter*].

TAYLOR, WILLIAM [of NORWICH].
Dr. Poem. Nathan the Wise...written originally in German 8° 1791
[Norwich]; 8° 1805.
[A translation of Lessing, Nathan der Weise.]
T. Iphigenia of Tauris 8° 1793; 8° 1794.
[A translation from Goethe.]

TENDUCCI, FERDINANDO.
O. Amintas, An English Opera (C.G. F. 15/12/1769) 8° 1769.
[See RICHARD ROLT, The Royal Shepherd. Music Rush.]

TERES, T.
T. Richard in Cyprus 8° [1769].

THELWALL, JOHN.
*O. The Incas; or, The Peruvian Virgin [see Biographia Dramatica, ii.
322].
Dr. Romance. The Fairy of the Lake [in Poems 8° 1801].

THOMAS, Mrs ELIZABETH.
Past. A Dramatick Pastoral Occasioned by the Collection at Glocester
on the Coronation Day. For Portioning Young Women of Virtuous Characters 8° 1762 [Glocester].

THOMPSON, BENJAMIN.
D. The Stranger...Translated from the German (D.L. S. 24/3/1798)
8° 1798.
[An alteration of A. v. Kotzebue, Menschenhass und Reue.]
D. La Perouse...from the German 8° 1799.
[A translation of A. v. Kotzebue's drama.]
T. The Robbers 8° 1800.
[A translation of Schiller, Die Räuber.]
D. The Happy Family...from the German of Augustus Von Kotze-
bue 8° 1799; 8° 1800 [Dublin].
T. Adelaide of Wulfingen...(Exemplifying the Barbarity which pre-
vailed during the thirteenth century.) From the German of
Augustus von Kotzebue 8° 1798.
D. Bianca Capello [a few scenes translated in The German Miscellany,
1796; from Meissner].
T. Don Carlos 8° 1798.
[A translation from Schiller.]
[For other translations in The German Theatre see the Hand-list
of Plays, 1800–1850.]

THOMPSON, EDWARD.
*F. The Hobby Horse (D.L. W. 16/4/1766) MS. Larpent 8. M.
[4/4/1766].
C. The Fair Quaker; or, The Humours of the Navy. Written by
Mr. Charles Shadwell and altered (D.L. T. 9/11/1773) 8° 1775;
8° 1775 [2nd; with many additions].
M. The Syrens (C.G. M. 26/2/1776) 8° 1776; Airs and Chorusses in
...The Syrens 8° 1776; MS. Larpent 16. M. [20/2/1776; as The
Syren].
[Music Fisher.]
*Int. St. Helena: or, The Isle of Love (Richmond 1776; D.L. W.
28/5/1777) MS. Larpent 13. S. [30/7/1776].
[B.O.] The Beggar's Opera (C.G. M. 17/10/1777) MS. of one new scene

in Larpent's collection 16. M. [15/10/1777; see also under *UN-KNOWN AUTHORS*].

[An alteration of Gay's ballad opera.]

THOMPSON, WILLIAM.
T.   Gondibert and Birtha 8° [1751].

THOMSON, ALEXANDER.
The German Miscellany; consisting of Dramas, Dialogues, Tales and Novels. Translated from that Language 12° 1796 [Perth].
C.   The East Indian...translated from the German of Augustus von Kotzebue 8° 1799.

THORNTON, BONNELL.
Comedies of Plautus, translated into familiar blank verse 8° 1769, etc.

TICKELL, RICHARD.
*Past. The Gentle Shepherd (D.L. M. 29/10/1781). The Select Songs of the Gentle Shepherd 8° 1784.
[Music T. Linley. An alteration from A. Ramsay, *The Gentle Shepherd.*]
C.O. Songs, Duos, Trios, Chorusses, &c., in...The Carnival of Venice (D.L. Th. 13/12/1781) 8° 1781.

TIGHE, EDWARD.
*T. The Force of Love 12° 1786 [*Dublin*].
[An alteration from N. Lee, *Theodosius.*]
*F. The Cut Miser 8° 1788.
[An alteration from H. Fielding, *The Miser.*]

TOLLET, ELIZABETH.
Poems on Several Occasions 12° 1755.
[Contains *Susanna.*]

TOMLINSON, ——.
*[F.] Contrariety [Stafford 1792?].

TOMS, EDWARD.
C.O. The Accomplish'd Maid (C.G. W. 3/12/1766) 8° 1767; MS. Larpent 8. L. [16/10/1766].
[An adaptation of C. Goldoni, *La Buona Figliuola*; music N. Piccini.]

TOOSEY, GEORGE PHILIP.
T.   Sebastian 8° 1772.

TOPHAM, EDWARD.
*F. Deaf Indeed (D.L. M. 4/12/1780) MS. Larpent 16. S. [29/11/1780].
F.   The Fool (D.L. F. 15/4/1785) 8° 1786; MS. Larpent 40. M. [1785].
*F. Small Talk; or, The Westminster Boy (C.G. Th. 11/5/1786).
*F. Bonds without Judgment; or, The Loves of Bengal (C.G. T. 1/5/1787) MS. Larpent 44. M. [1787].

TOWNLEY, Rev. JAMES.
F.   High Life Below Stairs (D.L. W. 31/10/1759) 8° 1759 [4 editions]; 8° 1775 [9th]; 8° [1787]; 8° [1795; 11th]; MS. Larpent 4. M. [23/10/1759].
*F. False Concord (C.G. T. 20/3/1764) MS. Larpent 7. L. [1764].
[Based on G. Colman, *The Clandestine Marriage.*]
*F. The Tutor (D.L. M. 4/2/1765) MS. Larpent 7. S. [26/1/1765]

TOWNLY, CHARLES [*?a pseudonym*].
[Pol.] The Courtesans: a Comedy...founded on truth 8° 1760.

TRIMMER, Mrs SARAH.
  D. The Little Hermit [in *The Juvenile Magazine* 1788].
TRUSLER, JOHN.
  F. The Country Election 8° 1768.
TURNER, Mrs MARGARET.
  Past. The Gentle Shepherd...By Allan Ramsay. Attempted in English
    8° 1790.
TYTLER, ALEXANDER FRASER.
  T. The Robbers...Translated from the German of Frederick
    Schiller 8° 1792; 8° 1795 [2nd]; 8° 1797 [3rd]; 8° 1800 [4th].
    [A translation of F. Schiller, *Die Räuber*.]
UNDERWOOD, T.
  *T. Belisarius 8° 1782.
  *F. The Country Wake 8° 1782 [*Madras*].
VALPY, Dr RICHARD.
  T. The Roses; or, King Henry the Sixth...Compiled principally
    from Shakespeare (Reading School, Oct. 1795) 8° 1795; 8° 1810
    [2nd].
  T. King John...Altered from Shakespeare (Reading School) 8° 1800.
    [For his later works see the Hand-list of Plays, 1800–1850.]
VANDERSTOP, CORNELIUS.
  Dr. Poem. The Gentle Shepherd...Done into English From the
    Original of Allan Ramsay 8° 1777.
VAUGHAN, THOMAS.
  [F.] Loves Vagaries; Or, The Whim of the Moment. A Dramatic
    Piece (D.L. M. 15/4/1776 as *Love's Metamorphoses*) 8° 1791.
    [Based on Popple.]
  F. The Hotel; or, The Double Valet (D.L. Th. 21/11/1776) 8° 1776;
    8° [1777]; MS. Larpent 12. S. [16/11/1776].
    [Based on C. Goldoni, *Il Servitore di due Padroni* with suggestions
    from *Arlequin valet de deux maîtres*.]
  *F. The Deception (D.L. Th. 28/10/1784) MS. Larpent 37. M. [1784].
VICTOR, BENJAMIN.
  C. The Two Gentlemen of Verona...with Alterations and Additions
    (D.L. W. 22/12/1762) 8° 1763.
    Original Letters, Dramatic Pieces, and Poems 3 vols. 8° 1776.
      [Contains: 1. *Altamira*; 2. *The Fatal Error*; 3. *The Fortunate
    Peasant: or Nature will Prevail*; 4. *The Sacrifice: or, Cupid's
    Vagaries*.]
VILLIERS, JOHN CHARLES.
  T. Chaubert; or The Misanthrope. A Tragic Drama 8° 1789.
WAKER, JOSEPH.
  *Past. Love in a Cottage 8° 1785.
WALDRON, FRANCIS GODOLPHIN.
  C. The Maid of Kent (D.L. M. 17/5/1773) 8° 1778; MS. Larpent
    13. M. [6/5/1773].
  *F. The Contrast; or, The Jew and the Married Courtezan (D.L.
    F. 12/5/1775).
  *C. The Richmond Heiress (Richmond 1777).
    [An alteration from Thomas D'Urfey.]

*F. Imitation; or, The Female Fortune Hunters (D.L. M. 12/5/1783).
Past. The Sad Shepherd 8° 1783.
[Int.] The King in the Country, A Dramatic Piece (Richmond and
Windsor) 8° 1789.
  [Based on Thomas Heywood, *Edward IV*.]
[Int.] The Prodigal. A Dramatic Piece (H.² M. 2/12/1793) 8° 1794;
MS. Larpent 25. S. [27/11/1793].
  [An adaptation of J. Mitchell, *The Fatal Extravagance*.]
C. Heigho for a Husband (H.² T. 14/1/1794) 8° 1794; MS. Larpent
26. S. [21/12/1793].
  [An alteration of *Imitation, supra*.]
*T.C. Love and Madness (H.² M. 21/9/1795) MS. Larpent 68. M.
[6/9/1795].
  [Based on *The Two Noble Kinsmen*.]
*C. 'Tis a Wise Child knows its own Father (H.² M. 21/9/1795) MS.
Larpent 14. S. [16/9/1795].
D. The Virgin Queen...attempted as a Sequel to Shakespeare's
Tempest 8° 1797.
[Burl.] The Man with Two Wives; Or, Wigs for Ever! A Dramatick
Fable (Royalty S. 24/3/1798) 8° 1798.
  [Music Sanderson.]
*C.O. The Miller's Maid (H.² Aug. 1804).
  [Ascribed to Waldron.]

WALKER, MAYNARD CHAMBERLAIN.
*C. The Benevolent Man; or, Medley Lovers (S.A. Dublin, F.
26/3/1773).

WALLACE, Lady EGLANTINE.
*C. Diamond cut Diamond 8° 1787.
  [An adaptation of *La Guerre Ouverte; ou, Ruse contre Ruse*.]
C. The Ton; or, Follies of Fashion (C.G. T. 8/4/1788) 8° 1788; MS.
Larpent 16. L. [1788].
C. The Whim 8° 1795 [*Margate*].
*T. Cortez [see *Biographia Dramatica*, ii. 131].

WALLIS, Dr GEORGE.
*C. The Leeds Merchant (Leeds 1776).
Sat. The Mercantile Lovers, A Dramatic Satire (York) 8° 1775; MS.
Larpent 12. L. [1775].
*T.[?] Alexander and Statira; or, The Death of Bucephalus (York)
[see *Biographia Dramatica*, ii. 14].

WALPOLE, HORACE, Earl of ORFORD.
T. The Mysterious Mother 8° 1768 [*Strawberry Hill*]; 8° 1781; 8°
1791 [*Dublin*].
[Int.] Nature will Prevail. A Dramatic Proverb (H.² W. 10/6/1778)
[printed in his *Works* 4° 1798 as a "Moral Entertainment"].
C. The Fashionable Friends (D.L. April 1802) 8° 1802.
  [Found among this author's papers.]

WALWYN, B.
Int. Chit-Chat; or the Penance of Polygamy (C.G. F. 20/4/1781) 8°
1781; MS. Larpent 24. M. [19/4/1781].
Burl. A Matrimonial Breakfast (Royalty 1787) 8° [1787].
  [Music Reeve.]

WARBOYS, THOMAS.
The Preceptor; A Comedy...and The Rival Lovers; A Farce 8°
1777.
[The first is an adaptation of D'Ancourt, *Le Besoin de l'Amour*,
the second an adaptation of Regnard, *La Sérénade*.]

WARNER, RICHARD.
Comedies of Plautus 8° 1769 etc.

WARWICK, Rev. THOMAS.
Dr. Poem. Edwy 8° 1784.

WATSON, GEORGE.
[T.] England Preserved: An Historical Play (C.G. Th. 26/2/1795) 8°
1795.

WATSON, WILLIAM.
*C.O. Granby enticed from Elysium 8° [1782?].

WEEKS, JAMES EYRE.
*C. The Prude 8° 1791 [*Dublin*].

WEST, Mrs JANE.
T. Edmund, surnamed Ironside 8° 1791 [*York*; printed with *Mis-
cellaneous Poems*].
Poems and Plays, 4 vols. 8° 1799–1805.
[Contain: 1. *Adela*; 2. *How Will It End?* before 1800.]

WEST, Rev. MATTHEW.
*T. Ethelinda 8° 1769.
*T. Pizarro 8° 1799.
[An adaptation of A. v. Kotzebue's drama.]
[For his later work see the Hand-list of Plays, 1800–1850.]

WEWITZER, RALPH.
P. Songs, Chorusses, and Recitative, in...the Magic Cavern, or
Virtues Triumph (C.G. M. 27/12/1784) 8° 1785.
P. Songs...in...The Gnome; or, Harlequin Under-ground (H.[1]
T. 5/8/1788) 8° [1788].

WHALLEY, Rev. THOMAS SEDGWICK.
T. The Castle of Montval (D.L. T. 23/4/1799) 8° 1799 [*bis*]; MS.
Larpent 37. S. [10/4/1799].

WHITE, JAMES.
C. The Clouds [of Aristophanes] 8° 1759.

WHITEHEAD, WILLIAM.
[For his earlier works see the Hand-list of Plays, 1700–1750.]
T. The Roman Father (D.L. S. 24/2/1750) 8° 1750 [*bis*]; 8° 1754 [in
Poems].
[Based on Corneille, *Horace*.]
T. Fatal Constancy 8° 1754 [in *Poems*].
T. Crëusa, Queen of Athens (D.L. S. 20/4/1754) 8° 1754; MS. Lar-
pent 5. L. [2/4/1754].
C. The School for Lovers (D.L. W. 10/2/1762) 8° 1762; 8° 1762
[*Dublin*].
[F.] A Trip to Scotland (D.L. S. 6/1/1770) 8° 1770.

WHITELEY, JAMES.
F. The Intriguing Footman; or, The Humours of Harry Humbug
(Shrewsbury, 15/6/1791) 8° 1791 (*Sheffield*).

WHYTE, ——.
 *C. The Confession (Edinburgh 1799).

WIGNELL, J.
 *Poems 8° 1762.
  [Contains: 1. *The Triumph of Hymen* (Bartholomew Fair, Shuter
  1761); 2. *Love's Artifice*, an alteration of W. Taverner, *The Maid
  the Mistress.* The latter was printed separately 8° [1762].]

WILD, JAMES.
 F. The Miser (C.G. T. 24/3/1789) 8° 1792.
  [An alteration of H. Fielding, *The Miser.*]

WILDER, JAMES.
 F. The Gentleman Gardener (Dublin) 12° 1751 [*Dublin*].
  [See the Hand-list of Plays, 1700–1750.]

WILLET, THOMAS.
 Burl. Buxom Joan (H.² Th. 25/6/1778) 4° 1778; MS. Larpent 19. M.
  [17/6/1778].

WILLIAMS, ANNA.
 Miscellanies in Prose and Verse 4° 1766.
  [Contains: *The Uninhabited Island*, a version of P. Metastasio,
  L'Isola disabitata.]

WILLIAMS, JOHN [pseud. ANTHONY PASQUIN].
 *Ent. The Indian Chief [see *Biographia Dramatica*, ii. 323].
 *C. The Unfortunate Beau (Capel-street, Dublin, T. 24/2/1784).
  [An alteration of C. Bullock, *Woman is a Riddle.*]
 [Sat.] The Royal Academicians, a Farce 8° [1786].

WILLIAMSON, ——.
 *C. The Lawyer (H.² T. 19/8/1783) MS. Larpent 33. M. [12/8/1783;
  as *The L., or A Suit for the Season*].

WILSON, Mrs ANN.
 Dr. Poem. Jephthah's Daughter 8° 1783.

WILSON, CHARLES HENRY.
 [D.] Poverty and Wealth, a Comedy...translated from the Danish 8°
  1799 [*bis*].

WILSON, RICHARD.
 Burlesque. The Rehearsal. By the Duke of Buckingham. Altered into
  an After-Piece (Edinburgh 1791?; H.² 1792) [in *A Collection of
  ...Farces* 12° 1786 vol. vi].

WILTON, ——.
 *C. The Contrast (Calcutta, Dec. 1789).

WISE, JOSEPH.
 [D.] The Coronation of David 8° 1766.
 Dr. Poem. Nadir 12° 1779.

WODHULL, MICHAEL.
 The Nineteen Tragedies and Fragments of Euripides, translated
  8° 1782.
 Hippolytus, and Iphigenia in Aulis...translated 12° 1786.

WOLCOT, Dr JOHN.
 *O. Nina (C.G. T. 24/4/1787) MS. Larpent 45. M. [1787].
  [An adaptation of B. J. Marsollier, *Nina, ou La Folle par amour.*]
 T. The Fall of Portugal 4° 1808.

WOOD, WILLIAM.
   Past. A Translation of...The Gentle Shepherd into English 8° [1785?].
   [C.O.] The Billet-Master; or, The Forgery: An Opera 8° 1787
     [Edinburgh].

WOODBRIDGE, ROBERT.
   F. The Pad (C.G. M. 27/5/1793) 8° 1793.

WOODFALL, HENRY SAMUEL.
   C. We have all our Deserts [see Biographia Dramatica, iii. 396].

WOODFALL, WILLIAM.
   T. Sir Thomas Overbury...Altered (C.G. S. 1/2/1777) 8° 1777; MS.
     Larpent 17. M. [23/1/1777].
     [An alteration of Savage's play.]

WOODS, WILLIAM.
   *F. The Volunteers; or, Britons strike Home (Hull 1778).
   F. The Twins; or, Which is Which?...Altered from Shakespeare's
     Comedy of Errors (Edinburgh c. 1780) 8° 1780 [Edinburgh].

WOODWARD, HENRY.
   *Int. Tit for Tat; or, A Dish of the Auctioneer's Own Chocolate (S.A.
     Dublin, April 1748).
   *[P.] Queen Mab...A New Entertainment in Italian Grotesque
     Characters (S.A. Dublin F. 5/2/1748, as Fairy Friendship, or The
     Triumph of Hibernia; D.L. W. 26/12/1750).
   *[Prel.] A Lick at the Town...A Dramatic Performance (D.L. S.
     16/3/1751).
   *P. Harlequin Ranger (D.L. Th. 26/12/1751).
   *[P.] The Genii...An Arabian Night's Entertainment (D.L. T.
     26/12/1752).
   *P. Harlequin Fortunatus (D.L. W. 26/12/1753).
   *P. Proteus; or, Harlequin in China (D.L. S. 4/1/1755).
   *F. Marplot in Lisbon (D.L. Th. 20/3/1755) 12° 1760 [Dublin].
     [An alteration of Mrs Centlivre's comedy.]
   *P. Mercury Harlequin (D.L. M. 27/12/1756).
   *P. Harlequin Dr. Faustus (C.G. 18/11/1766). L. 259.
   P. Songs...in the New Entertainment of Harlequin's Jubilee (C.G.
     S. 27/1/1770) 8° 1770.
   C. The Man's the Master (C.G. F. 3/11/1775) 8° 1775.
     [An alteration of D'Avenant's comedy.]
   Dr. Ent. The Seasons [see Mrs G. A. Bellamy, Apology for her Life,
     1785, vol. ii].

WORSDALE, JAMES.
   [For his earlier works see the Hand-list of Plays, 1700–1750.]
   [Pol.] Gasconado the Great 4° 1759.

WOTY, WILLIAM.
   The Poetical Works, 2 vols. 8° 1770.
     [Contain: 1. The Country Gentleman; 2. The Ambitious Widow.]

WRANGHAM, Rev. FRANCIS [pseud. S. FOOTE jun.].
   [Sat.] Reform. A Farce. Modernised from Aristophanes 8° 1792.

YEARSLEY, ANNE.
   [T.] Earl Goodwin, an Historical Play (Bath 1789) 4° 1791.

YEO, ——.
  *C. The Asiatic (Portsmouth F. 7/5/1790).

YOUNG, ——.
  *Int. The Lewes Maid; or, A Trip to Brighton (Lewes 1792).
  *Ent. The Haunted Village; or, The Way to be Happy (Gainsborough 1800).

YOUNG, Dr EDWARD.
  [For his earlier works see the Hand-list of Plays, 1700–1750.]
  T. The Brothers (D.L. S. 3/3/1753) 8° 1753.
        [This seems to have been in rehearsal at D.L. in 1726 (see Victor, *op. cit.* ii. 129); it is based directly on T. Corneille, *Persée et Démétrius*.]

UNKNOWN AUTHORS.
  *Ent. Abon Hassan (R.S. M. 10/6/1793).
  *[Ball.] Adelaide de Brabant; or, The Triumph of Virtue (C.G. S. 8/5/1784).
        [Styled a "Dramatic Romance" in the bills.]
  *Ball. Adelaide de Ponthieu (C.G. 1784).
  *Ent. Admiral Nelson's Triumph, or Buonaparte in The Dumps (Ast. Th. 4/10/1798).
  [Sat.] The Adventurers. A New Dramatic Piece 8° 1777 [*Canterbury*].
  *Ent. The Adventures of the Prince of Seville; or, The Prince Chimney-Sweeper, and Chimney-Sweeper Prince (R.G. M. 5/4/1790).
  M.D. The Air-Balloon [mentioned in *Biographia Dramatica*, ii. 10 as printed 8° 1784. No doubt this is an erroneous entry, Mary Alcock's poem called *The Air-Balloon; or, Flying Mortal* 4° 1784 being thus classed as a play].
  *Ent. Aladdin; or, The Wonderful Lamp (C.G. M. 29/12/1788).
        [Cp. *Aladdin* under *O'KEEFFE*.]
  M. Albion Restored, or Time Turned Occulist 8° 1758.
  *F. The Alchemist (D.L. S. 12/10/1782).
        [Evidently a new alteration of Jonson's comedy.]
  T. Alexander the Great...with Alterations (D.L. and C.G.) 8° 1770.
  *F. Alexander the Little (C.G. 1764).
  *Burlesque. Alexander the Little (C.G. M. 2/5/1791) MS. Larpent 55. M. [2/5/1791].
  T. Alfred, An Historical Tragedy 8° 1789.
  T. Alfred the Great, Deliverer of his Country 8° 1753.
  Ball. Sketch of Alfred the Great: or The Danish Invasion (S.W. M. 7/5/1798) 8° 1799.
  F. All in the Right: or the Cuckold in good earnest 8° 1761.
  C. All Pleas'd at Last 8° 1783 [*Dublin*].
  *M. Piece. All's not Gold that Glitters (S.W. M. 19/7/1790).
        [Described M. 27/8/1792 as "by Mr. Dibdin".]
  *Int. All up at Stockwell; or, The Ghost no Conjurer (D.L. April 1772).
  *T. Almira (Manchester) MS. Larpent 42. M. [1786].
  *Ent. Almoran and Hamet; or, The Fair Circassian (R.C. M. 1/4/1799).
  *Ball. Alonzo and Imogine; or, The Bridal Spectre (S.W. M. 8/5/1797).
  *C. The Alternative (Crow-street, Dublin, W. 20/1/1796).
  *Ent. The American Heroine (R.C. W. 30/6/1790).

*P. The American Heroine; or, Ingratitude Punished (H.¹ M. 19/3/1792).

*Ent. The American Heroine (Ast. T. 9/5/1797; translated from the French).

*Ent. The American Heroine; or, The Ungrateful Spaniard (S.W. M. 18/4/1796).

*C.O. The Amorous Alderman (S.A. Dublin M. 25/1/1773).
   [Music Dr Arne.]

F.   The Anatomist; or, The Sham Doctor (D.L. M. 15/4/1771) 8° [1771].
   [An alteration of T. Ravenscroft's comedy.]

C.   The Andrian of Terence 8° [1772; *Sherbourne*].

*C. Angelica; or, Quixote in Petticoats 8° 1758.
   [Based on Mrs Lennox, *The Female Quixote*.]

*F. The Anniversary (C.G. W. 29/3/1758) MS. Larpent 4. M. [as "a Sequel to Lethe"; 20/3/1758].

*Ball. Apelles and Campaspe (H.¹ S. 2/11/1782).

*M. Piece. The April Day (S.W. F. 27/9/1782).

*Ent. April Fool (S.W. M. 2/6/1788).

*Ball. Arden of Feversham (S.W. S. 18/5/1799).

M.   The Arcadian Nuptials (C.G. Jan. 1764).
   [A dialogue in this is printed in *A Favourite Collection of Songs …Book XIV* F. (1764) and in *The Gentleman's Magazine*, Jan. 1764, xxxiv. 38.]

*Prel. Arrived at Crow-Street; or, A Thespian from Tanderagee (Crow-street, Dublin, F. 1/3/1796).

Ent. Arthur and Emmeline…Abridged from the Masque of King Arthur. As altered from Dryden by David Garrick (D.L. M. 22/11/1784) 8° 1786; 12° 1789 [*Dublin*].

[Pol.] The Assembly: or, Scotch Reformation. A Comedy 12° 1752 [*Edinburgh*]; 8° 1766 [*Edinburgh*]; 12° 1766 [*Edinburgh*].
   [Attributed to A. Pitcairne.]

*Int. At Anchor in the Bay of Naples. MS. Larpent 27. S. [28/4/1794, for C.G.].

*Ent. The Austrian Peasant (S.W. M. 23/5/1791).

*E. The Author on the Wheel, or A Piece cut in the Green Room, MS. Larpent 20. S. [1785, for D.L.].

*M. Piece. L'Avare corrigé (R.G. M. 26/7/1790).

C.   The Babbler. 8° 1762.

*M. Piece. Bagshot-Heath Camp; or, The Line of March (R.S. W. 19/9/1792).

*Ball. Le Ballet des Sauteurs et Voltigeurs (S.W. W. 27/8/1788).

[Int.] The Barber's Petition. A Short Piece (C.G. F. 6/5/1796) MS. Larpent 29. S. [29/4/1796].

F.   Barnaby Brittle: or, A Wife at Her Wit's End…Altered from Moliere and Betterton. With Additions (C.G. W. 18/4/1781) 8° 1788.

*Ent. Baron Munchausen (S.W. M. 25/5/1795).

Sat. The Bastard Child, or a Feast for the Churchwardens 8° 1768.
   [Daniel Downright is the pseudonym of the author.]

D.   The Batchelors 8° 1799.
   [A translation from Iffland.]

*M. Int. The Bathing Machine; or, The Fisherman caught (Brighton 11/9/1796).

[Int.] The Battle of the Nile, A Dramatic Poem, on the Model of the Greek Tragedy 8° 1799.

*F. The Battle Royal (H.² 1785).
[See *Biographia Dramatica*, ii. 52.]

*M. Beard's Night (Hampstead 1760).
[Dryden's secular masque set by Dr Boyce, with other musical entertainments.]

*Burl. The Beau outwitted (R.C. M. 1/9/1788).

*Ser. Beauty and Virtue (D.L. 1762).

*B.O. The Beggar's Opera [altered "Preludio" MS. Larpent 15. L. (2/8/1781, for H.²)].

*B.O. The Beggar's Opera [altered "Prelude" MS. Larpent 24. M. (13/10/1781, for C.G.)].

[F.] The Belle's Association, or Female Orators MS. Larpent 15. L. (14/7/1780, for Liverpool).

[Pol.] The Belle's Stratagem: A Comedy 8° 1781.

C. The Belle's Stratagem; or The Female Fortune Hunters MS. Larpent 18. S. [12/8/1782, for Richmond].

Burlesque. The Benevolent Cut-throat [in *The Meteors* 8° 1800; reprinted in *The Spirit of the Public Journals*, vol. iv].

*Ball. The Bird Catchers (D.L. T. 27/11/1750).

*C. The Bird in a Cage; or, Money works Wonders (C.G. M. 24/4/1786).

*C. Piece. Birds of a Feather; or, Buz and Mum (S.W. M. 25/7/1796).
[Billed as "by Mr Moorhead".]

*M. Past. The Birth-Day (Royalty M. 23/6/1788).

*C. The Birth-Day 8° 1799.

*C.O. The Birth-Night 8° 1796.

*M. Piece. The Black and White Milliners (R.G. S. 2/8/1788).

*[M.D.] The Black Forest. A Dramatic Romance MS. Larpent 34. S. [17/11/1798, for C.G.].

*Int. The Blade Bone (H.² W. 20/8/1788).
[Acted also at D.L. Th. 30/4/1789. A Scene from *The Genius of Nonsense*.]

*[Pol] The Blessings of P × × × and a Scotch Excuse 8° 1763.

*O.F. The Blind Man, or The Manœuvre MS. Larpent 30. M. [14/6/1782, for H.²].

*T. A Bloody Plot Discovered 8° 1780.
[Ascribed to a Mr Ball.]

*P. Blue Beard; or, The Flight of Harlequin (C.G. W. 21/12/1791) MS. Larpent 24. S. [21/12/1791].

*M. Piece. The Blunt Tar (R.G. T. 28/6/1791).

*M. Int. The Bonny Lass of Leith; or, The Humours of Dugald McBickar (Edinburgh 1793).

*[F.] The Bourbon League. A Piece in Two Acts MS. Larpent 7. L. [8/3/1762, for C.G.].

[Sat.] The Bow-Street Opera...Written on the Plan of the Beggar's Opera 8° [1773]; 8° 1776 [4th].

*M. Piece. Boxing's the Rage (R.C. W. 4/11/1789).

*F. Bribery on Both Sides (C.G. T. 4/5/1784) MS. Larpent 36. M.

*Int. The Brilliants (C.G. 1799).

*Ent. The Bristol Sailor, or The Whimsical Ladies MS. Larpent 16. L. [1786; no theatre mentioned].

*F. The Bristol Tar, or A New Way to get rid of a Wife MS. Larpent
  56. M. [1/6/1792, for Bristol].
*[Prel.] Britain's Brave Tars!! Or, All for St. Paul's (C.G. T.
  19/12/1797).
      [This would seem to be the piece mentioned by O'Keeffe in his
      Recollections under the title of *All to St. Paul's*.]
*Ent. Britain's Defenders, or, A Fig for Invasion (S.W. M. 17/4/1797).
*Ent. Britannia's Relief (S.W. T. 16/6/1789).
*Int. British Loyalty, or A Squeeze for St. Paul's (D.L. Th. 30/4/1789).
*Burl. The British Peasant; or, The False Alaram (S.W. Th.
  25/4/1799).
*Int. The British Recruit (C.G. 1795) 8° 1795.
*Int. The British Sailor; or, The Fourth of June (C.G. F. 22/5/1789).
      [This was acted first at Bath, 18/4/1786.]
*[O.F.] The Broker bewitch'd 8° [1785?].
*Ent. Broom (S.W. M. 25/4/1791).
*Int. Buck's Interlude (C.G. 26/3/1761). L. 185.
*Int. Buck's Lodge (D.L. F. 14/5/1790).
[Sat.] The Bumbrusher: A Farce. Intended to be translated into
  Latin, and performed before the Masters and Fellows of the
  Colleges of the University of Cambridge 8° 1786.
*[Prel.] A Bundle of Prologues (D.L. April 1777).
      [Ascribed to *DAVID GARRICK*.]
T. Buthred (C.G. T. 8/12/1778) 8° 1779. L. 462.
      [Ascribed to one Johnstone.]
*[Pol.] The Cabal 8° 1763.
T. Cabal and Love...Translated from the German 8° 1795.
      [A literal rendering of F. Schiller, *Kabale und Liebe*.]
*C.O. Calcutta, or Twelve Hours in India MS. Larpent 48. M.
  [18/2/1788, for D.L.].
*P. The Caldron (D.L. 1785).
Int. The Cambro-Britons; or, Fishguard in an Uproar (C.G. W.
  31/5/1797) MS. Larpent 71. M. [17/5/1797].
*F. The Cantabs (C.G. M. 21/5/1787) MS. Larpent 46. M.
*[Pol.] The Canvass 8° 1765.
*Int. Capochio e Dorinna (M.G. Th. 28/7/1768).
      [Music Dr Arne.]
*O.F. The Captain MS. Larpent 15. L. [24/4/1781].
*Ent. The Caravan, or, The Victorious British Tar (R.G.M. 7/7/1788).
*Int. The Caravan, or Caravansera [advertised on 26/9/1791 as about
  to be produced at H.²].
T. The Carthusian Friar; or, The Age of Chivalry 8° 1793.
*[M.D.] Casimer the Great. A Play MS. Larpent 67. M. [25/5/1795,
  for H.²].
*Int. The Casino MS. Larpent 15. L. [1780; for Bath].
*[M.D.] The Castle of Otranto MS. Larpent 26. S. [13/11/1793, for
  Newcastle].
*P. The Castle of Wonders MS. Larpent 40. M. [1786, for C.G.].
*Ball. The Catalonian Marriage (C.G. T. 8/3/1763).
*Int. The Catch Club (H.² F. 22/8/1788).
[Pol.] The Cat let out of the Bag; or, A Play without a Plot. Being a
  Tragical, Comical, Farcical, Operatical, Burlettical, Pantomimical,
  Serious, Satirical, Nonsensical Pasticcio, Acted the Devil Knows
  where, by A Company of the Devil knows Who, and written by

Sir Drawcansir Slashthem, Bart. With Notes critical, philological, polemical, and political 8° 2971 [*sic*; "*Goathem and Dublin*"].

*Ent. The Ceinture, or Harlequin in the Dumps (S.W. M. 19/7/1790).

*T.C. Cenia 8° 1752.
[A translation by J. M. D. of Madame Graffigny's play.]

*C. Cheapside; or, All in the City (H.² 1783).

*Ent. Champ de Mars, or, The Royal Federation (S.W. M. 2/8/1790).
[An entertainment of the same name given at R.G. Th. 5/8/1790. Both purported to be reproductions of "the Grand National Fête" held at Paris on July the 14th of that year.]

Past. The Chase: A Pastoral Drama 4° 1772 [*Cambridge*].

*M. Piece. The Chimney-Sweeper Prince (R.G. T. 9/9/1788).

*F. The Choice; or, Merit before Money (C.G. M. 30/3/1772).

P. The Choice of Harlequin; or, The Indian Chief. A Pantomimical Entertainment (C.G. T. 26/2/1782) 8° 1782; Airs, Duetts, Trios, &c., in...The Choice of Harlequin: or, The Indian Chief 8° 1782 [4 editions].
[Contrived by Messink; music M. Arne.]

*Int. The Choice of Hercules (C.G. W. 14/3/1753).

*Burl. La Cicisbea alla Moda 4° 1759.

*D. The Circassian MS. Larpent 26. M. [19/11/1781, for D.L.].

*F. The Citizen's Daughter 12° [*c.* 1775].

*Int. The City Association; or, The National Spirit roused (H.² 1780).

T. Clavidgo...translated from the German 8° 1798.
[A translation from Goethe.]

*Int. The Clock-Case; or, Female Curiosity (C.G. 2/5/1777) MS. Larpent 16. M. [April 1777].

*Ent. The Clown turned Beau (S.W. M. 7/7/1788).

[Pol.] The Coach Drivers: A Political Comic-Opera 8° 1766; 8° 1766 [2nd; To which is subjoined, A Letter of Thanks to the Compilers of the Critical Review, for the Encomiums which they have let slip, on that Performance].

[Sat.] Coalition; A Farce. Founded on Facts, and lately performed, with the Approbation, and under the Joint Inspection of the Managers of the Theatre Royal 8° 1779.
[An attack on T. and R. B. Sheridan.]

*M. Piece. The Cobler and the Lottery Ticket (R.G. T. 10/4/1787).

T. Codrus (Manchester, 29/4/1774, as *Codrus, King of Athens*) 8° 1774.
[Attributed to Dorning Ramsbottom.]

C. The Coffee-House; or, Fair Fugitive...written by Mr. Voltaire. Translated from the French 8° 1760.

*F. Colin and Susan MS. Larpent 64. M. [12/5/1794, for C.G.].

*Dr. Poem. Comala (Hanover Square Rooms) 8° 1792.

*C. The Comedy of Errors...With Alterations and Additions MS. Larpent 7. L. [1/4/1762, for C.G.].

*C. The Comet; or, How to come at Her (H.² M. 10/8/1789) MS. Larpent 50. M. [5/8/1789].

*O.F. The Comical Resentment; or, Trick for Trick (C.G. M. 26/3/1759).

*Ent. The Comic Extravaganza MS. Larpent 5. M. [1760, for C.G.].

*[Pol.] Il Conclave del 1774 8° 1774.
[A reprint of abbé Sertori's satirical work with an English translation.]

*Int. The Congress of Critics [printed in *The General Advertiser*, 1783].

C. The Connaught Wife (S.A. Dublin M. 19/1/1767) 8° 1767 [*Dublin*].
     [An alteration of Hippisley, *A Journey to Bristol*; acted with sub-title, *Or, The Honest Munsterman*; attributed to *RYDER*.]

T. The Conquest of Corsica, by the French...By a Lady 8° 1771.

*Int. The Conquest of St. Eustacia (D.L. 31/3/1781) MS. Larpent 24. M. [27/3/1781].

*T. The Conspiracy of Gowrie 8° 1800.

Ent. The Constant Maid; or, Polly of Plympton...By the Author of The Birth-Day (Royalty 1787) 8° 1787.

*F. The Contented Cuckold (H.² M. 5/9/1763).

*Past. The Contrast [printed in *The General Review* 1752].

*Burl. The Coquette (H.² Th. 13/8/1761).
      [Music Galuppi.]

*C. Piece. The Coquette (S.W. M. 9/4/1792).

D. The Corsicans...Translated from the German 8° 1796; 8° 1799; 12° 1799 [*Dublin*].
     [A translation from A. v. Kotzebue.]

*Int. The Cottage Maid (C.G. F. 3/6/1791) Airs, Duets, Choruses, &c. in The C.M. 8° 1791. MS. Larpent 54. M. [21/5/1791].

T. The Count de Villeroi; or, The Fate of Patriotism 8° 1794.
     [Attributed to the Rev. John Haggitt.]

*F. The Counterfeit Captain, or Usurer outwitted MS. Larpent 27. M. [24/4/1781, for D.L.].

*F. The Counterfeit Heiress (C.G. F. 16/4/1762).
     [An adaptation of T. D'Urfey, *Love for Money*.]

*F. The Counterfeits (D.L. M. 26/3/1764).
     [Based on E. Moore, *Gil Blas*.]

B.O. The Country Coquet; or, Miss in her Breeches (D.L.) 8° 1755.

*Int. The Country Courtship (York 1773).

*Prel. The Country Fair (C.G. Sept. 1775).

*Ball. The Country Farmer deceived (C.G. W. 1/5/1751).

*O.F. The Country Mad-Cap in London (C.G. W. 12/12/1770).
     [An adaptation of H. Fielding, *Miss Lucy in Town*. This is evidently the same as *The Country Madcap* dated 1772 in *Biographia Dramatica*, ii. 136.]

*Ent. The Country Painters (R.G. W. 20/8/1788).

*B.O. The Country Wedding; or, Love in a Dale 8° 1750. [By J. W.]

[Pol.] Courage Rewarded; or The English Volunteer. A Political Drama...By Mr. A. L.... G.... 8° 1798.

*[Pol.] Court and No Country. A Seri-tragi-comi-farcical Entertainment 8° 1753 [*Dublin*].

*Prel. The Court of Apollo (D.L. Th. 20/5/1790).

*F. The Credulous Husband (H.² Th. 21/8/1766).

— The Critic; or, Tragedy rehearsed 8° 1780.
     [A "Literary Catchpenny."]

[Pol.] The Critic; or, Tragedy rehearsed 8° 1780.

F. The Critic anticipated; or, The Humours of the Green Room 8° 1779.

C. Cross Partners...By a Lady (H.² Th. 23/8/1792) 8° 1792; MS. Larpent 57. M. [19/8/1792].
     [Attributed without any sure evidence, to Mrs *ELIZABETH INCHBALD*.]

Dr. Fable. The Cry 12° 1754 [see *Biographia Dramatica*, ii. 145].

*Ent. Cupid Pilgrim (R.G. F. 22/5/1789; not first performance).

*Ball. Cupid's Gift (Ast. S. 22/8/1795).

*Int. A Cure for a Coxcomb; or, The Beau bedevill'd (C.G. T. 15/5/1792).

*Int. A Cure for Dotage (M.G. 1771) 8° 1771.

*D. Curiosity (C.G. T. 17/4/1798).

*Ent. The Custom of the Manor (S.W. M. 16/6/1766).
  [Evidently from C. Johnson, *The Country Lasses*.]

Dr. Romance. Cymon...Written originally by David Garrick, Esq....
  With Additional Airs, Chorusses, etc. To which is added, The Order
  and Description of the Grand Procession of the Hundred Knights
  of Chivalry, and Ancient Tournament (H.¹ S. 31/12/1791) 8° 1792;
  Songs, Duets, etc., in...Cymon 8° 1815.

*Ent. Cymon and Iphigenia (Ast. Th. 13/8/1795).

*D. Czartoriska MS. Larpent 64. [30/5/1794, for D.L.].

*M. Piece. Cymon and Iphigenia (R.C. M. 19/4/1790).

*D. Daniel in the Lion's Den (Doncaster 1793).
  [An adaptation of H. More, *Daniel* (see her *Sacred Dramas*).]

Past. Daphnis and Amaryllis 8° 1766 [*Exon.*].
  [A reprint of Harris' *The Spring*.]

*T. Darius MS. Larpent 1784. Extra.
  [This may be the *Darius* by the Rev. Dr Stratford mentioned in
  Biographia Dramatica, ii. 153.]

*C. Extravaganza. A Day of Taste; or, London Raree Show (C.G. Th. 20/3/1760).

*P. The Death of Captain Cook (C.G. M. 21/9/1789).

*Int. The Death of Captain Faulknor; or, British Heroism (C.G. T. 19/5/1795) MS. Larpent 65. M. [23/4/1795].

*P. The Death of General Wolfe (R.G. M. 9/8/1790).

*Ent. Deception (R.C. W. 11/6/1788).

*Ball. The Deserter (C.G. F. 13/11/1789).

*P. The Deserter of Naples (D.L. M. 2/6/1788).

P. Songs...in The Deserter of Naples; or, The Royal Clemency (Royalty M. 16/6/1788) 8° [1788].

*P. The Deserter of Naples; or, Royal Clemency (R.C. M. 17/8/1789).

*C. The Detection; or, A Sketch of the Times (H.² M. 13/11/1780).

*F. The Devil in the Wine-Cellar (H.² T. 25/7/1786).

*Ent. The Diamond Ring; or, the Jew Outwitted (R.G. M. 28/7/1788).

*F. The Disagreeable Surprise (Reading School 1798).

C. The Disappointed Coxcomb 8° 1765.
  [By "Bartholomew Bourgeois."]

*F. The Disputants. A Piece in Two Acts MS. Larpent 23. M. [12/5/1780, for H.²].

D. The Distressed Family 8° 1787.
  [A rendering of L. S. Mercier, *L'Indigent*.]

*C.O. The Distressed Knight; or, The Enchanted Lady [Crow-street, Dublin, S. 12/2/1791].
  [Music T. Giordani.]

*C. The Distres'd Wife MS. Larpent 17. M. [14/4/1777, for H.²].

*F. Doctor Last's Examination (H.² T. 14/8/1787).

D. Don Carlos...Translated from the German 8° 1798.
  [A literal translation of F. Schiller.]

*Int. Don Jerome's Trip to England (C.G. 1778).

*P. Don John; or, The Libertine Destroyed (D.L. F. 10/5/1782).

P. Don Juan; or, The Libertine Destroy'd: A Tragic Pantomimical Entertainment (Royalty M. 23/6/1788) 8° [1788; 3 editions].

P. Don Juan; or, The Libertine Destroyed: A Grand Pantomimical Ballet (D.L. T. 26/10/1790) 8° [1790].

*F. Don Quixote in England. As Alter'd from Mr. Fielding (D.L.M. 6/4/1752).

*P. Don Raymond, or The Castle of Lindenburgh MS. Larpent 71. M. [11/3/1797, for C.G.].

C. Dorval; or, The Test of Virtue...Translated from the French of Mr. Diderot 8° 1767.

*F. The Double Amour (H.² 1791) MS. Larpent. Extra [1791].

*C. The Double Marriage; or, The Husbands reformed (York 1768).

*C. Double Perplexity: or The Mysterious Marriages 8° 1787; 12° 1796.

C.T. The Downfall of the Association 8° 2771 [Winchester].

[Pol.] The Downfall of St. Stephens [printed in The General Advertiser 1784].

— Dramatic Dialogues for Young Persons 12° 1792.

*— A Dramatic Oglio MS. Larpent 29. M. [13/9/1782, for D.L.].

— Dramatic Pieces from the German 8° 1792 [Edinburgh].
    [Includes: 1. The Sisters; 2. The Conversation of a Father with his Children; 3. The Set of Horses.]

*Dr. Poem. The Dream of St. Cloud [in Poetry by an Artist] 8° 1797 [Edinburgh].

M. Airs, Duets, Chorusses, etc., in...The Druids...The words chiefly taken from Ben Jonson (C.G. S. 19/11/1774) 8° 1774.
    [Music Foster. Styled in the advertisements "A Pastoral Masque and Pantomime."]

Int. The Drunken News-Writer: A Comic Interlude (H.² 1771) 8° 1771.

*Ball. The Drunken Swiss (C.G. T. 12/10/1793).

*F. A Duke and No Duke 8° 1758.
    [An alteration of Nahum Tate's comedy.]

*T. The Duke of Lochford (Edinburgh 1799).

*P. The Dumb Cake; or, The Regions of Fancy (C.G. 1787).

*[Pol.] The Dutch Alliance. A Farce 8° 1759.

*Ent. The Dutch Tea Garden (R.C. Th. 17/7/1788).

*C. The Dutiful Deception (C.G. W. 22/4/1778).

*[T.] The Earl of Douglas. A Dramatic Essay 8° 1760.

*Ent. Easter Monday (S.W. M. 31/3/1777).

*F. Easter Monday; or, The Humours of the Forth 8° [1781; Newcastle].

*Ent. Easter Pastimes (D.L. M. 5/4/1790).

*C. The East Indian (H.² T. 16/7/1782) MS. Larpent 29. M. [2/7/1782].

*C. Eastward Hoe (D.L. M. 29/10/1751) 12° 1751.
    [An alteration of the comedy by B. Jonson, G. Chapman and J. Marston.]

T. Edmond, Orphan of the Castle 8° 1799.
    [Based on Clara Reeve's novel, The Old English Baron.]

Dr. Past. Edward and Egwina; or, The Feast of Ceres 8° 1776 [Salisbury].
    [Music Goss.]

*Ent. The Election (R.C. W. 30/6/1790).

*[Sat.] The Election. An Interlude 12° 1784.

*T. Elmira MS. Larpent 26. M. [19/3/1781, for Manchester].

*P. The Elopement (D.L. 26/12/1768).

*F. An Elopement, or The Liverpool Welcome MS. Larpent 19. S. [1784, for Liverpool].

*Prel. Elysium [printed 12° 1789 in *Sentimental Love*].

*C. The Embarassed Husband [printed in *The Lady's Magazine*, 1785, 1786 and 1787].

*D. The Emigrant in London 8° 1795 [French and English].

*T. Emilia Galotti (D.L. T. 28/10/1794) MS. Larpent 65. M. [21/10/1794].
    [A rendering of Lessing's tragedy.]

*P. The Emperor of the Moon (Patagonian 1777).

*M. Piece. England against Italy (S.W. M. 21/5/1787).

*[Prel.] England's Glory; or, The British Tars at Spithead (C.G. May 1795).

*[Int.] England's Glory; or, The Defeat of the Dutch Fleet by the gallant Admiral Duncan, on the memorable Eleventh of October (C.G. W. 18/10/1797).

*P. England's Joy (Ast. M. 4/5/1795).

*[Pol.] The English Britons. A Farce 8° 1763.

C. The Englishmen in Bordeaux...Written in French, by the celebrated Monsieur Favard...Translated by an English Lady now residing in Paris 8° 1764.

*F. The Englishman in Germany MS. Larpent 18. L. [13/1/1792, for Manchester].

*Droll. The English Sailors in America (C.G. Th. 20/3/1760).
    [Described as Mr Shuter's Droll. This seems to be the same as *G. A. STEVENS' The French Flogged* (Bartholomew Fair, 1760).]

C. The English Tavern at Berlin 8° 1789.

*Int. The Enraged Musician MS. Larpent 21. S. [17/4/1789, for H.²].

*Ball. Les Epoux de Tempe (H.¹ S. 26/1/1793).

*Int. The Escape (D.L. 1798).

*P. The Escape of Harlequin, Bill-Sticker, Cooper and Music Master (Ast. W. 5/7/1797).

*F. Esop (D.L. S. 19/12/1778).
    [An alteration of Sir John Vanbrugh's comedy, attributed to *T. SHERIDAN*.]

[Sat.] The Etymologist. A Comedy...Most Humbly Dedicated to the late Dr. Samuel Johnson's Negro Servant, to the August and Learned Company of Reviewers; To all the Commentators that ever wrote, are writing, or will write on Shakespeare; and particularly to that Commentator of Commentators, the Conjectural Inventive, and Collatitious G—— S——, Esq. 8° 1785.
    [A satire on George Steevens.]

*[O.F.] Execution; or, More frightened than hurt [advertised for C.G. in May 1785; see *More frightened than hurt, infra*].

*F. The Fabulist (York —).
    [See *Biographia Dramatica*, ii. 210.]

*P. The Fair (C.G. W. 7/2/1750).
    [Contrived by John Rich.]

*C.O. The Fair American (Crow-street, Dublin, S. 18/5/1771).

*C.O. The Fair Orphan (Lynn, by G. A. Stevens' company, 1771).

T. The Fair Parricide...Founded on a late Melancholy Event 8° [1752].

*C.O. The Fair Peruvian MS. Larpent 43. M. [1786, for C.G.].

*C. The Fair Refugee; or, The Rival Jews (H.² 1785) MS. Larpent 24. M. [1780].

*C.O. The Fair Venetian (Crow-street, Dublin, M. 18/3/1776). [Music Borghesi.]

P. The Songs and Descriptions of the Pantomime called The Fairy Favour: or Harlequin animated (D.L. M. 27/12/1790) 8° 1790.

*Int. The Fairy Favours, or The Nuptial Benison MS. Larpent 31. S. [8/5/1797, at D.L.].

*M. The Fairy Festival (D.L. S. 13/5/1797).

*P. Fairy's Fantasy (Ast. F. 10/4/1795).

Past. The Faithful Shepherd, A Dramatic Pastoral, Translated into English from the Pastor Fido of the Car. Guarini 8° 1782. [Attributed to William Grove.]

*Prel. The Fall of Martinico; or, Britannia Triumphant (C.G. 1794).

*Sat. The Fall of Public Spirit 8° 1757.

*Ent. The Fall of Rizzio (S.W. M. 25/5/1795).

C. False Shame...Translated from the German of Kotzebue 8° 1799.

[F.] The Family Party; A Comic Piece (H.² S. 11/7/1789) 8° 1789; 12° 1789 [Dublin].

[D.] The Family Picture. A Play. Taken from the French of M. Diderot's Pere de Famille. By a Lady 8° 1781.

F. The Farmer's Journey to London 8° 1769.

*F. The Faro Table (C.G. S. 4/4/1789). [An alteration of Mrs Centlivre, The Gamester.]

*F. The Fashionable Crop quizzed (Dublin 1792).

T. The Fatal Elopement [printed in The Lady's Magazine, 1799, 1800]. [A translation from Lessing.]

*C. The Father 8° 1770. [A translation of Diderot, Le Père de Famille.]

[D.] The Father of a Family. A Comedy...By Charles Goldoni, translated into English with the Italian Original 8° 1756. [The title gives the name of Goldoni's play—Il Padre di Famiglia.]

Int. The Father outwitted [printed in The Wits' Magazine, Oct. 1784]. [A translation from Lope de Vega.]

T. The Favourite 8° 1770. [Ascribed to James Scott; an alteration of Ben Jonson, Sejanus.]

*Ent. The Feast of Anacreon (C.G. Th. 14/5/1789).

*P. Ball. The Feast of Bacchus (C.G. F. 22/12/1758).

*Ent. The Feast of Thalia; or, A Dramatic Oglio (H.² W. 22/8/1781). [See CHARLES STUART, Ripe Fruit.]

C. The Female Adventurer; or, Stop her who can (C.G. Th. 29/4/1790). [An alteration of E. Moore, Gil Blas.]

*Ball. The Female Archer (C.G. W. 14/1/1767).

[Ent.] The Female Duellist. An After Piece (H.¹ W. 22/5/1793) 8° 1793; MS. Larpent 61. M. [12/5/1793]. [Music Suett. Based partly on Beaumont and Fletcher, Love's Cure.]

*Prel. The Female Orators (C.G. 12/5/1780) MS. Larpent 23. M. [7/5/1780].

*[Pol.] The Female Parliament. A Seri-Tragi-Comi-Farcical Entertainment. Never acted in Utopia before 12° 1754.

*F. The Female Pursuit (C.G. T. 11/5/1790).
    [An alteration of *The Female Adventurer*, *supra*.]
*Ent. The Female Soldier (S.W. M. 13/4/1789).
C.   The Financier 8° 1771.
    [A translation from St Foix. See *The Uneasy Man*.]
*Int. First Come First Served 8° 1797.
*[F.] The First of September, or Each Man his Bird. An Afterpiece
    MS. Larpent 22. S. [31/8/1789, for Liverpool].
*Dr. Romance. The Flesh and the Spirit MS. Larpent 64. M.
    [30/8/1794, for H.²].
*Ent. The Follies of a Night; or, Harlequin Rambler (S.W. M.
    29/4/1787).
*P. Extravaganza. The Folly of Age; or, The Accomplished Lady
    (C.G. F. 9/6/1797).
*F. Fondlewife and Letitia (Crow-street, Dublin, 1767; H.² F.
    14/8/1767).
    [An alteration of W. Congreve, *The Old Batchelour*.]
*Int. Forecastle Fun; or, Saturday Night at Sea (C.G. 1798).
*Domestic Tale. La Forêt noire; or, The Natural Son (S.W. M.
    27/8/1792).
*Int. Fortune's Wheel (H.¹ T. 7/5/1793) MS. Larpent 60. M. [4/5/1793].
*Ent. The Four Quarters of the World (R.G. T. 28/6/1791).
*Ent. The Fourth of June; or, Birth-Day Loyalty (S.W. W. 3/7/1792).
*C.O. France as it was (Bath, S. 7/3/1795).
    [An alteration of O'Keeffe's *Fontainebleau*.]
*D. French Faith [printed in *The Devil* 1786].
*Ent. French Gardeners (C.G. Th. 7/4/1763).
*Ent. The French Jubilee (R.C. T. 3/8/1790).
C.   The Frenchman in London...From the French of Monsieur De
    Boissy 8° 1755.
*F. The French Village surrender'd, or The Loyal Soldier MS. Lar-
    pent 62. M. [25/6/1794, for Bristol].
C.   The Friendly Rivals; or, Love the best Contriver 8° 1752.
*Ent. Friendly Tars (S.W. M. 2/6/1788).
*C. Friendship à la Mode (S.A. Dublin W. 30/5/1766) 8° 1766.
    [An alteration of Sir John Vanbrugh, *The False Friend*.]
*F. The Frolick; or, The Romp in Disguise MS. Larpent 20. S.
    [7/6/1786, for Bath].
    [The *Biographia Dramatica* chronicles a performance at Dor-
    chester in June 1792.]
*Int. The Frolics of an Hour (C.G. 16/6/1795) 8° 1795; MS. Larpent
    65. M. [7/6/1795].
*C.O. The Fugitives; or, Lovers' Stratagem (Crow-street, Dublin,
    T. 10/2/1778).
*Int. Fun and Frolic; or, The Sailor's Revels (C.G. 1799).
M. Piece. Songs, &c. in...Gaffer's Mistake; or, The Case is Altered
    (S.W. M. 4/5/1795) 8° 1795.
T.C. The Gallant Moriscoes; or, Robbers of the Pyrenees. A Dra
    matic Performance 8° 1795.
*Ball. The Gallant Peasants (C.G. T. 13/1/1767).
*Ent. Gallic Freedom; or, Vive la Liberte (R.C. F. 21/8/1789)
[Burl.] An English Musical Entertainment, called Galligantus (H.² M.
    17/9/1759) 8° 1758.
    [Described in the advertisements as "Taken from the Memoirs

of Jeferey ap Arthur, of Monmouth" and evidently satirising the bills of Lillo's *Arden of Feversham*.]

*Ent. Gambols (R.G. M. 23/6/1788).

*Ball. The Garland (C.G. F. 4/10/1765).

[Sat.] Garrick in the Shades; or, A Peep into Elysium. A Farce. Never offered to the Managers of the Theatres-Royal 16° 1779.

[Sat.] Garrick's Vagary; or, England run mad; with particulars of the Stratford Jubilee 8° 1769.

*T. The Gauntlet (Branderburgh House *c.* 1799).

[An adaptation, probably by Lady Craven, of Schiller's *Die Räuber*. See *The Robbers, infra*.]

*C. The Generous Rivals (Manchester M. 1/3/1773).

*M. Piece. The Generous Turk (R.G. M. 13/9/1790).

*P. The Genii of the Deep; or Harlequin in his Element (Ast. W. 10/7/1799).

*Int. The Genius of Glasgow (Glasgow 1792).

*O. The Georgian Princess MS. Larpent 37. S. [12/4/1799, for C.G.].

*F. George a Green, The Pindar of Wakefield (York 1775).

[An alteration from the anonymous *George a Green*.]

*M. George's Natal Day [printed 8° 1780 in *Original Poems by a Young Gentleman*].

T. Germanicus...By a Gentleman of the University of Oxford 8° 1775 [*bis*].

C. The Ghost (S.A. Dublin W. 2/12/1767) 8° 1767.

[This is an alteration of Mrs Centlivre's *The Man's Bewitched*. The *Biographia Dramatica* states it was acted in London as *The Witchcraft of Love*. This I have been unable to trace, but as *The Ghost; or, The Man Bewitched* it was performed at D.L. M. 10/4/1769, and at H.² T. 28/8/1787; while it was acted at C.G. W. 23/4/1783 as *The Ghost; or, The Devil to do about Her*.]

*P. The Giant Defeated; or, The Reward of Valour (C.G. F. 12/6/1789).

P. Gil Blas; or, The Fool of Fortune. A New Pantomimic Entertainment (Royalty 1788) 8° [1788].

[The pantomime is described as being by *BATES*, the music by W. Reeve, the scenery by Dixon.]

*C.O. The Gingerbread Nut; or, The Termagant tam'd 12° 1790 [*Dublin*].

*P. The Golden Dream (Ast. M. 1/4/1799).

*Ball. The Gondoliers (C.G. S. 19/1/1751).

*P. The Good and Bad; or, Jupiter's Vengeance (R.S. T. 9/7/1792).

*Ent. Good News for British Tars (R.G. M. 21/6/1790).

— The Governess; or, The Boarding School Dissected. A Dramatic Original in Three Acts. Wherein are exposed, in Dramatic Order, the Errors in the present Mode of Female Education, and a Method of correcting them, in order to form the Mind, and improve the Understanding 8° 1785.

*P. The Governor; or, The Creolian Insurrection (C.G. M. 1/4/1793).

*C. The Greek Slave; or, The School for Cowards (D.L. T. 22/3/1791) MS. Larpent 55. M. [14/3/1791].

[An alteration of Beaumont and Fletcher, *The Humorous Lieutenant*.]

*M. Piece. Le Grenadier (S.W. W. 27/8/1788).

*Burl. The Grey Mare's the Better Horse (S.W. M. 25/5/1795).

*F. The Grumbler (D.L. T. 30/4/1754) MS. Larpent 3. M. [22/4/1754].
    [An alteration of Sir Charles Sedley's play.]

*[Int.] Guy Fawkes; or, The Fifth of November. A Dramatic Sketch
    (H.² T. 5/11/1793) MS. Larpent 25. S. [30/10/1793].

*[F.] Hail Fellow well met. A Comic Sketch (C.G. T. 8/5/1792)
    MS. Larpent 58. M. [24/4/1792].
    [Described in the bills as *The Quip Modest called H. F. w. m.*;
    see *The Rights of Women.*]

Int. Half an Hour after Supper (H.² S. 23/5/1789) 8° 1789; MS. Lar-
    pent 48. M. [9/4/1789].

Ent. Songs, Duets, Finale, &c. in The Hall of Augusta; or, The Land
    we Live in (S.W. M. 1/4/1793) 8° 1793.

*P. Harlequin Amulet; or, The Magic of Mona (D.L. 23/12/1800)
    8° 1800.
    [Attributed to Powell.]

P. Songs, Duets, Choruses, &c. in...Harlequin and Faustus, or
    The Devil will have his Own (C.G. Th. 19/12/1793) 8° 1793; MS.
    Larpent 60. M. [14/12/1793].

*P. Harlequin and Oberon; or, Little Fanny's Love (C.G. M.
    19/12/1796) MS. Larpent 31. S. [10/12/1796].
    [This had also another sub-title, *The Chace to Gretna.*]

*P. Harlequin Captive; or, The Magic Fire (D.L. M. 18/1/1796) 8°
    1796; MS. Larpent 70. M. [6/1/1796].
    [Attributed to *WILLIAM LINLEY.*]

*P. Harlequin Emperor of the Moon (Ast. M. 9/8/1784).
    [Music Reeve.]

*P. Harlequin Enchanted (D.L. W. 25/4/1753).

*P. Harlequin Everywhere (Ast. T. 9/5/1797).

*P. Harlequin in Ireland; or, Apollo and Daphne (R.S.W. 19/9/1792).

*P. Harlequin Invincible (Ast. T. 25/8/1795).

*P. Harlequin Junior; or, The Magic Cestus (D.L. W. 7/1/1784).

*P. Harlequin Mariner (R.C. Th. 18/5/1797).

*P. Harlequin Mountebank (D.L. F. 14/5/1756).

P. Songs, Duets, Choruses, &c., in Harlequin Peasant; or, A Panto-
    mime Rehearsed (H.² F. 27/12/1793) 8° 1793; MS. Larpent 26. S.
    [21/12/1793].

*P. Harlequin Perambulator (Ast. M. 29/5/1797).

[Pol.] Harlequin Premier: A Farce, as it is daily acted 8° 1769
    ["Printed at Brentaforda, Capital of Barataria"].

*P. Harlequin Quack; or, The Modes of the Moderns (S.W. M.
    13/9/1762).

*P. Harlequin Rambler; or, The Convent in an Uproar (C.G. Th.
    29/1/1784).
    [This is probably by *O'KEEFFE.*]

*P. Harlequin Restored; or, Taste a la Mode.
    [The *Biographia Dramatica* states that this was acted at D.L. (no
    date given) and that the songs were printed in 8°. A pantomime
    styled *Harlequin Restored* was performed at S.W. F. 10/7/1767.]

[Pol.] The Harlequins. A Comedy. After the Manner of the Theatre
    Italien. As it is now acting with great Applause, by a Company
    of Gentlemen, for the Entertainment of their Friends at the Great
    Room in Drumcondra-Lane 8° 1753 [*Dublin*].

*P. Harlequin's Adventure; or, Half an Hour's Magic (S.W. W.
    21/9/1791).

*Ent. Harlequin's Campaign (S.W. T. 9/7/1793).

*P. Harlequin's Chaplet (C.G. M. 21/12/1789).
*P. Harlequin's Choice of the Beauties of the World (R.G. M. 20/7/1789).
*P. Harlequin's Frolick; or, A Voyage to Prussia (H.² F. 16/6/1757).
     [Described in the bills as "A Lilliputian Pantomime."]
*P. Harlequin's Frolicks (C.G. Th. 26/12/1776).
*P. Harlequin's Gambols (Royalty W. 23/6/1790).
*P. Harlequin's Jacket; or, The New Year's Gift (D.L. M. 2/1/1775).
*P. Harlequin Skeleton, or The Royal Chace (C.G. F. 16/7/1788).
*Ent. Harlequin's Medley (R.S. M. 6/5/1793).
*P. Harlequin's Mite, or, The Weird Sisters' Festival (Royalty M. 18/2/1799).
P.   Songs, Duets, Choruses, &c., in the New Pantomime called Harlequin's Museum, or, Mother Shipton Triumphant (C.G. Th. 20/12/1792) 8° 1792.
*P. Harlequin's Oddities; or, The Devil in a Bottle (Ast.W.17/5/1797).
*P. Harlequin Statue; or, The Jealous Farmer outwitted (C.G. W. 27/4/1763).
*P. Harlequin's Tour; or, The Dominion of Fancy (C.G. 1800) 8° 1800.
*P. Harlequin's Treasure; or, Jewels new set (C.G. T. 15/3/1796).
*Ent. Harlequin's Vagaries (R.S. T. 29/5/1792).
*P. Harlequin Touchstone MS. Larpent 21. S. [Nov. 1789, for C.G.].
*P. Harlequin's Vagaries (R.S. T. 29/5/1792).
*Ent. The Haunted Village (R.S. M. 9/4/1792).
*C. Heautontimoroumenos 8° 1777.
     [A translation of Terence.]
[Sat.] Hecate's Prophecy [printed in *Brief Remarks on the Original and Present State of the Drama* 8° 1758].
O.   Helvetic Liberty; or, The Lass of the Lakes 8° 1792.
*O.P. Henry and Louisa (Ast. T. 25/7/1797; "as in Paris").
P.   Hercules and Omphale (C.G. W. 19/11/1794) 8° 1795.
*P. Here, There and Everywhere (H.² W. 31/8/1785) MS. Larpent 20. S. [26/8/1785].
*P. The Hermit of the Alps; or, Harlequin Wanderer (Ast. M. 22/5/1797).
*Burlesque O. The Hermit; or, Quarter Day (Dublin 1792).
*Int. Hide and Seek; or, The Slippers (C.G. T. 24/2/1789) MS. Larpent 50. M. [Jan. 1789].
*F. Hobby Horses (H.² F. 31/7/1789).
*Int. The Hodge Podge; or, A Receipt to make a Benefit (H.² T. 28/8/1781) MS. Larpent 24. M. [25/8/1781].
*D. The Honest Criminal; or, Filial Piety 8° 1778.
     [A translation from the French by G. L.]
*F. Honesty is the Best Policy MS. Larpent 17. L. [10/5/1791].
     [This play was billed at C.G. in 1791 but was withdrawn.]
*Ent. Honi soit qui mal y pence; or, La Fille mal Gardu (Ast. Th. 2/5/1799).
Ent. Songs, &c. in The Honours of War; or, The Siege of Valenciennes (S.W. M. 12/8/1793).
*Ent. Hooley and Fairly; or, The Highland Laddie (S.W. M. 17/8/1789).
     [Apparently the same piece was acted at C.G. S. 28/4/1798; MS. Larpent 35. S. (18/4/1798).]

*F. The Hop; or, Who's afraid? MS. Larpent 55. M. [2/5/1791].
  [This was billed at D.L. in 1791 but was withdrawn.]
F. An Hour before Marriage...as it was Attempted to be Acted at
  the Theatre-Royal in Covent-Garden 8° 1772.
  [Based on Molière, Le Mariage forcé.]
*B.O. The Hovel (D.L. T. 23/5/1797) MS. Larpent 72. M. [18/5/1797].
*F. How to get married MS. Larpent 29. S. [19/4/1795, for
  Norwich].
*O. The Hue and Cry MS. Larpent 32. S. [11/10/1797, for C.G.].
*Int. The Humourists (D.L. 1754).
*[Pol.] The Humours of an Irish Court of Justice. A Dramatic Satire
  8° [1750].
*Burlesque. The Humours of Gil Blas (R.G. S. 2/8/1788).
  [See Gil Blas, supra.]
*M. Piece. The Humours of King Henry VIII and the Merry Cobler
  (Ast. T. 1/8/1797).
*Ent. The Humours of May Day (S.W. M. 28/5/1787).
*F. The Humours of Portsmouth; or, All is well that ends well 8°
  [1760].
*Ent. Hurly Burly (R.S. M. 9/4/1792).
  [See under JAMES COBB.]
*Ent. Huzza for Old England (S.W. Th. 26/9/1782).
C. The Hymeneal Party, or, The Generous Friends. By a Young
  Gentleman 8° 1789.
*T. Ignatius MS. Larpent 17. S. [20/12/1781, for Hull].
*Ent. The Incas of Peru; or, The Children of the Sun (S.W. F.
  9/4/1790).
*D. The Indian Captive; or, The Death of Ingomar (Dublin 1796).
*Dr. Tale. The Inheritance (printed in Tales, Romances etc. 12° 1786).
  [A translation from the French of Bret.]
*Prel. The Inquiry, or Cause of the present high Price of Provisions
  MS. Larpent 38. M. [1785; no theatre mentioned].
*C.O. The Interview MS. Larpent 15. L. [26/3/1784, for D.L.]
*B.O. The Intriguing Chambermaid (D.L. W. 3/11/1790).
  [An alteration of Fielding's play.]
*F. The Invasion 8° 1759.
*F. The Invisible Mistress (D.L. M. 21/4/1788).
  [An alteration of C. Bullock, Woman is a Riddle.]
*Int. Invitation à la Mode (Earl of Aldborough's private theatre,
  Stratford Place, 1791).
*Ent. The Invitation; or, Return of the Season (R.G. T. 10/4/1787).
O. Iphigenia in Aulis [printed in An Essay on the Opera 8° 1768
  (Glasgow)].
  [A translation of F. Algarotti, Iphigenia in Aulide, in Saggio
  sopra l'Opera in Musica.]
*Ball. The Irish Cake (R.C. M. 1/9/1788).
*F. Irish Hospitality (S.A. Dublin Th. 19/3/1767; D.L. S. 15/3/1766).
  [An alteration of Charles Shadwell's play.]
*C. Irish Promotion (Crow-street, Dublin, M. 14/2/1791).
*Ent. Irish Taylors (S.W. W. 5/10/1791).
*D. The Italian Husband MS. Larpent 66. M. [20/5/1795].
T. Ivar 8° 1785 [Exeter].
*— Jacob's Ramble. A Short Piece MS. Larpent 29. S. [29/4/1796,
  for C.G.].

*C. The Jealous Husband (C.G. M. 7/4/1777).
   [An alteration of J. Dryden, *The Spanish Fryar*.]
*Ent. The Jealous Lover cured [printed in *The Lady's Magazine*, 1788].
D. Jean Hennuyer, Bishop of Lizieux; or, The Massacre of St. Bartholomew 8° 1773.
   [Translated from the French.]
*F. Jehu (D.L. F. 19/2/1779) MS. Larpent 21. M. [17/2/1779].
*Burl. The Jew and the Gentile (R.C. Th. 24/9/1795).
*Ent. Jewish Courtship (D.L. M. 23/4/1787) MS. Larpent 44. M. [1787; as *A Specimen of Jewish Courtship. A Prelude to The Mistake of a Minute*].
*Int. Jewish Education (D.L. M. 19/4/1784).
*Int. The Jolly Crew; or, Tars at Anchor (C.G. 1799).
*Sac. D. Joseph sold by his Brethren 8° 1789.
— The Jubilee in Honour of Shakespeare. A Musical Entertainment ...with Additions (Waterford 1773) 12° 1773 [*Waterford*].
*[Pol.] The Junto; or, The Interior Cabinet laid open. A State Farce 8° 1778.
*Ent. Jupiter and Alcmena...interspersed with a Comic Piece call'd The Imprisonment of Harlequin (S.W. M. 16/4/1750).
*F. The Kept Mistress, or, The Mock Orators MS. Larpent 5. L. [7/4/1756, for D.L.].
C. A Key to the Lock...As it was damned at the Theatre Royal, in the Haymarket (H.² M. 18/8/1788) 8° 1788.
   [An adaptation of Sedaine, *La Gageure imprévue* (Paris, 1768).]
*Ent. The King and the Cobbler (R.G. M. 25/4/1791).
*T.C. The Knight of Malta (C.G. W. 23/4/1783).
   [An alteration of Beaumont and Fletcher's play.]
*Int. The Knights of the Post; or, The Blackamoor wash'd White (Newcastle 1797).
*Int. The Knowing Ones taken in (Edinburgh 1797).
   [An adaptation of Holman's *Abroad and at Home*.]
*T. The Labyrinth; or, Fatal Embarrassment 8° 1795 [*Dublin*].
   [A translation from T. Corneille, *Ariane* (Paris, 1762).]
*Ball. The Labyrinth (D.L. Th. 9/3/1797).
   [Contrived by Gentili.]
*F. Lady Pentweazel in Town (C.G. T. 27/3/1787).
*Local Extravaganza. The Land we live in (S.W. M. 5/9/1791).
   [See *The Hall of Augusta*.]
*M. Laoeudaimonos, or A People made happy (D.L. T. 19/5/1789) MS. Larpent 22. S. [19/5/1789].
*D. La Peyrouse MS. Larpent 77. M. [1781; no theatre mentioned].
   [This apparently is not now in the Larpent collection.]
*Ent. The Laplanders (R.G. M. 23/6/1788).
*Dr. Poem. Lavinia [see *Biographia Dramatica*, ii. 364].
T. Leander and Hero 8° 1769.
   [Attributed to *T. HORDE*.]
*F. The Legacy MS. Larpent 71. M. [20/6/1797, for H.²].
*F. A Lesson for Lawyers (D.L. T. 5/5/1789).
   [An alteration of Foote's *The Lame Lover*.]
C. The Liar 8° 1763.
*Burlesque. The Life and Death of Common-Sense (H.² T. 13/8/1782).
   [An alteration of H. Fielding, *Pasquin*.]

*Burlesque. The Life, Death, and Renovation of Tom Thumb [1785; see *Biographia Dramatica*, ii. 371].

*P. The Lilliputian Camp (D.L. F. 27/2/1767).

*O.F. Lingo's Wedding MS. Larpent 19. S. [1784; no theatre mentioned].

*O.F. Little Ben and Little Bob, or Huzza for Old England MS. Larpent 29. S. [12/5/1795, for C.G.].

*Ball. Little Peggy's Love (D.L. 1796).

*F. Live Lumber; or, The Unburied Dead (C.G. W. 30/3/1796).
    [An adaptation of *Bickerstaff's Unburied Dead*.]

*Operetta. The London 'Prentice (D.L. S. 23/3/1754).
    [Music de Fesch.]

*F. A Lounge at Brighton MS. Larpent 29. S. [Feb. 1795, for C.G.].

*C. Love and Friendship: or, The Lucky Recovery 8° 1754.

*F. Love and Honour; or, The Privateer 8° 1753 [*Ipswich*].

*O. Love and Honour; or, Britannia in full Glory at Spithead (C.G. F. 9/5/1794) MS. Larpent 27. S. [1/5/1794].

Ser. Love and Innocence, A Pastoral Serenata (M.G. 1789) 8° 1789.
    [Music James Hook.]

*O. Love and Loyalty MS. Larpent 28. S. [April 1795, for Norwich].
    [The Larpent MS. has a note, "by B. Lindor".]

*F. Love and Money (Norwich, 20/4/1795) L. 1066. [Advertised as "by a Lady of this city".]

*T. Love and Valour; or, The Two Noble Kinsmen (Richmond 1779).
    [An alteration of Shakespeare and Fletcher's play.]

*C. Love and Wine 8° 1754.

*C. Love at a Venture; or, The Rake Reclaimed (H.² 1782).

*C.O. Love conquers all, or The Cheshire Knight outwitted MS. Larpent Extra [1786, for T. R. Chester].

*C. Love in a Puddle [see *Biographia Dramatica*, ii. 387].

*C. Love in his Dotage; or, The Manchester Friends (Manchester 1773).

*Ent. Lovely Nancy (R.C. F. 20/6/1788).

*F. The Love Match (C.G. S. 13/3/1762) MS. Larpent 7. L. [8/3/1762].

*F. Lovers no Conjurors MS. Larpent 25. S. [25/6/1792, for H.²].

*— The Lovers of their Country; or, Themistocles and Aristides (H.² W. 14/2/1770).

*F. Lovers' Quarrels (C.G. Th. 11/2/1790).
    [An adaptation of Sir John Vanbrugh, *The Mistake*.]

*P. Love Triumphant (R.C. W. 11/6/1788).

[Sat.] Low Life above Stairs...As it is acted in most Families of distinction throughout the Kingdom 8° 1759 [3 editions].

*Ent. The Lucky Lovers (Manchester 1773).

*Ent. The Lucky Return (D.L. W. 30/5/1787).

*P. Lun's Ghost; or, The New Year's Gift (D.L. Th. 3/1/1782).
    [Based largely on *Harlequin's Jacket*, *supra*.]

*C. The Lyar 8° 1763.

*M. Lycidas 4° 1762.

*Past. Lynce and Pollidore (Vyse's Academy, Mitcham, Surrey, 1781) 8° 1781.

*Burl. The Mad Captain (Yarmouth 1769).
    [Ascribed to *G. A. STEVENS*.]

*Burl. The Madman (M.G. 1770) 4° 1770.

*— The Magic Chace (Liverpool, 27/6/1789).

*P. The Magic Feast (R.C. F. 3/7/1795).

Burl. Songs, &c. in The Magician: or, The Invisible Lover (S.W. 1797) 8° 1797.

*Ent. The Magician of the Grove (Hull, 1/1/1796).

*P. The Magician of the Mountain (D.L. 3/1/1763).
    [Contrived by Guerini.]

*P. The Magician of the Rocks; or, Harlequin in London (Royalty, S. 2/2/1799).

P. Songs, Recitations, etc., in The Magic Oak: or Harlequin Wood-cutter (C.G. T. 29/1/1799) 8° 1799 [bis].

P. The Magic of Orosmanes: or, Harlequin Slave and Sultan: A Pantomime, Drawn from Arabian Legends 8° 1785.

*Ent. The Magic World (R.G. F. 11/5/1787).

*— The Maid of Liverpool, or, The Loyal Tar MS. Larpent 19. L. [16/9/1799, for Liverpool].

D. The Maid of Marienburg...From the German of Kratter 8° 1798.

*F. The Maid of the Mill; or, The Country Revels...In which will be introduced a Musical Masque, call'd The Judgment of Paris (C.G. Th. 5/4/1750).
    [An adaptation of Beaumont and Fletcher's play.]

C.O. The Maid of the Vale 12° 1775 [Dublin].
    [An adaptation of C. Goldoni, La Buona Figliuola, attributed to HOLCROFT.]

*T. Malvina 8° 1786 [Glasgow].

*Prel. The Manager in Affliction (Ast. M. 6/4/1795).

*C. The Managers 4° 1768.

*Ent. The Mandarin; or, Harlequin Widower (S.W. M. 13/4/1789).

*Int. The Man like himself, or Stratford Wake MS. Larpent 20. S. [1785, for Manchester].

*F. The Man of Taste (D.L. T. 10/3/1752).
    [An alteration of James Miller's play.]

Burlesque. The Man of the Mill. A New Burlesque Tragic Opera. The Musick Compiled, and the Words written, by Seignior Squallini 8° 1765.

*Ent. The Marches Day 8° 1771 [Edinburgh].

*F. Marriage à la Mode (D.L. M. 24/3/1760).
    [An adaptation of Boden, The Modish Couple. Since there are several plays with this title, the theatrical record is confused; but the 1760 piece is distinct from the others. See also under A. MURPHY, What We Must All Come To.]

*Burl. Marriage by Comedy; or, Fashionable Playfolks (S.W. M. 16/5/1796).

*M. Piece. The Marriage by Stratagem; or, The Musical Amateur (R.G. M. 15/6/1789).

*C. The Married Man, or, The Closet Cordial MS. Larpent 40. M. [4/7/1786, for Bath].

*M. Sketch. Mars' Holiday (S.W. T. 14/8/1792).

*C. The Mask'd Friend (C.G. F. 6/5/1796) MS. Larpent 69. M. [29/4/1796].
    [An adaptation of Holcroft's Duplicity.]

*F. The Masquerade MS. Larpent 29. S. [21/3/1795, for Norwich].

*M. Piece. A Match at Gibraltar (R.C. Th. 3/7/1788).

*Int. Matrimony; or, The Sleep-Walker (C.G. S. 28/4/1798) MS. Larpent 72. M. [1798].

*Ball. Medea and Jason (H.[2] W. 8/8/1781).

    [Composed by "Novestris," according to the bills. This seems to have been a burlesque of the ballet at H.[1].]

*Ent. Medea's Kettle; or, Harlequin Renovated (S.W. M. 9/4/1792).

*P. The Medley; or, Cupid's Frolic (S.W. F. 14/6/1765).

*P. The Medley; or, Harlequin have at all (C.G. W. 14/10/1778).

C. Melite 12° 1776.

    [A translation of Corneille's comedy.]

*Int. Melocosmiotes (C.G. 1796).

*P. Mercury Harlequin in Ireland; or, The Rape of Colombine (Crow-street, Dublin, M. 16/5/1763).

    [Contrived by Messink.]

*Ent. Merlin; or, The Enchanter of Stonehenge (S.W. M. 20/4/1767).

*P. Merlin's Cave (C.G. F. 21/12/1750).

*Ent. Merlin's Cave; or, A Cure for a Scold (S.W. F. 26/9/1788).

*F. The Merry Counterfeit; or, The Viscount à la Mode (C.G. M. 29/3/1762).

*O. The Merry Making MS. Larpent 46. M. [7/5/1787, for H.[2]].

*C. The Merry Men of Kent MS. Larpent 17. L. [March 1789, for Manchester].

*F. The Merry Mourners MS. Larpent 55. M. [10/3/1791, for C.G.]

*Int. The Methodist Preachers (Richmond 1775).

[Sat.] An Improved Edition of the Songs in the Burletta of Midas, adapted to the Times 8° 1789.

*F. The Miller outwitted (C.G. S. 30/5/1752).

*M. Piece. The Milliner's Shop (R.G. M. 20/7/1789).

*Int. A Mirror for the Ladies MS. Larpent 15. S. [1/3/1779].

*P. Mirsa and Lindor (R.S. M. 2/6/1794).

*P. Mirth and Magic (Ast. W. 15/7/1795).

*M. Piece. The Miser (R.S. T. 5/11/1793).

*Int. The Mistakes of a Minute (D.L. M. 23/4/1787).

    [See *Jewish Courtship* and *A Specimen of Jewish Courtship*, as well as supplementary notes.]

*O.F. The Mistakes of a Day (Norwich 1787) MS. Larpent 45. M.

*Prel. Mistress Doggrell in her Altitudes; or, The Effects of a West India Ramble (H.[2] 1795) MS. Larpent 18. L. [20/4/1795].

*Int. Mistress Nonsuch's Nonsense [advertised at H.[2] in 1790].

*F. The Mock Orators (D.L. S. 10/4/1756).

T. The Modern Arria...translated from the German of F. M. Klinger 8° 1795.

*— A Modern Character 8° 1751.

    [Described as introduced into *Æsop* at H.[2].]

[Int.] Modern Comedy; or, It is all a Farce. A Dramatic Afterpiece 8° 1792

C. Modern Courtship 8° 1768.

C.O. Modern Honour; or, The Barber Duellist (S.A. Dublin F. 20/10/1775) 8° 1775 [*Dublin*].

*C. The Modern Wife (C.G. S. 27/4/1771) MS. Larpent 11. M. [15/4/1771].

    [An alteration of Gay's comedy.]

*Ball. Moggy and Jemmy (D.L. T. 5/2/1799).

Ent. Songs, &c. in Momus's Gift (S.W. M. 6/4/1795) 8° 1795 [together with *The Lord of the Manor; or, the Village Nuptials*].

*Prel. Monopoly MS. Larpent 29. M. [10/9/1782, for C.G.].

*Ent. The Monster of the Cave; or, Harlequin and the Fay (S.W. M. 23/4/1798).

*Ent. The Monster of the Woods (S.W. M. 13/4/1772).

*M. Piece. The Monster; or, The Wounded Ladies (R.G. S. 22/5/1790).

*Int. Mordecai's Beard (D.L. T. 20/4/1790) MS. Larpent 51. M. [20/4/1790].

*O.F. More Frightened than Hurt (H.² T. 16/8/1785).
    [See *The Execution, supra.*]

*[Sat.] More Kotzebue; or, My Own Pizarro...A Monodrama 8° 1799.

*C. More Ways than Means MS. Larpent 42. M. [1786; no theatre mentioned].

*— Moses and Shadrac. A Petit Piece MS. Larpent 16. S. [13/4/1780, for D.L.].

*Sac. D. Moses in the Bulrushes (Doncaster 1793).
    [An alteration of H. More's sacred drama.]

P. The Recitatives, Airs, etc., in the New Pantomimic Entertainment of Mother Shipton (C.G. W. 26/12/1770) 8° 1771 [*bis*].

*— Mother Shipton's Review of the Audience (C.G. M. 16/4/1787).

P. Sketch of The Mountain of Miseries; or, Harlequin Tormentor (S.W. 1797) 8° 1797.

*Dr. Ode. The Muse of Britain 4° 1785.

*Burlesque. Music Alamode, or Bays in Chromatics MS. Larpent 7. S. [29/3/1764, for D.L.].

*F. Mutual Inconstancy MS. Larpent 65. M. [24/4/1795, for Norwich].

*F. My Night-Gown and Slippers, or Tales in Verse MS. Larpent 19. L. [20/4/1797].

*F. The Nabob outwitted (Tewkesbury 1797).

*Int. Naples Bay; or, The British Seamen at Anchor (C.G. F. 2/5/1794).
    [Attributed to *J. CROSS.*]

C. Narcissus [printed in the translation of Rousseau's *Miscellaneous Works* 8° 1767].

*F. The Narrow Escape MS. Larpent 8. S. [4/11/1766, for D.L.].

[D.] Natalia and Menzikof; or, The Conspiracy against Peter the Great. A Tragedy 8° 1798.
    [A translation from Kratter.]

*C. The Natural Son MS. Larpent 65. M. [24/5/1794, for D.L.].

*— Nature will Prevail (D.L. W. 7/5/1788).

*Ent. Naval Gratitude; or, The Fleet under Weigh (R.C. Th. 18/5/1797).

*Prel. Naval Volunteers; or, Britain's Glory (C.G. Th. 7/5/1795).

D. The Negro Slaves...from the German 8° 1796.
    [A translation from Kotzebue.]

*Ent. Neptune's Friendship; or Harlequin Busy Body (R.G. T. 10/4/1787).

*Ent. Neptune's Levee; or, Harlequin in Spain (S.W. M. 2/5/1791).

*F. The Neuter MS. Larpent 40. M. [5/6/1786, for H.²].

*Int. New Gretna Green MS. Larpent 33. M. [23/8/1783, for H.²].

*— A New Divertisement MS. Larpent 62. M. [21/5/1794, for C.G.].

*— A New Drama MS. Larpent 58. M. [7/5/1792, for C.G.].

*Burlesque. The New Maid of the Oaks 8° 1778.
    ["By Ahab Salem."]

*Burlesque. The New Rehearsal MS. Larpent 8. S. [Oct. 1767, for D.L.].

*Prel. News from the Nile, or Laurels from Egypt MS. Larpent 34. S. [13/10/1798, for C.G.].

*C. New Ways to Catch Hearts MS. Larpent 31. M. [1783, for C.G.].

*Ball. P. New Wheat (Ast. M. 17/8/1795).

C. Nina; or, The Love Distracted Maid 8° 1787.
    [A translation of Marsollier, *Nina, ou La Folle par Amour*.]

D. The Noble Lie 8° 1799.
    [A translation from Kotzebue.]

*F. No Matter What (D.L. T. 25/4/1758).

*P. Nootka Sound; or, Britain prepared (C.G. F. 4/6/1790) MS. Larpent 53. M. [1/6/1790].

*Prel. No Play this Night MS. Larpent 32. S. [23/8/1797; marked "Not Licensed"].

*Ent. Norwood Gipsies (S.W. M. 31/3/1777).

P. Airs, Duets, &c., in the New Pantomime called The Norwood Gypsies (C.G. T. 25/11/1777) 8° 1777.
    [Music J. A. Fisher.]

*F. No Wit like a Woman's [D.L. T. 28/3/1769].
    [An adaptation of Molière, *George Dandin*.]

*F. Now's your Time, Taylors!! [advertised at C.G. in 1794] MS. Larpent 27. S. [14/4/1794; as *Now Taylors is your Time*].

*Int. Numpo's Courtship; or, Love makes a Painter (H.² M. 16/1/1758).

*Int. An Occasional Interlude, or The King of Denmark When in England MS. Larpent 9. M. [7/10/1768, for C.G.].

Dr. Poem. Oithona...Taken from the Prose Translation of the Celebrated Ossian (H.² 1768) 8° 1768.
    [Music Barthélémon.]

*M. Piece. Old Graspall outwitted (R.G. M. 5/7/1790).

*[Pol.] Old Interest. A Farce, of Forty Three Acts. Performed with great Disaffection at the Theatre in Oxford 8° 1753.

*— The Old Woman's Oratory (H.² M. 30/12/1751).

*Ent. Olympian Revels; or, Harlequin Mimus (R.C. Th. 25/5/1797).

*C. One Rake in a Thousand MS. Larpent 18. S. [1783; no theatre mentioned].

*F. The Opiate MS. Larpent 31. S. [24/10/1797, for D.L.].

*F. Opposition (H.² F. 6/8/1790).
    [An alteration of Crowne's *Sir Courtly Nice*; attributed to *RYDER*.]

*Ent. The Oracle of Delphi; or, Harlequin's Vagaries (S.W. Th. 28/3/1799).

*Ent. Oriental Magic; or, Harlequin Nabob (S.W. M. 20/4/1778).

*T. Oroonoko...altered from Southern 8° 1760.

T. The Orphan of China...translated from the French of M. de Voltaire 8° 1755.

*O. Orpheus and Eurydice (C.G. 1792).

P. The Airs, Duets, Choruses, and Argument, of the New Ballet Pantomime (taken from Ossian) called Oscar and Malvina; or, The Hall of Fingal (C.G. Th. 20/10/1791) MS. Larpent 23. S. [13/10/1791].

*Dr. Piece. Our Wooden Walls, or All to St. Paul's MS. Larpent 71. M. [8/12/1797].
    [Cp. *JOHN O'KEEFFE*.]

*M. Piece. The Palace of Mirth (S.W. M. 20/4/1778).
*D. Palladius and Irene 8° 1773.
C. Pamela. A Comedy by Charles Goldoni. Translated into English
with the Italian Original 8° 1756.
Ent. Songs, Recitatives, &c. in...Pandora's Box; or, The Plagues of
Mankind (S.W. F. 26/7/1793) 8° 1793; 8° 1795.
*F. The Paradox; or, Maid, Wife and Widow (C.G. T. 30/4/1799).
*Ent. The Paris Federation (Royalty, 1790).
*Ent. Paris in an Uproar; or, The Destruction of the Bastille (R.G. M.
17/8/1789).
[Past.] Parthenia: or, The Lost Shepherdess. An Arcadian Drama 8°
1764.
*P. Patient Griselda; or, The Mysterious King of Lombardy (S.W. M.
22/7/1799).
*C. The Patriot (H.² 1784).
[The *Biographia Dramatica* (iii. 131) states that this was first
advertised as *The Artful Patriot; or, The Rage of the People*.]
*[Pol.] Patriotism! A Farce. Acted by His Majesty's Servants 8° 1763.
*C. The Patron; or, The Disinterested Friend [on rehearsal at Edin-
burgh 1793].
*O.F. The Pedantic Apothecary Quizzed, or Lottery Prize 92,538
(private theatre, Fishamble-street, Dublin, 1794).
*Bell. The Pedlar tricked (C.G. M. 10/1/1763).
*Int. A Peep into Elysium; or, Foote, Shuter and Weston in the
Shades (H.² T. 10/8/1784) MS. Larpent 35. M. [17/8/1784].
*Ent. Penmaenmawr; or, The Wonders of Wales (S.W. T. 22/4/1794).
*Int. The Perplexed Lovers; or, The Double Marriage (Salisbury) 8°
1776 [*Salisbury*].
[Music selected by G. Gaudry.]
*P. Perseus and Andromeda; or, The Cheats of Harlequin (C.G. W.
9/10/1765).
C.O. The Peruvian...By a Lady (C.G. S. 18/3/1786) 8° 1786 [*bis*];
Airs...in...The Peruvian 8° 1786.
*T. Phaedra MS. Larpent 18. L. [7/2/1793; "For the Benefit of the
Literary Fund"].
T.   Phaedra...translated from Racine 12° 1776.
O.   Phaedra and Hippolitus (S.A. Dublin T. 6/3/1753) 8° 1753 [*Dublin*].
[Music Roseingrave; an operatisation of Edmund Smith's
tragedy (1709).]
*Past. Philander and Rose 12° 1785 [*Manchester*]; MS. Larpent 16. L.
[1785, as *P. and R., or The Bridal Day*, for the T.R. Manchester].
*[Pol.] The Philistines; or, The Scotch Tocsin sounded 8° 1793.
C.O. Phillis at Court (Crow-street, Dublin, W. 25/2/1767) 8° 1767;
12° 1767 [*Dublin*].
[Music T. Giordani. An alteration of R. Lloyd's *The Capricious
Lovers*.]
*D. Philoctetes in Lemnos 8° 1795.
*C. The Philosopher, or, The Turns of Fortune MS. Larpent 66. M.
[17/2/1795; no theatre mentioned].
[Sat.] The Philosopher's Opera 8° [1757].
*Ball. Pigmalion (D.L. F. 2/11/1750).
*P. Pigmy Revels; or, Harlequin Foundling (D.L. S. 26/12/1772).
Ent. A Pill for the Doctor: or, The Triple Wedding (Royalty, S.
17/4/1790) 8° 1790.

*[Pol.] The Planters of the Vineyard; or, The Kirk Sessions Con-
founded [see *Biographia Dramatica*, iii. 160].

*[Sat.] The Plotting Managers...By Peter Pindar, jun. 4° [?1787].

*Int. The Point at Herqui; or, British Bravery Triumphant (C.G. F.
15/4/1796) MS. Larpent 30. S. [7/4/1796].

Sat. The Polite Gamester; or, The Humours of Whist. A Dramatic
Satire, as Acted every Day at White's, and other Coffee-Houses
and Assemblies 8° 1753.
[This is but a later edition of *The Humours of Whist*.]

*F. The Politician, or No Matter What MS. Larpent 6. L. [15/4/1758,
for D.L.].

D. The Politician Reformed [printed in *An Appeal to the Publick
for the Judgment of a Certain Manager, with Original Letters and
the Drama, in One Act, which was refused Representation* 8° 1774].
[The *Appeal* is signed T. R.]

*P. Poluscenion (C.G. M. 8/6/1789).

Prel. Poor Covent Garden! or, A Scene Rehearsed...Intended for
the opening of the New Theatre Royal, Covent-Garden, This
Season 8° 1792.

*O.F. The Poor Sailor; or, Little Bob and Little Ben (C.G. F.
29/5/1795).
[Music T. Attwood.]

*C. The Portrait (H.² 1784).

*Burlesque. Precious Relics; or, The Tragedy of Vortigern Rehearsed.
A Dramatic Piece 8° 1796.

*F. The Prejudice of Fashion (H.² M. 22/2/1779) MS. Larpent 12. L.
[24/9/1776].

*O.F. The Press Gang; or, Love in Low Life (C.G. 1755) 8° 1755.
[See under *HENRY CAREY* in the Hand-list of Plays, 1700–
1750.]

*C.O. Primrose Green; or, Love in the Country (C.G. T. 24/5/1791)
MS. Larpent 24. S. [21/5/1790].

*Dr. Poem. The Princess of Zanfara 8° 1789.

*[Pol.] Principle and Practice Combined; or, The Wrongs of Man.
An Opera 8° 1792.

Ent. Songs, &c. in the Prize of Industry; or, The Village Rejoicing Day
(S.W. M. 8/7/1793) 8° 1793.

*C. The Prodigal; or, Marriage A-la-Mode 8° 1794.

*F. The Projectors, or Wit at a Pinch MS. Larpent 47. M. [1788, for
Bath].

*P. Prometheus (C.G. T. 26/12/1775).

*Ball. P. Provocation (C.G. M. 4/10/1790).
[Partly based on *Nootka Sound, q.v.*]

*Ent. The Prussian Camp (D.L. M. 9/1/1758).

*M. Piece. The Prussian Dragoon; or, The Termagant Mistress (R.G.
S. 2/8/1788).

*Ball. The Prussian Festival (C.G. 1791).

*[Sat.] The Public House; or, Consequential Landlord and his Cus-
tomers. A Farce, as it is performed every night in various parts of
London and Westminster 8° 1787.

D. Pygmalion...translated from Rousseau 4° 1779.

*C. The Quacks; or, The Credulous Man (D.L. M. 19/4/1784) MS.
Larpent 37. M. [12/4/1784].
[Ascribed to Jesse Foot.]

*C. Extravaganza. Queen Dido (S.W. M. 9/4/1792).

Ent. Les Quatres Fils d'Hemons; or, The Four Valiant Brothers (S.W. M. 2/6/1788) 8° 1788.

*Extravaganza. Queen Dido; or, The Trojan Ramblers (S.W. M. 9/4/1792).

*O. The Queen of Carthage [under this title Reed's *Dido* was revived with a few alterations in 1797].

*Int. The Quidnuncs 4° 1779.

*F. Quoz (Richmond F. 4/9/1789).

Sat. The Ragged Uproar; or, The Oxford Roratory 4° [1754].

T. Raymond 8° 1793.

Ball. P. Airs, Glees and Chorusses in a New Grand Ballet Pantomime of Action called Raymond and Agnes; or, The Castle of Linden-bergh (C.G. Th. 16/3/1797) 8° 1797.

[C.O.] The Reapers: or, The Englishman out of Paris. An Opera 8° 1770.
    [A rendering of Favart, *Les Moissonneurs*.]

*Sat. The Reasonable Animals (H.² 1780) 8° 1780.

*M. Piece. The Reasonable Fool (R.G. Th. 14/5/1789).

C. The Reasonable Lover MS. Larpent 12. L. [5/2/1776, for C.G.].

*Play. The Reception 8° 1799 [*Plymouth*].

*Int. The Recruit (Dumfries 1794).

*M. Piece. The Recruit (R.G. M. 1/9/1788).

*P. Redoutable Don Pierrot (R.G. M. 1/9/1788).

*F. The Reformed Coquette [printed in *The Lady's Magazine*, 1787 and 1788].

*C.O. Reformed in Time (C.G. W. 23/5/1798) 8° 1798; MS. Larpent 72. M. [9/5/1798].

*Ent. The Regions of Fancy; or, Harlequin's Home (S.W. M. 1/4/1782).

*[Sat.] The Reign of Hellebore 8° 1760.

*Int. The Relief of Williamstadt; or, Return from Victory (C.G. 1793).

*Int. The Rendezvous; or, Tars regaling (C.G. 1800).

O. The Revenge of Athridates (S.A. Dublin W. 12/12/1765) [printed as *Pharnaces: or, The R. of A.* 12° 1769 (*Dublin*)].
    [This is an alteration of Hull's *Pharnaces*, with music selected by Tenducci. It was acted also at the T.R. Edinburgh in 1769.]

*C.O. Richard II MS. Larpent 57. M. [8/12/1792, for C.G.].

*Int. The Richmond Gardener (Richmond 1790) MS. Larpent 23. S. [1/8/1790].

*F. The Rider; or, The Humours of an Inn 8° 1768.

*C. Ridicule, or Life's a Jest MS. Larpent 68. M. [8/2/1795].

*Burl. The Ridiculous Guardian (H.² Th. 30/7/1761) 4° 1761.

*Int. The Rights of Woman (C.G. T. 8/5/1792) MS. Larpent 58. M. [24/4/1792].
    [Billed as *The Retort Courteous called the R. of W.*; see *Hail Fellow well met.*]

*Burl. The Ring's End (R.C. F. 3/7/1795).

*Hist. Romance. The Rival Cavaliers, or Bertrand and Matilda (S.W. M. 18/5/1789).

*M. Piece. The Rival Favourites, or The Death of Bucephalus the Great.
    [In the Larpent collection is a printed copy (7. M.) dated 1765, for C.G.]

*M.D. The Rival Knights (C.G. Th. 9/10/1783).

Burl. Songs, &c. in The Rival Loyalists; or Sheelah's Choice (S.W. M. 12/5/1794) 8° 1794; 8° 1795.

*Ent. Rival Magic (R.G. M. 25/4/1791).

*C. The Rival Mother; or, The Sailors' Stratagem (Dublin 1789).

*Ent. The Rival Sorcerers; or, Harlequin Vanquisher (R.G. M. 16/8/1790).

Prel. The Rivals, or, The Green-Room Controversy (Salisbury 1776) 8° 1776 [*Salisbury*].

T. The Robbers...Translated and Altered from the German... With a Preface, Prologue and Epilogue, written by her Serene Highness, The Margravine of Anspach (Brandenburgh House 1797) 8° 1799.
> [An adaptation of F. Schiller, *Die Räuber*; ascribed to the Hon. Keppel Craven.]

*Int. Robin Bullcalf's Readings, or His Journey to London MS. Larpent 37. M. [9/5/1785, for D.L.].

*P. Robinson Crusoe; or, Harlequin Friday (D.L. M. 29/1/1781) 8° 1797.
> [Attributed to *R. B. SHERIDAN*.]

T. Rome Preserved 8° 1760.
> [A translation from Voltaire.]

*T. Romeo and Juliet...written originally in Spanish 8° 1770.

O. Rosamond...Altered from Mr. Addison (C.G. T. 21/4/1767) 8° 1767.
> [Music S. Arnold.]

*Past. D. The Rose Wreath, or Chaplet of Innocence MS. Larpent 17. S. [1781; no theatre mentioned].

*Ball. P. The Round Tower, or Irish Fidelity MS. Larpent 31. S. [17/11/1797, for C.G.].

*C. The Rover; or, The Banished Cavalier (C.G. S. 19/2/1757) 8° 1757.
> [An alteration of Mrs Behn's comedy.]

*[Sat.] Rowley and Chatterton in the Shades; or, Nugae Antiquae et Novae. A New Elysian Interlude 8° 1782.

Burl. The Royal Fugitives, or France in an Uproar (R.G. M. 18/7/1791) 8° 1791 [3 editions].

*Ent. The Royal Prisoners (S.W. Th. 26/9/1793).

*Ball. Rural Love (C.G. W. 12/12/1764).

*O. Rusticity [see *Biographia Dramatica*, iii. 234].

*Ent. The Sacrifice of Iphigenia (N.W. Clerkenwell 1750) 12° 1750.
> [Music Dr Arne. A ballet of the same name was given at Richmond S. 12/7/1766.]

P. Sketch of the Story, Scenery, and Songs, in Sadak & Kalasrade: or The Waters of Oblivion (S.W. M. 29/5/1797) 8° 1797.
> [Attributed to *T. J. DIBDIN*.]

*Ent. The Sailors' Contrivances (S.W. M. 7/7/1788).

*Int. The Sailor's Prize; or, May-Day Wedding (C.G. F. 1/5/1795) MS. Larpent 63. M. [28/4/1794].

*Int. The Sailor's Reception (Richmond S. 30/8/1766).

*Ent. St. George's Day; or, Britains rejoice (C.G. Th. 30/4/1789) MS. Larpent 17. L. [1789].

*Int. The St. Giles's Scrutiny; or, The Cries of London in a new Style (D.L. 1785) MS. Larpent 16. L. [31/3/1785].

*Ent. St. Monday (S.W. M. 16/6/1788).
*F. Sancho the Great [printed in *Will Whimsical's Magazine*, 1799].
Ent. Songs, Trios, Choruses, &c. in the Sans Culottes and the Grand
Culottes; or, The Invasion of Holland (S.W. S. 27/4/1793) 8° 1793.
Ent. The Savages; or, Harlequin Wanderer (S.W. M. 23/5/1792) 8° 1792.
*F. Scapin...altered from Otway, with several Additions (D.L. M.
30/4/1753).
*Int. The Scheming Valet [printed in *The Theatrical Museum*, 1776].
C. The School for Honour; or, The Chance of War...Translated
from the German 8° 1799.
[A translation of Lessing, *Minna von Barnhelm*.]
*C. The School for Husbands MS. Larpent 6. M. [16/1/1761, for C.G.].
*C. The School for Indifference [advertised at D.L. in 1787].
[Apparently an alteration of C. Cibber, *The Comical Lovers*.]
*C. The School for Ladies; or, The Levee of Lovers (H.² W. 5/4/1780).
[Pol.] The School for Scandal. A Comedy 8° 1779.
*[Pol.] The School for Scandal. A Comedy 8° 1784.
*[Sat.] The School for Scandal; or, Newspapers. A Comedy 8° 1792.
*Int. The School for Scandal Scandalized (York, 27/3/1779; C.G. S.
18/3/1780) MS. Larpent 13. L. [13/3/1779, for T.R. York. The
Larpent MS. is in the hand of *J. P. KEMBLE*, who may be the
author.]
*Ent. The School of Shakespeare; or, Humours and Passions (H.² T.
7/8/1781).
*Ball. The Scotch Ghost (D.L. 1796).
*C. The Scribler 12° 1751 [*Dublin*].
*F. The Secret Castle, or, Henry and Edwy (Manchester 1799) MS.
Larpent 36. S. [18/2/1799].
[Pol.] The Secret Expedition. A Farce...As it has been represented
upon the Political Theatre of Europe. With the Highest Applause
8° 1757 [*bis*].
T. Semiramis...translated from Voltaire 8° 1760.
*Burl. The Servant Mistress 8° 1770; 4° 1774.
[A version of *La Serva Padrona*, *q.v.* under Italian Operas.]
*Prel. Seventeen Hundred and Eighty One; or, The Cartel at Phila-
delphia (C.G. S. 28/4/1781) MS. Larpent 24. M. [1781].
*Int. Shakespeare's Choice Spirits; or, Falstaff in Pantomime (S.W.
M. 18/7/1768).
*C. The Sham Beggar 8° 1756 [*Dublin*].
[See *Biographia Dramatica*, iii. 262.]
*[Pol.] The Sham Fight; or, Political Humbug. A State Farce 8° 1756.
*Int. The Sham Ghost (R.G. Th. 7/10/1790).
*Dr. Fable. The Sheep, the Duck and the Cock 8° 1783 [*Bath*].
*Int. The She Gallant; or, Recruits for the King of Prussia (C.G. T.
20/3/1759).
*Ent. She's mad for a Husband (S.W. M. 20/4/1778).
*Ent. She would be a Soldier (R.G. M. 5/7/1790).
*O. The Shipwreck (Patagonian, 1780) 8° 1780.
[An adaptation of the Dryden-Shadwell *Tempest*, with music by
Smith.]
*Ent. The Shipwreck, or, Harlequin, Old Leo, and the Savages (S.W.
T. 10/7/1787).
*Ball. P. The Shipwreck; or, French Ingratitude (C.G. 1793).
*Ball. Sicilian Peasants (C.G. W. 29/12/1762).
*P. The Siege of Quebec; or, Harlequin Engineer (C.G. 1760).

*P. The Siege of Quebec (R.G. M. 31/5/1784).
[Sat.] The Siege of the Castle of Aesculapius. An Heroic Comedy, as it is Acted at the Theatre in Warwick-Lane 8° 1768.
Ent. The Siege of Troy; or, Famous Trojan Horse, A Grand Heroic, Serio-Comic, Tragic Spectacle (Ast.) 8° 1795.
*Ent. The Siege of Valenciennes (R.S. F. 6/9/1793).
*F. Sir Thomas Callicoe; or, The Mock Nabob (C.G. Th. 6/7/1758).
    [An alteration of Crowne's *Sir Courtly Nice*.]
*Ent. Six Spaniards (S.W. M. 28/5/1787).
T. Socrates...translated from Voltaire 8° 1760.
*Ent. The Soldiers' Festival (C.G. W. 21/4/1790).
*Ent. The Son of Neptune (S.W. M. 25/4/1791).
*Prel. The Sons of Anacreon (D.L. 1785).
*Burl. The Sons of Britannia (S.W. Sept. 1794).
*Ent. The Sorceress; or, Trick upon Trick (S.W. M. 31/3/1766).
C. The South Briton...Written by a Lady (S.A. Dublin 21/1/1773; C.G. T. 12/4/1774) 8° 1774.
*Int. The Spaniards dismayed; or, True Blue for Ever (C.G. 1780) 8° 1780.
    [Based on Henry Carey, *Nancy*.]
*Ball. The Spanish Coquettes (R.C. M. 1/9/1788).
*F. The Spanish Curate (C.G. S. 10/5/1783).
    [An alteration of Beaumont and Fletcher's comedy.]
*O.F. The Speechless Wife (C.G. Th. 22/5/1794).
*Ent. The Spirit of the Grotto; or, An Hour at Weybridge (S.W. M. 16/5/1796).
C. The Spiritual Minor 8° [1762].
Int. Spring Valley [printed in *The West Indian* 8° 1787].
C. The Squire Burlesqued; or, The Sharpers Outwitted 8° 1765.
    [By "Bartholomew Bourgeois."]
*F. The Stage Coach...altered (C.G. M. 16/4/1787).
    [An adaptation of Vanbrugh's comedy.]
*[Pol.] The State Farce; or They are all come Home 8° 1757; 8° 1758.
M. The Statute. A Pastoral Masque. As it is privately performed with great Applause 8° 1777.
*D. Stella...from the German 8° 1798.
    [A translation from Goethe.]
*Burl. The Stratagem. Taken from the Italian (H.² T. 23/6/1761).
    [Music Hasse.]
*Ball. P. The Strawberry Pickers (S.W. T. 29/3/1796).
C. The Students...Altered from Shakespeare's Love's Labours Lost, and Adapted to the Stage 8° 1762.
*C. The Students 8° 1779.
*M. The Sultan (C.G. W. 3/1/1759).
*Ent. The Surrender of Conde (S.W. M. 29/7/1793).
*Ent. The Surrender of Trinidad; or, Safe moor'd at Last (C.G. Th. 11/5/1797) MS. Larpent 71. M. [2/5/1797].
*Ent. The Surrender of Valenciennes (Doncaster, Nov. 1793).
*C. The Suspicious Brother MS. Larpent 49. M. [9/4/1789, for H.²].
C. The Swindler 12° 1785.
*F. The Swindlers (D.L. M. 25/4/1774) MS. Larpent 11. L. [1774].
*F. The Swop (H.² M. 22/6/1789) MS. Larpent 50. M. [14/5/1789].
F. The Sylph 8° 1771.
    [A translation from Saint-Foix; see *The Uneasy Man*.]

*P. Airs and Chorusses in...The Sylphs; or, Harlequin's Gambols
(C.G. M. 31/1/1774) 8° [1774].
  [Music Fisher.]
*O.F. The System of Lavater; or, The Knights of the Post (Edin-
burgh 1797).
  [See *The Knights of the Post.*]
*C. The Systematic or Imaginary Philosopher 8° 1800.
  [Ascribed to Lieut.-Col. Buckeridge.]
[Burlesque.] The Tailors. A Tragedy for warm Weather (H.² Th.
2/7/1767) 8° 1778.
*C. A Tale of the Castle; or, Who is she like? (Edinburgh 1793).
*F. The Talisman (H.² 1784) MS. Larpent 34. M. [1784].
Ent. Sketch of the Story, Scenery, &c....In the new Comic Entertain-
ment of The Talisman; or, Harlequin made Happy (S.W. 1796)
8° 1796.
*F. The Tamer Tam'd (D.L. S. 30/4/1757) MS. Larpent 5. S.
[25/4/1757].
  [An alteration of Fletcher's comedy.]
*F. The Tamer Tam'd (Brandenburgh House T. 9/6/1795).
*Int. Tars at Torbay; or, Sailors on Saturday Night (H.² 1799).
*[Sat.] Taste and Feeling (H.² F. 13/8/1790) MS. Larpent 22. S.
[5/8/1790].
*Int. Teague's Ramble to London (H.² 1770).
*M. Piece. The Temple of Plutus; or, The Miser Reformed (R.G.
M. 13/5/1791).
*Ent. The Termagant Wife (R.S. M. 1/7/1793).
*[Sat.] The Theatrical Manager 8° 1751.
T. Theodorick King of Denmark 8° 1752 (*Dublin*).
*Ent. The Thespian Panorama (Bath F. 6/3/1795).
*Int. They've bit the old one; or, The Scheming Butler (C.G. T.
1/5/1798) MS. Larpent 35. S. [21/4/1798].
*F. Thimble's Flight from his Shopboard (H.² T. 25/8/1789) 8°
[1790?; *Brighton*]; MS. Larpent 21. S. [14/8/1789].
*Ent. Thomas and Susan; or, The Fortunate Tar (Royalty 1787).
Pol. The Three Conjurers. A Political Interlude. Stolen from Shake-
speare. As it was performed at sundry Places in Westminster, on
Saturday, the 30th. of April, and Sunday, the 1st. of May. Most
humbly dedicated to that distressed and unfortunate Gentleman,
John Wilkes, Esq., Late Prisoner in the Tower 4° [1767].
Ent. The Times; or, A Fig for Invasion. A Musical Entertainment 8°
1797.
*Ent. The Tinker (R.G. M. 8/8/1791).
*P. Tippoo Sahib; or, British Valour in India (C.G. M. 6/6/1791).
*Ent. Tippoo Sahib, or, The Siege of Bangalore (R.S. M. 9/4/1792;
"A Whimsical, Oriental, Tragical, Comical, Pantomimical
Sketch").
*F. 'Tis an ill Wind that blows nobody good; or, The Road to Odiham
(D.L. M. 14/4/1788).
*C. 'Tis a strange World MS. Larpent 66. M. [17/4/1795, for
C.G.].
*Ent. Tit for Tat (S.W. M. 7/4/1777).
*C.O. Tit for Tat, or The Cadi gulled (Crow-street, Dublin, M.
20/1/1766).
*Int. The Tobacco Box; or, Soldier's Pledge of Love (H.²T. 13/8/1782).

*F. Tony Lumpkin's Ramble to London MS. Larpent 56. M [6/4/1792, for C.G.].

[See under *JOHN O'KEEFFE* for *Tony Lumpkin in Town.*]

*Prel. A Touch at the Times; or, A Ramble through London (H.[2] W. 20/8/1788) MS. Larpent 21. S. [1788, for D.L.].

*C. A Tour in Wales MS. Larpent 14. L. [30/6/1779, for H.[2]].

*Prel. Transformation (H.[2] T. 7/8/1787).

*Prel. Transformation; or, The Manager an Actor in spite of himself (D.L. W. 25/4/1787).

*— The Trial of Skill; or, The Statesman foil'd MS. Larpent 9. L. [11/6/1768].

*Play. Trials of the Heart (D.L. W. 24/4/1799) MS. Larpent 37. S. [20/4/1799].

*F. A Trip to Elysium (H.[2] W. 10/8/1791).

*C. A Trip to Ireland; or, The Tour Writer (Fishamble-street, Dublin, 8/2/1777).

*Ent. The Triumph of Cupid (Royalty T. 3/7/1787).

*P. The Triumph of Fidelity (Miniature Theatre, Rice's Rooms, Brewer-street, Golden-square, 1790).

*M. The Triumph of Friendship [printed in *The Oxford Miscellany*, 1752].

*T.C. The Triumph of Honour (H.[2] W. 13/8/1783).

[An alteration of Beaumont and Fletcher's drama.]

*Ent. The Triumph of Liberty, or, The Destruction of the Bastille (R.C. T. 18/8/1789).

P. Airs…in The Triumph of Mirth, or, Harlequin's Wedding (D.L. Th. 26/12/1782) 8° 1782.

[Music T. Linley.]

*Ent. True-Blue (Royalty) 8° 1787.

[An adaptation of Henry Carey, *Nancy.*]

D. True Patriotism; or Poverty Enobled by Virtue (Louth, F. 21/12/1798) 8° 1799.

*D. Truth and Filial Love 12° 1797.

F. Try Again (H.[2] S. 26/6/1790) 8° 1790; 12° 1790 [*Dublin*].

[Based on Fatouville, *La précaution inutile* (1692).]

*Dr. Poem. The Tryal of Abraham 8° 1790 [*Stamford*].

[Ascribed to one Farrer, of Oundle.]

*F. Tummus and Meary; or, The Adventures and Misfortunes of a Lancashire Clown (Manchester 1773).

Burl. The Tutor (D.L. F. 14/12/1759) 8° 1759.

[An adaptation of *Il Tutore* (Teatro di S. Bartolomeo, Naples, 1730); music A. Hasse.]

*P. The Twenty One Metamorphoses, or, Harlequin of Age (R.G. M. 8/9/1788).

*Int. Twisting and Twining; or, Tea's the Twaddle (H.[2] 1785) MS. Larpent 39. M. [8/2/1785; as *Tea's the Twaddle*].

*Ent. The Two Boat Makers (R.G. M. 7/7/1788).

D. The Two Friends; or, The Liverpool Merchant 8° 1800.

[A translation by C. H. from Beaumarchais.]

*Burl. The Two Nannys (R.G. W. 1/10/1788).

*F. The Two Socias (H.[2] F. 31/8/1792).

[An adaptation of Hawkesworth's *Amphitryon.*]

*Ball. The Tythe Pig (C.G. T. 12/5/1795).

*Ent. The Tythe Sheaf (R.G. T. 17/5/1791).

*Int. The Ugly Club...by Edmund Spenser the Younger (D.L. W. 6/6/1798) 8° 1798; MS. Larpent 33. S. [2/6/1798).

C. [The Uneasy Man] Three Comedies: The Uneasy Man, The Financier, and The Sylph. Freely Translated from Messrs. De St. Foix and Fagan 8° 1771.

*Int. The Unfeeling Parent; or, Secours Imprévu (Dublin 1793).

*Ent. The Union; or, St. Andrew's Day (C.G. 18/5/1790) MS. Larpent 54. M. [21/5/1791].

*F. The Universal Register Office MS. Larpent 6. S. [7/3/1761].

*C. The Unreserved Young Lady [printed in *The Lady's Magazine*, 1788].

*Ent. Ups and Downs, or The Farmer MS. Larpent 46. M. [1787; for Liverpool].

*F. The Usurers MS. Larpent 14. L. [14/7/1780].

[Pol.] Utrum Horum? A Comedy 8° 1797.

*Int. The Vanguard; or, British Tars regaling after Battle (C.G. F. 3/5/1799).

*O.F. The Venetian Tale MS. Larpent 32. S. [12/5/1797, for C.G.].

*Ent. Venus's Girdle; or, The World bewitched (S.W. M. 25/7/1796).

*Ent. The Victorious Tars (R.G. W. 14/9/1791).

*Int. The Village Conjurer...translated from J. J. Rousseau 12° 1767.

O. The Village Maid...by a Young Lady 8° 1792.

*F. The Villagers (D.L. 23/3/1756).
   [An alteration of C. Johnson, *The Village Opera*.]

*P. Village Romps (C.G. M. 9/12/1765).

*Ent. Vineyard Revels (S.W. M. 14/7/1777).

*P. Vintage (D.L. T. 24/2/1767).

*Ent. The Virgin Unmask'd 8° 1786.
   [An alteration of H. Fielding's comedy.]

*T. The Virgin Victim.

*M. Virtue and Beauty reconciled 4° [1762]; MS. Larpent 6. M. [23/2/1762, for D.L.].

*F. The Virtuoso MS. Larpent 4. L. [28/12/1751, for D.L.].

*Int. The Volunteer Returned [printed in *The Lady's Magazine*, 1784, 1785 and 1786].

*F. The Wager MS. Larpent 15. L. [7/2/1780, for Manchester].

*T. Wallace 8° 1799 [*Edinburgh*].

*C. Ways and Means (S.A. Dublin W. 7/12/1785).
   [Cp. under *GEORGE COLMAN the Younger*.]

*Ent. The Weird Sisters, or, Harlequin's Progress (R.S. M. 1/7/1793).

*Prel. Westminster Hall (H.² 16/8/1785).

*Int. Weston's Return from the Universities of Parnassus (H.² 1775).

*Piece. Wet Weather MS. Larpent 9. L.

*P. What you please (R.C. F. 20/6/1788).

*Ent. Which is the Real Dog; or, Harlequin Pointer (Royalty S. 2/2/1799).

*P. The Whim of the Moment (Ast. T. 6/6/1797).

*M. Piece. Whitsun Monday; or, A Cure for a Scold (S.W. T. 23/9/1788).

*P. Whittington and his Cat (Ast. M. 4/5/1795).

*C. Who is she like MS. Larpent 26. S. [9/3/1793, for Edinburgh].

*Ent. Who pays the Rent? or, The Landlord outwitted (S.W. M. 8/5/1797).
   [An adaptation of Sedaine, *Blaise le Savetier*.]

*C.O. Who's to have her? MS. Larpent 24. S. [4/1/1791, for Sheffield].
*Burl. The Widow and no Widow; or, The Faithful Irishman (S.W.
    M. 18/4/1796).
C.   The Widow of Wallingford...As it was performed in the Neigh-
    bourhood of Wallingford, by a Set of Gentlemen and Ladies 8°
    [1775].
*F. Will and no Will; or, Wit's last Stake (D.L. 24/4/1799).
    [An alteration of T. King's *Wit's Last Stake.*]
*C. The Will and the Deed MS. Larpent 31. S. [24/3/1797, for
    D.L.].
*Int. William and Susan; or, The Sailor's Sheet Anchor (H.² 26/8/1785)
    MS. Larpent 20. S. [20/8/1785].
Ent. Descriptive Sketch of the New Historical Entertainment of
    William Tell (S.W. M. 12/5/1794) 8° 1795.
    [Attributed to *HENRY SIDDONS*. It is billed occasionally
    with a sub-title, *Or, The Origin of Swiss Liberty.*]
*Ent. The Wish MS. Larpent 15. M. [22/4/1775, for D.L.].
*Dr. Sat. The Wishes MS. Larpent 29. M. [18/2/1782, for C.G.].
Ent. Songs, Recitatives, &c. in The Witch of the Lakes, or, Harlequin
    in the Hebrides (S.W. M. 16/6/1788) 8° 1793; The Witch of the
    Lakes 8° 1793.
*O.F. The Witch of the Wood; or, The Nutting Girls (C.G. T.
    10/5/1796) MS. Larpent 30. S. [6/5/1796].
*P. The Witches' Revels; or, The Birth of Harlequin (C.G. S.
    2/6/1798).
*Ent. The Witty Wife (R.G. M. 13/5/1791).
*C. Wives in Plenty; or, The More the Merrier (H.² S. 23/11/1793)
    MS. Larpent 26. S. [19/11/1793].
    [An alteration of Molloy, *The Coquet.*]
*Ent. The Wizard (S.W. M. 31/3/1777).
*P. Wizards of the Rocks (Richmond W. 31/8/1768).
P.   An Account of The Wonders of Derbyshire, introduced in the
    Pantomime Entertainment at the Theatre-Royal, Drury-Lane
    (D.L. F. 8/1/1779) 8° 1779; MS. Larpent 19. M. [2/1/1779].
    [Acted as *The W. of D., or, Harlequin in the Peak.*]
D.   The Writing Desk 8° 1799.
    [A translation from Kotzebue.]
*F. You may like it, or let it alone (Lord Delaval's private theatre
    Seaton Delaval, 1791).
*T. Zapphira 8° 1792.

II. *Italian Operas, Oratorios and Ballets performed at the Opera House*

Orat. Abimelech (H.¹ W. 16/3/1768) 8° 1768 4° [1768].
    [Music S. Arnold.]
Orat. Adam; or, The Fatal Disobedience [in *Poems* by Richard Jago
    8° 1784].
*P. Ball. Adelaide, ou La Bergère des Alpes (H.¹ S. 11/1/1794).
*O. Aci e Galatea MS. Larpent 67. M. [10/3/1795, for H.¹].
Ball. Adela of Ponthieu. A tragy-pantomime ballet (H.¹ Th. 17/4/1788)
    [in J. G. Noverre's *Works* 8° 1783].
    [This seems to have been presented first in 1782.]

*O. Adriano in Siria (H.¹ T. 20/2/1750).
    [Metastasio; music V. L. Ciampi.]
O. Adriano in Siria (H.¹ S. 26/1/1765) 8° 1765.
    [Metastasio; music J. C. Bach.]
C.O. L'Albergatrice vivace (H.¹ T. 16/12/1783) 8° 1783; MS. Larpent
    32. M. [13/12/1783].
    [Author unknown; original composer Luigi Caruso. Teatro di
    S. Samuele, Venice 1780.]
*C.O. L'Albero di Diana (H.¹ T. 18/4/1797).
    [Music Martini.]
*O. Alceste (H.¹ S. 23/12/1786) MS. Larpent 41. M. [23/12/1786].
O. Alceste ossia Il Trionfo dell' Amor conjugale [H.¹ Th. 30/4/1795]
    8° [1795]; MS. Larpent 67. M. [24/4/1795].
    [R. de Calsabigi; music C. Gluck.]
*C.O. Alcina (H.¹ Th. 28/3/1776) MS. Larpent 35. M. [16/3/1784, as
    Alina].
    [Music Gazaniga.]
O. Alessandro nell' Indie (H.¹ S. 11/12/1756) 8° 1756.
    [Altered from Metastasio; Pasticcio.]
O. Alessandro nell' Indie (H.¹ 13/10/1761) 8° 1761.
    [Altered from Metastasio; music G. Cocchi.]
O. Alessandro nell' Indie (H.¹ Nov. 1774) 8° 1774.
    [Metastasio, with alterations by G. G. Bottarelli; translation by
    Bottarelli jun.; music Corri.]
Orat. Alfred the Great (H.¹ S. 12/5/1753) 8° 1753; 8° 1754.
    [Music Dr Arne.]
Past. Ent. Le Ali d'Amore (H.¹ Th. 29/2/1776) 8° 1776; 8° 1777.
    [C. F. Badini; music V. Rauzzini.]
C.O. Gli Amanti gelosi (C.G. M. 17/12/1753) 12° 1753; 12° 1754.
    [G. Giordani; music G. Cocchi.]
C.O. Gli Amanti gelosi [The Jealous Lovers] (S.A. Dublin) 8° 1764
    [*Dublin*].
    [G. Giordani; music B. Galuppi and T. Giordani.]
C.O. Gli Amanti ridicoli [The Ridiculous Lovers] (H.¹ S. 5/11/1768)
    8° 1768.
    [Galuppi, altered by G. G. Bottarelli; music B. Galuppi and
    F. Alessandri.]
*Ball. L'Amant retrouvé (H.¹ T. 20/1/1795).
    [Composed by Onorati.]
C.O. L'Amor artigiano (H.¹ M. 3/8/1778).
    [Goldoni; music Gassmann; original music by J. Schuster.
    Teatro Giustiniani di San Moisè, autumn 1776.]
C.O. L'Amore contrastato, ossia La Molinarella (H.¹ S. 6/12/1794) 8ᵒ
    1794; MS. Larpent 17. L.
    [G. Palomba; music G. Paisiello. Teatro dei Fiorentini, Naples,
    summer 1788.]
C.O. L'Amor Costante [Love and Constancy] (C.G. M. 11/2/1754)
    8° 1754; MS. Larpent 4. S. [8/2/1754].
    [Music Leonard Lee.]
C.O. L'Amore Soldato (H.¹ T. 5/5/1778) 8° 1778; 8° 1780.
    [N. Tassi, with alterations by A. Andrei; music A. Sacchini.]
*C.O. L'Amor fra le Vendemmie (H.¹ T. 6/12/1796) MS. Larpent
    69. M. [2/12/1796].
    [Music P. Guglielmi.]

*Ball. L'Amour et Psyché (H.¹ T. 29/1/1788).

O. Andromaca (H.¹ T. 11/11/1755) 8° 1755; MS. Larpent "Extra" [11/11/1755].
    [Altered from A. Salvi, *Astianatte*; music Jomelli.]

O. Andromaca (H.² F. 28/5/1790) 8° [1790]; MS. Larpent 53. M. [1/6/1790].
    [C. F. Badini; music Nasolini.]

*O. Antigona (H.¹ Th. 17/4/1760) MS. Larpent 5. M. [1760].
    [Pasticcio.]

O. Antigona (H.¹ T. 24/5/1796) 8° 1796; MS. Larpent 69. M. [23/5/1796].
    [Music F. Bianchi.]

O. Antigono (H.¹ March 1757) 8° 1757.
    [Altered from Metastasio by G. Roccaforte; music N. Consorto.]

*O. Antigono (H.¹ Th. 28/3/1765).

O. Antigono (H.¹ T. 8/3/1774) 8° 1776.
    [Music T. Giordani.]

*Past. O. Apollo ed Issea (H.¹ T. 30/3/1773).
    [Music Pugnani.]

*C.O. L'Arbore di Diana MS. Larpent 19. L. [14/4/1797].

Burl. L'Arcadia in Brenta (C G. M. 18/11/1754) 8° 1755.
    [C. Goldoni; original music L. V. Ciampi. Bassano, autumn 1747.]

*C.O. L'Arcifanfano (H.¹ S. 25/11/1780) MS. Larpent 15. L. [1780].
    [C. Goldoni; original music by G. Scolari. Teatro di rua Dos Condes, Lisbon, 1768.]

*Ball. Ariadne et Bacchus (H.¹ T. 28/11/1797).
    [Composed by Gallet.]

O. Arianna e Teseo (H.¹ S. 20/12/1760) 8° 1761.
    [Altered from Francis Colman, *Ariadne in Crete*; pasticcio.]

*O. Armida (H.¹ T. 8/11/1774).

O. Armida (H.¹ Th. 25/5/1786) 8° 1786; MS. Larpent 41. M. [1786].
    [Music M. Mortellari.]

O. Armida (Pantheon S. 9/4/1791) 4° 1791.
    [G. Tonioli; translation by O'Reilly; music A. Sacchini.]

O. Arminio (H.¹ S. 1/3/1760) 8° 1760.
    [Antonio Salvi, with additions from Metastasio; pasticcio. Teatro Regio, Milan, 28/8/1730.]

O. Artaserse (H.¹ T. 29/1/1754) 8° 1754.
    [Altered from Metastasio; music G. A. Hasse.]

*O. Artaserse (H.¹ M. 13/1/1766).
    [Music G. A. Hasse.]

O. Artaserse (H.¹ T. 21/4/1772) 8° 1772.
    [Metastasio, altered by G. G. Bottarelli; translation by Carara; music arranged by T. Giordani.]

O. Artaserse (H.¹ 1779) 8° 1779.
    [Music Bertoni. All these four are more or less amended versions of Metastasio's *dramma per musica*.]

Orat. The Ascension (C.G. 1776) 4° 1776; MS. Larpent 13. S. [1776].
    [Music Hook.]

C.O. L'Assemblea [The Assembly] (H.¹ S. 28/3/1772) 8° 1772.
    [G. G. Bottarelli, based on C. Goldani, *La Conversazione*; music P. Guglielmi.]

O. Astarto Ré di Tiro (H.¹ S. 11/12/1762) 8° 1762; 8° [1770].
    [A. Zeno, adapted by G. G. Bottarelli; pasticcio.]

*O. Astarto Rè di Tiro (H.¹ S. 2/11/1776).
   [Pasticcio.]
O. Attalo (H.¹ S. 11/11/1758) 8° 1758.
   [Pasticcio.]
*O. Attilio Regolo (H.¹ S. 11/5/1754) MS. Larpent 3. M. [1753].
   [Metastasio; music Jomelli; original music Hasse. Dresden 1750.]
*O. Attilio Regolo (H.¹ S. 15/5/1762).
   [The above with new music by Jomelli.]
C.O. L'Avaro (H.¹ S. 14/6/1783) 8° 1783; MS. Larpent 15. L. [1783].
   [G. Bertati; music P. Anfossi. Teatro di S. Moisè, Venice,
   autumn 1775.]
C.O. L'Avaro deluso (H.¹T. 24/11/1778) 8° 1778; MS. Larpent 18. M.
   [23/11/1778].
   [G. Bertati, *Calandrano*, with translation by Mrs Rigaud;
   additions by A. Andrei; music A. Sacchini; original music by
   G. Gazzaniga. Teatro di S. Samuele, Venice, autumn 1771.]
C.O. Il Bacio (H.¹ T. 9/1/1776) 8° 1776.
   [C. F. Badini; music M. Vento.]
*C.O. Il Bacio (H.¹ T. 9/4/1782).
   [Music T. Giordani.]
Orat. Balaam 8° 1787 [with *Ruth*].
   [Rev. Charles Davy.]
*C.O. Il Barbiere di Siviglia (H.¹ Th. 11/6/1789) MS. Larpent 50. M.
   [9/6/1789].
   [An Italian adaptation of Beaumarchais' comedy.]
C.O. Il Barone di Torre Forte (H.¹ Th. 22/2/1781) 8° [1781]; MS. Lar-
   pent 15. L. [13/2/1781].
   [Music N. Piccinni.]
O. La Bella Arsene (H.¹ S. 12/12/1795) 8° 1795; MS. Larpent 67. M.
   [10/12/1795].
   [Altered from C. S. Favart by L. da Ponte; translation by G.
   Mazzinghi; music altered from Grétry by G. Mazzinghi.]
C.O. La Bella Pescatrice (Pantheon, Th. 24/3/1791) 4° 1791; 8° 1794;
   MS. Larpent 64. M. [17/3/1794].
   [S. Zini, altered by G. Mazzinghi; music P. Guglielmi. Teatro
   Nuovo sopra Toledo, Naples, 1789. The edition of 1794 contains
   alterations by L. da Ponte.]
*Orat. Belshazzar (C.G. W. 22/2/1758) MS. Larpent 15. L. [1782].
   [Händel's original oratorio "with Alterations and Additions."]
O. Berenice (H.¹ T. 1/1/1765) 8° 1764/5.
   [Pasticcio.]
*C.O. La Bergère costante (H.¹ T. 5/11/1782).
C.O. Bertoldo, Bertoldino e Cacasenno alla Corte del Ré Alboino
   (C.G.) 8° 1755; 8° 1762.
*C.O. Bertoldo (H.¹ M. 11/1/1760).
   [C. Goldoni, *Bertoldo, Bertoldino e Cacasenno*; music L. V.
   Ciampi. Teatro di S. Moisè, Venice, 1748.]
*Orat. Betulia Liberata (H.¹ Th. 25/2/1768).
   [Music Jomelli.]
*Ball. La Bontè de Seigneur (H.¹ S. 31/5/1788).
C.O. La Buona Figliuola (H.¹ T. 25/11/1766) 8° [1766]; 8° [1767; 3rd];
   8° 1775; 8° 1777.
   [C. Goldoni; music N. Piccini; original music by E. Duni.
   Parma 1756.]

*C.O. La Buona Figliuola (H.¹ T. 3/6/1783).

C.O. La Buona Figliuola maritata (H.¹ S. 31/1/1767) 8° 1767.
[C. Goldoni, altered by G. G. Bottarelli; original music by N. Piccinni. Teatro Formagliari, Bologna, May 1761.]

C.O. Il Burbero di buon Cuore (H.¹ S. 17/5/1794) 8° [1794]; MS. Larpent 63. M.
[L. da Ponte; music V. Martini. Burgtheater, Vienna, 4/1/1786.]

*O. Caio Mario (H.¹ S. 20/4/1776).
[Music N. Piccinni.]

C.O. La Calamita de' Cuori [The Magnet of Hearts] (H.¹ Th. 3/2/1763) 8° 1763.
[C. Goldoni, adapted by G. G. Bottarelli; music B. Galuppi. Teatro Nuovo di S. Samuele, Venice, 1752.]

C.O. La Cameriera accorta [The Artful Chambermaid] (C.G. M. 4/3/1754) 8° 1754.
[Music B. Galuppi.]

C.O. La Cameriera astuta (H.¹ T. 4/3/1788) 8° 1788; MS. Larpent 48. M. [1/3/1788].
[Music S. Storace.]

C.O. I Capricci del Sesso (H.¹ T. 13/5/1777).
[Music T. Trajetta.]

C.O. Il Capriccio dramatico (H.¹ S. 8/3/1794) 8° [1794]; MS. Larpent 63. M. [27/2/1794].
[Adapted by L. da Ponte from G. M. Diodati, L'Impresario in Angustie; translation by G. Mazzinghi; music D. Cimarosa.]

O.   Carattaco (H.¹ S. 14/2/1767) 8° 1767.
[G. G. Bottarelli; music J. C. Bach.]

C.O. Il Carnovale di Venezia (H.¹ T. 14/1/1772) 8° 1772.
[C. F. Badini; music P. Guglielmi.]

C.O. La Cascina [The Dairy-House] (H.¹ S. 8/1/1763) 8° 1763.
[C. Goldoni, adapted by G. G. Bottarelli; pasticcio; original music by G. Scolari. Teatro di S. Samuele, 1755.]

*O. Celopida (H.¹ S. 24/5/1766).

*C.O. La Chercheuse d'Esprit (H.¹ S. 23/12/1786).
[C. S. Favart. Foire St Germain, Paris, 20/2/1741.]

O.   Il Cid (H.¹ T. 19/1/1773) 8° 1773 [bis].
[G. Pizzi; music A. Sacchini. Teatro di Torre Argentina, Rome, 1769. Alterations in the Italian have been made by G. G. Bottarelli, whose son executed the translation into English.]

C.O. La Cifra (H.¹ S. 10/3/1798) 8° [1798].
[G. Petrosellini, altered by L. da Ponte; music Salieri.]

O.   Cimene (H.¹ T. 7/1/1783) 8° [1783].
[Probably B. Pasqualio; music G. Bertoni.]

*O. Cinna MS. Larpent 72. M. [1798].

O.   Il Ciro riconosciuto (H.¹ T. 16/1/1759) 8° 1759.
[Metastasio, with alterations; music G. Cocchi]

*C.O. La Cisra MS. Larpent 73. M. [8/3/1798].

O.   La Clemenza di Scipione (H.¹ S. 4/4/1778) 8° 1778.
[Music J. C. Bach; translation by F. Bottarelli.]

*O. La Clemenza di Tito (H.¹ T. 15/1/1760).
[P. Metastasio; music G. Cocchi. Teatro della Corte Cesarea Vienna, 4/11/1734.]

O.   La Clemenza di Tito (H.¹ T. 3/12/1765) 8° 1765.
[Music G. Cocchi.]

O. Cleonice Regina di Siria (H.¹ S. 26/11/1763) 8° 1763.
[Pasticcio.]

*Burl. La Comediante fatta Cantatrice (C.G. M. 12/1/1756).

O. La Conquista del Messico (H.¹ S. 4/4/1767) 8° 1767.
[G. G. Bottarelli; music M. Vento.]

*C.O. Il Consiglio imprudente (H.¹T.20/12/1796) MS.Larpent 69. M. [29/12/1796].

C.O. La Contadina in Corte [A Country Girl at Court] (H.¹ Th. 14/3/1771) 8° 1771; 8° 1782; MS. Larpent 14. L. [14/12/1779] and 10. L. [7/3/1771].
[Music A. Sacchini. Probably the opera acted at the Teatro Valle, Rome, 1765.]

C.O. Le Contadine bizarre (H.¹ T. 7/11/1769) 8° 1769; MS. Larpent 9. L. [28/10/1769].
[G. Petrosellini; music N. Piccinni. Rome, Capranica, Feb. 1763.]

C.O. I Contadini bizarri (H.¹ S. 1/2/1794) 8° [1794]; MS. Larpent 62. M. [31/1/1794].
[T. Grandi, with alterations by L. da Ponte; music G. Sarti and G. Paisiello.]

*C.O. Il Conte ridicolo (H.¹ T. 14/4/1795) MS. Larpent 67. M. [10/4/1795].
[Music G. Paisiello.]

C.O. La Contessina [The Proud Beggars] (H.¹ T. 11/1/1774) 8° 1774.
[Coltellini, altered by G. G. Bottarelli; music F. Gassmann.]

C.O. Il Convito [The Banquet] (H.¹ S. 2/11/1782) 8° 1782; MS. Larpent 15. L. [1782].
[F. Livigni, with alterations by A. Andrei; music Bertoni. Piccolo Teatro, Dresden, 1783.]

C.O. La Cosa Rara (H.¹ S. 10/1/1789) 8° 1789; MS. Larpent 22. S. [8/1/1789].
[L. da Ponte; music V. Martini. Vienna 17/11/1786.]

*O. Cosroe (H.¹ S. 24/11/1770).

C.O. La Costanza di Rosinella (H.¹ S. 31/3/1770) 8° 1770.
[Music P. Guglielmi.]

*O. Creso (H.¹ 1758).

O. Creso 8° 1767.
[G. Pizzi; music A. Sacchini; translation F. Bottarelli. Teatro di S. Carlo, Naples, 4/11/1765.]

O. Creso (H.¹ S. 8/11/1777) 8° 1777.

O. Creusa in Delfo (H.¹ T. 29/4/1783) 8° 1783; MS. Larpent 18. S. [1783].
[Music V. Rauzzini.]

Orat. The Cure of Saul (D.L. 27/4/1763) 4° 1763.
[At first with selections from G. F. Händel; later re-set by Dr Arnold.]

*[O.] Il Curioso Indiscreto MS. Larpent 36. M. [1784; no theatre mentioned].

Orat. The Death of Abel (H.¹ W. 24/2/1768) 4° 1768.
[Music N. Piccinni.]

*Orat. Debora e Sisara MS. Larpent 68. M. [1795].

O. Demetrio, Re di Siria (H.¹ T. 8/11/1757) 8° 1757.
[P. Metastasio; pasticcio. Vienna 4/11/1731.]

O.   Il Demofoonte (H.¹ T. 9/12/1755) 8° 1755.
     [P. Metastasio; music Jomelli. Padua, 13/6/1743.]
*O.   Il Demofoonte (H.¹ 1765).
     [Music M. Vento.]
O.   Il Demofoonte (H.¹ S. 28/11/1778) 8° 1778.
     [Music F. Bertoni.]
O.   Didone (H.¹ S. 5/1/1754) 8° 1754.
     [Altered from Metastasio; music V. Ciampi.]
O.   Didone abbandonata (H.¹ S. 14/3/1761) 8° 1761.
     [P. Metastasio; music D. Perez and B. Galuppi.]
O.   Didone abbandonata (H.¹ 1775) 8° [1775]; MS. Larpent 12. S.
     [1/5/1775].
     [Music A. Sacchini. The Larpent collection has also *Didone*
     42. M. (10/2/1786) and *La Didone* 74. M. (27/5/1799).]
*Ser. La Diffesa d'Amore (H.¹ S. 6/5/1775).
C.O. La Discordia conjugale (H.¹ 1791) 8° 1792; MS. Larpent 18. L.
     [1792].
     [Music G. Paisiello.]
C.O. Il Disertore (H.¹ S. 19/5/1770) 8° 1770.
     [C. F. Badini; music P. Guglielmi.]
*C.O. Il Disertore (H.¹ S.28/2/1789) MS. Larpent 49. M. [March 1789].
O.   La Disfatta di Dario (H.¹ S. 20/3/1762) 8° 1762.
     [Pasticcio.]
T.C.O. Don Giovanni (H.¹ S. 8/3/1794) 8° [1794].
     [L. da Ponte; pasticcio.]
C.O. La Donna di Spirito (H.¹ T. 23/5/1775) 8° 1775.
     [Music N. Piccinni.]
C.O. Le Donne vendicate [The Ladies revenged] (H.¹ T. 13/12/1768)
     8° 1769.
     [G. G. Bottarelli, based on Pizzi; music N. Piccinni.]
C.O. Il Duca d'Atene (H.¹ T. 9/5/1780) 8° 1780.
     [C. F. Badini; music G. Bertoni.]
C.O. I due Castellani burlati (H.² T. 2/2/1790) 8° 1790; MS. Larpent
     23. S. [1790].
     [F. Livigni; music Fabrizi. Teatro Marsigli, Bologna, autumn
     1785.]
C.O. Le due Contesse (H.¹ T. 4/11/1777) 8° 1771.
     [G. Petrosellini; music G. Paisiello. Teatro Valle, Rome,
     1776.]
*C.O. I due Gobbi (H.¹ T. 15/3/1796) MS. Larpent 31. S. [14/3/1796].
     [Evidently the same as *La Confusione nata della somiglianza,
     ossiano I due Gobbi*, the title under which Cosimo Mazzini's *La
     Somiglianza, ossiano I Gobbi* (Teatro Elettorale, Dresden, 4/12/1793)
     was performed at the Teatro Palla a Corda, Florence, in the spring
     of 1793. Music M. Portugallo.]
*Intermezzo. I due Svizzeri MS. Larpent 74. M. [14/5/1799].
*O. Elfrida (H.¹ S. 19/5/1798) MS. Larpent 73. M. [24/4/1798].
Orat. Elijah 4° 1789 [in *Miscellaneous Poetry*].
     [Thomas Skelton Dupuis; music Calcot.]
O.   Enea e Lavinia (H.¹ S. 5/5/1764) 8° 1764.
     [G. G. Bottarelli; music F. Giardini.]
O.   Enea e Lavinia (H.¹ Th. 25/3/1779) 8° 1779; MS. Larpent 20.
     [20/3/1779].
     [Music A. Sacchini.]

O.   Enrico (H.¹ T. 27/11/1753) 8° 1753.
      [F. Vanneschi; music B. Galuppi.]
O.   Erginda Regina di Norvegia (H.¹ S. 31/5/1760).
      [Music G. Cocchi.]
O.   Erifile (H.¹ S. 7/2/1778) 8° 1778; MS. Larpent 15. S. [1778].
      [Gamerra; translation by F. Bottarelli; music A. Sacchini.]
*O.   L'Eroe cinese (H.¹ S. 12/4/1766).
      [P. Metastasio; music B. Galuppi. Schönbrunn, spring 1752.]
O.   L'Eroe cinese (H.¹ S. 16/3/1782) 8° 1782; 8° 1784; MS. Larpent
      17. S. [14/3/1782].
      [Music V. Rauzzini.]
O.   Eumene (H.¹ S. 23/11/1765) 8° 1765.
      [Pasticcio.]
*O.   Euristeo (H.¹ T. 31/5/1757) MS. Larpent 5. L. [31/5/1757].
      [A. Zeno; music B. Galuppi. Vienna 17/5/1724.]
*Ball. Euthyme e Euchario (H.¹ Th. 13/3/1788).
O.   Evelina [The Triumph of the English over the Romans] (H.¹ T.
      10/1/1797) 8° 1797.
      [L. da Ponte, based on N. F. Guillard; music A. Sacchini.]
O.   Ezio (H.¹ S. 12/4/1755) 8° 1755.
      [P. Metastasio; music G. A. Hasse. Teatro delle Dame, Rome,
      26/12/1728.]
O.   Ezio (H.¹ S. 24/11/1764) 8° 1764/5 [bis].
      [Pasticcio; text altered from Metastasio.]
O.   Ezio (H.¹ S. 10/2/1770) 8° 1770.
      [Music P. Guglielmi.]
O.   Ezio (H.¹) 8° 1782.
Orat. The Fall of Egypt (D.L.) 4° 1774; MS. Larpent 15. M. [19/3/1774].
      [Dr Hawkesworth; music J. Stanley.]
*Burl. La Famiglia di Bertoldo alla Corte del Rè Alboino (C.G. M.
      9/12/1754) 8° 1754.
      [Music V. Ciampi.]
C.O. La Famiglia in Scompiglio, Or, The Family in an Uproar (H.¹
      S. 3/4/1762) 8° 1762.
      [Music G. Cocchi.]
O.   Farnace (H.¹ S. 21/4/1759) 8° 1759.
      [A. M. Lucchini; music D. Perez.]
*Ball. La Fête Provençal (H.¹ T. 22/5/1787).
*Ball. Les Fêtes de Tempe (H.¹ S. 1/3/1788).
*Ball. La Fête villageoise (Pantheon S. 31/12/1791).
*O.   Fetonte MS. Larpent 5. M. [1760].
*Ball. La Fille mal gardu (Pantheon S. 30/4/1791).
C.O. Il Filosofo di Campagna (H.¹ T. 6/1/1761) 8° 1761; MS. Larpent
      6. S. [1761].
      [C. Goldoni; music B. Galuppi. Teatro Regio-Ducal, Milan,
      summer 1750.]
*C.O. La Finta Principessa MS. Larpent 38. M. [1785].
C.O. La Finta Sposa [The Counterfeit Bride] (H.¹ Th. 14/4/1763) 8° 1763.
      [Pasticcio.]
*Past. O. La Forza d'Amore (H.² S. 19/1/1751).
C.O. La Frascatana (H.¹ T. 5/11/1776) 8° 1776; 8° 1781; 8° [1794];
      MS. Larpent 63. M. [June 1794].
      [F. Livigni, with alterations; music G. Paisiello. Teatro S.
      Samuele, Venice, 1774.]

*O. Le Gelosie Villane MS. Larpent 36. M. [1784].

*C.O. Il Geloso in cimento (H.¹ T. 4/2/1777).
[Music P. Anfossi. Burgtheater, Vienna, 25/5/1774.]

*O. Le Gemelle MS. Larpent 19. S. [1784].

O. La Generosità d'Alessandro (H.¹ T. 2/6/1789) 8° [1790]; MS.
Larpent 21. S. [May 1789].
[Adapted from P. Metastasio, *Alessandro nell' Indie*; music
Varchi and others.]

O. Germondo (H.¹ T. 21/1/1777) 8° 1776.
[C. Goldoni; music T. Trajetta. Venice 1739.]

C.O. Giannina e Bernardone (H.¹ T. 9/1/1787) 8° 1787; MS. Larpent
45. M. [5/1/1787].
[F. Livigni; music D. Cimarosa. Teatro S. Samuele, Venice,
autumn 1781.]

*Orat. Gioas Rè di Giuda (H.¹ Th. 22/3/1770).
[Music J. C. Bach.]

C.O. I Giuochi d'Agrigento (H.¹ T. 5/2/1793) 8° [1793].
[A. E. Pepoli; music G. Paisiello.]

*O. Giramondo MS. Larpent 20. S. [1787].

O. Giulio Cesare in Egitto (H.¹ Th. 1/3/1787) 8° 1787; MS. Larpent
47. M. [28/2/1787].
[Music Händel, selected by Dr Arnold.]

O. Giulio Sabino (H.¹ S. 5/4/1788) 8° 1788; MS. Larpent 42. M.
[30/3/1786] and 47. M. [22/3/1788].
[P. Giovannini; music G. Sarti. Teatro S. Benedetto, Venice,
1781.]

*P. Ball. Giustino I, Imperatore dei Romani (H.¹ S. 6/12/1794).

C.O. La Governante [The Duenna] (H.¹ S. 15/5/1779) 8° 1779; MS.
Larpent 15. S. [7/5/1779].
[C. F. Badini; music G. Bertoni.]

Orat. Hannah (H.¹ T. 3/4/1764) 4° 1764; MS. Larpent 7. M.
[1764].
[Music C. Worgan.]

O. Idalide (Pantheon S. 30/4/1791) 8° 1791; MS. Larpent 17. L.
[F. Moretti; translated G. Mazzinghi; music G. Sarti.]

O. Ifigenia in Aulide (H.¹ S. 16/1/1768) 8° [1768].
[G. G. Bottarelli; music P. Guglielmi.]

O. Ifigenia in Aulide (H.¹ S. 25/5/1782) 8° 1782; MS. Larpent 29. M.
[23/5/1782].
[V. A. Cigna, altered by A. Andrei; music G. Bertoni.]

O. Ifigenia in Aulide (H.¹ S. 24/1/1789) 8° 1789; MS. Larpent 22. S.
[21/1/1789].
[F. Moretti; music Cherubini.]

O. Ifigenia in Tauride (H.¹ Th. 7/4/1796) 8° 1796; MS. Larpent 69.
M. [4/4/1796].
[L. da Ponte; music C. Gluck.]

O. Ines de Castro. L. 1241 [18/1/1799, for H.¹]

*C.O. L'Innamorate del Cicisbeo (H.¹ Th. 2/4/1767) MS. Larpent 9. L.
[1767].

O. L'Ipermestra (H.¹ S. 9/11/1754) 8° 1754.
[Altered from Metastasio; music G. A. Hasse and Lampugnani.]

O. L'Ipermestra (H.¹ T. 28/11/1797) 8° [1797]; MS. Larpent 71. M.
[23/11/1797].
[Music G. Sarti and G. Paisiello.]

C.O. L'Isola di Alcina (Fishamble-street, Dublin) 8° 1777.

*C.O. L'Isola d'Amore (H.¹ T. 12/3/1776).
 [Music A. Sacchini.]
*C.O. L'Isola del Piacere (H.¹ T. 26/5/1795).
 [L. da Ponte; music V. Martini.]
Orat. Israel in Babylon (H.¹ F. 25/1/1765) 4° [1765].
 [Music G. F. Händel.]
*Orat. Israel in Egypt (C.G. F. 24/2/1758).
 [With "Alterations and Additions."]
*O. Issipile (H.¹ S. 18/3/1758) MS. Larpent 36. M. [1784].
 [Music G. Cocchi.]
*Ent. La Jardinière (H.¹ T. 5/6/1787).
Orat. Jephtha 4° [1752] 12° 1757 [in *Poems*].
 [Dr John Free; music Stanley.]
Orat. Judith (H.¹ F. 25/2/1765) 4° 1761 [as at D.L.]; 4° [1765]; 4° 1773.
 [Isaac Bickerstaffe; music Dr Arne.]
*O. Junius Brutus (H.¹ S. 12/1/1782) MS. Larpent 17. S. [1782; as
 Giunio Bruto].
 [Pasticcio.]
O. Leucippo (H.¹ T. 10/1/1764) 8° 1764.
 [G. G. Bottarelli; music M. Vento.]
C.O. La Locanda (H.¹) 8° 1792; MS. Larpent 17. L. [8/6/1791].
 [Bertati, with additions by G. Tonioli; music G. Paisiello.]
C.O. La Locandiera (H.¹ T. 15/1/1788) 8° 1788; MS. Larpent 48. M.
 [10/1/1788].
 [Music D. Cimarosa. The same as *L'Italiana in Londra*,
 Teatro Valle, Rome, 1778.]
*— Lucio Silla. A Piece in Three Acts MS. Larpent 33. M.
 [28/11/1783].
O. Lucio Vero (H.¹ S. 20/11/1773) 8° 1773; MS. Larpent 10. S.
 [8/10/1773].
 [A. Zeno, altered; music A. Sacchini and others.]
*C.O. Madame Ciana (H.¹ S. 13/1/1750) MS. Larpent 20. S.
 [G. Barlocci; original music G. Latilla. Teatro Valle, Rome,
 spring, 1738.]
Orat. Manasseh (Lock Hospital, 1766).
 [Music C. Worgan.]
C.O. La Marchesa Giardiniera (H.¹ T. 7/3/1775).
 [Music P. Anfossi.]
*C.O. Il Marchese Tulipano MS. Larpent 42. M. [17/1/1786].
*C.O. Il Marchese villano (H.¹ Th. 26/3/1778).
 [C. Goldoni, according to the bills; music N. Piccinni and
 G. Paisiello.]
C.O. Il Matrimonio segreto (H.¹ S. 11/1/1794) 8° [1794]; 8° [1796];
 8° [1798]; MS. Larpent 64. M. [9/1/1794].
 [G. Bertati; translated by G. Mazzinghi; music D. Cimarosa.
 Vienna, 7/2/1792.]
Orat. Medea 8° [1765].
 [Benjamin Stillingfleet.]
Ball. Historical Account of the Grand Tragic Ballet called Medea and
 Jason (H.¹ M. 26/3/1781) 4° 1781; Medea and Jason...Composed
 by Signor Vestris, Sen. 8° 1781.
O. Medonte (H.¹ Th. 14/11/1782) 8° 1782; MS. Larpent 74. M.
 [29/11/1798].
 [G. de' Gamerra; pasticcio.]
Burl. Il Mercato di Malmantile (H.¹ T. 10/11/1761).

[C. Goldoni; music B. Galuppi and D. Fischietti. Teatro S. Samuele, Venice, 1757.]

O. Mitridate (H.¹ T. 23/1/1781) 8° 1781; MS. Larpent 15. L. [1781].
 [Music A. Sacchini.]

C.O. La Modista Raggiratrice (H.¹ S. 16/4/1796) 8° 1796; MS. Larpent. 69. M. [14/4/1796].
 [G. Lorenzi; music G. Paisiello. Teatro de' Fiorentini, Naples. 1787.]

*C.O. La Moglie a Forza (C.G.) 8° 1754.

C.O. La Moglie fedele (H.¹ S. 27/2/1768) 8° 1768.
 [G. G. Bottarelli; music F. Alessandri.]

*C.O. La Molinarella (Pantheon S. 21/5/1791).

C.O. Il Mondo nella Luna (H.¹ S. 22/11/1760) 8° 1760.
 [C. Goldoni, with alterations; music B. Galuppi. Venice 1750.]

O. Montezuma (H.¹ T. 7/2/1775) 8° 1775.
 [Music A. Sacchini.]

Orat. Nabal (C.G. W. 21/3/1764) 4° 1764; MS. Larpent 7. S. [15/2/1764].
 [Dr T. Morell; music arranged by Smith to airs by Händel.]

*C.O. Nanetta e Lubino (H.¹ S. 8/4/1769) 8° 1769.
 [C. F. Badini; music G. Pugnani.]

Past. O. Nerina (H.² S. 16/2/1751).

O. Nerone (H.¹ T. 13/11/1753) 8° 1753.
 [Pasticcio.]

*O. Nina (H.¹ Th. 27/4/1797).
 [Music Paisiello.]

C.O. Ninetta, o Chi dell' altrui si veste presto si spoglia (H.² S. 16/1/1790) 8° 1790; MS. Larpent 50. M. [30/12/1789].
 [Music D. Cimarosa.]

O. Nitteti (H.¹ T. 19/4/1774) 8° 1774; MS. Larpent 38. M. [1785].
 [P. Metastasio, altered by G. G. Bottarelli; translated by F. Bottarelli; music A. Sacchini. Vienna 1756.]

*C.O. Le Nozze de Contadini Spagnuoli (H.¹ Th. 28/5/1795) MS. Larpent 18. L. [20/5/1795].

*C.O. Le Nozze di Dorina (H.¹ M. 1/2/1762).
 [Music B. Galuppi.]

C.O. Le Nozze di Dorina (H.¹ 1793) 8° [1793]; MS. Larpent 60. M. [26/2/1793] and 66. M. [10/6/1795].
 [Music G. Sarti, S. Storace and V. Martini.]

*O. Odenato e Zenobia (H.¹ T. 11/6/1793) MS. Larpent 60. M. [10/6/1793].
 [Music G. Sarti and others.]

*Ent. Les Offrandes à l'Amour (H.¹ T. 18/12/1787).

O. L'Olimpiade (H.¹ T. 10/2/1756) 8° 1756.
 [P. Metastasio; music B. Galuppi.] Milan, 1747.

O. L'Olimpiade (H.¹ S. 27/4/1765) 8° 1765.
 [Music Dr Arne.]

O. L'Olimpiade (H.¹) 8° 1783.
 [Pasticcio.]

O. L'Olimpiade (H.¹ Th. 8/5/1788) 8° 1788; MS. Larpent 48. M. [3/5/1788].
 [Music D. Cimarosa.]

Past. Ent. L'Omaggio (H.¹ T. 5/6/1781) MS. Larpent 17. L. [4/6/1781; as L'Omaggio Festa Teatrale Giardino] and 17. L. [1791].
 [Music F. Bianchi and others.]

O.   Orfeo (H.[1] S. 7/4/1770) 8° 1771; 8° 1773.
      [Calsabigi, altered by G. G. Bottarelli; music C. Gluck, J. C.
      Bach and P. Guglielmi.]
O.   Orfeo (H.[1]) 8° 1780; 8° 1785.
      [R. de' Calsabigi, with alterations by A. Andrei; music J. C.
      Bach, C. Gluck and P. Anfossi.]
*O. Orione (H.[1] S. 24/5/1777).
      [Music J. C. Bach.]
O.   Orione, o sia Diana vendicata (H.[1] 19/2/1763) 8° 1763.
      [G. G. Bottarelli; music J. C. Bach.]
C.O. Il Padre e il Figlio Rivali (H.[1] T. 13/2/1770) 8° 1769.
      [G. G. Bottarelli from G. Petrosellini, *Incognita perseguitata* and
      G. Casori, *Amore industrioso*; music T. Giordani.]
Orat. Paradise Lost (C.G. F. 29/2/1760) 4° 1760.
      [B. Stillingfleet; music Smith.]
Orat. The Passion (C.G.) 4° 1770.
C.O. La Pastorella nobile (Pantheon S. 17/12/1791) 8° 1791; MS. Lar-
      pent 17. L. [1791].
      [S. Zini; music P. Guglielmi. Teatro del Fondo di Separazione,
      Naples, 1788.]
*P. Ball. Paul et Virginie (H.[1] Th. 26/3/1795).
C.O. Le Pazzie d'Orlando (H.[1] S. 23/2/1771) 8° 1771; MS. Larpent
      9. S, [16/2/1771].
      [C. F. Badini; music P. Guglielmi.]
*Orat. I Pellegrini (H.[1] Th. 5/4/1764).
O.   Pelopida (H.[1] 24/5/1766) 8° 1766.
      [Music F. H. Barthélémon.]
O.   Penelope (H.[1] S. 11/1/1755) 8° 1754.
      [P. A. Rolli; music B. Galuppi.]
O.   Perseo (H.[1] S. 29/1/1774) 8° 1774.
      [G. G. Bottarelli "from an original Manuscript by Signor
      Gamerra"; music A. Sacchini.]
*C.O. La Pescatrice (H.[1] T. 28/4/1761).
      [C. Goldoni; music G. Bertoni. Teatro S. Samuele, Venice,
      1751. Dr Burney (*Hist. Music*, iv. 476) has a note on this opera,
      declaring that "it must have been chiefly by Galuppi and Latilla,
      as there were no other masters at this time who wrote so well in
      this style." Bertoni's name is definitely mentioned in the news-
      paper advertisements.]
*P. Pigmalion (H.[1] Th. 5/6/1788).
O.   Piramo e Tisbe (H.[1] 16/3/1775) 8° 1776; MS. Larpent 69. M.
      [Feb. 1796].
      [Coltellini; music V. Rauzzini.]
O.   Piramo e Tisbe (H.[1]) 8° 1781.
Orat. The Prodigal Son (C.G.) 4° 1773.
      [Music Dr Arnold.]
*O. Il Pittor Parigino MS. Larpent 39. M. [1785].
C.O. Il Puntiglio amoroso (H.[1] T. 7/12/1773) 8° 1773.
      [Music B. Galuppi, Buranello and others.]
*Int. Pygmalion MS. Larpent 71. M. [8/6/1797].
O.   Quinto Fabio (H.[1] S. 22/1/1780) 8° 1780; 8° 1782; 8° 1791; MS.
      Larpent 17. L.
      Altered from A. Zeno, *Lucio Papirio*, by A. Andrei; translated
      by Povolesi; music G. Bertoni.]

O. Il Ratto della Sposa (H.¹ S. 26/3/1768) 8° 1768.
   [G. Martinelli and G. G. Bottarelli; music P. Guglielmi.]
Orat. Rebecca (C.G.) 4° 1761; MS. Larpent 5. M. [Jan. 1761].
   [Music Smith.]
C.O. Il Rè alla Caccia (H.¹ Th. 2/3/1769) 8° 1769.
   [G. G. Bottarelli; translated by F. Bottarelli; music F. Alessandri.]
Orat. Redemption (D.L.) 8° 1786.
   [Music Dr Arnold.]
*O. La Regina di Golconda (H.¹ Th. 18/3/1784).
   [Music V. Rauzzini.]
O. Il Rè Pastore [The Royal Shepherd] (H.¹ S. 22/1/1757) 8° 1757;
   MS. Larpent 5. L. [18/1/1757].
   [Altered from Metastasio; music G. A. Hasse.]
O. Il Rè Pastore (H.¹ Th. 7/3/1765) 8° 1765.
   [Music F. Giardini.]
O. Il Rè Pastore (H.¹) 8° 1778.
   [Music T. Giordani.]
Orat. The Resurrection (C.G.) 8° 1771.
   [Music Dr Arnold.]
C.O. Il Rè Teodoro in Venezia (H.¹ T. 18/12/1787) 8° 1787; MS. Lar-
   pent 44. M. [7/12/1787].
   [G. B. Casti; music G. Paisiello. Burgtheater, Vienna, 23/8/1784.]
O. Ricimero (H.¹ T. 18/2/1755) 8° 1755.
   [Music B. Galuppi.]
O. Rinaldo (H.¹ S. 22/4/1780) 8° 1780.
   [G. de' Gamerra; music A. Sacchini.]
C.O. I Rivali delusi [The Disappointed Rivals] (H.¹ T. 6/1/1784) 8°
   1784; MS. Larpent 35. M. [5/1/1784].
   [Music G. Sarti.]
*O. Rosmira (H.¹ S. 7/5/1757) MS. Larpent 5. L. [1757].
   [Music F. Giardini.]
Orat. Ruth 4° 1763.
Orat. Ruth 4° 1769 [in *Original Poems*].
   [By a lady—C. R.]
Orat. Ruth 8° 1778 [in *Works*].
   [H. Brooke.]
Orat. Ruth 8° 1787 [in *Letters upon Subjects of Literature*].
   [Rev. Charles Davy.]
Orat. The Sacrifice: or, Death of Abel (H.¹ W. 8/2/1764) 4° [1764].
   [Music Dr Arne.]
Orat. Samson (C.G. W. 6/3/1765) 4° 1765.
C.O. La Schiava (H.¹ W. 4/11/1767) 8° 1772; 8° 1784.
   [This is fundamentally the same as *Gli Stravaganti* (Rome
   1/1/1764); music N. Piccinni. Alterations were made in the text
   by G. G. Bottarelli, and in the music by A. Andrei.]
C.O. Gli Schiavi per Amore (H.¹ T. 24/4/1787) 8° 1787; MS. Larpent
   45. M. [23/4/1787].
   [Fundamentally the same as *Le Gare generose* (Naples 1786) by
   G. Palomba; music G. Paisiello.]
*C.O. La Scuola de' Gelosi MS. Larpent 42. M. [4/3/1786].
C.O. La Scuola dei Maritati (H.¹ S. 21/2/1795) 8° [1798].
   [L. da Ponte; music V. Martini.]
O. Semiramide o La Vendetta di Nino (H.¹ S. 26/4/1794) 8° 1794.
   [Music F. Bianchi.]

O. Semiramide riconosciuta (H.¹ S. 9/2/1771) 8° 1771; MS. Larpent
   11. M. [1771].
   [P. Metastasio; altered by G. G. Bottarelli; music G. Cocchi.
   Teatro S. Benedetto, Venice, 1756.]
O. Senoscrita (H.¹ T. 21/2/1764).
   [Music D. Perez and N. Piccinni.]
C.O. La Serva Padrona [The Servant Mistress] (H.¹ F. 27/4/1750)
   8° 1794.
   [G. A. Federico; original music G. B. Pergolesi. Teatro S.
   Bartolomeo, Naples, 28/8/1733.]
C.O. Le Serve Rivali [The Rival Servant-Maids] (H.¹ S. 3/6/1769) 8°
   1769.
   [P. Chiari; music T. Trajetta. Teatro S. Moisè, Venice, autumn
   1766.]
O. Sesostri (H.¹ Th. 10/3/1768) 8° 1768.
   [Text by G. G. Bottarelli "taken from an old Book"; music P.
   Guglielmi.]
O. Siface (H.¹ T. 8/12/1767) 8° 1767.
   [Pasticcio.]
C.O. Il Signor Dottore (H.¹ 2/3/1767) 8° 1767.
   [C. Goldoni; music D. Fischietti. Teatro S. Moisé, Venice
   autumn 1758.]
O. Silla (H.¹ S. 29/11/1783) 8° 1783.
O. Siroe (H.¹ T. 14/1/1755) 8° 1755.
   [Altered from Metastasio; music Lampugnani.]
*O. Siroe (H.¹ T. 13/12/1763).
   [Pasticcio.]
O. Sofonisba (H.¹ T. 21/1/1766) 8° 1765.
   [G. G. Bottarelli; music M. Vento.]
*O. Sofonisba (H.¹ S. 14/11/1772).
   [Pasticcio.]
*O. Il Soldano generoso (H.¹ S. 1/1/1780).
   [Pasticcio.]
O. Solimano (H.¹ T. 31/1/1758) 8° 1758; MS. Larpent 5. S.
   [31/1/1758].
   [Pasticcio.]
O. Il Solimano (H.¹ T. 14/5/1765).
   [Pasticcio.]
Orat. Solomon (C.G. F. 15/3/1765) 4° [1765].
Orat. Solomon's Temple 12° 1797 [in *Masonic Miscellanies*].
*Ser. Le Speranze della Terra, ovvero Il Tempio di Destino (H.¹
   19/9/1761).
   [G. G. Bottarelli; music G. Cocchi.]
*C.O. Lo Speziale (H.¹ S. 6/5/1769).
   [C. Goldoni; music D. Fischietti. Teatro S. Samuele, Venice,
   1755.]
*C.O. La Sposa fedele (H.¹ T. 31/10/1775) MS. Larpent 12. S.
   [27/10/1775].
   [P. Chiari; pasticcio. Venice 1767.]
C.O. La Sposa in Equivoco (H.¹ Th. 22/3/1798) MS. Larpent 34. S.
   [21/3/1798].
C.O. Gli Stravaganti o sia I Matrimoni alla Moda [The Humourists]
   (H.¹ T. 21/10/1766) 8° 1766.
   [Pasticcio. See *La Schiava, supra.*]

C.O. Lo Studente alla Moda (C.G. F. 18/1/1754) 8° 1754; MS. Larpent 4. S. [9/1/1754].
    [Altered from G. Palomba, *La Violante*; music G. B. Pergolesi.]

Orat. Susannah (C.G. F. 9/3/1759) MS. Larpent 5. L. [1755].
    [With "Alterations and Additions."]

O. Tamerlano (H.¹ Th. 6/5/1773) 8° 1773.
    [G. G. Bottarelli; translated by F. Bottarelli; music A. Sacchini.]

*O. Telemaco (H.¹ S. 15/3/1777).
    [Music T. Trajetta.]

*M. Ent. Il Tempo della Gloria (H.¹ W. 31/1/1759).
    [Music G. Cocchi.]

O. Teodelinda (H.¹ T. 16/4/1793) 8° [1793]; MS. Larpent 60. M. [18/3/1793].
    [G. Boggio; music G. Andreozzi. Torino 1789.]

*C.O. Il Tesoro (H.¹ T. 14/6/1796).
    [Music Mazzinghi.]

Orat. Theodora (C.G. F. 16/3/1750) 4° 1749; 4° 1759.
    [Thomas Morell; music G. F. Händel.]

O. Tigrane (H.¹ Oct. 1767) 8° 1767.
    [Pasticcio.]

O. Tito Manlio (H.¹ S. 10/4/1756) 8° 1756.
    [Music Abos.]

O. Tito Manlio (H.¹ S. 7/2/1761) 8° 1761.
    [Music G. Cocchi.]

O. Tolomeo (H.¹ S. 2/1/1762) 8° 1765.
    [Pasticcio.]

C.O. I Traci Amanti (H.¹ T. 16/2/1796) 8° 1796; MS. Larpent 69. M. [15/2/1796].
    [G. Palomba; music D. Cimarosa. Teatro Nuovo, Naples, 1793.]

C.O. Trakebarne gran Mogol (H.¹ S. 1/11/1766).
    [Pasticcio.]

*C.O. I tre Gobbi Rivali (H.¹ M. 9/3/1761).

Past. Il Trionfo d'Amore (H.¹ T. 9/3/1773) 8° 1773.
    [Translated by F. Bottarelli.]

O. Il Trionfo d'Arianna (H.¹ S. 17/1/1784) 8° 1784; MS. Larpent 35. M. [1784].
    [C. G. Lanfranchi-Rossi; music P. Anfossi.]

C.O. Il Trionfo della Costanza (H.¹ Th. 19/12/1782) 8° 1783 [*bis*]; MS. Larpent 17. S. [1782].
    [C. F. Badini; music P. Anfossi.]

*O. Il Trionfo di Camilla (H.¹ S. 31/3/1750) MS. Larpent 7. S. [1765].
    [Music V. Ciampi.]

Orat. The Triumph of Time and Truth (C.G. F. 10/2/1758) 4° 1757.
    [Music G. F. Händel.]

Orat. The Triumph of Truth 4° 1767 [in *Works*].
    [George Jeffreys.]

C.O. Il Tutor burlato (H.¹ S. 17/2/1787) 8° 1787; MS. Larpent 43. M. [16/2/1787].
    [Music G. Paisiello.]

C.O. Il Tutore e la Pupilla (H.¹ S. 13/11/1762) 8° 1762.
    [G. G. Bottarelli; pasticcio.]

C.O. Gli Uccellatori (H.¹ T. 18/12/1770) 8° [1771].
    [C. Goldoni. Venice 1759.]

O.   L'Usurpator innocente (H.² T. 20/4/1790) 8° 1790; MS. Larpent 51. M. [6/4/1790].
   [Altered from P. Metastasio, *Demofoonte*; music Frederici.]

C.O. I Vecchi burlati (H.¹ Th. 27/3/1783) 8° 1783; MS. Larpent 30. M. [1783].
   [Music P. Anfossi.]

O.   La Vendemmia (H.¹ S. 9/5/1789) 8° 1789; MS. Larpent 22. S. [8/5/1789].
   [G. Bertati; music Gazzaniga. Teatro della Pergola, Florence, 12/5/1778.]

C.O. La Vera Costanza (H.¹ T. 20/1/1778) 8° 1778.
   [Music P. Anfossi.]

O.   La Vestale (H.¹ T. 6/2/1776) 8° 1776.
   [C. F. Badini; music M. Vento.]

*O. La Vestale (H.¹ T. 1/5/1787) MS. Larpent 45. M. [1787].
   [Music V. Rauzzini.]

C.O. I Viaggiatori felici (H.¹ T. 11/12/1781) 8° 1782; 8° 1785; MS. Larpent 15. L. [6/12/1781].
   [F. Livigni; music P. Anfossi. Venice, Oct. 1780.]

C.O. I Viaggiatori ridicoli tornati in Italia [The Ridiculous Travellers return'd to Italy] (H.¹ T. 24/5/1768) 8° 1768.
   [G.G.Bottarelli;translation by F.Bottarelli;musicP.Guglielmi.]

C.O. Le Vicende della Sorte; or, The Turns of Fortune (H.¹ T. 6/11/1770) 8° 1770.
   [G. Petrosellini; original music N. Piccinni. Teatro Valle, Rome, 3/1/1761.]

C.O. La Villana riconosciuta (H.¹ T. 24/3/1789) 8° 1789; MS. Larpent 21. S. [23/3/1789].
   [Music D. Cimarosa.]

*C.O. La Villanella rapita MS. Larpent 23. S. [24/2/1790].

O.   Virginia (H.¹ Th. 15/3/1787).

C.O. Vittorina (H.¹ T. 16/12/1777) 8° 1777.
   [C. Goldoni; translated by F. Bottarelli; music N. Piccinni.]

O.   Vologeso (H.¹ T. 13/11/1759) 8° 1759.
   [Altered from A. Zeno, *Lucio Vero*; pasticcio.]

O.   Zanaida (H.¹ S. 7/5/1763) 8° 1763.
   [G. G. Bottarelli; music J. C. Bach.]

C.O. Zemira e Azore (H.¹ T. 23/2/1779) 8° 1779; 8° 1781; 8° 1783.
   [Translation into Italian by Verazzi of *Zémire et Azor* (Fontainebleau 9/11/1771) by Marmontel with music by Grétry. The English translation is by Mrs Rigaud, and alterations in the Italian have been made by C. F. Badini.]

O.   Zenobia (H.¹ T. 10/1/1758) 8° 1758.
   [Altered from Metastasio; music G. Cocchi.]

O.   Zenobia in Palmira (H.¹ S. 6/12/1794).
   [Music P. Anfossi.]

Orat. Zimri (C.G. W. 12/3/1760) 4° 1760; MS. Larpent 5. M. [Jan. 1760].
   [Dr Hawkesworth; music Stanley.]

C.O. I Zingari in Fiera (H.¹ T. 14/5/1793) 8° 1794; MS. Larpent 62. M. [14/5/1793] and 68. M. [9/1/1795].
   [Translated by F. Panormo; music G. Paisiello.]

SUPPLEMENTARY TO CHAPTER I

Introductory: The Audience.

THE gradually extending scope of theatrical activities during the second half of the eighteenth century is now only beginning to be fully realised. While provincial performances had had a long and not wholly undistinguished career from the days of the Elizabethan strollers, it was not until this half century that permanent and properly equipped playhouses outside of London established themselves under competent management. A general picture of the conditions under which the wandering players worked has been given us[1]; Tate Wilkinson's attractive adventures have been chronicled[2]; use has been made of Roger Kemble's journal of 1766-8[3]; and new light has been thrown on the peregrinations of John Ward, grandfather of Mrs Siddons[4].

This extension of provincial playing is paralleled by an equally noteworthy development of amateur theatricals, both among the wealthier aristocrats capable of building their own private stages and among the humbler—if no less ambitious— apprentices in their public halls or tavern rooms. Even the "rules" of such amateur groups were formulated and printed[5], and London's theatrical lion, David Garrick himself, did not disdain to attend their productions[6]. Further informa-

---

[1] Apart from articles and books referred to in vol. ii, see F. T. Wood, "Strolling Actors in the Eighteenth Century" (*Englische Studien*, 1931/2, lxvi. 16–53): this article makes use of some interesting manuscript material.

[2] F. T. Wood, "Some Aspects of Provincial Drama in the Eighteenth Century" (*English Studies*, 1932, xiv. 65–74).

[3] Herschel Clay Baker, "Strolling Actors in Eighteenth-Century England" (*University of Texas Studies in English*, 1941, pp. 100–20).

[4] Cecil Price, "John Ward, Stroller" (*Theatre Notebook*, Jan. 1946, i. 10–12); James G. McManaway, "The Two Earliest Prompt Books of *Hamlet*" (*Papers of the Bibliographical Society of America*, 1949, xliii. 1–34).

[5] Ifan Kyrle Fletcher, "The Rules of a Private Theatre" (*TLS*, Dec. 21, 1935).

[6] Sybil Rosenfeld ("David Garrick and Private Theatricals," *NQ*, Oct. 25, 1941, clxxx. 230–1), noting the theatrical activities of the Earl

tion on some of the private performances has lately been presented[1]. What seems to have escaped comment hitherto is the interesting fact that, under the direction of one enthusiast, the modern open-air method of production was anticipated. When Lady Craven gave her play *The Statue Feast* at Benham House in 1782, *The London Chronicle*[2] informs us that the stage was set in a wood—

the trees formed a canopy, and the darkness and stillness of the night were favourable to the lights and the dresses[3].

The Theatre.

The actual structure of the provincial playhouses is being keenly studied not only from such documentary evidence as exists but from the extant relics of theatres built during these years[4]; and at the same time information is being gathered concerning the work of the scenic artists who worked in them. Besides Loutherbourg and Capon, the names of diverse painters, designers and machinists have been recorded, and it is noteworthy that their efforts came increasingly to be deemed worthy of mention, first in the bills, and eventually even in the text of the plays themselves. Richards and Carver, Greenwood, Malton, Catton, Bugarlo, French, Edwards and Marinari were thus credited for their scene designs, Carbonel (or Cabanel) for machine effects and

of Essex (at Cassiobury Park), William Hanbury (at Kelmarsh, Northants), Sir Watkin Williams Wynne (at Wynnstay) and Oldfield Bowles (at North Aston, Oxon), expresses the belief that Garrick never acted on amateur boards and rarely could be persuaded to attend a performance. J. Paul de Castro (*ib.* April 25, 1942, vol. clxxxii), referring to an anecdote in Mrs Bellamy's *Apology for Her Life* (1785), suggests that at least once he consented to appear with amateurs: but it should be noted that on this occasion the place of performance was the house of a fellow-actor, Thomas Sheridan, and the object was to bring out or to test a young actress. Garrick's general interest in school plays, however, is documented by T. H. Vail Motter ("Garrick and the Private Theatres," *ELH*, 1944, xi. 63–75).

[1] See the correspondence in *NQ*, 12th series, xi, Oct. 21, 1922 and following; H. Askew, "Private Theatricals in the Eighteenth Century" (*ib.* clxiv, June 17, 1933).

[2] lii, Aug. 1, 1782.

[3] It seems probable that the Benham House endeavour was inspired by continental example (Austrian in particular).

[4] Richard Southern, *The Georgian Playhouse* (1948).

Johnston for dress designs[1]. Recent research in this subject has amply proved that realism and spectacularism were the twin aims of the more important among these designers. William Capon[2], preceded by the less well-known Michael Angelo Rooker[3], stressed the former, with special reference to historical accuracy; while Loutherbourg sought to use realistic methods for more showy ends. The craggy reaches of Derbyshire and the exciting pictures of the East which returning travellers proudly displayed came alike as apt material to his hands[4]. The *Wonders of Derbyshire* was a famous Drury Lane production of 1779. Six years later, at Covent Garden, appeared *Omai*, the central figure of which was a South Sea Islander who had but recently arrived in England. Based on authentic material supplied by John Webber, who had accompanied Cook on his third voyage, Loutherbourg and his assistants presented to admiring eyes a richly ornamented panorama of oriental wonders[5].

Comment on the gradual attempt to establish correctness of costume has already been given elsewhere[6], but it is important to note here that the earlier tentative experiments first passed beyond the vogue of novelty during this half century. "The true starting point in this matter of the historic dressing of plays," it has been said[7], "is the theatrical winter season of 1762–63"; and for this statement there seems ample justification. The stage, clinging as always to traditionalism, no doubt still presented relics of ancient

[1] Russell Thomas, "Contemporary Taste in the Stage Decorations of London Theatres, 1770–1800" (*Modern Philology*, 1944–5, xlii. 65–78). See also Mitchell Wells, "Spectacular Scenic Effects in Eighteenth-Century Pantomime" (*Philological Quarterly*, 1938, xvii. 67–81).

[2] Responsible for *Macbeth* (1794), *The Cherokee* (1794), *The Iron Chest* (1796), *Vortigern* (1796), *The Plain Dealer* (1796) and *De Montfort* (1800).

[3] Chief designer at the Haymarket from 1778.

[4] See Wallace Cable Brown, "The Near East in English Drama, 1775–1825" (*Journal of English and Germanic Philology*, 1947, xlvi. 63–9).

[5] William Huse, "A Noble Savage on the Stage" (*Modern Philology*, 1935–6, xxxiii. 303–16). On spectacular effects under Sheridan's regime see also G. H. Nettleton, "Robinson Crusoe: Sheridan's Drury Lane Pantomime" (*TLS*, Dec. 25, 1943 and Jan. 1, 1944).

[6] See vol. ii, p. 414.

[7] Donald T. Mackintosh, "New Dress'd in the Habits of the Times" (*TLS*, Aug. 25, 1927).

theatrical fashions, but the road towards Charles Kean was now firmly and definitely set.

The Actors.

The actors of this period have attracted some attention. Dominated by a new belief in intuitive identification of the actor with his part, a fresh histrionic standard was set up by Garrick and Macklin towards the middle of the century[1]. Later came an inevitable reaction, when John Philip Kemble and Mrs Siddons sought to impose the classically grand style on the theatre[2]; but their endeavours could not prevent the explosive and clamorous success of Edmund Kean in the early years of the nineteenth century.

[1] Lily B. Campbell, "The Rise of a Theory of Stage Presentation in England during the Eighteenth Century" (*PMLA*, 1917, xxxii. 163–200); Earl R. Wasserman, "The Sympathetic Imagination in Eighteenth-Century Theories of Acting" (*Journal of English and Germanic Philology*, 1947, xlvi. 264–72). See also George Winchester Stone, Jr., "The God of His Idolatry: Garrick's Theory of Acting and Dramatic Composition with Especial Reference to Shakespeare" (*Adams Memorial Studies*, 1948, pp. 115–28).

[2] See Herschel Baker, *John Philip Kemble: The Actor in His Theatre* (1942) and Naomi Royde-Smith, *The Private Life of Mrs Siddons: A Psychological Investigation* (1933).

SUPPLEMENTARY TO CHAPTER II

THE theatre of the second half of the eighteenth century made but sad contributions to tragedy, but that was not for lack of will. The desire to produce noteworthy plays deserving to stand alongside the serious masterpieces of the past was widespread, and tragedy's aims, its essential being, were eagerly and animatedly discussed[1]. Always, however, the creative writers failed to achieve their ends; the classical style no longer possessed vital force, while the newer romantic style, whether seeking for the depiction of the real or striving after the impossible, had not attained sureness of touch or a definite orientation.

At the same time, even although nothing of consequence artistically was produced during these years, the changing tastes and the enlargement of influences have much of interest. Partly inspired by Garrick, a fresh attitude developed towards Shakespeare. This Elizabethan poet, whose strength gave him a charmed life even during the time when stricter neo-classic theory was bound to find him a very faulty artist, now was enskyed as a god. Rising opposition to the alteration of his plays is evident as the century passed its half-way mark and by its last years, despite continued tampering with the text, the principle of Shakespeare-not-rewritten was established at least as an ideal[2]. Valuable work has recently been accomplished in the study of Garrick's acting versions[3], and that prime sign of Shakespeare idolatry, the famous Stratford

[1] Clarence C. Green well surveys the critical debate in *The Neo-classic Theory of Tragedy in England during the Eighteenth Century* (1934).
[2] R. W. Babcock, "The Attack of the Late Eighteenth Century upon Alterations of Shakespeare's Plays" (*Modern Language Notes*, 1930, xliv. 446–51).
[3] George Winchester Stone, Jr., "Garrick's Handling of *Macbeth*" (*Studies in Philology*, 1941, xxxviii. 609–28); "Garrick's Long Lost Alteration of *Hamlet*" (*PMLA*, 1934, xlix. 890–921); "Garrick's Presentation of *Antony and Cleopatra*" (*Review of English Studies*, 1937, xiii. 20–38); "*A Midsummer Night's Dream* in the Hands of Garrick and Colman" (*PMLA*, 1939, liv. 467–82).

"Jubilee," with the *Jubilee* playlet which Garrick later put on the Drury Lane stage, has been set in the place it deserves[1].

Earlier classical French influence was, naturally, on the decline, even although a few stray versions of works by Racine and Corneille still made their appearance, but Voltaire began to make a deeper impression than he had done before 1750[2].

What was new was the vast impress of the German drama[3], and concerning this perhaps sufficient has been said in the text, but note should be made of the fact that the truly extraordinary wave of popularity which came with the introduction of these German plays, associated with the eager filching of latest Parisian successes, points the way clearly towards early nineteenth-century theatrical conditions. Holcroft's account of the way in which he seized upon whatever he could capture in the playhouse of *Le Mariage de Figaro* and of the haste with which he converted the mutilated French original into an English play reads as though it were an event of 1820, and the excited perusal of the German dramas reminds us of the rapid growth during the romantic period of the unacted and often unactable poetic drama designed for perusal in the study, rather than for representation on the stage[4].

Naturally, the tragedies written during these years have received less attention than other forms of drama, but at least a few of the authors have been separately studied. The significance of Edward Moore's *The Gamester* has been more

---

[1] For references see supplementary notes to the Hand-list. I have not seen W. P. Harberson, *Elizabethan Influence on Late XVIII Century Tragedy* (1927).

[2] R. S. Crane, "The Diffusion of Voltaire's Writings in England, 1750–1800" (*Modern Philology*, 1923, xx. 261–74), and see references in vol. ii, p. 73. Edith Wray presents a brief list of "English Adaptations of French Drama between 1780 and 1815" (*Modern Language Notes*, 1928, pp. 87–90).

[3] The general non-dramatic influence of German literature is surveyed by F. W. Stokoe in *German Influence in the English Romantic Period 1788–1818* (1926). See also Violet Stockley, *German Literature as known in England, 1750–1830* (1929).

[4] In connection with the influence of Metastasio an essay by A. Sägesser, *John Hoole, his Life and Tragedies* (1922) may be consulted.

fully stressed[1]. That Home's ever famous *Douglas* has not been completely forgotten is shown by its revival at the Edinburgh Festival in 1950[2], while the significance of Jephson's works has been signalised by the appearance of a critical volume devoted to the life and activities of this author[3].

[1] John Homer Caskey, *The Life and Works of Edward Moore* (1927). Note should be taken of the considerable continental popularity of this play. Gottlieb Fritz has a study of *Die Spieler im deutschen Drama des achtzehnten Jahrhunderts* (1896). In France the play appeared as *Le joueur* in 1762 and an "imitation" by B. J. Sauvin was issued in 1768 (*Beverley, tragédie bourgeoise*).

[2] St Vincent Troubridge and L. R. M. Strachan (*NQ*, Sept. 13 and 20, 1941, clxxxi) have notes on the contemporary popularity of this drama. Allusion should have been made in the text to A. E. Gipson, *John Home* (1917), which pays particular attention to the *Douglas* controversy.

[3] Martin Severin Peterson, *Robert Jephson, 1736–1803* (1930). Edward Jerningham also has a biographical study accorded to him (Lewis Bettany, *Edward Jerningham and his Friends* (1919)).

SUPPLEMENTARY TO CHAPTERS III AND IV

REFERENCE to several recent studies of Shakespeare's stage career during the latter half of the eighteenth century have been made above[1]; fundamentally the most important aspect of Shakespearian influence during this period is the sudden and enthusiastic revival of interest in the comedies[2].

In the extension of continental influence many dramatists contributed, but none was more important than the eager Thomas Holcroft[3]. Always on the look-out for things novel and revolutionary, he was responsible for introducing to the English stage several of the latest dramatic forms. The fortunes of Destouches and Favart in this country have recently been surveyed[4], and some attempt is now being made to explore in detail the indebtedness of particular plays to their French (and other) sources[5].

Sentimentalism, because it was the greatest force in the theatre of this time, has been the subject of much speculation[6]. The work of the two chief exponents of this style—Cumberland and Kelly—has now been examined[7]. So far as

[1] Pp. 57, 369. Alfred Loewenberg has an interesting article on *Midsummer Night's Dream Music in 1763* (*Theatre Notebook*, April 1946, i. 23–6).

[2] On the continuing vogue of the "Beaumont and Fletcher" plays see Donald J. Rulfs, "Beaumont and Fletcher on the London Stage 1776–1833" (*PMLA*, 1948, lxiii. 1245–64). R. G. Noyes carries the story of Jonson's plays down to 1776 (*Ben Jonson on the English Stage, 1660–1776* (1935)). Emmett L. Avery has some supplementary notes ("Ben Jonson in the Provinces," *NQ*, Oct. 2, 1937, clxxiii).

[3] Elbridge Colby discusses this subject in "Thomas Holcroft: Translator of Plays" (*Philological Quarterly*, 1924, iii. 228–36).

[4] Ira O. Wade, "Destouches in England" (*Modern Philology*, 1931–2, xxix. 27–47); Alfred Iacuzzi, *The European Vogue of Favart* (1932).

[5] Willard Austin Kinne has a most useful study of *Revivals and Importations of French Comedies in England 1749–1800* (1939). Among essays on individual plays may be noted that by Kathleen M. Lynch on "*Pamela nubile, L'Écossaise and The English Merchant*" (*Modern Language Notes*, 1932, xlvii. 94–6).

[6] Besides the references given in vol. ii, pp. 179–80, note may be taken here of B. Sprague Allen, "The Dates of *Sentimental* and its Derivatives" (*PMLA*, 1933, xlviii. 303–7) and Samuel P. Chew, Jr., "*The Dupe*: A Study in the 'Low'" (*Philological Quarterly*, 1939, xviii. 196–203).

[7] In addition to the essays on Cumberland contributed by S. T. Williams (*supra*, pp. 125 and 126) Wylie Sypher has a study in "The

the latter is concerned, a peculiar dichotomy has been observed—his critical principles conflicting constantly with his
practice[1]. Similar dichotomy, it is claimed[2], distinguished
their companion, Thomas Holcroft. An examination of his
career does seem to show that this dramatist would indeed
have preferred to pen comedies with a satirical touch but that,
despite his prepossessions, he found himself forced to drift
along in the strong sentimental current of his age. In this he
was in a position similar to that of others less fully identified
with the sentimental style.

Goldsmith and Sheridan, of course, hold a peculiar position
in the dramatic literature of this age, and the latter, in particular, has evoked much interested speculation during recent
years[3]. Attention, too, has been given to some of their
companions. Arthur Murphy's endeavour to combat sentimentalism has been chronicled[4]. It has been suggested,
with justice, that in this author's career the early influence of
Foote yielded later to the influence of Fielding and that

West-Indian as a 'Character' in the Eighteenth Century" (*Studies in
Philology*, 1939, xxxvi. 503–20), which shows how this type was evolved
out of contemporary accounts of life in the West Indies.

[1] Mark Schorer, "Hugh Kelly: His Place in the Sentimental School"
(*Philological Quarterly*, 1933, xii. 389–401).

[2] Virgil R. Stallbaumer, "A Satirist in the Stream of Sentimentalism"
(*ELH*, 1936, iii. 31–62).

[3] In addition to the biographical-critical studies mentioned in the text
should be noted R. Crompton Rhodes, *Harlequin Sheridan* (1933), W. A.
Darlington, *Sheridan* (1933), and Lewis Gibbs, *Sheridan* (1947). Miriam
Gabriel and Paul Mueschke ("Two Contemporary Sources of Sheridan's
The Rivals," *PMLA*, 1928, xliii. 237–50) argue that this play was inspired
by Garrick's *Miss in Her Teens* and Colman's *The Deuce is in Him*.
Alfred Lowenberg ("The Songs in 'The Critic'", *TLS*, March 28, 1942)
draws attention to the significance of the folio *Favorite Airs in the Critic*
(1779). In "Sheridan's Share in *The Stranger*" (*Modern Language Notes*,
1930, xlv. 85–6) Dougald MacMillan suggests that Sheridan did no more
than cut Benjamin Thompson's version and add a few songs and dances.
Among Goldsmith studies reference may be made to J. Harrington
Smith, "Tony Lumpkin and the Country Booby Type in Antecedent
English Comedy" (*PMLA*, 1943, lviii. 1038–49) which interestingly
discusses characters in Shadwell's *The Lancashire Witches*, Steele's *The
Tender Husband*, Cibber's *Woman's Wit*, Dryden's *The Wild Gallant* and
Fielding's *The Lottery*.

[4] J. Homer Caskey, "Arthur Murphy and the War on Sentimental
Comedy" (*Journal of English and Germanic Philology*, 1931, xxx. 563–77).
The Dramatic Career of Arthur Murphy (1946) is surveyed by Howard
Hunter Dunbar. J. H. Caskey has also an interesting article on "Arthur
Murphy's Commonplace-book" (*Studies in Philology*, 1940, xxxvii. 598–
609).

"it was Murphy who most persistently, from the sixth to the last decade of the eighteenth century, led the fight against sentimental comedy." His companion, George Colman the Elder, has also been graced with a modern biography[1], as has the latter's son, George Colman the Younger[2]—that author whose now long-forgotten works must, in the opinion of a critic in 1795, "remain as long as taste, sensibility, and invention have any power to delight, or claim to be gratified, amongst the first in estimation for elegance of sentiment and strength of dialogue." Garrick's importance as a playwright, often obscured because of his powers as an actor, has rightly been emphasised[3], and there is now a similar volume for Samuel Foote[4].

Pantomimes, preludes and miscellaneous dramatic "entertainments" played a considerable role on the eighteenth-century stage[5], and as these more and more captured public attention there was a corresponding reaction in the direction of "closet drama." That the vogue for German drama aided the latter seems certain, but rightly a recent study of this subject has emphasised that, several decades before Schiller and Kotzebue impinged themselves on the English consciousness, plays were being written rather for perusal than for performance[6].

[1] Eugene R. Page, *George Colman the Elder: Essayist, Dramatist, and Theatrical Manager, 1732–1794* (1935). For some additional information see Howard P. Vincent, "Christopher George Colman, 'Lunatick'" (*Review of English Studies*, 1942, xviii. 38–48).

[2] Jeremy F. Bagster-Collins, *George Colman The Younger 1762–1836* (1946). Howard P. Vincent has a note on "George Colman the Younger: Adopted Son" (*Philological Quarterly*, 1936, xv. 219–20).

[3] Elizabeth P. Stein, *David Garrick, Dramatist* (1938).

[4] Mary Megie Belden, *The Dramatic Work of Samuel Foote* (1929). Edward H. Weatherby ("Foote's Revenge on Churchill and Lloyd," *Huntington Library Quarterly*, 1945–6, ix. 49–60) shows how in the revised version of *Taste* (preserved only in the Larpent manuscript) this gusty author replied in kind to the strictures in Robert Lloyd's *The Actor* and in Charles Churchill's *The Rosciad*. W. K. Wimsall ("Foote and a Friend of Boswell's," *Modern Language Notes*, 1942, lvii. 325–35) discusses the original or originals of *The Nabob*.

[5] Charles Read Baskerville has an essay on this subject, "Play-Lists and Afterpieces of the Mid-Eighteenth Century" (*Modern Philology*, 1925–6, xxiii. 445–64).

[6] Stephen A. Larrabee, "The 'Closet' and the 'Stage' in 1759" (*Modern Language Notes*, 1941, lvi. 282–4).

SUPPLEMENTARY TO APPENDIX A

IN addition to the summary notes on the various playhouses, the following may be recorded:

Drury Lane. This theatre was altered in 1762 and again (by the Adams brothers) in 1775. The diary of William Hopkins, the prompter, records in the latter year that "the House has been quite altered since last Season, and is now fitted up in the most elegant Manner possible by the Adams's &c.—and is the compleatest Theatre in Europe." See Dougald MacMillan, *Drury Lane Calendar 1747–1776* (1936).

Covent Garden. The reconstruction carried out in 1792 was under the direction of Holland. On this house see H. Saxe Wyndham, *The Annals of Covent Garden Theatre from 1732 to 1897* (2 vols. 1906).

The Little Theatre in the Haymarket. In 1765, when this house became a Theatre Royal, there were extensive alterations and further alterations were carried out in 1797. See Cyril Maude, *The Haymarket Theatre* (1903).

The King's Theatre in the Haymarket. The old theatre was altered in 1782; the new, built in 1790, was the work of the architect Novosielski.

The Pantheon. The original structure, designed by Wyatt, was built in 1772, and already in 1788 operas were being given there. Altered in 1790, there was a complete reconstruction, under Wyatt, in 1793.

Royal Grove. "Astley's" started as early as 1768. The building was altered in 1772 and 1778, and was destroyed by fire in 1794. A new house was erected in 1795. Besides the titles recorded in the text should be noted that of the *Royal Amphitheatre* (R.A.).

Sadler's Wells. This theatre was reconstructed in 1778.

SUPPLEMENTARY NOTES TO THE
HAND-LIST OF PLAYS, 1750–1800

Apart from a few corrections, the principal entries in these supplementary notes present: (1) indication of authorship of plays previously placed under "Unknown Authors"; (2) notes regarding sources of plays translated or adapted from foreign dramas; (3) inclusion of several previously unrecorded titles, chiefly provincial productions. In addition to Dougald MacMillan's important analysis of the contents of the Larpent collection, these notes are heavily indebted to various studies, in particular: F. T. Wood, "Unrecorded Eighteenth Century Plays" (*NQ*, 1936, clxx. 56–8; 1938, clxxiv. 383–4), Dougald MacMillan, *Drury Lane Calendar 1747–1776* (1938) and "Unrecorded Eighteenth Century Plays" (*NQ*, 1936, clxx. 193–4), F. E. Budd, "Four Unrecorded Plays" (*TLS*, June 22, 1933), Frances S. Miller, "Notes on Some Eighteenth-Century Dramas" (*Modern Language Notes*, 1937, lii. 203–6), Emmett L. Avery, "The Summer Theatrical Seasons at Richmond and Twickenham, 1746–1753" (*NQ*, 1937, clxxiii. 290–4, 312–15, 328–32), F. T. Wood, "Theatrical Performances at Bath in the XVIII Century" (*NQ*, 1947, cxcii. 477–8, 486–90, 539–41, 552–8; 1948, cxciii. 38–40, 92–3, 253–5), Sir St Vincent Troubridge, "Late XVIIIth Century Plays" (*Theatre Notebook*, 1946, i (5), 62). A few production dates will be found to differ from MacMillan's: those given here have all been checked.

In these notes references to pages in the main Hand-list are given in the left-hand margin. The plus sign (+) indicates a new entry or additional information regarding performances or printed texts; an "equals" sign (=) is used to indicate authorship. Thus "+*BADDELEY, ROBERT*" means that this writer's name does not appear in the main list; "+Gil Blas" indicates that a fresh title is being added to the works of an author already included; "+8° 1792" presents an additional published text; "=*J. C. CROSS*" added to a play in the "Unknown Authors" section means that that play was written by J. C. Cross. In certain instances the = sign is used to refer to other titles in this "Unknown authors" section, and for these, since no playwrights' names are mentioned, the variant titles alone are recorded: thus the entry in the supplementary notes "Who is she like? [= *A Tale of the Castle*]" is employed to convey the information that a manuscript play in the Larpent collection, entitled *Who is she like?* is identical with *A Tale of the Castle* acted at Edinburgh in 1793. Note should be taken of the fact that, whereas "*UNKNOWN AUTHORS*" is used as a reference in the main Hand-list, this has been contracted to "*UA*" in the supplementary notes.

p. 233] *ANDREWS, M. P.*
  Summer Amusement. [+8° 1784 (4th).]
  The Enchanted Castle. [+L. 752, as *The Castle of Wonders* (*UA*).]

p. 234] *ARNE, T. A.*
  The Cooper. [*Le Tonnelier*, music by Audinot, was originally produced in Paris in 1761, and in 1765 appeared in its final, and more popular, version.]

  ARNOLD, S. J.
  Who Pays the Reckoning? [+*Songs, Duets, Chorusses, &c. in W. P. the R.* 8° 1795.]
  The Irish Legacy. [L. 1176, as *The Legacy* (*UA*).]

  ATKINSON, J.
  A Match for a Widow. [*L'Heureuse Erreur* was produced in Paris in 1783.]

p. 235] *AYSCOUGH, G. E.*
  Semiramis. [Voltaire's play was produced in Paris in 1748.]

  +*BADDELEY, ROBERT.*
  F. The Swindlers (D.L. M. 25/4/1774). L. 374 (*UA*).

p. 236] *BATE, H.*
  The Dramatic Puffers. [+L. 583 (7/2/1782).]

  BATES, ——.
  +Gil Blas (Royalty, 1788). See *UA*.

  +*BENNETT, J.*
  P. The Magic Oak (Norwich, 25/5/1793).
  P. The Pit of Acheron (Norwich, 18/5/1795).

  BERKELEY, G. M.
  Nina. [Acted C.G. 24/4/1787. An adaptation of *Nina, ou la folle par amour* (Paris, 1786) by B. J. Marsollier.]

  +*BERNARD, JOHN.*
  Ent. The Bristol Sailor, or The Whimsical Ladies (Bath, 9/5/1786). L. 732 (*UA*). [Peculiarly, a play called *The British Sailor* (*UA*) appeared at Bath on 18/4/1786: perhaps they were the same.]

p. 237] *BICKERSTAFFE, I.*
  The Maid of the Mill. [+8° 1767; 8° 1783.]
  Daphne and Amintor. [+8° 1778.]
  The Plain Dealer. [+8° 1786 (new).]
  The Absent Man. [Based on Regnard, *Le Distrait* (Paris, 1697).]
  +Sacred D. Judith...As Performed in the Church at Stratford upon Avon 8° 1769. See *ITALIAN OPERAS.*

The Ephesian Matron. [+Ranelagh House, 12/5/1769.]
He wou'd if he Cou'd. [+Ranelagh House, 28/5/1770, as *The Maid the Mistress*.]

p. 238]   The Sultan. [An adaptation of Favart, *Soliman Second* (Paris, 1761), music by Gibert.]

BIRCH, S.
Fast Asleep. [+L. 1182, as *The Opiate* (*UA*).]
Albert and Adelaide. [+L. 1236, as *The Black Forest* (*UA*). *Airs, Chorusses, &c. &c. in A. & A.* 8° 1798.]

BOADEN, J.
Aurelio and Miranda. [Original title, *The Monk*.]

p. 239]   *BONNOR, C.*
The Manager an Actor in spite of himself. [*La Fête de Campagne* was produced in Paris in 1784.]

BOULTON, T.
The Guinea Outfit. [+8° 1782.]

+*BREREWOOD, FRANCIS.*
C. The Retaliation (*c.* 1764). MS. sold in 1918. [See "Two Unknown Plays," *TLS*, Aug. 22, 1918.]

p. 240]   *BROOKE, F.*
Rosina. [An adaptation of Favart, *Les moissonneurs* (Paris, 1768).]

p. 241]   *BURGOYNE, J.*
The Lord of the Manor. [An adaptation of Marmontel, *Silvain* (Paris, 1770).]
Richard Cœur de Lion. [An adaptation of J. M. Sedaine's similarly titled play (Paris, 1784).]

BURKE, Miss.
The Ward of the Castle. [+*Songs, Duets, Choruses, &c. in The W. of the C.* 8° 1793.]

CAPELL, E.
Antony and Cleopatra. [For an examination of this production see George W. Stone, Jr., "Garrick's Presentation of *Antony and Cleopatra*" (*Review of English Studies*, 1937, xiii. 20–38).]

p. 242]   *CAREY, G. S.*
The Magic Girdle. [An adaptation of J. B. Rousseau, *La Ceinture magique* (Versailles, 1701).]

CELISIA, D.
Almida. [*Tancrède* was produced in Paris in 1760.]

p. 243]   *CIBBER, Mrs S.-M.*
The Oracle. [*L'Oracle* was produced in Paris in 1740.]

CLARKE, G. S.
Œdipus. [A translation of Sophocles' play.]

CLELAND, J.
Titus Vespasian. [An adaptation of Metastasio, *La clemenza di Tito* (1734).]
Tombo-Chiqui. [An adaptation of Delisle, *L'Arlequin sauvage* (Paris, 1721).]

CLIVE, C.

The Rehearsal. [+12° 1753 (Dublin).]

+Oa. The London 'Prentice (D.L. S. 23/3/1754). [See *UA*. For arguments in favour of Kitty Clive's authorship see P. J. Crean in *NQ*, Nov. 12, 1932.]

The Island of Slaves. [An adaptation of Marivaux, *L'Isle des esclaves* (Paris, 1725).]

COBB, J.

The Contract. [An adaptation of Marivaux, *La fausse suivante* (Paris, 1724).]

The Wedding Night. [+*Songs, Duetts, Trios, &c. in The W.N.* 8° 1780.]

p. 244] Love in the East. [+L. 796, as *Calcutta; or, Twelve Hours in India (UA).*]

The Doctor and the Apothecary. [An adaptation of G. Stephanie, *Doktor und Apotheker* (Vienna, 1786), music by C. Ditters von Dittersdorf. Additional music was provided by Stephen Storace.]

The Siege of Belgrade. [Music by Stephen Storace.]

p. 245] *COLLIER, Sir G.*

Selima and Azor. [An adaptation of *Zémir et Azor* (Fontaine-bleau, 1771) by J. F. Marmontel, music by Grétry.]

+*COLLINS, JOHN.*

A Cure for a Coxcomb (C.G. T. 15/5/1792). See *UA* and supplementary notes.

p. 246] *COLMAN, G.*

The English Merchant. [An adaptation of Voltaire, *L'Écossaise* (Paris, 1760).]

The Portrait. [An adaptation of Anseaume, *Le Tableau parlant* (Paris, 1769), music by Grétry.]

The Fairy Prince. [An alteration of Ben Jonson, *Oberon.*]

The Spleen. [Advertised for S. 24/2/1776 but not performed till a fortnight later.]

The Sheep Shearing. [An alteration of part of Shakespeare's *Winter's Tale.*]

The Spanish Barber. [An adaptation of Beaumarchais, *Le barbier de Séville* (Paris, 1775).]

+The Distress'd Wife (1777). See *UA.*

p. 247] The Genius of Nonsense. [+*Songs, Duetts, Trios, &c. in The G. of N.* 8° 1781.]

Fatal Curiosity. [An alteration of Lillo's play.]

Ut Pictura Poesis! [L. 1826, as *The Enraged Musician (UA).*]

COLMAN, G., The Younger.

+F. The Female Dramatist (H.¹ 16/8/1782). L. 598. (3/8/1782).]

Ways and Means. [+L. 755, as *More Ways than Means (UA).*]

The Battle of Hexham. [+12° 1790 *(Dublin)*.]

+F. My Nightgown and Slippers, or, Tales in Verse (D.L. 28/4/1797). 8° 1797. L. 1165 [printed copy]. See *UA.*

25-2

p. 248]   Blue-Beard. [Based on Sedaine, *Raoul Barbe-Bleue* (Paris, 1789), music by Grétry. The original title of Colman's play was *Female Curiosity; or, Bluebeard's Marriage*.]

Blue Devils. [Based on Patrat, *L'Anglais* (Paris, 1781).]

CONWAY, H. S.
False Appearances. [An adaptation of Louis de Boissy, *Les dehors trompeurs* (Paris, 1740).]

COOKE, W.
The Capricious Lady. [An alteration of *The Scornful Lady*.]

+*COWDROY, W.*
Love Conquers All (1786). See *UA*.

COWLEY, H.
The Belle's Stratagem. [R. Crompton Rhodes (*Review of English Studies*, 1929, v. 129–42) discusses the Dublin piracies in relation to the authorised text and shows that a late Lacy edition (1866) seems to be taken from the authoress's original draft.]

The World as it Goes. [Possibly no changes were made when the title was altered to *Second Thoughts are Best*.]

p. 249]   More Ways than One. [+L. 640, as *New Ways to Catch Hearts* (*UA*).]

CRADOCK, J.
Zobeide. [An adaptation of Voltaire, *Les Scythes* (Paris, 1767).]

CRAVEN, E.
The Sleep-Walker. [An adaptation of Pont-de-Veyle, *Le Somnambule* (Paris, 1739).]

The Statue Feast. [An adaptation of Molière, *Don Juan* (Paris, 1665).]

The Princess of Georgia. [+L. 1251, as *The Georgian Princess* (*UA*).]

p. 250]   *CROSS, J. C.*
The Apparition. [+L. 1038, as *The Flesh and the Spirit* (*UA*).]

The Charity Boy. [L. 1139 (for H.²), L. 1142 (for D.L.).]

An Escape into Prison. [+L. 1184, as *The Hue and Cry* (*UA*) —the title of Mrs Inchbald's play of which this is an alteration.]

+Ball. P.   Julia of Louvain; or, Monkish Cruelty (R.C. Th. 18/5/1797). See under *Circusiana*.

+Ball. P.   The Round Tower; or, The Chieftains of Ireland (C.G. T. 24/11/1797). L. 1186, as *The R.T., or Irish Fidelity* (*UA*). And see under *Circusiana*.

Harlequin and Quixotte. [+L. 1189 (15/12/1797).]

Joan of Arc. [+*Airs, Duets, and Chorusses, in...J. of A.* 8° 1798.]

+Int.   They've bit the old one (C.G. T. 1/5/1798). See *UA*.

The Genoese Pirate. [Originally acted at R.C., 9/4/1798, as *Black Beard; or, The Captive Princess*. See under *Circusiana*.]

p. 251] *CUMBERLAND, R.*
Amelia. [The 1771 text is as the play was acted, D.L. 14/12/1771.]
+F. The Squire's Return (private, Kelmarsh, Northampton-shire, Nov. 1772).
The Princess of Parma. [I. K. Fletcher (*TLS*, March 15, 1934) describes a MS. part book recently discovered. For the exact date of performance see William Van Lennep (*TLS*, Oct. 24, 1936).]
The Election. [For a part manuscript see I. K. Fletcher, as above.]
+Prel. The Critic (C.G. 20/3/1779). L. 472 [15/3/1779]. [Possibly by R. C.]

p. 252] The Natural Son. [+L. 1026, as revised for D.L. 10/6/1794.]
The Country Attorney. [+L. 779 (25/6/1787).]
+C.O. Richard the Second. L. 963, for C.G. see *UA*. [Licence refused. Larpent states that this was by R. C.]
The Wheel of Fortune. [Original title, *The Philosopher, or The Turns of Fortune.*]

p. 253] *DAVIDSON, A.*
Maria. [See R. W. Babcock, "Eighteenth-century Comic Opera Manuscripts" (*PMLA*, 1937, liii. 907–8).]

+*DAVY, Rev. CHARLES.*
Balaam (1787). See *ITALIAN OPERAS.*

DELPINI, CARLO.
[For pantomimes "composed" by this performer see, in *UA*, *Blue Beard* and *The Four Quarters of the World.*]

p. 254] *DENIS, C.*
The Siege of Calais. [An adaptation of Belloy, *La Siège de Calais* (Paris, 1765).]

DENT, J.
+The Two Nannys (R.G. W. 1/10/1788). See *UA*.

DERRICK, S.
Sylla. [The original *Sylla*, music by Graun, was produced in Berlin in 1753.]

DIBDIN, C.
[See E. R. Dibdin, *A Charles Dibdin Bibliography* (Liverpool, 1937).]
The Wedding Ring. [*Il Filosofo di Campagna*, music by Galuppi, was produced in Venice in 1754.]
The Deserter. [*Le Déserteur* was produced in Paris in 1769.]
The Cobler. [Based on M. J. Sedaine, *Blaise le savetier* (Paris, 1759).]

p. 255] Rose and Colin. [An adaptation of M. J. Sedaine, *Rose et Colas* (Paris, 1764).]
The Wives Revenged. [An adaptation of M. J. Sedaine, *Les Femmes vengées* (Paris, 1775).]
Annette and Lubin. [*Annette et Lubin* was produced in Paris in 1762.]
The Islanders. [Based on Saint-Foix, *L'Isle sauvage* (Paris, 1743) and Framéry, *La Colonie* (Paris, 1775).]

p. 256] None so Blind as those who won't see. [This is probably L. 594, *The Blind Man, or The Manœuvre* (*UA*).]

+The Milk Maid (Sheffield, 14/11/1787).

+A Cure for a Coxcomb (C.G. T. 15/5/1792). See *UA* and supplementary notes.

Hannah Hewitt. [The songs are printed in the author's *Chorus of Melody*.]

DIBDIN, T. J.

[See James Sandoe, "Some Notes on the Plays of T. J. Dibdin" (*University of Colorado Studies*, 1940, i. 205–20].

+Ent. Something New (written by 1792; acted that year in the Masons' Hall, Elgin, according to the author's *Reminiscences* (1827), i. 81–2 and 146).

+Ba. The Rival Loyalists; or Sheelah's Choice (S.W. M. 12/5/1794). *Songs, &c. in the R.L.* 8° 1794; 8° 1795. See *UA*. [Music by Reeve.]

The Mad Guardian. [In the *Reminiscences* placed before *The Rival Loyalists*: it may have appeared by 1793.]

+Ba. The Village Ghost (S.W. *c.* 1794). [See *Reminiscences*, i. 189. Music by Reeve.]

+Ba. Gaffer's Mistake (S.W. *c.* 1794). See *UA*. [Music by Levesque.]

+P. The Death of David Rizzio (S.W. *c.* 1795). [Music by Reeve.]

+Ba. The Prospect of Peace (S.W. *c.* 1795). [Music by Reeve.]

+Ba. A Pennyworth of Wit (S.W. *c.* 1795). [Music by John Davy.]

+P. The Ruins of Paluzzi; or, The Black Penitent (S.W. *c.* 1796).

+Ba. The Magician; or, The Invisible Hand (S.W. *c.* 1796).

+P. Alonzo and Imogine; or, The Bridal Spectre (S.W. M. 8/5/1797). See *UA*. [Although 1797 is the earliest date I have found, the *Reminiscences* (i. 189) suggest an original performance in 1796.]

+Ball. Chevy Chace (S.W. *c.* 1796).

+P. Sadak and Kalasrade; or, The Waters of Oblivion (S.W. *c.* 1796).

+P. The Talisman; or, Harlequin made Happy (S.W. 1796) 8° 1796. See *UA*.

+P. John of Calais (S.W. *c.* 1796).

+Ba. Jane of Pentonville (S.W. *c.* 1796).

+P. Harlequin and Hudibras (*c.* 1796). [According to the *Reminiscences* (i. 190) purchased by S.W. but not acted.]

+P. The Pyramids; or, Harlequin in Egypt (*c.* 1796). [Also purchased but not acted.]

+Ba. Blindman's Buff; or, Who pays the Reckoning (R.A *c.* 1796).

+Ent. The Lover's Trial or The Whirligig (*c.* 1796). [The *Reminiscences* (i. 196) say that this and the following were produced "at an equestrian theatre in the Lyceum."]

+Ent. The Auctioneer (*c.* 1796). [See above.]

+Ba. The Glazier (R.A. *c.* 1796).

+P. The Pirates; or, Harlequin Woodcutter (R.A. *c.* 1797).

+Ba. Two Sides of the Question (R.A. *c.* 1797).

The Mouth of the Nile. [+L. 1227, as *News from the Nile, or Laurels from Egypt* (*UA*).]

The Birth-Day. [An adaptation of Kotzebue, *Der Bruderzwist* (1797).]

+The Magic Oak (C.G. T. 29/1/1799). See *UA*. [Written in association with *CHARLES FARLEY*.]

The Horse and the Widow. [An adaptation of Kotzebue, *Die Wittwe und der Reitpferd*.]

p. 257]   +P. The Volcano; or, Rival Harlequins (C.G. 23/12/1799). L. 1272 [12/12/1799]. *Songs, Recitatives, &c. in The V.* 8° 1799. [Written in association with *CHARLES FARLEY*.]

DODD, J. S.
Gallic Gratitude. [An adaptation of La Font, *La Naufrage* (Paris, 1710).]

DOSSIE, R.
The Statesman Foil'd. [+L. 283, as *The Trial of Skill; or, The Statesman foil'd* (*UA*).]

DOWNMAN, H.
+— The Dramatic Works of M. de Voltaire 8° 1781 (2 vols.). [In association with *DAVID WILLIAMS*.]

+DUPUIS, THOMAS SKELTON.
Elijah (1789). See *ITALIAN OPERAS*.

p. 258]   DUTTON, T.
Pizarro in Peru. [A translation of Kotzebue, *Die Spanier in Peru, oder Rollas Tod*.]

+EDWIN, JOHN.
Ent. Lingo's Opinions on Men and Manners (C.G. 10/4/1787) L. 767. [Printed in John Williams, *The Eccentricities of John Edwin* (1791), but without any precise indication of authorship.]

p. 259]   +FARLEY, CHARLES.
+P. The Magic Oak (C.G. T. 29/1/1799). See *UA* and *T. J. DIBDIN*.

+P. The Volcano (C.G. 23/12/1799). See *T. J. DIBDIN*.

FEILDE, M.
[Dougald MacMillan, p. 98, gives this author's name as Peilde, but the *Biographia Dramatica* is the authority for Feilde.]

FERRIAR, J.
The Prince of Angola. [An alteration of Southerne, *Oroonoko*.]

+FIELDING, HENRY.
C. The Fathers: or, The Good-Natur'd Man (D.L. 30/11/ 1778). 8° 1778. L. 461 [25/11/1778].

FOOTE, S.
Taste. [+L. 93, as *The Virtuoso*, dated 28/12/1751.]

The Englishman in Paris. [L. 100, epilogue and additions.]

+F. The Diversions of the Morning (D.L. 17/10/1758). L. 149. [This is an altered version of the similarly titled entertainment acted in 1747.]

p. 260]   The Minor. [L. 177 is a printed copy for D.L., where the play was acted on 22/11/1760.]

The First Act of Taste. [As *Tragedy à la Mode* in Tate Wilkinson, *The Wandering Patentee* (1795), i; as *Lindamira* in Thomas Matthews, *Thespian Gleanings* (1805).]

+The Comic Theatre. Being a Free Translation of all the Best French Comedies. 12° 1762 (5 vols.). [Contains: (1) *The Young Hypocrite*, from Destouches, *La fausse Agnès*; (2) *The Spendthrift*, from Destouches, *Le Dissipateur*; (3) *The Triple Marriage*, from Destouches, *Le triple mariage*; (4) *The Imaginary Obstacle*, from Destouches, *L'Obstacle imprévu*; (5) *The Sisters*, from Destouches, *La belle orgueilleuse, ou, l'enfant gâté*; (6) *The Libertine, or, The Hidden Treasure*, from Destouches, *Le Trésor caché*; (7) *The Legacy; or, The Fortune-Hunter*, from Destouches, *Le Dépot*; (8) *The Generous Artifice; or, The Reformed Rake*, from Destouches, *Le jeune homme à l'épreuve*; (9) *The Whimsical Lovers; or, The Double Infidelity*, from Destouches, *L'Amour usé*; (10) *The Blunderer*, from Molière, *L'Étourdi*; (11) *The Amorous Quarrel*, from Molière, *Le Dépit amoureux*; (12) *The Conceited Ladies*, from Molière, *Les Précieuses ridicules*; (13) *The Forced Marriage*, from Molière, *Le Mariage forcé*; (14) *The Man-Hater*, from Molière, *Le Misanthrope*; (15) *The Gentleman Citizen*, from Molière, *Le bourgeois gentilhomme*; (16) *The Faggot-Binder*, from Molière, *Le Médecin malgré lui*. Foote had little to do with the translations in this volume.]

The Lyar. [An adaptation of Corneille, *Le Menteur*.]

The Orators. [Originally advertised as *A Course of Comic Lectures on English Oratory*: see *Public Advertiser*, April 30, 1762.]

+C. Doctor Last in his Chariot (H.² W. 21/6/1769). See *I. BICKERSTAFFE*.

+[Burlesque.] Wilkes. An Oratorio. As Performed at The Great Room in Bishopsgate-Street. 8° 1769.

Piety in Pattens. [Also called *The Handsome Housemaid*.]

p. 261]   *FRANCIS, ——.*

The Enchanted Wood. [A play of this title was given at Bath on 20/11/1785: it is possible that the performance marks an early production of Francis's drama.]

FRANCIS, P.

Eugenia. [Based on Mme Graffigny, *Cénie* (1750).]

FRANCKLIN, T.

The Earl of Warwick. [An adaptation of J. F. de La Harpe, *Le Comte de Warwick* (Paris, 1763).]

+—— The Tragedies of Sophocles. 8° 1759 (2 vols.).

Matilda. [An adaptation of Voltaire, *Le Duc de Foix* (Paris, 1752).]

The Contract. [An adaptation of Destouches, *L'Amour usé* (Paris, 1741).]

+*FREE, Dr JOHN.*
Jephtha (1752). See *ITALIAN OPERAS.*

p. 262] +*GARDNER,* ——.
P. The Vineyard Revels; or, Harlequin Bacchus (Canterbury, 24/2/1791).

GARRICK, D.
The Fairies. [Garrick repudiated the authorship of this play. It may have been by the composer J. C. Smith.]
The Guardian. [Based on B. C. Fagan, *La Pupille* (Paris, 1734).]
Harlequin's Invasion. [A manuscript of this in the Boston Public Library has been published by E. P. Stein, 1926.]

p. 263] Neck or Nothing. [+L. 260, as *The Narrow Escape (UA).* An adaptation of Le Sage, *Crispin rival de son maître* (Paris, 1707).]
Cymon. [+8° 1791, with additional airs for revival on 31/12/1791.]
A Peep behind the Curtain. [+L. 271, as *The New Rehearsal (UA).*]
The Jubilee. [After having been lost for over a century, three manuscripts have recently come to light: (1) L. 298, printed by E. P. Stein (1926); (2) a version discovered by R. Crompton Rhodes and formerly in his possession; and (3) a copy in my possession. These vary slightly from one another. See my article, "Garrick's Lost *Jubilee*" (*The Times*, July 25, 1927) and R. C. Rhodes, "Garrick and Shakespeare's Birthday" (*Birmingham Post*, April 23, 1932).]
Albumazar. [For an earlier version see the Hand-list of Plays, 1700–1750.]
A Christmas Tale. [*La Fée Urgèle* was produced at Fontainebleau in 1765.]
The Meeting of the Company. [L. 378 printed by E. P. Stein (1926).]

p. 264] *GEISWEILER, M.*
Crime from Ambition. [A translation of W. A. Iffland, *Verbrechen aus Ehrsucht* (1784).]
Joanna of Montfaucon. [A translation of A. F. von Kotzebue, *Johanna von Montfaucon* (printed 1800).]
The Noble Lie. [A translation of A. F. von Kotzebue, *Die edle Lüge* (1792).]
Poverty and Nobleness of Mind. [A translation of A. F. von Kotzebue, *Armuth und Edelsinn* (1793).]

GENTLEMAN, F.
Sejanus. [An alteration of Ben Jonson's play.]
Richard II. [This version of Shakespeare's drama probably appeared at Bath on 17/3/1755.]
The Tobacconist. [An alteration of part of Ben Jonson, *The Alchemist.*]
Oroonoko. [An alteration of Southerne's play.]

p. 265]   *GOLDSMITH, O.*

The Good Natur'd Man. [+12° 1768 (*Dublin*); 12° 1770 (*Dublin*).]

She Stoops to Conquer. [+12° 1773 (*Dublin*); 12° 1773 (*Belfast*); and several subsequent Dublin editions. For an examination of L. 349 in relation to the printed texts see K. C. Balderston, "A Manuscript Version of *She Stoops to Conquer*" (*Modern Language Notes*, 1930, xlv. 84–5) and C. O. Parsons, "Textual Variations in a Manuscript of *She Stoops to Conquer*" (*Modern Philology*, 1942–3, xl. 57–69).]

The Grumbler. [L. 354 printed by A. I. Perry (1931).]

GRAVES, R.

The Coalition. [The *Biographia Dramatica* says this was acted at Bath, but I can find no record in the bills.]

+*GREEN, Mrs.*

F. Everybody to their own liking (Bath, 6/9/1756).

p. 266]   +*GRETTON, JOHN.*

M. A Masque for the Marriage of the Prince of Wales (C.G. 6/6/1795). L. 1087. [Music by Spofforth.]

GRIFFITH, E.

The School for Rakes. [Based on P. A. C. Beaumarchais, *Eugénie* (Paris, 1767).]

The Barber of Seville. [An adaptation of P. A. C. Beaumarchais, *Le barbier de Séville* (Paris, 1775).]

The Times. [An adaptation of C. Goldoni, *Le bourru bienfaisant* (Paris, 1771).]

+*GRIFFITHS, Miss.*

Cross Partners (H.¹ Th. 23/8/1792). See *UA* and supplementary notes.

GROVE, W.

The Faithful Shepherd. [A translation of G. B. Guarini, *Il Pastor fido*.]

+*HAGGITT, Rev. JOHN.*

The Count de Villeroi. 8° 1794. See *UA*.

HAMILTON, C.

The Patriot. [An adaptation of P. Metastasio, *Temistocle* (Vienna, 1736).]

HARRIS, J.

Daphnis and Amaryllis. [+4° 1763 (*Salisbury*).]

p. 267]   *HAWKESWORTH, J.*

[For *The Fall of Egypt* (1774) and *Zimri* (1760) see under *ITALIAN OPERAS*.]

Oroonoko. [An alteration of Southerne's play.]

HAYLEY, W.

+*— The Afflicted Father 8°. [? 1770.]

+*— The Happy Prescription. [8° 1785 (*Calcutta*).]

The Two Connoisseurs. [+8° 1785 (*Calcutta*).]

Marcella. [L. 847 for D.L. and L. 849 for C.G. The two houses acted this in rivalry (D.L. S. 7/11/1789 and C.G. T. 10/11/1789).]

p. 268] *HERON, R.*

Pizarro. [An adaptation of *Die Spanier in Peru* (1796).]

HIFFERNAN, P.

The Earl of Warwick. [An adaptation of J. F. de La Harpe, *Le Comte de Warwick* (Paris, 1763).]

National Prejudice. [An adaptation of Favart, *L'Anglois à Bordeaux* (Paris, 1763).]

p. 269] *HOARE, P.*

The Cave of Trophonius. [+*Songs...in The C. of T.* 8° 1791. An adaptation of *La grotta di Trofonio* (Vienna, 1785), by G. B. Casti. Original music by Salieri arranged by Stephen Storace.]

Dido. [+L. 943 (10/5/1792). An adaptation of Metastasio, *Didone Abbandonata* (1724).]

p. 270] A Friend in Need. [An adaptation of *Le Comte d'Albert* (Fontainebleau, 1786) by J. M. Sedaine, music by Grétry.]

Sighs. [An adaptation of A. F. von Kotzebue, *Armuth und Edelsinn* (1795).]

HOLCROFT, T.

[See E. Colby, "A Bibliography of Thomas Holcroft" (*Bulletin of New York Public Library*, 1922).]

The Follies of a Day. [An adaptation of Beaumarchais, *Le mariage de Figaro* (Paris, 1784).]

p. 271] The Choleric Fathers. [+*Songs...in The C.F.* 8° 1785 (*bis*).]

Theatre of Education. [A translation of Mme de Genlis, *Le théâtre d'éducation* (1779).]

The German Hotel. [An adaptation of J. C. Brandes, *Trau', Schau', wem!* (1769), later called *Der Gasthoff*.]

The School for Arrogance. [Also attributed to Marshall on first production. An adaptation of Destouches, *Le Glorieux* (Paris, 1732).]

The Deserted Daughter. [+L. 1077, as *Tis a Strange World* (*UA*). Based on Diderot, *Le père de famille* (Paris, 1761).]

Knave or Not? [Based on C. Goldoni, *La Serva Amorosa* (1752) and *Il Padre di Famiglia* (1750).]

He's Much to Blame. [Original title, *The Disloyal Lover*. Based on Goethe, *Clavigo* (1774) and Pont-de-Veyle, *Le complaisant* (Paris, 1732).]

p. 272] *HOOLE, J.*

Timanthes. [Based on Metastasio, *Demofoonte* (1733).]

The Works of Metastasio. [Contains: (1) *Artaxerxes* (from *Artaserse*, 1730); (2) *The Olympiad* (from *Olimpiade*, 1733); (3) *Hypsipile* (from *Issipile*, 1732); (4) *Titus* (from *La clemenza di Tito*, 1734); (5) *Demetrius* (from *Demetrio*, 1731); (6) *Demophoon* (from *Demofoonte*, 1733).]

Dramas. [This contains the above, and adds: (1) *The Dream of Scipio* (from *Il sogno di Scipione*, 1735); (2) *Achilles in Scyros* (from *Achille in Sciro*, 1736); (3) *Adrian in Syria* (from *Adriano in Sirio*, 1731); (4) *Dido* (from *Didone abbandonata*, 1724); (5) *The uninhabited Isle* (from *L'isola disabitata*, 1752); (6) *The Triumph of Glory* (from *Il trionfo della* gloria, 1748); (7) Zenobia (from Zenobia, 1740); (8) The-mistocles (from Temistocle, 1736); (9) Siroes (from Siroe, 1726); (10) Regulus (from Attilio Regolo, 1740); (11) Romulus and Hersilia (from Romolo ed Ersilia, 1765); (12) The Dis-covery of Joseph (from Giuseppe riconosciuto, 1733).]

p. 274] HULL, T.

All in the Right. [An adaptation of Destouches, Le triple mariage (Paris, 1716).]

Henry the Second. [+8° 1775.]

p. 275] +ILIFFE, ——.

[See The Ugly Club under UA. Kemble has written in his copy "Iliffe is the real Name of the Authour."]

INCHBALD, E.

[See G. L. Jonghin, "An Inchbald Bibliography" (University of Texas Studies in English, 1934, pp. 59–74).]

A Mogul Tale. [+12° 1788 (Dublin).]

The Widow's Vow. [+L. 736 (5/6/1786) as The Neuter (UA) 12° 1786 (Dublin). An adaptation of Patrat, L'heureuse erreur (Paris, 1783).]

The Midnight Hour. [An adaptation of Dumaniant, La guerre ouverte (Paris, 1786).]

Animal Magnetism. [+12° 1788? (Dublin).]

The Child of Nature. [An adaptation of Mme de Genlis, Zélie, ou l'ingénue (1781).]

The Married Man. [An adaptation of Destouches, Le philo-sophe marié (Paris, 1727).]

The Hue and Cry. [An adaptation of Dumaniant, La nuit aux aventures (Paris, 1787).]

Next Door Neighbours. [+12° 1791 (Dublin). Based on L. S. Mercier, L'indigent (printed 1722) and Destouches, Le dissipateur (1736).]

Young Men and Old Women. [+L. 952, as Lovers No Conjurers (UA). An adaptation of Gresset, Le méchant (Paris, 1747).]

+Cross Partners (H.² Th. 23/8/1792). See UA and supple-mentary notes.

Wives as they Were. [+12° 1797 (Dublin).]

Lovers' Vows. [An adaptation of A. F. von Kotzebue, Das Kind der Liebe (1790).]

The Wise Men of the East. [An adaptation of A. F. von Kotzebue, Das Screibepult (printed 1800).]

+JAGO, RICHARD.

Abimelech (1784). See ITALIAN OPERAS.

p. 276] JAMES, C.

Tarare. [The original French play was produced in Paris in 1787.]

+JEFFREYS, GEORGE.

The Triumph of Truth (1767). See ITALIAN OPERAS.

JENNER, C.

The Man of Family. [Based on Diderot, Le père de famille (Paris, 1761).]

JEPHSON, R.
>Braganza. [+12° 1775 (*Dublin*).]

p. 277] The Count of Narbonne. [+12° 1782 (*Dublin*); 8° 1787.]
>The Hotel. [An alteration of T. Vaughan, *The Hotel.*]
>The Campaign. [Larpent has a note (L. 703), "the poetry by
>Sᵣ Nathaniel Barry."]
>Julia. [+12° 1788 (*Dublin*).]

JOHNSTONE, J.
>The Disbanded Officer. [An adaptation of Lessing, *Minna
>von Barnhelm* (1763).]

p. 278] *KELLY, H.*
>False Delicacy. [+12° 1770 (*Dublin*).]
>A Word to the Wise. [+12° 1770 (*Dublin*).]
>Clementina. [+12° 1771 (*Dublin*).]
>The School for Wives. [+12° 1774 (*Belfast*).]
>The Romance of an Hour. [+12° 1775 (*Dublin*). Based on
>J. F. Marmontel, *Coralie.*]
>The Man of Reason. [+L. 401, as *The Reasonable Lover*
>(*UA*).]
>[For *The Prince of Agra* (C.G. 1774) see *Sir W. ADDING-
>TON.*]

+KEMBLE, ELIZABETH.
>Past. Philander and Rose (Manchester, 25/4/1785). Songs,
>12° 1785 (*Manchester*). L. 689. See *UA*.

KEMBLE, J. P.
>Oh! It's Impossible. [An alteration of Shakespeare, *The
>Comedy of Errors.*]
>The Maid of Honour. [An alteration of Massinger's play.]
>Coriolanus. [An alteration of Shakespeare's play.]
>The Farm House. [An alteration of Charles Johnson, *The
>Country Lasses.*]
>King Henry V. [An alteration of Shakespeare's play.]
>Macbeth. [An alteration of Shakespeare's play.]
>Lodoiska. [+L. 1029, as *Czartoriska* (*UA*). An adaptation
>of the musical drama by J. C. B. Dejaure (Paris, 1791).]

p. 279] +Otway's Tragedy of Venice Preserved (D.L. 21/10/1795).
>8° 1795; 8° 1811.
>The Plain Dealer. [An alteration of Wycherley's comedy.]
>The Merry Wives of Windsor. [An alteration of Shakespeare's
>comedy.]
>Celadon and Florimel. [An alteration of C. Cibber, *The
>Comical Lovers.*]
>Much Ado about Nothing. [An alteration of Shakespeare's
>comedy.]

KENRICK, W.
>Falstaff's Wedding. [+12° 1766 (*Dublin*).]
>The Duellist. [+12° 1774 (*Dublin*).]
>The Lady of the Manor. [+12° 1779 (*Dublin*).]

KING, T.
>Wit's Last Stake. [Based on J. F. Regnard, *Le légataire
>universel* (Paris, 1708).]

+Hurly Burly (D.L. 1785). See *J. COBB.*

[*Lovers' Quarrels, or, Like Master like Man*, an alteration of part of J. Vanbrugh, *The Mistake*, is printed in *The London Stage* (1824–7), vol. iii.]

KNAPP, H.
The Exciseman. [L. 535 (2/11/1780), untitled.]

p. 280]   *LAWRENCE, R.*
Gortz of Berlingen. [A translation of Goethe, *Götz von Berlichingen* (1773).]

LEE, H.
Throw Physic to the Dogs! [L. 1221, original title, *Jack of All Trades.*]

LEE, J.
Romeo and Juliet. [An alteration of Shakespeare's play.]

p. 281]   +*LEFTLEY, F.*
Clavidgo. 8° 1798. See *UA.*

LENNOX, C.
Philander. [+12° 1758 (*Dublin*).]
+The Greek Theatre, 3 vols. 8° 1759. [Contains, by this authoress, Sophocles' *Œdipus, Electra* and *Philoctetes.*]

LEWIS, M. G.
The Minister. [A translation of F. Schiller, *Kabale und Liebe* (1784).]
Rolla. [A translation of A. F. von Kotzebue, *Die Spanier in Peru* (1796).]
The East Indian. [An adaptation of A. F. von Kotzebue, *Die Indianer in England* (1789).]

LILLO, G.
Arden of Feversham. [L. 867 presents an altered version of Lillo's play, probably about 1790: printed copy with manuscript changes.]

+*LINDOE, ——.*
The Norwich Lass (Norwich, 15/5/1793).
Forget and Forgive; or, The Road to Happiness (Norwich, 26/5/1794).

LINLEY, W.
+P. Harlequin Captive (D.L. M. 18/1/1796). See *UA.*
The Honey Moon. [See R. W. Babcock, "Eighteenth-century Comic Opera Manuscripts" (*PMLA*, 1937, liii. 907–8).]
p. 282]   The Ring. [+*Songs, Duets, &c. in The R.* 8° (1800).]

LLOYD, H. E.
The Nephews. [An adaptation of *Die Mündel* (1785).]

LLOYD, R.
The New School for Women. [A translation of *La nouvelle école des femmes* (Paris, 1758).]
The Death of Adam. [A translation of *Der Tod Adams* (1757).]
The Capricious Lovers. [*Le caprice amoureux* was produced in Paris in 1755.]

LOGAN, J.
Runnamede. [Probably produced in Edinburgh in 1784. *Tancrède* appeared in Paris in 1760.]

LONSDALE, M.
+P. Alfred the Great: or The Danish Invasion (S.W. M. 7/5/1798). See *UA*.
+Ent. Baron Munchausen (S.W. M. 25/5/1795). See *UA*.

p. 283] *LOVE, J.*
The Ladies Frolic. [This may be the same as *The Fine Lady's Frolic*, acted at Hull, 3/1/1777.]
Rule a Wife. [+8° 1786 (in *The New English Theatre*, vol. iii).]

LUDGER, C.
The Lawyers. [A translation of A. W. Iffland, *Die Advokaten* (1796).]
The Peevish Man. [A translation of A. F. von Kotzebue, *Üble Laune* (1799).]
The Reconciliation. [A translation of A. F. von Kotzebue, *Die Versöhnung* (1798).]

McDONALD, A.
Vimonda. [This was first performed in Edinburgh.]

p. 284] *MACKLIN, C.*
Covent Garden Theatre. [See Esther M. Raushenbush, "Charles Macklin's Lost Play about Henry Fielding" (*Modern Language Notes*, 1936, li. 505–14).]
Love A-la-Mode. [+12° 1784 (? *Dublin*, pirated); 12° 1785 (in *A Volume of Plays as performed at the Theatre, Smoke-Alley, Dublin*). The first act was printed in *The Court Miscellany*, 1766. See W. Matthews, "The Piracies of Macklin's *Love A-la-Mode*" (*Review of English Studies*, 1934, x. 311–18).]
The Married Libertine. [+L. 184, as *The School for Husbands* (*UA*).]
The True-born Irishman. [L. 274 is the text of *The Irish Fine Lady*, as acted at C.G. +12° 1793 (*Dublin*).]
The Man of the World. [There are three Larpent manuscripts: (1) L. 311 (2/8/1770 for H.², licence refused); (2) L. 500 (4/12/1779 for C.G., licence refused); (3) L. 558 (10/5/1781 for C.G., licensed). See Dougald MacMillan, "The Censorship in the Case of Macklin's *The Man of the World*" (*Huntington Library Bulletin*, No. 10, Oct. 1936, 79–101).]

McLAREN, A.
The Highland Drover. [This and *The Scottish Volunteers* are two separate plays.]

p. 285] *MACREADY, W.*
The Village Lawyer. [An adaptation of Brueys, *L'avocat Patelin* (Paris, 1706).]
The Irishman in London. [This was apparently acted as *The Happy Africans* at Manchester on 4/10/1796.]

p. 287] *MEYERS, —.*
Zelma. [+*Airs, Duets, Choruses, &c. in Z.* 8° 1792.]

+*MONRO, THOMAS.*
    T. Philoctetes in Lemnos...to which is prefixed a Green
    Room Scene. 8° 1795.

p. 288] *MOORE, E.*
    Gil Blas. [+12° 1751 (*Dublin*).]
    The Gamester. [+8° 1776; 8° 1784.]

MORE, H.
    A Search after Happiness. [See C. L. Shaver, "The Publica-
    tion of Hannah More's First Play" (*Modern Language Notes*,
    1947, lxii. 343).]

MORELL, T.
    +Theodora (C.G. F. 16/3/1750). See *ITALIAN OPERAS.*
    +Nabal (C.G. W. 21/3/1764). See *ITALIAN OPERAS.*

MORRIS, E.
    The Adventurers. [Original title, *The Travellers.*]

+*MORRIS, Captain THOMAS.*
    T. Phaedra. L. 1004 [? 1793].

MORTON, T.
p. 289]   Zorinski. [+L. 1081, as *Casimer the Great* (*UA*).]

MOUBRAY, ——.
    [Dougald MacMillan gives this author's name as Maubray:
    the *Biographia Dramatica* is the authority for Moubray.]

MURPHY, A.
    The Orphan of China. [An adaptation of Voltaire, *L'Orphélin
    de la Chine* (Paris, 1755).]
    The Way to Keep Him. [Based on Moissy, *La nouvelle école
    des femmes* (Paris, 1758). The enlarged version has bor-
    rowings from La Chaussée, *Le préjugé à la mode* (Paris,
    1735).]

p. 290]   The Old Maid. [Based on Fagan, *L'étourderie* (Paris, 1737).]
    The Citizen. [Based partly on Destouches, *La fausse Agnès*
    (Paris, 1759).]
    No One's Enemy but his Own. [An adaptation of Voltaire,
    L'indiscret (Paris, 1725).]
    What We Must All Come To. [Frequently acted as *Marriage
    à la Mode*, sometimes with sub-title, *or Conjugal Douceurs.*]

MURRAY, C.
    +Ent. The Norfolk Lass (Norwich, 26/4/1784).

NEUMAN, H.
    Self-Immolation. [A translation of A. F. von Kotzebue, *Der
    Opfertod* (1798).]

p. 291] *NOEHDEN, G. H.*
    Fiesco. [A translation of Schiller, *Die Verschwörung des Fiesko*
    (1783).]
    Don Carlos. [A translation of Schiller, *Don Carlos* (1787).]

O'BEIRNE, T. L.
    The Generous Impostor. [An adaptation of Destouches, *Le
    dissipateur* (Paris, 1736).]

+ *O'BRIEN, Mrs MARY.*
> C.O. The Temple of Virtue. [See R. W. Babcock, "Eight-
> eenth-century Comic Opera Manuscripts" (*PMLA*, 1937,
> liii. 907–8).]

O'BRIEN, W.
> Cross Purposes. [Based on La Font, *Les trois frères rivaux*
> (Paris, 1713).]
> The Duel. [An adaptation of M. J. Sedaine, *Le philosophe sans
> le savoir* (Paris, 1765).]

O'BRYEN, D.
> A Friend in Need is a Friend Indeed. (+L. 626 (27/6/1783).]

p. 292] *O'KEEFFE, J.*
> The She Gallant. [+12° 1767 (*Dublin*).]
> The Son in Law. [Apparently the first authorised text is that
> in *Cumberland's British Theatre*, xxxi.]
> The Agreeable Surprise. [+12° 1783 (*Newry*) and, first
> authorised text, *Cumberland's British Theatre*, xxxi.]

p 293] The Young Quaker. [First authorised text in *Cumberland's
> British Theatre*, xxxvii.]
> The Birth-Day. [An adaptation of Saint-Foix, *Le rival supposé*
> (Paris, 1747).]
> Peeping Tom of Coventry. [+*Airs...in P.T. of C.* 8° 1785
> and *Cumberland's British Theatre*, xxi (first authorised text).]
> Omai. [+ *Songs...in O.* 8° 1785.]
> The Farmer. [+L. 786, as *Ups and Downs* (*UA*).]

p. 294] Modern Antiques. [+L. 893, as *The Merry Mourners* (*UA*).]
> The Irish Mimic. [+L. 1069, as *A Lounge at Brighton* (*UA*).]
> Merry Sherwood. [+L. 1099, as *The Merry Forester*.]

p. 295] The Wicklow Gold Mines. [+L. 1117, as *The Lad of the Hills*.]
> She's Eloped. [+L. 1212, as *Quarter Day*.]
> All to St. Paul's. [This is the same as *Britain's Brave Tars*
> (*UA*) and *Our Wooden Walls* (*UA*).]

OLIPHANT, R.
> +[F.] The First of September. See *UA*.

p. 296] + *PALMER, JOHN.*
> The Rose Wreath (Bath, 16/6/1781). See *UA*.

p. 298] *PILON, F.*
> +A Lecture on Heads, Written by George Alexander Stevens,
> with Additions by Mr Pilon; As Delivered by Mr Charles
> Lee Lewis (? C.G. 26/6/1780) 8° 1788. L. 527 [25/6/1780].

PLUMPTRE, A.
> The Count of Burgundy. [A translation of A. F. von Kotzebue,
> *Der Graf von Burgund* (1798).]
> The Natural Son. [A translation of A. F. von Kotzebue,
> *Das Kind der Liebe* (1790).]
> The Force of Calumny. [A translation of A. F. von Kotzebue,
> *Der Verläumder* (1795).]
> La-Peyrouse. [A translation of the similarly titled drama
> (1798) by A. F. von Kotzebue.]
> The Spaniards in Peru. [A translation of A. F. von Kotzebue,
> *Die Spanier in Peru* (1796).]

The Virgin of the Sun. [A translation of A. F. von Kotzebue, *Die Sonnen-Jungfrau* (1791).]

The Widow and the Riding Horse. [A translation of A. F. von Kotzebue, *Die Wittwe und das Reitpferd*.]

PLUMPTRE, B.
The Foresters. [A translation of A. W. Iffland, *Die Jäger* (1785).]

p. 299] *PORTER, S.*
Lover's Vows. [A translation of A. F. von Kotzebue, *Das Kind der Liebe* (1790).]

POTTER, R.
+The Tragedies of Sophocles. 4° 1788.

+*POWELL, THOMAS [pseud. T. DE MONMOUTH].*
T. Edgar and Elfrida. 8° [*c.* 1792].

PRATT, S. J.
The Fair Circassian. [+L. 576, as *The Circassian* (*UA*).]

p. 300] *PYE, H. J.*
[See also the Hand-list of Plays, 1800–1850.]

+*RAMSBOTTOM, DORNING.*
Codrus (Manchester, 29/4/1774).

RANNIE, J.
[See also the Hand-list of Plays, 1800–1850.]

REED, J.
The Register-Office. [+12° 1760 (*Dublin*). L. 189, as *The Universal Register Office* (*UA*), was not given a licence; the accepted text is in L. 196.]

p. 301] *RENDER, W.*
Count Benyowsky. [A translation of A. F. von Kotzebue, *Graf Benjowsky* (1795).]

REYNOLDS, F.
The Will. [+L. 1158, as *The Will and the Deed* (*UA*).]

+*RHODES, EBENEZER.*
T. Alfred, An Historical Tragedy (Sheffield, 28/10/1788) 8° 1789. See *UA*. [See F. T. Wood, "The Authorship of an Eighteenth Century Play" (*NQ*, April 5, 1947, cxcii.)]

RICH, JOHN.
The Spirit of Contradiction. [A variant title appears in L. 173, *The House Tyrant; or, Love and Discretion*. Based on C.-R. Dufresny, *L'esprit de contradiction* (Paris, 1700).]

p. 302] *RICHARDS, ——.*
The Device. [+*Airs, Duet, & Finale, in The D.* 8° 1777. See R. W. Babcock, "Eighteenth-century Opera Manuscripts" (*PMLA*, 1937, liii. 907–8).]

ROBINSON, ——.
The Test of Love. [+*Songs…in The T. of L.* 8° 1787.]

ROBSON, H.
[Dougald MacMillan gives this author's name twice as Robinson; this seems to be an error.]

p. 303]   *ROSE, J.*
The Prisoner. [L. 959 gives original titles, *The Dungeon of Death* and *Clara, or The Maid of Chili*.]

ROWE, H.
+Macbeth, A Tragedy. 8° 1799 (*York: bis*).

RYDER, T.
+The Connaught Wife (S.A. Dublin, M. 19/1/1767). See *UA*.

p. 304]   *RYLEY, S. W.*
The Civilian. [Acted at Manchester, 13/5/1789.]

ST JOHN, J.
The Island of St. Marguerite. [Licence was refused for the original text (L. 845), but approved for L. 848. The original title was *The Iron Mask*.]

SCHOMBERG, R.
The Death of Bucephalus. [See *The Rival Favourites* (*UA*).]

p. 305]   *SHARPE, J.*
Laura. [+L. 889, as *Who's to have her* (*UA*).]

SHERIDAN, F.
+C. A Trip to Bath. [Printed by F. Rae, in *Sheridan's Plays as he wrote them* (1902).]

SHERIDAN, R. B.
[See R. Crompton Rhodes, *The Plays and Poems of Richard Brinsley Sheridan*, 3 vols. 1928.]
The Rivals. [The Larpent manuscript (L. 383) has been edited by R. L. Purdy (1935). This play was acted at Portsmouth, F. 28/6/1782, as *The Rivals; or, The Devonshire Maccaroni*.]
St Patrick's Day. [The text in *Cumberland's British Theatre* (*c.* 1831) has importance.]
The School for Scandal. [The chief texts are: 12° 1780 (*Dublin*); 12° 1781 (*Dublin*; 3 editions); 12° 1782 (*Dublin*; 2 editions); 12° 1783 (*The Real and Genuine School for Scandal*); 12° 1783 (*Dublin*); 12° 1786 (*Dublin*); 12° 1787 (*Dublin*); 12° 1788 (*Dublin*); 8° 1823. The supposed "first" of Dublin, formerly dated 1777, is now supposed to be *c.* 1799.]
The Camp. [The 1833 *Cumberland's British Theatre* text should be noted. F. W. Bateson ("Notes on the Text of Two Sheridan Plays," *Review of English Studies*, 1940, xvi. 312–17) discusses the Larpent manuscript, notes that the newspapers definitely give this play to Sheridan and suggests that *T. HULL* may have been a collaborator.]

p. 306]   The Critic. [F. W. Bateson (*loc. cit.*) discusses the Larpent text, which he thinks represents the first acting version: the second and third acts are similar to those in the Framton Court manuscript printed by F. Rae (*Sheridan's Plays as he wrote them*, 1902). The 1781 Becket text was apparently authorised: a prompt book at Harvard belongs to 1782; the version in *Cumberland's British Theatre* (1827) corresponds

to a production at C.G. 15/12/1826. The probability is that
the 1781 text was never used for performance.]

+ The Storming of Fort Omoa. [An interlude in *Harlequin
Fortunatus* (D.L. 3/1/1780). See *H. WOODWARD*: this
pantomime was given originally in 1753.]

+ P. Robinson Crusoe; or Harlequin Friday (D.L. M.
29/1/1781). A Short Account of the Situations and Incidents exhibited in the Pantomime of R.C. 8° 1797. See
UA. [See G. H. Nettleton, "Robinson Crusoe: Sheridan's
Drury Lane Pantomime" (*TLS*, Dec. 25, 1943, Jan. 1,
1944). Music by T. Linley.]

Pizarro. [An adaptation of A. F. von Kotzebue, *Die Spanier
in Peru* (1796).]

T. SHERIDAN.
[*The Brave Irishman* in L. 120 (18/2/1755) has a text markedly
different from that of 1737.]

+ *SMART, CHRISTOPHER.*
Hannah (H.¹ T. 3/4/1764). See *ITALIAN OPERAS.*

p. 309]   *STEVENS, G. A.*
+ M. Albion Restored, or Time Turned Occulist. 8° 1758.
See *UA*.
+ The Mad Captain (Yarmouth, 1769). See *UA*.
+ C.O. The Fair Orphan (Lynn, 1771). 8° 1771. See *UA*.
+ Ent. A Lecture on Heads (C.G.? 26/6/1780). See *F.
PILON.*

STILLINGFLEET, B.
+ Paradise Lost (C.G. F. 29/2/1760). See *ITALIAN
OPERAS.*

STOCKDALE, P.
Amyntas. [An adaptation of Tasso, *Aminta* (1573).]

p. 310]   *STORACE, S.*
La Serva Padrona. [The original Italian play was produced
in 1733.]
The Coquet. [An adaptation of Goldoni, *La cameriera
spiritosa.*]

+ *STRATFORD, AGNES.*
The Labyrinth. 8° 1795. See *UA*.

STRATFORD, T.
[For *Darius*, see *UA*.]

STUART, C.
The Box-Lobby Loungers. [L. 777, as *The Lobby Lounger*.]
The Irishman in Spain. [Dougald MacMillan, in notes under
L. 915 and L. 917, observes that there seems to be some
confusion in the dates, unless a performance was allowed
"before the revision was submitted in a clean state to the
Examiner."]

p. 311]   *TAYLOR, W.*
Iphigenia of Tauris. [Goethe's *Iphigenie auf Tauris* appeared
in 1786.]

THOMPSON, B.
  The Stranger. [A translation of A. F. von Kotzebue, *Menschenhass und Reue* (1789).]
  La Perouse. [A translation of A. F. von Kotzebue, *La Peyrouse* (1798).]
  The Robbers. [A translation of F. Schiller, *Die Räuber* (1781).]
  The Happy Family. [A translation of A. F. von Kotzebue, *Die silberne Hochzeit.*]
  Adelaide of Wulfingen. [A translation of A. F. von Kotzebue, *Adelheid von Wulfingen* (1789).]
  Don Carlos. [A translation of F. Schiller, *Don Carlos* (1787).]

THOMPSON, EDWARD.
  The Fair Quaker. [An alteration of Charles Shadwell, *The Fair Quaker of Deal.*]
  +C.O. Love's Labour's Lost. [On the Folger manuscript (1772) of this version of Shakespeare's comedy see G. W. Stone, Jr., "Garrick and an Unknown Operatic Version of *Love's Labour's Lost*" (*Review of English Studies*, 1939, xv. 323–8).]

p. 312] *THOMSON, A.*
  The German Miscellany. [Contains *The Indians of England*, a version of A. F. von Kotzebue, *Die Indianer in England* (1789).]

+*TIMAEUS, J. J. K.*
  Cabal and Love, 8° 1795. See *UA*.

TOWNLEY, J.
  High Life Below Stairs. [A. Murphy, in his *Life of Garrick*, 1801, i. 343, ascribes this farce to *DAVID GARRICK*.]

p. 313] *WAKER, J.*
  Love in a Cottage. [See R. W. Babcock, "Eighteenth-century Comic Opera Manuscripts" (*PMLA*, 1937, liii. 907–8).]

WALDRON, F. G.
  The Contrast. [A play of this title was acted at Manchester, 17/1/1774: it is probably Waldron's.]

p. 314] Imitation. [+L. 599, as *The Belle's Stratagem* (*UA*).]
  The Sad Shepherd; with a Continuation 8° 1783. [An attempt to complete Jonson's pastoral.]
  The Prodigal. [Original title, *The Perils of Penury.*]
  Love and Madness. [+*Songs...in...L. and M.* 8° 1795.]

+*WALKER, B.*
  D. Palladius and Irene. [8° 1773. See *UA*. The Fordham University copy has a note "written by Mr B. Walker": see J. E. Tobin, "Three Eighteenth Century Plays" (*NQ*, Jan. 1, 1944, clxxxvi).]

WALLACE, Lady E.
  The Whim. [L. 1093 (7/9/1795, for Margate) was refused a licence; L. 1104 is a printed copy.]

p. 315] *WATSON, G.*
  England Preserved. [+L. 1057, as *King Henry the Third.*]

WEST, M.
Pizarro. [An adaptation of A. F. von Kotzebue, *Die Spanier in Peru* (1796).]

WHITEHEAD, W.
The Roman Father. [+12° 1750 (*Dublin*).]
Crëusa. [+12° 1755 (*Dublin*).]
The School for Lovers. [Based on Fontenelle, *Le testament* (Paris, 1758).]

p. 316]   +WILLIAMS, DAVID.
The Dramatic Works of M. de Voltaire 8° 1781. See *H. DOWNMAN*.

WILSON, R.
+Westminster Hall (H.² 16/8/1785). See *UA*.
+The Union (C.G. 18/5/1790). See *UA*.

WOLCOT, J.
Nina. [The French original, with music by Dalayrac, was produced in Paris in 1786. Music for English production adapted by W. T. Parke.]

p. 317]   WOODS, W.
The Volunteers. [+L. 453 (5/8/1778, for York).]
+Int. Hallow Fair; or, The School for Lasses. [L. 653; given at Edinburgh for Woods' benefit on 17/4/1784, and probably by him.]

WOODWARD, H.
[See the Hand-list of Plays, 1700–1750.]
A Lick at the Town. [+L. 92.]
Harlequin's Jubilee. [+L. 304.]

YEARSLEY, A.
Earl Goodwin. [+L. 846.]

p. 318]   YEO, ——.
The Asiatic. [The bills say "with considerable Alterations and Improvements"—but there is no record of a production earlier than 1790.]

UNKNOWN AUTHORS.
+The Alarm (York, 30/3/1776).
Albion Restored [=*G. A. STEVENS*].
+P. Alexander the Great; or, The Conquest of Persia (D.L. 12/2/1795). 8° [1795]. [According to the *Biographia Dramatica*, this was "composed" by J. D'Egville, with music by Krazinski Miller; the description of the action "was written by Mr Kemble, and distributed gratis at the theatre."]
Alfred. [=*E. RHODES*. Based on a play by D'Arnaud.]
Alfred the Great. [=*M. LONSDALE*.]
Alonzo and Imogine. [=*T. J. DIBDIN*.]

p. 319]   +Ancient and Modern Fashions (Bath, 14/3/1797).
At Anchor in the Bay of Naples. [=*Naples Bay; or, The British Seamen at Anchor*.]
The Babbler. [An adaptation of Voltaire, *L'Indiscret* (Paris, 1725).]
Baron Munchausen. [=*M. LONSDALE*.]

+The Bashful Virgin (Bath, 21/5/1760).

The Batchelors. [A translation of A. W. Iffland, *Die Hage-stolzen* (1793).]

p. 320]   The Beggar's Opera. [See *G. COLMAN*. L. 572 (13/10/1781) is a prelude to *The B.O.* "to be acted as The Lady's Opera" (C.G. 16/10/1781, as *The Lady's Opera*). *The Beggar's Opera Reversed* was given at Doncaster, 17/10/1781. L. 565 contains the Colman alteration.]

The Belle's Stratagem. [=*F. G. WALDRON, Imitation*, 1783.]

The Black Forest. [=*S. BIRCH, Albert and Adelaide*, 1798. A play of this title, possibly the same, was acted at Ponte-fract, 13/8/1795.]

+Bladud, or Harlequin at Bath (Bath, 20/9/1777).

The Blind Man. [=*C. DIBDIN, None so Blind as those who won't see*, 1782.]

Blue Beard. [Composed by Carlo Delpini, music by Grétry.]

+Botany Bay (Liverpool, 3/8/1791).

The Bourbon League. [L. 210, licence refused.]

+The Brickdustman (Canterbury, 25/1/1773).

The Bristol Sailor. [=*J. BERNARD*.]

p. 321]   Britain's Brave Tars. [=*J. O'KEEFFE* and see *Our Wooden Walls*.]

Cabal and Love. [This seems to have been translated by *J. J. K. TIMAEUS*.]

Calcutta. [=*J. COBB, Love in the East*, 1788.]

Casimer the Great. [=*T. MORTON, Zorinski*, 1795.]

The Casino. [With sub-title, *or, London trip'd down to Bath*.]

The Castle of Otranto. [=*H. SIDDONS, The Castilian Romance*, 1794.]

The Castle of Wonders. [=*M. P. ANDREWS, The En-chanted Castle*, 1786.]

p. 322]   +The Cave of Hecate (Bath, 28/1/1797).

The Choice of Hercules. [+L. 99, as *Hercules's Choice of Pleasure and Virtue*, an oratorio.]

The Circassian. [=*S. J. PRATT, The Fair Circassian*, 1781.]

Clavidgo. [A translation of Goethe, *Clavigo* (1774), by "F. L.," apparently F. Leftley.]

The Coffee-House. [A translation of Voltaire, *L'Écossaise* (Paris, 1760).]

Colin and Susan. [=*The Speechless Wife*.]

The Comical Resentment. [F. T. Wood records at Yarmouth, 2/1/1758, *The Comical Reconcilement*: this sounds like an error for "*Resentment*."]

p. 323]   The Corsicans. [A translation of A. F. von Kotzebue, *Die Korsen* (1799).]

+Courage and Constancy (Bristol, 8/9/1766).

+The Crisis; or, What You Please (Town Malling, 27/3/1775).

Cross Partners. [Kemble has written in his copy, "Miss Griffiths" (q.v.). An adaptation of Destouches, *L'amour usé* (Paris, 1741).]

p. 324] A Cure for a Coxcomb. [Songs by *JOHN COLLINS* and *CHARLES DIBDIN.*]

Curiosity. [An adaptation of J. A. Gruttschreiber, *Siri Brahe* (1794), based on a play attributed to Gustavus III, King of Sweden.]

Czartoriska. [=*J. P. KEMBLE, Lodoiska*, 1794.]

+ Darby in America (Leeds, 11/7/1792).

+ Days of Old (Leicester, 8/12/1797). [Possibly this is Cumberland's *The Days of Yore.*]

The Devil in the Wine-Cellar. [+L. 741, as *The Walking Statue, or The D. in the W.C.* An alteration of Aaron Hill, *The Walking Statue.*]

The Disagreeable Surprise. [Possibly this is *R. SICKLEMORE, Saltimbanco; or, The D.S.*, 1797.]

+ Int. The Disaster; or, The Farmer in Distress (Manchester, 24/2/1779).

The Distress'd Wife. [Possibly by *G. COLMAN the Elder.* An alteration of Gay's comedy.]

+ The Doctor in the Dumps (Scarborough, 18/8/1798).

Doctor Last's Examination. [Evidently part of *S. FOOTE, The Devil upon Two Sticks*, 1768.]

p. 325] Don Raymond. [=*Raymond and Agnes.*]

Dorval. [A translation of Diderot, *Le fils naturel* (Paris, 1757).]

+ Down with the Dutch (Scarborough, 7/8/1798).

+ The Dutchmen Tricked (Liverpool, 29/9/1784).

The East Indian. [This has been ascribed to Frances (Burney) D'Arblay.]

p. 326] + The Enchanted Cavern (Portsmouth, F. 11/3/1791).

+ The Enchanted Flute. [See R. W. Babcock, "Eighteenth-century Comic Opera Manuscripts" (*PMLA*, 1937, liii. 907–8).]

The Englishmen in Bordeaux. [A translation of C. S. Favart, *L'anglais à Bordeaux* (Paris, 1763).]

The Enraged Musician. [=*G. COLMAN the Elder, Ut Pictura Poesis*, 1789.]

+ Evil Spirits (Leicester, 6/2/1775).

+ The Fair Maid of Kent. [See R. W. Babcock, "Eighteenth-century Comic Opera Manuscripts" (*PMLA*, 1937, liii. 907–8).]

The Fair Orphan. [=*G. A. STEVENS.*]

The Fair Peruvian. [=*The Peruvian.*]

p. 327] The Fair Refugee. [The date 1780 is that given to it by J. P. Collier, who adds that it was licensed 12/4/1784.]

The Fairy Favours. [Evidently=*The Fairy Festival.*]

False Shame. [A translation of A. F. von Kotzebue, *Falsche Shaam* (1798).]

+ Family Distress; or, Self Immolation. 8° 1799. [A translation of A. F. von Kotzebue, *Der Opfertod* (1798).]

+ The Farmer Deceived (Faversham, 24/6/1779).

The Faro Table. [+L. 820, as *The Pharo Table.*]

+ The Fashionable Wife (York, 7/5/1782).

p. 328] + A Fig for the French (Portsmouth, F. 11/1/1782).

The Financier. [A translation of Saint-Foix, *Le financier* (Paris, 1761).]

The First of September. [=*ROBERT OLIPHANT.*]

The Flesh and the Spirit. [=*J. C. CROSS, The Apparition,* 1794.]

+The Florists' Feast (Bath, 9/4/1765).

The Four Quarters of the World. [Composed by Carlo Delpini.]

+The French Invasion (Manchester, Feb. 1783).

The Frenchman in London. [A translation of de Boissy, *Le Français à Londres* (Paris, 1727).]

The Frolick. [Original title, *The Oxford Scholar.*]

Gaffer's Mistake. [=*T. J. DIBDIN.*]

Galligantus. [This is evidently the *Galigantus* given at D.L. for one night only, 14/4/1760.]

p. 329]   The Georgian Princess. [=*E. CRAVEN, The Princess of Georgia,* 1799.]

+The German Baron (Norwich, 21/4/1784). ["By a Gentleman of Norwich."]

+The Gladiator (Norwich, 8/4/1786).

+The Grateful Lion (Manchester, 3/4/1793).

p. 330]   Hail Fellow well met. [There are two main puzzles concerning this piece. It was advertised, but it seems very doubtful whether it was actually produced. Secondly, in some advertisements the title of "The Quip Modest" is given as *The Rights of Man.* A third problem arises from the fact that a play called *The Rights of Man,* by *W. F. SULLIVAN,* was acted at Buxton in 1791 and later (F. 9/8/1792) at H.[1]]

+Harlequin at Amsterdam (York, 20/3/1797).

+Harlequin Fortunatus (Wakefield, 13/9/1793). See *H. WOODWARD.*

+Harlequin Foundling (Wakefield, 11/9/1784).

+Harlequin from the Moon (Brighton, 12/9/1775). See *Harlequin Emperor of the Moon,* above, and *J. LOVE,* 1763.

+Harlequin Hero (Leicester, 23/2/1795). [Perhaps =*M LONSDALE, Mago and Dago,* 1794.]

+Harlequin in the Moon (Liverpool, 14/1/1799). See above.

+Harlequin in the Oven (Aylsham, 24/5/1779).

Harlequin Mariner. [A pantomime of this title was given at Bath on 13/11/1788.]

+Harlequin Negro (Birmingham, 13/8/1795).

+Harlequin Salamander (York, 1/2/1766).

+Harlequin's Animation (York, 24/4/1781).

p. 331]   +Harlequin's Museum; or, Mother Shipton Triumphant. [+L. 964 (12/12/1792).]

Harlequin Skeleton. [A pantomime of this title was given at Liverpool on 16/7/1774.]

+Harlequin's Revels at Portsdown Fair (Portsmouth, M. 26/11/1781).

+Harlequin Traveller (York, 2/3/1782).

p. 332]   The Hue and Cry. [=*J. C. CROSS, An Escape into Prison,* 1797.]

+Hull Fair (Hull, 10/10/1774). [Evidently altered as *Leeds Fair* (Leeds, 10/7/1775).]

The Invisible Mistress. [Presumably the same play was acted under this title at Leeds on 21/7/1788.]

+Irish Darby in Leeds (Leeds, 18/6/1792). [Evidently the same as *Irish Darby in Doncaster* (Doncaster, 10/10/1792).]

Jacob's Ramble. [= *A Ramble to Bath.*]

p. 333]   +Jason and Medea (Norwich, 16/4/1791). [This may have been *Medea and Jason* (see *infra*) or else R. Glover's *Medea.*]

+The Jovial Coopers (Norwich, 27/3/1759).

The Kept Mistress. [= *The Mock Orators.*]

The Labyrinth. [= *AGNES STRATFORD.*]

The Legacy. [= *S. J. ARNOLD, The Irish Legacy,* 1797.]

p. 334]   Little Ben and Little Bob. [= *The Poor Sailor.*]

The London 'Prentice. [See *C. CLIVE.*]

A Lounge at Brighton. [= *J. O'KEEFFE, The Irish Mimic,* 1795.]

Love conquers all. [= *W. COWDROY.* Original title, *The Use of the Globe; or, The World Full of Love.*]

Lovers no Conjurors. [= *E. INCHBALD, Young Men and Old Women,* 1792.]

+The Lovers of Columbine (Liverpool, 1/11/1786).

p. 335]   The Magician. [= *T. J. DIBDIN.*]

The Magic Oak. [= *C. FARLEY and T. J. DIBDIN.* The latter contributed songs to this piece.]

The Maid of Marienburg. [A translation of F. Kratter, *Das Mädchen von Marienburg* (1795).]

The Maid of the Vale. [*La Buona Figliuola* was produced in Rome in 1760. See R. W. Babcock, "Eighteenth-century Comic Opera Manuscripts" (*PMLA*, 1937, liii. 907–8).]

+The Man-hater...The School for Husbands...The School for Wives...Love is the Best Doctor...The Hypocondriac. 12° 1771 (*Berwick*: in 5 parts). [Translations of five Molière plays.]

The Masquerade. [Acted at Norwich 13/4/1795, when it was said to be "by a gentleman of this city."]

p. 336]   The Merry Mourners. [= *J. O'KEEFFE, Modern Antiques,* 1791.]

Mirth and Magic. [An entertainment of this title was acted at Hull on 8/1/1790.]

The Mistakes of a Minute. [+L. 766.]

The Mistakes of a Day. [Dougald MacMillan, under L. 760, notes that J. P. Collier conjectured that the author might be J. H. Colls.]

+The Misrepresentor Represented. A Comedy, not performed in this Kingdom since 1715. 8° 1755 (*Dublin*).

The Mock Orators. [= *The Kept Mistress.*]

+Mock Pamela; or, A Kind Caution to all Country Coxcombs (Richmond, S. 4/8/1750).

+Modern Education (private, Wavendon, 18/8/1789).

Monopoly. [Acted at C.G. 23/9/1782.]

p. 337]   More Ways than Means. [= *G. COLMAN the Younger, Ways and Means*, 1788.]

Moses and Shadrac. [Acted at D.L. 17/4/1780.]

My Night-Gown and Slippers. [= *G. COLMAN the Younger.*]

Naples Bay. [= *At Anchor in the Bay of Naples.*]

Narcissus. [A translation of Rousseau, *Narcisse* (1752).]

The Narrow Escape. [= *D. GARRICK, Neck or Nothing*, 1766.]

Natalia and Menzikof. [A translation of F. Kratter, *Alexander Menzikof* (1794).]

The Negro Slaves. [A translation of A. F. von Kotzebue, *Die Negersclaven* (1796).]

The Neuter. [= *E. INCHBALD, The Widow's Vow*, 1786.]

New Gretna Green. [= *C. STUART, Gretna Green*, 1783.]

+A New Comic Scene to the Comedy of the Minor, written by Mr Foote 8° 1761.

A New Divertissement. [Acted at C.G. 26/5/1794.]

p. 338]   +A New Scene for the Comedy, call'd the Knights: or, Fresh Tea for Mr Foote 8° 1758.

The New Rehearsal. [= *D. GARRICK, A Peep behind the Curtain*, 1767.]

News from the Nile. [= *T. J. DIBDIN, The Mouth of the Nile*, 1798.]

New Ways to Catch Hearts. [= *H. COWLEY, More Ways than One*, 1783.]

The Noble Lie. [A translation of A. F. von Kotzebue, *Die edle Lüge* (1792).]

+The Noble Pilgrim (Walsingham, 9/8/1791).

No Matter What. [= *The Politician.*]

+The Old Fairy of the Woods (Bath, 25/12/1756).

One Rake in a Thousand. [Acted at Bristol, 16/8/1783.]

The Opiate. [= *S. BIRCH, Fast Asleep*, 1797.]

The Orphan of China. [A translation of Voltaire, *L'Orphélin de la Chine* (Paris, 1755).]

Our Wooden Walls. [= *J. O'KEEFFE, Britain's Brave Tars*, 1797.]

p. 339]   Palladius and Irene. [= *B. WALKER.*]

Pamela. [A translation of C. Goldoni, *Pamela nubile* (1750).]

The Peruvian. [= *The Fair Peruvian.* An adaptation of Favart, *L'amitié à l'épreuve* (Fontainebleau, 1770, with music by Grétry). J. Hook added new music for the English production.]

Phaedra (1793). [= *T MORRIS.*]

Philander and Rose. [= *E. KEMBLE.* Acted at Manchester, 25/4/1785.]

Pigmy Revels. [See also *Harlequin Foundling.*]

p. 340]   +The Player's Looking Glass (Richmond, M. 9/9/1751).

+The Pleasures of the Town (Norwich, 18/4/1757).

The Politician. [= *No Matter What.*]

The Poor Sailor. [= *Little Ben and Little Bob.*]

+The Power of Magic (York, 22/1/1783).

+The Privateer Invasion (York, 28/1/1779).

Pygmalion. [A translation of Rousseau, *Pygmalion* (Paris, 1775).]

p. 341] +Ralph's Ramble; or, O! Rare London (D.L. 19/4/1766). L. 254 (5/4/1766).
+A Ramble to Bath (C.G. 6/5/1796). [=*Jacob's Ramble.*]
The Reasonable Lover. [=*H. KELLY, The Man of Reason,* 1776.]
+The Rhinoceros (Wakefield, 6/9/1775).
Richard II. [=*R. CUMBERLAND,* 1792.]
+The Rights of Man. [See *Hail Fellow well met.*]
The Rights of Woman. [Although advertised, this play does not seem to have been acted.]
The Rival Favourites. [An alteration of *R. SCHOMBERG, The Death of Bucephalus* (1765).]

p. 342] The Rival Loyalists. [=*T. J. DIBDIN,* 1794.]
The Robbers. [A translation of Schiller, *Die Räuber* (1781).]
Robinson Crusoe; or, Harlequin Friday. [See the description of a pantomime of this title acted at Newcastle and printed 8° (1791, *Newcastle*).]
Rome Preserved. [A translation of Voltaire, *Rome sauvée* (Paris, 1752).]
Romeo and Juliet. [This seems to be a translation of Lope de Vega, *Castelvines y Monteses.*]
Rosamond. [An alteration of this play by Addison was given at D.L. 22/4/1765.]
The Rose Wreath. [Acted at Bath, 16/6/1781. Evidently by *J. PALMER.*]
The Round Tower. [=*J. C. CROSS,* 1797.]
+The Royal Hostages (Liverpool, 27/2/1793).
+The Rush Light (Swansea, 21/10/1795).
+The Sailor's Distress (Bristol, 16/8/1765).

p. 343] The School for Honour. [A translation of Lessing, *Minna von Barnhelm* (1763).]
The School for Husbands. [=*C. MACKLIN, The Married Libertine,* 1761.]
+Scotch Œconomy. [See R. W. Babcock, "Eighteenth-century Comic Opera Manuscripts" (*PMLA,* 1937, liii. 907–8).]
Semiramis. [A translation of Voltaire, *Sémiramis* (Paris, 1748).]

p. 344] +The Siege of Warsaw (Manchester, 15/12/1794).
+A Specimen of Jewish Courtship (D.L. 23/3/1787). [L. 765 shows that this was a "prelude" to *The Mistakes of a Minute.*]
The Speechless Wife. [=*Colin and Susan. +Songs, Duets, Choruses, &c. in The S.W.* 8° 1794.]
+The Spell (Bath, 8/5/1756).
+The Spendthrift's Folly and Fortune (Wolverhampton, 18/4/1751).
Stella. [A translation of Goethe, *Stella* (1776).]
The Stratagem. [A burletta called *La Stratagemma, or The Stratagem* was acted at M.G. 26/7/1759.]

The Suspicious Brother. [= *Try Again.*]

The Swindlers. [=*R. BADDELEY.*]

+ The Sword of Peace; or, A Voyage of Love (D.L.). 8° 1789; 12° 1790 (*Dublin*).

The Sylph. [A translation of Saint-Foix, *Le Silphe* (Paris, 1743).]

p. 345]   The Tailors. [= *Wet Weather.*]

A Tale of the Castle. [= *Who is she like?*]

The Talisman (S.W. 1796). [= *T. J. DIBDIN.*]

+ Tea's the Twaddle. [= *Twisting and Twining.*]

+ The Theatrical Museum: or, Fugitive Repository: Being a Collection of Interludes 8° 1776.

They've bit the old one. [=*J. C. CROSS,* 1798.]

'Tis a strange World. [=*T. HOLCROFT, The Deserted Daughter,* 1795.]

+ Ton and Antiquity 8° 1795 (*Oxford*). [By "T. S.," possibly *T. STREATFIELD.*]

p. 346]   Tony Lumpkin's Ramble to London. [Acted at C.G. 10/4/1792.]

+ The Touchstone of Truth (York, 22/4/1779).

The Trial of Skill. [=*R. DOSSIE, The Statesman Foil'd,* 1768.]

The Triumph of Fidelity. [See a play of the same name by *T. HARPLEY.*]

Try Again. [= *The Suspicious Brother.*]

+ Tully's Rambles (C.G. 29/4/1794) L. 1020.

Twisting and Twining. [= *Tea's the Twaddle.*]

The Two Friends. [A translation of Beaumarchais, *Les deux amis* (Paris, 1770).]

+ Two Knights from the Land's End (Twickenham, T. 20/8/1751).

The Two Nannys. [=*J. DENT,* music by Reeve.]

p. 347]   The Ugly Club. [= —— *ILIFFE.*]

The Uneasy Man. [A translation of Fagan, *L'Inquiet* (Paris, 1737). For the sources of the two other plays see the titles listed separately.]

The Union. [=*R. WILSON.*]

The Universal Register Office. [=*J. REED, The Register-Office,* 1761.]

Ups and Downs. [=*J. O'KEEFFE, The Farmer,* 1787.]

+ Valentia. [See R. W. Babcock, "Eighteenth-century Comic Opera Manuscripts" (*PMLA,* 1937, liii. 907–8).]

The Venetian Tale. [= *T. E. HOOK, Diamond cut Diamond,* 1797.]

The Village Conjurer. [A translation of Rousseau, *Le devin du village* (Fontainebleau, 1752).]

The Virtuoso. [=*S. FOOTE, Taste,* 1752.]

+ The Vision of an Hour (York, 7/3/1789).

Westminster Hall. [=*R. WILSON.*]

Wet Weather. [= *The Tailors.*]

+ We Two. [Leeds, 25/7/1783.]

What you please. [See R. W. Babcock, "Eighteenth-century Comic Opera Manuscripts" (*PMLA,* 1937, liii. 907–8).]

+The White Fox (Pontefract, 21/7/1779).

+Who'd have thought it? (Bath, 19/2/1763). [This cannot be the similarly named play by J. Cobb, who was only seven years old in 1763.]

Who is she like? [=*A Tale of the Castle.*]

p. 348]   Who's to have her? [=*J. SHARPE, Laura*, 1791.]

+The Widower (Yarmouth, 23/12/1785).

+The Widow of the Rocks (Brighton, 28/9/1797).

The Will and the Deed. [=*F. REYNOLDS, The Will*, 1797.]

The Wish. [Genest records a performance on 2/5/1775, but this is not apparently to be found in the advertisements.]

The Wishes. [Acted at C.G. on 3/10/1782.]

+The Witches of the Rocks (Deal, 24/3/1787).

The Witch of the Wood. [+*Airs, Duetts, Trios and Chorusses in The W. of the W.* 8° 1796.]

+The World turn'd Upside Down (York, 19/3/1777).

The Writing Desk. [A translation of A. F. von Kotzebue, *Das Schreibepult* (printed 1800).]

+The Yorkshire Hoyden (Liverpool, 28/8/1797).

+La Zingara; or, The Gipsey (M.G. 25/8/1773). [Music by Barthélemon.]

ITALIAN OPERAS, &c.

p. 349]   Alceste (1795). [Originally presented at Vienna, 26/12/1767.]

Alessandro nell' Indie (1761). [+L. 201, printed copy.]

L'Amor contrastato. [There are two Larpent manuscripts— L. 1047 and L. 1048.]

L'Amor Costante. [+L. 107, printed copy, Amsterdam, 1752.]

p. 350]   L'Arcadia in Brenta. [Although an original production in 1747 has been recorded, the first certain date is Venice 1749.]

Arianna e Teseo. [+L. 180, printed copy.]

Armida (1791). [Originally presented at Milan in 1772.]

Artaserse (1754). [Originally presented at Venice in 1730.]

p. 351]   Il Barbiere di Siviglia. [+8° 1789. Libretto by G. Petrosellini, music Paisiello; St Petersburg, 1782.]

Bertoldo. [Both the *Bertoldo* operas are the same, by C. Goldoni.]

p. 352]   Il Burbero di buon Cuore. [The name V. Martini, here as elsewhere, stands for Martin y Soler.]

Caio Mario. [+L. 411.]

+The Choice of Hercules. [See *UA.*]

La Cifra. [+L. 1198. Originally presented at Rome in 1780.]

Cinna. [Libretto by L. da Ponte.]

p. 353]   La Contessina. [Originally presented at Neustadt in 1770.]

La Costanza di Rosinella. [Libretto by P. Chiari; Venice, 1767. This is the same as *La Sposa fedele.*]

+La Creanza. 8° [1762, *Dublin*, Ital. and Eng.; a comic opera as it was to be acted at Smock Alley, Dublin, 27/2/1762.]

Creso (1777). [+L. 439.]

p. 354] Don Giovanni. [+L. 1013.]
    Elfrida. [Libretto by R. de Calsabigi, music by Paisiello; Naples, 4/11/1792.]

p. 355] L'Eroe cinese. [Original music by J. Bonno.]
    Evelina. [+L. 1152.]
    Ezio (1755). [At Rome in 1728 the music was by Pietro Auletta; Hasse's score was used at Dresden, 20/1/1755.]
    La Famiglia di Bertoldo. [+L. 116, printed copy, Amsterdam, 1754. See *Bertoldo*.]
    La Finta Principessa. [Acted at H.^{1} on 2/4/1785. Music by Cherubini.]

p. 356] Il Geloso in cimento. [Libretto by G. Bertati.]
    Germondo. [+L. 423.]
    I Giuochi d'Agrigento. [+L. 968.]
    Hannah. [Text by Christopher Smart.]
    Ifigenia in Aulide (1789). [Presented at Turin, Feb. 1788.]
    +L'Inglese in Italia (H.^{1} 18/5/1786). L. 733 (17/5/1786). [By C. F. Badini.]

p. 357] L'Isola d'Amore. [Originally presented at Rome in 1766.]
    Issipile. [The two operas of 1758 and 1784 seem to be separate; the latter was printed 8° 1784.]
    Il Marchese Tulipano. [Acted at H.^{1} on 24/1/1786, as *Le finte contesse*. Libretto by P. Chiari, music by Paisiello; Rome, 1766.]
    Medonte. [Twice represented in the Larpent collection— L. 1235 and L. 1238.]

p. 358] +Merope. [+L. 1174 (3/6/1797), for H.^{1}]
    La Moglie a Forza. [+L. 102, printed copy, Amsterdam, 1752.]
    Nina. [+L. 1164 (25/4/1797). Libretto by G. B. Lorenzi; Naples, 1789.]
    L'Olimpiade. [Originally presented at Vicenza in 1784.]

p. 359] Orione. [The *Orione* of 1777 is a revival of the opera of 1763.]
    Penelope. [A revival of the opera of 1741.]
    Piramo e Tisbe. [+L. 1114.]
    Quinto Fabio. [Originally presented at Milan in 1778.]

p. 360] Il Ratto della Sposa. [Originally presented at Venice in 1765.]
    La Regina di Golconda. [+L. 648, as *Alina, o sia, La R. di G.*]
    Rinaldo. [+L. 520.]
    La Scuola dei Maritati. [+L. 1053.]
    Semiramide. [Libretto by L. da Ponte, from F. Moretti; Naples, 1790.]

p. 361] Senoscrita. [+L. 234.]
    Il Soldano generoso. [+L. 502.]
    La Sposa fedele. [See *La Costanza di Rosinella*.]

p. 362] Lo Studente alla Moda. [L. 103 is a printed copy. Amsterdam, 1752.]
    Il Tesoro. [+L. 1136.]
    Tito Manlio. [Originally presented at Naples in 1751.]
    +Le Trame deluse. L. 934 [8/2/1792, for H.^{1}].
    Gli Uccellatori. [Music by F. L. Gassmann.]

p. 363]   La Vera Costanza. [Libretto by F. Puttini; Teatro delle
Dame, Rome, 2/1/1776.]

La Vestale. [Original title in L. 773, *Emilia*.]

La Villanella rapita. [Loewenberg gives H.[1] 27/2/1790, but
this I have not been able to verify. This is evidently the
opera by G. Bertati, music by Bianchi, produced at Venice
in 1783.]

Virginia. [+L. 731.]

Zemira e Azore. [+L. 469.]

Zenobia in Palmira. [+L. 1049. Libretto by G. Sertor;
Venice, 26/12/1789.]

I Zingari in Fiero. [Libretto by G. Palomba; Naples,
21/11/1789.]

INDEX
OF PERSONS AND SUBJECTS

[A final volume in this series will present a general comprehensive index of all the English plays catalogued in this and the other Hand-lists. Consequently the present index is concerned only with persons and subjects.]